Introduction and contents

As a child I lived on a farm in Yorkshire, where almost everything we ate was home-grown and full of flavour. We ate simply, but wonderfully well. The milk, cream and butter came from our own cows and at a very early age I learned how to milk a cow and churn the butter. We ate our own poultry and cured our own bacon, then hung the hams from the oak beams in the kitchen.

When my mother wasn't making bread, cakes or pies, which were baked in the oven that was heated by the flames of the open wood fire, she was busy making cream cheese, bottling our own fruit or blackberries we had picked from the hedgerows, or making apple jelly or jam in our old copper preserving pan—I liked the jam days best of all for the sweet smell, in spite of the constant buzzing of the wasps.

Watching my mother cook I learned to bake and knead and mix ingredients at about the time I was learning to read. I couldn't have had a better teacher, for my mother had the most important asset any cook can have—she loved food. She was also an inventive cook. My father would bring in a hare or pheasant that he had shot and my mother, who always had the imagination to adapt a recipe, would make it into a superb dish.

In *The Essential Cookbook* I have tried to show how easy it is to prepare the raw ingredients and to cook them in the most suitable way. Each cooking method – boiling and steaming, stewing and casseroling, grilling, frying and sautéing, roasting and baking—is described in detail, and each of these sections is preceded by a contents list in the form of a chart.

On the charts the recipes are divided into first courses, main courses, light lunch or supper dishes, accompaniments and desserts, and there are suggestions wherever necessary for what to serve with each dish. There is also a miscellaneous section, which includes cakes, pastries, bread, snacks and such breakfast dishes as porridge.

Once you have understood the reasons behind the basic cooking techniques you should be able to tackle any recipe, however complicated, for even the elaborate dishes of the haute cuisine are just a combination of a number of simple operations.

The Essential Cookbook will be, I hope, a springboard to start you off on a lifetime of good, exciting and creative cooking.

Kitchen equipment

The choice of cooking equipment is enormous and the less experienced cook can be forgiven for not knowing quite what to buy. Although the following list is basic, there may be items in it that are irrelevant to your style of cooking. If, for example, you rarely bake cakes and biscuits there will be no need for you to buy such a wide range of baking tins. Specialist utensils, such as those required for making sauces or steaming (for example a vegetable steamer) are described in the appropriate sections.

It is more economical in the long run to buy the best-quality kitchen equipment, for only such equipment can be expected to survive high temperatures, constant cleaning and hard wear.

For cutting, stirring and beating

Good kitchen knives are a sound investment, and those made of carbon steel are still the best because they can be kept very sharp. Stainless steel, however, is easier to keep clean.

Keep knives away from other cutlery—for example on a knife-rack—for safety and to prevent them from being blunted on other implements. Wash carbon steel knives immediately after use and rub them lightly with fine wire wool or soap-filled pads to keep them bright and shiny. If knives become badly discoloured, rub them with a damp cloth and scouring powder, then rinse and dry them immediately or they will rust.

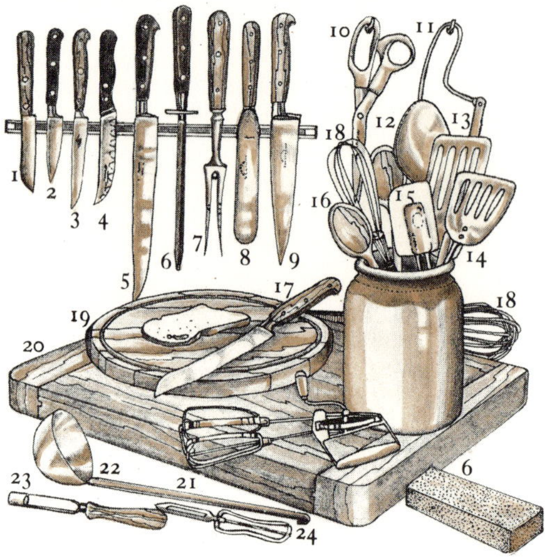

1 Paring knife for peeling vegetables, preparing garnishes or boning fish. 2 Chopping knife. 3 Filleting knife with flexible blade. 4 Small, stainless steel serrated tomato knife. 5 Carving knife. 6 Carborundum or steel. 7 Carving fork with guard. 8 Palette knife. 9 Chopping knife. 10 Kitchen scissors. 11 Meat saw. 12 Long-handled kitchen spoon. 13 Fish slice. 14 Slotted turner. 15 Rubber spatula. 16 Wooden spoons. 17 Stainless steel serrated bread knife. 18 Wire whisks in graduated sizes. 19 Bread board. 20 Chopping board. 21 Rotary beater. 22 Ladle. 23 Stainless steel apple corer. 24 Swivel-bladed knife—good for chocolate curls as well as for peeling vegetables.

Pots and pans

Good pans are designed for utility rather than for appearance. They are made from high-quality metals that conduct heat evenly. The inexpensive and more decorative pans that abound in many hardware shops are a waste of money because inferior metals conduct heat poorly. This causes the base of the pan to overheat—burnt milk and ruined sauces too often confirm this.

Aluminium pans with heavy bases last a lifetime, but they discolour when they are used for boiling water. Add a little vinegar to the pan or bring back the shine by using soap-filled steel-wool pads. Stainless steel pans are equally durable and always stay shiny.

Amongst the other types of pans available, the heavy enamelled ones are excellent for making casseroles but are too heavy for general use. Take care not to chip the enamel, because once damaged, the lining cannot be replaced. Non-stick pans are useful for heating milk and for making scrambled eggs, but the coating wears off eventually.

You can also buy handsome copper pans, but they need relining from time to time. To clean a copper crêpe pan, just wipe it with kitchen paper. Other copper pans can be cleaned with steel-wool pads.

Store all pans without their lids on to prevent them from smelling musty.

1 Copper crêpe pan. 2 Cast-iron or aluminium frying-pans of different sizes. 3 Iron omelette pan. 4 Fish kettle with rack and lid—also useful for puddings, hams, galantines. 5 Non-stick milk saucepan. 6 Stainless steel or aluminium saucepans of various sizes, with lids. 7 Large, deep aluminium pan (good for cooking shellfish and pasta). 8 Double saucepan. 9 Sauté pan, a straight-sided, heavy-based pan with lid. 10 Pressure cooker 11 Enamelled casseroles of various sizes with well-fitting lids.

How to season a new cast-iron omelette or crêpe pan

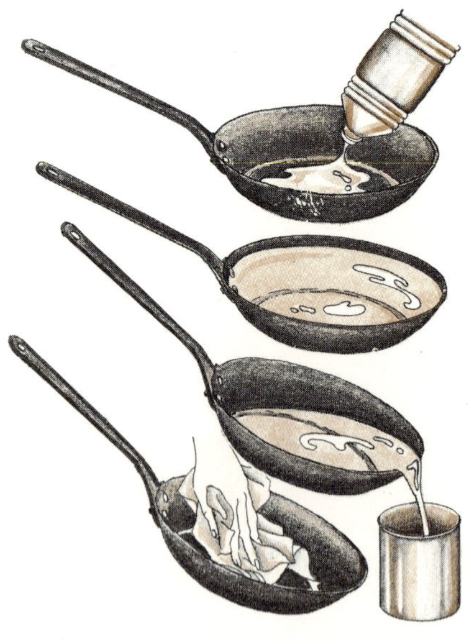

Fill the pan with oil and heat it slightly. Turn the heat off and allow the oil-filled pan to stand for twenty-four hours. Pour off the oil and wipe the pan with kitchen paper to remove any excess grease. Never wash the inside of the pan—just wipe it with kitchen paper. If the pan becomes very dirty, rub it all over with salt, wipe with a damp cloth and then oil lightly. Wash the underside of the pan after use, to prevent dirt accumulating.

Baking utensils and moulds

1 Bun or muffin trays. 2 Cast-iron baking sheets to fit oven. 3 Cooling rack. 4 Oval ovenproof dishes of different sizes. 5 Rectangular hinged tin. 6 Pie plates of different sizes. 7 Fluted biscuit cutters. 8 Three-way spring-form cake tin. 9 Plain biscuit cutters. 10 Plain flan rings of various sizes. 11 Mousse or jelly moulds. 12 Bombe mould. 13 Tartlet tins. 14 Flan case with removable base for tarts and fruit flans. 15 Porcelain crinkle-edged flan dishes. 16 Soufflé dishes of various sizes. 17 Oval ovenproof casseroles. 18 Swiss roll tins of different sizes. 19 Roasting tins to fit oven. 20 Charlotte mould. 21 Marmite pot. 22 Individual soufflé or ramekin dishes. 23 Sandwich cake tins of different sizes. 24 Pie dishes of different sizes. 25 Loaf tins.

Other useful equipment

1 Mandolin or coleslaw grater. 2 Conical strainer. 3 Corkscrew. 4 Wire sieves in different sizes. 5 Wire salad basket. 6 Potato masher. 7 Garlic press. 8 Can opener. 9 Mincing machine. 10 Colander. 11 Pestle and mortar. 12 Juice extractor. 13 Cheese mill. 14 Grater. 15 Sugar sifter. 16 Food mill. 17 Sugar thermometer. 18 Metal skewers. 19 Trussing needle. 20 Weighing scales. 21 Measuring jug. 22 Copper bowl for whisking egg whites. 23 Set of measuring spoons. 24 Flour dredger. 25 Funnel. 26 Pastry brush. 27 Pudding basins in various sizes. 28 Set of graduated mixing bowls. 29 Basting syringe. 30 Rolling-pin. 31 Large forcing bag with nozzles. 32 Marble slab or pastry board. You will also need: Aluminium foil in two sizes; greaseproof paper; clear plastic film; kitchen paper towels; baking parchment; muslin; string; rubber bands and a roll of polythene bags with bag fasteners.

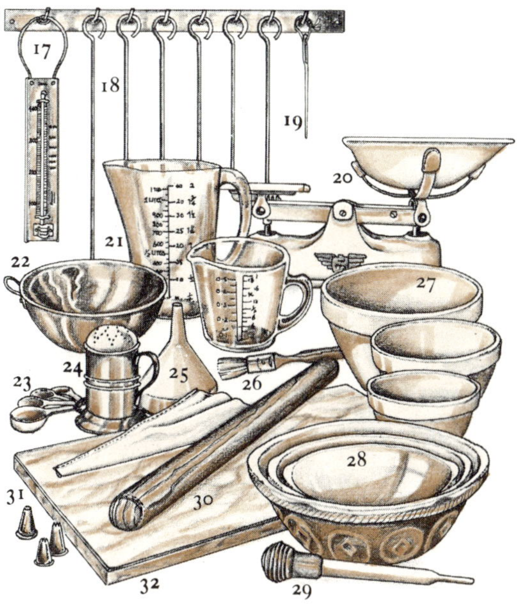

Electrical equipment

Of all the electrical gadgets available the only really essential one is the liquidizer. It eliminates many tedious kitchen chores such as crumbing bread and puréeing vegetables and fruit, and it saves time when making hollandaise sauce or mayonnaise.

The hand-held electric beater is useful for mixtures that need to be beaten over hot water or ice for a long time.

A coffee-grinder is necessary if you wish to serve really fresh coffee. If you keep the grinder very clean and free of ground coffee, it can also be used for grinding nuts and making breadcrumbs in small quantities.

Although it is possible to have all these gadgets incorporated in one large all-purpose kitchen mixer, the convenience of the hand-held beater cannot be matched by the fixed-head machine.

1 Liquidizer. 2 Coffee-grinder. 3 All-purpose kitchen mixer. 4 Hand-held beater.

Buying and storing

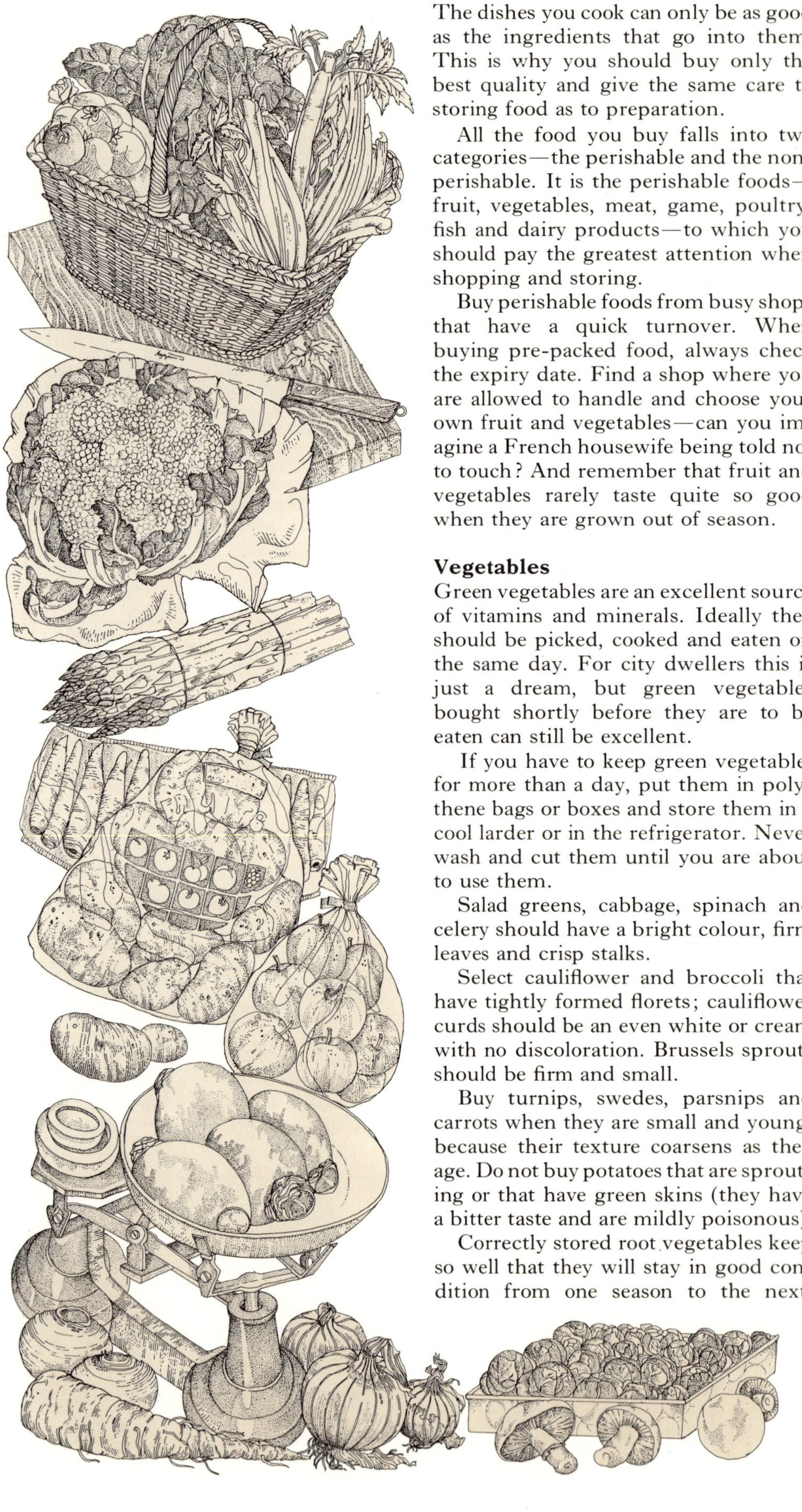

The dishes you cook can only be as good as the ingredients that go into them. This is why you should buy only the best quality and give the same care to storing food as to preparation.

All the food you buy falls into two categories—the perishable and the non-perishable. It is the perishable foods—fruit, vegetables, meat, game, poultry, fish and dairy products—to which you should pay the greatest attention when shopping and storing.

Buy perishable foods from busy shops that have a quick turnover. When buying pre-packed food, always check the expiry date. Find a shop where you are allowed to handle and choose your own fruit and vegetables—can you imagine a French housewife being told not to touch? And remember that fruit and vegetables rarely taste quite so good when they are grown out of season.

Vegetables

Green vegetables are an excellent source of vitamins and minerals. Ideally they should be picked, cooked and eaten on the same day. For city dwellers this is just a dream, but green vegetables bought shortly before they are to be eaten can still be excellent.

If you have to keep green vegetables for more than a day, put them in polythene bags or boxes and store them in a cool larder or in the refrigerator. Never wash and cut them until you are about to use them.

Salad greens, cabbage, spinach and celery should have a bright colour, firm leaves and crisp stalks.

Select cauliflower and broccoli that have tightly formed florets; cauliflower curds should be an even white or cream with no discoloration. Brussels sprouts should be firm and small.

Buy turnips, swedes, parsnips and carrots when they are small and young, because their texture coarsens as they age. Do not buy potatoes that are sprouting or that have green skins (they have a bitter taste and are mildly poisonous).

Correctly stored root vegetables keep so well that they will stay in good condition from one season to the next. Because they require cool, dry conditions a garden shed is the best place to store them. If you grow your own vegetables you may keep potatoes and turnips outdoors packed in earth "pies"—the vegetables neatly stacked, covered with straw and then with soil. In the same way carrots can be layered in sand in a clean dustbin or similar container. In the kitchen, root vegetables keep better on a vegetable rack than in the refrigerator.

Buy asparagus that has tightly closed tips and fleshy stalks. The stalks vary in size and colour from the gigantic, pale, mauve-tipped asparagus to the slimmer, green, delicately flavoured variety. A type of asparagus called sprue has thin, green, hard stalks and an excellent flavour. Cheap and plentiful at the height of its season, it can be made into soup or cooked with scrambled eggs.

A globe artichoke should have firm, green, overlapping, fleshy leaves in a tight rosette. If the leaves have spread and are discoloured the artichoke will be tough.

It is often difficult to find ripe avocados on the day you want them, so to avoid disappointment buy them in advance, slightly under-ripe, and let them ripen in a warm kitchen. To test for ripeness, gently press the stalk end; if it gives slightly the pear is ripe.

Of all the vegetables that fall into the category of pods and seeds, sweetcorn is the one that deteriorates fastest after harvesting. Young corn is naturally sweet, but shortly after the cob is cut off the stalk the sugar begins to convert into starch, so cook corn as soon as you can after buying it.

Fresh young peas taste best—they are sweet, not starchy, and have smooth, well-filled pods. French beans and runner beans should be bright green and so fresh that they break with a snap when you bend them.

The vegetable fruits—marrows, courgettes, cucumbers, aubergines, peppers and tomatoes—should be firm, smooth-skinned and bright. If they are in good condition when you buy them they will keep well in the refrigerator for at least three to four days.

The most delicious mushrooms are the wild ones, which you pick yourself in fields and woods or buy in a few specialist shops. The variety most commonly sold, however, is the commercially grown white mushroom. There is usually a choice between button or open mushrooms. Button mushrooms look attractive in casseroles, but the open mushrooms have a better flavour. Mushy, decayed mushrooms are dangerous to eat. Wild mushrooms in particular do not keep well.

Buy onions that are firm and without shoots. They keep well on a vegetable rack or hung in a dry, cold shed. If your kitchen is small and warm, refrigerate onions; humidity and warmth will make them sprout. Use spring onions within a day or two of purchase or, if you want to keep them longer, put them in a polythene bag and refrigerate. Garlic bulbs keep best strung up like onions in a cold shed, but if you have to keep them in the kitchen for any length of time they should be stored in the refrigerator. Leeks are best when they have long, slender stems, more white than green. They should be eaten fresh but can be stored for up to two days in the refrigerator.

Use fresh herbs during the short season when they are available; they are incomparably superior to the dried or frozen ones. Buy fresh herbs in small quantities for use that day, and make sure they are truly fresh; limp, discoloured leaves mean loss of flavour. If you have bought more than you can use, put them in polythene bags in the refrigerator, where their freshness will be preserved a few days longer. They can also be dried successfully. Such herbs as mint and rosemary will survive a day or two in a cool place if the stems are kept in water.

Fruit

When buying fruit remember that, generally speaking, small is delicious; overgrown fruit is often tasteless. Keep unripe fruit in a brown paper bag at room temperature. Look at them every day and when they are ripe use them immediately or put them in the refrigerator.

Apples and pears that are firm and free from bruises will keep well in a cold larder or in a refrigerator.

Select grapefruit, oranges and lemons that have smooth skins and are heavy for their size. Green patches indicate that they are not ripe and, therefore, may be sour. Lemons with thin skins are usually the most juicy. All citrus fruit can be refrigerated for a few weeks.

Buy bananas that are yellow, not those that are turning black. Do not refrigerate them or they will darken. Bananas ripen quickly so use them within a few days of purchase.

Although the sweetest melons are those that are ripened on the vine, you can buy under-ripe ones that will mature well in the kitchen. If necessary you can store ripe melons for up to a week in the refrigerator. Avoid buying melons at the end of their season, because they may rot before they ripen. When a melon is ripe it smells fragrant and "gives" at the stalk end. Chill it whole, and only cut it just before serving. Once a melon has been cut, wrap it in clear plastic film or enclose it in a polythene bag, and keep it in the refrigerator.

Soft fruit—berries and currants—are best when eaten or cooked within two days of picking, so if you buy them from a shop, use them as quickly as possible. Do not wash soft fruit until just before you use them.

When buying peaches, nectarines, plums and cherries, choose unblemished fruits. If the shopkeeper insists on selecting your fruit for you, tell him when you want to eat it and be warned that, as often as not, any fruit he says is ready for eating will probably need to be ripened for a further day or two.

Green figs are not unripe purple figs—they are a different variety. All figs sold in shops are ready to eat, because they must always ripen on the tree.

Grapes should be plump and covered with a bloom (a light powdery deposit). Eat ripe grapes immediately or store them for up to twenty-four hours in the refrigerator. Wash grapes in cold water just before eating them.

Pineapples are sold in various stages of ripeness. A ripe pineapple will have a strong fragrance and well-rounded "eyes", and if a leaf in the crown is tugged it will come out easily. Keep an unripe pineapple in a warm kitchen, away from sunlight, for a few days until it ripens.

Buying and storing

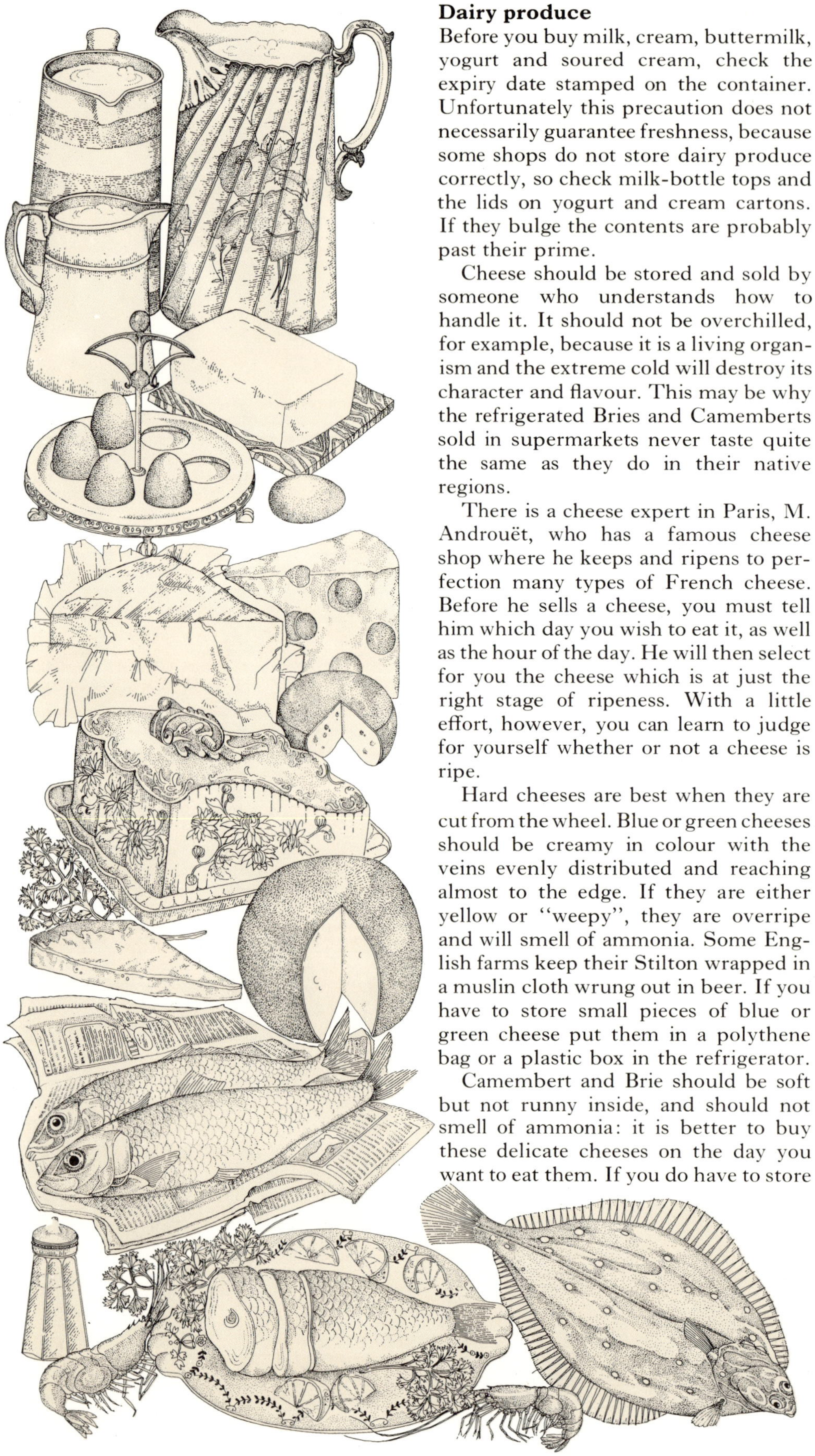

Dairy produce
Before you buy milk, cream, buttermilk, yogurt and soured cream, check the expiry date stamped on the container. Unfortunately this precaution does not necessarily guarantee freshness, because some shops do not store dairy produce correctly, so check milk-bottle tops and the lids on yogurt and cream cartons. If they bulge the contents are probably past their prime.

Cheese should be stored and sold by someone who understands how to handle it. It should not be overchilled, for example, because it is a living organism and the extreme cold will destroy its character and flavour. This may be why the refrigerated Bries and Camemberts sold in supermarkets never taste quite the same as they do in their native regions.

There is a cheese expert in Paris, M. Androuët, who has a famous cheese shop where he keeps and ripens to perfection many types of French cheese. Before he sells a cheese, you must tell him which day you wish to eat it, as well as the hour of the day. He will then select for you the cheese which is at just the right stage of ripeness. With a little effort, however, you can learn to judge for yourself whether or not a cheese is ripe.

Hard cheeses are best when they are cut from the wheel. Blue or green cheeses should be creamy in colour with the veins evenly distributed and reaching almost to the edge. If they are either yellow or "weepy", they are overripe and will smell of ammonia. Some English farms keep their Stilton wrapped in a muslin cloth wrung out in beer. If you have to store small pieces of blue or green cheese put them in a polythene bag or a plastic box in the refrigerator.

Camembert and Brie should be soft but not runny inside, and should not smell of ammonia: it is better to buy these delicate cheeses on the day you want to eat them. If you do have to store them, keep them wrapped in several layers of muslin in a cool place.

Keep such crumbly cheeses as Cheshire and Caerphilly wrapped in foil. Plastic bags make cheese sweat. Grated Parmesan cheese will keep for a week or two in a screw-top jar. The hard cheeses and cream cheeses can be successfully refrigerated.

Keep butter in its wrapper or in a covered dish in the refrigerator away from other foods because it absorbs strong flavours. If you leave it in a warm place for any length of time, it will turn rancid.

Whenever possible buy eggs directly from a farm or from a supplier who stamps the cartons with a date before which the eggs must be sold. If you are doubtful about the freshness of an egg, place it in a bowl of water. The egg will sink to the bottom if it is sound; if it sits right up, or floats, discard it. Never store a dirty egg because the dirt will be absorbed through the porous shell. Keep eggs in the refrigerator or in a cold larder and bring them out an hour or two before they are to be used for cooking. Eggs used for frying, however, may be taken straight from the refrigerator.

Fish and shellfish
If you do not get fish fresh from the sea or river, make sure you buy from a fishmonger who receives a daily supply. Fish is so good when it is fresh, but so objectionable when it is not that it is better to buy frozen fish rather than "fresh" fish of uncertain age.

Fresh fish has clear, bright, bulging eyes and shiny, tight scales. If the fish smells strongly and its scales are falling off, then it is not fresh. Look for red-pink gills and flesh that is resilient to the touch. Never buy a fish about which you have any doubts. Do not, for example, buy a sea bass with sunken eyes just because you have decided to serve bass for dinner.

When buying smoked fish, be sure that it is firm, dry, glossy skinned and sweet-smelling. Smoked fish can be kept in an airtight container and refrigerated for up to a week.

Although it is best to buy fresh fish the day it is to be eaten, it will keep for a day or two if promptly gutted, sprinkled with salt, wrapped in foil or in clear plastic film and refrigerated. Oily fish, such as herring, deteriorates more quickly than white fish, so cook it at once.

Molluscs must be bought alive and cooked on the same day. Clams, mussels, oysters and scallops should have tightly closed shells. Scallops can also be bought ready for eating—they should have very white flesh and a bright orange roe.

Among the crustaceans, fresh crabs should have rough shells and lobsters springy tails and uncluttered shells—encrustations are a sign of age. Shrimps should be dry and firm to the touch.

Meat
Beef and lamb should be firm, odourless, medium-red in colour, and well marbled—this shows that the fat content is high and, therefore, the meat will be tender. Veal should be very pale pink and odourless. High-grade pork is close grained, pale pink and odourless.

Poultry
Such poultry as chicken, turkey and goose should have white, unwrinkled skin, a plump, firm breast and clear, bulging eyes. The feathers, if they have not been plucked, should be soft and full. The feet should also be soft and flexible. When buying a fresh, unplucked chicken be sure that it is hung for no more than three days before it is drawn. Once drawn, cook the chicken within twenty-four hours, or store it in the refrigerator for up to three days.

The underbill of a fresh, young duck is flexible and soft. There should be plenty of flesh on the breast and the skin should be thin. Duck can be stored in the refrigerator for up to three days.

When you buy pre-wrapped, oven-ready poultry, remove the wrapping, then store the giblets and the bird separately in the refrigerator.

Although guinea-fowl is now bred for the table it was once a game bird. It is available oven-ready and frozen from many shops, but a fresh bird must be hung (before plucking and drawing) for at least two days in warm weather and longer when it is cooler.

Game birds
Game birds can only be bought in season, although frozen birds are sometimes available from specialist shops out of season. The most commonly available in shops are pheasant, partridge and grouse. Choose birds with feathers and feet intact so that you can judge their age. This is important for determining the method of cooking. A young bird has pliable, soft feet, hardly formed spurs, pointed wing feathers and a supple breastbone. An old bird has scaly legs, fully formed spurs, rounded wing feathers and a firm breastbone.

Game birds should be hung in a cool, dry, airy place, uncleaned, with feathers intact for one to two weeks depending on how warm or cold the weather is and how high you like them. Generally, these birds are ready to be cooked when the feathers pull out easily. When drawn and trussed they will keep for two to three days in the refrigerator.

Game
Skin and clean rabbits soon after killing. Use a young rabbit for roasting and an old one for stewing. To test for age, hold the ear of the rabbit with both hands and twist. If the ear tears, the animal is young.

Only young hare is worth eating, so test it for age as you would a rabbit. Hang it for four days, head down, without cleaning. Skin and clean the hare and cut into joints, saving as much blood as possible for cooking. Use immediately or refrigerate for no longer than two days.

Dust venison with flour and pepper (to keep the flies away) and hang it for seven to ten days in a cool, dry, airy place. A good animal will have a certain amount of fat around the haunches, especially if it is young. It is interesting to note that the meat will need to be well hung if the hunt was long. The violent exercise makes the flesh tougher than if the animal had been taken by surprise. When you buy venison from a reputable butcher it will almost certainly have been hung and will be ready for cooking. If you are given venison, check the age of the animal and ask when it was killed.

Venison, particularly an older animal, requires marinading from one to four days before it is cooked and is best stewed; roast only very young animals.

Freezing

Home freezing is one of the simplest and most convenient ways of preserving food. The home freezer will safely store whole meals prepared at leisure, left-overs that would otherwise be wasted, stocks, sauces and soups useful for quick meals, inexpensive seasonal fruit and vegetables and meat and poultry bargains.

To get the best out of your freezer, however, you must put in the best—good-quality food, well prepared and correctly wrapped.

Food must be packed in airtight, moisture-proof wrappings or it will become dry and lose its flavour. Worse still, it will pick up the flavours of other foods. Some foods, such as small fish and various fruits and vegetables, may be tray-frozen before they are packed. Spread them out on a tray, without touching each other, freeze, then pack and seal in airtight containers. They can then be removed from the container individually.

Heavy-duty plastic bags are suitable for most foods. Use a straw to suck all the air out of the bag, then seal it quickly with wire fasteners or special freezer sealing tape.

Heavily waxed cartons and plastic boxes are excellent for fruit, vegetables, cooked foods, sauces and liquids. Allow about half an inch (1 cm) in a one-pint (575-ml) container for the expansion of liquids.

Pastry, pies, desserts and any dishes that will be reheated in the oven can be frozen in aluminium foil dishes.

For such dishes as lasagne or goulash, line a baking dish with freezer foil, allowing enough foil to cover the food completely. Place the food in the dish, freeze it, then remove the food from the dish, cover the top with foil and return it to the freezer. To reheat, peel off the foil and put the frozen block back into the original container.

Freezer foil is particularly useful for wrapping such awkwardly shaped food as cutlets or a rack of lamb.

Always keep an up-to-date record of the contents of your freezer and label anything that goes into it. Using a soft wax marking pencil and special low-temperature adhesive labels, state the contents of each package and the number of servings. Remember to include the date on the label because all food will deteriorate or lose flavour if kept too long in the freezer.

Fish and shellfish

Only freeze really fresh seafood. Tray-freeze small fish and shellfish. Cut larger fish into steaks—wrap each piece separately before packing in boxes, bags or foil. Cook such shellfish as lobster and crab before freezing. Do not, however, cook shrimps before freezing them because they become tough. Shell oysters, clams and scallops, then pack them in their own liquor.

The maximum storage life for	
White fish	6 months
Oily fish, shellfish	3 months
Molluscs	6 months
Cooked fish dishes	3 months

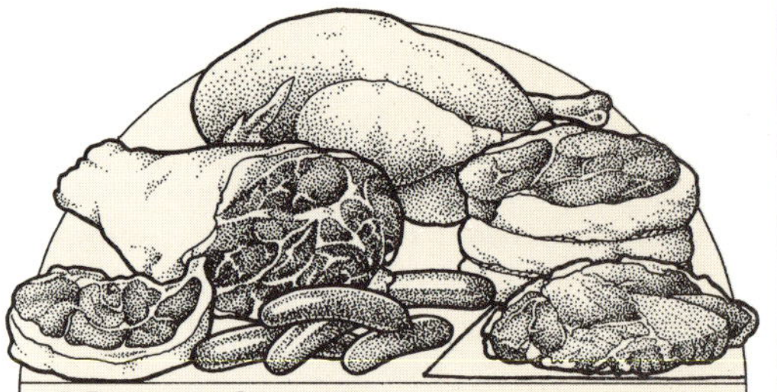

Meat and poultry

To freeze escalopes, lamb cutlets, fillet steaks, hamburgers or any other individual pieces of meat, wrap the pieces singly in double layers of foil or greaseproof paper. The thawing time for individual servings is usually one to two hours. Large pieces of raw meat should be thawed in the refrigerator for twenty-four hours. If poultry is frozen whole, remove the giblets and wrap them separately in a moisture-proof wrapping before putting them back inside the bird. Do not stuff a bird before freezing it. To save space, halve or joint a bird.

The maximum storage life for	
Beef, lamb	6–9 months
Pork, veal	3–4 months
Offal	1–2 months
Mince, sausages	1–2 months
Poultry	9 months
Hare, rabbit, venison	6 months
Cooked dishes	2–3 months

Vegetables

According to some experts almost all vegetables should be blanched prior to freezing to retard enzyme activity, which causes loss of nutrition and flavour. Others say that for such vegetables as broad beans, peas and corn on the cob, blanching is unnecessary as long as they are absolutely fresh. Try both methods and see which you prefer. Such vegetables as Brussels sprouts and artichoke hearts can be tray-frozen.

To freeze fresh herbs, wash and dry them, tie into bundles and freeze in sealed, airtight polythene bags.

The maximum storage life for	
Vegetables	12 months

Fruit

Discard fruit that have bruises, or any that are under-ripe or overripe. Such fruit as berries can be frozen in dry sugar, in syrup, or as a purée. They can also be tray-frozen, without sugar. Large fruits must be stoned or cored and pared and the stalks removed before freezing.

The maximum storage life for	
Fruit with sugar	12 months
Fruit with no sugar, and purées	6 months

Dairy produce

Double cream (but only to be used for beating or for making ice-cream), butter, margarine, and cooking fats freeze well. Grated cheese freezes well, but not soft cheeses.

Eggs cannot be frozen in their shells. Break them and beat them lightly adding half a teaspoon of salt or one teaspoon of castor sugar to two eggs. Or store separated, adding salt or sugar only to the yolks.

The maximum storage life for

Eggs, unsalted butter	6 months
Double cream, salted butter, soft cheese, ice-cream	3 months
Cheese (hard or grated)	6 months

Bread dough and pastry

Knead unrisen yeast dough once, then put it in a large, greased plastic bag, tie loosely and freeze.

Unbaked yeast dough for rolls should be allowed to rise then knocked down, re-kneaded and shaped into rolls. Grease the rolls, tray-freeze then pack in a plastic bag. Tray-freeze unbaked biscuits then pack.

Pastry with a high fat content freezes well. If you are making a filled pie, brush the pastry base with egg white and the top crust with fat. Slit the top crust just before baking. Unbaked frozen pies taste better than pies baked prior to freezing.

Maximum storage life for

Bread dough	10 days
Bread dough for rolls	7 days
Unbaked biscuits	2 months
Baked pastry	6 months
Pastry dough	9 months
Uncooked fruit pie	4–6 months

Bread, cakes and biscuits

Freshly baked bread should be cooled for three hours prior to freezing. It will keep for six months in the freezer, but begins to lose its flavour after two months. Wrap cakes in plastic or greaseproof paper then pack them in cartons. Iced cakes can be frozen provided the icing is made with butter and icing sugar. Freeze the cake before wrapping it.

Tray-freeze cooked biscuits then pack in polythene bags.

The maximum storage life for

Baked bread	2–6 months
Cakes	2–6 months
Iced cakes	2 months
Baked biscuits	3 months

Stocks, sauces, soups

Chill stocks, sauces and soups quickly over iced water then skim off any fat. Leave room in the storage container for expansion. Add such ingredients as cream and final seasonings to soups and sauces just before serving. Because you often require only a little stock to flavour a sauce or stew, freeze it in ice-cube trays first, then transfer the cubes to a bag.

The maximum storage life for

Stocks, sauces, soups	4 months

Stews

When freezing stews, use salt, pepper, herbs and spices sparingly because seasonings intensify during freezing. Remove any bay leaves or bouquet garni from a dish before freezing it. Remember to slightly undercook any dish that will require heating before serving. Foods to be reheated straight from the freezer should be put in the oven for twice the normal reheating time, at 350°F (180°C, Gas Mark 4), or reheated in a double saucepan on the top of the cooker.

The maximum storage life for

Stews	2 months

Foods that do not freeze well

The foods that can never be frozen successfully include salad vegetables—lettuce, cress, cucumber, chicory, endive, celery and tomato (except in stews and casseroles or as a purée)—uncooked potatoes and other root vegetables, kale, marrow and other vegetable fruit.

The fruits that do not freeze well are avocados and bananas, which turn black, and pears, which lose their delicate flavour and texture.

Fresh milk, single cream, soured cream and yogurt separate if frozen; custards also tend to separate. Cottage cheese becomes rubbery.

Mayonnaise and other egg-based sauces do not freeze well because the oil separates from the egg yolk.

It is not a good idea to freeze fried foods—they become tough and dry.

The whites of hard-boiled eggs become leathery in the freezer, and clear jellies lose their texture. Carbonated drinks may explode at low temperatures.

Thawing

All foods, with the exception of raw vegetables, can be thawed slowly, either at room temperature or in the lower part of the refrigerator. Stews and casseroles, pies and such dishes as cauliflower cheese can go straight from the freezer into the oven.

Basic preparation

What would be your reaction if you were presented with a duck—bill, feathers and all—by a proud hunter who wanted it for dinner? Or, even more alarming, if you were given a lively, wriggling eel? You may well be a good cook, but the chances are you do not have the first idea how to deal with such foods in their natural state.

Today most people buy fish and meat that has been prepared by the fishmonger or butcher, and are helpless on the rare occasions when they are confronted by the "real thing". This may also be true of some fruit and vegetables; others are so common that we all know how to prepare them, although it may not always be in the quickest and simplest way.

The squeamish may find some aspects of basic preparation unpleasant, especially where game and poultry are concerned. It is true, however, that the more experienced you become in drawing a chicken or skinning a rabbit, for example, the quicker the whole operation becomes.

This section will teach you how to handle anything—from a live crab to a French bean—and to know how to have it ready for cooking in the minimum time, with the least effort and waste.

Fish

One of the greatest delights is the sight of a well-arranged fishmonger's slab. The variety of shapes, sizes, colours and markings of the many kinds of fish is overwhelming.

Although it is possible to have almost any fish prepared by your fishmonger, it is well worth learning how to deal with a fish that has just been caught. You never know when you might receive a gift of freshly caught trout, or, if you are lucky, a salmon. And the flavour of a fresh fish is incomparably better than that of any fish you might find in a shop.

If you are baking or grilling a whole fish, it can be stuffed after it has been gutted. Put the stuffing in the stomach cavity of a round fish and use cocktail sticks to keep the slit closed. To stuff a flat fish use a sharp knife to make a slit down the middle of the back, then tuck the stuffing between the fillets and the backbone. It is also possible to stuff fillets. Those taken from flat fish are simply folded round a roll of stuffing. Fillets of round fish may be sandwiched together with the stuffing mixture.

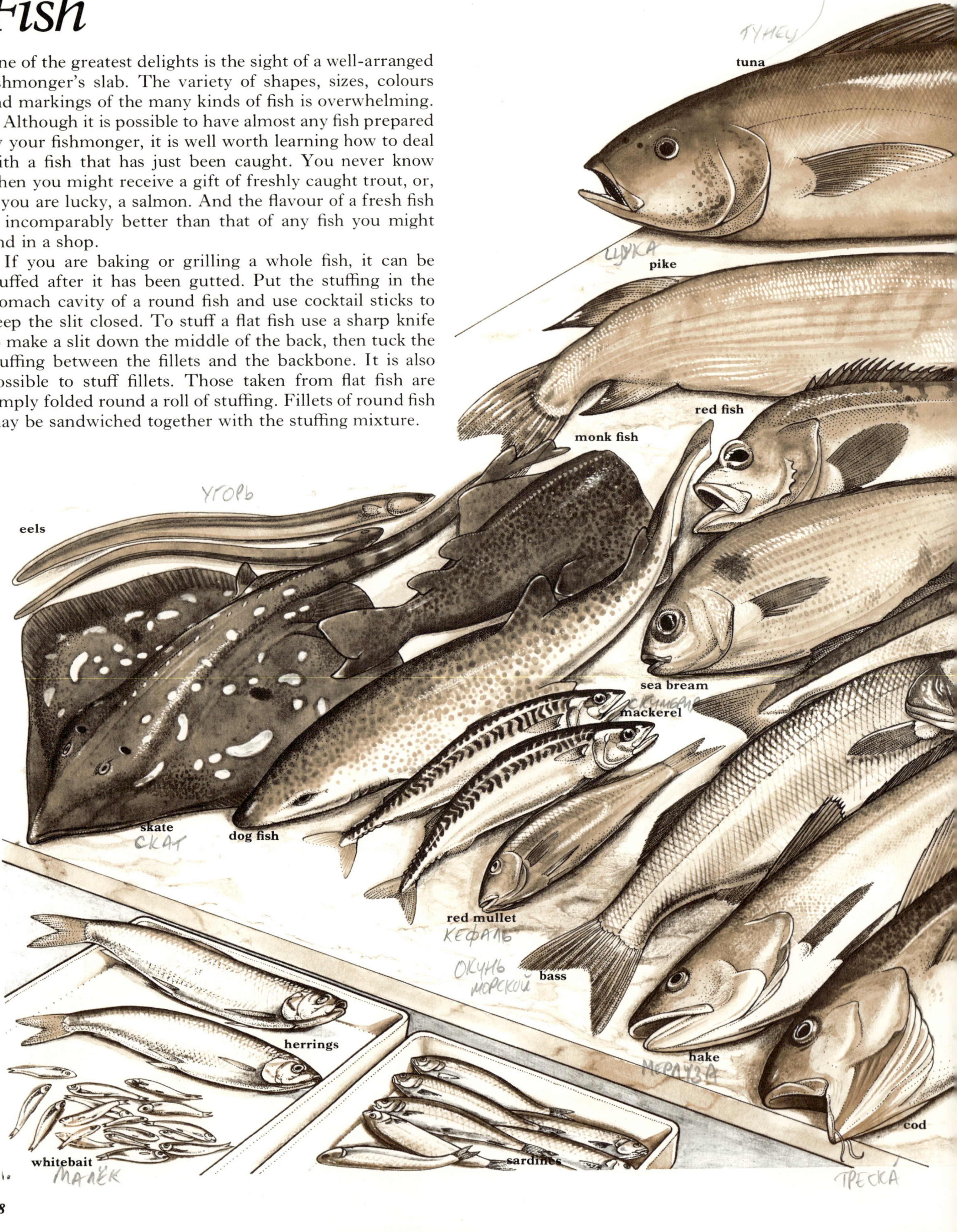

salmon
salmon trout
bream
trout
whiting
John Dory
brill
flounder
turbot
dab
Dover sole
plaice

Fish

For preparation, fish are usually divided into two groups —flat fish, for example plaice and sole, and round fish, of which cod, mackerel and herrings are the most common. Fish within a group can generally be prepared in the same way, with the obvious exception of eel, a round but otherwise unique fish.

Many fish are smoked, salted, pickled or dried. Dried salt cod must be soaked in cold water for two days. The water should be changed regularly—about three times a day. At the end of the soaking time the fish will have swollen to twice its size and is then ready for cooking.

Such smoked fish as trout and mackerel need only to be skinned. No other preparation is required.

Round fish

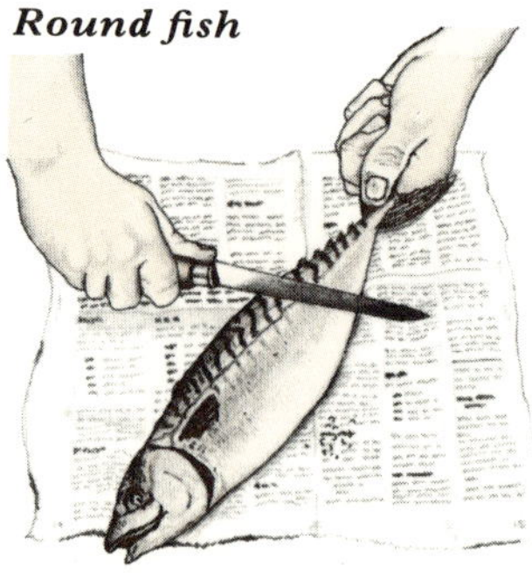

To scale the fish, hold it by the tail and scrape towards the head with the back of a knife.

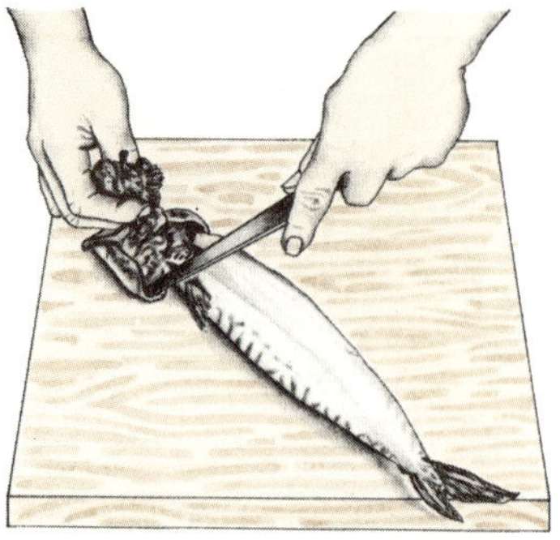

Lift the gill flap and slit the skin underneath. With the point of a knife, scrape out the gills.

Using sharp scissors, snip off the fins as close to the skin surface as possible.

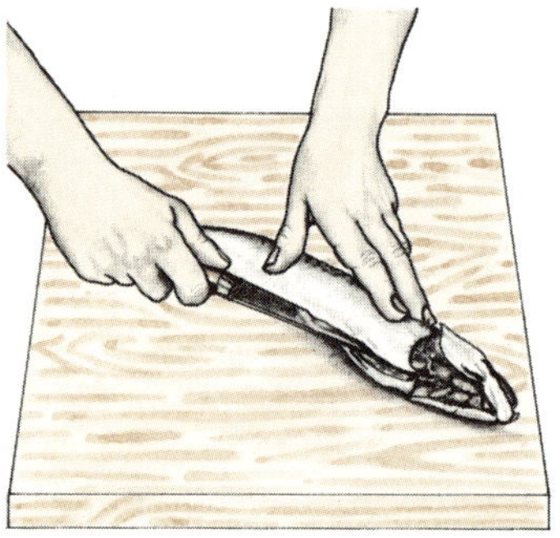

Now hold the fish firmly and slit the stomach. Using a teaspoon, scrape out the entrails.

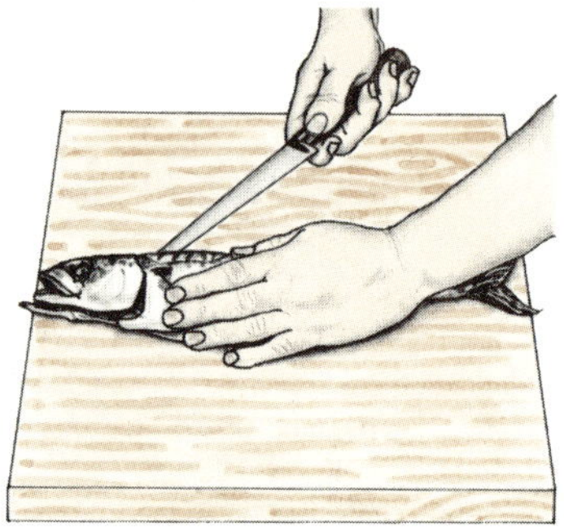

Turn the fish round and slit it right along the backbone, from the gill flap to the tail end.

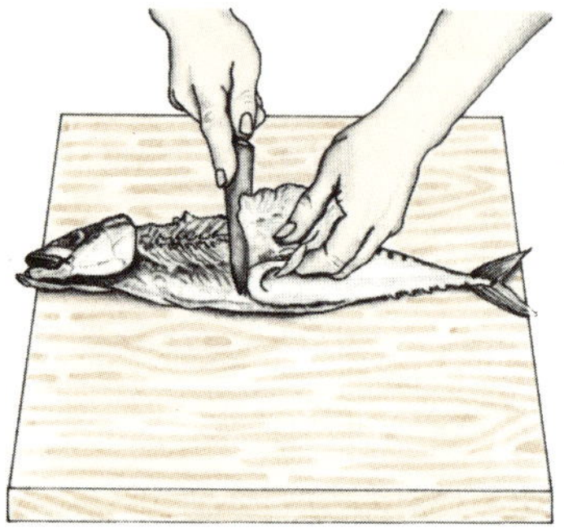

Keeping the knife flat against the backbone cut out the fillet with clean, sweeping strokes.

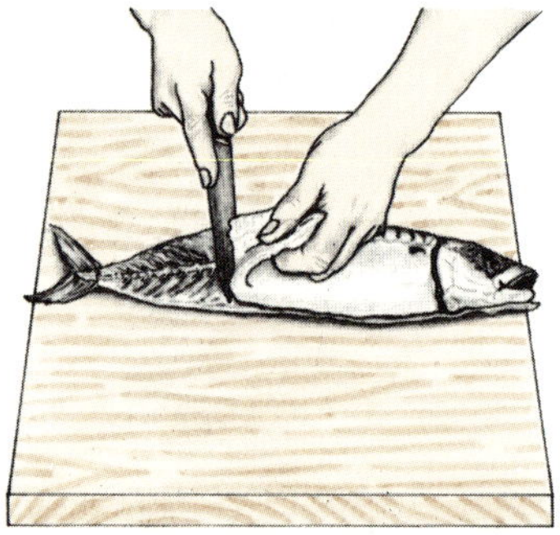

Turn the fish over and cut out the other fillet. Reserve the bones, head and tail for stock.

To skin the fillet, hold one end firmly and run the knife-blade between the skin and flesh.

Small round fish

Small round fish come in the category of oily fish. They include smelts, sardines, pilchards, sprats, whitebait and anchovies. Anchovies are almost always bought filleted and canned, and whitebait are never washed or cleaned. Just pick out any bad or damaged ones. Because small round fish have such small scales they require very little preparation: just wipe them over with a damp cloth, cut the heads off, squeeze out the entrails and leave on the tail.

Cut the head off below the gills and squeeze the body until all the entrails come out.

Herring

Herring is a round fish that also comes into the category of oily fish. It is available fresh and smoked. When a herring is smoked it is called a kipper. Herrings are full of tiny bones, and only some of these can be removed before cooking or smoking. The bones are a nuisance, but the flavour of the fish more than compensates for this. Fresh herring is the fish that is most often pickled in many European cuisines.

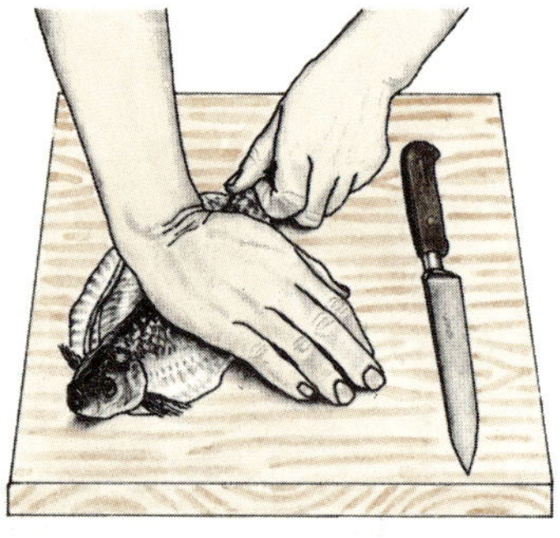

Slit the fish down its belly and lay it down skin-side up. Press down on its back to open it out.

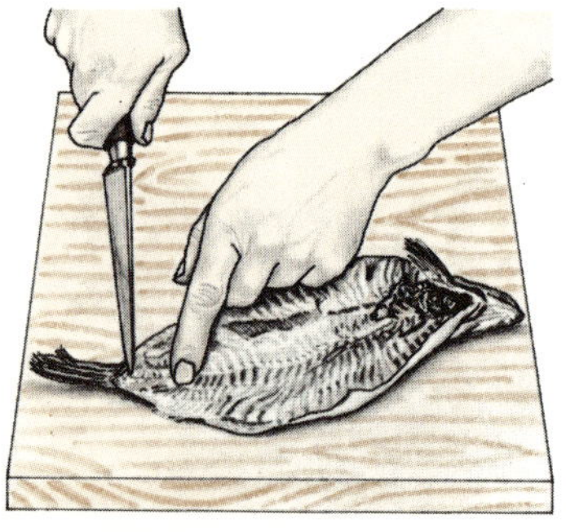

Cut the backbone just above the tail. Using the point of the knife, gently loosen the bone.

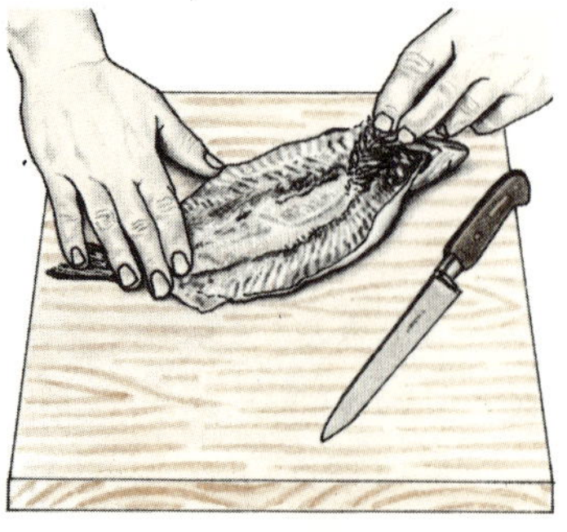

You should now be able to pull the backbone out easily, then lift out the side bones.

Eel

Although the eel is categorized as a round fish it is different from all other fish in shape and method of preparation. An eel must be alive when you buy it and killed and skinned only hours before you cook it. Once the eel has been killed it will keep on wriggling until you have almost finished preparing it. The skin should peel off easily in one piece, but the eel is slippery and slimy, so dip your hand in salt or wrap the part you are holding in newspaper to get a firm grip.

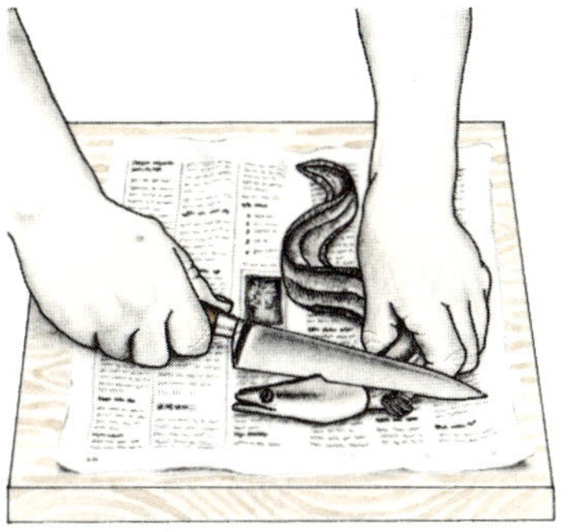

Hold the eel firmly just below the head and cut the head off with a clean, sharp movement.

With the point of a sharp knife, make a small cut at the neck end of the eel to loosen the skin.

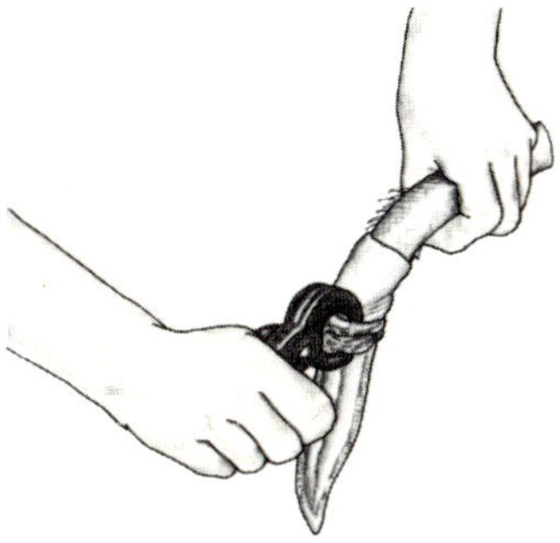

Grasp the neck skin firmly with pincers and tug hard—it should come away in one piece.

Flat fish

A flat fish is easily recognizable because it has a flattened body and both eyes are on the same side of its head. Flat fish include brill, turbot, flounder, plaice, halibut, dab and the various types of sole. They all have fairly similar shapes and are therefore cleaned, gutted, skinned and filleted in the same way. Skate is also a flat fish, but it is different from other flat fish because the body part is inedible and only the wings are eaten.

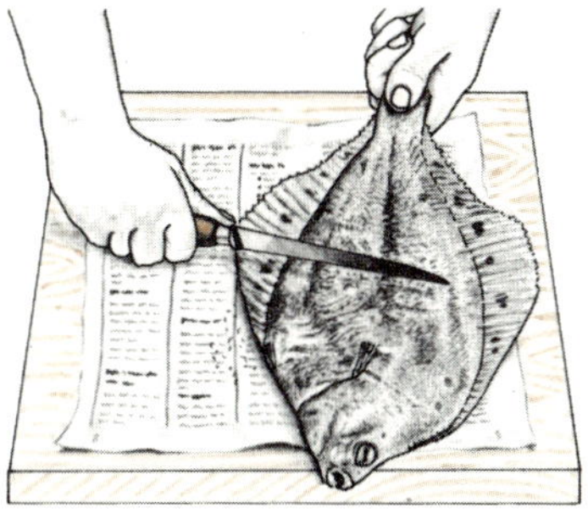

To scale a flat fish, grasp it by the tail and run the back of a knife from the tail to the head.

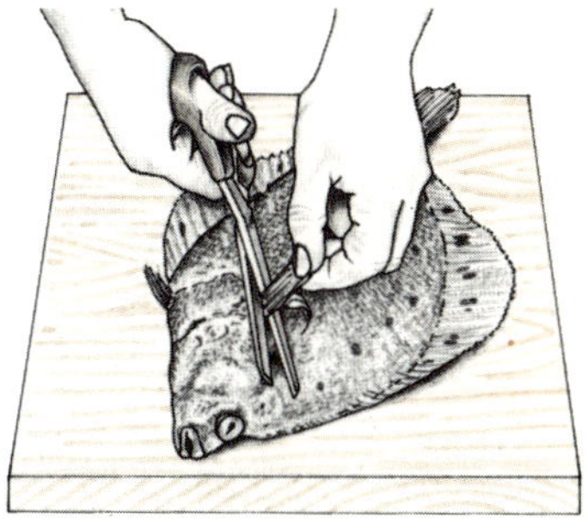

With a sharp pair of kitchen scissors, snip off the dorsal fins on each side of the body.

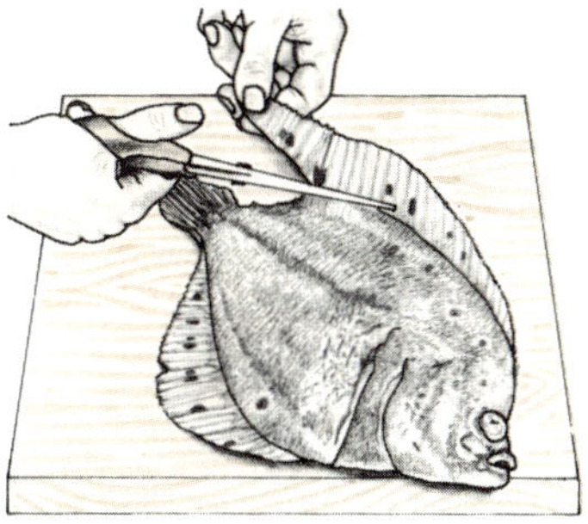

Now cut off the side fins, which surround the body. Follow the contours of the fish's shape.

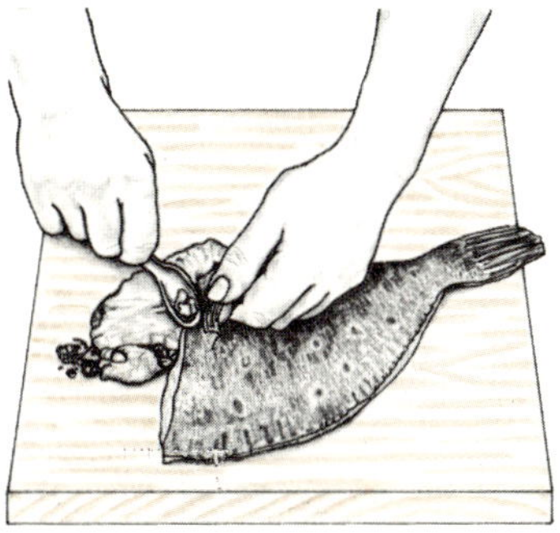

With a sharp knife, cut the head off, and then scoop out the gills with a teaspoon.

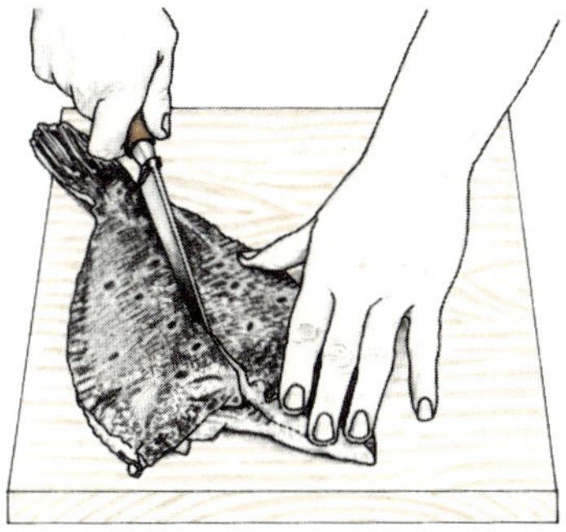

Hold the fish down flat with one hand and make a slit down the backbone from top to tail.

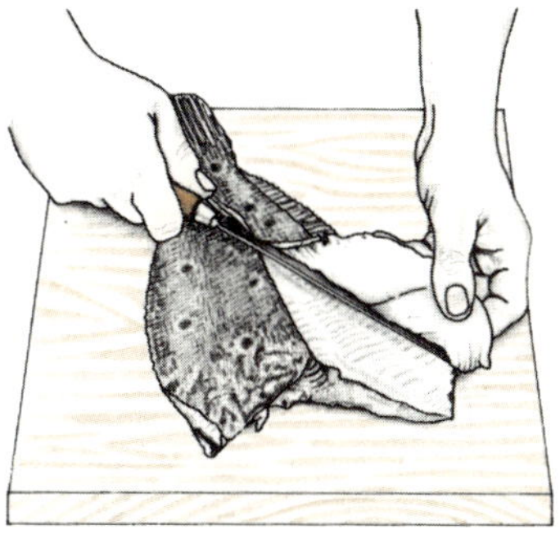

Keeping the knife flat against the bones, work the flesh away from the bones to make a fillet.

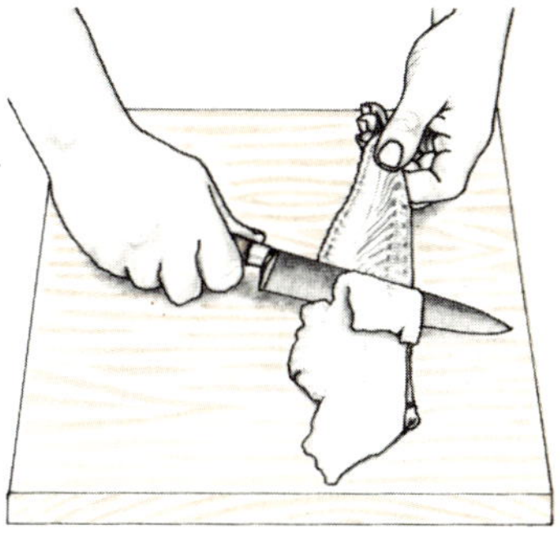

Hold the tail end of one fillet firmly and scrape the flesh away from the skin.

Sole

Sole is a flat fish with an oval-shaped body. The flesh is white and the skin varies in colour from light sand to muddy brown. There are three main types of sole—lemon sole, Torbay sole (witch) and Dover sole. Dover sole is considered the best of the three, and is said to have the finest flavour of any white fish. For this reason it should be cooked simply and served with subtle sauces and plain vegetables to enhance its delicate flavour.

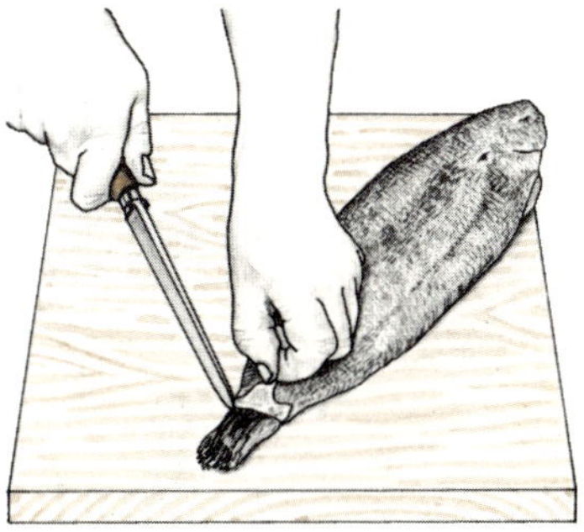

One method of skinning Dover sole is to make a small nick in the tail end of the skin.

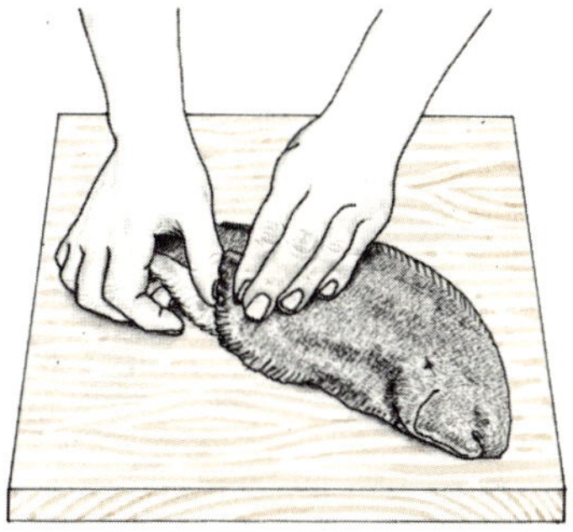

Beginning at the sides of the fish, start carefully easing the skin away from the flesh.

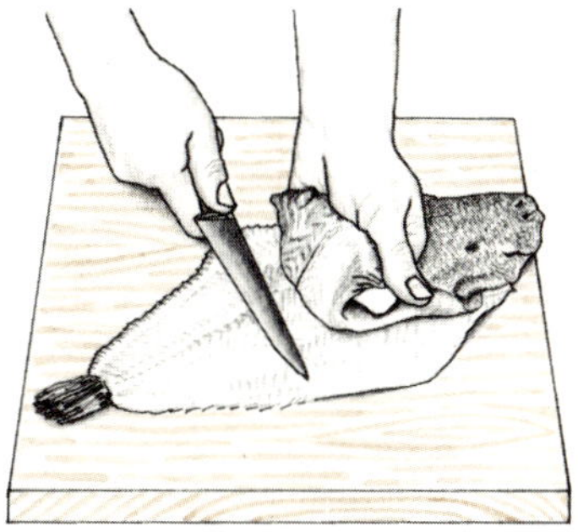

When the side skin has been eased away, pull the skin off sharply from the tail end.

Shellfish/molluscs

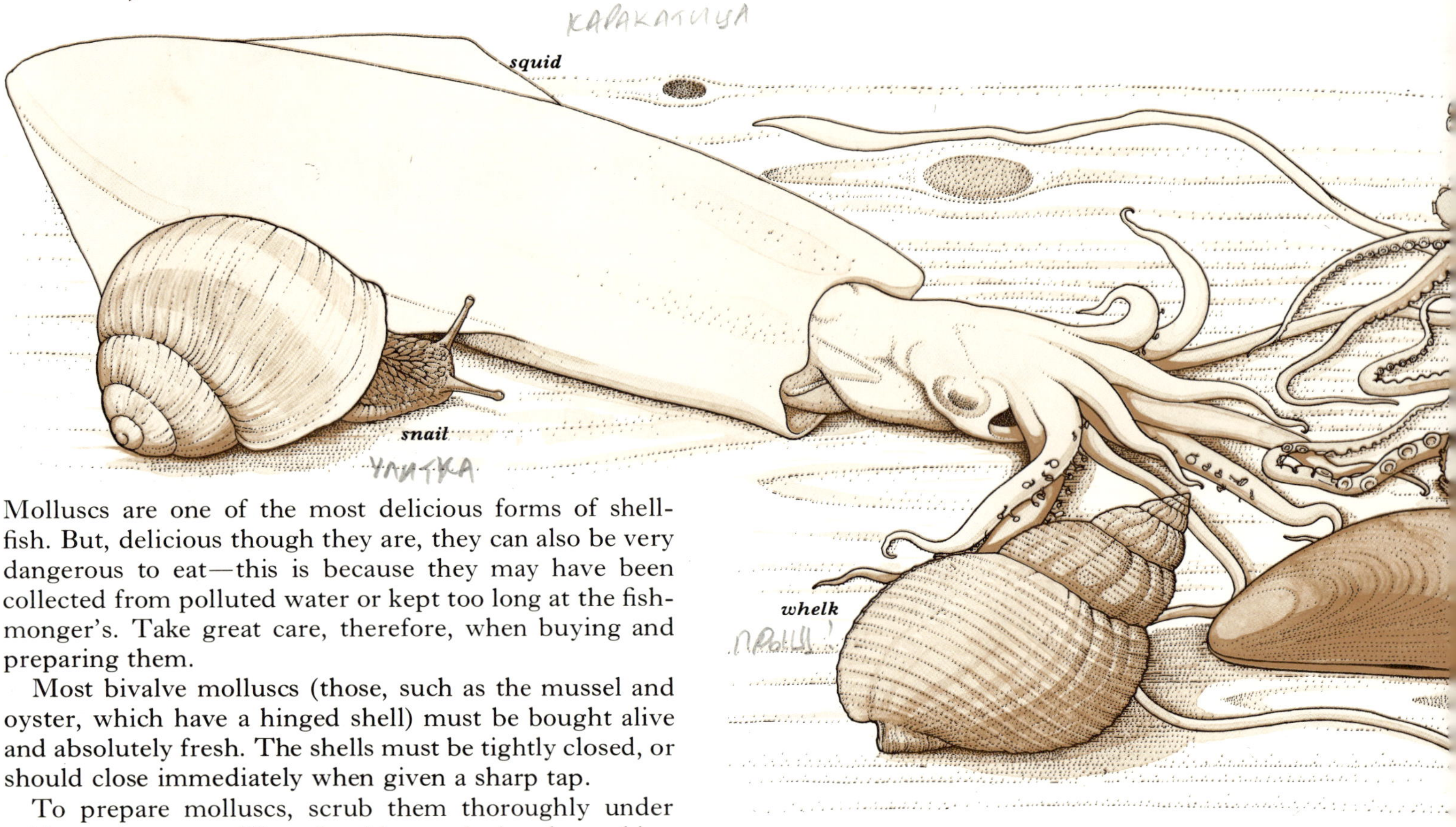

Molluscs are one of the most delicious forms of shellfish. But, delicious though they are, they can also be very dangerous to eat—this is because they may have been collected from polluted water or kept too long at the fishmonger's. Take great care, therefore, when buying and preparing them.

Most bivalve molluscs (those, such as the mussel and oyster, which have a hinged shell) must be bought alive and absolutely fresh. The shells must be tightly closed, or should close immediately when given a sharp tap.

To prepare molluscs, scrub them thoroughly under cold running water. They should open during the cooking period; discard any that remain closed.

Univalve molluscs, such as whelks, have one shell, which is open at the base. They can often be bought cooked, but if you buy them uncooked they must be alive. To test them, gently prod the flesh through the open end. If the whelk retreats into its shell, it is alive; if it remains inert, it is dead and should be discarded. Soak whelks and winkles in water for several minutes, rinse, then drop them into a pan containing boiling salted water for twenty minutes. Use a needle to remove them from their shells.

Snails are univalve land molluscs, and they too can be dangerous to eat because they quite happily feed off plants that are poisonous to us. If you can obtain live snails, gather them during the winter, when they are hibernating. Or, at other times of the year, starve them for up to ten days before cooking them.

To prepare snails for cooking, soak them in a bowl of salted water for four hours, changing the water every half hour. While the snails are soaking make a court bouillon with equal quantities of wine and water. Strain the court bouillon into another saucepan and let it cool.

Put the snails into the court bouillon and bring it to the boil. Simmer for three hours. Remove the snails from the pan and ease them from their shells, using a needle or a sharp-pointed knife. Cut off the membrane and the black part of each snail.

Octopus and squid are shell-less molluscs and are prepared in a totally different way to other molluscs.

Preparing oysters

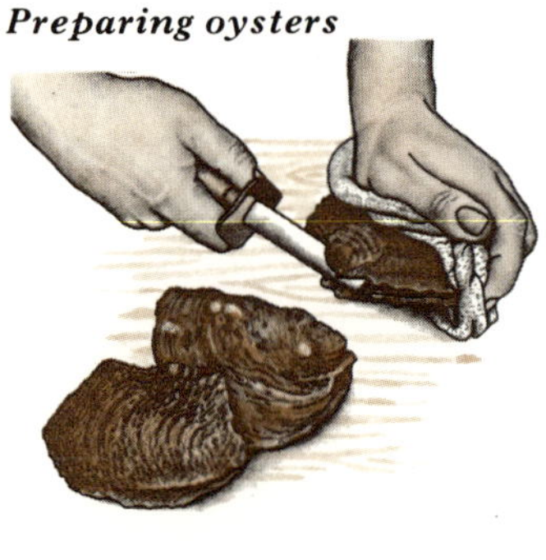

Scrub the oyster shell thoroughly to remove all the grit. Insert an oyster knife into the hinged part of the shell and prise it open.

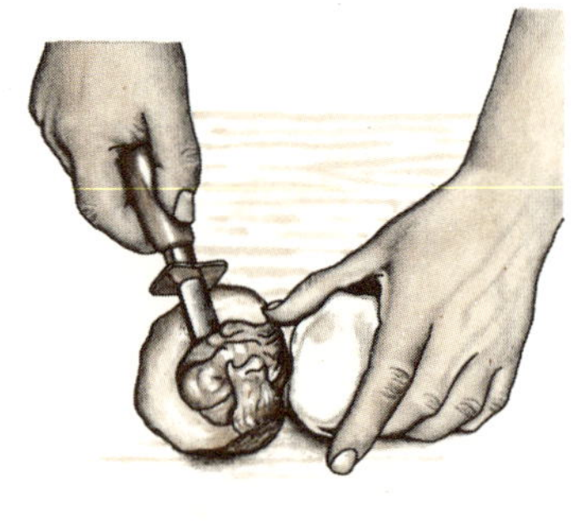

When the two shells have come apart, cut the oyster flesh off the flat shell, making sure you do not waste any flesh.

Preparing mussels

Mussels must be scrubbed very thoroughly. The small "beard" coming out of one side must be cut off before cooking.

If any mussels remain open after washing, tap them sharply. This should make them close: discard any that do not.

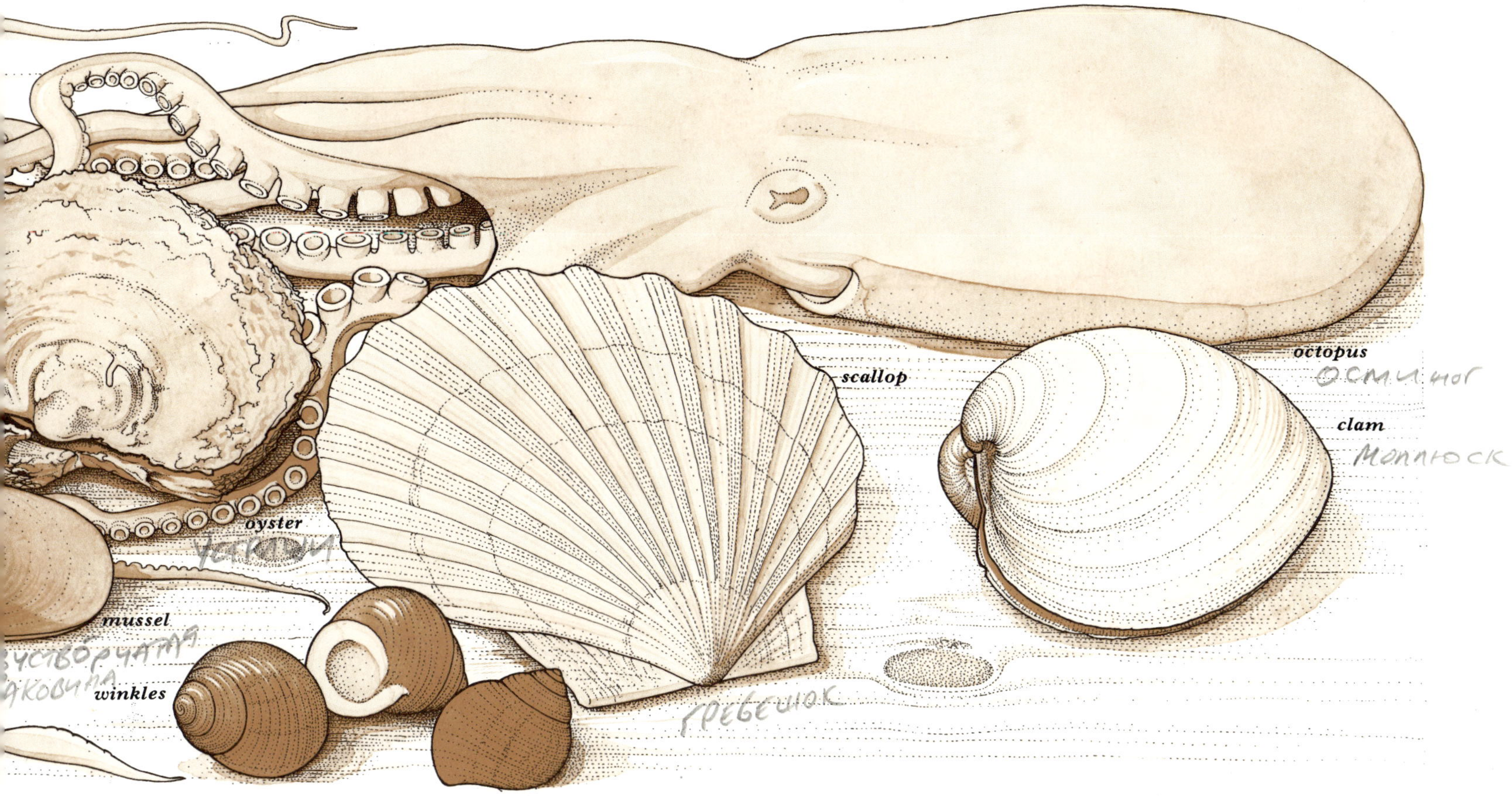

Preparing scallops

Lay the scrubbed scallops on a baking sheet, not touching each other, and heat in a low oven for 2 minutes or until they open.

Cut through the hinge with a sharp knife and pull the shells apart. Cut the scallop flesh from the flat shell.

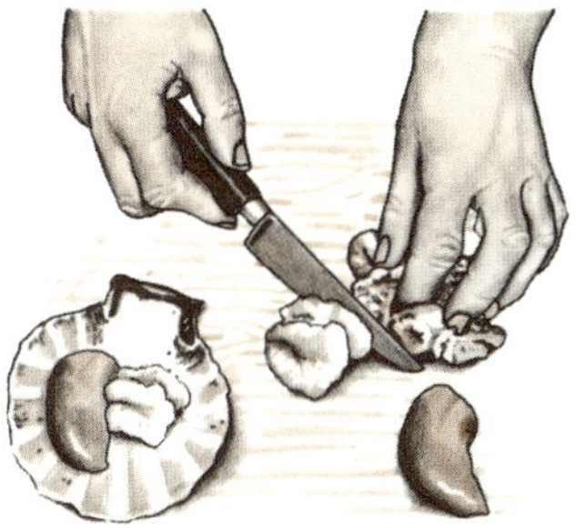

With a small, sharp knife, cut off the inedible parts from the scallop flesh—the beard-like fringe and the intestinal cord.

Preparing clams

Scrub the clam shells thoroughly with a stiff brush. Open them through the hinge with a knife and remove the flesh.

Preparing squid

Hold the squid's body and pull the head end out. Most of the gut—a milky substance—will come out easily with it.

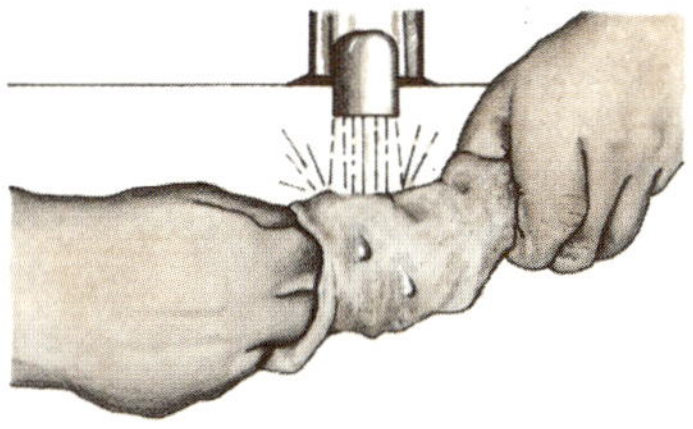

Wash the body under cold running water. Insert your fingers into the body and carefully remove the coral and ink sac.

The squid has only one bone, and that will pull out easily. Cut the tentacles off below the eyes and discard the head and bone.

Preparing winkles

The winkle is very small, so nothing larger than a pin should be used to prise it out of the shell.

Shellfish/crustaceans

The term crustacean is applied to shellfish that have jointed shells, rather like suits of armour. They include crab, lobster and shrimp.

In their natural state crustaceans vary in colour from pale grey to blackish-blue—ideal camouflage in their habitat, the sea. But once cooked their colour undergoes a dramatic change, ranging from pale pink to deep coral.

Like molluscs, crustaceans can be dangerous to eat; the only way you can ensure that they will do you no harm is to buy from a reliable fishmonger who sells only the freshest seafood. Most crustaceans can be bought either cooked or alive.

The killing of crab, lobster and crawfish (which is prepared in the same way as lobster) is worth special mention for it is thought that they are more sensitive to pain than other shellfish. It is believed that the most painless way of killing a crab is to drive a sharp instrument through the nerve centre. Unless you know exactly where the nerve centre lies, however, and can be sure of killing the crab at once, this is not recommended. The most practical method for the cook is to drop the live crab or lobster into fast-boiling water, but if the lobster is to be grilled, the point of a sharp knife must be driven through its head—the exact spot is conveniently marked by a cross—and death is instantaneous.

The stomach sac and intestine of lobster and crab must be discarded. The red coral of lobster is edible.

Crayfish are sometimes gutted before they are cooked. Wash them thoroughly under cold running water, then twist off the central tail fin—the intestine will come away with it. Have ready a pan of fast-boiling water, drop in the crayfish, cover with a lid and boil for about seven minutes. Alternatively, after the crayfish has been cooked, prise open the tail shell, lift out the meat and remove the dark, string-like intestine. To extract the meat from the claws, cut off the movable claw, and with a sharp knife loosen and remove the meat.

Shrimps, prawns and Dublin Bay prawns are often sold ready cooked. If they are alive, however, cook them, like crayfish, in boiling water. Shrimps and prawns will be ready in five minutes; Dublin Bay prawns require fifteen minutes. To prepare shrimps and prawns, twist and pull off the tail, snap off the head, then peel off the shell.

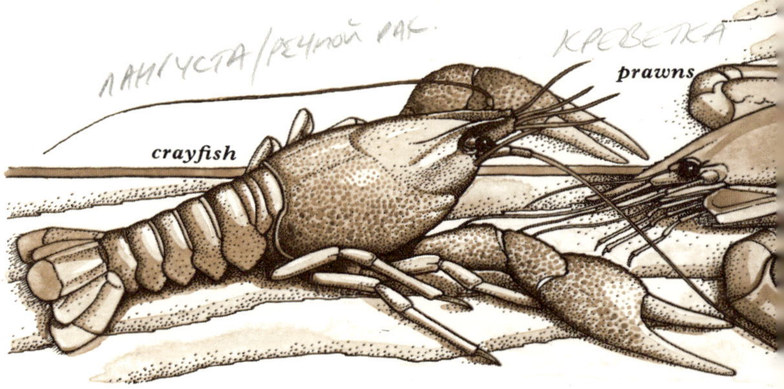

Preparing crab

To kill a crab, lay it on a wooden board with the underside facing upwards. Drive a skewer between the eyes and through its brain.

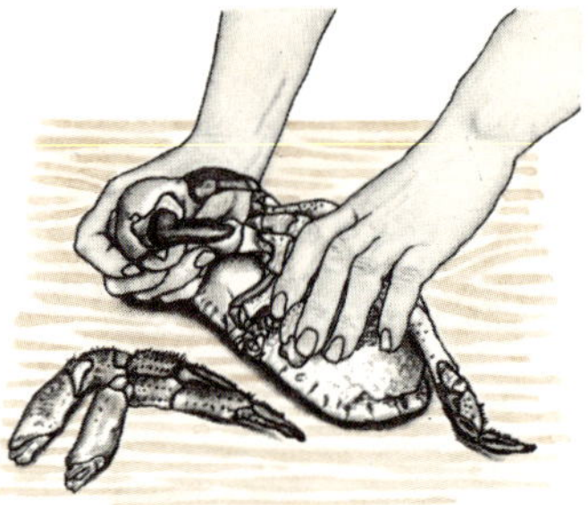

The flesh is removed after the crab has been boiled. Begin by twisting off all the legs and the two large claws.

Using the back of a knife or a small hammer, crack the claws in several places. Remove the meat and discard the shell.

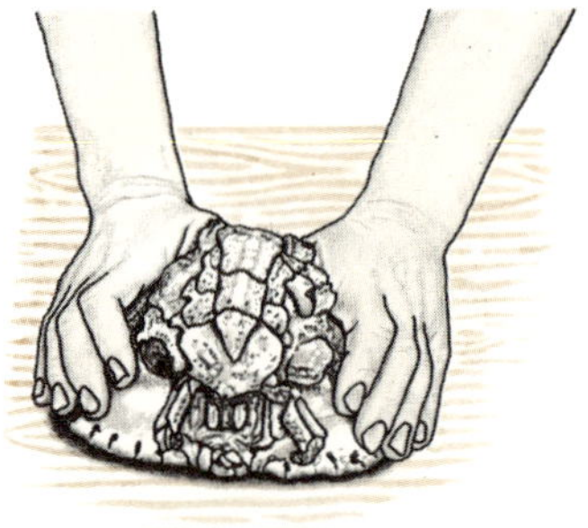

Lay the crab on its back. Hold it with both hands. Press the body upwards with your thumbs until it comes away from the shell.

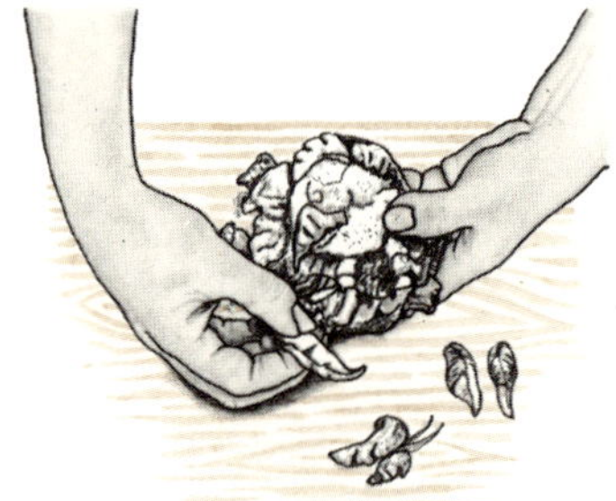

There are three inedible parts, which must be removed from the body—the lungs, the sac behind the head, and any green matter.

Using a teaspoon, scrape the meat out of the main part of the body into a bowl. Keep the white and brown meat in separate bowls.

With the teaspoon, scrape all the brown meat out of the shell. Wash the shell under cold running water and pat it dry.

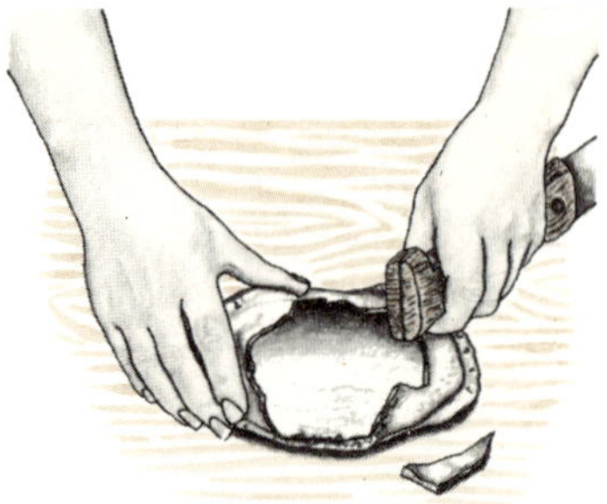

Using a small hammer, lightly break off the rough edges and trim the edge of the shell into a uniform shape.

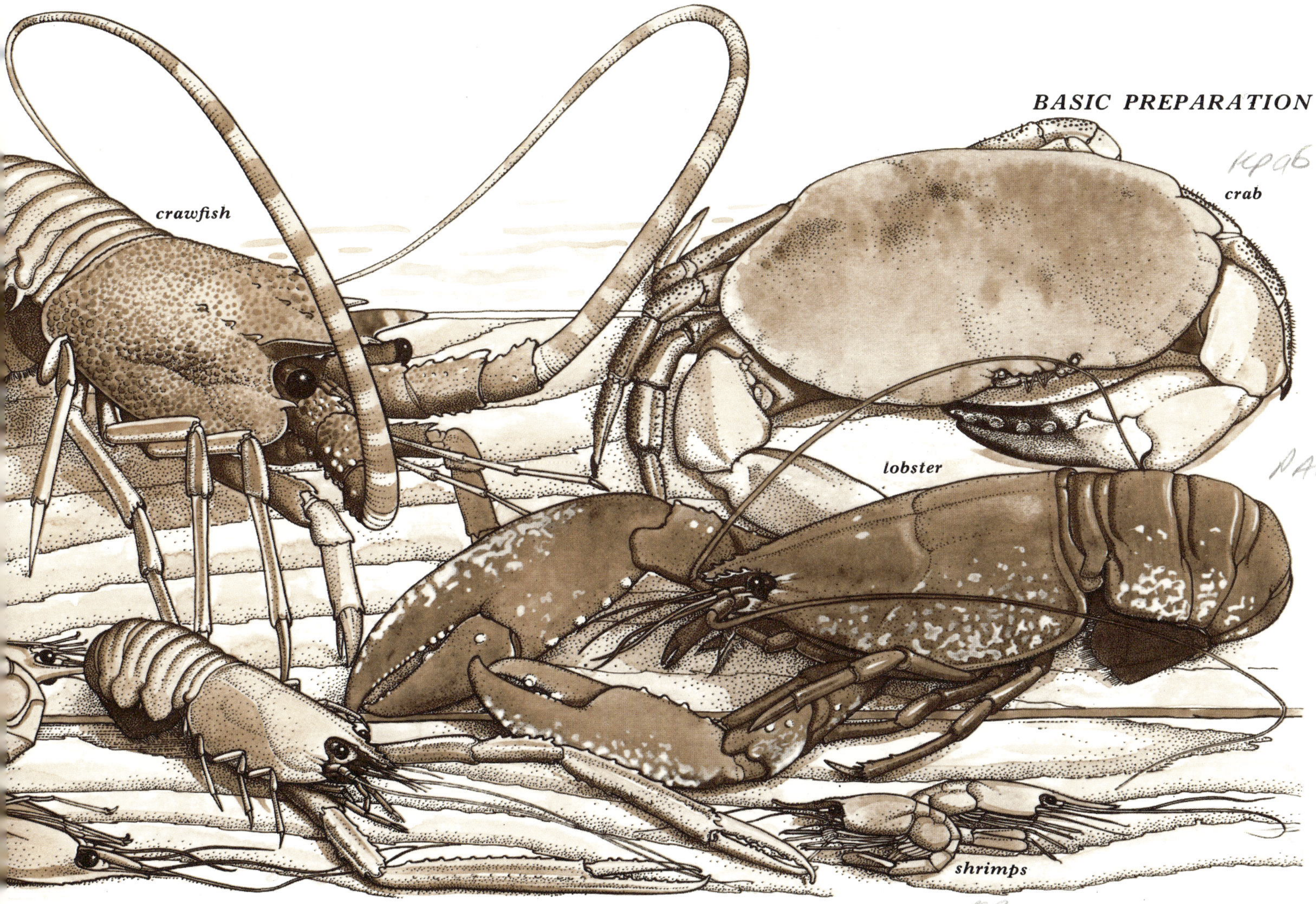

Preparing lobster

To kill a lobster, drive the point of a knife through the brain, which lies under the cross where the body meets the head.

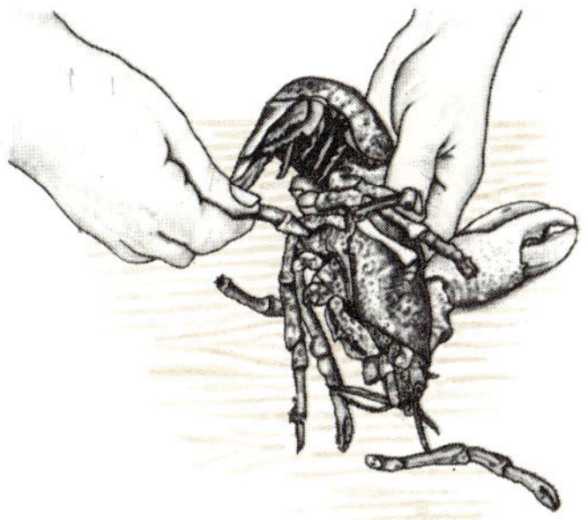

Hold the lobster firmly by the body and twist off the two large claws and small pincers. Remove the meat from these first.

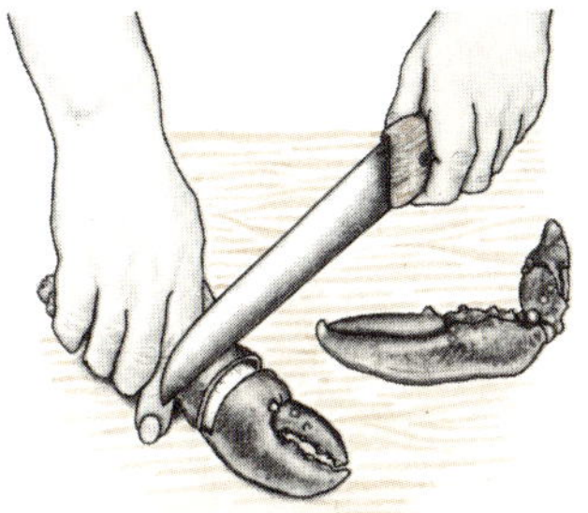

Using a hammer or a lobster cracker, crack the large claw shells. Remove any small shell particles before taking out the meat.

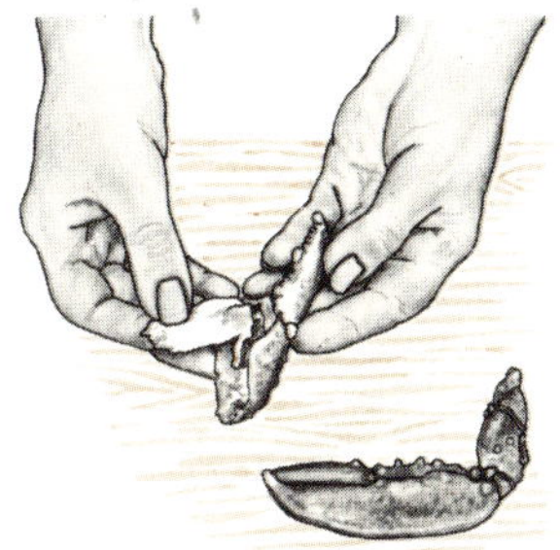

Extract the meat from the claws, using the point of a knife if it does not come out easily. Then remove the membrane.

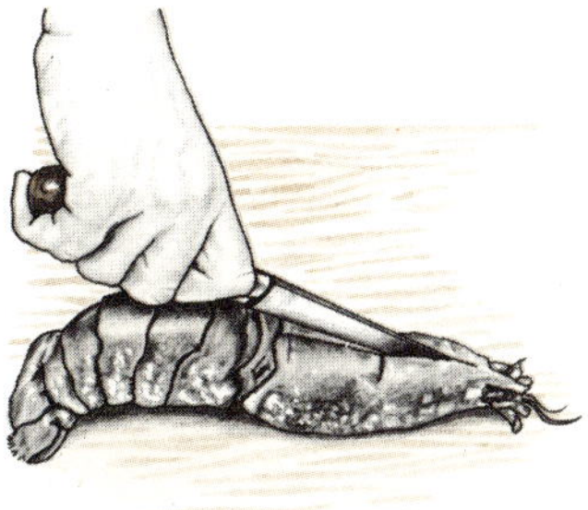

Lay the main body of the lobster on its stomach. Using a very sharp knife, split the lobster in half down the centre of the back.

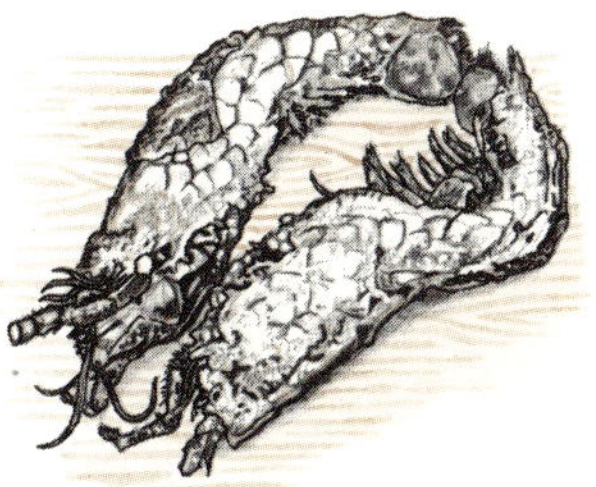

Separate the two halves; remove and discard the black intestinal cord, the gills and the stomach sac. The greenish liver is edible.

Preparing prawns and shrimps

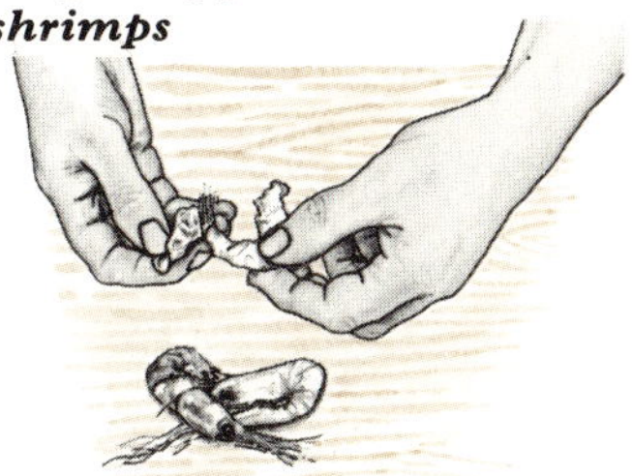

To shell prawns and shrimps, twist the tail and pull it off. Open up the body shell, to which the legs are attached, and peel it off.

Preparing crayfish

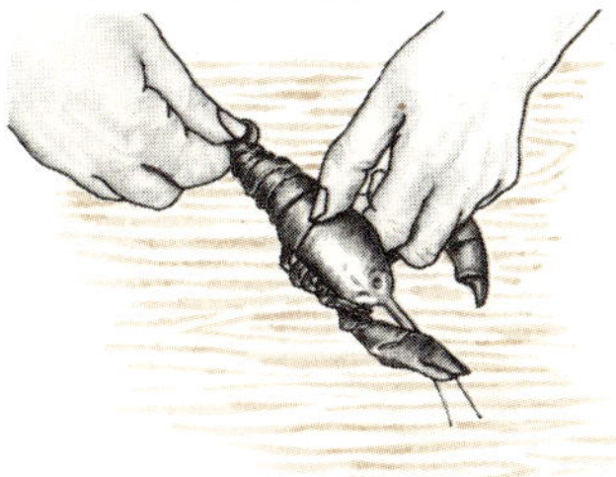

Crayfish may be gutted before being cooked. Grip the middle tail fin, twist and pull to remove the gut. Drop into boiling water.

Poultry and game birds

All poultry and game birds, unless they are bought oven-ready, must be hung, plucked and drawn before they are cooked.

Poultry—chicken, duck, turkey, goose and guinea-fowl—is traditionally plucked before it is hung by its feet. Game birds—pheasant, partridge, pigeon, grouse, quail, snipe, mallard, teal and woodcock—are hung by their necks unplucked.

Hanging times vary according to the bird, its age and the weather. A young chicken should be hung for one day only. A duck or goose needs two days, and a turkey or guinea-fowl must be hung for about three to five days.

Game is nearly always hung until the flesh is "high" and has developed a strong flavour. If after about three days the feathers above the bird's tail come out easily when pulled, it is, according to most tastes, ready for cooking.

In warm weather hang all birds for shorter periods, but remember that an older bird must be hung for longer than a young one or the flesh will not be tender.

Poultry and game birds are plucked in the same way. Any stubborn feathers can be singed off and the quill ends removed with tweezers.

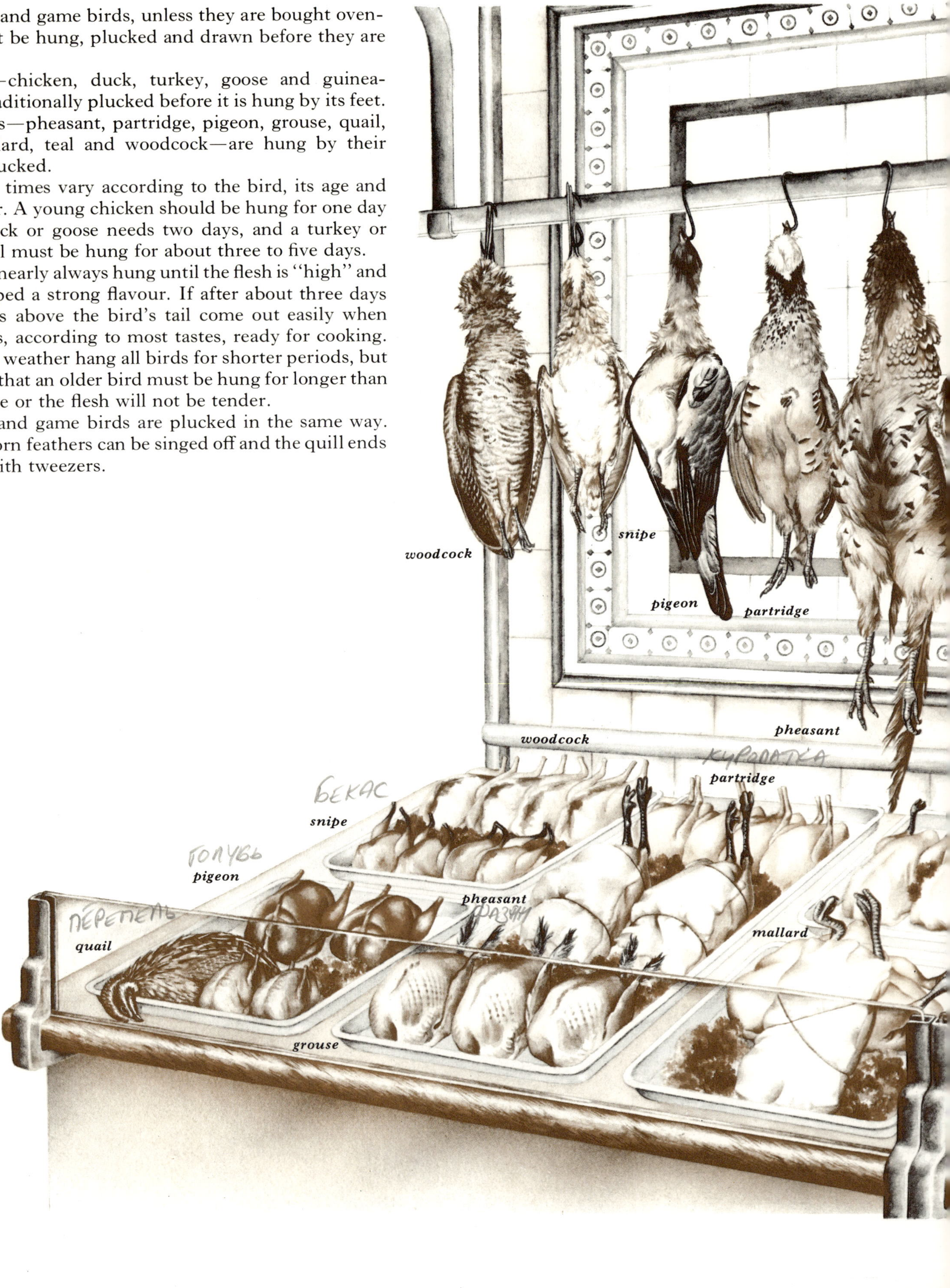

teal
grouse
mallard
guinea-
fowl
chicken
duck
goose
turkey
teal
duck
goose
turkey
guinea-fowl
chicken
I Jacob

Poultry and game birds

Drawing a bird is not a complicated process—it is just a matter of cutting off its head and feet and removing its entrails. (If a game bird is to be roasted, however, the feet are usually left on.) The bird's intestines are discarded, but the heart, gizzard and neck are kept for making stock or gravy. The liver is not used in stock but can be mixed into the stuffing. Before using the liver the gall bladder must be cut away from it. If the gall bladder breaks while you are doing this, discard the whole liver because it will taste unpleasantly bitter. The leg tendons are removed by making a slit in the side of the leg, just below the drumstick. Use a skewer to hook out the four or five tendons.

Plucking a bird

Plucking is done in the same way for all poultry and game birds. Lay the bird down on a table with the feet pointing towards you. Hold the bird firmly by the feet and begin plucking from under the wing towards the breast. Pull the feathers away from the direction of growth. If the bird is old, it can be plunged into boiling water for one minute (no more) to facilitate plucking: but if you do this the bird must be cooked at once or it will decompose.

Cleaning a bird

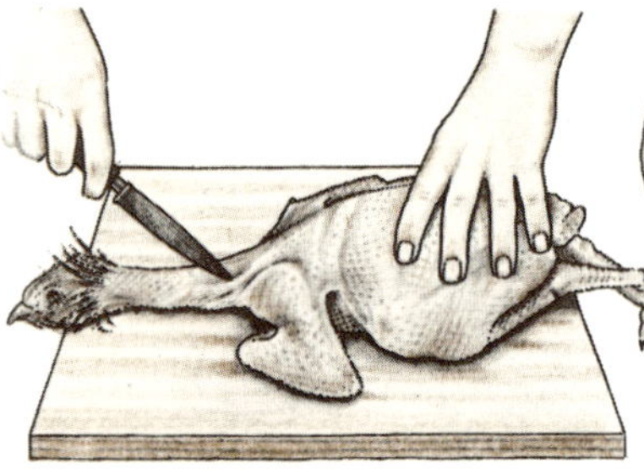

Using a small, very sharp knife, make a slit from the base of the neck to the base of the head and open up the slit.

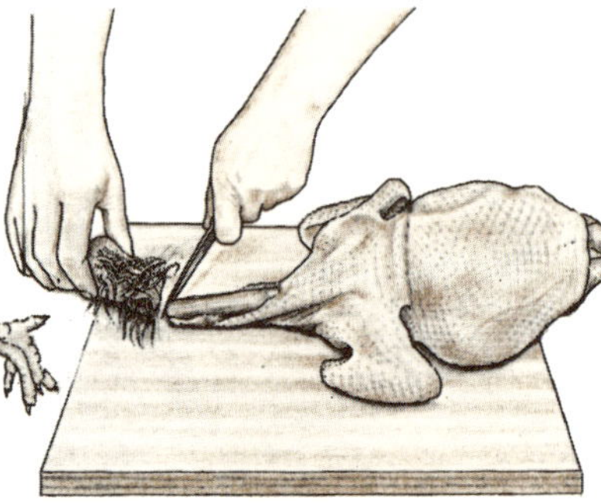

Stretch the neck slightly by pulling the head. With a sharp movement, cut off the head cleanly at the top of the neck.

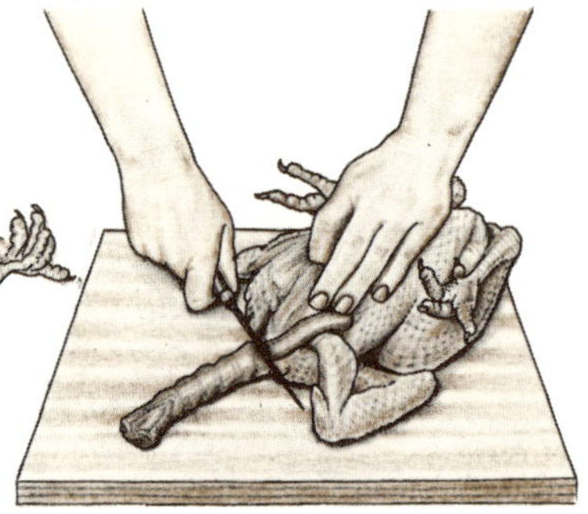

Pull the neck skin right back and scrape off the fat. Pull the neck and cut it off at the base. Reserve it for making stock.

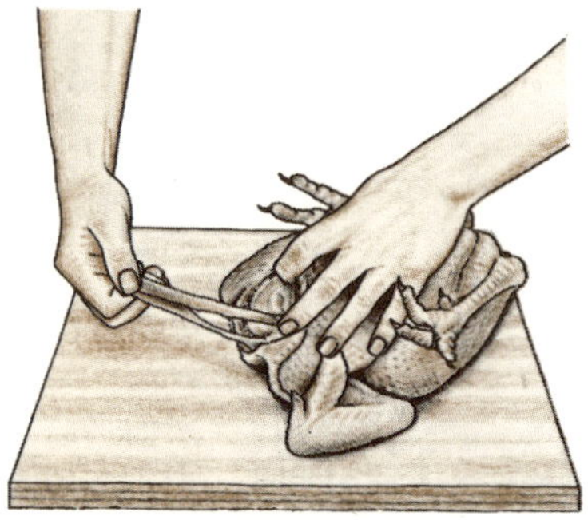

Hold the bird firmly and pull out the windpipe, crop and any fat from inside the neck cavity.

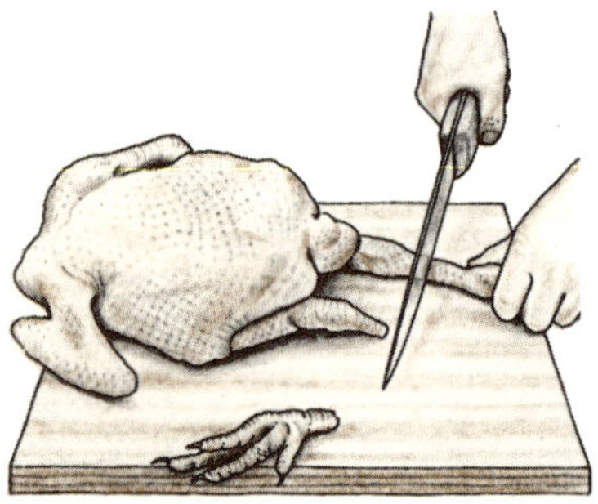

Turn the bird around and cut the skin around the base of the knee joint. Twist and pull off the lower part of the leg and tendons.

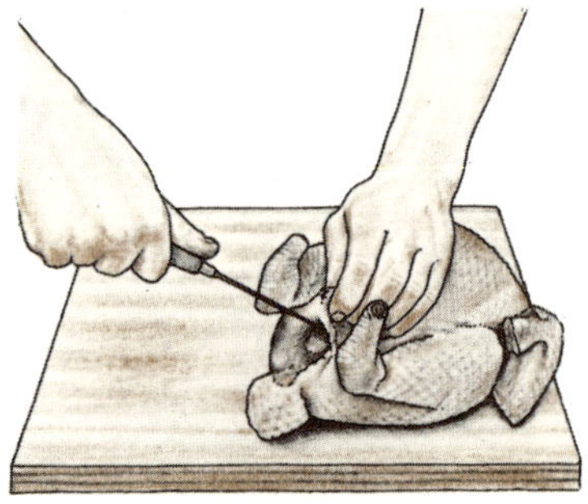

Make a short slit in the vent to increase the cavity opening. You can also make a slit above the vent to tuck the tail in later.

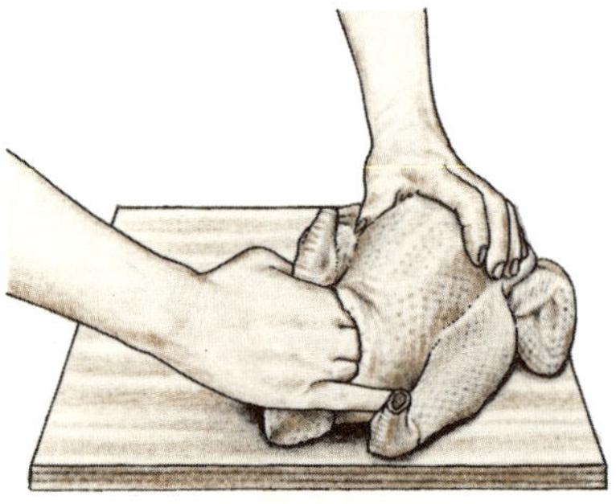

Insert your fingers, keeping them near the breastbone, and dislodge the entrails. Take great care not to break the gall bladder.

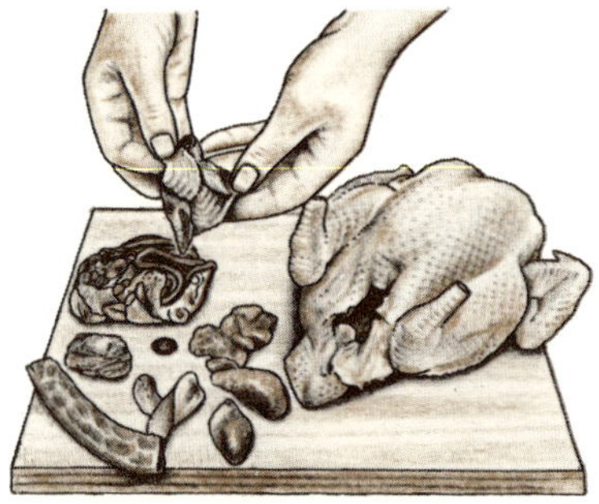

Carefully pull out all the entrails: the stomach, heart, intestines and liver. Cut the gall bladder away from the liver.

Jointing a bird

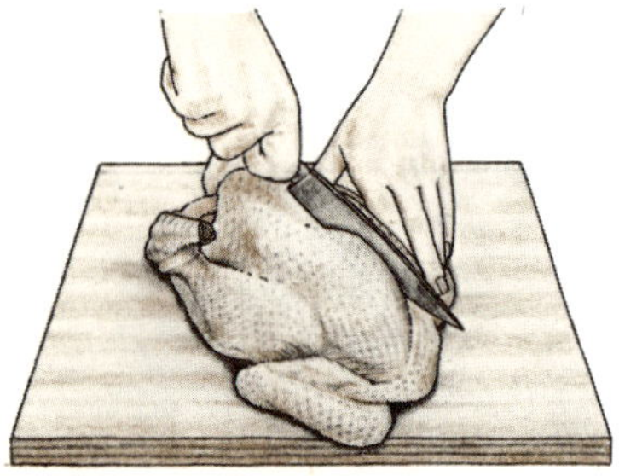

Using a very sharp carving knife, split the chicken through the breastbone right down the centre.

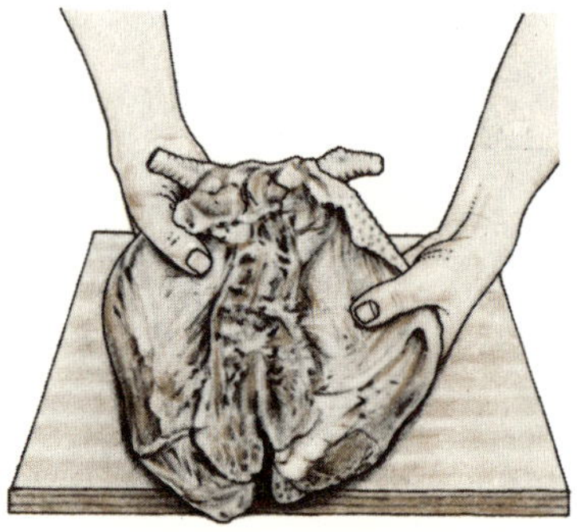

Open out the two halves and lay the chicken skin-side down on the table. Cut through the backbone.

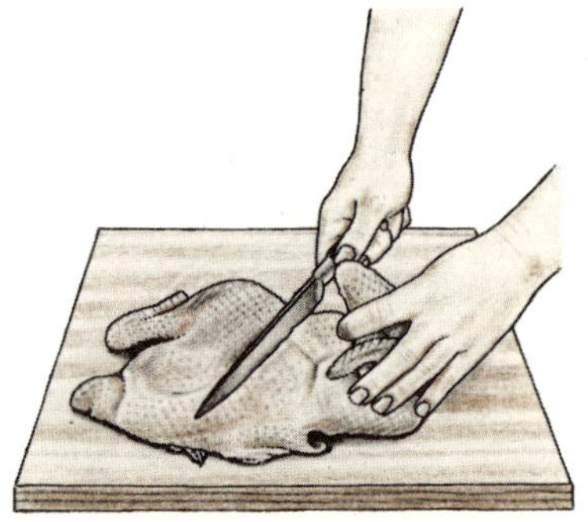

With a sharp knife, cut the thigh away from the wings and breast of the chicken.

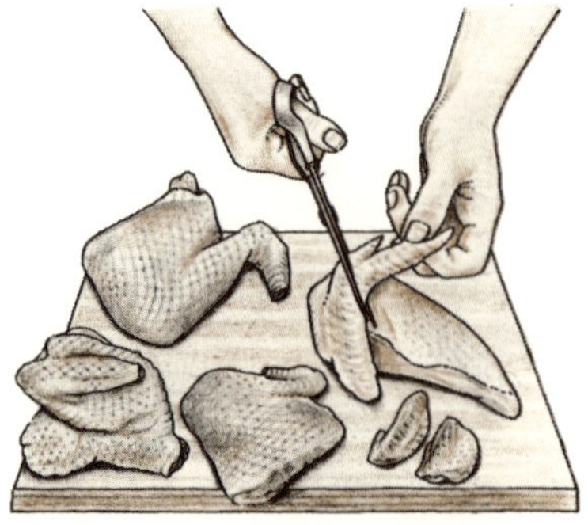

Use kitchen scissors to cut off the wings and cut the rest of the chicken into smaller pieces.

Trussing a bird

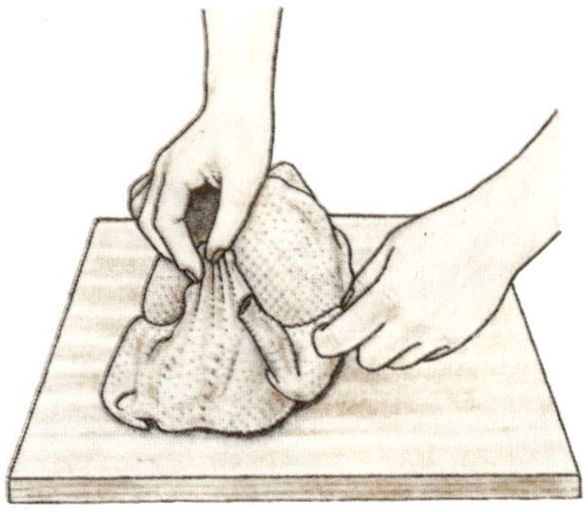

Place the bird on its breast and fold over the neck skin. Pull and stretch the skin over the back.

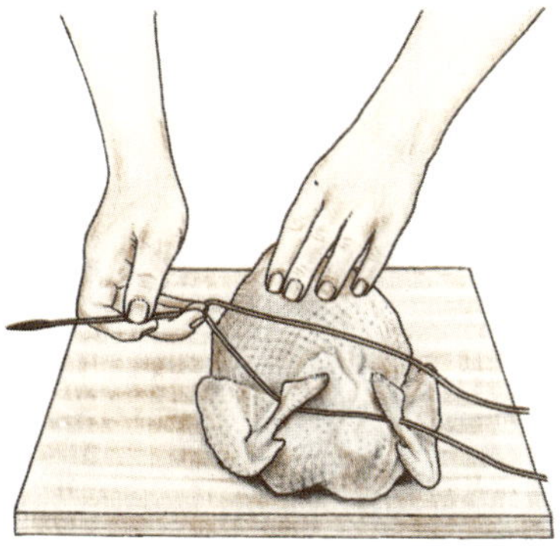

Bend the wings back to hold the neck skin in place and tie them with trussing string.

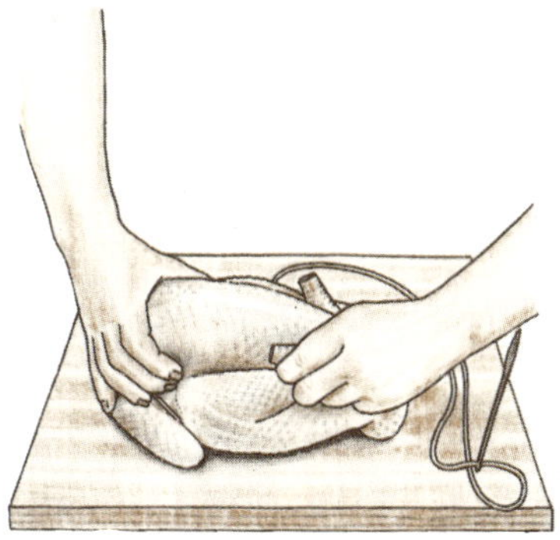

Turn the chicken over and push the legs together to plump up the breast.

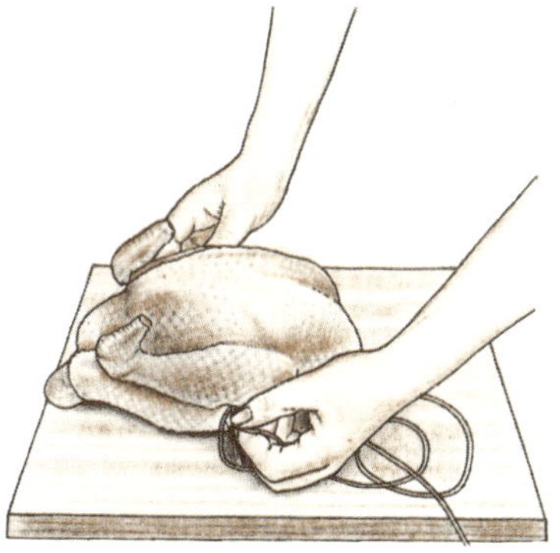

Push the threaded trussing needle into the fleshy part of one thigh and push it through the body.

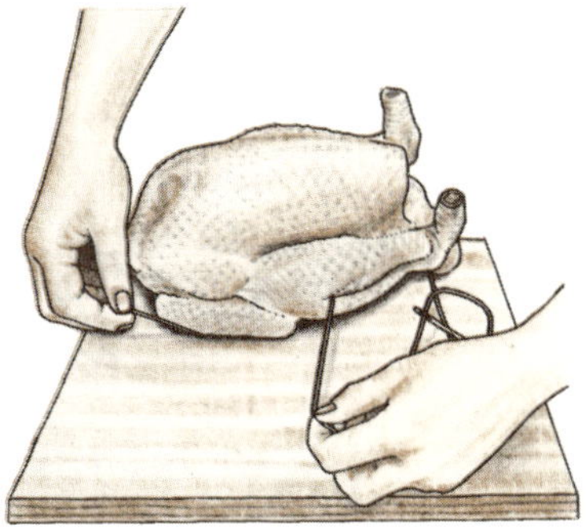

The needle and thread should come out of the other thigh in exactly the same place.

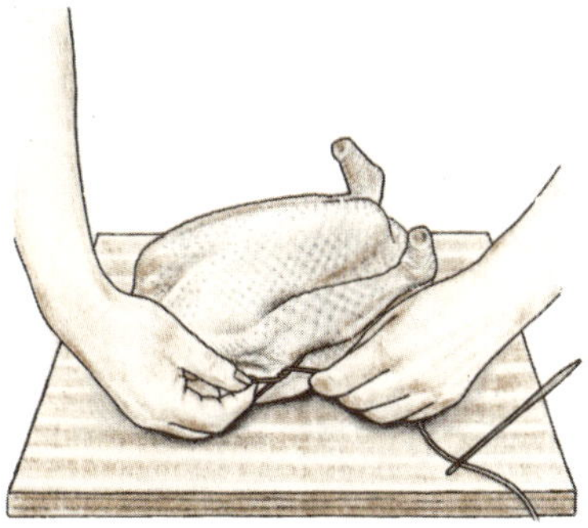

Pass the loose end of string from the other thigh under the body and tie with the other end.

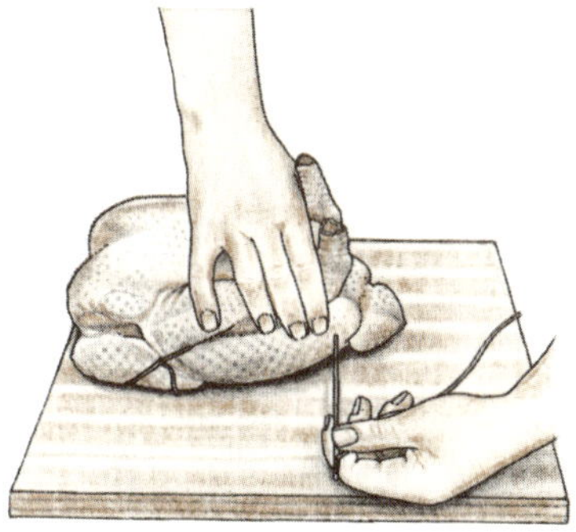

Pass the threaded needle through just under the parson's nose and pull the two ends together.

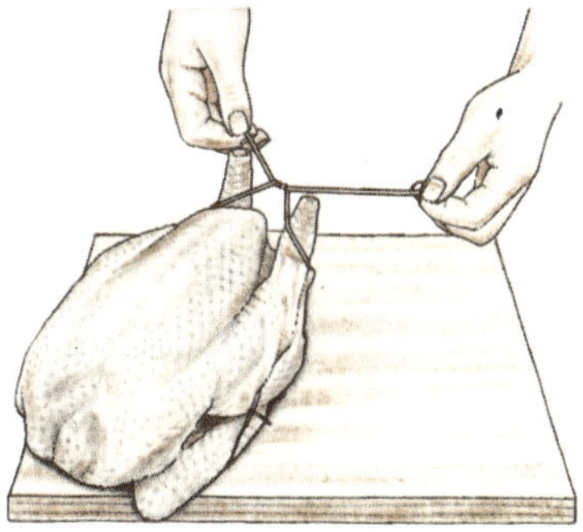

Use the two loose ends of string to tie the back legs together firmly in place.

Boning a bird

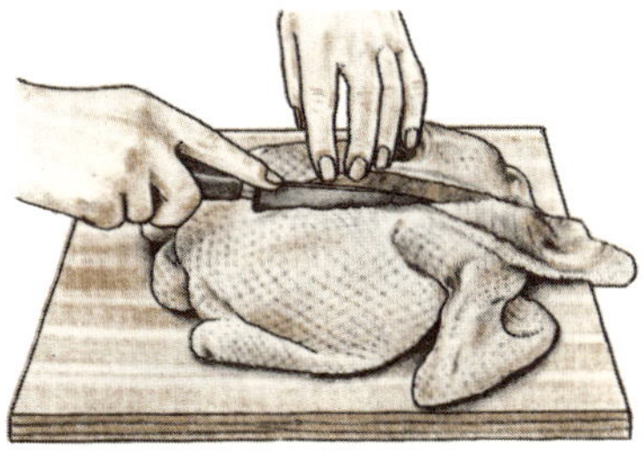

Lay the bird breast-side down on the work surface. With a very sharp knife, make a cut along the backbone, piercing the skin.

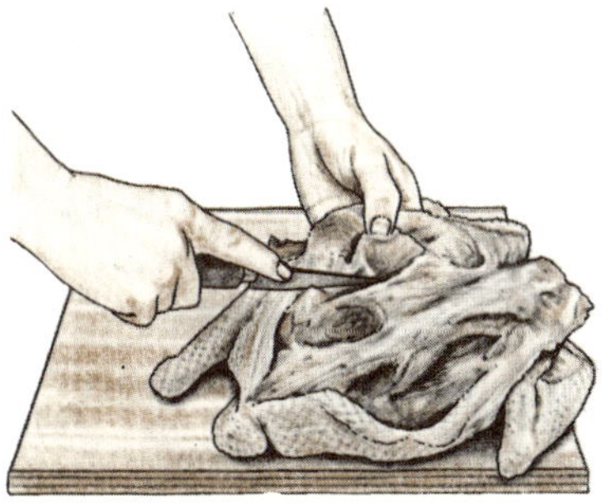

Resting the knife against the bone and keeping it flat, work the flesh away from the backbone on both sides.

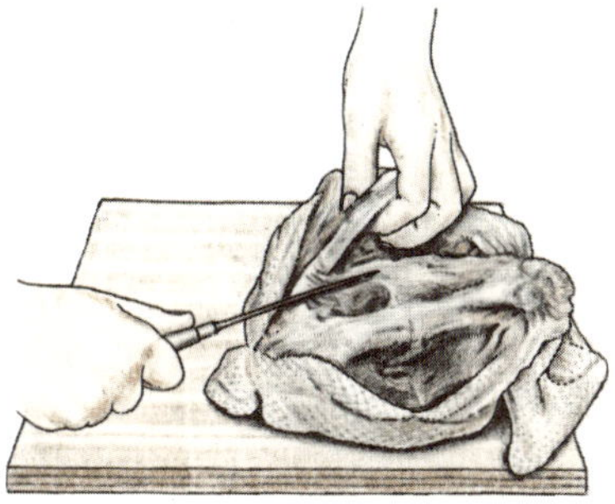

Trim the flesh away from the thigh bone and lift out the thigh bone. Be very careful not to pierce the flesh.

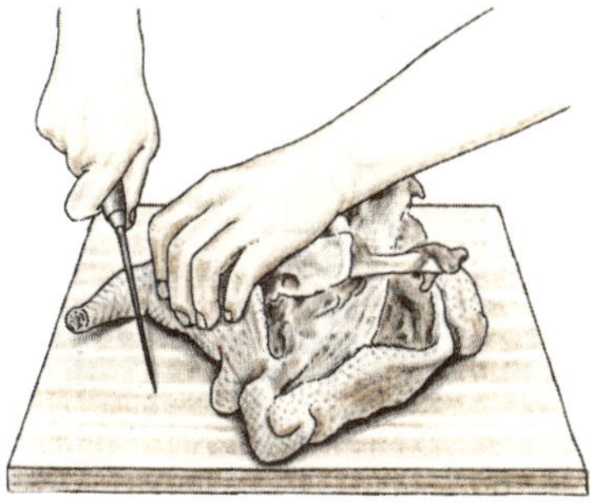

With a clean, sharp movement, chop the leg off at the knee joint. The wings are left intact to give the chicken a better shape.

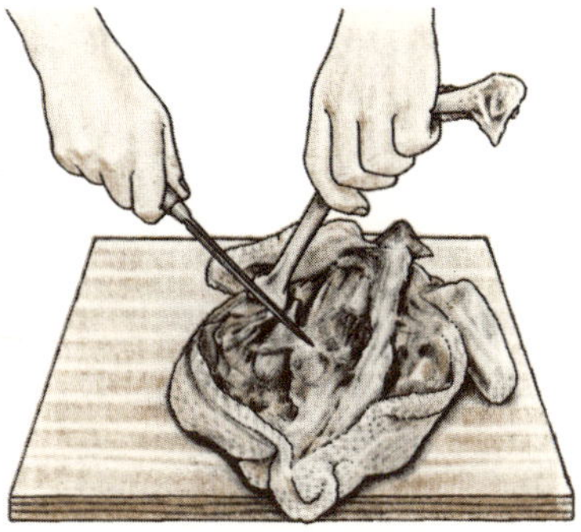

With the edge of the knife, scrape all the meat from the leg bone. Lift out the leg bone and reserve with the other bones for stock.

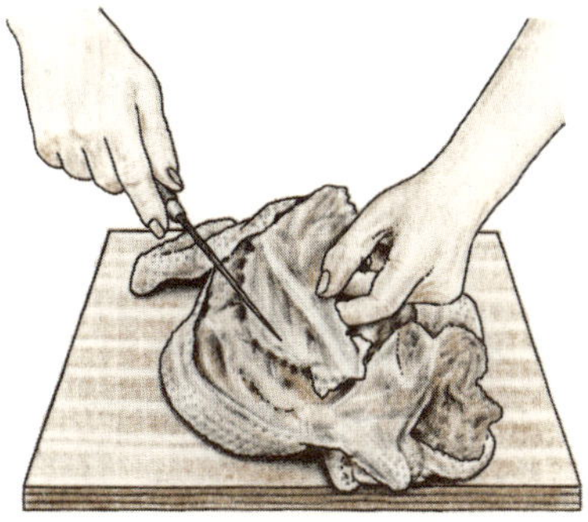

Very carefully scrape the meat off the rib cage. Great care must be taken at this stage as very little flesh covers this part.

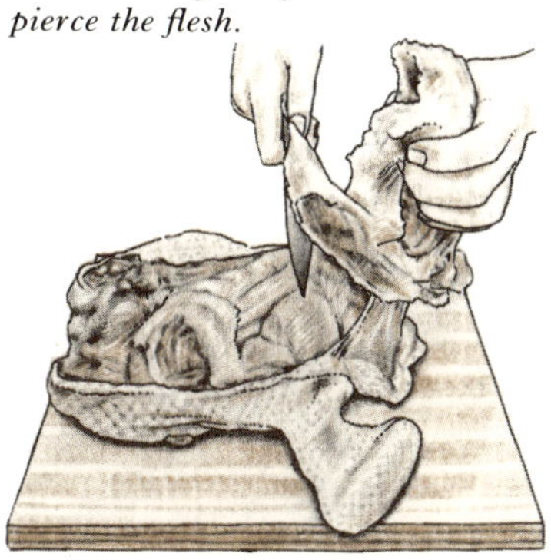

When all the meat has been scraped off, lift out the carcass. The chicken is now ready for stuffing.

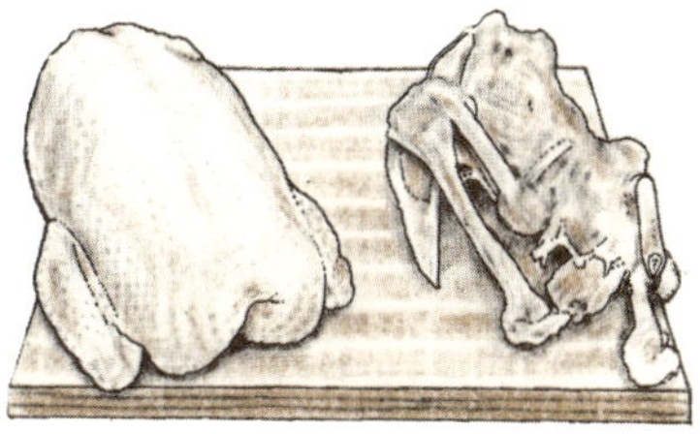

Stuff the bird, fold the sides over, tuck in the ends and sew into place. Plump the bird into shape ; it can now be cooked.

Meat and game

A good butcher will do most of the preparation of meat for you. There will be occasions, however, when he may be too busy or when at the last moment you decide you want to bone and stuff a joint or turn a rack of lamb into a crown roast.

Some cuts of meat require little preparation, others much time-consuming trimming, cutting, beating or sewing. But whatever the task there is no doubt that practice will bring perfection.

Boning and rolling is one of the jobs that is much less complicated than it looks. Although meat cooked on the bone has more flavour, a boned and rolled joint has the advantage that it can be stuffed and is much easier to carve.

Other preparations that you can easily learn to do yourself include paunching and skinning a hare or rabbit, making noisettes of lamb or a crown roast from two best ends.

You can also learn to salt or pickle meat. Such pieces of beef as silverside, brisket, flank and tongue are soaked (for several days, or in some cases, weeks) in a brine solution before being cooked, or they may be pickled in a similar solution to which such spices as mace, ginger and cloves are added. In the days before refrigeration, salting and pickling was a way of preserving meat. Today it is done purely for the delicious flavour it gives the meat.

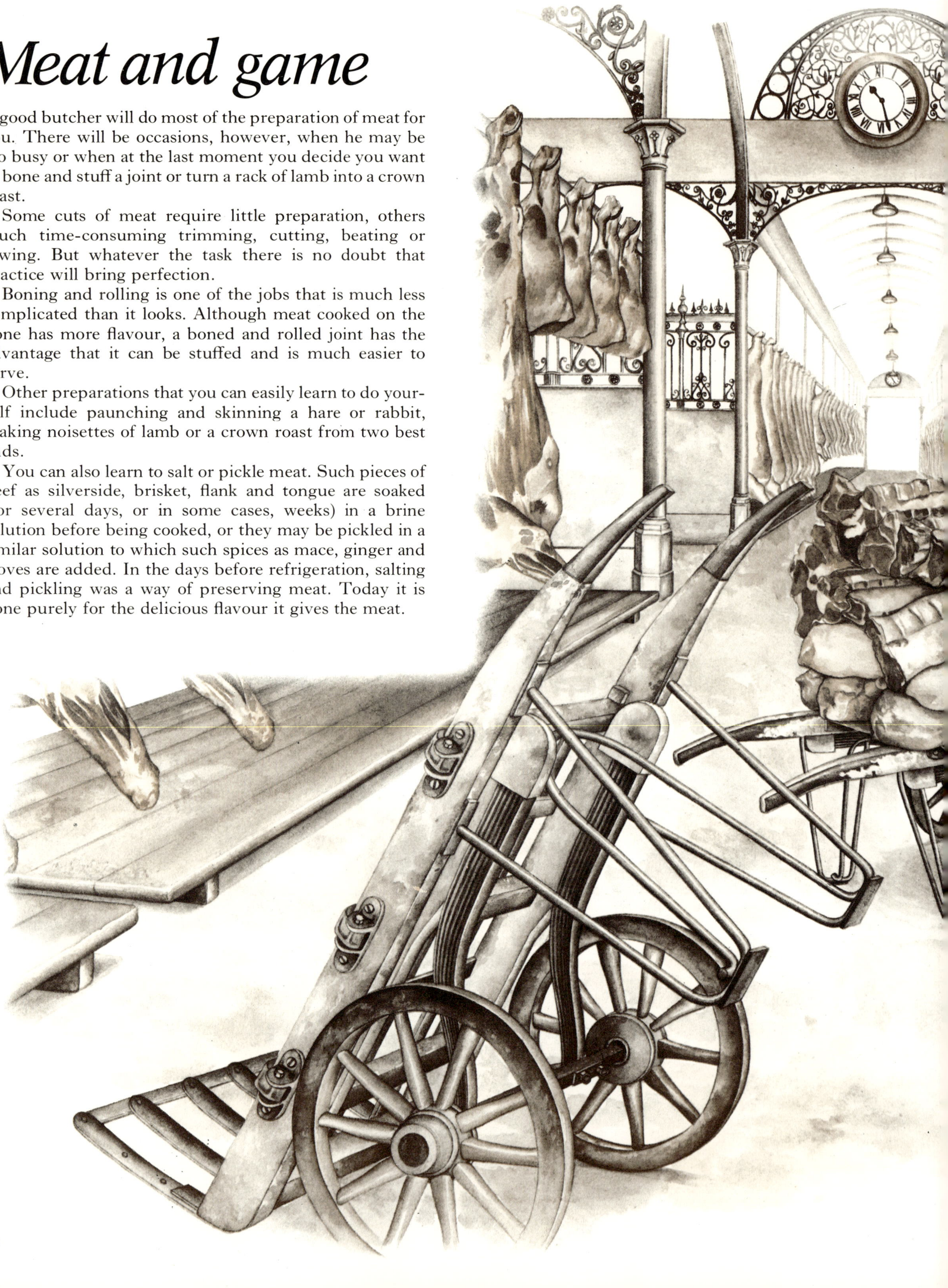

Ingrid Jacob

Beef and veal

Traditionally such joints as sirloin of beef and shoulder of veal are boned and rolled before being roasted. To prevent a lean joint, such as fillet, from drying out, lard it with thin strips of pork fat or fat bacon. Use a special larding needle and thread the fat through the surface of the meat.

To tenderize beef, marinate it in beer for up to twenty-four hours. For two pounds (900 g) of stewing steak use three-quarters of a pint (450 ml) of beer, four fluid ounces (125 ml) of corn oil, two tablespoons of lemon juice mixed with salt, sugar, garlic and mustard to taste.

If you have a mincer, make your own mince—it is the only way to control the balance of lean meat and fat.

Larding a fillet

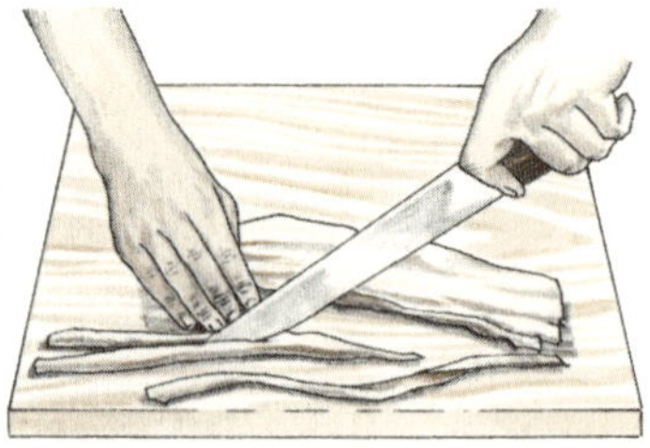

To lard a fillet of beef, take a piece of back fat and cut it into thin, even-sized strips. Clip one strip on to a larding needle.

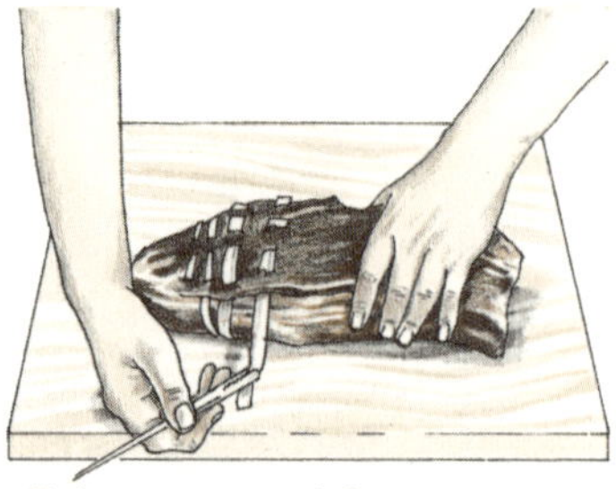

Being very careful not to tear through the surface of the meat, thread the needle and fat in and out of the fillet.

Tournedos

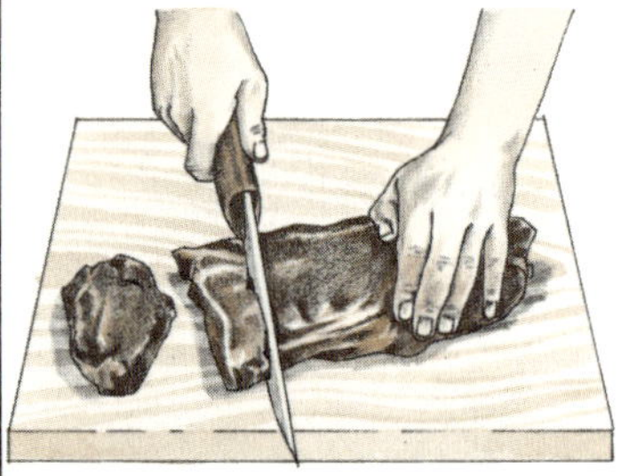

To make tournedos, cut a beef fillet into thick steaks. Cut strips of back fat wide and long enough to fit around the steaks.

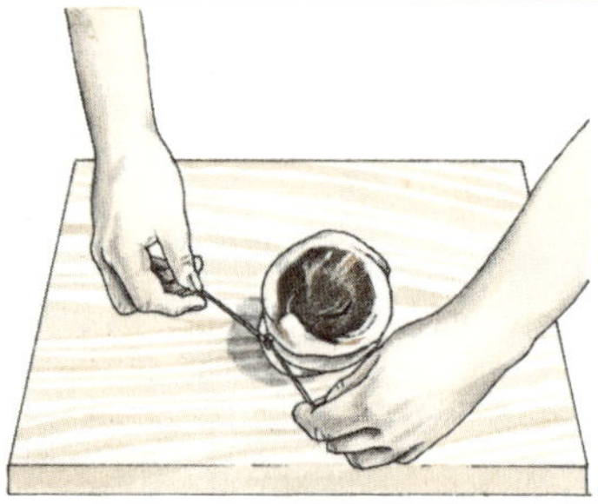

Shape each steak into a round and tie a piece of the fat securely around the steak, fastening it on with trussing string.

Veal escalopes

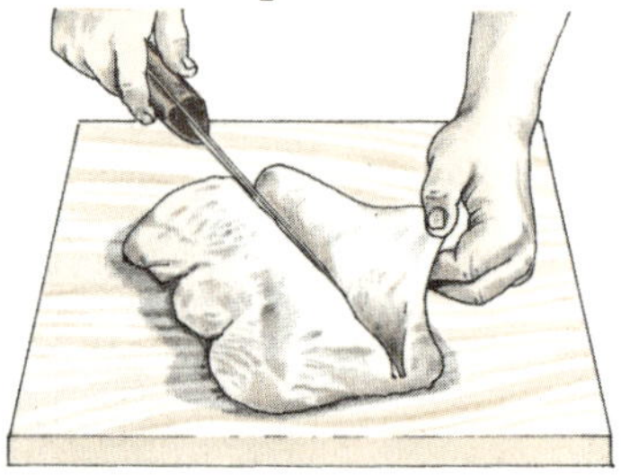

With a long, very sharp meat knife, cut an even slice from a piece of veal fillet.

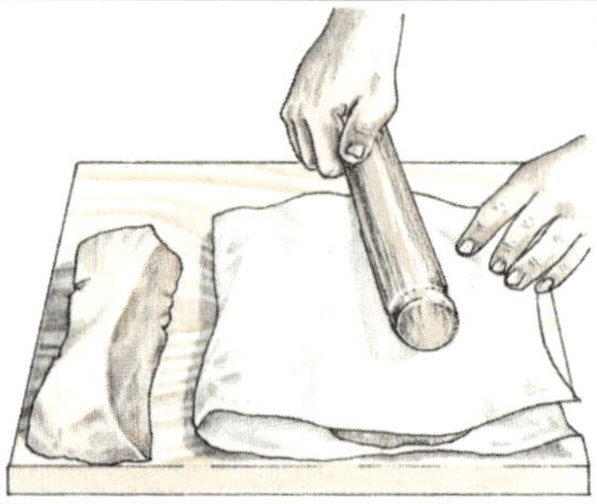

Place the slice of fillet between two sheets of greaseproof paper and beat it with a blunt object until it is paper thin.

Boning sirloin

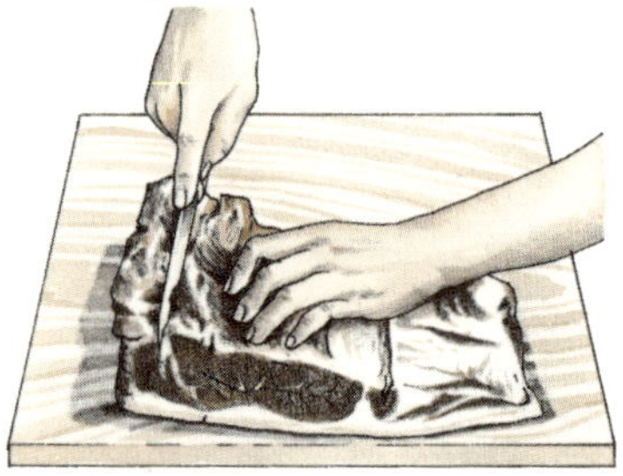

Take a wing rib of beef (a sirloin without the fillet) and lay it on its fatty side. Cut out the undercut.

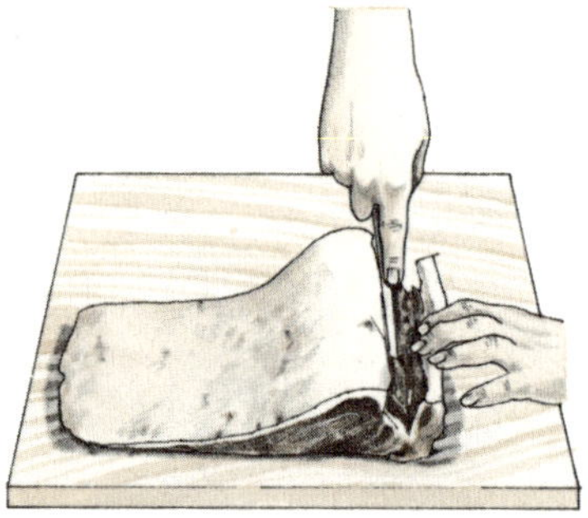

Turn the meat over. Cut down the other side of the chine bone, pulling it away from the meat.

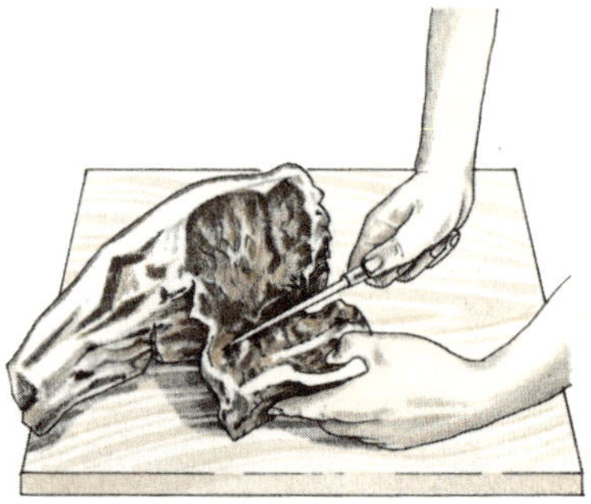

Turn the meat over on its side and cut away more of the flesh, keeping the blade of the knife flat against the bone.

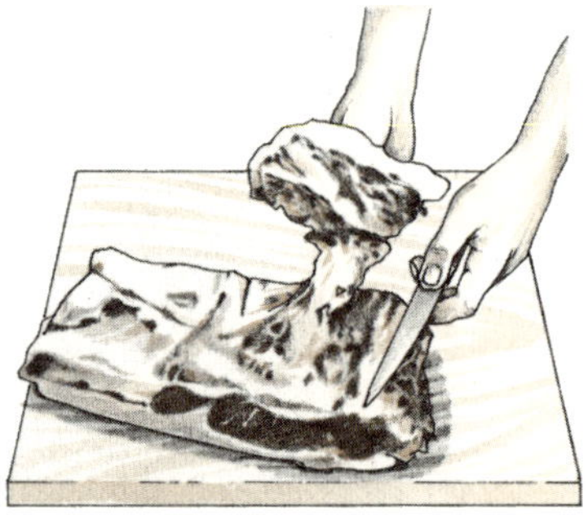

Turn the meat over, laying it fat-side down. Cut away the last pieces of meat and fat from the bone and pull the bone right off.

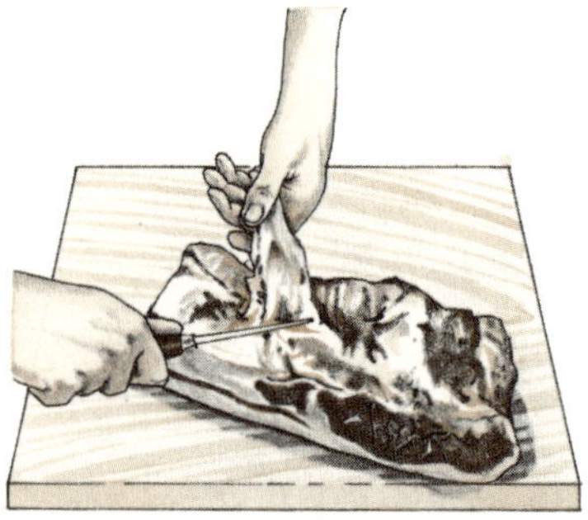

Depending on the size of the sirloin, there will be either three or four rib bones in the meat and these must be cut out.

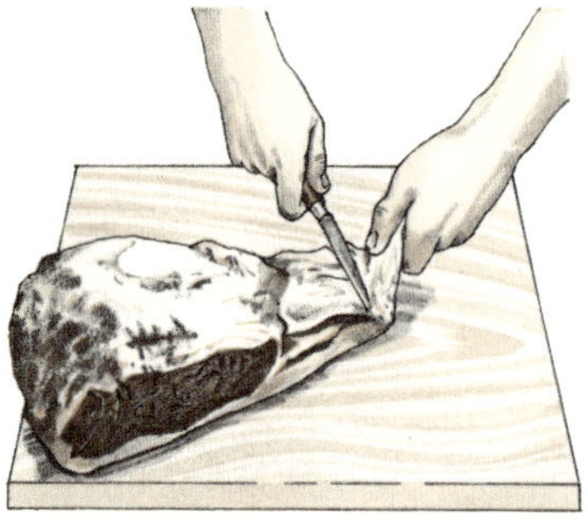

Turn the meat around and cut and scrape the meat and fat from the rib bones as you pull them out.

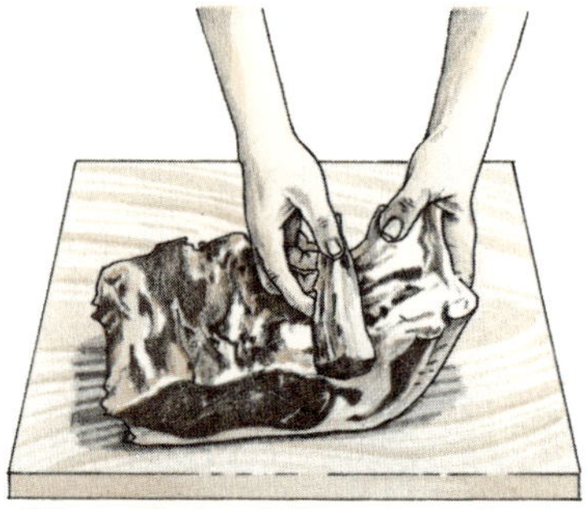

When all the rib bones have been cut out, put the undercut on top of the meat and pack it in.

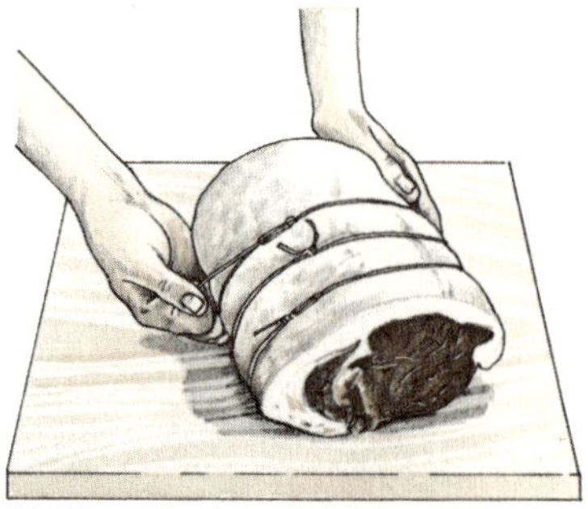

Roll up the boned sirloin and tie the roll in several places with trussing string.

Boning veal breast

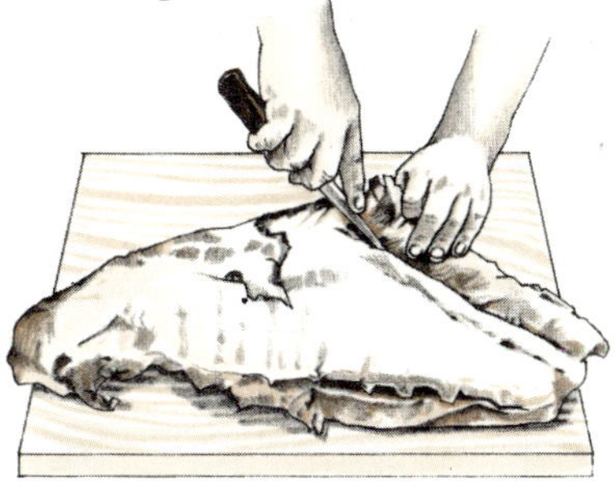

Lay the veal breast fat-side down. Make a slit along the length of the skirt and pull it back.

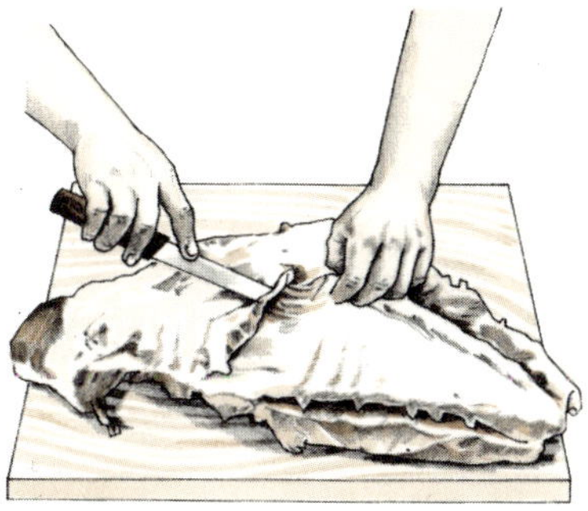

Trim the surplus fat from the surface of the meat.

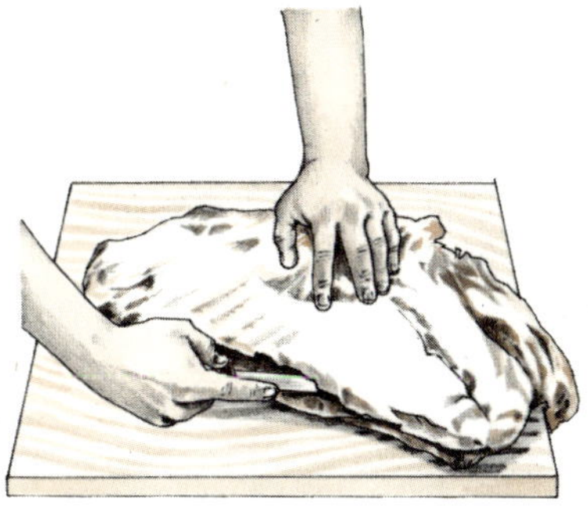

Keeping the knife flat against the underside of the rib bones, begin slitting the meat through the middle.

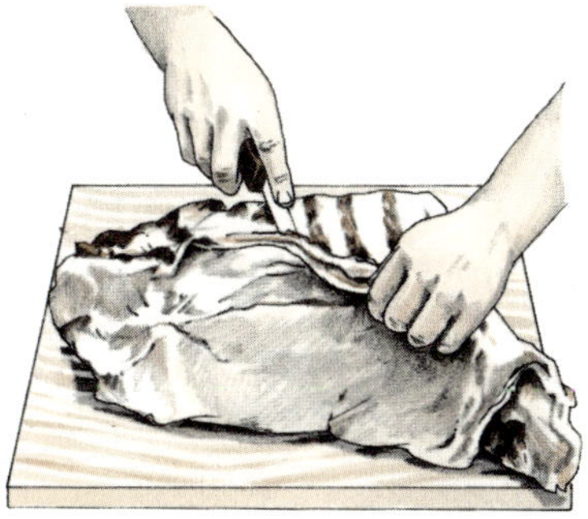

Hold the meat on its side and continue slitting the meat down the middle, cutting right against the rib bones.

As you continue cutting down into the meat, the meat will fall to one side, leaving the ribs bare.

Continue cutting right down until the whole rib section can be pulled away from the meat.

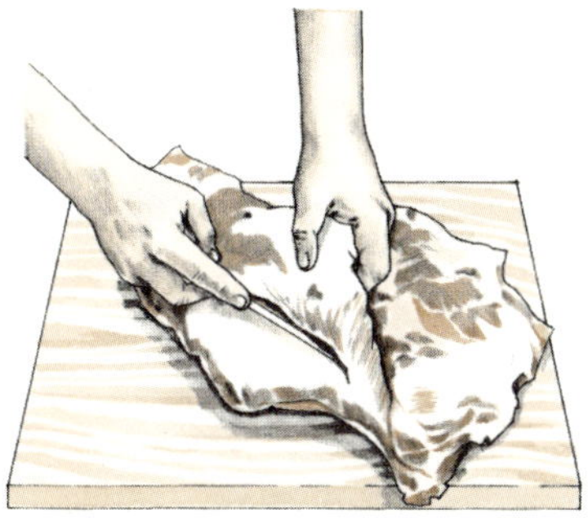

Begin cutting through the middle of the meat as before, separating the meat from the fat. Remove excess fat.

Stop cutting before you get to the other side of the meat. Open the meat out like a book. It can now be stuffed and rolled.

Boning a veal loin

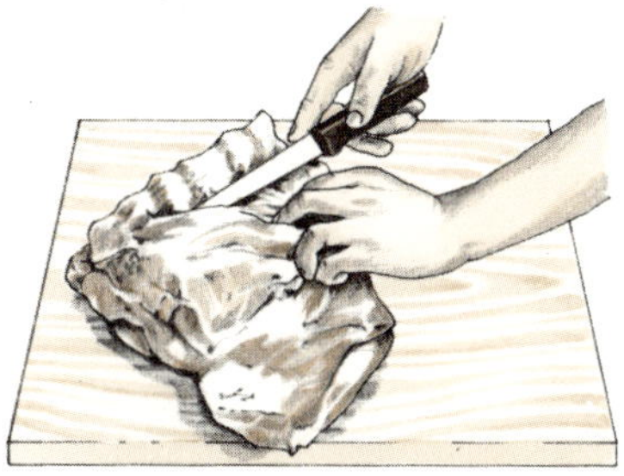

Cutting close to the bone, begin loosening the fillet away from the chine bone.

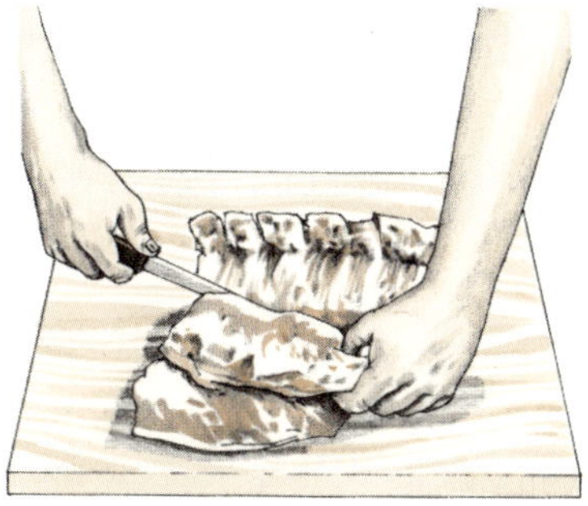

Continue cutting down the chine bone, pulling the fillet away gently as you cut.

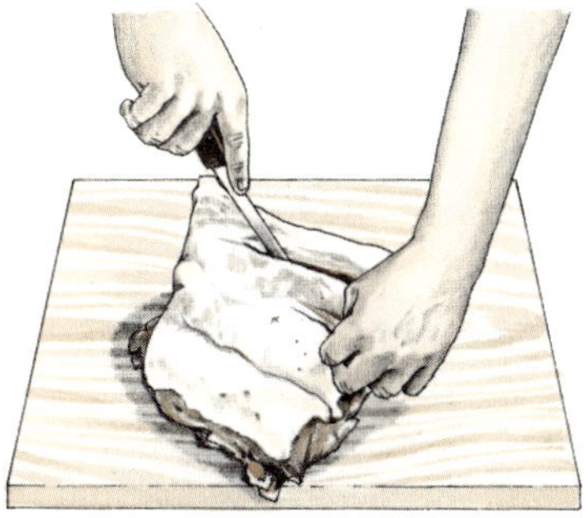

Turn the meat over so the fatty side is uppermost. Make a cut through the other side of the chine bone.

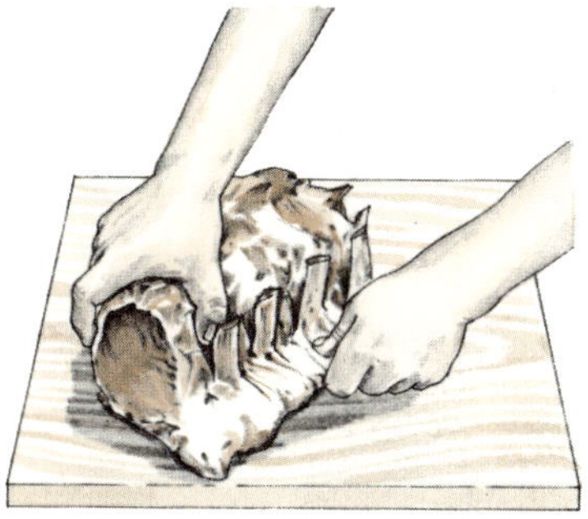

Hold the meat down and move the bone back and forth to loosen it from the meat.

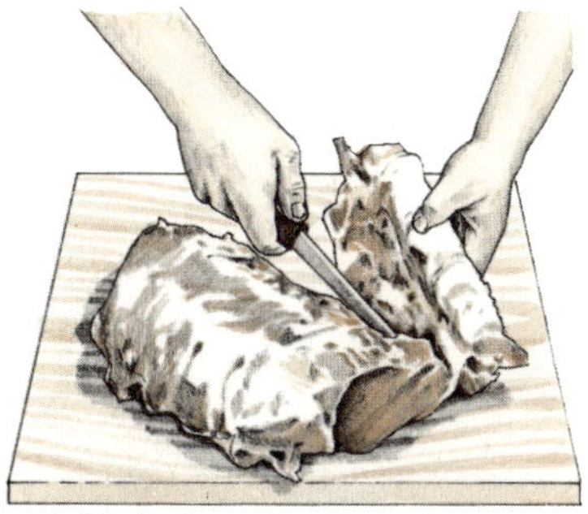

Hold the bone firmly and cut it right away from the meat.

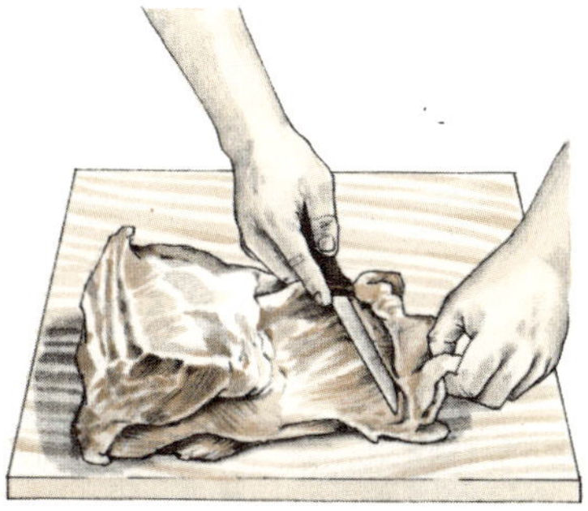

Trim off the back gristle and all surplus fat from the meat.

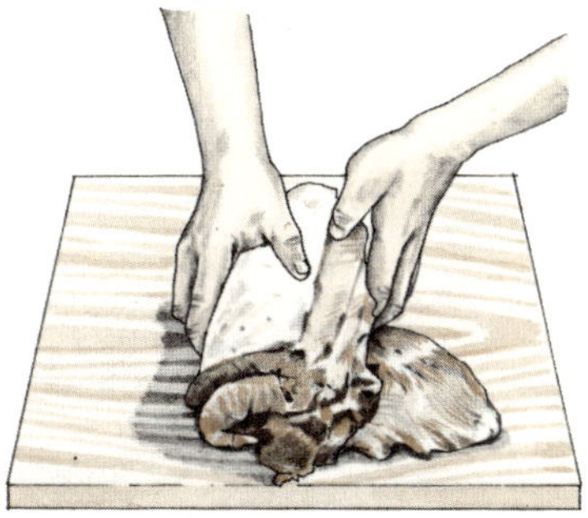

Roll the meat up and plump it into shape. The roll should be fairly tight.

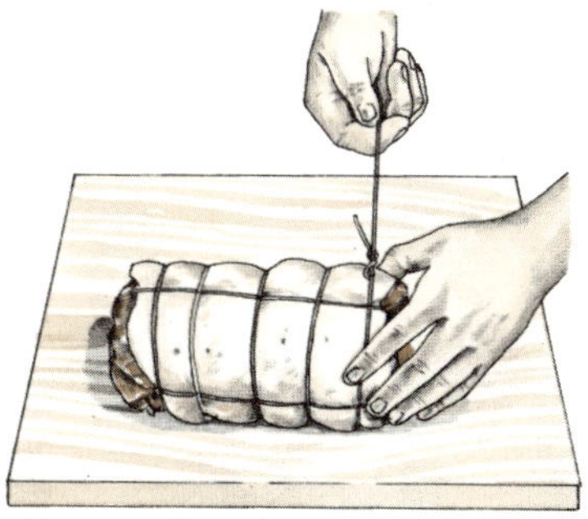

Tie the roll up in several places across and lengthways.

Mutton and lamb

Lamb is the flesh of a sheep aged between about three and twelve months old. The flesh of an older animal is known as mutton. The most popular cuts of lamb for roasting or braising are the leg, shoulder and breast, which may be cooked on the bone or boned and rolled.

Loin and chump chops and cutlets may be fried or grilled, but before cooking nick the fat that surrounds the meat so that the meat does not curl up as it cooks.

Two impressive dishes, crown roast and guard of honour, are prepared by sewing together two best ends of lamb. Each best end is made up of about eight cutlets or ribs. Scrape the fat and gristle from the narrow end of each bone to form the "prongs" of the crown and the "crossed swords" of the guard of honour.

Noisettes

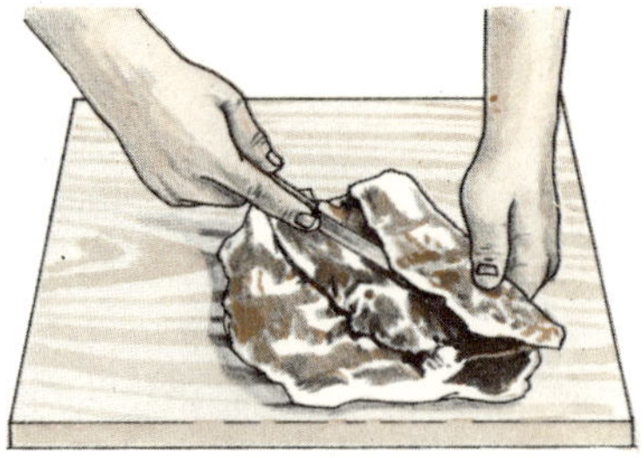

To make noisettes, carefully cut the chine bone from a loin of lamb and reserve for stock.

Using a sharp knife, trim the fat from the thin end of the loin to make a thin, even layer.

Now beat the layer of fat with a blunt instrument, a rolling pin for example, to flatten it.

Roll the meat up tightly so that it is completely enclosed by the layer of fat.

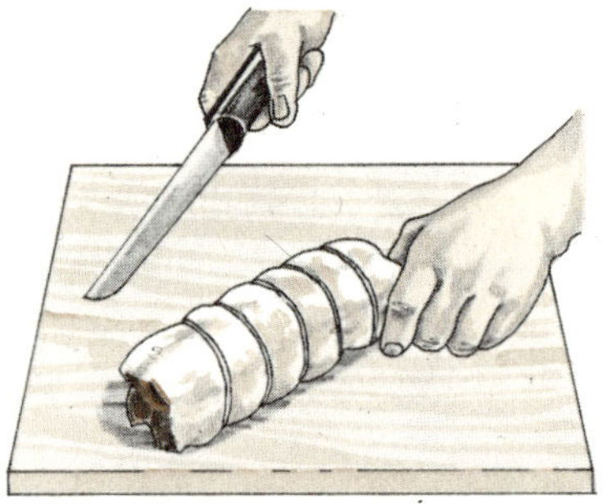

Tie the roll up at regular intervals with trussing string or strong button thread.

With a very sharp knife, cut the meat in thick slices between the string to make the noisettes.

Crown roast and guard of honour

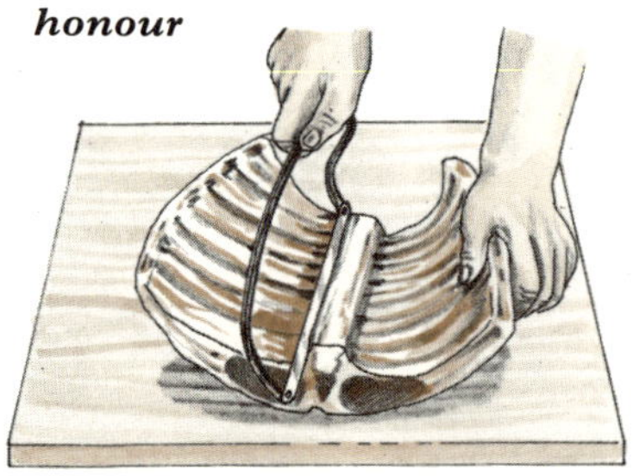

Lay the best end of lamb fat-side down on a wooden board and saw either side of the chine bone with a meat saw to loosen it.

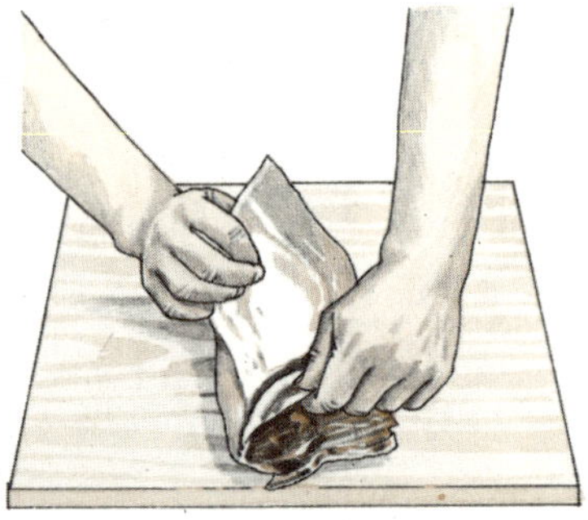

Bend the meat inwards and, holding one end firmly, peel off the surface layer of skin. It should come away easily.

Cut out the loosened chine bone. Cut down the middle of the meat right to the other side and separate the two halves.

With a sharp-pointed knife, trim the fat and skin from the end of the rib bones. This is known as "French trimming".

Tie the two halves together by passing trussing string through the top and bottom of the end ribs and tying a knot.

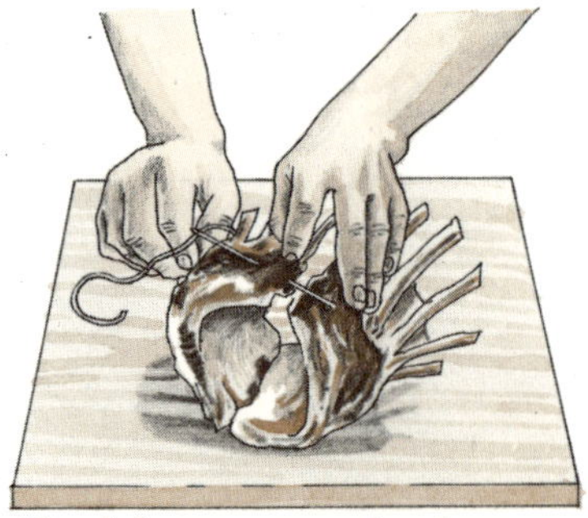

Bend the meat around to form a circle and sew it up with trussing string to keep the circle together.

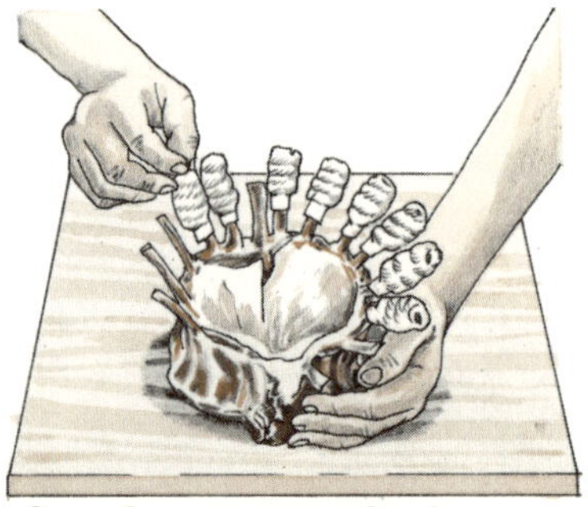

Once the crown roast has been cooked, it is traditionally garnished with a paper frill on top of each rib bone.

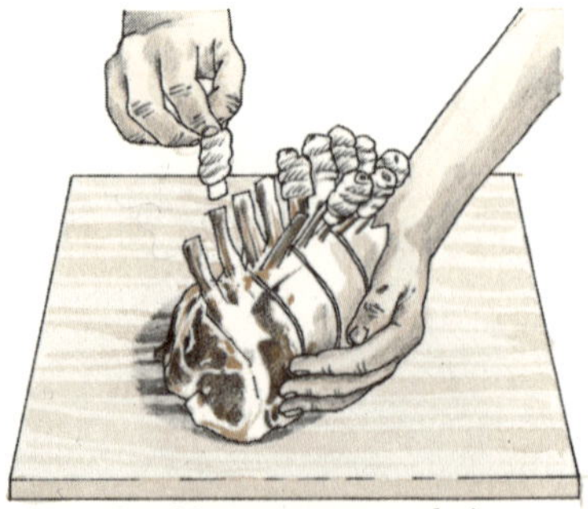

Guards of honour are made in the same way except that the two halves are sewn and tied together with the bones crossing.

Boning a shoulder of lamb

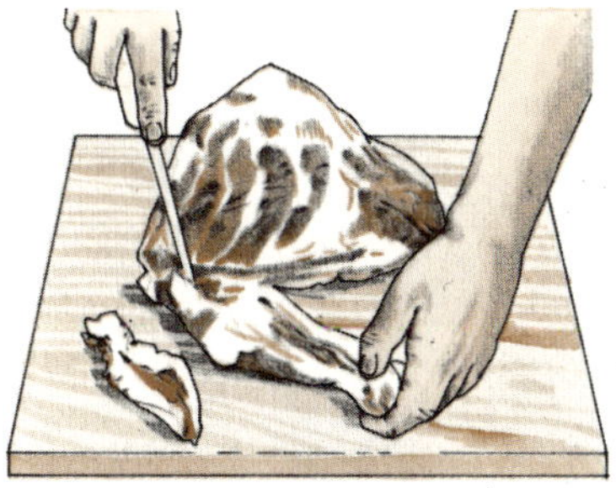

Trim off the fat from the shoulder. Hold the meat by the shoulder bone and loosen the meat from the bone and joint.

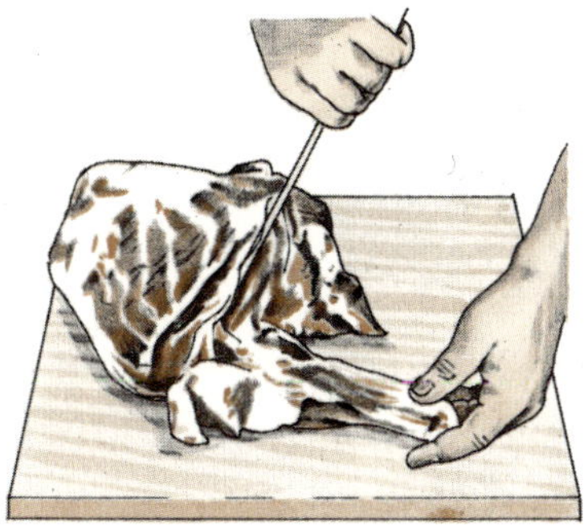

With a very sharp knife, cut through the joint and bend the bone back until the joint cracks.

Slice through any meat and fat between the bone and the body of the meat and pull out the shoulder bone.

Being very careful not to break through the surface of the skin, loosen the meat all around the middle bone.

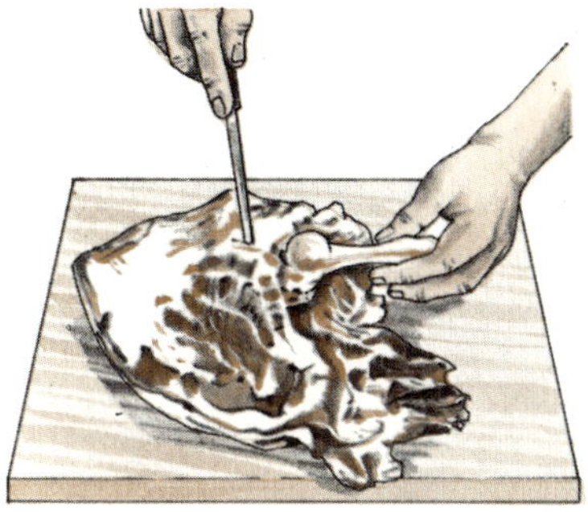

Cutting off the meat and fat as you go, pull out the middle bone.

Keeping the knife as close as possible to the bone, loosen the meat from the shoulder blade.

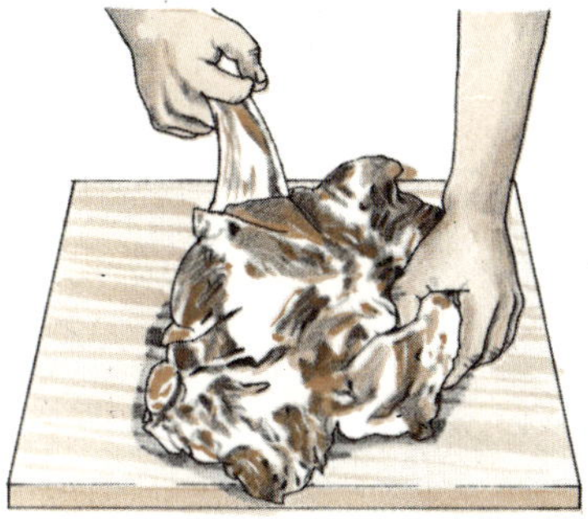

Hold one end of the shoulder blade bone firmly and pull it out.

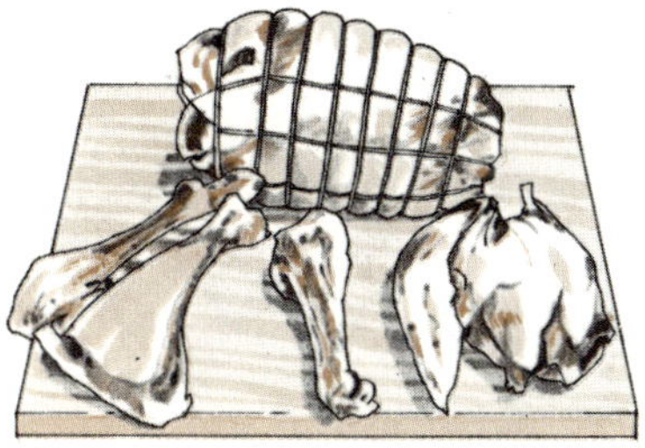

Roll up the meat, fat-side outwards, and tie the roll with trussing string. Reserve all the bones for stock.

Boning a leg of lamb

Hold the leg of lamb firmly at the shin end. With the point of a knife, loosen and lift out the aitchbone.

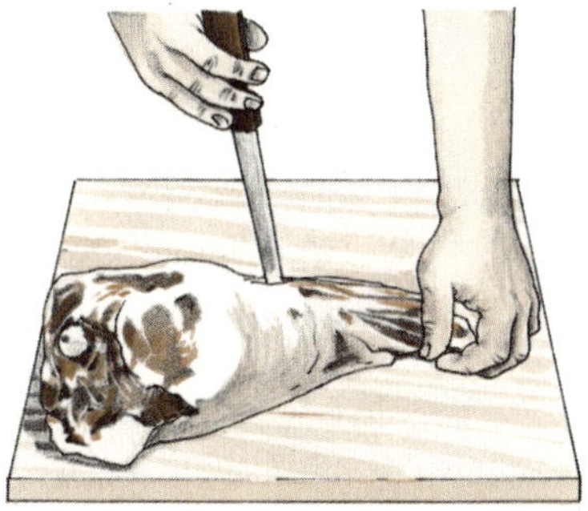

Turn the leg around and, with the point of the knife, cut round the shin bone to loosen it.

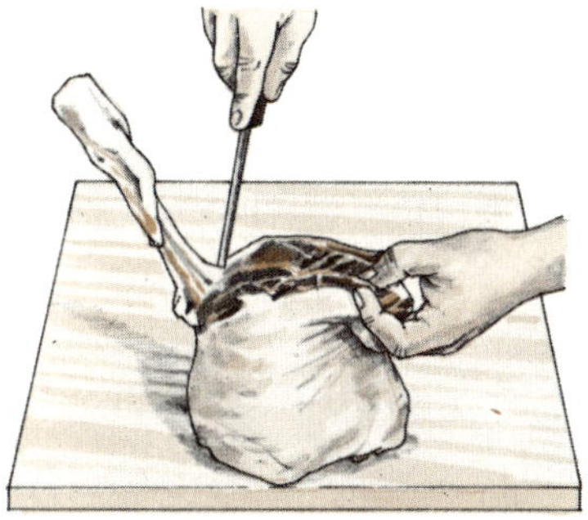

Lift the whole shin bone out of the leg, cutting close to the bone as you pull it out.

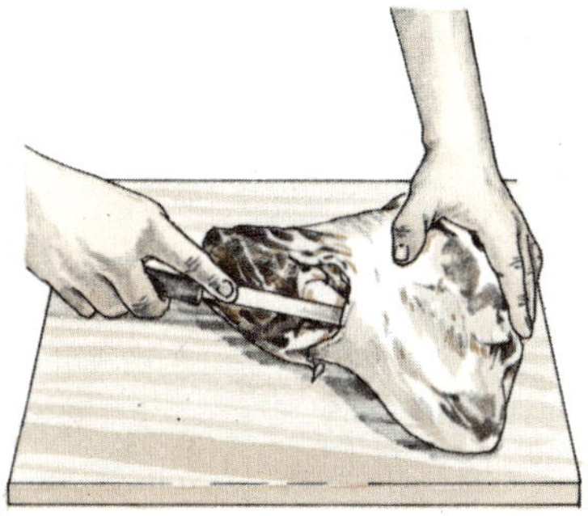

Keeping the knife close against the bone, tunnel into the leg to loosen the middle bone. Be careful not to break the skin.

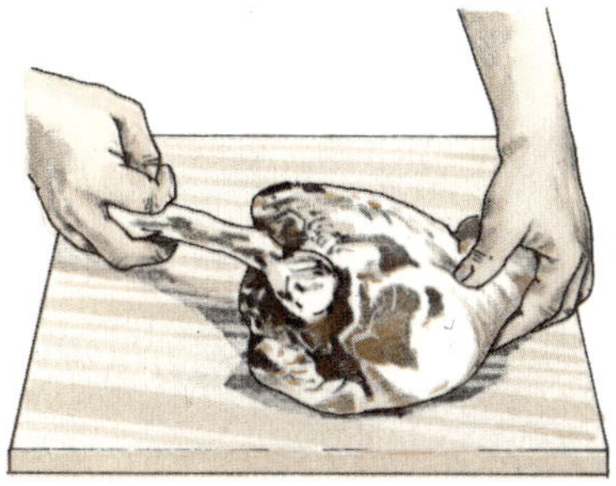

Loosen the middle bone from the cavity left by the aitchbone as well, and then pull out the whole bone from the leg.

Trim around the small bone at the shin end and pull it out. This is the last bone in the leg.

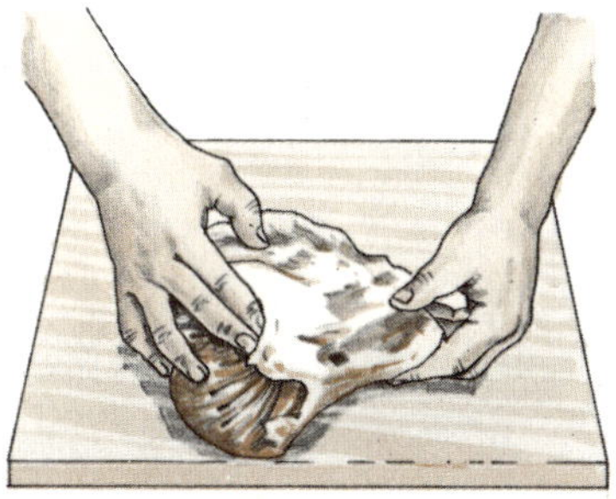

Push the shin end of the meat into the cavity left by the bone, tucking it in neatly.

Plump the meat into shape and tie it securely at regular intervals with trussing string.

Pork

To prepare pork for roasting you must either remove the skin altogether, or score it deeply and rub with salt and fat for deliciously crisp crackling. When you are cooking a pork chop or gammon steak, make several nicks in the fat to prevent it from curling up during cooking.

A bacon or gammon joint should be soaked in cold water for at least two to three hours and preferably overnight before cooking, to reduce its saltiness. Remove the skin after boiling and, if you like, score the joint, stud it with cloves, cover it with brown sugar and bake it.

Bacon rashers that are to be fried should have their rinds removed. Store the rinds in the refrigerator and use them to add flavour to soups and casseroles.

Bacon rolls

To make bacon rolls first cut the rind off with kitchen scissors and then cut away any gristle with a sharp knife.

Using a round-bladed knife and being careful not to tear the bacon, pull and stretch it, roll it up and fasten if necessary.

Pork escalopes

Lay the pork fillet on a wooden board and slit it down the middle to just past the centre.

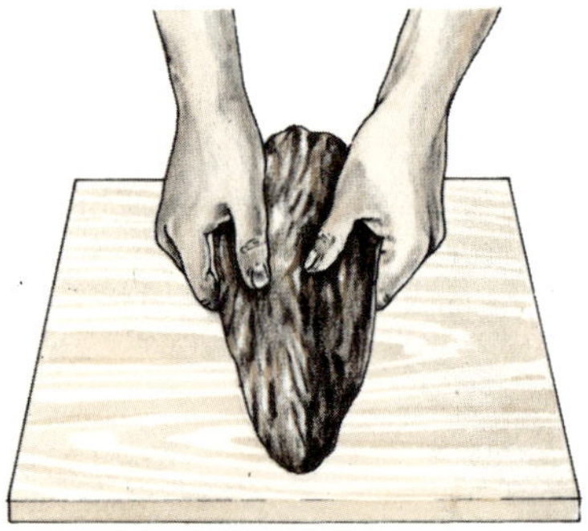

Open the fillet out like a book and lay it between two sheets of greaseproof paper.

Pound the fillet with a blunt instrument, a rolling pin, for example, until paper thin.

Remove and discard the greaseproof paper—the fillet is now ready to be cooked.

Gammon

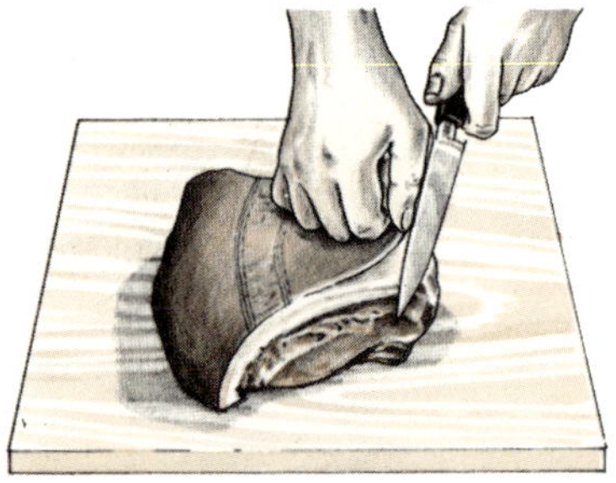

Put the cooked gammon, skin-side up, on a wooden board and make a small cut to get a grip on skin.

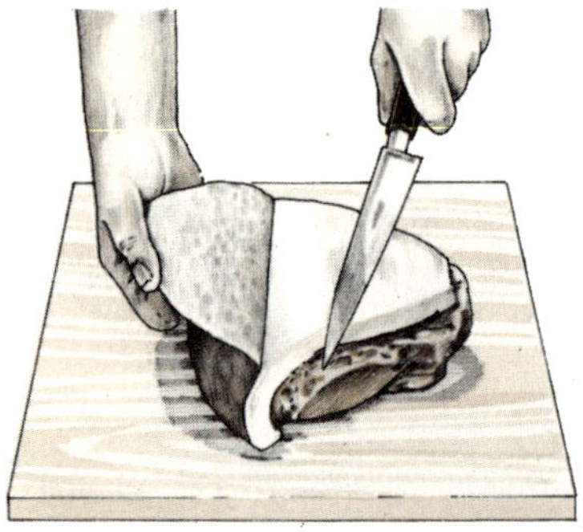

Grip the piece of cut skin firmly and pull, cutting it as you go, until it all comes off.

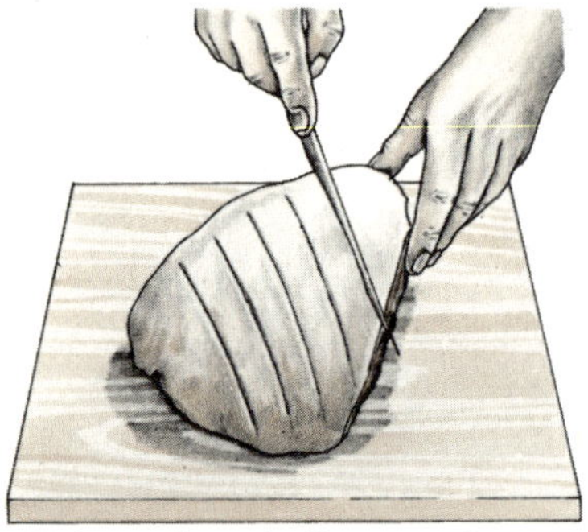

Using a sharp knife, score the surface of the fat diagonally in parallel lines.

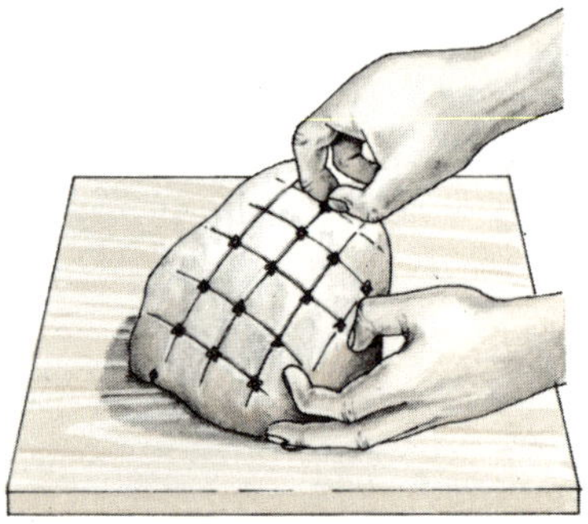

Turn the gammon round and score it the other way to make diamond shapes. Stud with cloves.

Pork chop

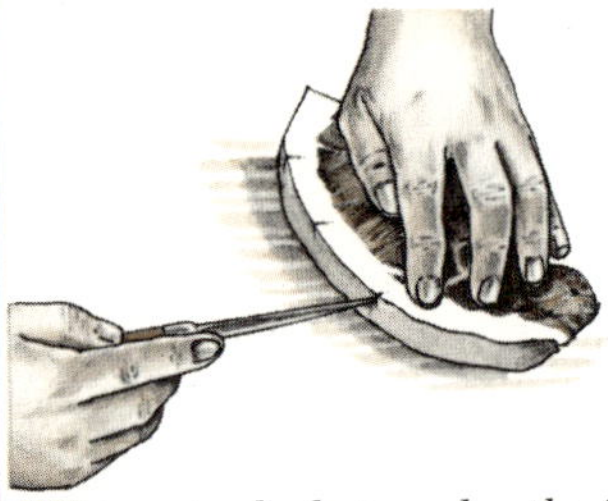

When a pork chop cooks, the fat surrounding it shrinks and the meat tends to curl up. Nick the fat all round to prevent this.

Crackling

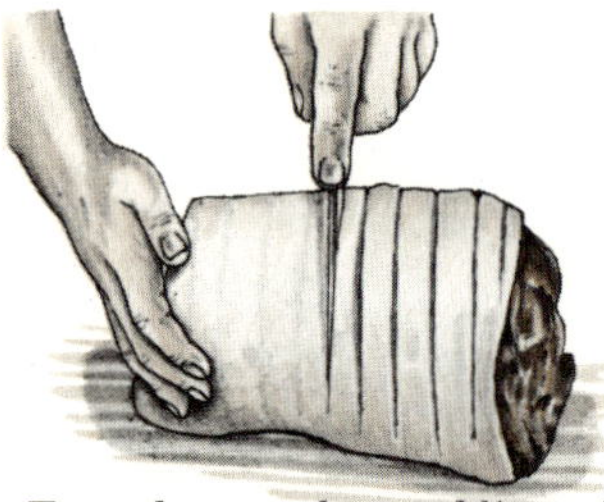

To make sure the crackling will be crisp all the way through, score the surface of the skin in close parallel lines.

Suckling pig

Suckling pig is sold ready for cooking. The entrails will have been removed, the feet cut off and the body cleaned. All you have to do is cover the ears and leg ends with foil to prevent them burning, and put a piece of wood in the mouth.

Game

Hare and rabbit are prepared in the same way, except that a rabbit should be cooked as soon as possible after it has been killed (unless it is a wild rabbit, in which case it should be "paunched", or gutted, then hung for about four or five days), whereas a hare should be hung for a week to ten days before being drawn. The blood of the hare is often used to thicken the gravy if the hare is being jugged or roasted, so hang the hare over a bowl and add a few drops of vinegar to the blood that is collected to stop it coagulating.

There are two methods of skinning a hare or rabbit. You can either lay the animal on a table, where it may be skinned according to the instructions below, or you can push a meat hook through the animal's back legs and hang it up with a bowl under its head. Using a sharp knife cut the skin down the back of each hind leg and round the thighs, and ease the skin away from the flesh. To remove the rest of the skin, pull it down over the animal's body and front legs. Cut off and discard the head with the skin.

Venison is drawn and then hung for one to two weeks. The meat is very lean and dry and should be marinated and larded or barded if it is to be roasted.

Hare and rabbit may also be marinated before cooking, to give the meat better flavour and to ensure that it will be tender. Use a deep dish so that the flesh can be completely submerged in the liquid.

Skinning and jointing rabbit

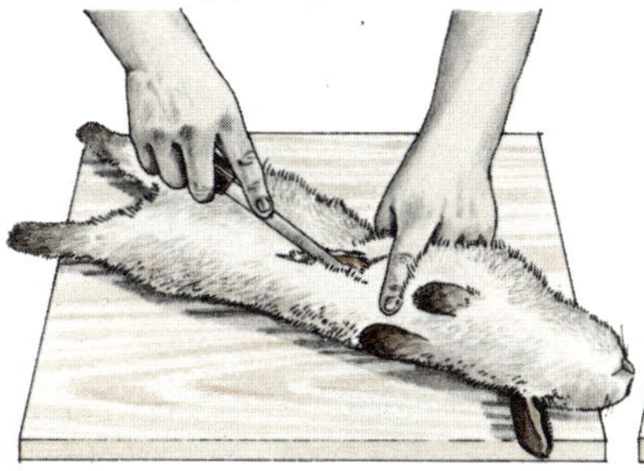

If the rabbit has not been paunched by the butcher, slit it along the stomach. Pull out the intestines and stomach.

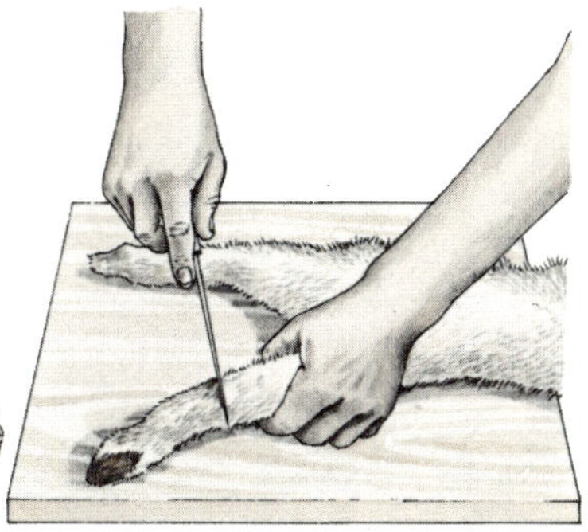

Slit the fur and skin all round half-way up the leg.

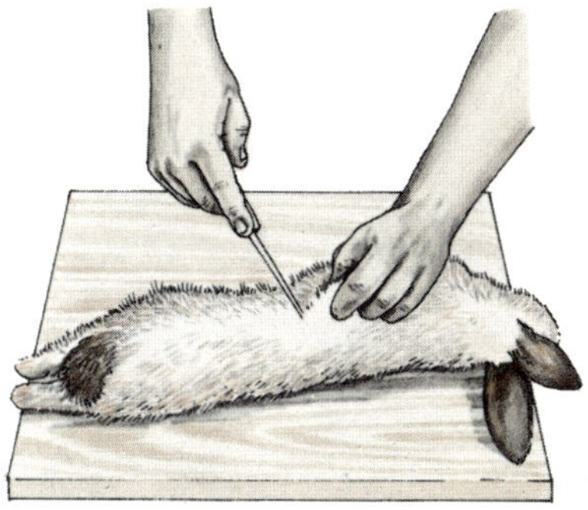

With the point of a sharp knife, make a small incision in the middle of the spine to get a firm grip on the fur.

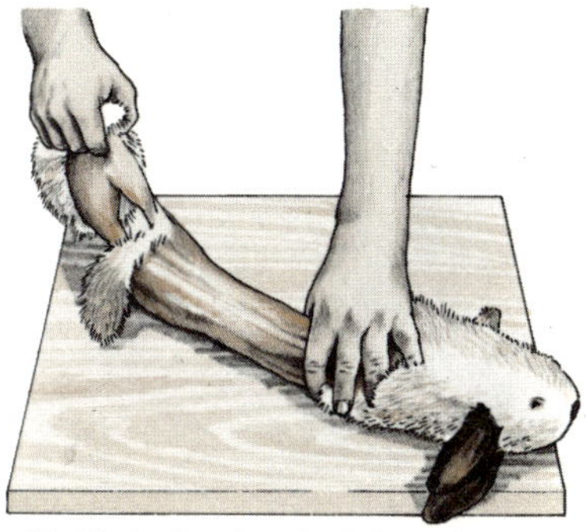

Hold the head end of the rabbit with one hand. Take hold of the fur at the incision with the other and pull the skin off.

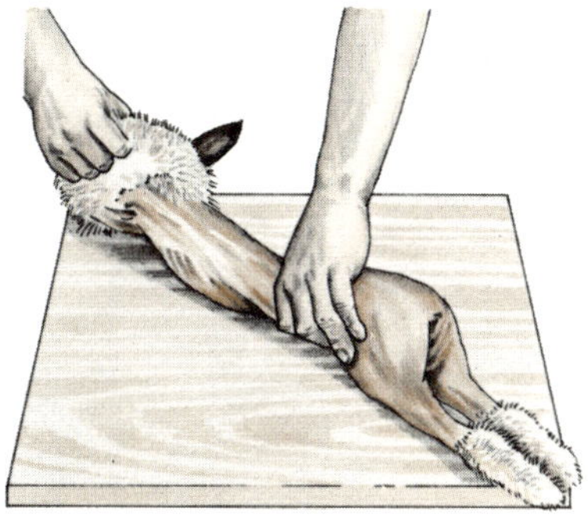

Turn the rabbit around and pull the fur off the upper part of the body in the same way. Pull right up to the end of the head.

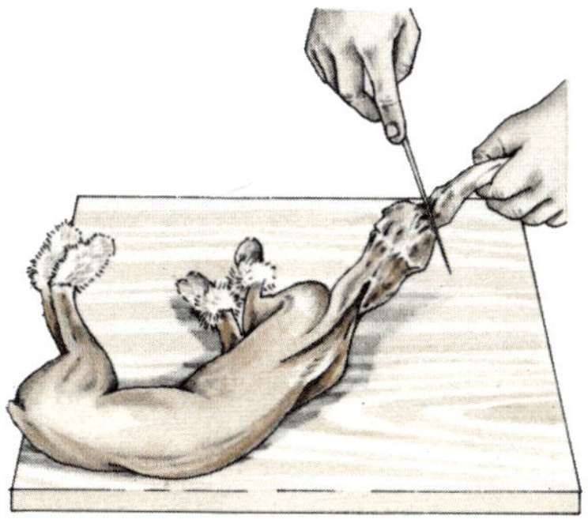

Cut through the skin attaching the fur to the head and pull the fur right off.

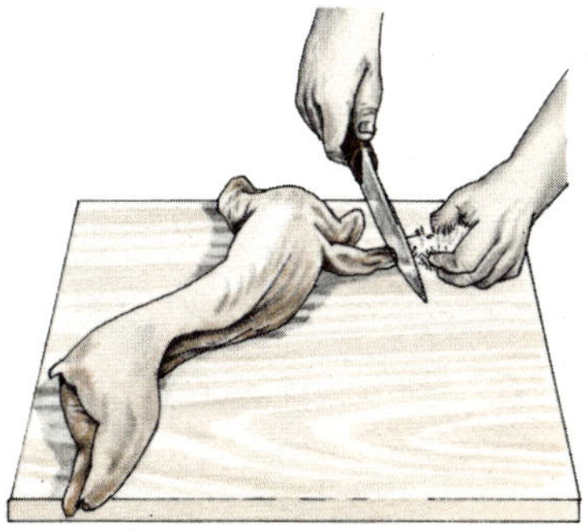

Cut off the head and then cut off the feet and discard.

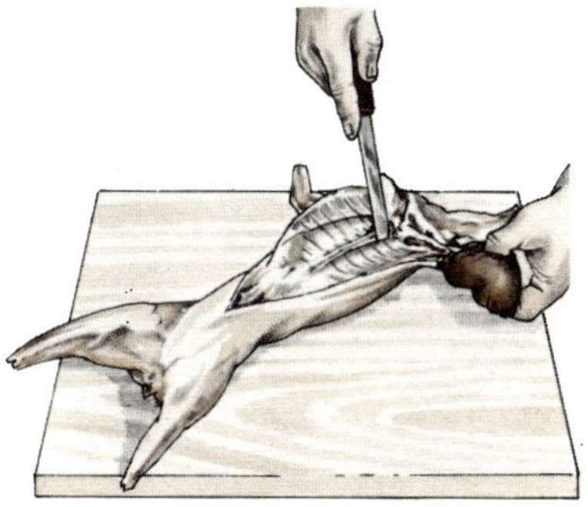

Slit the front open (continuing from the paunch slit) up to the neck, open up the body and remove the heart and lungs.

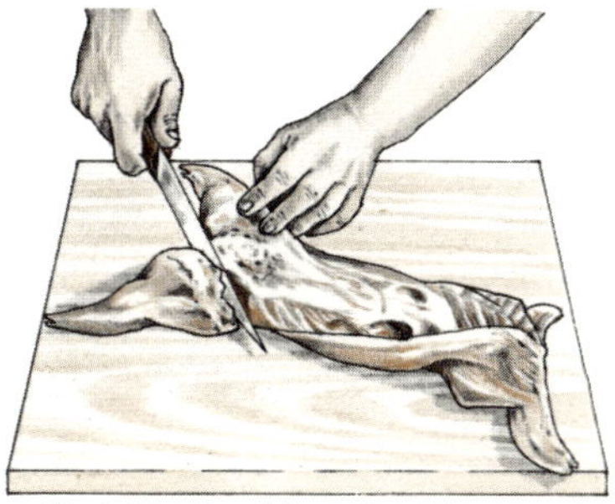

To joint the skinned rabbit, begin by cutting off the hind legs.

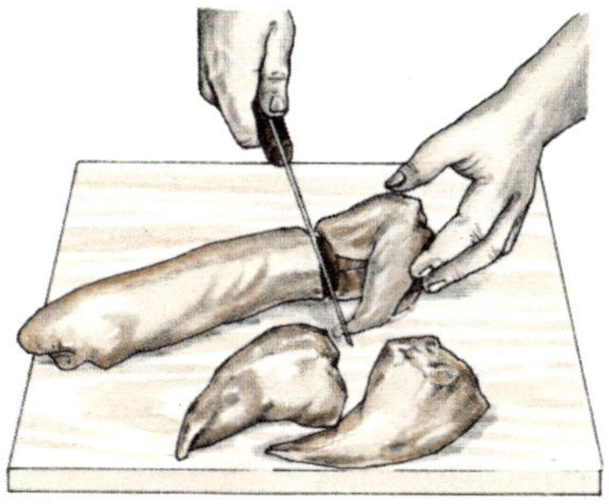

Cut off the forequarters—that is, the front legs and upper part of the body.

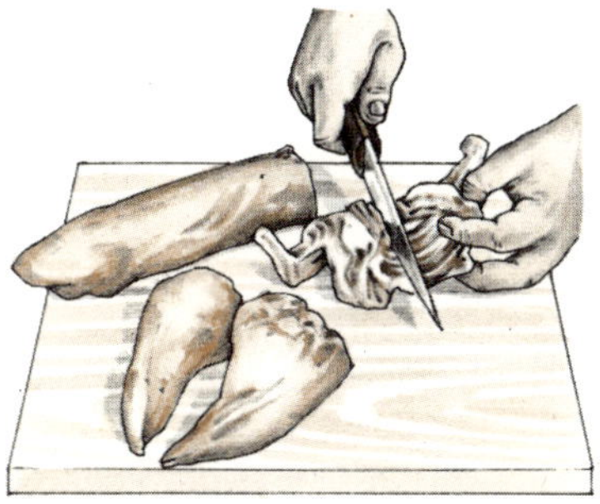

Split the forequarters in half down the middle.

Cut the saddle across into serving pieces.

Offal

All the edible parts that are left when an animal or poultry carcass has been cut up into joints are known as offal. Because it is extremely perishable, offal should always be eaten as soon as possible after the animal or bird has been killed.

Tripe, which is the lining of an ox's stomach, is nearly always sold blanched and ready for cooking.

Sweetbreads should be soaked in salted water and blanched after soaking. Brains should be soaked in salted or acidulated water, and ox heart in water to which a little vinegar has been added, for several hours.

The best sweetbreads, brains and livers are those of calves, although chicken livers are also delicious. Calves and lambs both provide delicately flavoured kidneys and the most tender hearts come from lambs.

Calves' feet and pigs' trotters are cooked and eaten either hot or cold, or are used to make a highly concentrated stock. Lambs' and sheep's heads are also used for making stock, but pigs' and calves' heads are usually used for making brawn. Calves' heads may also be boiled and eaten hot or cold. Before cooking a head scrub it thoroughly and soak it in salted water for at least thirty minutes.

Ox tail, which can be used to make a wonderfully rich casserole, ox cheek, and ox tongue (a delicacy when pickled in brine) are also categorized as offal.

Liver

Lay the liver on a wooden board and clean it thoroughly by wiping it all over with a damp cloth.

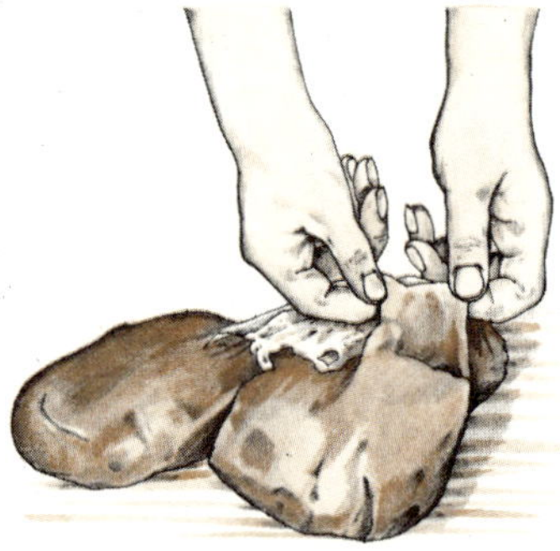

Carefully peel off all the skin from the liver—it should come away quite easily.

With a sharp knife, cut off the fat, gristle and core. Ox liver is coarse and has the strongest flavour. Use for stewing.

Wash the liver in cold water then wipe it dry. Cut the liver—the slices should be very thin for frying and grilling.

Kidney

Kidneys are surrounded by a layer of fat, which is usually removed before cooking : the fat is used as suet.

The next step is to remove the skin : insert the point of a knife between the skin and flesh and loosen the skin at this point.

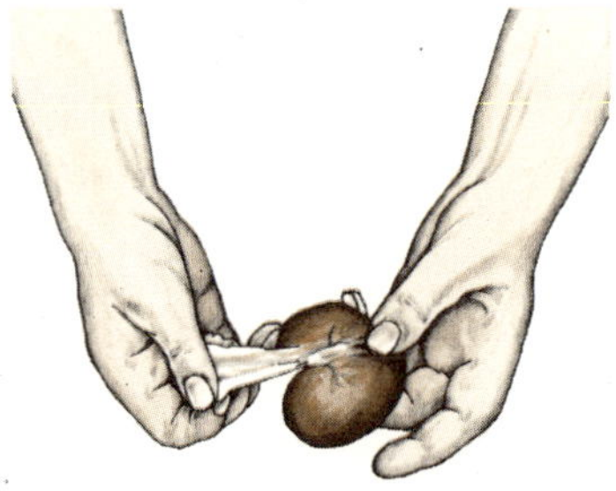

Pull the loosened piece of skin down towards the core, and do the same on the other side of the kidney.

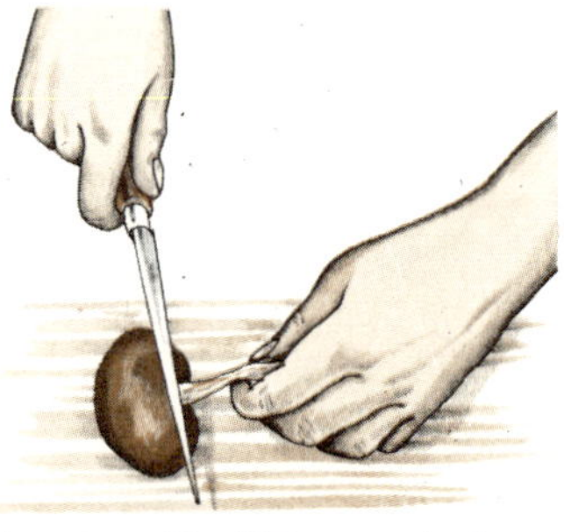

The skin will still be attached to the central core—pull it right to the edge of the core and cut it off.

Cut the kidneys across in half—this can be done with a pair of scissors or a knife

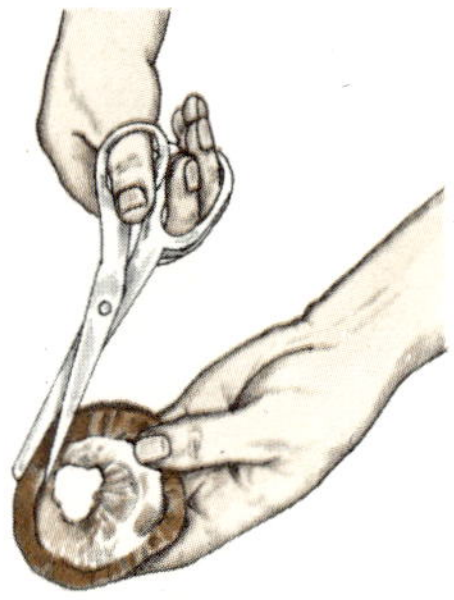

Cut out every part of the central core with a pair of scissors.

The core of the ox kidney is removed in the same way, usually with a pair of scissors.

When the preparation is finished, the kidneys should be neatly trimmed and have a hole where the core was removed.

Ox heart

The ox heart is the largest edible heart sold by the butcher—it usually weighs about four pounds (2 kg).

Rinse the heart under cold running water and pat dry. With scissors, snip out the very tough artery stumps and tendons.

Because ox heart is quite tough it needs to be stewed or casseroled for several hours. Wash it well before cooking.

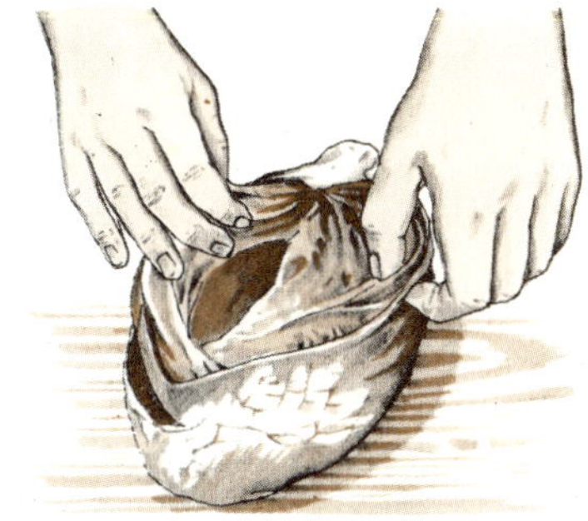

Drain the washed heart and pat it dry. It can now be stuffed, or cut into pieces and stewed, braised or casseroled.

Sweetbreads

Soak sweetbreads in a bowl of cold water for about 2 hours to remove all the blood.

Put the sweetbreads in a pan of cold salted water and bring to the boil. Drain off the water, repeat the process and drain.

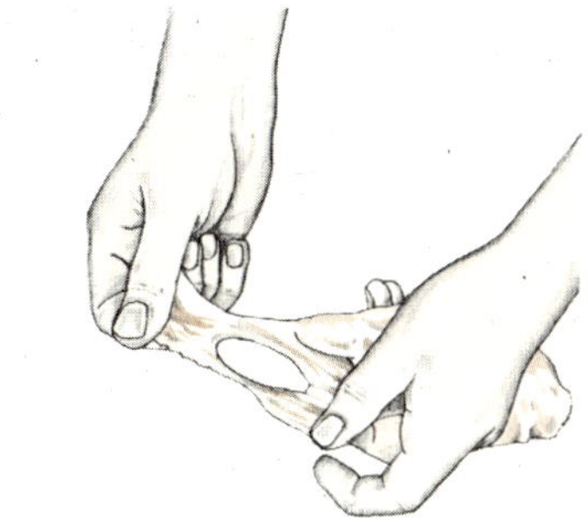

When the sweetbreads are cool enough to handle, pull off all the skin, veins and membranes.

The prepared sweetbreads can now be cooked in stock for about 20 minutes, and then finished off by frying.

Pigs' trotters

Pigs' trotters are sold cleaned by the butcher, and the usual serving is one per person. They can be boiled or stewed whole, or split in half. After cooking, they may be finished off by being dipped in egg and breadcrumbs and fried. Trotters can also be boned, stuffed and baked or grilled.

Because of their high gelatine content, pigs' trotters are often used in stocks and to make brawns and aspics.

Oxtail

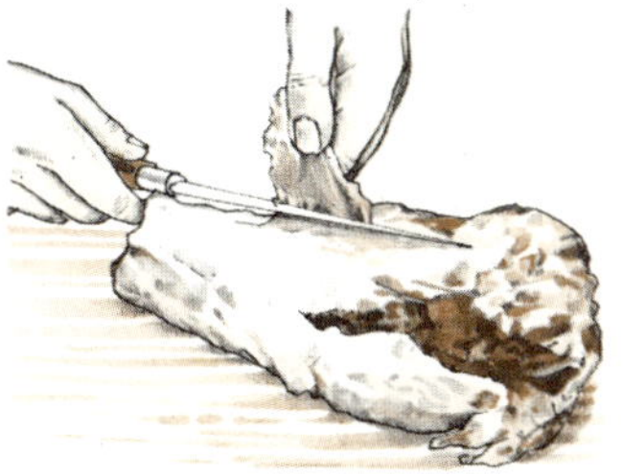

Trim as much fat as possible from the oxtail and cut it into pieces. Generally, one whole oxtail will serve four people.

Oxtail is usually stewed or made into casseroles and soups. It requires long, slow cooking—anything from 3 to 5 hours.

Tripe

Tripe is the lining of the ox's stomach. It is always sold partially prepared by the butcher : that is, cleaned, blanched and half-cooked. In addition to this preparation, tripe should be cooked in milk (flavoured with onions and herbs) for about 2 hours, depending on how long the butcher has already cooked it. After cooking, cut up the tripe and serve with a sauce.

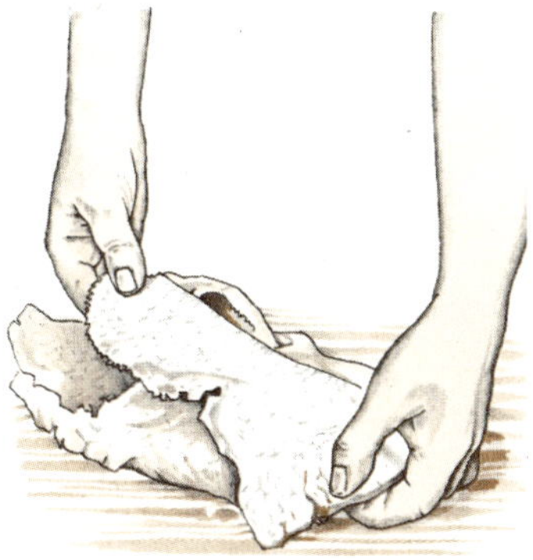

Brains

Brains must be soaked in cold salted or acidulated water for 3 to 4 hours before cooking.

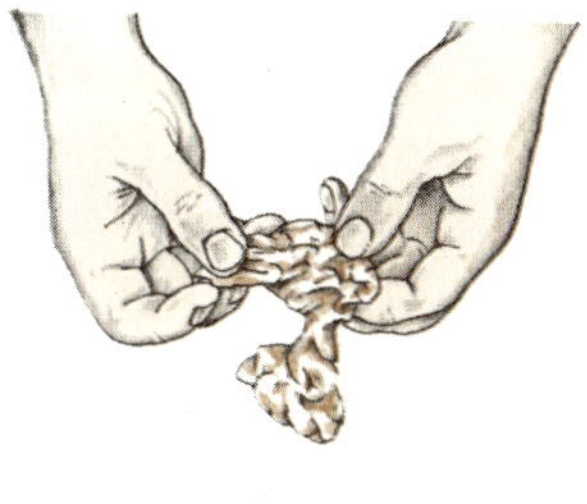

Remove the brains from the water and pat them dry. Pull off all the skin and membranes.

Vegetables

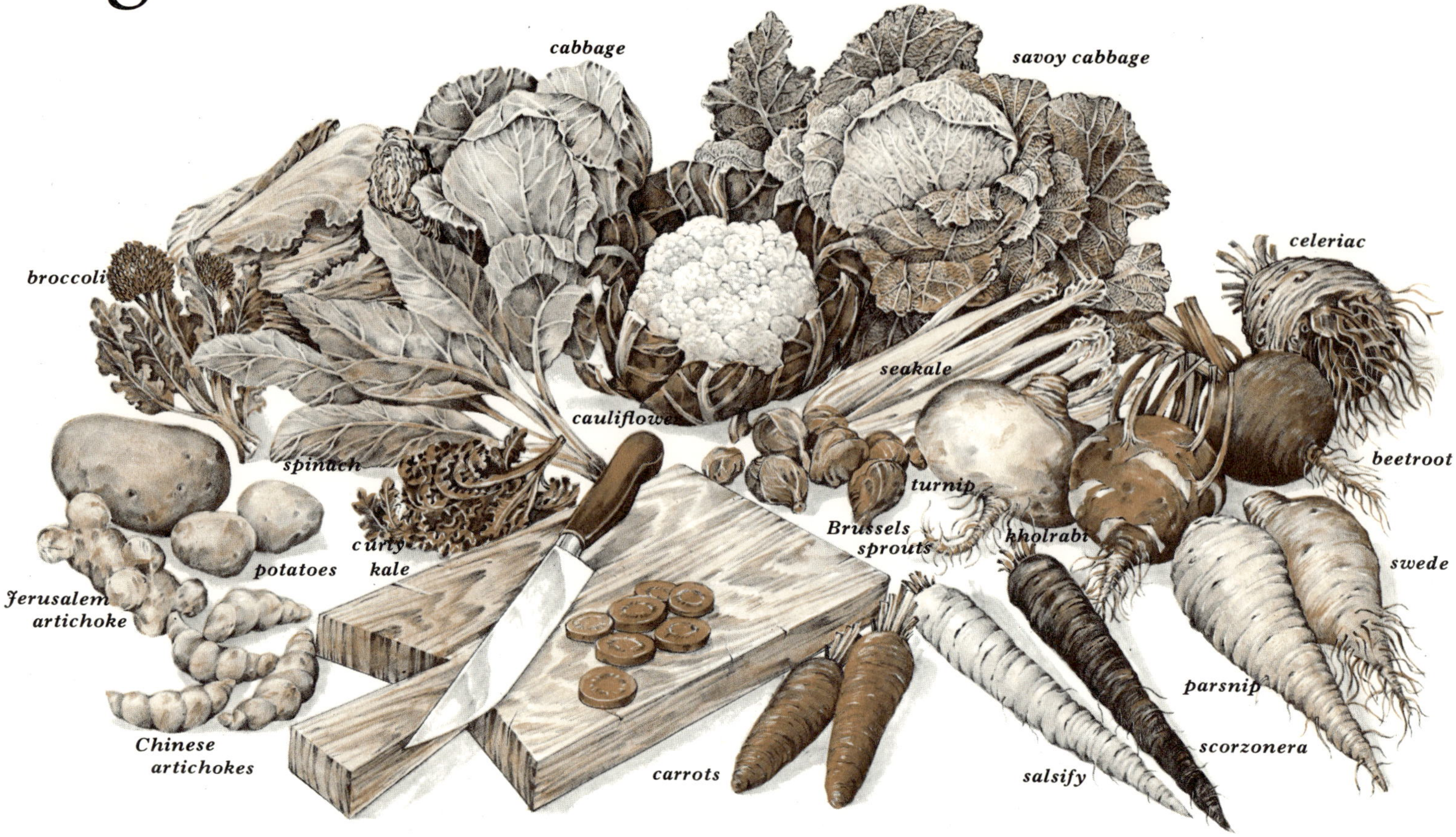

All vegetables must be prepared in some way even if they are going to be eaten raw, but do not prepare them too far in advance, for once peeled or cut they quickly lose their freshness. The exceptions to this rule are vegetables that are marinated, dried pods and seeds that are soaked prior to cooking and such vegetables as aubergine and cucumber, which are degorged (sliced or chopped and layered with salt in a colander, left for about thirty minutes and then rinsed).

Many vegetables lose flavour and nutrients by being peeled and cut. So before preparing a vegetable consider whether it is really necessary. There is, for example, no reason to peel mushrooms, baby carrots or new potatoes.

Always wash vegetables, even if they appear to be clean, under cold running water using a nylon pan scourer or nail brush to scrub them if necessary. Vegetables you grow yourself must also be washed thoroughly; any soil clinging to the skin, even in minute particles, will give an unpleasant, gritty texture. Slugs, caterpillars and many other small insects are masterly at hide-and-seek, so swirl leaf vegetables vigorously in a bowl of cold, well-salted water.

There are a great many machines on the market to slice, shred, dice and even peel your vegetables for you, and although they save time you can manage perfectly well without them. All you really need is a sharp vegetable knife, a parer, a stout wooden chopping board, a grater and perhaps a mandolin.

Tubers

A tuber is the natural swelling of an underground stem. The most important tuber is the potato, which, at its best, requires little preparation—a good scrub and it is ready to be boiled or steamed. The yam, or sweet potato, is easier to peel after it has been cooked, but is otherwise prepared and cooked in the same way as the potato. Two other vegetables in this group are Jerusalem and Chinese artichokes. When young, they need only be scrubbed and any discoloured patches scraped off.

To make game chips, cut a potato into paper-thin slices, using a mandolin or a knife.

Scrub Jerusalem artichokes in cold water, then scrape or peel away any discoloured patches.

Put the prepared artichokes into a bowl of acidulated water to prevent discoloration.

Brassicas

The most common brassicas are cabbage (green, red and white), Brussels sprouts, cauliflower, broccoli (white, purple and green sprouting) and kale. Chinese cabbage, a relative newcomer to Western markets, is becoming increasingly popular for its delicate flavour and lack of odour when it is cooked. All brassicas should have their stalks and coarse outer leaves trimmed. Wash cauliflower and broccoli carefully and leave to soak in cold salted water for a few minutes to get rid of any grubs.

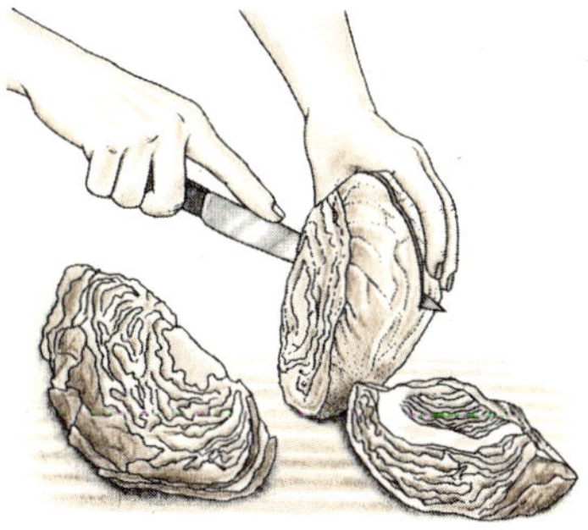

Remove the coarse outer leaves of the cabbage, then cut it into quarters and slice out the core.

To shred cabbage, hold one quarter firmly and slice it thinly down its length.

To prepare Chinese cabbage, cut off the coarse outer leaves and slice it crossways into shreds.

To make a whole cauliflower cook faster remove a wedge from the core or cut a cross in the base.

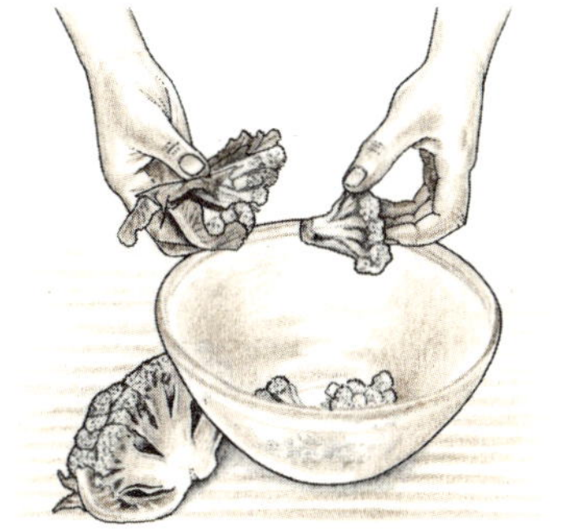

To separate a cauliflower into florets, first cut it in half then break it apart.

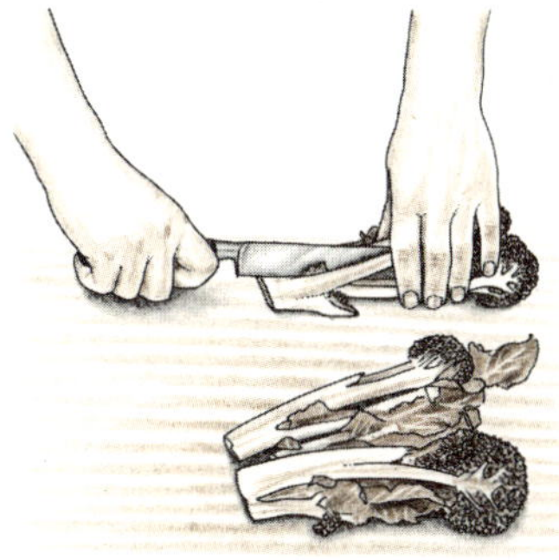

To prepare green sprouting broccoli, trim the stem then make a slit in the thicker end.

Remove the coarse outer leaves of Brussels sprouts. Trim and cut a cross in the centre of the base.

Root vegetables

Such root vegetables as turnips, swedes and celeriac should be peeled thickly. To obtain the best flavour from salsify and scorzonera, however, do not peel or scrape until the vegetables are cooked. To prepare beetroot, cut off the top, leaving about one inch (2 cm) of stem, then wash with the utmost care—if the skin is pierced the beetroot will "bleed" during cooking.

Cook small root vegetables whole; larger ones are diced or cut into chunks or julienne strips.

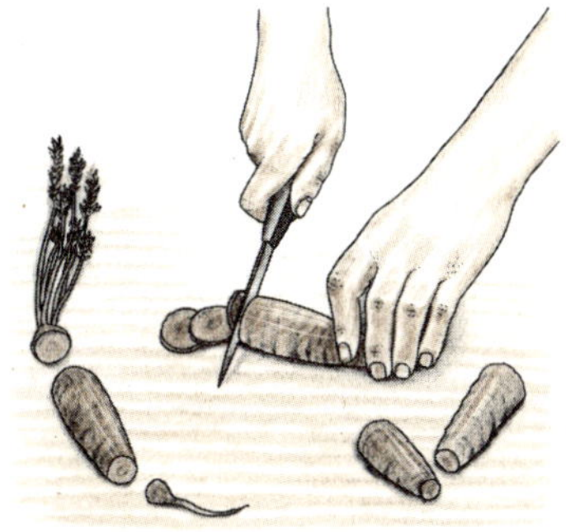

Before slicing carrots into rounds, scrub them then cut off the top end and trim the root end.

To make julienne strips, cut the carrot in half lengthways, then cut each half into strips.

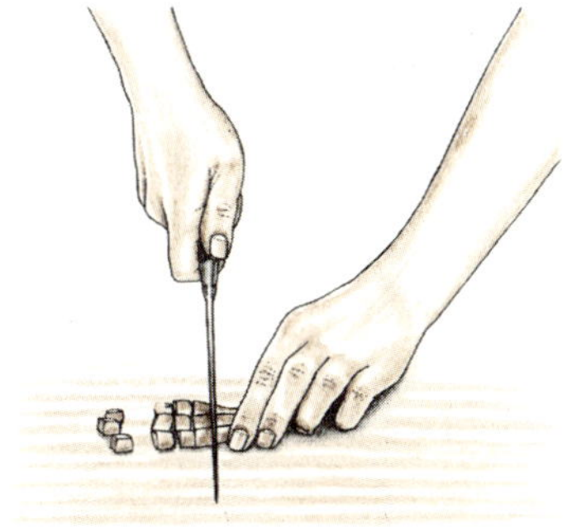

To dice carrots, cut them up as for julienne strips, and then slice the strips across.

Chop celeriac into manageable pieces, peel it thickly, then slice finely.

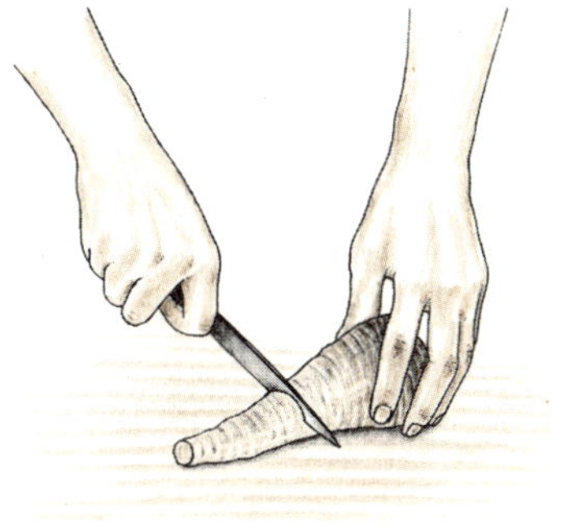

Peel the parsnip, cut off the pointed end and cut the thicker end in half before cooking.

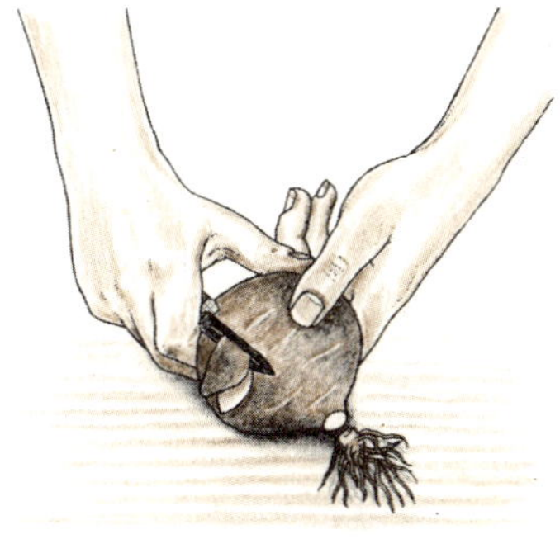

Remove the leaves, stalk and tapering root end of kohlrabi before peeling thickly.

Root ginger should be peeled thinly with a very sharp knife, then sliced, chopped or grated.

Vegetables

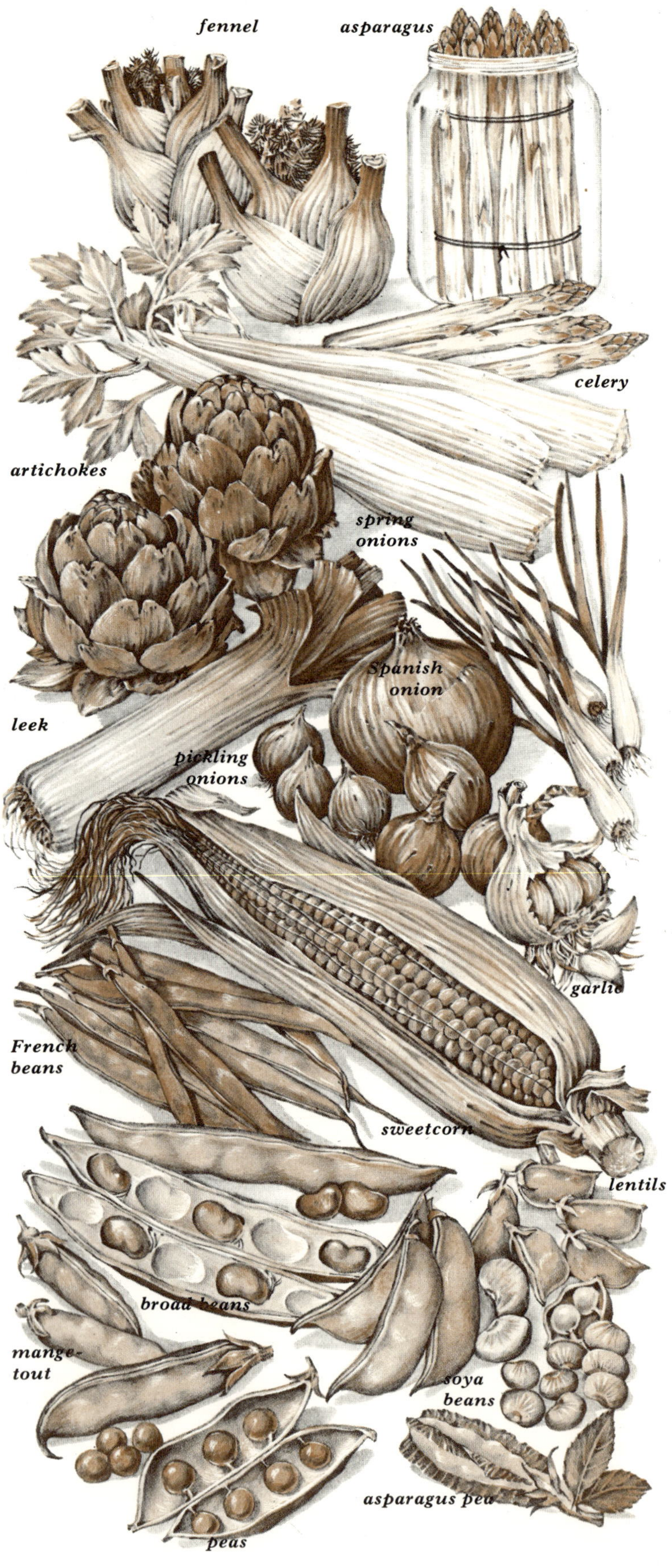

Stalks and shoots

Celery, asparagus and globe artichokes are the best-known vegetables in this category. Others include seakale, Florence fennel and cardoons. To prepare seakale stalks, trim the root, wash under cold running water and tie in bundles for cooking. Trim the top stalks of Florence fennel and cut a slice from the base. Scrub it thoroughly before cooking. Cardoons are grown only for their leaf-stems : discard the tough outer stalks and remove the "strings" from the remaining stalks.

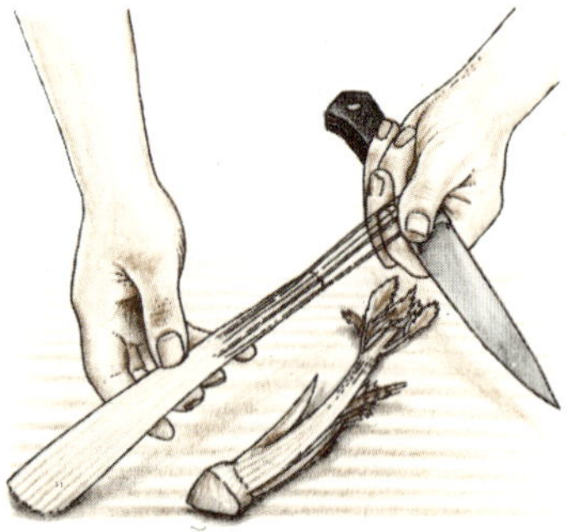

Trim the root end and any damaged stalks from celery, and remove the strings.

With a sharp knife, cut off the woody part at the base of the asparagus stalks.

Scrape the white part of the stalk, then tie the stalks in bundles for cooking.

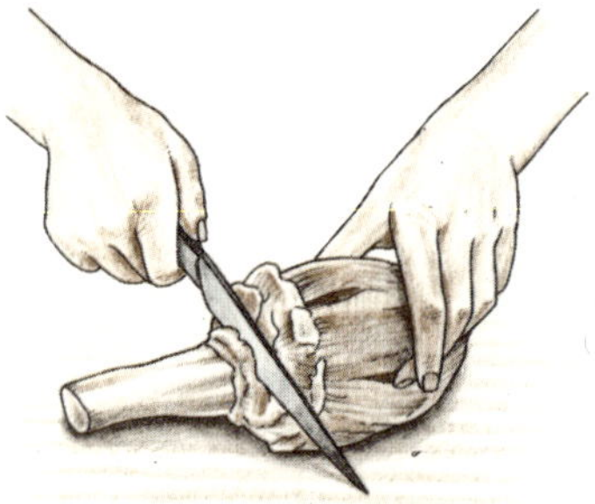

Break off the tough outer leaves of the artichoke, then slice off the stalk and trim the base.

Cut off the top third of the artichoke, snip tops off the leaves and rub with lemon.

Hold the artichoke in one hand and pull out the prickly leaves surrounding the choke.

Using a metal teaspoon, scrape out the hairy choke. Sprinkle the inside with lemon juice.

The onion family

The onion family includes garlic, leeks, shallots, spring onions and chives, as well as many other varieties. They are invaluable as flavourings—few savoury dishes would be complete without a touch of onion or garlic. If the onion has too strong a flavour, blanch it in boiling water for three minutes. Although a garlic press is an invaluable kitchen aid, perfectionists argue that it impairs the flavour of the garlic—they prefer to use a spoon or knife to crush it with a little salt.

Slice off the root end and coarse green leaves of the leek. Slit lengthways to the centre.

Spread the leaves apart and hold under fast-running water to remove all the dirt and grit.

Coarsely chop a garlic clove, sprinkle over a little salt and crush to a paste with a spoon.

To make onion rings, cut the onion across into thin slices and push out into rings.

To chop an onion, peel and halve it, retaining the root end. Slice horizontally up to the root end.

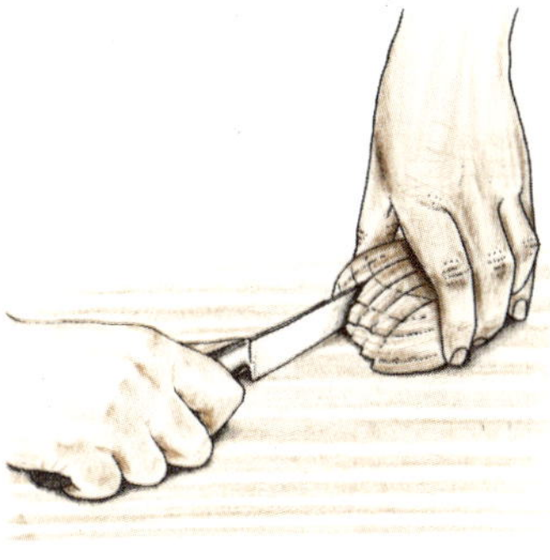

Turn the onion round and slice at right angles to the first cuts, up to the root end.

Turn the onion round once more and slice it across the previous cuts to make dice.

Pods and seeds

Pods and seeds is a category that covers a great many vegetables that are prepared in different ways. Some, such as lentils, split peas and dried beans, are bought dried and must be soaked before cooking. Others, for example peas and broad beans, must be removed from their pods, whereas mange-tout peas, French and runner beans are cooked and eaten, pods and all. Unless they are dried, pods and seeds are best eaten young, when they are sweet and tender and before they become coarse.

Peel back the husks right down to the stalk end and cut them off. Tear off the silk.

To remove corn from the cob, cook the cob, then scrape the kernels off with a blunt knife.

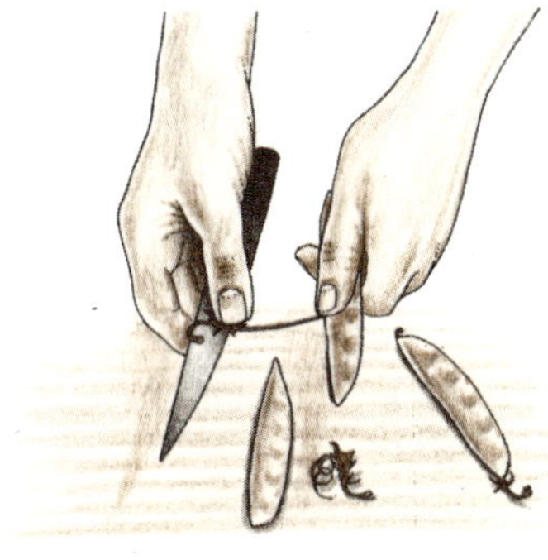

Young mange-tout peas need only be washed, topped and tailed; older ones require stringing.

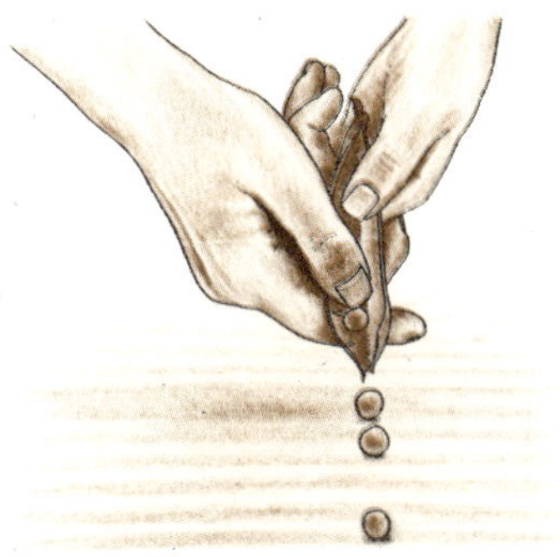

Press the pea pod gently to split it open. Run your thumb along the inside to dislodge the peas.

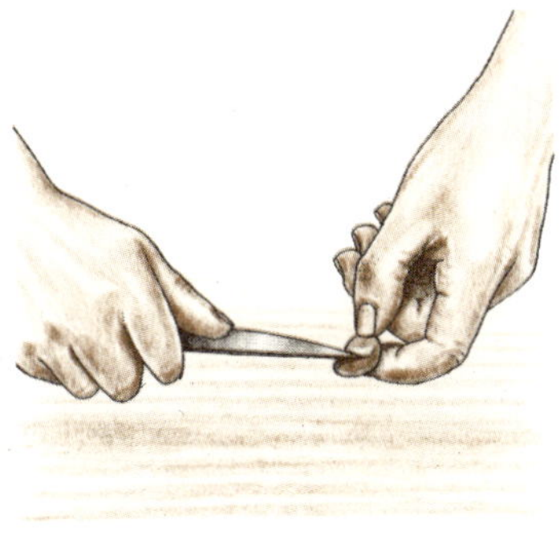

Tough broad beans usually have their skins peeled off. It is easier to do this after cooking.

Young French, green and runner beans need only be topped and tailed before cooking.

To remove the strings from older, larger beans, cut through the stalk end and pull off the strings.

Vegetables

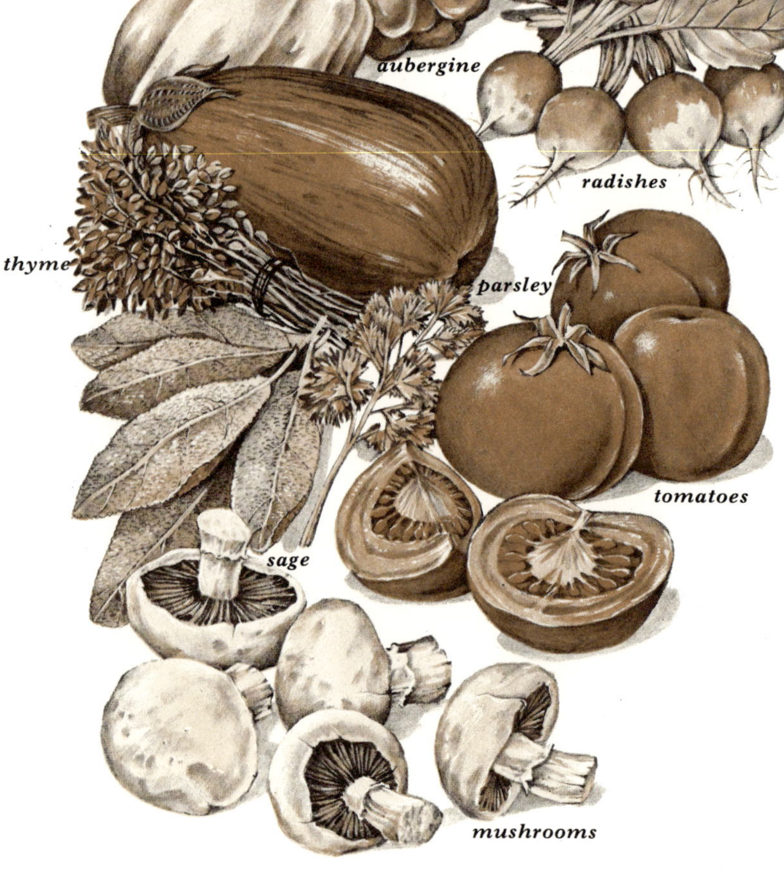

Mushrooms

Mushrooms are wild or cultivated, large or small, flat or round, and their colour varies from black to palest cream. They are used in soups and stews, as a vegetable accompaniment or garnish, or stuffed as a main dish. Remove the stalks from old, tough mushrooms, then peel the caps, if necessary. Young mushrooms keep their stalks; cook them whole and unpeeled. When mushrooms are cooked as part of a dish, remember that they give out a lot of juice, so reduce the cooking liquid accordingly.

To prepare mushrooms, wipe them clean, wash them only if necessary, trim stalks and slice.

Salad vegetables

The most popular salad vegetables are radish, endive, chicory, cress and lettuce—the crisp-hearted cabbage type, the long and crisp Cos type, and the soft, round cabbage type. Most salad vegetables are eaten raw, but some, for example chicory and endive, may also be cooked. All salad vegetables are prepared in the same way; trim the root end and any damaged or yellowing leaves; wash the leaves in cold water, and then drain thoroughly.

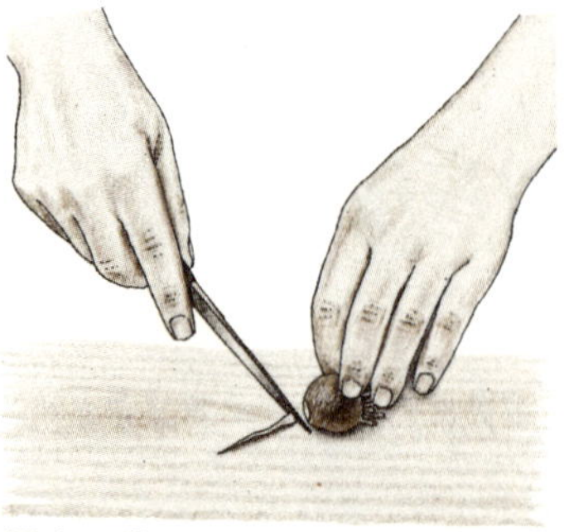

Trim off all but a short end of the leaf stalks, then slice off the root end.

Vegetable fruit

Vegetable fruit are those vegetables that are classified as fruit but are cooked and eaten as vegetables. The one thing they have in common is seeds. Marrow, peppers and pumpkin always have their seeds removed before cooking; chillies, tomatoes, cucumbers and courgettes are sometimes seeded, but aubergines never are. With the exception of chillies, all vegetable fruit can be stuffed and baked. Aubergines, courgettes, cucumbers and marrow can be degorged to remove excess liquid.

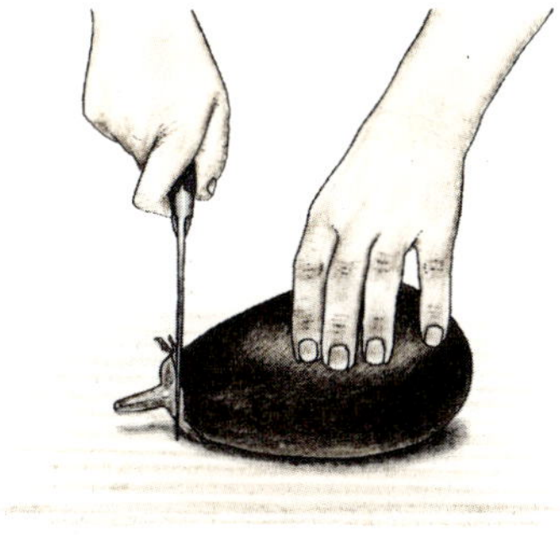

Wipe the aubergine clean with a damp cloth, then use a sharp knife to cut off the stalk end.

Chop or slice the aubergine, or halve it, according to the recipe. The seeds are edible.

Layer the aubergine with salt in a colander and weigh down with a plate. Leave for 30 minutes.

One method of peeling a tomato is to dip it in boiling water to loosen the skin.

Another method is to spear the tomato on a fork and hold it over heat until the skin splits.

Cut carefully around the stem of the pepper. Remove the stem—the core should come away with it.

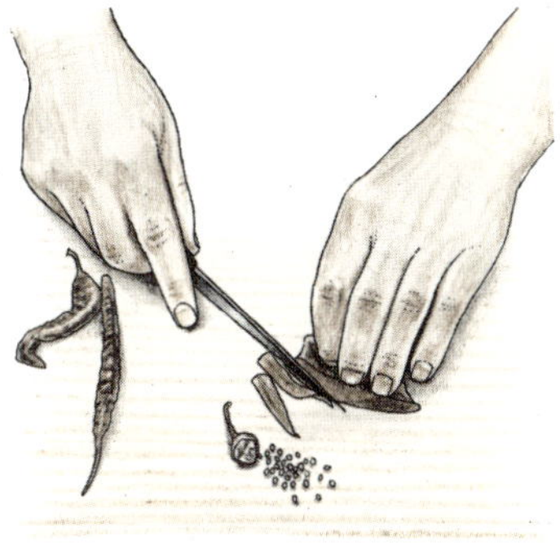

Cut off the stalk end and slit the chillies in half to take out the seeds (the hottest part).

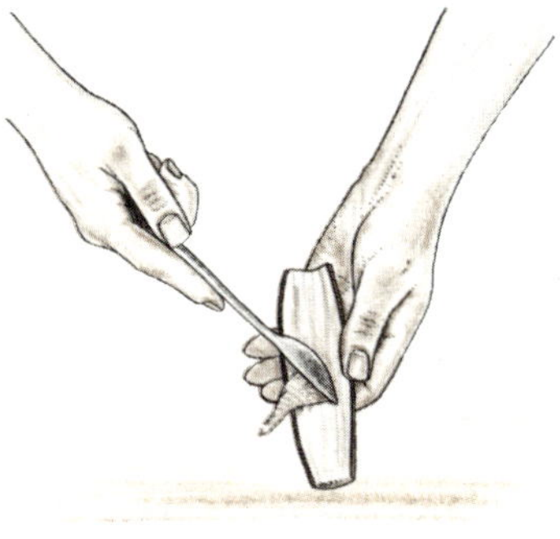

To remove seeds from courgettes, cut in half lengthways and run a teaspoon down the middle.

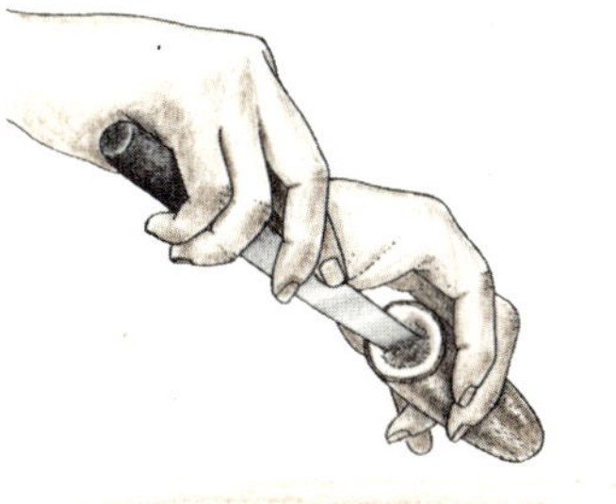

Or remove seeds by cutting courgettes into lengths and scooping them out with a knife.

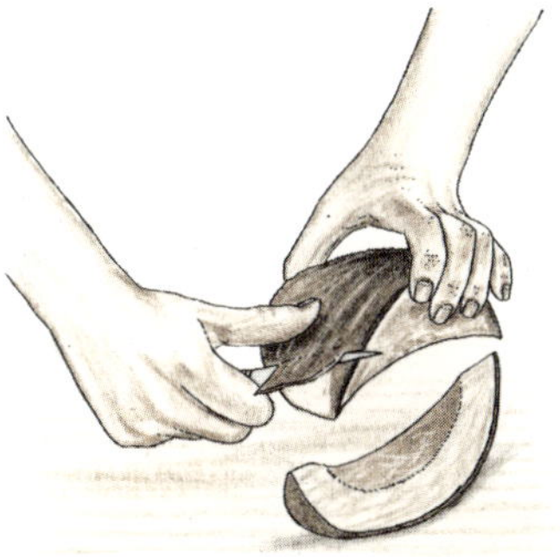

Cut the pumpkin into manageable pieces, peel it and scoop out all the seeds and strings.

Cut the marrow in half lengthways and use a large metal spoon to scoop out all the seeds.

Fresh herbs need little preparation—just wash and dry them and remove any leaves that have become yellow. When adding herbs to a dish, chop them finely or use whole leaves or sprigs. Alternatively, for stocks, stews or casseroles, make a traditional bouquet garni by tying together a bunch of herbs—parsley, bay and thyme are the ones most commonly used, but such herbs as tarragon, savory, chervil and burnet may also be included.

A quick way of chopping parsley is to use a small food mill.

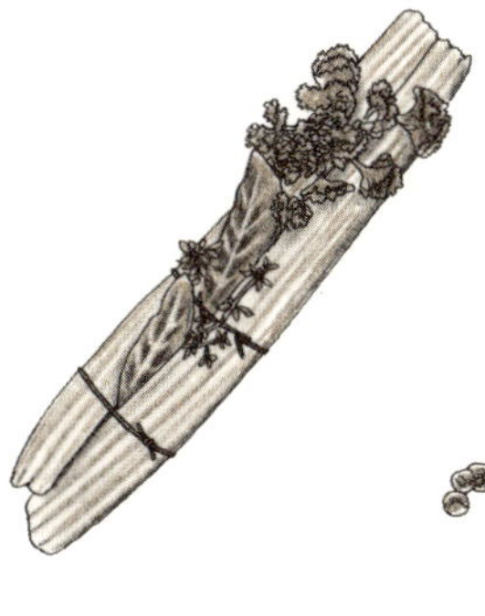

A bouquet garni can be made by tying a few herbs in a bunch, encasing them in a split leek or enclosing them in a small piece of muslin.

Fruit

Wash fruit that is to be eaten unpeeled under running water, to ensure that all traces of dirt or chemical sprays have been removed. Such soft fruit as strawberries, raspberries or currants, however, should be washed only if it is absolutely necessary.

Hull all berries before they are served, and strip currants from their stalks—just run a fork down the length of each stalk and the currants will come away easily.

Some fruit, for example apples and bananas, discolour when they have been peeled and sliced. To prevent discoloration, sprinkle the cut fruit with a little lemon juice.

If grapes or peaches are difficult to peel, dip them in a bowl of boiling water for a minute or less. Then dip them in cold water and peel immediately.

Several kinds of nuts also have skins that are hard to remove. Shelled almonds and pistachios should be dropped into boiling water for a few minutes; the skins can then be rubbed off without any trouble.

To peel chestnuts, first cut a cross on the flat side of the nut or slit it at the pointed end. Put the nuts in a pan of cold water and boil them for two to three minutes. Use a spoon to lift a few nuts at a time out of the water and shell and peel them while they are still hot. Alternatively, slit the shells and bake the chestnuts in a 400°F (200°C, Gas Mark 6) oven for ten minutes.

Toast shelled hazelnuts under a grill, then rub them together in a paper bag; the skins will soon come off.

A mature coconut (the only kind available away from the tropics) has a hard, tough shell. To open it, puncture the three dark spots, or "eyes", with a skewer or any other strong, sharp instrument. Strain out the liquid and tap the coconut sharply with a hammer; it should break in half. If it does not break put the coconut into a 400°F (200°C, Gas Mark 6) oven for fifteen minutes. Then take it out, put it on a board and give it a sharp tap with a hammer. It will split in half and the flesh will come away from the shell. To grate the coconut, peel away the brown skin and use a hand grater.

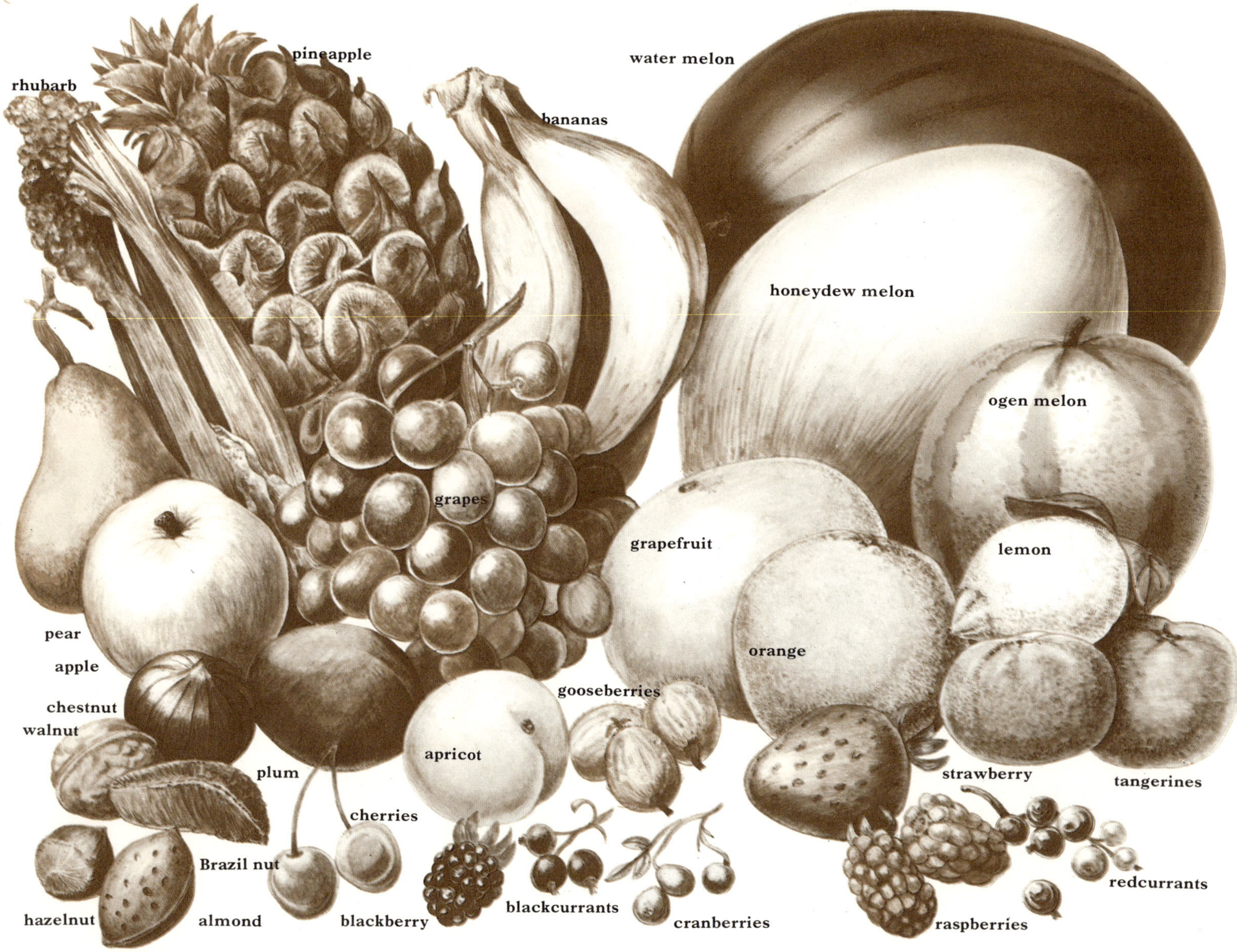

How to prepare fruit and nuts

To prepare fruit you need very little equipment—just a few sharp knives of various sizes and a chopping board. Other pieces of equipment that are not essential but which you may wish to buy include a special scoop for making melon balls, and a cherry stoner, although cherry stones and grape pips can be removed with a hair grip.

Small hard-shelled nuts should be cracked open with nutcrackers, but to break a coconut you will need a hammer.

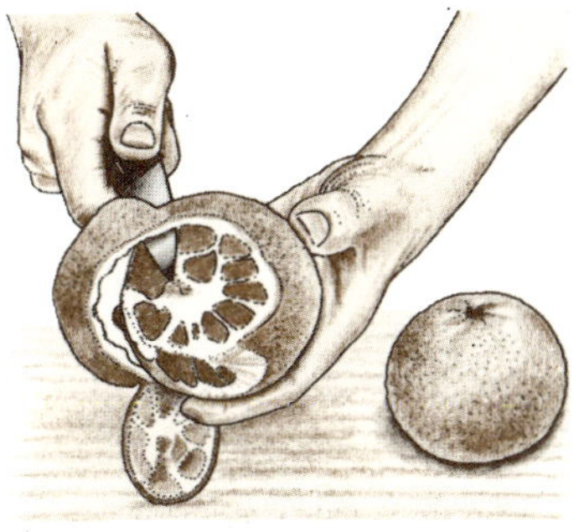

To peel an orange, turn the fruit while cutting away strips of peel and pith with a sharp knife.

Remove any remaining pith, then cut through the membranes to release the orange segments.

Cut the melon in half, remove the seeds, then use a special scoop to cut out the melon balls.

The best way to peel a pineapple is to cut it diagonally, removing the skin and the "eyes" together.

Cut the pineapple into slices, then use an apple corer to remove the hard centre from each slice.

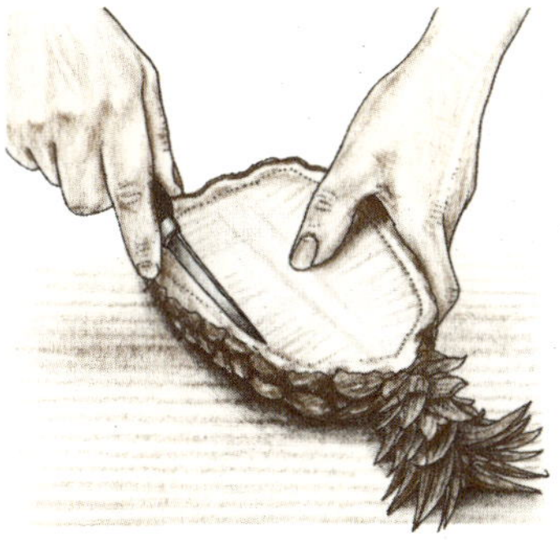

Another way to serve pineapple is to cut the fruit in half and remove all the flesh from both halves.

Cut the flesh into pieces and remove the core, then pile all the flesh into one of the empty shells.

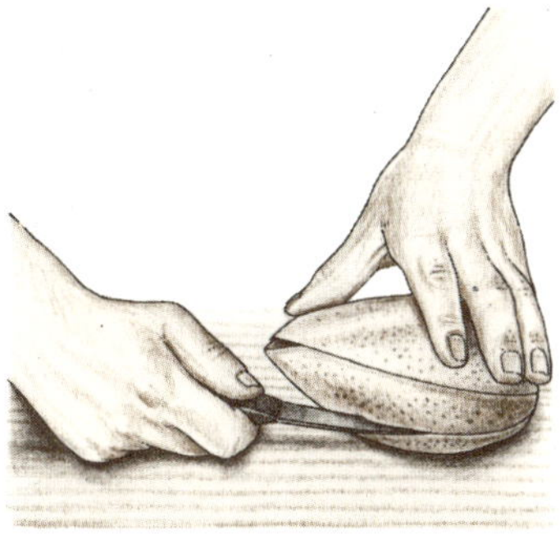

To prepare a mango cut it into three, keeping the knife as close as possible to the stone.

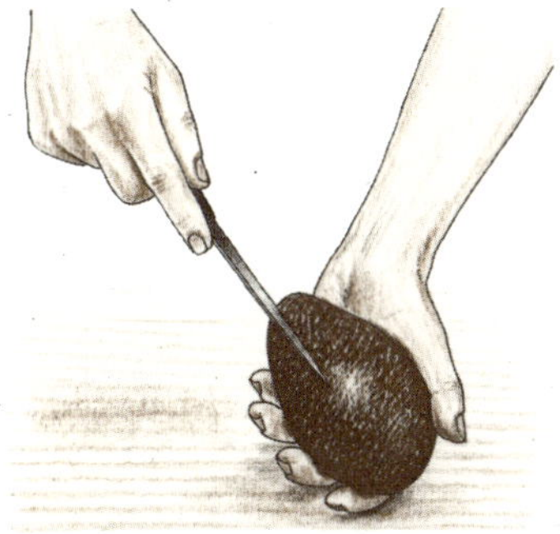

Slice an avocado pear in half, cutting round the central stone. Remove the stone and serve.

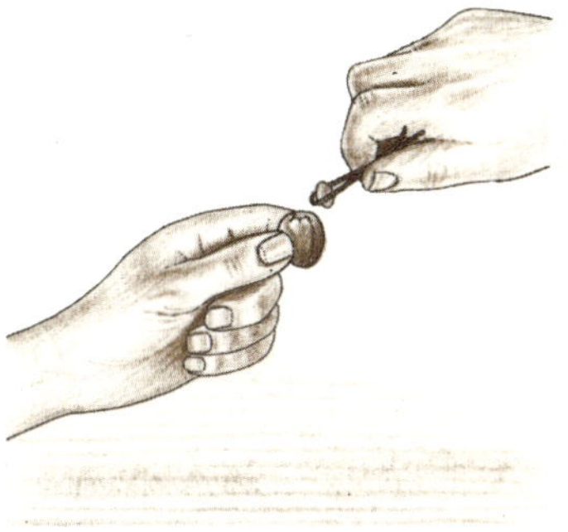

Insert a clean hair grip into the stem end of a cherry, hook it round the stone and lift it out carefully.

To prepare a strawberry, pull the stalk and the soft central core will come away with it easily.

Use a pair of nutcrackers to shell such small nuts as almonds, hazelnuts, walnuts and Brazil nuts.

To release the liquid from a coconut, puncture the three "eyes" with a strong, sharp instrument.

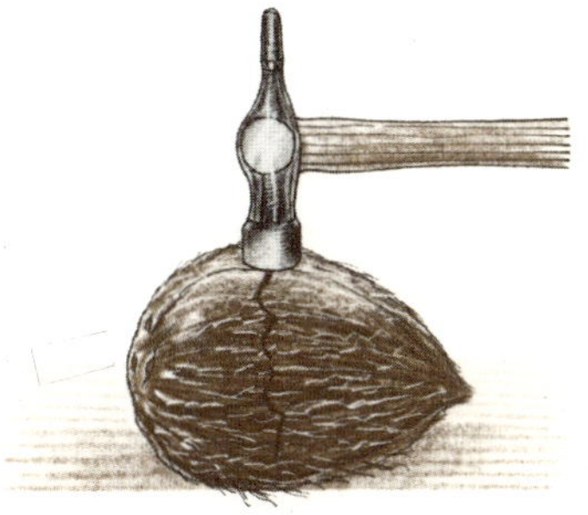

Having strained out the liquid, crack open the coconut by tapping it sharply with a hammer.

Before peeling a chestnut cut a cross in the side, immerse in water and boil for a few minutes.

Cereals

Pastry-making is an art and a science. The art lies in the lightness of your touch, and the science in the correct combination and proportion of ingredients. With a few exceptions pastry dough should be mixed as lightly as possible to introduce air into the mixture; too much handling or a "heavy" hand knocks out the air. (It is the air in the dough that expands with the heat of the oven and makes pastry light.)

There are nine main types of pastry: shortcrust, rich shortcrust, pâte sucrée (French flan pastry), flaky, puff, strudel, choux, hot-water crust and suet crust. With the exception of the last four, the rules for making the different types of pastry are basically the same.

If possible, always work in a cool kitchen with cool ingredients.

Use sifted plain flour unless otherwise instructed. Self-raising flour or the addition of baking powder to plain flour makes a spongy pastry, which is unsuitable for most purposes. When you are making a savoury cheese dough, however, add a very small amount of baking powder to lighten the pastry.

Butter is the best fat to use for making a rich, light pastry, but hard margarine or a mixture of butter or hard margarine and vegetable lard may be used instead. Pastry made entirely with lard, for example hot-water crust, is only suitable for savoury pies.

The consistency of the fat is important; it should be kept at room temperature until it is cool and firm. If the fat is cold and hard you will find it difficult to rub it into the flour evenly; if it is too warm and soft the mixture will have the texture of a paste rather than that of breadcrumbs and the result will be streaky, unmanageable dough.

Use your fingertips to rub the fat into the flour. Or, if the weather is warm, start by using a knife or pastry blender, then use your fingertips to bring the dough together after the water has been added.

Water is generally used to bind the dough, but milk or a mixture of milk and water may be used. Sprinkle the liquid, all at once, over the flour and butter mixture. If you pour it into the centre your pastry may be streaky. The amount of water you add is important; if you use too little, the dough will crack and become difficult to roll out. The cracks let the air out when the dough is baked and this makes the pastry heavy. If too much water is added, the dough will be sticky and too soft to handle; add more flour to redress this and you will unbalance the proportion of fat to flour—the result will be pastry that is tough and hard.

When the dough is ready, shape it into a ball and put it in a covered bowl in the refrigerator for at least thirty minutes. The longer you chill it—up to twelve hours—the easier the pastry will be to handle. Remove the dough from the refrigerator one hour before using it.

Shortcrust and rich shortcrust pastry may be flavoured with herbs, garlic, cheese, ground or finely chopped nuts and orange or lemon rind. A teaspoon of lemon juice added to shortcrust, flaky or puff dough lightens the pastry.

Roll pastry dough on a lightly floured, cool, smooth surface. A marble slab or wooden board is ideal. Use a heavy rolling pin without handles and make light, short movements from the centre out. Turn the dough but not the rolling pin. Rest the rolled-out dough for five minutes before using; this prevents shrinkage during baking.

Before baking pastry cases, chill them in the refrigerator for at least thirty minutes.

When a weight of pastry is called for in a recipe—for example six ounces (175 g) of shortcrust—this refers to the amount of flour used and not the total weight of the finished dough.

Shortcrust pastry

This amount of pastry will line one 9-inch (23-cm) flan dish or ring.

MAKES 6 OUNCES (175 G)

6 oz (175 g) flour
Pinch salt
3 oz (75 g) butter
2 to 3 tablespoons iced water

Sift the flour and salt into a bowl and add the butter. Cut the butter into the flour, then lightly rub it in with your fingertips until the mixture resembles breadcrumbs. Sprinkle in most of the water, then mix it in with a knife, adding a little more if necessary. Give the dough a final mix with your fingertips to bring it together. Shape it into a ball, cover and chill.

Cut the butter into the flour.

Rub it in with your fingertips.

Rich shortcrust pastry

This amount of pastry will line one 11-inch (28-cm) flan tin.

MAKES ½ POUND (225 G)

½ lb (225 g) flour
Pinch salt
6 oz (175 g) butter
1 egg yolk mixed with 2 to 3 tablespoons iced water

Sift the flour and salt into a bowl and add the butter. Cut it into small pieces with a knife, and then lightly rub it into the flour until the mixture resembles breadcrumbs. Add the egg and water mixture and mix it in, adding a little more water if necessary. Give the dough a quick, final mix with your fingertips. Shape into a ball, cover and chill.

Almond pastry

This is a difficult pastry to roll out. It is easier to press it into the tin with your fingertips.

MAKES ¼ POUND (125 G)

¼ lb (125 g) flour
3 oz (75 g) butter, cut into small pieces
2 oz (50 g) sugar
1 egg yolk
2 oz (50 g) ground almonds
Few drops almond essence

Sift the flour into a mixing bowl. Rub in the butter until the mixture resembles breadcrumbs. Mix in the remaining ingredients until a smooth dough is formed.

Shape the dough into a ball, wrap it in greaseproof paper and chill in the refrigerator for 1 hour.

Pâte sucrée

This amount of pastry will line one 11-inch (28-cm) flan tin. Pâte sucrée is sometimes called French flan pastry.

MAKES 6 OUNCES (175 G)

6 oz (175 g) flour
3 oz (75 g) softened butter, cut into pieces
1 oz (25 g) castor sugar
1 oz (25 g) icing sugar
3 egg yolks
Vanilla essence

Sift the flour on to a marble slab or wooden board. Make a well in the centre and put in the butter, sugar, egg yolks and a few drops of vanilla essence.

With the fingertips of one hand, mix the butter, sugar, yolks and essence together, gradually drawing in the flour. When all the flour has been drawn in, flatten the dough with the heel of your hand to make it smooth, then draw it up together again. Repeat the process no more than six times.

Wrap the dough in greaseproof paper and let it rest for at least 40 minutes before using.

Mix the butter, eggs and sugar together, drawing in the flour.

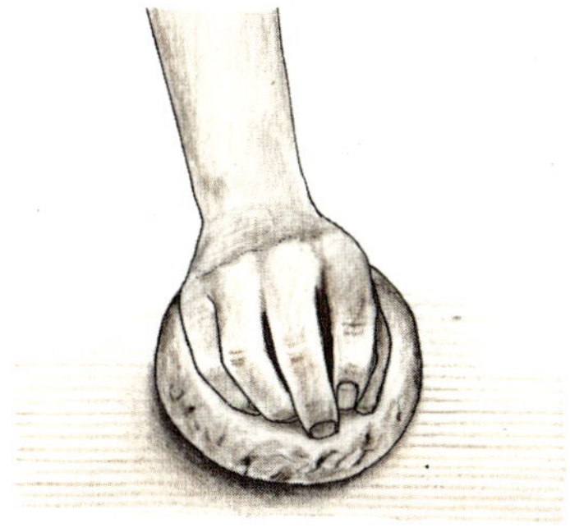

Flatten the dough with the heel of your hand several times.

Flaky pastry

MAKES 6 OUNCES (175 G)

6 oz (175 g) flour
Pinch salt
2 oz (50 g) butter
2 oz (50 g) vegetable lard
3 to 4 tablespoons iced water

Sift the flour and salt into a bowl. Cut half the butter into the flour then rub it in with your fingertips. Mix in the water to make a dough, adding more if necessary. Shape the dough into a ball and chill.

Roll out the dough into an oblong. Cut half the lard into small pieces and dot it over two-thirds of the dough. Fold the unused one-third of dough upwards, and the top third downwards and over. Turn the dough so that the open end faces you and roll it out into an oblong. Cut up the remaining butter, dot it over the dough and repeat the process. Cut up the remaining lard and repeat the process.

If the dough looks very streaky roll it out and fold it once more. Wrap the dough in greaseproof paper and chill before using.

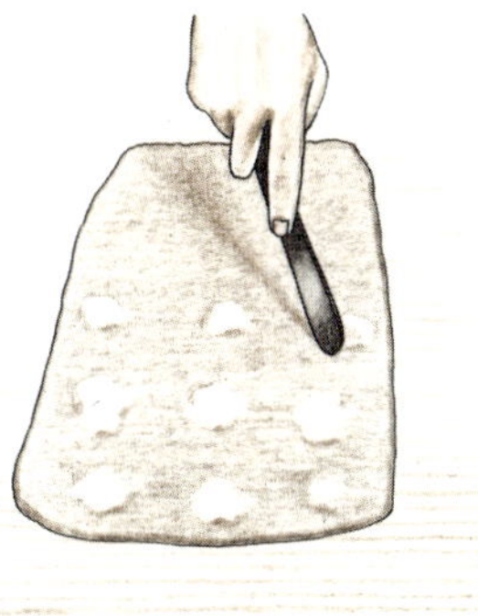

Dot the butter over two-thirds of the rolled-out dough.

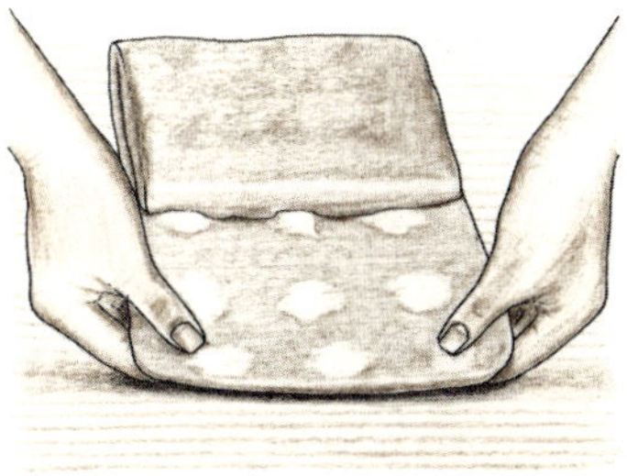

Fold the dough in three and seal the edges before rolling out.

Puff pastry

This amount of pastry will make six 3-inch (8-cm) bouchée cases.

MAKES 6 OUNCES (175 G)

6 oz (175 g) flour (strong white flour is preferable)
Pinch salt
6 oz (175 g) butter
1 teaspoon lemon juice
About 4 fl oz (125 ml) iced water

Sift the flour and salt into a bowl and add a walnut-sized piece of the butter. Cut it into small pieces then lightly rub it into the flour with your fingertips. Mix in the lemon juice and most of the water to make a firm dough, adding a little more water if necessary. Turn the dough out on to a lightly floured slab or board and knead it very gently, for the shortest time possible, until the dough is smooth.

Roll the dough out into a square about $\frac{1}{2}$ inch (1 cm) thick. Place the remaining butter between two sheets of greaseproof paper and beat it (no more than two or three times) until it is pliable but not soft. Remove the paper and place the butter in the centre of the dough. Wrap the dough up like a parcel to enclose the butter. Wrap the parcel in greaseproof paper and chill for 15 minutes.

Remove the dough from the refrigerator, unwrap it and place it on the board or slab, the join facing upwards. Flatten it slightly with the rolling pin, then roll it out to an oblong about $\frac{1}{2}$ inch (1 cm) thick. Turn the dough so that the short end is facing you. Fold the bottom third over towards the middle. Bring the top third down over the folded third to make three layers of dough. Turn the dough round so that the open edges are facing you and seal the edges by pressing lightly with the rolling pin. Roll the dough out into an oblong again and fold as before. Wrap the dough in greaseproof paper and chill for 15 minutes.

Repeat the rolling and folding process another four times. Chill the dough for at least 20 minutes before using.

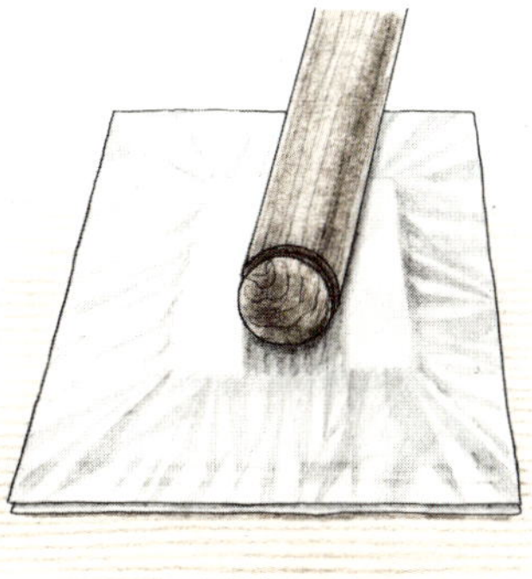

Put the butter between sheets of paper and beat to flatten.

Put the butter on the rolled-out dough and fold in the sides.

Fold the dough in three and turn the open edges towards you.

Roll the dough out, fold it again and repeat four times.

Cereals/pastry

Pour the flour into the liquid.

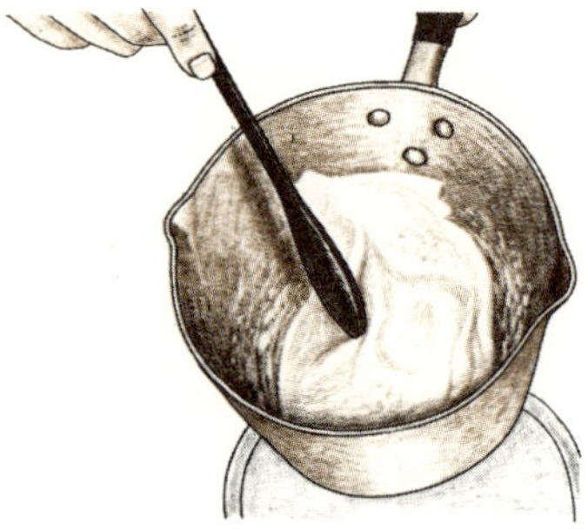

Beat until smooth and glossy.

Choux pastry
This amount of pastry will make eighteen 4-inch (10-cm) éclairs.

MAKES FIVE OUNCES (138 G)

$\frac{1}{2}$ pint (300 ml) water
$\frac{1}{4}$ lb (125 g) butter, cut into pieces
5 oz (150 g) flour
3 eggs

Put the water and butter into a saucepan over moderate heat. When the butter has melted bring the mixture to the boil. Remove the pan from the heat and let the bubbles subside. Add the flour all at once, stirring quickly until the dough is smooth and leaves the sides of the pan. Cool the dough slightly, then beat in the eggs one at a time. Continue beating vigorously until the dough is glossy. Use immediately.

Strudel pastry
This amount of pastry will make one 6-foot (2-metre) strudel. Once stuffed and rolled it may be cut to fit your baking sheets.

MAKES TEN OUNCES (275 G)

10 oz (275 g) sifted flour
Pinch of salt
1 egg, lightly beaten
7 fl oz (200 ml) lukewarm water
2 tablespoons melted butter

Sift the flour and salt into a mixing bowl. In another mixing bowl, beat the egg, water and butter together with a fork. Stir the liquid into the flour with a wooden spoon to make a soft dough. Place the dough on a lightly floured board or slab and knead it well for about 10 to 15 minutes or until it is smooth and shiny.

The dough will stick to your fingers and be difficult to knead. The technique is to lift the dough with a twist and throw it on to the board, gather it up and throw it again. Continue doing this until the dough ceases to be sticky and becomes smooth and elastic. Shape the dough into a ball, place in a bowl, cover and set aside in a warm, draught-free place for 30 minutes.

Useful baking equipment

The use of a pastry blender instead of your fingertips to mix butter and flour together results in a much lighter and crisper pastry.

Fluted and plain biscuit cutters and a pastry wheel make uniform shapes for biscuits and scones, and a pastry brush is invaluable for glazing pastry, breads and scones.

A pie funnel placed under a pastry lid allows the steam to escape as the pie bakes and so avoids a soggy crust.

For other useful baking equipment, see page 9.

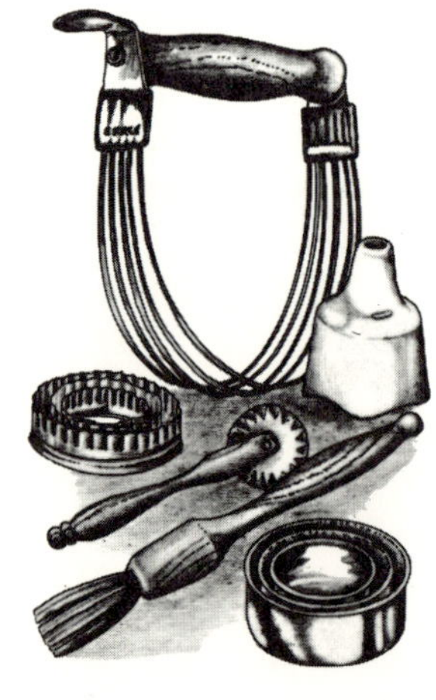

Hot-water crust

MAKES THREE-QUARTER POUND (350 G)

$\frac{3}{4}$ lb (350 g) flour
Pinch of salt
6 fl oz (175 ml) water
3 oz (75 g) lard, cut into pieces

Sift the flour and salt into a bowl and make a well in the middle. Put the water and lard into a small saucepan over moderate heat. When the lard melts, bring the mixture to the boil. Take the pan off the heat and pour the contents into the middle of the flour. Working very quickly, mix the dough with a wooden spoon and then with your hands until it is smooth. It must be used while still warm or the lard will solidify and the dough will become brittle and impossible to mould.

Suet crust
This amount of suet crust will line and cover a $2\frac{1}{2}$- to 3-pint ($1\frac{1}{4}$- to $1\frac{1}{2}$-litre) pudding bowl.

MAKES ONE POUND (450G)

1 lb (450 g) self-raising flour
Pinch of salt
5 oz (150 g) fresh white breadcrumbs
10 oz (275 g) shredded suet
Iced water

Sift the flour and salt into a bowl and stir in the breadcrumbs and suet. Very lightly rub the suet into the flour mixture with your fingertips for just a few minutes. Using a spoon, mix to a spongy dough with a little water. Shape into a ball and use immediately.

Basic pasta dough
Pasta is the Italian name for a dough made with flour, water and eggs or just with flour and water. Spinach, which is sometimes added to the dough, gives it an interesting green colour and good flavour.

The dough is cut to whatever shape is required to make such dishes as ravioli and cannelloni.

MAKES ONE POUND (450 G)

1 lb (450 g) strong white flour
1 teaspoon salt
4 eggs
4 tablespoons water

Put the flour and salt on a pastry board or work surface and make a well in the centre. In a bowl beat the eggs with the water then pour the mixture into the well. Using your hands, combine the flour with the egg mixture until a dough is formed. The dough should be stiff so add more flour if necessary. Shape the dough into a ball then knead it for about 10 minutes or until it is smooth and elastic.

Sour cream pastry
This pastry can be used to make savoury meat loaves, to cover meat pies and to make savoury pasties. If you add a little sugar and grated lemon rind, you can also use it for sweet pies and tartlets.

MAKES SIX OUNCES (175 G)

6 oz (175 g) flour
Pinch of salt
3 oz (75 g) butter
1 small egg yolk
2 tablespoons soured cream
1 to 2 tablespoons iced water

Sift the flour and salt into a large mixing bowl. Add the butter and cut it into small pieces with a knife. Using your fingertips, lightly rub the butter into the flour until the mixture resembles fine breadcrumbs.

In a small bowl, mix the egg yolk with the soured cream and a little of the water.

Make a well in the centre of the flour mixture and add the egg yolk mixture. Mix it into the flour with a knife, then knead the dough lightly, just enough to bring it together.

Shape the dough into a ball and wrap it in greaseproof paper. Chill the dough in the refrigerator for 40 minutes before using.

Cream cheese pastry
This amount of pastry will make about 40 small pies or tarts.

MAKES SIX OUNCES (175 G)

6 oz (175 g) cream cheese
6 oz (175 g) butter
6 oz (175 g) self-raising flour
Salt

Cream the cheese in a bowl. Beat in the butter and mix in the flour and salt.

Knead the dough lightly, shape it into a ball with well-floured hands and chill in the refrigerator for 2 hours.

Cereals/bread

In the past everyone baked their own bread and thought nothing of it. Twentieth-century housewives with less time on their hands have welcomed the factory-made loaf, however, and the art of bread-making has almost been forgotten. For many people the smell and taste of home-made bread has become part of a nostalgic memory.

Today, an interest in healthy eating, a longing for the forgotten flavours of home baking and boredom with the tastelessness of manufactured bread is bringing the home-made loaf back into favour. Bread-making is one of the most exciting and satisfying culinary experiences, yet it is not a complicated process. Simply follow the basic rules and work in a warm, draught-free room, using warm utensils and ingredients.

Yeast is a living organism which, given the right conditions, produces carbon dioxide, the gas that causes bread to rise. Warmth is required to activate yeast—between 75° and 85°F (24° and 29°C) is ideal. A little sugar—a quarter teaspoon for half an ounce (15 g) of yeast—will quicken the process, but too much will slow it down.

Bread can be made from fresh or dried yeast. Fresh yeast should be an even grey-beige colour; it should break with a clean edge and crumble easily. If it is streaky or sour-smelling it is past its best and must be thrown away. Fresh yeast will keep in a plastic bag in the refrigerator for up to a week. Dried yeast will keep in a screw-top jar in a cool cupboard for up to six months.

Mix dried yeast with a little lukewarm water or milk and a quarter teaspoon of sugar and leave it in a warm, draught-free place for about fifteen minutes or until it is frothy and puffed up. This process is necessary to dissolve the granules of dry yeast, but it may also be used as a precaution with fresh yeast to make sure it is still "live".

If a recipe specifies one ounce (25 g) of fresh yeast, use half that quantity of dried yeast. One ounce (25 g) of yeast will raise two pounds (900 g) of flour in about one and a half to two hours.

The all-purpose plain and self-raising flours that are used to make cakes and biscuits are unsuitable for making bread. This is because their gluten content is not sufficiently high; it is the gluten in the flour which makes the dough elastic and springy. Strong white, wholewheat or wholemeal, granary and rye are the main types of flour used for bread-making. Rye, which has a low gluten content, makes a flatter, heavier loaf that is popular in such countries as Norway, Sweden and Germany.

Salt is added to the flour to bring out the flavour of the bread—use about one teaspoon to every pound (450 g) of flour. Never add salt directly to the yeast because it slows down its growth.

Use lukewarm water or milk, or a mixture of both, to bind the flour into a dough. If the liquid is too hot it will kill the yeast. The amount of liquid required varies with the kind of flour used, because some flours absorb more than others.

Eggs are sometimes added to a white dough (for example brioche) to make it richer and to give it a yellow colour.

Although butter or oil are not essential ingredients, they can be added to a bread dough to help it to expand more easily and to improve its flavour. The bread will also stay fresh longer. Rub the butter into the flour, or melt it and add it with the liquid. Stir oil into the liquid before adding it to the flour.

Apart from the small amount of sugar that is "fed" to the yeast to help activate it, a certain amount can also be added to the flour to sweeten or to improve the flavour of the bread. Honey can be used instead of sugar; its hygroscopic properties improve the keeping quality of the bread.

Such additional ingredients as dried fruit, cheese, herbs, garlic and malt can be added to the dough to make sweet or savoury breads. They are generally mixed in with the flour, with the exception of malt, which goes in with the liquid.

When all the ingredients have been mixed together, shape the dough into a ball, turn it out on to a floured board and knead it for at least ten minutes. Kneading is vital for two reasons: it distributes the ingredients evenly to make a smooth-textured, evenly risen bread, and it develops the gluten content in the flour. It also reduces the stickiness of the dough.

After kneading the dough, shape it into a ball and place it in a large, lightly greased bowl. Cover the bowl with plastic wrap or a damp cloth and set it aside for the dough to rise in a warm, draught-free place until it has doubled in bulk—it will take up to two hours. The time the dough takes to rise depends on the ingredients used and the weather. If, however, it rises too quickly the texture of the bread may be uneven.

As soon as the dough has doubled in bulk, turn it out of the bowl and punch it to knock out the air pockets, then knead it again for two to three minutes.

Bread dough can be baked in tins, or shaped into rolls, a plait, or a ball with a cross cut on top, and baked on a baking sheet. Having shaped the dough, or put it in a tin, leave it to rise for up to one hour. It must double in bulk, and, if it is in a bread tin, it should rise to the top of the tin. Then brush the top lightly with salted water, egg yolk or milk or a mixture of both, or with melted butter, and sprinkle over coarse salt, nuts, or poppy seeds. For how to bake bread and for bread recipes see page 198.

Yeast dough is also used to make flat bread or pitta. The ingredients are plain flour (white or wholemeal), yeast, water, salt and sometimes a little oil and the proportions and the preparation of the dough are the same as for ordinary bread. Punch the dough down, divide it into pieces, then roll out into rounds. Dust with flour, cover and leave to prove. Set the oven at its highest. Heat lightly oiled baking sheets for ten minutes, slip the dough on to them and bake for six to ten minutes or until puffed up but not coloured. Cool on a rack.

Cereals/bread

Basic bread dough

MAKES ONE LARGE LOAF

$\frac{3}{4}$ oz (20 g) fresh yeast
1 tablespoon plus 1 pinch sugar
$\frac{3}{4}$ pint (450 ml) lukewarm water
1$\frac{1}{2}$ lb (700 g) strong white or wholewheat flour
2 teaspoons salt
$\frac{1}{2}$ oz (15 g) butter

Mash the yeast with the pinch of sugar and 2 tablespoons of the water in a small bowl until smooth. Set aside in a warm, draught-free place for 15 minutes or until the mixture is puffed up and frothy.

Sift the flour and salt into a mixing bowl and rub in the butter. Stir in the sugar and make a well in the centre. Pour in the yeast mixture and the remaining water and mix to a dough. When the dough comes away from the sides of the bowl, turn it out on to a floured surface and knead for 10 minutes, or until it is smooth and elastic.

Put the dough in a lightly oiled bowl and cover with a damp cloth. Set aside in a warm, draught-free place for 1 to 1$\frac{1}{2}$ hours, or until doubled in bulk.

Turn the dough out of the bowl and knead it for about 3 minutes. Either shape the dough and put it on a greased baking sheet, or put it in a greased loaf tin. Set aside in a warm place for at least 30 minutes, or until it has doubled in bulk or risen to the top of the tin. The dough can now be glazed and baked.

See page 198 for instructions on baking bread.

Let the yeast mixture rise.

Pour it into the flour mixture.

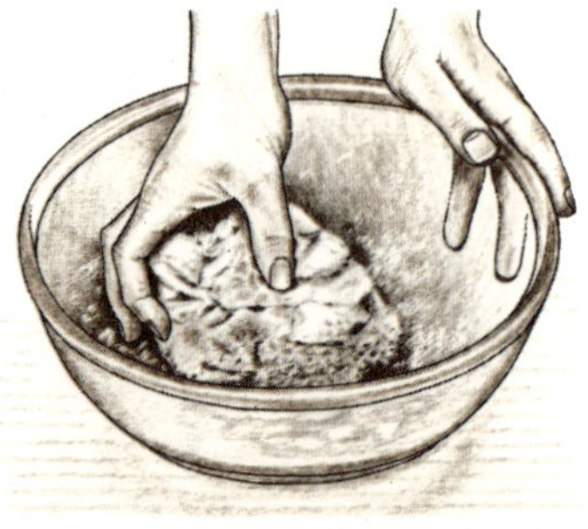

Mix to a dough with your hands.

Knead the dough for 10 minutes.

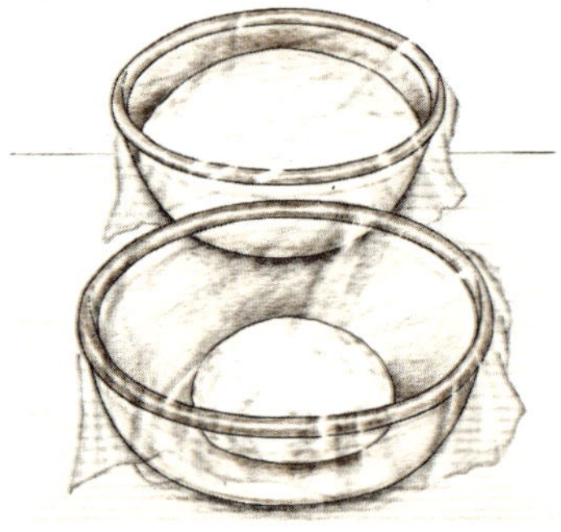

Let the dough double in bulk.

Shape it and let it rise again.

Breadcrumbs, bread cases and croûtons

Breadcrumbs should always be made with bread that is at least one day old. Fresh white breadcrumbs are used for making meat loaves, stuffings and bread sauce. To make breadcrumbs, cut off the crusts, then rub the bread through a sieve, pull it apart with your fingers or a fork, or use a liquidizer. Fresh breadcrumbs will not keep and must be used immediately.

Dry white breadcrumbs are used to coat food that is to be fried. Put fresh breadcrumbs on a baking tray and cook them in a very low oven, 250°F (130°C, Gas Mark $\frac{1}{2}$), until they are dried but not brown. Dried breadcrumbs can be stored in a screw-top jar for several weeks.

Dry brown breadcrumbs are used to cover a gratin. Take several crusts of bread and brown them in a 325°F (170°C, Gas Mark 3) oven. Place the browned crusts on a pastry board and crush them with a rolling pin or in a liquidizer. If the crumbs are not to be used immediately store them in an airtight container.

Bread cases make unusual and delicious containers for all sorts of foods. To make them, follow the step-by-step instructions on this page.

Croûtons are made from toasted or fried cubes or thin slices of bread. The smaller cubes are used as a garnish for soups or added to a dressed green salad just before serving. The larger slices are used to put under a steak or chop. To make fried croûtons, trim the crusts, cut the bread into cubes and fry in butter, bacon fat or oil.

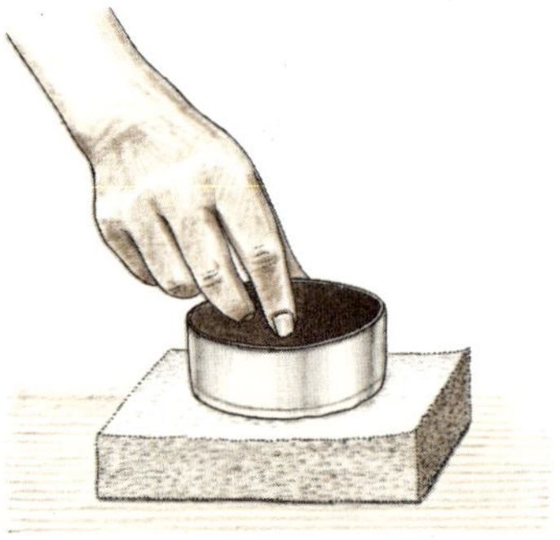

Cut a circle out of a very thick piece of bread with a round biscuit cutter.

Cut out a smaller circle, not quite to the bottom, or scrape the bread out with a knife.

To make large bread cases, cut the crust off a large oblong loaf and slice in half.

With a knife, scrape the insides out of each half to make two bread cases.

Eggs and dairy produce

Eggs

Keep eggs at room temperature (70° to 75°F/21° to 24°C) for an hour or two before using them, except when they are needed for frying, when they may be taken straight from the refrigerator.

Although it is possible to buy a special gadget for separating egg whites from egg yolks, the three-bowl method is still the most successful. Have ready three bowls, one of which should be large and deep and in which the whites can be beaten. This bowl should be made of copper, glazed earthenware or glass, but not of plastic or aluminium, which have a detrimental effect on the colour and volume of the beaten whites. Wash the bowls and whisk thoroughly before using them. If you cannot be sure that every trace of grease has been removed, rub all round with a lemon slice or some vinegar, then rinse and dry.

To separate an egg, give it a sharp tap in the middle of its side against one of the smaller bowls. Then, holding the egg in both hands with the cracked side uppermost and the wider end lower than the pointed end, ease the two halves of the shell apart. While you are doing this some of the egg white will slip into the bowl. To finish separating the egg, tip the yolk from one half of the shell to the other until there is no white left in the shell. Tip the egg yolk into the bowl that has not yet been used, transfer the egg white into the larger, deep bowl, then begin the process again with another egg. This process may seem tedious, but it helps you to discover a bad egg before it taints the others in the bowl.

If, while you are separating an egg, the yolk breaks, try and remove any that has fallen into the white, using the broken eggshell to scoop it up. If this fails, tip the whole egg into an airtight container and store it in the refrigerator to be used for another purpose. The reason for this is that egg whites will not whip to several times their original volume if they come into contact with even a trace of the fat from the broken yolk.

The traditional way to beat egg whites, and one the purists say is the most effective, is to use a copper bowl and a wire whisk. If you do not have either a copper bowl or the endurance to use a wire whisk, a rotary electric beater will do; the result may not be quite as good but it will be adequate.

To whip egg whites in the traditional way, take a thin wire whisk and with a relaxed wrist and light touch beat steadily until the whites become foamy. Increase the tempo and beat more vigorously until they stand in stiff, glossy peaks. Overbeating will make them dry.

Use three bowls when cracking eggs to prevent yolks mixing with whites.

Dairy produce

Before beating double cream (single cream cannot be beaten), particularly in warm weather, chill the cream, the bowl in which it is to be beaten and the wire whisk (a rotary or electric beater may also be used). Then beat the cream until it thickens and forms soft, glossy peaks when you lift the beater. Check frequently to see if the cream is thick enough. If you overbeat cream it will turn into butter.

All eggs used in the recipes in this book are standard eggs that weigh about two ounces (50 g) each.

Clarified butter

Butter is clarified to clear it of impurities, salt and milk solids. The result is a pure fat that, when heated, does not burn as easily as butter and is therefore more useful for frying at higher temperatures. Clarified butter is also used in such recipes as potted shrimps and *cervelles au beurre noir* (brains in black butter).

To clarify butter, put it in a pan over very low heat and let it melt. When it has melted cook it for thirty seconds without colouring. Remove any scum from the surface, take the pan off the heat and strain the butter into a bowl through a sieve lined with muslin. Put the bowl aside for a few minutes to allow any sediment to settle at the bottom, then pour the butter into a clean bowl, leaving the sediment behind. The butter is now clarified and ready for use, or it can be stored in an airtight container in the refrigerator.

Butter curls and moulds

To make butter curls, dip a butter curler into warm water then run it along the top of a slab of firm, but not frozen, butter. Butter moulds and stamps must be dipped first in boiling water then in iced water before use. When using a mould, cut the butter into squares the same size as the mould.

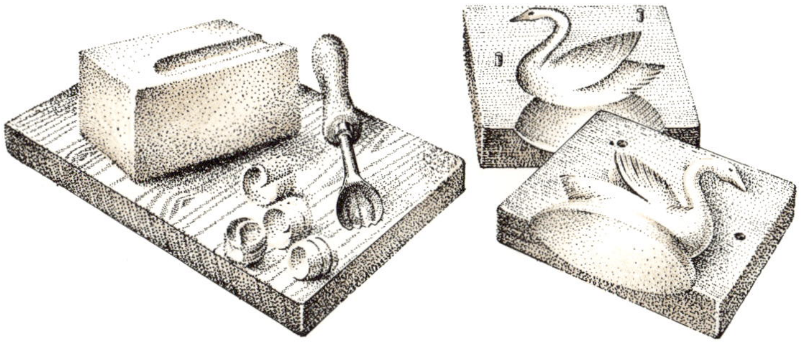

To present butter attractively, use a butter curler or butter moulds.

The heart of good cooking

Stock is to the cook what foundations are to the builder, for so many of the great dishes of Western cooking are based on this simply made yet indispensable liquid.

There is something marvellously rewarding about making stock. You put a few bones in a pan of water, add some meat and vegetable trimmings and a few herbs and simmer until all the flavour of the ingredients has been extracted. Thus with very little effort you have created something valuable out of almost nothing.

Stock makes a homely soup seem luxurious. It is an essential part of all brown sauces and some white sauces. It is used in stews, casseroles and many dishes where the food is braised, poached or sautéed. As Mistress Margaret Dods, a nineteenth-century Scottish cook, wrote, stock is a "floating capital subservient to many purposes", and it does indeed give us much interest.

Stocks

It is a great pity that the art of making good stock has been abandoned by so many cooks in favour of the stock cube.

Home-made stock is so easy to make—bones, meat and vegetables (or vegetables alone) are simmered in water until all their flavour has been extracted. Strained, cooled and any fat skimmed off, the stock is then ready to be used as the base for countless soups, sauces and gravies, and for all kinds of casseroles, stews and savoury pies. And, apart from the culinary considerations, making your own stock is an economy no cook can afford to ignore. So much of the debris of cooking—fish and meat bones, game and poultry carcasses and vegetable peelings—is there waiting to be turned into delicious and nourishing stock. To throw it away is a wasteful and unnecessary extravagance.

The stock pot, however, should never be treated as a garbage bin for kitchen waste. You should give the same careful thought to choosing the ingredients for a stock as you would for a stew. And you should also take into consideration how the stock is going to be used. White stocks, for example, are used for making cream sauces, white stews and soups.

It is a good idea to freeze bones or poultry carcasses until there are enough of them to make the preparation of stock worth while. But if you need to make a stock and have no leftover bones, or not enough of them, you can buy them from the butcher; or you can use a piece of stewing meat such as flank, shin or silverside, rich in gelatine, which gives taste to a stock.

A simple household stock can be made from the bones of cooked meat and chicken, bacon rinds, mushroom peelings and stalks, carrots, onions and leeks. A small piece of beef shin or stewing veal added to the pot will give body to the liquor and will improve its flavour and colour.

Only a little salt should be added to a basic stock because the stock will become unpleasantly salty if it has to be reduced in volume by boiling.

Stock can be kept in the refrigerator for about one week provided it is well covered.

Points to remember when making stock:

Never add cooked vegetables or gravies to the stockpot.

Use unpeeled onions for making brown stock, and peeled onions for light stock.

Always put the ingredients into cold water and bring it slowly to the boil, then simmer on a very low, even heat.

Remove as much scum as possible before the stock comes to the boil. Do not leave or store stock in a warm place because it will soon turn sour.

Household stock

MAKES 1 QUART (1 LITRE)

3 lb (1½ kg) cooked meat bones
½ lb (225 g) stewing steak or beef or veal shin
Chicken carcass and giblets (but not the liver)
A few bacon rinds
2 quarts (2 litres) water
Mushroom peelings and stalks
2 onions, sliced
2 carrots, sliced
2 leeks, sliced
1 celery stalk, sliced
Bouquet garni

Saw the bones into short lengths. Put them into a pot and brown them slightly without adding any fat. Add the meat, chicken carcass, giblets and bacon rinds. Pour on the water and bring it slowly to the boil, skimming off the scum as it forms.

Add the vegetables and the bouquet garni. Partly cover the pan and simmer very gently for 3 hours.

Strain the stock into a large bowl through a sieve lined with wet muslin. Discard the contents of the sieve. When the stock is cool, cover it and refrigerate.

Bone stock

MAKES 3 PINTS (1½ LITRES)

4 lb (2 kg) beef marrow bones, sawn into short lengths
3 quarts (3 litres) water
1 lb (450 g) beef shin or veal knuckle and stewing veal
¼ lb (100 g) bacon trimmings
2 onions, sliced
2 carrots, sliced
1 celery stalk, sliced
Mushroom trimmings and stalks
2 leeks, cut in half
Bouquet garni

Wrap the bones in muslin to prevent the loss of the marrow and put them into a large pot. Pour in the water and bring it slowly to the boil. As it begins to boil, skim off the scum. Add the remaining ingredients, half cover the pot and simmer gently for 1 hour. Remove the vegetables, because all their flavour will have been extracted, and continue simmering for a further 2 hours. Do not let the stock boil quickly or it will become cloudy. Strain the stock into a bowl through a colander lined with wet muslin. When the stock is cool, cover it and put it in the refrigerator.

Other bone stocks:

Brown stock

Brown stock is made in the same way, except that the bones are browned in dripping in a roasting tin before being put into the stock pot.

White stock

Use veal bones and ½ pound (225 g) of stewing veal instead of the beef.

Game bird or chicken stock

For stock made with only the carcass, proceed as for bone stock but cook for only 1 hour. The best chicken stock, however, is made from a jointed boiling fowl, which should simmer for 3 hours. A good chicken stock can also be made from chicken wings, necks and backs.

Vegetable stock

Vegetable stock is used for many delicately flavoured soups.

MAKES 3 PINTS (1½ LITRES)

1 oz (25 g) butter
1 lb (450 g) carrots, cut into large pieces
1 lb (450 g) onions, peeled and cut into large pieces
6 celery stalks, cut into large pieces
½ lb (225 g) turnips, peeled and cut into large pieces
1 leek, sliced
Bouquet garni
6 peppercorns
2 teaspoons salt
3 quarts (3 litres) hot water

Melt the butter in a large pan or casserole. Add the vegetables and cook them over low heat, stirring frequently, until they are brown. Add the remaining ingredients and the water and bring it to the boil. Partially cover the pan and simmer for 3 hours. The liquid should have reduced to about one-third of its original volume. Pour the stock into a bowl through a colander lined with wet muslin. Cool the stock, then store it in the refrigerator until it is needed.

Pot au feu

In most French households a pot au feu is cooked every week. This provides a stock that is full of body, as well as delicious boiled meat, which is served either hot or cold.

If the meat is to be served hot, remove some of the stock (it may require seasoning) to serve with it. The vegetables from the pot may be served with the meat along with jacket potatoes, horseradish, mustard, gherkins and a salad.

If the meat is to be served cold, let it cool in the stock and serve it sliced the next day with a potato salad dressed with a vinaigrette to which chopped capers, shallots and parsley have been added. Garnish the dish with quartered hard-boiled eggs. Serve it as a main course or as an hors d'oeuvre.

Traditionally a pot au feu is cooked in a deep earthenware marmite, but an enamel or stainless-steel pot will do just as well.

SERVES SIX

2 lb (900 g) beef flank
½ lb (225 g) beef shin
1 lb (450 g) veal knuckle, cut into pieces
½ lb (225 g) ox liver (optional)
1 lb (450 g) oxtail, cut into pieces and soaked in cold water for 2 hours
3 quarts (3 litres) cold water
2 onions, halved
2 leeks, halved
2 carrots
1 celery stalk
½ lb (225 g) turnip or swede, peeled
1 tomato, halved
Bouquet garni
2 teaspoons salt
4 peppercorns

Put all the meats into a pot. Pour in the water and very slowly bring it to the boil, skimming off the scum as it rises to the top. The scum will be quite thick and will continue to surface as the water begins to simmer. When the scum is sparse and white add the vegetables and seasonings. Partly cover the pan and simmer very gently for 3 hours.

Remove the pan from the heat and take out all the vegetables and meat. Strain the stock into a bowl through a colander lined with wet muslin. Skim the fat off the top using kitchen paper to absorb the grease or, if the stock is not to be used at once, leave it to cool, then refrigerate and remove the layer of solidified fat before reheating.

Stocks

Fish stock
Fish stock is used to make sauces that are required to coat a finished fish dish. This is suitable for sole, plaice, whiting and turbot. If the fishmonger is filleting fish for you be sure to ask for the heads and bones—and some extra ones if you feel you will need them.

MAKES ABOUT 1 QUART (1 LITRE)

1 lb (450 g) fish bones, from sole, plaice, turbot or whiting
1 onion, sliced
½ oz (15 g) parsley or parsley stalks
1 oz (25 g) butter
Strips of lemon peel
2 fl oz (50 ml) white wine
6 peppercorns
1 teaspoon salt
1 quart (1 litre) cold water

Break the bones into pieces and put them into a pan with all the other ingredients. Partly cover the pan and simmer the stock for 20 minutes. Pour the stock through a sieve. Cool the stock and then keep in the refrigerator until it is needed.

Court bouillon
This is basically a seasoned, acidic liquid in which such large whole fish as salmon and turbot are cooked. The simplest court bouillon is strained sea water to which vinegar or lemon juice has been added.

MAKES 1½ QUARTS (1½ LITRES)

¼ pint (150 ml) white wine
2 quarts (2 litres) water
2 onions, peeled
½ lb (225 g) carrots, sliced
1 bay leaf
1 large thyme sprig
1¼ oz (30 g) salt
¼ pint (150 ml) tarragon vinegar
1 oz (25 g) parsley, with stalks
12 peppercorns

Put all the ingredients into a saucepan and bring to just under boiling point. Simmer gently for 1 hour. Strain, cool and refrigerate until needed.

To clarify stock
Stock is clarified to make clear, sparkling aspics, consommés and chaudfroids. The ingredients used include a small amount of minced raw beef, which helps the clarification process and enriches the stock. A stock can be clarified without the beef, but it will be less tasty.

½ lb (225 g) stewing steak, minced
1½ pints (900 ml) cold stock
2 fl oz (50 ml) sherry or wine (optional)
1 egg shell, broken up
1 egg white, whipped until frothy

Put the meat, stock, wine, if you are using it, and the egg shell into a large pan. Add the egg white and whisk steadily. Stop whisking when the stock comes to the boil. Without disturbing the crust that will have formed on the top, allow the stock to rise in the pan, then remove the pan from the heat. Line a colander with a piece of clean muslin that has been scalded and then wrung out. Gently tip the crust into the colander and pour the stock slowly through it.

Aspic
Make the stock for the aspic in the same way as bone stock, but use a calf's foot and a chicken carcass instead of the marrow bones. For a fish aspic make a strong fish stock using only sole bones.

MAKES ABOUT 1 QUART (1 LITRE)

1 quart (1 litre) stock
2 fl oz (50 ml) sherry
2 fl oz (50 ml) white wine
2 tablespoons wine vinegar
2 oz (50 g) gelatine, dissolved in a little of the stock
2 egg whites, whipped until frothy

Put the stock, sherry, wine, vinegar and gelatine in a large pan. Add the egg whites and whisk steadily. Stop when the stock boils and rises in the pan. Draw the pan aside, then return it to the heat and allow the stock to boil and rise in the pan again. Repeat this once more. Do not disturb the crust that will have formed on the top.

Remove the pan from the heat. Line a colander with a piece of clean muslin that has been scalded and then wrung out. Gently tip the crust into the colander and pour the stock slowly through it.

Let the aspic cool and use it when it is on the point of setting.

Soups

A soup can be delicious or dreadful, depending on the amount of care, time and effort you are prepared to devote to its preparation.

One of the nicest things about soups is their variety—they range from thin and delicate, like a consommé, to rich and creamy, like crème Crécy, and can be made from almost any ingredients that have enough flavour.

Soup is usually served as a first course, but a thick soup makes an excellent light lunch. Some soups, such as pot au feu, can be eaten as a complete meal, with the broth being served as the first course and the ingredients—meat and vegetables—as the main course.

There are many types of soups, but for convenience they can be divided into two groups—thin soups and thick soups. The thin soups include consommés and broths and the thick soups include creams, veloutés, purées and bisques. In addition, there are soups that do not fit into any category—a fruit soup, a beer soup and a gazpacho. When you have mastered the techniques of making these soups, you can experiment with all kinds of ingredients to create soups in a variety of flavours and textures.

A garnish can alter the taste of a soup and add texture. It can make a thin soup more filling and a plain soup more fancy. The simplest garnishes are chopped fresh parsley, chives, basil, mint and watercress, slices of lemon or orange, grated cheese, croûtons and whipped or soured cream. More elaborate garnishes are choux pastry puffs, quenelles, dumplings and tiny meatballs.

Clear, sparkling consommés are made from well-flavoured stocks that have been clarified with egg whites and shells.

THIN SOUPS

Consommé Madrilène

Serve this consommé hot, or well chilled with lemon quarters. If the chicken stock is not strong enough to set, add 1 to 1½ teaspoons of gelatine to every pint (575 ml) of stock.

SERVES FOUR

1 quart (1 litre) chicken stock, made from fresh chicken or from chicken wings and necks
¾ lb (350 g) ripe tomatoes, finely chopped
6 oz (170 g) minced beef
2 egg whites, whipped to a froth
Pinch cayenne pepper
Salt and pepper

Combine the cold stock, tomatoes, beef and egg whites in a large saucepan. Bring the mixture to the boil over moderate heat, whisking constantly. Allow the soup to rise up the sides of the pan as it boils, then turn down the heat to low and simmer very, very gently for 30 minutes. Add the cayenne and season to taste.

Remove the pan from the heat and strain the soup through a sieve lined with wet muslin. Serve the soup hot, or cool and then chill the consommé in the refrigerator before serving.

Consommé aux profiteroles

SERVES FOUR

Make this consommé in the same way as the Madrilène, but add a little fresh tarragon with the other ingredients to the stock. After straining the soup, put it back into the saucepan, which has been rinsed out.

Meanwhile, make up half a recipe of choux pastry and stir in 1 ounce (25 g) of finely grated Parmesan cheese. Pipe or spoon the pastry into pea-sized balls on to a greased baking sheet and bake in a hot oven, 400°F (200°C, Gas Mark 6), for 5 to 8 minutes or until golden. Serve the choux puffs separately with the hot consommé.

Game consommé

One stewing partridge or pheasant or two pigeons may be used to make this well-flavoured consommé. Serve it with fried croûtons.

SERVES SIX

1 oz (25 g) butter
1 onion, sliced
½ lb (225 g) stewing veal, cut into small cubes
1 onion, unpeeled and cut in half
3 carrots
1 celery stalk
Bouquet garni
1 teaspoon salt
8 peppercorns
1 stewing game bird
3 pints (1½ litres) cold water

Melt the butter in a large saucepan. Add the sliced onion and fry, stirring, until golden. Add the veal and continue frying until it is slightly browned.

Stir in the rest of the vegetables, the bouquet garni, salt and peppercorns and the game bird. Pour over the water and bring it slowly to the boil. Skim off the scum, partly cover the pan and simmer very gently for 3 hours.

Strain the liquid through a sieve lined with wet muslin. Cool and then chill the consommé. Remove any fat.

To serve, reheat the consommé, adjusting the seasoning if necessary.

Bortsch

Chilled Bortsch makes a refreshing start to a summer meal. A few chopped chives sprinkled on the soured cream adds flavour and makes an attractive garnish.

SERVES FOUR

1 quart (1 litre) clarified beef stock
¾ lb (350 g) beetroot, peeled and grated
Salt and pepper
¼ pint (150 ml) soured cream

Put the stock into a saucepan, add the beetroot and simmer gently for 30 minutes. Strain the soup through a sieve lined with wet muslin. Season to taste. Chill the bortsch and serve topped with soured cream.

Soups

Scotch broth

Broths are seldom thickened or clarified. They usually thicken naturally from being cooked with such ingredients as rice, pasta, potatoes, beans or barley.

SERVES SIX

2 lb (900 g) neck of mutton, trimmed of excess fat and cut into small pieces
3 pints (1½ litres) water
2 tablespoons pearl barley, blanched for 1 minute and drained
2 leeks, diced
2 carrots, diced
2 small turnips, diced
1 onion, diced
2 celery stalks, diced
Salt and pepper
Chopped parsley

Put the meat into a large saucepan. Pour over the water and bring it to the boil, skimming off any scum as it rises. Add the barley and simmer for 20 minutes. Put in the vegetables and seasoning, cover the pan and simmer the broth for 1 hour.

Remove the meat from the pan. Take the meat from the bones and discard the bones. Skim off the fat from the surface of the broth with a metal spoon, or by touching the surface of the soup with kitchen paper. Return the meat to the pan. Serve hot, garnished with the parsley.

Minestrone

SERVES SIX

½ lb (225 g) haricot beans, soaked overnight in cold water and drained
3 pints (1½ litres) beef stock
2 tablespoons olive oil
½ lb (225 g) onions, chopped
¼ lb (125 g) celery, chopped
1 garlic clove, crushed
1 lb (450 g) canned Italian tomatoes
2 oz (50 g) parsley, finely chopped
½ small cabbage, finely chopped
2 courgettes, cut into small cubes
Salt and pepper
Parmesan cheese

Place the beans in a large saucepan with the stock. Bring the stock to the boil, reduce the heat to low and simmer for 1 hour.

Heat the oil in a frying-pan, add the onions and celery and fry them until the onions are transparent but not brown. Stir in the garlic and fry for a few seconds. Scrape the contents of the frying-pan into the stock. Add the tomatoes and half the parsley and simmer for 15 minutes. Add the cabbage and courgettes and cook for a further 15 minutes.

Add the seasoning. Sprinkle the remaining parsley over the soup and serve it with the Parmesan cheese handed round in a separate bowl.

Potage bonne femme

This soup may be served with a dish of fried croûtons. A little cream may be stirred into the soup just before serving.

SERVES FOUR

2 oz (50 g) butter
¾ lb (350 g) leeks, white part only, chopped
1 lb (450 g) potatoes, peeled and chopped
1½ pints (875 ml) stock
Salt and pepper
½ teaspoon sugar
A few parsley sprigs

Melt the butter in a large saucepan and cook the leeks gently until they are softened. Add the potatoes, stock, salt, pepper and sugar. Bring the stock to the boil, skimming off any scum as it rises. Reduce the heat and simmer for 20 minutes.

Adjust the seasoning, if necessary, and add the parsley before serving.

Thin mushroom soup

SERVES FOUR

1 oz (25 g) butter
1 lb (450 g) mushrooms, very thinly sliced
1 garlic clove, crushed
1 quart (1 litre) chicken or veal stock
2 fl oz (50 ml) sherry

Melt the butter in a large saucepan and add the mushrooms and garlic. Cook gently for a few minutes, stirring constantly, then add the stock. Bring the stock to simmering point and simmer for 1 minute. Remove the pan from the heat, add the sherry and serve.

French onion soup

SERVES FOUR

2 oz (50 g) butter
3 large onions, preferably Breton, peeled and thinly sliced
1 quart (1 litre) chicken or beef stock
Salt and pepper
12 French bread slices
¼ lb (125 g) grated Gruyère cheese

Melt the butter in a large saucepan. Add the onions and fry them for about 15 minutes, or until they are soft and lightly browned. Add the stock and salt and pepper to taste. Simmer very gently for 30 minutes.

Preheat the oven to 475°F (240°C, Gas Mark 9). Place the bread slices on a baking sheet and bake until they are evenly browned on both sides.

Pour the soup into a casserole or into 4 individual ovenproof soup bowls. Float the toast on the top, sprinkle with the cheese and bake in the oven for about 10 minutes, or until the cheese is golden brown on top.

Clam chowder

If fresh clams are not available use two 14-ounce (400-g) cans of minced clams. Measure the liquid in the cans and make it up to 1 pint (575 ml) with water to use in the recipe.

SERVES EIGHT

¼ lb (125 g) fat bacon or salt pork
2 large onions, peeled and chopped
1 lb (450 g) peeled potatoes cut in ½-inch (1-cm) cubes
½ pint (300 ml) water
1 quart (2 lb/900 g) clams, chopped
1 pint (600 ml) milk
1 oz (25 g) butter
Salt and pepper

Cut the fat into cubes and cook it in a casserole over low heat until it is rendered down and quite liquid. Be careful not to burn the fat.

Add the onions and fry them until they are soft and translucent. Add the potatoes and water and cook for 10 minutes. Add the clams, milk, butter and seasoning. Cook for a further 10 minutes, or until the potatoes are tender. Serve hot.

THICK SOUPS

Cream of watercress soup

This basic recipe can be used for such other leafy vegetables as lettuce (use 2 or 3 heads) and spinach (use 1 lb/450 g fresh spinach). Cream of watercress soup is particularly good served with fried croûtons and lemon slices floated on top.

SERVES FOUR

1½ oz (40 g) butter
1 onion, peeled and chopped
4 large bunches watercress, washed, shaken dry and chopped
1 oz (25 g) flour
1 quart (1 litre) milk
Salt and pepper
2 teaspoons arrowroot
4 fl oz (125 ml) cream

Melt the butter in a large saucepan. Add the onion and cook over low heat until soft but not brown. Add the watercress, cover the pan and cook gently for 5 minutes. Remove the pan from the heat and stir in the flour.

Scald the milk (bring it to just under boiling point) and pour it slowly into the pan, stirring constantly. Cook the soup for 15 minutes, stirring occasionally.

Remove the pan from the heat. Either blend the soup in a liquidizer or rub it through a sieve. Return the soup to the pan.

In a small bowl, mix the arrowroot with the cream until smooth. Add a few spoonfuls of soup to the arrowroot and cream mixture then stir it into the soup in the saucepan. Bring the soup to the boil, simmer for 1 minute and serve immediately.

Cream of fish soup Normandy

SERVES SIX

½ lb (225 g) white fish (cod, haddock or whiting)
1 onion, peeled
1 celery stalk
2 tomatoes, skinned and seeded
¼ pint (150 ml) dry white wine
Bouquet garni
1½ pints (900 ml) water
½ lb (225 g) shelled shrimps
1 slice of fresh white bread, crumbled
Salt and pepper
¼ pint (150 ml) double cream
1 tablespoon chopped parsley

Put the fish, onion, celery, tomatoes, wine, bouquet garni and water into a large saucepan and bring to the boil. Reduce the heat and simmer for 30 minutes.

Strain the liquid into another saucepan. Remove all the bones from the fish. Blend the fish and vegetables with some of the liquid in a liquidizer, or rub the mixture through a sieve. Stir the mixture into the liquid in the saucepan. Add the shrimps, breadcrumbs and seasoning and bring the soup to the boil. Remove the pan from the heat and stir in the cream. Garnish with parsley and serve.

Cream of asparagus soup

The recipe can also be made with mushrooms (¾ lb/350 g), cauliflower (1 head) or celery (1 head). Because celery is so stringy, however, it cannot be liquidized. Either rub it through a sieve or use a vegetable mill.

Cream of chicken soup can be made from the basic chicken stock using the same method but omitting both the asparagus and the onion.

This soup can be served chilled or hot.

SERVES FOUR

30 asparagus spears
1 quart (1 litre) chicken stock
1 small onion, peeled and chopped
1½ oz (40 g) butter
1 oz (25 g) flour
Salt and pepper
¼ pint (150 ml) cream

Cut the asparagus into small pieces and reserve a few of the best tips for the garnish. Put the stock, asparagus and onion in a large pan and simmer for 25 minutes.

Remove the pan from the heat and either blend the soup in a liquidizer or rub it through a sieve.

Wash and dry the saucepan and return it to the heat. Put in the butter and when it has melted remove the pan from the heat and stir in the flour. Gradually stir in the soup. Season to taste, return the pan to the heat and bring the soup to the boil, stirring constantly. Simmer for 2 minutes.

Meanwhile, cook the reserved asparagus tips in a little water until tender and add them to the soup with the cream just before serving.

Soups

Cream of avocado soup

This soup is eaten cold, and because avocados discolour, it should be served soon after it is made.

SERVES SIX

3 ripe avocados
2 teaspoons lemon juice
1 quart (1 litre) chicken stock
¼ pint (150 ml) cream
Salt and pepper
Cayenne pepper
1 tomato, skinned, seeded and diced

Cut the avocados in half and scoop out the flesh into a liquidizer, or sieve and sprinkle with the lemon juice. Add some of the stock and either blend in the liquidizer or rub through the sieve.

Stir in the remaining stock, the cream and seasoning, adding just a pinch of cayenne. Garnish with the diced tomato.

Cream of cauliflower soup

This recipe can be used for carrots (Crème Crécy), celeriac, fennel, sorrel, Jerusalem artichokes, turnips and spinach.

SERVES FOUR

2 oz (50 g) butter
¾ lb (350 g) cauliflower florets
1 small onion, chopped
1 pint (575 ml) white stock
½ pint (300 ml) béchamel sauce
¼ pint (150 ml) cream
Salt and pepper

Melt the butter in a large pan. Add the cauliflower florets and the onion and cook for a few minutes until the onion is softened. Add the stock and simmer for about 15 minutes, or until the cauliflower is tender. Remove the pan from the heat. Blend the soup in a liquidizer or rub through a sieve.

Return the soup to the pan. Stir in the béchamel sauce, cream, and salt and pepper to taste. Reheat the soup and serve.

Chicken and mushroom velouté

Velouté is the French word for "velvety". It is the name of a sauce that is based on a roux but which is made with stock instead of milk. Cucumber, celery, chestnuts or white asparagus can be substituted for the mushrooms.

SERVES FOUR

1 pint (575 ml) chicken velouté
1 pint (575 ml) chicken stock
½ lb (225 g) white mushrooms, chopped
¼ pint (150 ml) cream
Salt and white pepper
2 oz (50 g) cooked chicken, shredded
2 oz (50 g) cooked ham, shredded

Combine the velouté and stock in a large saucepan, add the mushrooms and bring to the boil. Reduce the heat and cook, stirring, for 10 minutes. Remove the pan from the heat and either blend the mixture in a liquidizer or rub it through a sieve.

Return the soup to the pan, stir in the cream and season to taste. Reheat the soup but do not let it boil. Garnish with the strips of chicken and ham.

Purée Saint Germain

Puréed soups are usually made from pulses, which thicken while cooking, or from puréed vegetables. They are often finished with an egg and cream liaison before serving, or thickened and enriched with the addition of beurre manié—a paste made from equal quantities of flour and butter—which is added a small piece at a time to the soup.

SERVES SIX

1 lb (450 g) split green peas
1 quart (1 litre) salted water
2 oz (50 g) fatty bacon or bacon fat
½ pint (300 ml) beef stock
Bouquet garni
Pepper
1 tablespoon beurre manié
Fried croûtons

Soak the peas in cold water for 2 to 3 hours. Drain the peas and put them in a large saucepan with the salted water. Bring the water to the boil, skimming off any scum. Partly cover the pan and cook for 2 to 3 hours, or until the peas are tender. Remove the pan from the heat and drain the peas. Blend the peas in a liquidizer or rub them through a sieve.

In a large saucepan fry the fat until it is rendered down. Add the puréed peas, stock, bouquet garni and pepper and simmer for 15 minutes. Remove the bouquet garni, stir in the beurre manié, a small piece at a time, and serve at once with fried croûtons.

Purée of lentil soup

Lentil soup is delicious on a cold day, and it is also rich in iron. Yellow split peas and white haricot beans can be substituted for the lentils.

SERVES FOUR

½ lb (225 g) red lentils, picked over and washed
1 quart (1 litre) stock
1 onion, peeled and stuck with 2 cloves
1 carrot
Bouquet garni
Salt and pepper
1 rasher streaky bacon, chopped
1 oz (25 g) butter

Put the lentils in a large saucepan with the stock and bring to the boil, skimming off any scum as it rises. Add the onion, carrot, bouquet garni, seasoning and bacon and simmer gently, covered, for 1 hour.

Take the pan off the heat and remove and discard the bouquet garni, onion and carrot. Blend the soup in a liquidizer or rub it through a sieve. Pour it back into the saucepan and bring to the boil. Add the seasoning, stir in the butter and serve.

Tomato soup

Canned tomatoes may be used for this recipe if fresh ones are not available.

If the soup does not taste strongly enough of tomato, add some tomato purée.

SERVES FOUR

2 lb (900 g) very ripe tomatoes, halved
1 onion, peeled and diced
2 teaspoons salt
2 teaspoons arrowroot
1½ pints (900 ml) milk or half milk, half stock
1 oz (25 g) butter
¼ teaspoon ground mace
1 teaspoon chopped fresh chervil or parsley

Put the tomatoes, onion and salt in a large saucepan. Cook, covered, for 10 minutes, or until the onion is very soft. Remove the pan from the heat and either blend the mixture in a liquidizer or rub it through a sieve. Return the purée to the pan.

Mix the arrowroot with a little of the milk. Stir it into the sieved tomato with the remaining milk. Cook, stirring, until the mixture is smooth. Stir in the butter, mace and chervil or parsley. When the soup is heated through, serve immediately.

Crème vichyssoise

SERVES FOUR

2 oz (50 g) butter
6 leeks, white part only, thinly sliced
3 potatoes, peeled and sliced
1 quart (1 litre) chicken stock
Salt and white pepper
¼ pint (150 ml) cream
Chopped chives

Melt the butter in a large pan. Add the leeks, cover the pan and cook over moderate heat for about 15 minutes or until they are softened. Shake the pan gently from time to time to prevent the leeks from sticking. Be careful not to let them brown.

Add the potatoes and stock and bring to the boil, stirring. Reduce the heat and simmer for 30 minutes.

Remove the pan from the heat and either blend the soup in a liquidizer or rub it through a sieve. Season to taste.

Cool the soup and stir in the cream. Put the soup in the refrigerator to chill. Serve very cold, garnished with chives.

Fresh green pea and lettuce soup

In the summer fresh peas and lettuce can make a very refreshing soup, especially if made with young peas from the garden.

SERVES FOUR

¼ lb (125 g) butter
2 lb (900 g) green peas, shelled
1 cabbage lettuce, washed and shredded
Salt and pepper
1 teaspoon sugar
1 quart (1 litre) water

Melt the butter in a large saucepan and add the peas, lettuce, salt, pepper and sugar. Cover and cook gently for 5 minutes, shaking the pan. Add the water and cook for 15 minutes.

Remove the pan from the heat and either blend the soup in a liquidizer or rub it through a sieve. Return the soup to the pan. Adjust the seasoning, reheat the soup and serve.

Soup normande

The thinly sliced potatoes disintegrate during the cooking period and thicken the soup.

SERVES SIX TO EIGHT

2 oz (50 g) butter
3 leeks, thinly sliced
2 small white turnips, peeled and thinly sliced
½ lb (225 g) potatoes, peeled and thinly sliced
3 pints (1½ litres) beef stock
¼ lb (125 g) dried Lima beans, cooked, or fresh Lima beans
Salt and pepper
½ pint (300 ml) milk
2 tablespoons double cream

Melt the butter in a large saucepan. Add the leeks and turnips and fry very gently for 2 to 3 minutes without browning them. Add the potatoes and continue to cook until they are soft.

Add the stock and Lima beans and season to taste. Bring the soup to the boil then add the milk. Simmer over low heat for 20 minutes, or until the Lima beans are tender. Stir in the cream and serve.

Lobster bisque

Add a little beurre manié if the soup is too thin.

SERVES SIX

1 lobster, killed but not cooked
1 tablespoon butter
1 tablespoon oil
¼ lb (125 g) each of celery, carrots and onion, finely chopped
Bouquet garni
1 garlic clove
1 pint (575 ml) chicken stock
14 oz (400 g) canned tomatoes
¼ pint (150 ml) dry white wine
2 tablespoons tomato purée
Salt and pepper
Cayenne pepper
¼ pint (150 ml) double cream
2 tablespoons brandy

Break off the lobster's tail. Cut the body into quarters. Discard the sac near the eyes. Reserve any coral. Crack the claws.

In a heavy saucepan melt the butter with the oil. Add the lobster pieces, tail, claws and vegetables and fry, stirring, for 3 to 4 minutes. Add the bouquet garni, garlic, stock, canned tomatoes and wine and bring to the boil. Stir in the coral, if any, and the tomato purée. Cover the pan and simmer for 40 minutes.

Remove the claws and tail from the soup and set aside. Put the lobster carcass in a food mill and push through as much as you can, then liquidize in batches. Return the soup to the saucepan, season to taste, add the cream and bring it to the boil.

Remove the tail and claw meat from the shells. Cut the lobster meat into cubes and add them to the bisque. Pour the brandy into a small saucepan and heat it gently. Ignite it and when the flames have died down, stir it into the soup and serve.

Clam bisque

If fresh clams are not available use canned clams (two 14-ounce/400-g cans), and add them to the soup with the clam juice, rice and tomatoes. Oysters, cockles and mussels may be prepared in exactly the same way. This is a very rich and delicious soup.

SERVES FOUR

12 clams
2 oz (50 g) butter
1 onion, peeled and chopped
1 garlic clove, peeled and chopped
1 teaspoon fresh thyme
2 teaspoons flour
14 oz (400 g) canned tomatoes
Salt and pepper
¼ pint (150 ml) white wine
½ pint (300 ml) cream

Open the clams over a bowl and reserve all the juice and meat.

Melt the butter in a large saucepan and add the onion, garlic and thyme. Fry, stirring, until the onion is soft, then add the clams and cook for 5 minutes. Stir in the flour, tomatoes, seasoning, and clam juice. Bring to the boil. Remove the pan from the heat. Either blend the soup in a liquidizer or rub it through a sieve. Put the soup back into the pan. Add the wine and cream, adjust the seasoning and heat thoroughly before serving.

Soupe à la bière

SERVES FOUR

1 quart (1 litre) beer
¼ lb (100 g) sugar
4 egg yolks
3 tablespoons soured cream
Salt and pepper
Cinnamon
4 slices French bread

Put the beer and sugar into a large saucepan over moderate heat. Stir until the sugar dissolves and remove the pan off the heat.

In a small bowl beat the egg yolks with the soured cream and a little hot beer, then stir it into the rest of the beer. Add the salt, pepper and cinnamon to taste. Return the pan to a low heat. Heat the soup thoroughly but do not let it boil.

Put one slice of bread into each soup bowl, pour the soup over the bread and serve.

Gazpacho

This is always a welcome summer soup. Serve with hot herb bread and black olives.

SERVES SIX

2 lb (900 g) tomatoes, skinned and chopped
1 cucumber, peeled and chopped
1 green pepper, cored, seeded and chopped
2 garlic cloves, chopped
8 fl oz (225 ml) water
5 tablespoons olive oil
4 fl oz (125 ml) wine vinegar
Salt
2 slices fresh white bread

Mix all the ingredients together in a bowl and either blend in a liquidizer for a short period or rub through a fairly coarse sieve. Serve chilled.

Apricot soup

Fruit soups can be made with any fruit or combination of fruits. The fruit may be puréed or finely sliced and the soup may be served hot or well chilled.

SERVES FOUR

1½ lb (700 g) apricots, stoned and sliced
Rind and juice of 1 orange
2 teaspoons lemon juice
2 fl oz (50 ml) white wine
1½ pints (900 ml) water
2 level teaspoons arrowroot
Castor sugar
4 tablespoons whipped cream
A few pistachio nuts, chopped

Put the apricots into a saucepan with a strip of orange rind, the orange and lemon juice, wine and water. Simmer the mixture for 8 to 10 minutes.

In a small cup, mix the arrowroot with 2 tablespoons of water. Remove the pan from the heat and stir in the arrowroot. Return the pan to the heat and bring the soup to the boil, stirring.

Add the sugar to taste. Pour the soup into bowls, garnish with the cream and sprinkle the nuts on top. Serve immediately.

Sauces

Sauces are divided into two categories—savoury and sweet. Among the savoury sauces pride of place naturally goes to the classic sauces—brown (espagnole, demi-glace), white (béchamel and velouté), butter (hollandaise and béarnaise) and cold (mayonnaise and vinaigrette)—and the sauces derived from them. Then there are the dessert sauces and those miscellaneous sauces that do not fit into any particular category.

Most sauces freeze well, including the sensitive butter sauces. A butter sauce should be thawed first and then reheated in a double saucepan. While the sauce is reheating it must be stirred frequently to prevent curdling. Do not freeze mayonnaise as it will separate. Some sauces will keep for up to a week in the refrigerator, but those made with eggs, cream or milk should not be kept for more than three days.

The utensils and tools required for sauce-making can usually be found or improvised in most kitchens. A bowl set over a pan of simmering water, for example, can be substituted for a double saucepan, and a roasting tin filled with hot water makes an adequate bain-marie.

Useful tools include a variety of whisks and beaters, a pestle and mortar, a conical strainer and, best of all, a liquidizer.

For savoury sauces the simplest ingredient is the residue—juices and scrapings—left in a pan after sautéing, grilling, frying or roasting poultry or meat.

Strong, well-flavoured, degreased stocks are essential for certain sauces. They can be made in advance and kept in the refrigerator (remove the top layer of fat only just before using) for up to a week.

Wines and stronger liquors are useful flavourings, particularly when the stock is lacking in body and taste. And to enrich a sauce and improve its consistency there are egg yolks, butter and cream.

The consistency of a sauce varies, depending on how it is to be used; thin for pouring, thicker for coating and thicker still for binding.

One of the simplest ways of thickening a sauce is by reduction. The sauce is boiled or simmered, uncovered, until it is reduced by evaporation. Another common method of thickening is with a roux. Roux is flour cooked in fat, and depending on how long it is cooked and the colour it acquires, it is called white, blond or brown. When making a roux remember that the amount of fat used should always be slightly more than the amount of flour.

Arrowroot and potato flour are often used to thicken sauces. Just over two tablespoons of flour will thicken one pint (575 ml) of thin liquid. Mix the flour in two tablespoons of cold water, stir it into the boiling liquid and cook for a few seconds.

Beurre manié, or kneaded butter, is made from equal quantities of butter and flour kneaded together to make a paste. Form the paste into small pellets and add them one by one to the simmering sauce, stirring constantly. Two ounces (50 g) of beurre manié thickens one pint (575 ml) of thin liquid.

Egg yolks can be used on their own or in combination with butter or cream to thicken sauces. Combine the egg yolks with a little cold stock or milk, then mix in a few tablespoons of the hot sauce. Add the egg mixture to the hot sauce and, stirring constantly, cook it over very low heat until it thickens. If you allow the sauce to boil the eggs will curdle. The addition of a little flour to the egg yolks will help to prevent this. Four egg yolks will thicken one pint (575 ml) of liquid.

Egg yolks combined with butter thicken such sauces as hollandaise and béarnaise and, when combined with oil, thicken a mayonnaise.

Blood (from the animal that is being cooked) is used to thicken some sauces, mainly in game dishes. It is added just before the dish is served. Strain the blood into a bowl, mix in a few spoonfuls of hot sauce and then stir it into the casserole. Simmer (never boil) for two minutes and remove the casserole from the heat.

Although it is essential for a good cook to know how to make the grand sauces, they are not always suitable—for reasons of economy, time and health—for everyday cooking. Often the simple gravy made from pan juices and scrapings of roasted or fried meat is delicious.

To make a deglazed sauce, remove the meat or poultry

from the pan. Remove all the fat. Return the pan to the top of the stove and pour in between two and four fluid ounces (50 and 125 ml) of water. Stir and scrape the bottom of the pan and bring the gravy to the simmer. Season and serve. A little wine or stock can be used instead of water.

To make a gravy, remove the meat or poultry from the roasting pan. Tip off all but a tablespoon of the fat into a bowl. Return the pan to the heat on top of the stove. Stir in two teaspoons of flour and brown over medium heat. Add half a pint (300 ml) of stock, or stock and the water in which the vegetables were cooked. Stir well, scraping all the sediments in the pan, and cook until thickened. Strain the gravy into a warmed sauce boat.

When the poured-off fat (dripping) from the meat has set in the bowl, separate it from any jellied stock or juices which are at the bottom. To these add any juice which is left after the meat has been carved. Save these juices to make any future gravies and sauces.

To keep a sauce hot, put it in a bain-marie or keep it in a double saucepan. The water should be hot, but on no account should it be allowed to simmer or boil.

To prevent a skin forming on the sauce you can either stir it every few minutes or lay a piece of greaseproof paper or plastic film gently on the surface. If the sauce is very thick rub the surface all over with a knob of butter.

Sauces that contain eggs sometimes curdle either because they have been brought to the boil, because they have been overbeaten, or because too much oil or butter has been added initially. If a hollandaise or béarnaise sauce curdles, start again with a clean bowl and another egg yolk. Begin beating the egg yolk and slowly blend in the curdled sauce a teaspoon at a time, increasing the amount as the sauce "takes" until it is all incorporated. A curdled mayonnaise can be revived in the same manner.

A curdled custard, if caught in time, can be stabilized by folding a little whipped cream into it. Or, if that fails, it can be resuscitated in the liquidizer, but the sauce will not be quite as smooth and thick as it should be.

Sauces

The brown sauces

The most important of the brown sauces are sauce espagnole and sauce demi-glace. Both are made from a strong bone stock in which the bones have been previously browned. The stock must be strained, chilled and the fat removed before it is used.

Sauce espagnole

MAKES ABOUT 1 QUART (1 LITRE)

3 oz (75 g) dripping or butter
¼ lb (100 g) onions, sliced
¼ lb (100 g) carrots, sliced
¼ lb (100 g) bacon, chopped
4 parsley stalks, chopped
2 oz (50 g) flour
3 pints (1½ litres) brown bone stock
2 teaspoons tomato purée
½ pint (300 ml) white wine
2 thyme sprigs
1 bay leaf
2 fl oz (50 ml) sherry
Salt and pepper

Melt the fat in a large saucepan. Add the onions, carrots, bacon and parsley and cook, stirring, until the vegetables are softened.

Stir in the flour, reduce the heat to very low, and cook, stirring, for 10 minutes or until the mixture is a rich brown.

Gradually pour in the stock, stirring constantly. Add the tomato purée and wine and, still stirring, bring the liquid to the boil. Add the herbs and simmer, uncovered, very gently—the liquid should barely shudder—for 2 hours or until the sauce is reduced by just over one-third. Using a metal spoon, skim frequently while it is cooking.

Remove the pan from the heat and pour the sauce through a fine strainer. Allow the sauce to cool, cover it and then refrigerate.

When the sauce is quite cold remove the fat from the top. The sauce is now ready to use as a base for other sauces. If you are going to use the sauce as it is, return it to a pan and bring it to the simmer. Stir in the sherry and add seasoning to taste.

Sauce demi-glace

MAKES ABOUT ½ PINT (300 ML)

½ pint (300 ml) sauce espagnole
½ pint (300 ml) bone stock
2 fl oz (50 ml) Madeira
Salt and pepper

Put the sauce and stock in a saucepan and bring them to the boil. Lower the heat and simmer, uncovered, for 30 minutes or until the liquid is reduced by half. Pour in the Madeira and season to taste. Strain the sauce. The sauce is now ready to use, but if you are using it as a base for another sauce leave out the seasoning.

Madeira or red wine sauce

MAKES ABOUT ¾ PINT (450 ML)

8 fl oz (225 ml) Madeira or red wine
½ pint (300 ml) demi-glace sauce
Salt and pepper

In a small saucepan bring the wine to the boil and cook until it is reduced by half. Stir in the demi-glace and the seasoning to taste. Simmer for 10 minutes and serve.

Sauce bordelaise

This is another red wine sauce traditionally served with steaks and roast beef.

MAKES ¼ PINT (150 ML)

½ oz (15 g) butter
1 oz (25 g) shallots, chopped
4 fl oz (125 ml) red wine
6 peppercorns
1 thyme sprig
¼ pint (150 ml) demi-glace sauce
½ oz (15 g) beef marrow, cut into small pieces

Melt the butter in a small saucepan. Add the shallots and cook them until they are softened. Add the wine, peppercorns and thyme and continue cooking until the wine is reduced by half. Add the demi-glace and simmer for 15 minutes. Remove the pan from the heat. Skim off the fat and strain the sauce. Pour the sauce into the top part of a double boiler.

Add the marrow and stir to dissolve it over very low heat for 10 minutes.

Sauce bigarade

This is a red wine sauce suitable for serving with game birds.

MAKES ¾ PINT (450 ML)

½ oz (15 g) butter
1 oz (25 g) shallots, chopped
2 fl oz (50 ml) red wine
1 bay leaf
Rind and juice of 1 orange
¼ pint (150 ml) demi-glace
1 teaspoon redcurrant jelly

Melt the butter in a small saucepan. Add the shallots and cook until they are softened. Add the wine and bay leaf and continue cooking until the wine is reduced by one-third. Add the juice and half the rind of the orange, and the demi-glace sauce. Simmer for 5 minutes.

Shred the remaining orange rind very thinly. Blanch it for 5 minutes and drain.

Strain the sauce and return it to the pan with the blanched orange rind and the redcurrant jelly. Bring the sauce slowly to the boil, stirring, until the jelly has dissolved.

Sauce Robert

MAKES ½ PINT (300 ML)

½ oz (15 g) butter
1 tablespoon chopped onion
2 fl oz (50 ml) wine vinegar
8 fl oz (225 ml) demi-glace sauce
3 gherkins, finely chopped
2 teaspoons French mustard
1 teaspoon chopped parsley

Melt the butter in a small saucepan. Add the onion and fry it gently until it is softened. Pour in the vinegar and continue cooking until it is reduced by half. Add the demi-glace sauce and simmer for 15 minutes. Stir in the rest of the ingredients.

The white sauces

The basic white sauces are béchamel and velouté. Béchamel is made with a white roux and milk and velouté is made with a golden roux and stock.

Sauce béchamel

MAKES ABOUT ½ PINT (300 ML)

½ pint (300 ml) milk
1 mace blade
1 bouquet garni
4 white peppercorns
1 shallot, sliced
¾ oz (20 g) butter
¾ oz (20 g) flour
Salt

Put the milk, mace, bouquet garni, peppercorns and shallot in a small saucepan and place it over a very low heat for 5 minutes to infuse. Strain the milk and set aside.

Melt the butter in a small pan. Stir in the flour and remove the pan from the heat. Gradually stir in the strained milk. Beat well to prevent lumps forming then cook, stirring constantly, over moderate heat until the sauce boils. Season to taste.

Cream sauce

To ½ pint (300 ml) of béchamel sauce add 2 fluid ounces (50 ml) of cream and season with a squeeze of lemon juice and a pinch of cayenne pepper.

Sauce mornay

For a stronger flavour a pinch of cayenne pepper or a teaspoon of French mustard may be added to the sauce.

MAKES ½ PINT (300 ML)

½ pint (300 ml) béchamel sauce
2 oz (50 g) grated Parmesan or Gruyère cheese
2 fl oz (50 ml) cream

Heat the béchamel sauce in a small pan. Add the cheese and stir until it has dissolved. Stir in the cream and serve.

Mushroom sauce

MAKES ABOUT ¾ PINT (450 ML)

1 oz (25 g) butter
¼ lb (100 g) mushrooms, sliced
Salt and pepper
Cayenne pepper
½ pint (300 ml) béchamel sauce
2 fl oz (50 ml) cream

Melt the butter in a small frying-pan. Add the mushrooms and fry quickly, shaking the pan, for 2 to

3 minutes. Season to taste.

Have the béchamel sauce hot in a saucepan. Remove the pan from the heat and add the mushrooms and their cooking liquid. Stir in the cream and serve.

Sauce velouté

MAKES ABOUT 1½ PINTS (900 ML)

3 oz (75 g) unsalted butter
1½ oz (40 g) flour
1½ pints (900 ml) chicken stock
2 fl oz (50 ml) cream
Salt and pepper
1 teaspoon lemon juice

Melt half the butter in a saucepan. Add the flour and mix it in to form a roux. Cook the roux, stirring constantly, over very low heat for 5 to 7 minutes until it becomes straw coloured.

Add the stock gradually, stirring constantly. Bring the sauce to the boil, reduce the heat and simmer gently for 5 minutes. Stir in the cream and simmer for a further 2 minutes. Add seasoning to taste and the lemon juice. Stir in the butter in small pieces and serve.

Sauce suprême

MAKES ABOUT 1 PINT (575 ML)

3 egg yolks
4 tablespoons double cream
¾ pint (450 ml) velouté sauce
Salt and pepper

In a small bowl, mix the yolks with the cream. Heat the sauce in a double saucepan. Draw the pan off the heat and add a few tablespoons of the sauce, a spoonful at a time, to the egg mixture. When well mixed pour the egg mixture into the sauce and whisk until it is smooth and velvety. Serve the sauce hot.

Sauce normande

This is a sauce to serve with sole or other white fish.

MAKES ABOUT ½ PINT (300 ML)

½ pint (300 ml) velouté sauce
1 egg yolk
1 oz (25 g) butter, cut into small pieces
Lemon juice
Salt and pepper

Heat the velouté sauce in a double saucepan. Put the egg yolk in a small bowl. Beat a few spoonfuls of the sauce, a spoonful at a time, into the egg. When well mixed pour the egg mixture into the sauce and mix well. Whisk in the butter, one piece at a time. Stir in the lemon juice and seasoning to taste.

Sauce poulette

MAKES ABOUT ½ PINT (300 ML)

½ pint (300 ml) velouté sauce
1 tablespoon chopped parsley
1 teaspoon lemon juice
1 egg yolk
2 tablespoons cream

Heat the velouté sauce in a double saucepan. Stir in the parsley and lemon juice. In a small bowl combine the egg yolk with the cream. Beat a little of the hot sauce, a spoonful at a time, into the egg mixture. Pour the egg mixture into the sauce. Whisk until the sauce is thick and smooth.

The butter sauces

The basic butter sauces are hollandaise and béarnaise. Delicate and delicious, they can turn the simplest vegetable dish, poached fish or grilled steak into something special. They require care in making, however, and have the unhappy knack of curdling when you least expect it. Butter sauces must always be made in a double saucepan as too much heat causes curdling.

Sauce hollandaise I

MAKES 6 FLUID OUNCES (175 ML)

3 to 4 oz (75 to 100 g) butter
2 egg yolks
Salt and pepper
1 tablespoon white wine vinegar or lemon juice

Using a palette knife work the butter until it is slightly soft. In a small bowl or in the top pan of a double saucepan mix the egg yolks with a teaspoon of the softened butter and a pinch of salt and pepper. Add the vinegar or lemon juice. Place the bowl over a pan of water or set the pan over the bottom half of the double saucepan. The water must be hot but not boiling. Stir the mixture with a whisk until it has thickened. Gradually add the butter, half a teaspoon at a time, stirring constantly. Season to taste. The sauce should be smooth and thick.

Sauce hollandaise II

This version is made in a liquidizer.

MAKES ABOUT ½ PINT (300 ML)

½ lb (225 g) butter
4 egg yolks
2 tablespoons lemon juice
¼ teaspoon salt

Melt the butter in a saucepan over low heat. Do not allow it to colour. Put the egg yolks, lemon juice and salt into the liquidizer. Cover the container and blend at low speed for 20 seconds. Uncover and pour in the hot butter in a steady stream while the motor is running. When the butter is used up switch off the motor. Pour the sauce into a bowl and stand it in a bain-marie of hot water until ready to use.

Sauce mousseline

MAKES ABOUT ¾ PINT (450 ML)

Prepare ½ pint (300 ml) of hollandaise sauce. Fold in ¼ pint (150 ml) whipped cream.

Sauce maltaise

MAKES ABOUT ½ PINT (300 ML)

Prepare ½ pint (300 ml) of hollandaise sauce. Mix in the juice and finely grated rind of ½ orange.

Sauce béarnaise

MAKES 6 FLUID OUNCES (175 ML)

4 tablespoons white wine
2 tablespoons white wine vinegar
1 bay leaf
1 mace blade
½ teaspoon dried thyme
1 shallot
4 peppercorns
2 egg yolks
¼ lb (100 g) butter, softened
2 teaspoons chopped tarragon
Salt and pepper

Put the vinegar and wine, bay leaf, mace, shallot, thyme and peppercorns into a small pan. Bring the liquid to the boil and cook until it is reduced to 2 tablespoonfuls. Strain the vinegar and set aside.

In the top of a double saucepan or in a small bowl, mix the egg yolks with 1 teaspoon of the butter and a pinch of salt. Pour the vinegar on to the egg mixture and stir to mix. Place the double saucepan, or bowl, over the heat—the water must be hot but not boiling—and whisk the egg mixture until it has thickened.

Gradually add the rest of the butter in half-teaspoonfuls, stirring constantly, until the sauce is like whipped cream. Add the chopped tarragon and seasoning.

Sauce batarde

MAKES ¾ PINT (450 ML)

¼ lb (125 g) butter
1 oz (25 g) flour
½ pint (300 ml) boiling water
2 egg yolks mixed with 1 tablespoon of cold water
1 to 2 teaspoons lemon juice
Salt

Melt 1 ounce (25 g) of the butter in a small saucepan. Stir in the flour to make a roux. Pour in the water gradually, stirring constantly, to prevent lumps forming. Draw the pan off the heat and beat in the egg yolk and water mixture. Add the remaining butter a small piece at a time. Stir in the lemon juice and salt.

Stand the saucepan in a bain-marie to keep the sauce hot.

Sauce ravigote

MAKES ABOUT ½ PINT (300 ML)

2 shallots, finely chopped
4 tablespoons vinegar
½ pint (300 ml) sauce batarde
1 teaspoon each of chopped parsley, chervil and tarragon
2 teaspoons chopped capers
2 teaspoons French mustard

In a small saucepan bring the shallots and the vinegar to the boil. Cook them until the vinegar is reduced by half. Set aside.

Put the sauce batarde into a bowl. Mix in the chopped herbs, capers and mustard. Strain the vinegar into the sauce and mix.

Sauces

White wine sauce

This sauce can also be made with red wine.

MAKES ABOUT $\frac{1}{2}$ PINT (300 ML)

1 oz (25 g) butter
$\frac{1}{2}$ oz (15 g) flour
$\frac{1}{4}$ pint (150 ml) well-flavoured white stock (fish or chicken)
3 fl oz (75 ml) dry white wine
4 fl oz (125 ml) cream
1 tablespoon lemon juice
Salt and pepper
1 oz (25 g) butter

In a small saucepan make a roux with the butter and flour. Draw the pan off the heat and gradually stir in the stock and wine, taking care to avoid lumps. Bring to the boil, stirring constantly. Add the cream, lemon juice and seasoning. When the sauce has thickened, remove the pan from the heat and stir in the butter in small pieces. Use at once or keep hot in a bain-marie.

Beurre noir

This sauce is served with fish, eggs and vegetables. Lemon juice can be substituted for the vinegar.

MAKES 4 FLUID OUNCES (125 ML)

1 tablespoon vinegar
Salt and freshly ground black pepper
$\frac{1}{4}$ lb (100 g) unsalted butter
1 tablespoon chopped parsley

In a small saucepan, boil the vinegar and seasoning until it is reduced by half. In another small saucepan, melt the butter and cook until it is dark brown but not black. Stir in the reduced vinegar and parsley and pour the sauce over the food.

Sauce mayonnaise

If you wish to keep the mayonnaise for a few days, stir 2 tablespoons of boiling water into the finished sauce. This will prevent the mayonnaise from separating.

MAKES ABOUT $\frac{1}{2}$ PINT (300 ML)

2 egg yolks
$\frac{1}{2}$ teaspoon salt
$\frac{1}{2}$ teaspoon French mustard
$\frac{1}{2}$ pint (300 ml) olive oil
2 teaspoons wine vinegar or the juice of $\frac{1}{2}$ lemon

Using a wooden spoon, mix the egg yolks well with the salt and mustard in a mixing bowl. With the oil in a measuring jug begin pouring it on to the yolks, drop by drop, beating all the time. Continue pouring and beating, adding the oil more quickly as the mayonnaise thickens. When all the oil has been incorporated the sauce will be very thick and glossy. Carefully fold in the vinegar or lemon juice.

To make mayonnaise in a liquidizer, first blend the egg yolks and salt together, then slowly, drop by drop, begin to add the oil, gradually pouring in a steady stream. Finally add vinegar or lemon juice and mustard.

Thousand island dressing

MAKES ABOUT $\frac{1}{2}$ PINT (300 ML)

8 fl oz (225 ml) mayonnaise
4 tablespoons tomato ketchup
2 tablespoons chopped green pepper
2 tablespoons chopped green olives
1 tablespoon chopped parsley
1 tablespoon finely chopped onion
1 hard-boiled egg, chopped

Combine all the ingredients well.

Aioli or garlic mayonnaise

MAKES ABOUT $\frac{3}{4}$ PINT (450 ML)

4 to 6 garlic cloves
Salt
2 egg yolks
$\frac{3}{4}$ pint (450 ml) olive oil
Pepper
Lemon juice

Crush the garlic with a little salt in a mortar. Beat in the egg yolks. Then, beating steadily, add the olive oil drop by drop. When the sauce thickens add the oil a little faster. Season with pepper and lemon juice.

Mayonnaise for coating

MAKES $\frac{3}{4}$ PINT (450 ML)

2 teaspoons powdered gelatine
$\frac{1}{4}$ pint (150 ml) aspic, hot
$\frac{1}{2}$ pint (300 ml) mayonnaise

Dissolve the gelatine in the aspic and cool the mixture. Whisk it into the mayonnaise. Use the mayonnaise as it begins to set.

Sauce tartare

MAKES ABOUT $\frac{1}{2}$ PINT (300 ML)

6 fl oz (175 ml) mayonnaise
2 fl oz (50 ml) double cream, whipped until thick
2 teaspoons lemon juice
1 teaspoon chopped chives
1 tablespoon chopped capers
1 tablespoon chopped gherkins

Put all the ingredients in a small mixing bowl and beat well until they are thoroughly combined.

Sauce verte

MAKES $\frac{1}{2}$ PINT (300 ML)

10 watercress sprigs
4 parsley sprigs
4 tarragon sprigs
10 spinach leaves
Salt
$\frac{1}{2}$ pint (300 ml) mayonnaise

In a small saucepan boil the watercress, parsley, tarragon and spinach for 3 minutes in a little salted water. Drain the herbs and spinach, reserving 1 tablespoon of the liquor. Rub the greens through a sieve.

Mix the purée into the mayonnaise with the reserved tablespoon of cooking liquor.

Brown chaudfroid sauce

Brown chaudfroid sauce is used for coating duck and game.

MAKES ABOUT 1 PINT (575 ML)

$\frac{3}{4}$ pint (450 ml) demi-glace sauce
2 teaspoons gelatine
4 fl oz (125 ml) aspic jelly
2 fl oz (50 ml) sherry or port

Warm the demi-glace. Dissolve the gelatine in the aspic jelly over low heat and add it to the demi-glace with the wine. Stir the sauce while it is cooling to prevent a skin forming. When it begins to set it is ready to be used.

White chaudfroid sauce

A white chaudfroid sauce is used for coating fish or chicken. Fawn chaudfroid sauce, made with a velouté instead of béchamel, is used to coat veal and lamb.

MAKES ABOUT 1 PINT (575 ML)

2 teaspoons gelatine
2 fl oz (50 ml) warm fish or chicken aspic
$\frac{3}{4}$ pint (450 ml) béchamel sauce
2 fl oz (50 ml) cream
Salt and pepper

Soften the gelatine in the warm aspic and add it to the béchamel with the cream. Season to taste. Stir frequently while the sauce is cooling to prevent a skin forming. When the sauce is thick it is ready to be used.

Sauce vinaigrette or French dressing

The classic proportions of a vinaigrette are three parts oil to one of vinegar. The proportions, however, depend on the strength of the vinegar and may be altered.

Use a good-quality olive oil, or a groundnut oil, or a combination of oils, and a wine, herb or cider vinegar, or lemon juice. A finely chopped garlic clove, one teaspoon of Dijon mustard and one tablespoon of chopped fresh tarragon, chives, thyme or parsley can also be added.

MAKES 4 FLUID OUNCES (125 ML)

2 tablespoons good wine vinegar or lemon juice
$\frac{1}{4}$ teaspoon salt
Freshly ground pepper
6 tablespoons oil

Place the vinegar, salt and pepper in a salad bowl. Beat in the oil, add the salad ingredients and toss.

English salad dressing

MAKES ABOUT $\frac{1}{4}$ PINT (150 ML)

Yolks of two hard-boiled eggs
Salt and pepper
2 tablespoons olive oil
2 teaspoons Worcestershire sauce
2 teaspoons vinegar
$\frac{1}{2}$ teaspoon dry mustard
2 spring onions, finely chopped, or 2 teaspoons chopped chives
4 fl oz (125 ml) cream or yogurt

In a small bowl, crush the egg yolks well with a fork. Add the salt and pepper. Beat in the oil drop by drop, then the Worcestershire sauce, vinegar, mustard and the onions or chives. With a wooden spoon, gradually beat in the cream.

Miscellaneous sauces

Tomato sauce

MAKES ABOUT 1 PINT (575 ML)

½ oz (15 g) butter
1 tablespoon olive oil
2 onions, sliced
1½ lb (700 g) chopped tomatoes
1 teaspoon salt
1 teaspoon sugar
Parsley
1 garlic clove
2 basil sprigs, chopped
2 tablespoons tomato purée

Melt the butter with the olive oil in a wide, shallow pan. Cook the onions gently until they are soft and golden. Stir in the remainder of the ingredients and simmer over low heat for 20 minutes. Put the sauce through a food mill and adjust the seasoning.

Bread sauce

MAKES ABOUT ½ PINT (300 ML)

1 onion, peeled and studded with 2 cloves
½ bay leaf
1 mace blade
4 peppercorns
½ pint (300 ml) milk
6 tablespoons fresh white breadcrumbs
Salt
1 tablespoon cream
½ oz (15 g) butter

Put the onion, bay leaf, mace blade, peppercorns and milk in a saucepan over low heat to infuse for 10 minutes. Strain the milk and return it to the pan. Increase the heat and bring the milk to the boil. Stir in the breadcrumbs and simmer over low heat until the sauce becomes thick. Remove the pan from the heat. Season and stir in the cream and butter.

Mint sauce

MAKES 2 FLUID OUNCES (50 ML)

1 large handful mint leaves
2 tablespoons boiling water
3 tablespoons wine vinegar
Salt
1 tablespoon castor sugar

Wash and dry the mint leaves. Chop them very finely or purée them in a mortar. Put the puréed mint into a bowl, pour in the boiling water to "set" the colour. Stir in the vinegar, salt and sugar.

Apple sauce

MAKES ABOUT ½ PINT (300 ML)

1 lb (450 g) tart apples, peeled and cored
2 strips orange peel
3 tablespoons water
1 to 2 tablespoons sugar
½ oz (15 g) butter

Put the apples in a saucepan with the orange peel and water. Cover the pan tightly and cook over low heat for about 15 minutes or until the apples are soft and fluffy. Stir in the sugar to taste and then add the butter.

Cumberland sauce

MAKES ABOUT ¾ PINT (450 ML)

½ lb (225 g) redcurrant jelly
Rind and juice of 2 oranges
Rind and juice of 1 lemon
2 fl oz (50 ml) port
1 tablespoon vinegar
1 teaspoon Dijon mustard
2 teaspoons arrowroot

In a small saucepan, dissolve the redcurrant jelly with the fruit juice and rind. Bring the mixture to the boil, reduce the heat and simmer for 5 minutes. Stir in the port, vinegar and mustard.

Mix the arrowroot with a tablespoon of cold water and stir it into the sauce. Simmer for 2 seconds and serve cool.

Cranberry and orange sauce

MAKES ABOUT 1½ PINTS (900 ML)

1 lb (450 g) cranberries
Rind and juice of 1 orange
½ pint (300 ml) water
½ lb (225 g) castor sugar

Put all the ingredients together in a deep saucepan. Cover and cook over very low heat for 10 minutes. Serve cool.

Dessert sauces

Chocolate sauce

MAKES ½ PINT (300 ML)

¼ lb (100 g) dark chocolate broken into pieces
1 oz (25 g) vanilla sugar
1 teaspoon cocoa powder
½ pint (300 ml) water
Rum to taste (optional)

Break up the chocolate and put it into a saucepan with the sugar, cocoa and half the water. Stir over low heat until the chocolate has dissolved, then bring it to the boil. Reduce the heat and simmer for 2 minutes. Add the remaining water and simmer for 10 to 15 minutes or until the sauce is glossy and syrupy. Stir in the rum if you are using it.

Fruit sauce

Depending on the tartness of the fruit, more or less sugar will be required for this sauce.

MAKES ½ PINT (300 ML)

1 lb (450 g) fresh or frozen raspberries, strawberries, peaches or redcurrants
1 teaspoon lemon juice
¼ lb (100 g) icing sugar

Crush the fruit or purée it in a liquidizer and then rub it through a sieve. Stir in the lemon juice and sugar to taste.

Butterscotch sauce

For a variation add 1 ounce (25 g) of chopped walnuts to the sauce after you have taken it off the heat.

MAKES ABOUT ½ PINT (300 ML)

3 oz (75 g) butter
½ lb (225 g) brown sugar
1 tablespoon light syrup (any commercial brand)
¼ pint (150 ml) double cream

Melt the butter in a saucepan over low heat. Stir in the sugar, syrup and cream. When the sugar has dissolved, bring the mixture to the boil. Remove the pan from the heat. Cool slightly before serving.

Custard sauce

Custard sauce can be flavoured with coffee, chocolate or cooking essences.

Whipped cream can be added to the custard once it has cooled.

MAKES ½ PINT (300 ML)

2 egg yolks
½ oz (15 g) vanilla sugar
½ pint (300 ml) milk

In a small bowl, beat the egg yolks with a fork. Dissolve the sugar in the milk in the top of a double saucepan. The water in the lower pan should be hot but not boiling. When the milk is hot pour it on to the egg yolks. Mix well and return the mixture to the pan. Stir over the hot water until the custard thickens sufficiently to coat the back of a wooden spoon.

Sauce sabayon

If it is made with brandy or rum, sabayon sauce makes an excellent accompaniment for Christmas pudding and mince pies.

MAKES ¼ PINT (150 ML)

3 egg yolks
2 oz (50 g) castor sugar
3 tablespoons sherry or marsala

In the top of a double saucepan, beat the egg yolks with the sugar until pale and frothy. Stir in the wine and bring the water in the lower pan to the boil, whisking constantly until the sauce is thick. Serve the sauce at once, or cool it and then place the top part of the pan over ice and whisk until it is cold.

Brandy butter

A teaspoon of finely grated orange rind gives brandy butter extra flavour, and helps lighten the richness. For rum butter use a fine, dark-brown sugar and a little grated lemon rind.

MAKES ½ POUND (225 G)

¼ lb (100 g) unsalted butter
¼ lb (100 g) castor sugar
4 tablespoons brandy

Have ingredients at room temperature. Cream the butter until white and fluffy. Gradually beat in the sugar and then the brandy, a little at a time. Pile into a serving dish and stand in a cool place to set.

The methods

Boiling and steaming, stewing and casseroling, grilling, frying and sautéing, roasting and baking—these are the basic methods of cookery. Some types of food, such as most cakes or pastry, can be made only by one method—they need the enveloping heat of the oven. Most foods, however, may be cooked either in an oven, or below or above the heat, and your choice of method depends on the available cooking equipment and the quality of the food.

On the following pages each cookery method is described and recipes are given for cooking every type of food by that method. When a dish must be cooked by a combination of methods the recipe will be found under the method that forms the main part of the cooking.

All metric equivalents in the recipes are approximate, and centigrade conversions have been made to the nearest round figure. Tablespoons and teaspoons are standard British measures. Amounts given are for level spoonfuls.

Boiling and steaming

Boiling is such a traditional English method of preparing food that the French often attach the label *à l'anglaise*—the English way—to boiled dishes. The term boiling is not, however, a truly accurate description of what actually takes place, for most foods would fall to pieces and lose all their flavour were they to be cooked in fast-boiling liquid. Although the liquid is initially brought to the boil, the heat is then lowered and the food is simmered or poached—the liquid stays well under boiling-point.

Fast boiling is recommended, however, when liquid is to be reduced and thickened, and for syrups and preserves.

Steaming, on the other hand, is one of the better ways of cooking such delicate foods as fish and vegetables as well as some grains, such as couscous and occasionally rice.

Although it is useful to have special equipment for steaming, you can improvise with a colander or strainer fitted over a saucepan and covered with a tight-fitting lid.

A steamer that opens like a flower and fits inside most saucepans is very useful for cooking vegetables. A version of the double saucepan with a perforated pan which fits on top is useful for steaming puddings and is available with a double tier for steaming more than one pudding at a time.

The Chinese use a many-tiered bamboo steamer; rice is boiled in the bottom pan and the steam is used to cook a whole array of dishes in separate baskets, which fit one on top of the other.

Fish kettles can also be fitted with a steaming rack, which holds the fish above the water.

Always bring the water to the boil in the pan before fitting the perforated top in place, and remember that steamed vegetables need to cook for about four to five minutes longer than boiled vegetables.

Some vegetables—asparagus, cauliflower and broccoli, for example—may be steam-boiled (there is a special pan for asparagus). Bring a small amount of water to the boil in a saucepan. Stand the vegetables in the pan, cover with a lid and simmer—the stalks will boil in the water while the more delicate heads cook in the steam.

Fish and shellfish		*Poultry and game birds*
Soused herrings 77 Buttered rye or granary bread 198 ***Bourride 78*** French bread	***Salmon trout in aspic 77*** Sauces: Mayonnaise, Verte 68 Salads: Tomato, Green 213	***English boiled chicken 83*** Glazed carrots 91, Brussels sprouts 92, Potato croquettes 151
Haddock crêpes 78 ***Salmon mousse 78*** Melba toast 81	***Trout in cider 77*** Sauce hollandaise 67 Boiled fennel 92, Casseroled celery 120	***Chicken à la king 84*** Boiled rice 97, Croûtons 158, Noodles 97
Gefillte fish 78 ***Kipper pâté 79*** Melba toast 81	***Sole Véronique 77*** Steamed courgettes, Mashed potatoes 93	***Chicken poached in cider 84*** Deep-fried parsley 153, Potatoes à la dauphinoise 180, French beans 92
Quenelles 79 Serve on croûtons 158 ***Jellied eels 79*** Buttered brown bread 198	***Fillets of sole florentine 78*** Tomato salad 213	***Chicken fricassée 84*** Boiled rice 97, Crusty noodles 158
Moules marinières 80 Garlic bread 189 ***Coquilles St Jacques 80***	***Steamed fish mould with anchovy sauce 79*** Alternative sauces: Mornay, Mushroom 66 Boiled spinach 92, Peas 93, Baked potatoes 180	***Chicken with spicy mayonnaise 84***
Scallops à la provençale 80 ***Dressed crab 80*** Salads: Green, Tomato 213	***Crayfish with butter sauce 80***	***Chicken salad 84***
Potted shrimps 81 Melba toast 81, Buttered brown bread ***Snails à la bourguignonne 81***	***Lobster mayonnaise 81*** Salads: Potato 93 Chicory, orange and watercress 213	***Chicken and pineapple salad 84***
Poached salmon 76 ***Poached salmon trout 76*** Sauces: Hollandaise, Mousseline 67, Mayonnaise, Verte 68 Salads: Rice 212, Green 213 Boiled new potatoes 93		***Chicken chaudfroid 85*** Salads: Rice 212, Celery, apple and walnut 213
		Chicken florentine 85 Sauté potatoes 151
Sweet-sour pungent fish, Steamed sea bass 77 Serve as part of a Chinese meal or with Stir-fried bean sprouts 153		***Duck galantine 85*** Salads: Chicory, orange and watercress, Waldorf 213

Meat and game

- **Salt beef and dumplings 86** Horseradish sauce 89, Mustard
- **Ham boiled in cider 86** Salads: Kidney bean 93, Avocado 213, Rice 212
- **Steak and kidney pudding 88** Mashed potato 93, Bubble and squeak 152 Glazed carrots 91, Cabbage 92
- **Boiled shoulder of mutton 88**
- **Boiled bacon with lentils 88**
- **Cold pressed ox tongue 89** Cumberland sauce 69 Salads: Courgette 92, Russian, Spinach and mushroom 212
- **Dolmas 89** Sauté potatoes 151
- **Sweetbread vol-au-vents 89**
- **Veal galantine 89** Sauces: Horseradish 89, Verte 68 Salads: Avocado, Tomato 213, Spinach and mushroom 212

Vegetables

- **Artichokes with prawn-mushroom mayonnaise 91**
- **Salad nicoise 92**
- **Butter beans with garlic 93**
- **Butter bean and mackerel salad 93**
- **Steamed stuffed cabbage 91**
- **Boiling and steaming chart 92-3**
- **Brussels sprouts with curried almonds 91**
- **Brussels sprouts with chestnuts 91**
- **Petits pois à la française 91**
- **Cauliflower salad 91**
- **Boiled chicory 91**
- **Glazed carrots 91**
- **Carrot and parsnip purée 91**
- **Courgette salad 92**
- **Marrow in caraway sauce 92**
- **Spinach purée 92**
- **Boiled fennel 92**
- **Beetroot salad 92**
- **Mashed potatoes 93**
- **Potato salad 93**
- **Kidney bean salad 93**
- **Lentil salad 93**

Fruit

- **Pommes aux fruits glacés 96**
- **Rødgrød med fløde 96**
- **Strawberry mousse 96** Cream, Macaroons 192
- **Fresh fruit compote 94** Custard sauce 69, Cream
- **Fresh peaches in vanilla syrup 94** Sauce sabayon 69
- **Pears in red wine 94** Whipped cream
- **Oranges in caramel 95**
- **Cherries jubilee with vanilla ice-cream 95**
- **Rhubarb fool 95**
- **Summer pudding 96** Cream
- **Danish apple cake 96** Cream
- **Blackcurrant mousse 96** Butter biscuits 191
- **Blackcurrant kissel 96**

Cereals

- **Spaghetti with pesto 97** Green salad 213
- **Noodles Alfredo 97** Green salad 213
- **Ravioli 97** Tomato sauce 69 Green salad 213
- **Gnocchi di semolina 98** Tomato sauce 69 Green salad 213
- **Polenta 98** Tomato sauce 69
- **Christmas pudding 98** Brandy or rum butter 69, Cream
- **Creamed rice pudding 99** Fresh fruit compote 94
- **Orange sponge pudding 99** Custard
- **Boston steamed bread 99**
- **Porridge 99** Cream

Eggs and dairy produce

- **Eggs in crispy rolls 100** Sauce: Mornay 66
- **Eggs florentine with ham 100**
- **Taramasalata eggs 100**
- **Eggs in aspic 100**
- **Swiss fondue 101**
- **Curried eggs 101** Mint chutney 152, Sautéed bananas 154
- **Charlotte russe 101**
- **Lemon mousse 101**
- **Chocolate mousse 101** Cream
- **Crème brulée 102**
- **Zabaglione 102**
- **Bavarois 102**
- **Jamaican rum custard 103**
- **Oeufs à la neige 103**
- **Austrian chocolate pudding 103** Chocolate sauce 69

First courses
Main courses
Light lunch-supper dishes
Accompaniments
Desserts
Miscellaneous

Fish

Boiling, or poaching, and steaming are the first stage in preparing many classic fish and shellfish dishes. The methods of boiling such shellfish as lobster and crab are given in the section on preparation, because in most cases this is part of their basic preparation.

There are two ways of poaching whole fish—on top of the stove or in the oven. Fish is poached in a fish kettle or in a large pan deep enough to ensure that it will be covered in liquid. If a pan is used wrap the fish in muslin, leaving enough cloth at both ends to make it easy to lift out the fish after it is cooked.

Cut a fish in half if it is too large for the pan and poach the two halves separately. Once cooked they can be put together on the serving dish, the join covered with a sauce or a garnish.

To poach a whole fish put it in enough court bouillon, salted water, fish stock or wine to barely cover it and bring it slowly to just under boiling point. Reduce the heat to low and simmer, allowing eight minutes per pound (450 g) for fish up to six pounds (3 kg) in weight and five to six minutes to the pound (450 g) for fish up to twelve pounds ($5\frac{1}{2}$ kg) in weight.

Large pieces of such fish as turbot, skate and cod can be poached in the same way. The cooking time is the same as

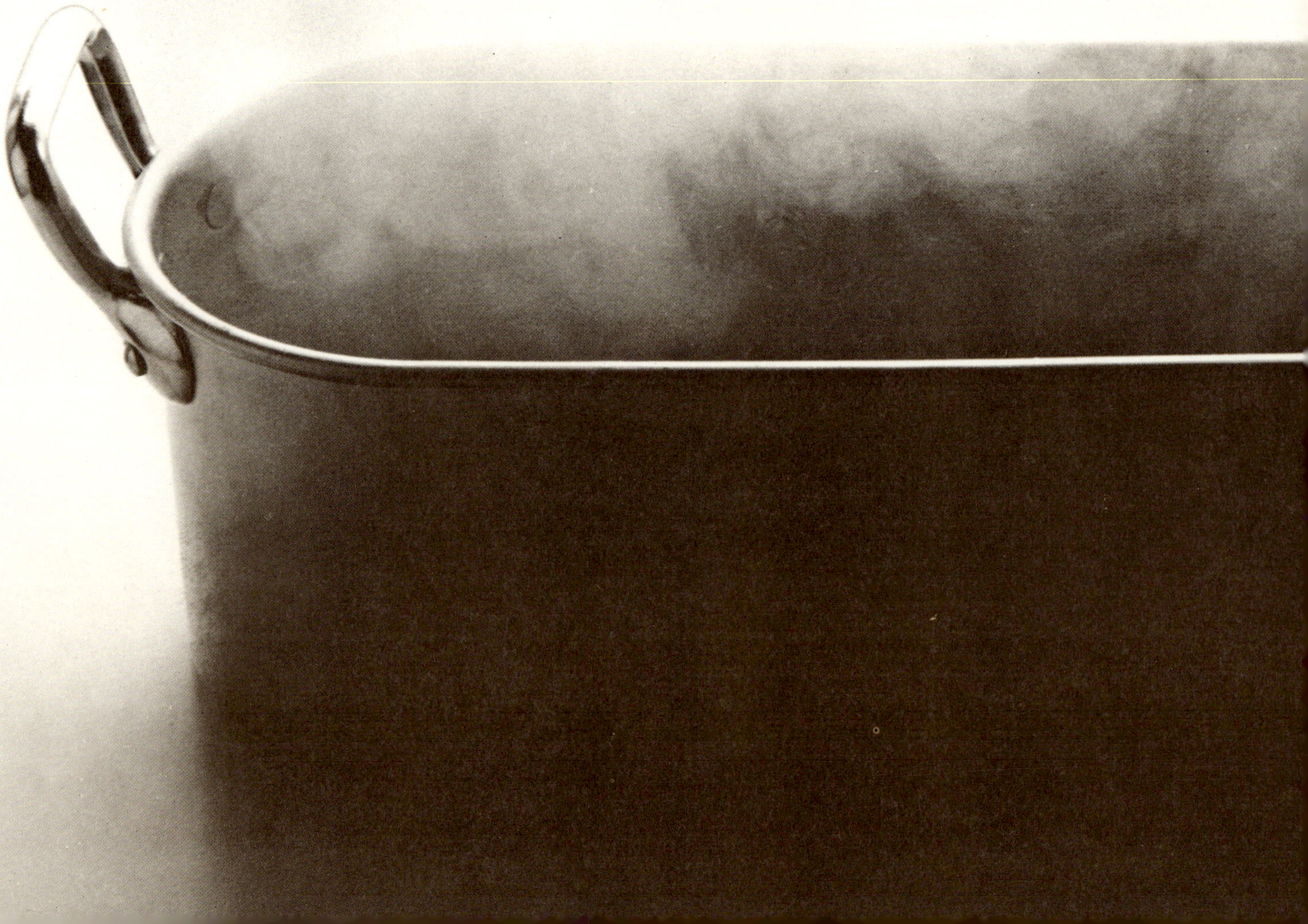

for a whole fish. Small whole fish such as plaice, sole or whiting will take about ten minutes. Poach fish in the oven —the liquid must come to the simmer first—at a temperature of 350°F (180°C, Gas Mark 4).

To test a fish to see if it is cooked, insert the point of a sharp knife into the flesh near the backbone. If the flesh lifts easily from the bone and is no longer translucent but quite white (or pink if the fish is salmon) and curd-like and flakes easily, the fish is cooked.

If the fish is to be skinned it is easier to do it while it is still hot.

Au bleu is an excellent way of cooking whole, delicate fish. Only freshwater fish are cooked *au bleu* and then only when they have been freshly caught and are still alive.

Immediately the fish is taken from the water, knock it on the head. Remove its gut through the smallest incision possible. Cut off the gills, but do not wash or scale the fish. Put the fish into a saucepan and sprinkle it with a little boiling vinegar. This sets the blue colour of the skin. Pour in boiling court bouillon to cover and poach gently for eight to ten minutes. Fish, particularly trout, cooked in this way are usually served simply with steamed potatoes, melted butter and lemon wedges. They can also be served cold with a vinaigrette or mayonnaise dressing.

Fish

When cooking fish fillets and steaks, the court bouillon should be boiling when the fish is put in so that the liquid seals the unprotected flesh. Then reduce the heat to very low so that the liquid barely simmers. When poaching such delicate fish as sole it is best to cook the fillets in the oven in a buttered ovenproof dish. The cooking time is the same whether you poach the fish in the oven or on top of the stove—eight to ten minutes for fillets; ten to fifteen minutes for steaks, depending on their size and thickness. Test the fish with the point of a knife—if the flesh flakes easily it is ready.

To steam fish fillets place them on a buttered soup plate. Season the fillets and sprinkle them with a little milk or lemon juice. Cover the fillets with greaseproof paper and place a second buttered plate, upturned, over them. Put the plates on top of a pan of simmering water and cook for fifteen minutes, or until the fish is cooked and the flesh flakes easily.

Poached salmon I

This is a method of cooking salmon that is used by the fishermen in Scotland. If the salmon is being served hot it may be garnished with lemon wedges, parsley sprigs and thinly sliced cucumber that has been marinated in seasoned vinegar, and accompanied by a hollandaise sauce or melted butter.

To serve the salmon cold, lay thinly sliced cucumber in overlapping slices down the centre of the fish. Cover lightly with almost set aspic. When set carefully transfer the fish on to a bed of watercress, parsley or lettuce. Serve with home-made mayonnaise.

To poach fish weighing up to 6 pounds (3 kg), bring the liquid very slowly to the boil and simmer for 12 minutes. Turn off the heat and leave the fish in the covered pan for 20 minutes.

SERVES FOURTEEN TO SIXTEEN

1 salmon, about 12 pounds (5½ kg), cleaned
About 3 quarts (3 litres) court bouillon

Place the fish on the rack in a fish kettle. Pour over enough cold court bouillon to cover the fish and bring it very slowly to the boil. Reduce the heat to low and simmer for 20 minutes. Turn off the heat and leave the fish in the covered pan for another 20 minutes (if it is to be served hot) or until it is quite cold.

Lift the fish carefully out of the kettle on the rack and slide it on to a serving dish. If it is to be served hot remove the skin from the upperside of the fish—the fish will become cold if you turn it over to remove the skin from the underside—leaving the head and tail intact, and brush it all over with melted butter. Garnish and serve.

If the salmon is to be served cold, remove the entire skin, leaving the head and tail intact. With a sharp knife cut along the backbone, easing the flesh off the bone. Using a pair of scissors, snip the backbone just below the head and just above the tail. Carefully remove the backbone.

Coating fish with aspic

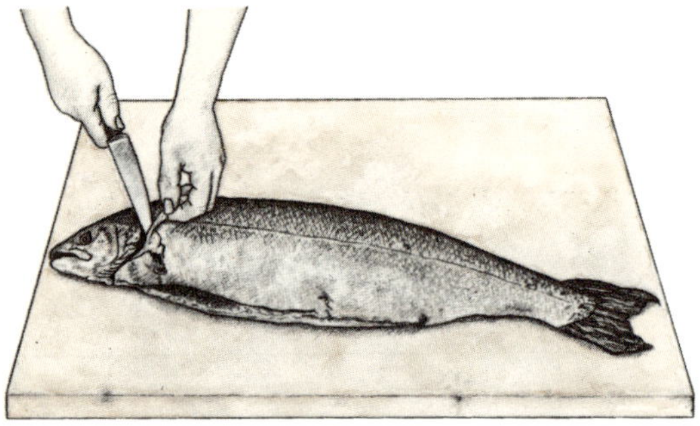

Place the cooked salmon on a board and skin it.

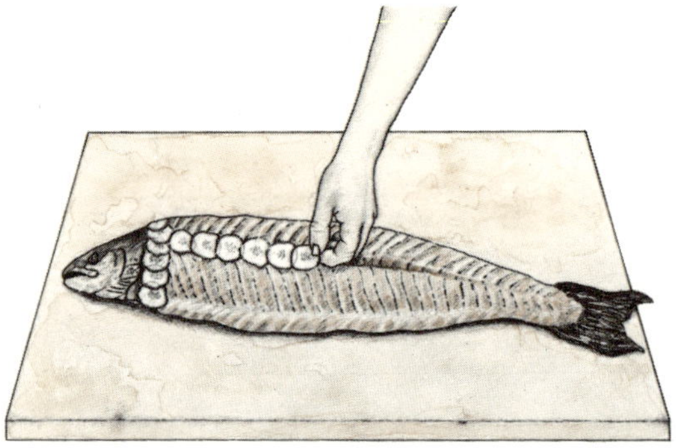

Decorate the skinned salmon with sliced cucumber.

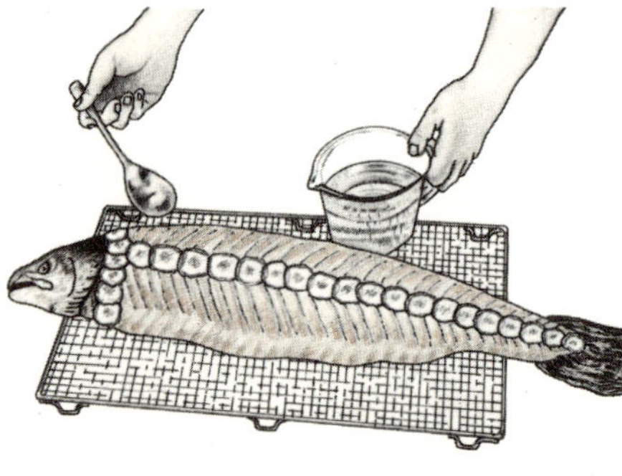

Spoon some cool aspic over the fish and garnish.

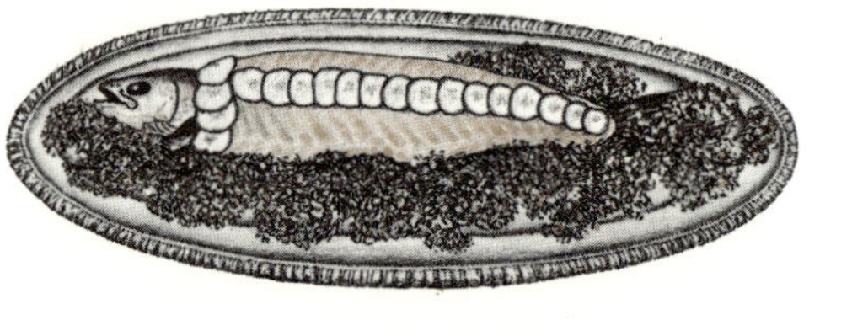

When the aspic has set, put the fish on a platter.

Poached salmon II

If the salmon is to be served cold, strain the cooking liquid and boil rapidly to reduce by half, then stir 2 tablespoons of it into 8 fluid ounces (225 ml) of mayonnaise to serve with the fish.

SERVES SIX TO EIGHT

5-lb (2½-kg) salmon, cleaned, with the head and tail left on
3 lemons, sliced
6 black peppercorns
1 teaspoon dried dill
1 teaspoon salt
1 small onion, thinly sliced
1 bay leaf, crumbled
½ pint (300 ml) dry white wine

Lay the lemon slices over the bottom of a large, heavy flameproof casserole to completely cover the base. Add the peppercorns, dill, salt, onion rings and bay leaf. Lay the salmon on top and pour the wine over it. Cover the casserole and bring the wine to the boil. Reduce the heat to very low and simmer for 40 minutes, or until the flesh flakes easily when tested with the point of a sharp knife. Remove the casserole from the heat. Very carefully lift the salmon out of the casserole and peel off the skin. Place the salmon on a serving dish and allow it to cool completely before serving.

Poached salmon trout

SERVES FOUR TO SIX

Butter
3- to 4-lb (1½- to 2-kg) salmon trout, cleaned
14 fl oz (400 ml) white wine
Bouquet garni
Salt and pepper
1 oz (25 g) beurre manié
¼ pint (150 ml) cream

Preheat the oven to 350°F (180°C, Gas Mark 4).

Butter a baking dish, put the fish into it, curving it to fit in. Pour the wine over the fish. Add the bouquet garni and seasoning. Cover the dish with buttered foil or greaseproof paper and place it in the oven.

Poach the fish, basting frequently, for 1 hour or until it is done. Test by inserting the point of a sharp knife into the flesh near the spine. If the flesh flakes easily, the fish is ready.

Remove the dish from the oven, lift out the fish carefully, place it on a heated serving dish. Keep it warm.

Strain the cooking liquid into a pan and bring it to the boil. Add the beurre manié, a little at a time, stirring constantly. Stir in the cream, adjust the seasoning if necessary and simmer for 1 minute. Serve immediately.

Salmon trout in aspic

SERVES FOUR TO SIX

3-lb (1½-kg) salmon trout, poached, skinned, the backbone removed and chilled (see previous recipe)
1½ pints (900 ml) fish aspic, cooled
1 cucumber, thinly sliced
6 prawns, cooked
Fresh or dried dill weed
1 lemon, cut into slices
Mayonnaise or sauce verte

Place the salmon on a rack and carefully spoon a thin layer of cool aspic over it.

Pour a thin layer of aspic on to a serving platter and put it in the refrigerator to chill. When the aspic has set, lift the salmon trout on to it. Garnish the edges of the dish with the cucumber slices and spoon a little of the aspic over them. Return the dish to the refrigerator to chill.

Decorate the salmon with the prawns, dill and lemon slices. Serve with the mayonnaise or sauce verte.

Trout in cider

SERVES FOUR

½ pint (300 ml) dry cider
1 tablespoon wine vinegar
Bouquet garni
1 onion, sliced
Salt and pepper
4 trout, cleaned and washed
½ pint (300 ml) hollandaise sauce

Put the cider, vinegar, bouquet garni, onion and the seasoning in a large sauté pan and bring to the boil. Add the trout, reduce the heat, cover the pan and simmer gently for 10 minutes.

Lift the trout carefully on to a serving dish and serve immediately, with the hollandaise sauce in a separate bowl.

Sweet-sour pungent fish

Hoisin is a thick, spicy sauce made from soya beans and spices. It is available in Chinese food stores and in some of the larger supermarkets.

SERVES FOUR

1 cucumber
2 carrots
1-inch (2-cm) piece root ginger
1 pickled gherkin
1 onion, finely grated
Salt
2 tablespoons sugar
4 fl oz (125 ml) wine vinegar
2 tablespoons plus 1 teaspoon cooking oil
3 lb (1½ kg) red snapper
1 tablespoon hoisin sauce
2 teaspoons cornflour
2 garlic cloves, crushed
Pepper

Slice the cucumber in half lengthways, remove the soft pulp and seeds and cut into 2-inch (5-cm) long matchsticks. Cut the carrots into matchsticks of the same size. Slice the ginger and gherkin into even finer strips and put them all into a bowl with the grated onion. Sprinkle with 1 teaspoon of salt and set aside for 10 minutes. Drain off the liquid. Mix the sugar, vinegar and 4 fluid ounces (125 ml) of water together and pour the mixture into the bowl. Let the vegetables marinate for 30 minutes.

Bring 2 quarts (2 litres) of water to the boil in a fish kettle. Add 2 tablespoons of salt and 2 tablespoons of oil. Place the fish carefully in the kettle. When the water comes back to the boil, cover and turn off the heat. Leave the fish in the water for 30 minutes.

Meanwhile drain the vegetables, reserving the marinade.

In a small bowl combine the marinade and the hoisin sauce. Mix the cornflour with a tablespoon of cold water and stir it into the marinade mixture.

Heat the teaspoon of oil in a small saucepan. Add the garlic and fry for 1 minute. Add the marinade mixture and simmer, stirring, for 2 to 3 minutes.

Gently lift the fish on to a serving dish, sprinkle with salt and pepper, cover with the marinaded vegetables and spoon the sauce over the top. Serve immediately.

Steamed sea bass

The time taken to steam a whole 2-pound (1-kg) fish is about 15 minutes. A 4-pound (2-kg) fish will take about 20 to 25 minutes.

SERVES FOUR

1 sea bass, about 2 lb (900 g), cleaned and scaled, with head and tail intact
1 tablespoon dry sherry
3 tablespoons vegetable oil
2 tablespoons finely shredded fresh root ginger
2 spring onions, sliced
3 tablespoons soy sauce
1 teaspoon sugar
1 tablespoon chopped coriander leaves

Lay a piece of buttered greaseproof paper on the steaming tray of a fish kettle and place the fish on top of it. Sprinkle the bass with sherry.

Bring the water in the fish kettle to the boil and fit in the tray. Be sure the fish is lying above the water and not in it. Reduce the heat to moderate and steam the fish for 15 minutes.

Meanwhile, heat a small frying-pan over high heat for 15 seconds. Add the oil and swirl to coat the bottom of the pan. Add the ginger and cook for 1 minute. Add the spring onions, soy sauce and sugar. Stir and cook for 1 minute.

Lift the fish out of the kettle and lay it on a heated serving dish. Pour the sauce over the fish and garnish with the coriander leaves.

Soused herrings

All oily fish are suitable for sousing as the vinegar or lemon juice offsets the oiliness. Either wine or cider may be used instead of the water and such herbs as tarragon, dill or mace may be included in the marinade.

SERVES SIX

6 fresh herrings, cleaned, with heads and tails removed
Salt
A pinch of mace
4 allspice berries
1 small dried red chilli
1 clove
6 black peppercorns
1 onion, sliced
1 bay leaf
¼ pint (150 ml) wine vinegar
¼ pint (150 ml) water

Preheat the oven to 300°F (150°C, Gas Mark 2).

Split and bone the herrings. Season lightly with the salt on the fleshy sides. Roll up the fish starting at the tail end, skin side outermost. Lay the rolls side by side in an ovenproof dish. Add the spices, arrange the onion and bay leaf on top, pour over the vinegar and water, adding more if necessary, so that the herrings are just covered. Cover the dish with foil and bake for 1½ hours.

Remove the dish from the oven and allow the herrings to cool in the cooking liquid. Keep the dish in the refrigerator for 2 days before serving.

Sole Véronique

SERVES SIX

1½ lb (700 g) sole fillets, skinned and trimmed, bones reserved
Butter
¼ pint (150 ml) white wine
¼ pint (150 ml) water
2 shallots, sliced
1 bay leaf
½ pint (300 ml) béchamel sauce
2 tablespoons double cream
Salt and pepper
6 oz (175 g) white grapes, peeled and pips removed

Preheat the oven to 350°F (180°C, Gas Mark 4).

Place the fish and fish bones in a buttered ovenproof dish with the wine and water, shallots and bay leaf and put in the oven for 15 minutes or until cooked.

Remove the dish from the oven, take out the fillets and keep warm. Turn off the oven. Strain the cooking liquid into a small pan and bring it to the boil. Cook until the liquid is reduced to 3 tablespoonfuls.

Meanwhile heat the béchamel sauce. Add the reduced fish liquid, the cream and salt and pepper to taste. Stir to mix thoroughly.

Wrap the grapes in foil and place them in the turned-off oven for 1 to 2 minutes or until they are warm.

Arrange the fish fillets on a heated serving dish, leaving a space down the centre. Coat the fillets with the sauce and arrange the grapes in the middle. Serve immediately.

Fish

Fillets of sole florentine

SERVES FOUR

1 lb (450 g) fresh spinach or ¾ lb (350 g) frozen leaf spinach
½ pint (300 ml) mornay sauce
Grated nutmeg
Salt and pepper
8 sole fillets, skinned, washed and dried, bones reserved
¼ pint (150 ml) dry white wine or cider
1 oz (25 g) Parmesan cheese, grated

Preheat the oven to 350°F (180°C, Gas Mark 4).

Wash the spinach thoroughly or thaw it slightly and cook it in a saucepan without any additional water. Press the spinach between two plates to drain thoroughly, then put it in a baking dish and mix in 4 tablespoons of the mornay sauce and a pinch of grated nutmeg. Season to taste. Set aside and keep warm.

Put the sole fillets in a buttered ovenproof dish. Bring the wine or cider to the boil and pour it over the fillets. Cover with the reserved bones and poach in the oven for 15 minutes. Discard the bones and arrange the fillets on top of the spinach in the baking dish. Carefully drain the cooking liquid into a small saucepan and boil it until it has reduced by half. Stir the reduced liquid into the remaining mornay sauce. Cook the sauce for a few minutes to reduce it a little and season to taste. Pour the sauce over the fish, sprinkle the Parmesan over the top and put under a hot grill for 4 to 5 minutes, or until the top is lightly browned.

Bourride

SERVES FOUR TO SIX

2 leeks, chopped
1 large onion, chopped
2 large tomatoes, chopped
3 lb (1½ kg) white fish, cut into steaks
3 garlic cloves
4 strips thinly pared orange rind
Bouquet garni
2½ pints (1¼ litres) water
Salt and pepper
1 lb (450 g) potatoes, boiled
½ pint (300 ml) aioli sauce
8 to 12 slices French bread, fried in olive oil

Put the vegetables in a large saucepan. Put the fish on top. Add the garlic, orange rind, bouquet garni, water, salt and pepper—be careful with the seasoning because the stock will be much reduced later. Bring to the boil. Reduce the heat and simmer for 10 to 15 minutes or until the fish is cooked.

Transfer the fish to a warm tureen. Arrange the potatoes around the fish and keep warm.

Raise the heat and boil the remaining ingredients in the saucepan until about 1 pint (575 ml) of liquid is left. Remove the pan from the heat and strain the liquid. Rinse out the pan.

Put half the aioli into a large mixing bowl. Pour in the hot liquid gradually, stirring to mix. Return the mixture to the clean pan and cook very gently, without letting the soup boil, for a few minutes or until it thickens slightly.

Put the fried bread in the tureen on top of the fish and pour in the soup.

Serve immediately with the remaining aioli sauce.

Haddock crêpes

SERVES FOUR

1½ lb (700 g) smoked haddock
¼ pint (150 ml) milk
2 fl oz (50 ml) water
2 oz (50 g) butter
¼ lb (100 g) mushrooms, sliced
1 oz (25 g) flour
2 fl oz (50 ml) cream
Rind and juice of 1 lemon
1 tablespoon chopped parsley
8 pancakes, kept warm
1 lemon, cut into wedges

Poach the haddock in the milk and water for 10 minutes. Strain off the liquid and reserve it. Flake the fish into a mixing bowl, discarding all the skin and bones.

Melt 1 ounce (25 g) of the butter in a small saucepan and fry the mushrooms until soft. Add to the haddock.

In another small saucepan, melt the remaining butter, make a roux with the flour and stir in the reserved cooking liquid and cream. Cook the sauce, stirring constantly, until it has thickened. Add the lemon juice, rind and the parsley. Mix into the bowl.

Preheat the oven to 400°F (200° C, Gas Mark 6).

Lay the pancakes on your working surface. Place some of the haddock mixture along one end of each pancake and roll it up. Arrange the pancake rolls in a heatproof dish. Cover the dish with buttered foil and place it in the oven for 10 minutes to reheat. Serve with the lemon.

Salmon mousse

If the mousse is to be kept for a day or two, seal the top with a layer of aspic jelly.

SERVES FOUR

¾-lb (350-g) salmon steak, poached, skinned, boned and flaked
½ pint (300 ml) béchamel
½ teaspoon dried dill weed
Salt and pepper
2 level teaspoons gelatine
1 teaspoon lemon juice
¼ pint (150 ml) double cream, whipped
2 egg whites, whisked until stiff
¼ cucumber, sliced thinly and blanched

Blend the salmon in a liquidizer with the béchamel sauce until it is smooth. Scrape the mixture into a bowl and season to taste.

In a cup, soften the gelatine in 2 tablespoons of water. Put the cup in a pan of simmering water until the gelatine dissolves. Stir the gelatine into the salmon mixture with the lemon juice. Fold in the cream and the egg whites.

Divide the mixture between 4 ramekin dishes or use a 1½-pint (900-ml) soufflé dish. Put the mousse into the refrigerator until it has set. Garnish with cucumber slices.

Gefilte fish

Gefilte fish is a traditional East European Jewish dish, served on feast days. It may be served as a first course or as a main dish.

SERVES FIFTEEN TO TWENTY

6 lb (3 kg) fish fillets—a mixture of carp, whiting and bream—heads, tails, bones and skin removed and reserved
4 onions, sliced, plus 2 onions, chopped
2 large carrots, thinly sliced

Soused herrings is a dish made all over the world in various forms. Serve as a first course.

4 teaspoons sugar
Salt and pepper
3 eggs
2 tablespoons matzo meal
4 fl oz (125 ml) cold water

Mince the fish fillets very finely. Put the heads, tails, bones and skin in a saucepan and add the sliced onions, carrots, sugar, and plenty of salt and pepper. Just cover with water and bring to the boil. Reduce the heat to low.

Meanwhile, place the eggs and the remaining 2 onions in a liquidizer and blend well. Fold them into the minced fish. Add the matzo meal and season well with salt and pepper. Fold in the cold water. Wet your hands and shape the mixture into balls. Drop the balls on to the fish trimmings and liquid and reduce the heat to very low. Cover the pan and simmer for 2 hours, removing the scum occasionally.

With a slotted spoon, remove the balls from the broth and arrange them on a serving dish. Garnish the balls with the sliced carrot. Strain the cooking liquid into a bowl. Put the balls and the strained broth into the refrigerator to chill.

Serve the gefilte fish with the jellied broth.

Steamed fish mould with anchovy sauce

SERVES FOUR TO SIX

¾ lb (350 g) whiting or any other similar white fish
1 oz (25 g) butter
1 oz (25 g) flour
4 fl oz (125 ml) milk
4 eggs, beaten
Tabasco sauce
Salt
Lemon juice
Anchovy sauce, made with ½ pint (300 ml) velouté sauce and 2 teaspoons anchovy essence, kept hot

Skin the fish and mince or chop it finely. Melt the butter in a saucepan. Stir in the flour and cook for a few seconds. Add the milk, stirring, to make a thick paste, or panade. Remove the pan from the heat and set aside to cool.

When the panade is cool, beat in the fish. Beat in the eggs a little at a time. Push the mixture through a sieve or blend it in a liquidizer until it is smooth. Add a few drops of Tabasco sauce, salt and lemon juice to taste.

Lightly grease a 1-pint (575-ml) fish or ring mould. Put the fish mixture into the mould and cover it with a piece of greaseproof paper. Put the mould in a steamer or stand it on a rack in a large pan. Cover the pan and steam over gently boiling water for 45 minutes.

Lift out the mould and turn the mixture out on to a heated dish. Coat with the hot anchovy sauce and serve.

Kipper pâté

This is an easy-to-make and economical first course. Serve it with toast made with brown bread.

SERVES FOUR

2 kippers (or smoked mackerel), skinned and boned
¼ lb (100 g) butter, softened
Juice and rind of 1 lemon
Pepper
1 hard-boiled egg, chopped

Put the kippers in a frying-pan and pour over enough boiling water to cover them. Put the pan over very low heat for 10 minutes.

Drain the kippers and remove any small bones. Put the flesh into a liquidizer with the butter, lemon juice and rind and a pinch of pepper and blend. When the mixture is well blended add the hard-boiled egg and blend again just long enough to mix thoroughly.

Pack the pâté into ramekin dishes and put them in the refrigerator to chill for at least 1 hour before serving.

Quenelles

Quenelles are a kind of dumpling made from meat, poultry, game or seafood. Depending on the size, quenelles are used as a garnish or served as a first or main course.

Fish quenelles are traditionally made with pike, but whiting, hake or cod can be used just as successfully. Serve the quenelles with ½ pint (300 ml) of velouté sauce to which 6 oz (175 g) of finely chopped shrimps have been added, or with a mornay sauce.

SERVES FOUR

½-lb (225-g) pike, skinned and boned
Salt and pepper
Grated nutmeg
3½ oz (90 g) butter
½ oz (15 g) flour
2 fl oz (50 ml) milk
1 whole egg plus 1 yolk
3 tablespoons double cream

Pound the fish with a pestle in a mortar or with the end of a rolling pin in a mixing bowl until smooth, or put the fish through a mincer. Season to taste.

Melt 1 ounce (25 g) of the butter in a saucepan, stir in the flour and gradually add the milk to make a panade, or thick paste. Set it aside to cool.

When the panade is cold, work in the fish then add the remaining butter, the whole egg and egg yolk. Beat the mixture thoroughly, using an electric beater. Beat in the cream a little at a time. Put the mixture in the refrigerator to chill for 1 hour.

Put the mixture in a piping bag fitted with an éclair or plain nozzle. Cut off 2-inch (5-cm) lengths with a knife. Arrange the quenelles in a buttered sauté pan. Bring some salted water to the boil and gently pour in enough to cover the quenelles. Place the pan over low heat and simmer very gently for 10 minutes.

Lift out the quenelles with a slotted spoon. Drain on kitchen paper and serve.

Jellied eels

SERVES FOUR

2 lb (900 g) eels, prepared and cut into 2-inch (5-cm) pieces
1 pint (575 ml) fish stock
1 teaspoon lemon juice
1 onion stuck with 1 clove
Bouquet garni
1 tablespoon chopped parsley
Salt and pepper

Put the eels into a large pan with the stock, lemon juice, onion and bouquet garni and bring to the boil. Reduce the heat, cover the pan and simmer for 30 minutes. Remove the pan from the heat and let the eels cool in the cooking liquid.

Lift the eel pieces out of the pan and arrange them in a large soufflé dish. Strain the cooking liquid, add the parsley, season to taste and pour it over the eels. Put the dish in the refrigerator to chill.

Remove the dish from the refrigerator. Run a knife round the edges of the dish to loosen the jelly and turn it out on to a platter. Cut the jelly into squares and serve.

Shellfish

Moules marinières

SERVES FOUR

3 quarts (6 lb/3 kg) mussels, cleaned
2 shallots, finely chopped
Freshly ground black pepper
6 fl oz (175 ml) dry white wine
Bouquet garni
1 tablespoon beurre manié
1 tablespoon chopped parsley

Put the mussels into a large saucepan with the shallots, pepper, wine and bouquet garni. Cover the pan and bring to the boil, shaking the pan occasionally. Reduce the heat and simmer for 5 minutes. Discard any mussels that do not open.

Remove the pan from the heat and strain the liquid into a saucepan. Put the mussels into a deep serving dish and keep warm. Put the saucepan on the heat, stir in the beurre manié, a little at a time, and bring the sauce to the boil.

Add the parsley. Pour the sauce over the mussels and serve immediately.

Coquilles St Jacques

If you want to serve Coquilles St Jacques as a main course use 8 large scallops to fill 4 large shells.

SERVES FOUR

6 scallops, prepared and removed from their shells (reserve 4 deep shells)
4 fl oz (125 ml) white wine
1 lemon slice
1 onion slice
6 white peppercorns
Salt
1 bay leaf
½ pint (300 ml) mornay sauce made with 1 oz (25 g) each of Parmesan and Gruyère cheese

Put the scallops in a small pan with the wine, lemon, onion, peppercorns, salt and bay leaf and bring to the boil. Reduce the heat, cover the pan and simmer for 5 minutes.

Remove the scallops from the pan and set aside. Strain the liquid and return it to the pan. Return the pan to the heat and bring the liquid to the boil. Continue to boil until the liquid is reduced to 2 tablespoons. Stir the mornay sauce into the reduced liquid and adjust the seasoning.

Preheat the grill to a medium heat.

Cut the scallops into quarters and place them in the reserved shells. Cover the scallops with the sauce and brown them lightly under the grill.

Scallops à la provencale

SERVES FOUR

6 scallops, prepared and removed from their shells (reserve 4 deep shells)
2 fl oz (50 ml) water
2 teaspoons lemon juice
1 slice onion
1 bay leaf
1½ oz (40 g) butter
2 oz (50 g) button mushrooms, quartered
½ oz (15 g) flour
2 fl oz (50 ml) white wine
1 garlic clove
Salt and pepper
2 teaspoons tomato purée
2 tomatoes, peeled, seeded and chopped
1 lb (450 g) potatoes, boiled and puréed with 1 tablespoon butter
1 oz (25 g) grated Gruyère cheese

Put the scallops in a small pan with the water, lemon juice, onion and bay leaf and bring to the boil. Reduce the heat, cover the pan and simmer for 5 minutes. Strain the contents of the pan; put the scallops in a bowl and reserve the liquid.

Melt the butter in another small saucepan. Add the mushrooms and fry them for 1 minute. Remove the mushrooms and set aside. Stir the flour into the butter and allow it to colour slightly. Stir in the white wine and the strained stock from the scallops. Crush the garlic with some salt and add it to the sauce with the tomato purée, tomatoes, mushrooms and seasoning. Simmer the sauce, stirring, for 5 minutes. Remove the pan from the heat and pour the sauce over the scallops.

Preheat the grill to medium.

Put the mixture into the reserved shells. Pipe the potato purée round the edge of the shells. Sprinkle the cheese over the top and brown under the grill.

Dressed crab

Serve dressed crab as a main dish with a variety of salads.

SERVES THREE TO FOUR

4-lb (2-kg) crab, cooked and prepared
Vinaigrette dressing
2 tablespoons fresh breadcrumbs
1 to 2 tablespoons cream
Salt and pepper
Cayenne pepper
Lemon juice
1 egg yolk, hard boiled
1 tablespoon chopped parsley
Lettuce leaves, torn into pieces
½ pint (300 ml) mayonnaise

Wash the crab shell thoroughly and dry it well. Put all the white meat into a bowl, mix in a spoonful of vinaigrette and set aside.

In another bowl, beat the brown meat with the breadcrumbs, adding some of the cream if the mixture is too dry. Season to taste with salt, pepper, cayenne and a few drops of lemon juice.

Pile the white crab meat into the middle of the shell. Arrange the brown meat on either side. Sieve the egg yolk and arrange it in 2 stripes dividing the white meat from the brown. Arrange the parsley in the same way. Lay the crab on lettuce leaves and serve with the sauce.

Crayfish with butter sauce

Crayfish has a very delicate flavour and is at its best when cooked very simply. The Scandinavians cook crayfish in a court bouillon and serve them piled up on a large platter with a bowl of melted butter flavoured with dill.

Eat the crayfish with your fingers. Separate the tail from the body. Discard the body—the meat is in the tail. Use your hands to open the tail shell and lift out the meat.

SERVES FOUR

Court bouillon
48 crayfish, prepared
½ lb (225 g) butter
1 tablespoon chopped dill weed
Lemon juice
Salt
White pepper

Half-fill a very large saucepan with court bouillon and bring to the boil. Add the crayfish, one or two at a time so as to not let the liquid go off the boil. Boil for 7 minutes.

Meanwhile, in a small saucepan melt the butter. Stir in the dill weed, and the lemon juice, salt and pepper to taste. Pour the butter into a bowl.

Lift out the crayfish. Arrange them on a platter and serve with the butter.

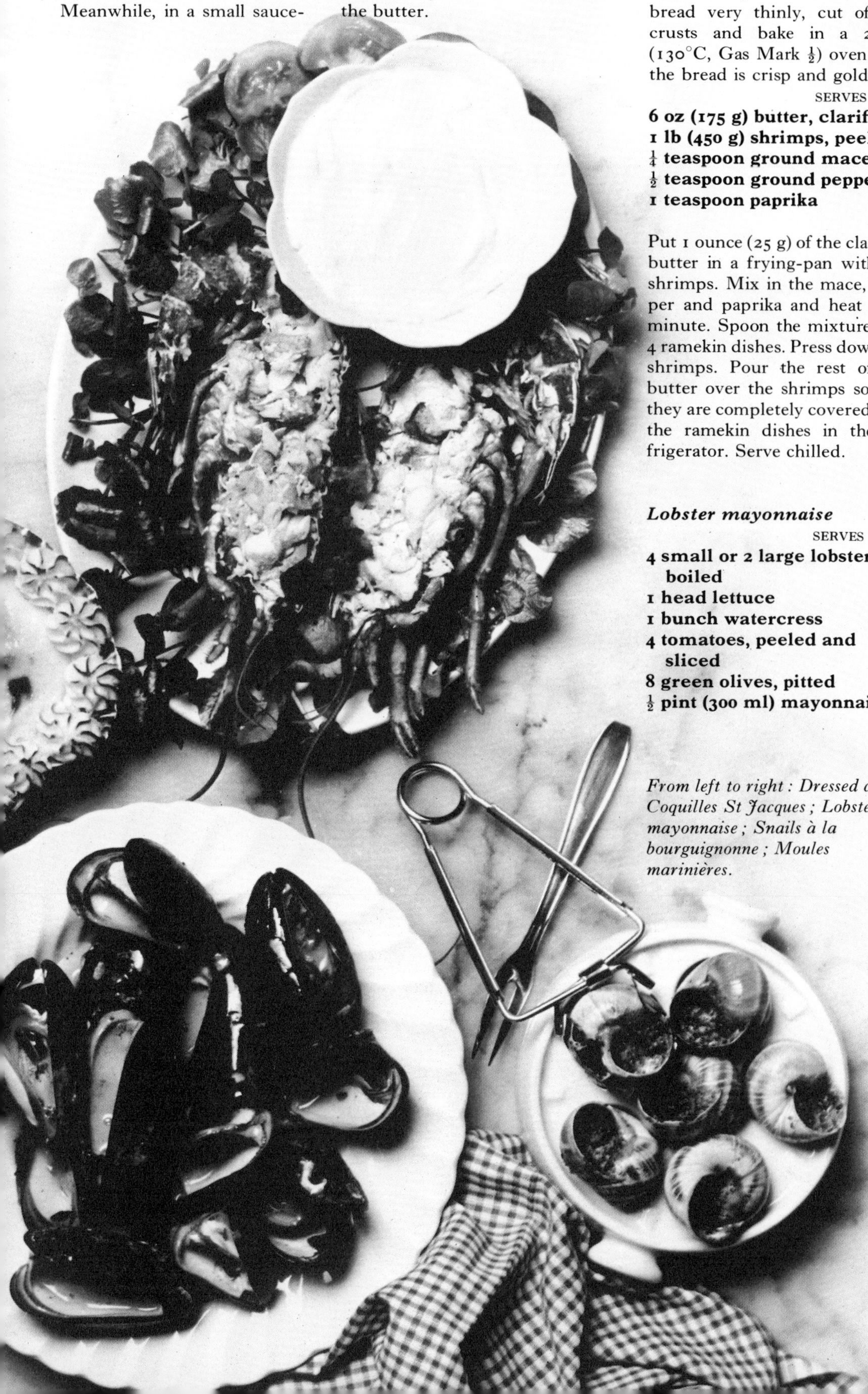

Potted shrimps

Serve potted shrimps as a first course with lemon quarters and melba toast or thinly sliced, buttered brown bread. To make melba toast, slice white or brown bread very thinly, cut off the crusts and bake in a 250°F (130°C, Gas Mark ½) oven until the bread is crisp and golden.

SERVES FOUR

6 oz (175 g) butter, clarified
1 lb (450 g) shrimps, peeled
¼ teaspoon ground mace
½ teaspoon ground pepper
1 teaspoon paprika

Put 1 ounce (25 g) of the clarified butter in a frying-pan with the shrimps. Mix in the mace, pepper and paprika and heat for a minute. Spoon the mixture into 4 ramekin dishes. Press down the shrimps. Pour the rest of the butter over the shrimps so that they are completely covered. Put the ramekin dishes in the refrigerator. Serve chilled.

Lobster mayonnaise

SERVES FOUR

4 small or 2 large lobsters, boiled
1 head lettuce
1 bunch watercress
4 tomatoes, peeled and sliced
8 green olives, pitted
½ pint (300 ml) mayonnaise

From left to right: Dressed crab; Coquilles St Jacques; Lobster mayonnaise; Snails à la bourguignonne; Moules marinières.

Split the lobsters in half. Crack the claws. Lift out the tail meat and cut it into slices. Wipe the shells with a little oil to make them shiny.

Put the tail meat back into the shells, red side uppermost. Place the claw meat in the top part of the shells. Arrange the lobster on a bed of lettuce and watercress. Garnish with sliced olives and tomatoes. Serve with the mayonnaise, well chilled in a separate bowl.

Snails à la bourguignonne

There are special dishes for holding the snails for the final heating in the oven. These are dented so that the snails do not tip over and the butter does not run out.

SERVES FOUR

2 dozen Roman snails, prepared
4 fl oz (125 ml) white wine
2 fl oz (50 ml) stock
1 onion
1 carrot
Bouquet garni
Salt
6 oz (175 g) unsalted butter, softened
1 shallot, finely chopped
1 garlic clove, crushed
Freshly ground pepper
1 tablespoon chopped parsley

Put the snails in a saucepan with the wine, stock, onion, carrot, bouquet garni and salt and bring to the boil. Cover the pan and simmer for 3 hours. Cool the snails in the cooking liquid.

Remove the snails from their shells and cut off the membrane and black part. Boil the empty shells in water with a few soda crystals for 30 minutes. Rinse the shells well and dry them. Set aside.

In a small bowl combine the butter, shallot, garlic, pepper, salt and parsley. Shape the butter into a block or roll and put it in the refrigerator to chill.

Preheat the oven to 400°F (200°C, Gas Mark 6).

Put the snails in their shells and cover them with a piece of butter the size of a hazelnut or larger, stuffing it in until the butter is level with the rim of the shell. Put the snails in a dish, open ends uppermost, and heat them in the oven for 5 to 6 minutes.

Poultry and game birds

Chicken and small turkeys are the kinds of poultry most often cooked by boiling, or poaching, although duck is occasionally cooked in this manner. The Chinese and Japanese often steam chicken and duck, but this is not a feature of Western cooking. Game birds are rarely, if ever, boiled or steamed.

Poultry may be poached either on top of the stove or in the oven. Use a large saucepan or casserole with a tight-fitting lid. If you are using frozen poultry be sure that it is completely thawed before cooking—a large chicken can take up to a day and a half to thaw in the refrigerator, and a small or medium-sized turkey up to two days.

You can poach either a boiling fowl or a roasting chicken. A boiling fowl is older and tougher than a roasting chicken and therefore requires a longer cooking time to make it tender.

To poach a chicken or turkey, put the bird and its giblets into a large saucepan or casserole. Add two teaspoons of salt, two onions (halved or quartered), two carrots (halved), a bouquet garni or bay leaf and a few peppercorns. (These flavourings are sufficient for a medium to large chicken, but may of course be varied according to taste.) Pour in enough cold water to just cover the chicken—or use stock, wine or either of these mixed with water. Bring the liquid to the boil over high heat, skimming the fat and scum from the surface. Reduce the heat to low, cover the pan and simmer, allowing forty-five minutes for a two-and-a-half- to three-pound (1- to 1½-kg) chicken, one hour for a three- to four-pound (1½- to 2-kg) chicken and one and a quarter hours for a four- to six-pound (2- to 3-kg) chicken. A five- to six-pound (2½- to 3-kg) boiling fowl will take about two to three hours and a medium-sized turkey—ten to twelve pounds (4½ to 5½ kg)—will take about one and three-quarter hours. To test if the bird is cooked, pierce the plumpest part of the thigh with a skewer or fork; the juices that run out should be clear, not pink.

When the bird is cooked, lift it out of the pan. Strain the cooking liquid, skimming off any surface fat, and reserve it for stock.

To poach the bird in the oven, put it in a flameproof casserole, cover it with cold water, add the flavourings and salt and bring to the boil over high heat. Cover the casserole and put it into a 350°F (180°C, Gas Mark 4) oven for the same amount of time as on top of the stove.

Chicken pieces can also be poached in the same way as a whole chicken. Allow about thirty to forty minutes for legs and about twenty to twenty-five minutes for breasts.

If you poach a chicken in the correct way it will be succulent and full of flavour, and can be used in a number of different dishes—for example, chicken à la king, chicken and pineapple salad and chicken chaudfroid.

English boiled chicken

This traditional English recipe can be varied by the addition of ½ pound (225 g) of button mushrooms, which should be sautéed in butter for about five minutes. Drain and add them to the sauce at the same time as the parsley, cream and lemon rind.

This dish may also be served with plain boiled rice.

SERVES FOUR TO SIX

4- to 5-lb (2- to 2½-kg) chicken, poached and kept hot, cooking liquid reserved
12 parsley sprigs
8 bacon rolls
1 oz (25 g) butter
1 oz (25 g) flour
2 fl oz (50 ml) cream
Grated rind of ½ lemon

Put 1 pint (575 ml) of the cooking liquid into a saucepan and bring to the boil over moderately high heat. Boil briskly until the liquid has reduced to about ¾ pint (450 ml). Remove the pan from the heat and set aside.

Meanwhile, put the parsley sprigs into a small pan of boiling salted water and simmer for 5 minutes. Drain the parsley, then rub it through a strainer into a bowl to make a purée and set aside.

Thread the bacon rolls on to a skewer and set aside.

Melt the butter in a saucepan. Add the flour and mix it in to form a roux. Cook the roux, stirring constantly over very low heat, for 5 to 7 minutes, until it becomes straw-coloured.

Remove the pan from the heat and gradually stir in the reduced cooking liquid. Return the pan to the heat and cook, stirring constantly, until the sauce thickens. Remove the pan from the heat and stir in the parsley purée, the cream and the lemon rind.

While you are making the sauce, preheat the grill to moderately high and grill the bacon rolls, turning them occasionally, for 3 to 5 minutes or until they are cooked. Remove the bacon rolls from the skewer.

Carve the chicken into serving pieces and arrange them on a heated serving dish. Spoon over a little of the sauce and pour the rest into a sauce boat. Garnish with the grilled bacon rolls and serve immediately.

Poultry and game birds

Chicken à la king

This dish may be served on a bed of rice or on croûtons, or in hollowed-out baked bread cases or rolls.

SERVES FOUR TO SIX

4-lb (2-kg) chicken, poached and cooled
2 oz (50 g) butter
2 green peppers, cored, seeded and finely sliced
½ pound (225 g) button mushrooms, finely sliced
1 oz (25 g) flour
½ teaspoon paprika
1 teaspoon salt
½ pint (300 ml) poaching liquid, strained
¼ pint (150 ml) cream
1 teaspoon lemon juice
2 tablespoons dry sherry

Skin the chicken. Remove the flesh from the bones and cut it into small dice.

Melt the butter in a large saucepan. Add the green peppers and mushrooms and fry gently, stirring, until they are softened. Stir in the flour, paprika and salt. Gradually add the reserved poaching liquid and cream, and bring the mixture to the boil, stirring constantly. Reduce the heat to low and cook the sauce for 2 to 3 minutes, stirring constantly, until it has thickened.

Stir in the chicken dice, lemon juice and sherry. Simmer over low heat, stirring occasionally, for about 5 minutes or until the chicken is heated through.

Chicken poached in cider

SERVES FOUR

3- to 3½-lb (1½-kg) chicken, jointed, or 4 chicken breasts
½ pint (300 ml) cider
1 small onion
3 peppercorns
3 tarragon sprigs
2 dessert apples, cored and sliced
2 teaspoons cornflour
¼ pint (150 ml) cream
Lemon juice
Salt and pepper

Put the chicken into a saucepan. Add the cider, onion, peppercorns and tarragon sprigs. Set the pan over high heat and bring to the boil. Reduce the heat to low, cover the pan and simmer for 30 minutes.

Add the apple slices to the saucepan, reserving about 8 for the garnish. Simmer the chicken for a further 10 minutes, or until it is cooked through. Remove the pan from the heat and transfer the chicken pieces and apple slices to a warmed serving dish.

Mix the cornflour with the cream, then stir the mixture into the pan juices. Return the pan to moderate heat and bring to the boil, stirring constantly. Simmer for 1 minute, stirring. Strain the sauce over the chicken pieces, set the dish aside and keep hot.

Put the reserved apple slices into a pan of boiling water to which a drop or two of lemon juice has been added. Blanch them for 1 minute then drain. Garnish the dish with the apple slices and serve.

Chicken fricassée

Serve the fricassée with plain boiled rice or buttered noodles, and a mixed green salad.

SERVES FOUR

1 oz (25 g) butter
1 oz (25 g) flour
¾ pint (450 ml) chicken stock or white wine and stock mixed
Salt and white pepper
Grated nutmeg
15 small or pickling onions
½ lb (225 g) button mushrooms
3 egg yolks
3 tablespoons cream
1 teaspoon lemon juice
3½- to 4-lb (1½- to 2-kg) chicken, poached, skinned, jointed and kept hot
Fried croûtons
1 tablespoon chopped fresh parsley

Melt the butter in a saucepan. Stir in the flour to form a roux. Cook the roux, stirring constantly, over very low heat for 5 to 7 minutes or until it is straw-coloured. Add the stock gradually, stirring constantly. Season with salt, pepper and a pinch of nutmeg.

Add the onions and simmer for 10 minutes, then add the mushrooms and simmer for a further 10 minutes.

Combine the egg yolks, cream and lemon juice in a small bowl. Stir in a little of the hot sauce, then pour the mixture into the saucepan, stirring constantly. Cook over very low heat, stirring, without letting the sauce boil. Check the seasoning.

Arrange the chicken pieces on a heated platter. Pour over the sauce, garnish with croûtons and chopped parsley and serve.

Chicken with spicy mayonnaise

SERVES FOUR TO SIX

4-lb (2-kg) chicken, poached and cooled
½ pint (300 ml) mayonnaise, well seasoned with salt, pepper and mustard
2 teaspoons curry paste or powder
2 tablespoons whipped cream
2 tablespoons apricot jam, sieved
2 teaspoons lemon juice
½ lb (225 g) long-grain rice, cooked and cooled
2 oz (50 g) slivered almonds, toasted
2 pickled gherkins, finely chopped
1 red pepper, cored, seeded and finely shredded
1 cucumber, finely sliced
2 tablespoons vinegar

Skin the chicken. Remove the flesh from the bones and cut it into small pieces.

Mix the mayonnaise, curry paste or powder, cream, jam and lemon juice together in a large bowl. Stir in the chicken pieces until they are well coated.

Arrange the cold rice in a layer on a serving platter. (If you prefer, make a rice mould by pressing the hot cooked rice into a 9-inch/23-cm ring mould, refrigerating it until chilled, then unmoulding it on to a platter.)

Arrange the chicken mayonnaise mixture over the rice or in the centre of the rice ring and scatter the toasted almonds, chopped gherkins and shredded pepper on top.

Put the cucumber slices into a pan of boiling water and blanch them for 1 minute. Drain them, then mix them with the vinegar. Set aside for 10 minutes. Drain off the vinegar, and arrange the cucumber slices around the rice. Chill for 30 minutes before serving.

Chicken salad

SERVES SIX

4- to 5-lb (2- to 2½-kg) chicken, poached and cooled
3 hard-boiled eggs, separated
2 oz (50 g) mild Cheddar, diced
1 head celery, chopped
2 large oranges, peeled and sliced
1 green dessert apple, cored, diced and mixed with 1 teaspoon lemon juice
2 oz (50 g) chopped walnuts
¼ pint (150 ml) vinaigrette dressing
6 large radishes, thinly sliced
1 bunch watercress

Skin the chicken, cut the meat into dice and put them into a mixing bowl. Chop the egg whites and add to the bowl.

Add the cheese, celery, oranges, apple and walnuts to the chicken. Mash the egg yolks to a paste in a small bowl, gradually incorporating the vinaigrette. Pour the dressing over the chicken and toss the salad to coat well.

Arrange the salad decoratively in a serving dish. Garnish with the radish slices and watercress.

Chicken and pineapple salad

SERVES SIX

4- to 5-lb (2- to 2½-kg) chicken, poached and cooled
1 large fresh pineapple
¼ pint (150 ml) mayonnaise
¼ pint (150 ml) soured cream
Rind and juice of ½ lemon
2 celery stalks, diced
Salt and pepper
Walnuts or blanched almonds

Skin the chicken, cut the flesh into neat, bite-sized pieces and put them in a large bowl.

Halve the pineapple. Using a serrated knife, remove the flesh from the skin, leaving the shell intact. Remove the core and chop the flesh into bite-sized pieces and add them to the chicken.

Mix the mayonnaise, soured cream and lemon rind and juice together. Add 6 tablespoons of the mayonnaise mixture and the celery to the chicken and pineapple in the bowl. Season to taste and mix well.

Pile the mixture into the pineapple shells and arrange the shells on a serving platter. Spoon over the remaining mayonnaise mixture and garnish with the walnuts or almonds.

Chicken chaudfroid

SERVES SIX TO EIGHT

8 large chicken breasts, skinned, boned, poached and cooled in the cooking liquid
$\frac{1}{2}$ pint (300 ml) chaudfroid sauce, cooled
1 tablespoon gelatine, softened in 2 tablespoons hot water
1 quart (1 litre) reserved cooking liquid, degreased and clarified
Cucumber peel, cut into strips
Lemon juice
4 stuffed olives, sliced
Lemon wedges
Watercress sprigs

Put the chicken breasts on a rack over a plate and spoon the cool chaudfroid sauce over them. Refrigerate until the sauce sets.

Stir the softened gelatine into the clarified cooking liquid. Pour half of the liquid into a Swiss roll tin and refrigerate until the aspic has set. Reserve the remaining liquid aspic and keep it cool so that it sets very lightly.

Decorate the chicken breasts with the cucumber peel and olives, then coat them with some of the reserved, lightly set aspic. Return the rack to the refrigerator until the aspic sets.

Arrange the chicken breasts on a serving dish. Chop the aspic in the Swiss roll tin and decorate the dish with it. Garnish with lemon wedges and watercress.

Chicken florentine

SERVES FOUR

3- to $3\frac{1}{2}$-lb ($1\frac{1}{2}$-kg) chicken, jointed, or 4 chicken breasts
1 tablespoon lemon juice
4 fl oz (125 ml) chicken stock
2 fl oz (50 ml) dry white wine
Salt and pepper
1 lb (450 g) fresh leaf spinach, washed thoroughly and trimmed
$1\frac{1}{2}$ oz (40 g) butter
2 oz (50 g) flour
$\frac{1}{2}$ pint (300 ml) milk
4 tablespoons cream
Grated nutmeg
3 oz (75 g) grated Gruyère
2 tablespoons fresh white breadcrumbs

Put the chicken, lemon juice, stock, wine and seasoning into a saucepan over high heat and bring to the boil. Reduce the heat to low, cover the pan and simmer for 30 to 40 minutes or until the chicken is cooked.

Meanwhile, put the spinach into a large pan, add salt to taste and cook covered, without adding any water (there is enough trapped in the leaves after washing), over moderately high heat for 5 to 6 minutes. Remove the pan from the heat and drain the spinach thoroughly, using two plates to squeeze out excess moisture. Spread the spinach over the bottom of a medium-sized ovenproof casserole. Set aside and keep hot.

When the chicken pieces are cooked, remove the pan from the heat. Lift out the chicken pieces, skin them and arrange them on top of the spinach. Strain the cooking liquid into a bowl.

Preheat the oven to 350°F (180°C, Gas Mark 4).

Melt the butter in a saucepan. Add the flour and mix it in to form a roux. Cook the roux, stirring constantly, over very low heat for 5 to 7 minutes, or until it becomes straw-coloured.

Gradually stir in the milk and bring to the boil. Cook for 1 to 2 minutes, stirring constantly, until the sauce thickens. Stir in the reserved cooking liquid, cream, and a little nutmeg. Stir in 2 ounces (50 g) of the grated cheese and simmer gently until it melts. Season to taste, and pour the sauce over the chicken.

Sprinkle the remaining grated cheese and the breadcrumbs over the sauce. Bake in the oven for 15 minutes.

Meanwhile, preheat the grill to moderately high. Remove the dish from the oven and place it under the grill for 2 to 3 minutes, or until the top is golden and bubbling.

Duck galantine

Chicken can be used instead of the duck, using marjoram instead of sage.

SERVES SIX TO EIGHT

1 duck, about 6 lb (3 kg), boned, with the wings and legs intact
1 lb (450 g) cooked tongue
1 lb (450 g) cooked ham
6 to 7 black olives, pitted and chopped
$\frac{1}{2}$ oz (15 g) pistachio nuts, blanched
$\frac{1}{4}$ pint (150 ml) warm meat aspic

STUFFING

1 oz (25 g) butter
2 onions, chopped
1 lb (450 g) minced veal
3 oz (75 g) soft white breadcrumbs
2 teaspoons dried sage
1 egg
$\frac{1}{4}$ pint (150 ml) double cream
Salt and pepper

First, prepare the stuffing. Melt the butter in a frying-pan. Add the onions and fry them until they are softened. Remove the pan from the heat and transfer the onions to a large bowl. Combine the remaining stuffing ingredients with the onions until they are thoroughly mixed.

Lay the duck on a board, skin-side down and open it out flat. Spread the stuffing over the duck, to within about 1 inch (2 cm) of the edges. Cut the tongue and ham into strips and arrange them over the stuffing with the olives and nuts.

Bring the outside edges of the duck's skin to the centre and re-form into the original shape. Sew up securely, using a trussing needle and strong thread. Enclose the duck in greaseproof or waxed paper, then in muslin, tying each end securely with string and sewing up the join.

Put the duck into a large pan or fish kettle of boiling salted water. Cover the pan and simmer for $1\frac{1}{2}$ to 2 hours.

Remove the duck from the pan and set it aside to cool, still in the muslin wrapping. When it is cool refrigerate the duck until it is very cold before unwrapping.

Brush the duck with the aspic, applying 2 or 3 coats and allowing one coat to set before applying the next one. Serve cold.

Duck galantine

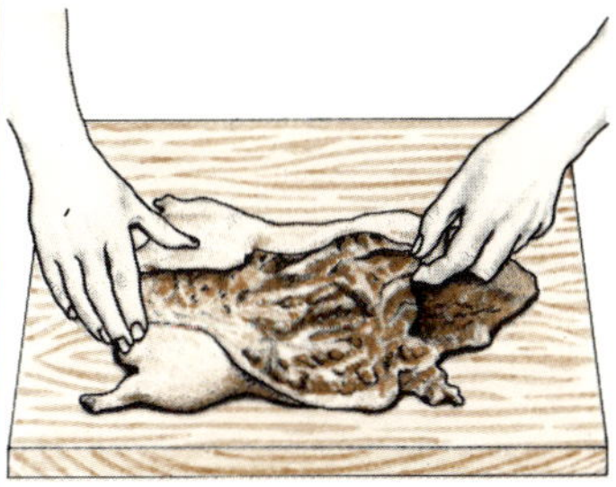

Lay the duck on a board, skin-side down, and open it out.

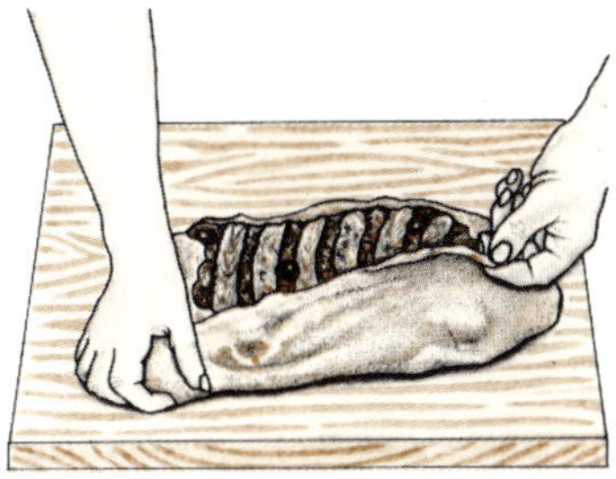

Spread with the stuffing, ham, tongue, olives and nuts.

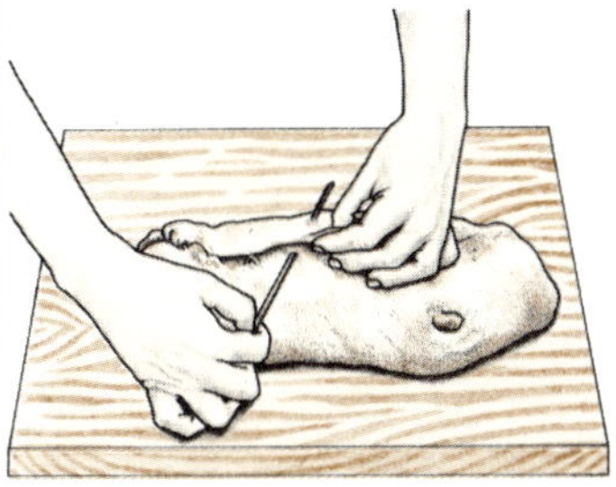

Bring the edges together, reshape the duck and sew it up.

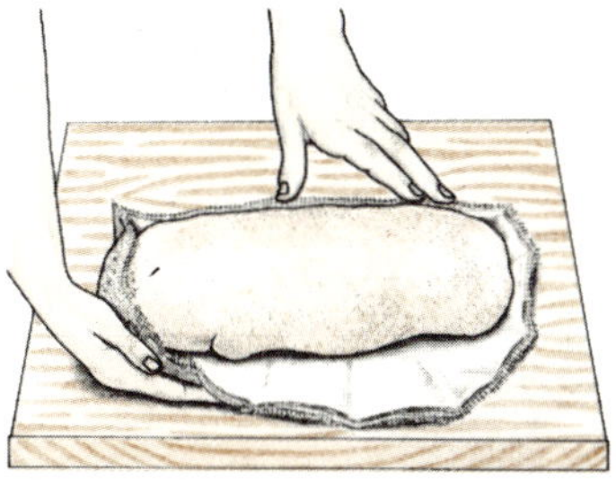

Enclose the duck completely in greaseproof paper and muslin.

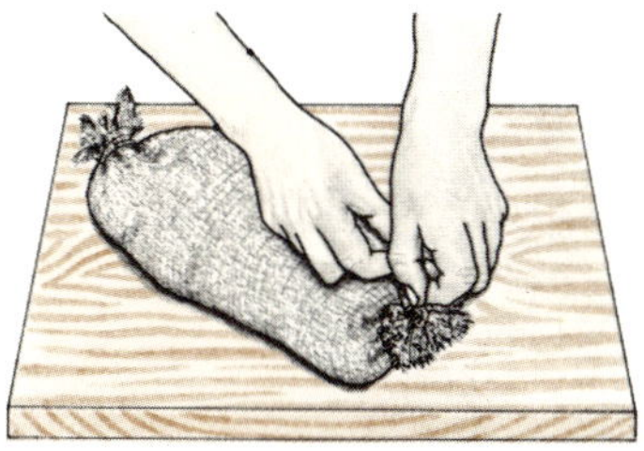

Tie the ends of the parcel up and sew up the centre join.

Meat and game

Boiling is not a method of cooking that is immediately associated with meat: yet some of the most delicious meat dishes are cooked by boiling. There are some famous examples from many countries: bollito from Italy, pot au feu from France, Boston boiled dinner from the United States, Wiener tafelspitz from Austria and boiled beef and dumplings from England.

Steaming meat, on the other hand, is unusual outside Chinese and Japanese cuisines. There are, however, a very few exceptions—the most common one being steak and kidney pudding.

Game is rarely boiled or steamed.

Both salted and unsalted meat can be boiled. The minimum cooking time is twenty-five minutes per pound (450 g) plus twenty-five minutes for salted meat and twenty minutes per pound (450 g) plus twenty minutes for unsalted meat. But some cuts of meat may need up to double that time if the meat is to be really tender. Test the meat to see if it is done by piercing it with a skewer. If the skewer penetrates to the centre easily the meat is cooked.

To boil meat, put the joint into a large saucepan and pour in enough cold water to cover it. Bring the water slowly to the boil, skimming the scum as it rises. Add some onion, root vegetables (see the recipes that follow) and a bouquet garni. Cover the pan and simmer very gently until the meat is tender. Top up with boiling water from time to time, if necessary.

Salt beef and dumplings

Plenty of hot English mustard or piquant horseradish sauce may be served with this dish.

Salt beef may also be served cold. Let the meat cool in the cooking liquid then remove it from the pan. Cover the meat and chill it in the refrigerator. Slice the beef thinly and serve it with a variety of salads.

SERVES SIX TO EIGHT

4 lb (2 kg) salt silverside or topside of beef
Bouquet garni
6 peppercorns
½ lb (225 g) suet-crust pastry, with 2 teaspoons chopped fresh herbs mixed in
6 onions, halved
6 carrots, halved
½ lb (225 g) turnips, cubed

Put the beef into a large saucepan, just cover with cold water and set over moderate heat. Bring to the boil, skimming the scum from the surface. Add the bouquet garni and peppercorns to the pan. Reduce the heat to low, cover the pan and simmer very gently for 2 hours, adding more boiling water if necessary.

Meanwhile, form the pastry dough into small walnut-sized dumplings and set them aside.

Remove the bouquet garni from the pan and skim any fat or scum from the surface. Add the vegetables, cover the pan and simmer for a further 15 minutes. Add the dumplings, cover the pan and cook for a final 20 minutes, or until the meat and dumplings are cooked.

Remove the meat from the pan and put it on a warmed serving dish. Surround it with the vegetables and dumplings. Skim the fat from the surface of the cooking liquid, strain it and serve separately in a sauce boat.

To salt beef or tongue

1 gallon (4 litres) water
2 lb (900 g) cooking salt
½ oz (15 g) saltpetre
½ oz (15 g) demerara sugar
4 to 6 lb (2 to 3 kg) tongue or joint of beef

Put the water in a large pan, add the salt, saltpetre and sugar and boil for 30 minutes. Skim, then allow to cool completely. Put the tongue or meat in a large, deep bowl or casserole and cover with the brine. Leave for 4 to 5 weeks for an ox tongue, 1 to 2 weeks for beef. Turn every 2 days. Remove the meat from the brine and rinse. The meat is now ready to be cooked.

To pickle beef or tongue

½ lb (225 g) salt
½ oz (15 g) saltpetre
½ oz (15 g) demerara sugar
1 teaspoon ground mace
1 teaspoon ground ginger
½ teaspoon ground cloves
½ teaspoon black pepper
½ teaspoon ground cinnamon
4 to 6 lb (2 to 3 kg) tongue or joint of beef

In a bowl mix together the salt, saltpetre, sugar and spices. Put the tongue or meat on a large serving dish and rub the mixture in well all over. Turn the meat each day: ox tongue can be left for 2 weeks, beef for 6 days.

Ham boiled in cider

Hams are usually boiled, even if they are to be finished by baking or glazing in the oven. If you are using a home-cured salted ham, it must be soaked overnight in water before cooking.

SERVES FOUR TO SIX

3-lb (1½-kg) gammon or ham
1 quart (1 litre) cider
1 onion, halved
1 carrot, halved
4 tablespoons breadcrumbs, toasted

Put the ham, cider, onion and carrot into a large saucepan over moderate heat. Bring to the boil, skimming the fat and scum from the surface. Reduce the heat to low, cover the pan and simmer for 1¼ hours (or allow 25 minutes per pound/450 g), until the ham is cooked. Remove the pan from the heat and let the ham cool in the cooking liquid. When the liquid is cold transfer the ham to a board.

Skin the ham, then press the breadcrumbs into the skinned side. It is now ready to be served.

Salt beef and dumplings, dolmas and steak and kidney pudding.

Meat and game

Steak and kidney pudding

SERVES FOUR

¾ lb (350 g) suet-crust pastry
1½ lb (700 g) lean stewing beef, cut into cubes
½ lb (225 g) ox kidney, cut into cubes
1 onion, finely chopped
1 oz (25 g) flour, seasoned with salt, pepper and paprika
1 teaspoon dried mixed herbs or 2 teaspoons chopped fresh herbs
1 tablespoon Worcestershire sauce
¼ pint (150 ml) beef stock

Roll out the pastry dough on a floured surface to a circle about 10 inches (25 cm) in diameter. Cut a right-angled segment out of the circle and set it aside. Moisten the cut edges of the dough circle with water, press them together then lift the dough and put it into a 1-quart (1-litre) pudding basin. Press it down lightly and trim with a sharp knife. Keep the trimmings.

Toss the beef, kidney and onion in the seasoned flour and put them in the basin. Sprinkle the herbs over the meat and pour in the Worcestershire sauce and stock (the stock should come half-way up the sides of the basin, so add more stock if necessary).

Lightly knead the remaining dough segment and trimmings and roll out to a circle large enough to cover the basin. Dampen the edges of the dough in the basin, then carefully place the circle over the top, trimming off any excess dough. Press the edges together to seal the pudding.

Dip a large piece of cloth in boiling water, wring it out and sprinkle it lightly with flour. Tie the cloth over the basin making a 1-inch (2-cm) pleat in the centre of the top to allow for expansion. Tie the cloth in place with string. (Aluminium foil can be used instead of cloth, if you prefer.)

Put the basin into a large pan of boiling water—the water must come half-way up the side of the basin. Reduce the heat to moderately low, cover the pan tightly and steam steadily for 4 hours. Add more boiling water to the pan as it evaporates. Alternatively use a steamer.

Remove the basin from the pan and take off the cloth. Tie a clean napkin around the basin and transfer it to a warmed serving dish. Serve immediately.

Boiled shoulder of mutton

Mutton is out of favour these days, which is sad because it is far more tasty than lamb.

SERVES FOUR TO SIX

4 lb (2 kg) boned and rolled shoulder of mutton
Salt and pepper
2 onions
2 carrots
2 celery stalks, halved
Bouquet garni
½ lb (225 g) turnips, chopped
¼ lb (100 g) dried butter-beans, soaked overnight in cold water and drained
2 teaspoons cornflour
¼ pint (150 ml) yogurt
2 tablespoons redcurrant jelly

Put the mutton into a large saucepan, just cover with cold salted water and bring to the boil, skimming any scum from the surface. Add the onions, carrots, celery and bouquet garni. Reduce the heat to low, cover the pan and simmer very gently for 1 hour. Season to taste and add the turnips and beans. Simmer covered for a further 40 to 45 minutes.

Remove the pan from the heat and transfer the meat to a warmed serving dish. Arrange the cooked vegetables around it and keep hot.

Strain the cooking liquid into a small saucepan. Set the pan over high heat and boil briskly until the liquid has reduced to about ½ pint (300 ml), skimming the fat from the surface.

Mix the cornflour, yogurt and redcurrant jelly together, then stir the mixture into the liquid. Bring to the boil, stirring and cook for 1 to 2 minutes.

Pour a little of the sauce over the mutton. Serve the remainder in a warmed sauce boat.

Boiled bacon with lentils

SERVES SIX

2-lb (900-g) bacon joint, soaked in cold water overnight and drained
1 oz (25 g) dripping
2 onions, chopped
Pepper
1 lb (450 g) brown lentils, soaked in cold water for 1 hour and drained
1 carrot
1 celery stalk
2 garlic cloves
Bouquet garni
1 oz (25 g) butter, melted
2 tablespoons chopped parsley

Put the bacon into a saucepan and just cover with cold water. Set the pan over high heat and bring the water to the boil, skimming the fat and scum from the surface. Remove the pan from the heat, drain the bacon then rinse it in cold water.

Melt the dripping in a large saucepan. Add the onions and fry them, stirring, until they are golden. Put the bacon into the pan and add plenty of freshly ground black pepper, the lentils, vegetables, garlic, bouquet garni and enough cold water to cover. Cover the pan, and cook over low heat for 2 hours.

Remove the pan from the heat. Transfer the bacon to a plate. Remove and discard the carrot, celery, garlic and bouquet garni. Strain the remaining contents of the pan and reserve the lentils. Discard the cooking stock. Toss the lentil mixture in the butter and transfer to a warmed serving dish. Slice the bacon and arrange around the lentils. Sprinkle with parsley and serve.

Steak and kidney pudding

Cut a segment from the circle.

Ease the dough into the basin.

Press the cut edges together.

Pour the stock over the meat.

Use the segment to make a lid.

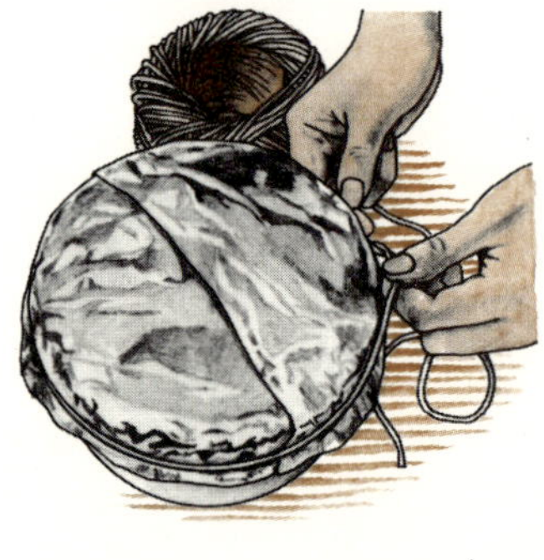

Tie on the covering with string.

Cold pressed ox tongue

SERVES EIGHT TO TEN

4- to 6-lb (2- to 3-kg) salted ox tongue, soaked in cold water for 24 hours and drained
2 carrots, halved
2 onions, halved
1 celery stalk, cut into short lengths
Bouquet garni
8 peppercorns

Wash the tongue and put it into a large saucepan. Cover completely with cold water and bring to the boil slowly, skimming the fat and scum from the surface. Add the vegetables, bouquet garni and peppercorns, cover the pan and simmer very gently for about 4 hours, or until the tongue is cooked and the small bones at the root can be pulled out easily. If they do not come out easily, simmer the tongue for a further 30 minutes and check again.

Remove the pan from the heat and leave the tongue to cool in the cooking liquid. Drain and transfer the tongue to a board. Discard the cooking liquid. Skin the tongue, trim the root and remove all the gristle and bones.

Roll up the tongue and fit it into a deep 8-inch (20-cm) cake tin (it should be a tight fit, so squeeze it in). Cover the tongue with a plate and stand a heavy weight on top (use a pan full of water if you do not have any other heavy object). Set aside in a cool place for 12 hours, or overnight.

Run a knife around the edge of the tin to loosen the tongue, then invert it on to a serving plate. Serve thinly sliced.

Dolmas

SERVES SIX

1 medium-sized cabbage, washed and trimmed
1 tablespoon butter
1 onion, finely chopped
2 lb (900 g) minced lamb
2 oz (50 g) cooked rice
2 tablespoons pine nuts, blanched and chopped
1 tablespoon chopped fresh mint
1 pint (575 ml) beef stock
Salt and pepper
2 tablespoons flour
½ pint (300 ml) tomato sauce

Put the cabbage into a pan of boiling salted water and blanch for 3 minutes. Remove the pan from the heat and drain the cabbage. Carefully remove the leaves, one by one. (If they are difficult to remove, blanch the cabbage again.) Remove the hard core and tough stalk.

Meanwhile, melt the butter in a small saucepan and fry the onion until it is golden. Remove the pan from the heat.

Mix the meat, fried onion, rice, pine nuts, mint and three tablespoons of the stock together in a bowl and season well.

Put a tablespoon of the meat mixture on each cabbage leaf at the stalk end. Fold the sides inwards and then roll the leaf up to enclose the filling completely. Gently coat the rolls in the flour, then arrange them in a heavy-based flameproof casserole as tightly packed as possible to prevent them unwinding. Pour over the remaining stock (the rolls should be covered, so add more if necessary). Set the casserole over high heat and bring to the boil. Reduce the heat to low, cover the pan and simmer for 40 minutes.

Preheat the oven to 350°F (180°C, Gas Mark 4).

Using a slotted spoon, transfer the dolmas to an ovenproof dish and pour over the tomato sauce. Put the dish into the oven and bake for 20 minutes.

Pressed ox tongue

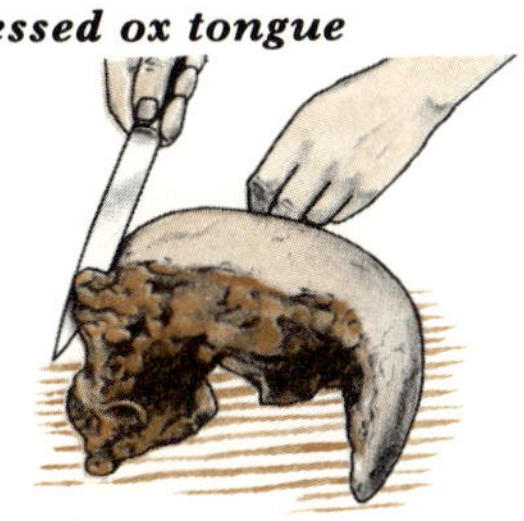

Trim off the root end and all the fat, bones and gristle.

Hold the tongue by the root end and peel off all the skin.

Curl the tongue into a cake tin—it should be a tight fit.

Cover the tin with a plate and stand a heavy weight on top.

Sweetbread vol-au-vents

SERVES FOUR

1 lb (400 g) calf's sweetbreads, prepared and blanched for 10 minutes
½ pint (300 ml) stock
1 teaspoon lemon juice
1 bay leaf
½ oz (15 g) butter
3 oz (75 g) mushrooms, chopped
½ oz (15 g) flour
1 oz (25 g) black olives, pitted and sliced
5 tablespoons cream
Salt and pepper
8 vol-au-vent cases, baked and kept hot

Cut the sweetbreads into pieces and put them into a large saucepan. Add the stock, lemon juice and bay leaf and bring to the boil. Reduce the heat to low, cover the pan and simmer for 10 minutes. Remove the pan from the heat and transfer the sweetbreads to a plate. Strain the stock.

Melt the butter in a saucepan. Add the mushrooms and cook, stirring, for 2 minutes. Stir in the flour. Add half the reserved stock gradually, stirring constantly, and bring to the boil. Cook the sauce for 2 to 3 minutes or until it thickens. Stir in the sweetbreads, olives and cream and season to taste. Simmer gently over low heat until the sweetbreads are heated through.

Spoon the mixture into the hot vol-au-vent cases and serve.

Veal galantine

Serve the galantine thinly sliced with horseradish sauce, or sauce verte, and pickles. To make horseradish sauce mix 1 tablespoon of freshly grated horseradish into ¼ pint (150 ml) stiffly whipped cream. Mix in 1 teaspoon of lemon juice and season with salt, pepper and sugar.

SERVES SIX TO EIGHT

3 lb (1½ kg) breast of veal, boned and fat trimmed
Salt and pepper
1 onion, finely chopped
½ lb (225 g) sausage meat
½ lb (225 g) minced ham
1 teaspoon chopped parsley
1 teaspoon chopped basil
½ teaspoon chopped oregano
2 tablespoons brandy
1 tablespoon pistachio nuts
3 thick slices ham
2 quarts (2 litres) stock
4 fl oz (125 ml) meat aspic

Lay the veal out flat on a board, fat side down. Season well.

Mix the onion, sausage meat, minced ham, the salt and pepper, herbs and brandy together in a bowl until they are well blended. Spread the stuffing over the veal to within ½ inch (1 cm) of the edges. Sprinkle the pistachio nuts over the stuffing. Put the ham slices on top down the length of the meat. Roll up tightly and tie securely with string. Enclose the veal in greaseproof or waxed paper, then in muslin, tying each end securely with string and sewing up the centre join.

Put the veal into a large pan, pour in the stock, cover the pan and simmer over low heat for 2 hours.

Remove the veal from the pan and set it aside to cool. Tighten and re-tie the cloth and put the veal on a board. Cover it with another board, put a heavy weight on top and leave it overnight. Then put it in the refrigerator.

Unwrap the veal and remove the string. Brush the veal with aspic, applying 2 or 3 coats and allowing one coat to set before applying the next one. Allow the final coat to set before serving.

Vegetables

Vegetables, particularly those that grow above ground, require careful cooking if their goodness is not to be lost. Boiling has one great disadvantage—the vitamins and flavours contained in vegetables are often cooked out completely and thrown away with the water; so steam vegetables whenever it is practicable.

There are two ways of steaming vegetables; you can use a flower steamer, which is specially designed for vegetables, or a saucepan with a steamer attachment. Be sure that the water is boiling before putting the vegetables in the steamer.

If you have to boil a vegetable use as little water as possible, bring it to the boil, then reduce the heat and simmer. Choose a saucepan with a tight-fitting lid, although greens usually retain their colour better if cooked uncovered. To keep such vegetables as cauliflower and chicory white, add a few drops of lemon juice to the water. Always keep the cooking liquid; you can use it for making stocks and soups.

Most vegetables should be slightly undercooked—they are at their most delicious when they are slightly crisp; there is nothing more distasteful than limp, soggy vegetables.

Because cooking times are affected by such variables as the age and size of the vegetables, and whether they are cut or whole, the times given in the chart overleaf are only approximate.

Artichokes with prawn and mushroom mayonnaise, lentil salad and steamed stuffed cabbage

Brussels sprouts with curried almonds

SERVES FOUR TO SIX

2 oz (50 g) butter
2 oz (50 g) slivered almonds
1 level teaspoon Madras curry powder
2 lb (900 g) Brussels sprouts, boiled and drained

Melt the butter in a large frying-pan and add the almonds. Fry, stirring constantly, until they are golden. Add the curry powder and stir well. Add the sprouts to the pan, stir well to coat with the almond mixture and serve.

Brussels sprouts with chestnuts

SERVES FOUR TO SIX

1 lb (450 g) chestnuts, blanched and peeled
1 pint (575 ml) vegetable stock
1 celery stalk
1 teaspoon sugar
2 lb (900 g) Brussels sprouts, steamed and kept warm
1 oz (25 g) butter
Salt and pepper

Put the chestnuts into a saucepan with the vegetable stock, celery and sugar and simmer for 35 to 40 minutes, or until tender.

Drain the chestnuts and discard the celery stalk. Add the butter to the pan and melt it over low heat. Return the chestnuts to the pan, add the sprouts and seasoning to taste and serve.

Petits pois à la française

SERVES FOUR

6 tablespoons water
3 oz (75 g) butter
3 lb (1½ kg) peas, shelled
12 spring onions, chopped
1 medium-sized crisp lettuce heart, shredded
2 teaspoons sugar
½ teaspoon salt
¼ teaspoon black pepper
Bouquet garni
2 teaspoons beurre manie

Put the water and butter in a large saucepan over moderate heat. When the butter has melted, add all the remaining ingredients except the beurre manié. Cover the pan with a tight-fitting lid and cook for about 10 minutes, or until the peas are tender. Shake the pan occasionally.

If there is too much liquid left in the pan, add the beurre manié, a little at a time, until it thickens. Remove the bouquet garni before serving.

Cauliflower salad

SERVES FOUR

1 cauliflower, boiled in florets with 2 sprigs of rosemary and drained
¼ pint (150 ml) vinaigrette
2 tomatoes, skinned, seeded and chopped

Put the cauliflower florets into a salad bowl and toss with the vinaigrette dressing and tomatoes. Serve hot or cold.

Steamed stuffed cabbage

SERVES FOUR

1 white cabbage, boiled for 10 minutes and drained

STUFFING

2 oz (50 g) butter
1 large onion, chopped
½ lb (225 g) mushrooms, chopped
1 lb (450 g) cooked ham, finely chopped
6 tablespoons cooked long-grain rice
Salt and pepper
Grated nutmeg
4 fl oz (125 ml) chicken stock
½ pint (300 ml) tomato sauce

Cut out the centre of the cabbage in a circle and scoop out the centre to form a cavity.

Melt the butter in a saucepan and fry the onion until soft. Add the mushrooms and cook for 4 minutes. Add the ham, rice and seasonings, moisten with chicken stock and mix well to combine.

Spoon the stuffing into the cavity. Place the cabbage in a buttered heatproof bowl, cover with foil and steam over boiling water in a covered pan for 45 minutes.

Remove the pan from the heat. Lift out the cabbage, put it on a heated serving dish and serve with the tomato sauce.

Boiled chicory

SERVES FOUR

½ pint (300 ml) water
1 teaspoon sugar
½ teaspoon salt
8 heads chicory, washed and trimmed
2 oz (50 g) butter
Juice of ½ lemon
2 tablespoons chopped parsley

Bring the water to the boil in a large saucepan with the sugar and salt. Add the chicory, butter and lemon juice, cover and cook for 15 to 20 minutes, or until the chicory is tender. Drain thoroughly, reserving the cooking liquid. Arrange the chicory in a heated serving dish and keep hot.

Put the cooking liquid back into the pan and boil to reduce by half. Pour the liquid over the chicory, sprinkle with parsley and serve.

Artichokes with prawn and mushroom mayonnaise

SERVES FOUR

½ pint (300 ml) sauce verte
6 oz (175 g) peeled cooked prawns
¼ lb (100 g) button mushrooms, quartered
4 globe artichokes, chokes removed, cooked and cooled

Put the sauce in a bowl. Stir in the prawns and mushrooms and adjust the seasoning. Pile the mixture into the centre of each artichoke.

To eat, dip the outer leaves in the sauce in the centre of the artichokes then eat the bottom with a knife and fork.

Glazed carrots

SERVES FOUR

1½ lb (700 g) small carrots, trimmed
¼ pint (150 ml) water
1 oz (25 g) butter
1 teaspoon sugar
Salt and pepper
1 tablespoon chopped parsley

Put the carrots into a saucepan with the water, butter, sugar and salt and pepper to taste. Cut out a circle of greaseproof paper to fit inside the saucepan. Grease the paper with a teaspoon of butter and place, greased side down, over the carrots. Cover the saucepan with a tight-fitting lid and simmer for 20 minutes. Turn the carrots out into a serving dish, sprinkle with the parsley and serve.

Carrot and parsnip purée

SERVES FOUR

1 lb (450 g) mature carrots, peeled, boiled, drained and mashed
1 lb (450 g) parsnips, peeled, boiled, drained and mashed
Salt and pepper
1 egg yolk
2 oz (50 g) butter, melted
¼ teaspoon grated nutmeg

Beat all the ingredients together to form a smooth purée. Pile into a serving dish and serve at once, or brown quickly under a hot grill before serving.

Vegetables

Courgette salad

SERVES FOUR TO SIX

1½ lb (700 g) baby courgettes, cut into rounds, boiled, drained and chilled
¼ lb (100 g) button mushrooms, sliced
1 small onion, chopped
1 tablespoon chopped tarragon
¼ pint (150 ml) vinaigrette dressing

Put all the ingredients into a salad bowl, toss well and serve.

Marrow in caraway sauce

SERVES FOUR

1 marrow, peeled, seeded and cut into large cubes
Salt
1 oz (25 g) butter
1 oz (25 g) flour
½ pint (300 ml) chicken or veal stock
2 teaspoons caraway seeds
1 tablespoon white wine vinegar
Pepper

Put the marrow cubes in a colander, sprinkle with 2 tablespoons of salt and set aside for 15 minutes. Rinse off the salt and drain the marrow well.

Melt the butter in a large saucepan and stir in the flour to make a roux. Gradually stir in the stock and cook, stirring, until the sauce has thickened. Add the caraway seeds, vinegar, marrow and seasoning to taste. Cover the pan and simmer over very low heat for 20 minutes.

Spinach purée

This spinach purée can be served as a vegetable accompaniment or used as a filling for pancakes, with a cheese sauce poured over the pancakes.

SERVES FOUR

2½ lb (1 kg) spinach, prepared, cooked and drained
1 oz (25 g) butter
2 tablespoons cream
Grated nutmeg
Salt and pepper

Chop the spinach finely or blend it in a liquidizer. Put it in a saucepan, stir in the butter, cream, nutmeg and seasoning to taste. Heat thoroughly and serve.

Boiled fennel

SERVES FOUR

4 heads of fennel, cut into quarters, boiled in acidulated water and drained
2 oz (50 g) butter
2 oz (50 g) grated Parmesan cheese
Salt and pepper

Place the fennel in a large saucepan and add the butter, cheese and seasoning. Cook over low heat for 5 to 6 minutes.

Beetroot salad

SERVES FOUR

4 tablespoons soured cream
1 tablespoon mayonnaise
1 tablespoon lemon juice
1 teaspoon horseradish sauce
Salt and freshly ground black pepper
1 tablespoon chopped fresh chives
1 lb (450 g) cooked beetroots, skinned and cut into large dice
2 hard-boiled eggs, chopped

Put the soured cream, mayonnaise, lemon juice, horseradish, salt, pepper and chives in a salad bowl. Beat with a wooden spoon until thoroughly mixed. Add the beetroot and toss gently to coat. Sprinkle over the chopped egg and serve.

Salad niçoise

SERVES FOUR TO SIX

1 lettuce heart, torn into pieces
1 Spanish onion, finely sliced
½ lb (225 g) French beans, cooked whole
3 tomatoes, quartered
1 red pepper, thinly sliced
1 green pepper, thinly sliced
2 hard-boiled eggs, sliced
8 black olives, pitted and halved
4 anchovy fillets, chopped
¼ pint (150 ml) vinaigrette flavoured with garlic

Put the lettuce, onion, beans, tomatoes, peppers and eggs in a large salad bowl. Scatter the olives and anchovies on top. Pour the dressing over the salad just before serving.

Boiling and steaming times

Chicory

Chicory is always boiled, never steamed. Plunge in a pan of boiling water to which 2 teaspoons of sugar and 1 teaspoon of lemon juice have been added. Should be tender but still firm—test through the base.
Boiling 15–20 min

Broccoli—white and purple
Cauliflower

Use no more than 1 inch (2 cm) of water in the pan when boiling florets.

A whole broccoli or cauliflower should be steamed. Use a steamer or trim the base so it will stand in the saucepan and pour in 1 inch (2 cm) of boiling water, adding more as it steams away.
Boiling 10–25 min
Steaming 15–25 min

Calabrese

Separate the stalks and use very little water as the vegetable tends to become waterlogged.
Boiling 10–15 min
Steaming 15–20 min

Cabbage, Kale

Cabbages are usually quartered, sliced or shredded before cooking. They should be slightly crisp at the end of the cooking time. Add 1 tablespoon of vinegar or lemon juice to the water when boiling red cabbage. Red cabbage and kale are not usually steamed.
Red quartered
Boiling 35–40 min
Green and white, quartered, and kale
Boiling 10–15 min
Steaming 15–20 min

Brussels sprouts

Boil Brussels sprouts whole in very little salted water.
Boiling 10 min
Steaming 15 min

Spinach

Spinach is never steamed. Boil it in plenty of salted water, then drain and press. Or cook it without water; there is enough trapped in the leaves after washing. Shake the washed spinach gently and put it in the pan with a little salt, cover the pan tightly and cook over moderate heat.
Boiling 7–10 min

Asparagus

Tie stalks in bundles of 10 to 12. To boil, prop upright with foil in a saucepan, fill with boiling water to just below tips and cover. The water must not touch the tips. To steam, use a steamer or asparagus pan or place in a glass jar, half fill with boiling water and cover with perforated foil. Stand jar in saucepan of boiling water. The stalks should be tender but not limp. Test in the middle of the stalk.
Boiling 10–15 min
Steaming 15–20 min

Globe artichoke

Cook whole or remove choke first and halve the cooking times. The leaves should pull out easily. The water must be boiling before the artichokes are put in the pan.
Boiling 35–40 min
Steaming 40–45 min

Celery, fennel

Celery and fennel stalks are usually cut into lengths and the hearts quartered before being cooked. Use plenty of salt when boiling. When cooked, they should be tender but not limp.
Boiling 10–20 min
Steaming 20 min

Bean sprouts

Steam bean sprouts or simmer them in a very little salted water, but for only 2 minutes or they will loose their crunchy texture.
Boiling 2 min
Steaming 2 min

Broad beans

Very young broad beans are usually boiled or steamed in their pods. Shell mature beans first, add 10 minutes to the cooking time and remove the skin after cooking if touch. The beans should be very tender.
Boiling 10–20 min
Steaming 15–25 min

Dried beans

Depending on age (old beans are soaked for a longer period) soak dried beans in a pan or bowl of boiling water for between 1 and 3 hours, or soak them overnight in cold water. Then boil them in salted water until they are tender.
Boiling 40–180 min

Lentils·split peas

Lentils and split peas do not have to be soaked, but it shortens the cooking time considerably.
Boiling 60 min

French beans, runner beans

Cook runner beans 5 minutes longer than French beans because they are tougher. Cook them whole or sliced.
Boiling 5–10 min
Steaming 10–15 min

Mange-tout

Boil mange-tout peas in salted water or steam with a little butter. They should be slightly crisp when cooked.
Boiling 4–5 min
Steaming 5–6 min

Peas

Boil peas in lightly salted water to which a teaspoon of sugar and a few mint leaves may be added. When very young they may be cooked in their pods.
Boiling 5–10 min

Sweetcorn

Sweetcorn is not usually steamed. Plunge into a large pan of fast-boiling water to which a little sugar (never salt as this toughens the kernels) has been added.
Boiling 5–6 min

Leek

Leeks can be boiled or steamed whole, halved, split lengthways down the middle or cut into lengths or rings. Cook until tender.
Boiling 10–20 min
Steaming 15–25 min

Onion

Boil or steam onions until they are very tender. The cooking times are for whole onions. Halve the times for small onions, spring onions and shallots.
Boiling 20–30 min
Steaming 30–40 min

Beetroot

Boil or steam beetroot whole, and skin after cooking. Do not trim the root end until after cooking or the beetroots will "bleed" into the cooking liquid. Cook until very tender.
Boiling 90–120 min
Steaming 120 min

Carrot

Cook carrots whole or sliced, and, unless very old, do not peel them before cooking. They should be just tender. Add a little sugar with the salt to the water.
Boiling 15–30 min
Steaming 20–40 min

Celeriac

Peel and dice celeriac or cut into strips and add at least 2 teaspoons of lemon juice to the water.
Boiling 10–30 min
Steaming 35–40 min

Kohlrabi

Peel kohlrabi and cook whole when small; otherwise slice or dice.
Boiling 20–25 min

Parsnip

Cook whole or in thick slices. If old, cut out tough central core.
Boiling 20–35 min
Steaming 35–40 min

Salsify, scorzonera

Peel and cook whole, or cut into lengths before cooking.
Boiling 15–20 min
Steaming 20–30 min

Swede

Peel swedes and cut into cubes or dice; boil until very tender.
Boiling 30–40 min

Turnip

Turnips are always peeled before cooking, and can be boiled or steamed whole or sliced.
Boiling 15–25 min
Steaming 20–30 min

Potato

Cut large potatoes into quarters or smaller pieces; boil new potatoes whole. Scrub, or peel before or after cooking. Add the potatoes to a pan of cold salted water and bring to the boil slowly.
Boiling 20–40 min

Jerusalem artichoke

Peel after cooking. Boil in water or in milk and water. Should be just tender when cooked.
Boiling 15–20 min
Steaming 20 min

Courgette, Marrow, Cucumber

Cook courgettes unpeeled unless old with tough skins; cook whole or sliced. Overboiling makes them soggy.

Halve marrow or cut into pieces. Cook peeled or unpeeled. Add between 10 and 20 minutes to the cooking time shown. Cucumber, although more generally eaten raw, can be boiled or steamed in the same way as courgettes.
Boiling 10–15 min
Steaming 10–20 min

Mushrooms

Not usually boiled, mushrooms are often steamed for garnishes.
Steaming 15–20 min

Mashed potatoes

There are many different flavourings you can add to mashed potatoes to make them more interesting: grated nutmeg; finely chopped spring onions; grated orange rind or grated cheese.

SERVES FOUR

1½ lb (700 g) potatoes, cut into quarters, cooked, peeled and drained
1½ oz (40 g) butter
¼ pint (150 ml) hot milk or cream
Salt and pepper

Put the potatoes in a large saucepan and put the pan over moderate heat. Shake the pan over the heat for a few minutes to dry the potatoes out. Mash the potatoes in the pan, gradually adding the butter and the milk. Season to taste and finish off by beating the potatoes with a wooden spoon.

Potato salad

This salad is delicious served with cold meats

SERVES FOUR

1½ lb (700 g) boiled potatoes, cut into cubes and kept hot
6 spring onions or a bunch of chives, chopped
¼ pint (150 ml) vinaigrette dressing
1 tablespoon French mustard
Salt and freshly ground pepper

Put the hot potatoes in a salad bowl. Mix the remaining ingredients in a small bowl and pour the dressing over the potatoes. Toss and serve hot or cold.

Butter-beans with garlic

SERVES FOUR

1 lb (450 g) butter-beans, cooked and drained
1 oz (25 g) butter, melted
2 garlic cloves, crushed
1 teaspoon salt
1 tablespoon chopped parsley
1 teaspoon lemon juice
Freshly ground pepper

Put the beans in a saucepan over low heat. Add the butter, garlic, salt, parsley, lemon juice and pepper. Stir until the mixture is hot and serve at once.

Kidney bean salad

SERVES SIX

1 lb (450 g) kidney beans, cooked and drained
1 onion, very thinly sliced
6 tablespoons vinaigrette dressing
1 teaspoon French mustard

Put the beans and onion in a salad bowl. Mix the vinaigrette dressing with the mustard and spoon it over the vegetables. Toss well before serving.

Lentil salad

Serve lentil salad as a first course with brown bread and butter or as a winter salad.

SERVES FOUR

½ lb (225 g) green or orange lentils, cooked, puréed and cooled
1 garlic clove, crushed
4 tablespoons vinaigrette dressing
1 tablespoon lemon juice
Salt and pepper
1 onion, very finely chopped
3 gherkins, finely chopped
2 tomatoes, thinly sliced
2 hard-boiled eggs, thinly sliced
10 black olives, pitted

Mix the lentil purée with the garlic, vinaigrette, lemon juice, salt and lots of pepper. Add the onion and gherkins. Place in a serving dish and garnish with the tomato and egg slices and black olives.

Butter-bean and mackerel salad

SERVES FOUR

4 fl oz (125 ml) soured cream
2 teaspoons lemon juice
2 teaspoons paprika
Salt and freshly ground black pepper
2 teaspoons finely grated orange rind
2 shallots, very finely sliced
½ lb (225 g) cooked butter-beans
1 smoked mackerel, skinned, boned and flaked

Put the soured cream, lemon juice, paprika, salt, pepper and orange rind in a salad bowl and stir well. Add the remaining ingredients, toss gently and serve.

Fruit

Fruit make some of the most delightful and refreshing desserts from the simplest compotes to the most elaborate charlottes. In midsummer during the height of the soft fruit season less-than-perfect fruit may be used to make compotes, sorbets and purées for the freezer. A dried fruit compote has the advantage that it can be made at any time of the year. A mixture of dried fruit and apples or pears is also delicious. For four servings, soak one pound (450 g) of mixed dried fruit in wine, wine and brandy or rum mixed, or in water overnight. Simmer in the soaking liquid for twenty minutes or until the fruit are soft. Add sugar if you prefer a sweeter dessert. Chill the compote well and serve it with cream.

Fresh fruit compote

Serve the compote well chilled with cream or custard.

SERVES FOUR

6 oz (175 g) sugar
½ pint (300 ml) water
2 lb (900 g) fresh mixed fruit (plums, cherries, gooseberries, apricots, redcurrants and blackcurrants), pitted and prepared
2-inch (5-cm) piece cinnamon stick
1 level teaspoon arrowroot
4 tablespoons white wine

Put the sugar and water in a saucepan, stir to dissolve the sugar, and boil for 5 minutes. Add the fruit to the syrup with the cinnamon and simmer gently for 5 minutes. Using a slotted spoon remove the fruit to a serving dish.

Blend the arrowroot with the wine in a cup and stir it into the syrup. Increase the heat and boil for 1 minute. Remove the pan from the heat and let the syrup cool. Strain the syrup over the fruit.

Fresh peaches in vanilla syrup

Apricots may be substituted for the peaches. Use 2 pounds (900 g) of apricots, ¾ pound (350 g) of vanilla sugar and 1½ pints (900 ml) of water.

Serve well chilled with cream.

SERVES SIX

6 large peaches
½ lb (225 g) vanilla sugar
1 pint (600 ml) water

Put the peaches in a large bowl and cover with boiling water. Leave for 2 minutes, then drain and peel. Cut the peaches in half and remove and discard the stones.

Dissolve the sugar in the water in a large saucepan. Add the peach halves, cover the pan and simmer gently for 5 minutes, or until the peaches are just tender. Using a slotted spoon remove the peaches from the syrup and arrange them in a serving dish. Increase the heat and boil the syrup rapidly until it reduces and thickens a little, then pour it over the fruit.

Serve cold.

Pears in red wine

Serve the pears chilled with whipped cream.

SERVES SIX

½ lb (225 g) castor sugar
¼ pint (150 ml) water
¾ pint (450 ml) red wine
1-inch (2-cm) piece cinnamon stick
6 firm pears
1 lemon

Dissolve the sugar in the water over low heat. Add the wine and cinnamon stick and bring to the boil. Reduce the heat and simmer for 10 minutes.

Meanwhile peel the pears, leaving the stalks attached and making sure the bases are flat enough for them to stand upright. Rub the pears all over with the lemon to prevent them discolouring. Place the pears close together, upright, in a large saucepan. Pour in the simmering wine syrup. Cover the pan and poach gently, basting occasionally, for 30 to 90 minutes or until the pears are tender.

Using a slotted spoon, lift the pears from the pan and arrange

them, standing upright, in a serving dish.

Remove and discard the cinnamon. Increase the heat and boil the syrup until it is reduced and has the consistency of a fairly heavy syrup.

Spoon the syrup over the pears. Put the pears in the refrigerator to chill, basting the fruit with the syrup occasionally.

Oranges in caramel

SERVES FOUR

5 large oranges
¼ lb (100 g) castor sugar

Peel 4 oranges, taking great care to remove the pith as well. Shred the peel of 1 orange finely and set aside. Slice the oranges, removing the pips, and put the slices together again in their original shape. Arrange them in a serving dish.

Put the sugar into a small, heavy saucepan and stir over low heat until it has melted and is caramel in colour. Initially the sugar will be lumpy, but it will become smooth as it turns into a syrup.

Draw the pan off the heat and stir in 4 tablespoons of water. Return the pan to the heat and stir until the caramel is dissolved in the water. Remove the pan from the heat and stir in the juice from the remaining orange and the shredded peel. Let the syrup cool before pouring it over the oranges. Serve chilled.

Cherries jubilee with vanilla ice-cream

SERVES SIX

½ lb (225 g) sugar
1 pint (575 ml) water
Salt
1½ lb (700 g) cherries, pitted
2 teaspoons cornflour
Vanilla ice-cream
Up to ¼ pint (150 ml) brandy

Dissolve the sugar in the water over low heat. Add a pinch of salt and bring to the boil. Add the cherries, reduce the heat to low, cover the pan and simmer gently for 8 to 10 minutes or until they are tender. Drain the cherries. Return the syrup to the pan and boil it rapidly until it is reduced to ½ pint (300 ml).

Combine the cornflour with a little cold water and add it to the syrup very gradually. Simmer, stirring, for 2 minutes. Add the cherries and remove the pan from the heat.

Spoon the ice-cream into a bowl or into individual serving dishes.

Warm the brandy in a ladle or in a small pan, pour it on to the cherry mixture and ignite with a match. Pour the flaming cherries over the ice-cream and serve.

Refreshing, colourful and simple, these fruit desserts are the perfect ending to a meal. On the top shelf: oranges in caramel and cherries jubilee. On the lower shelf: pears in red wine.

Rhubarb fool

All fruit fools are made in the same way, but some fruits require no preliminary cooking before they are puréed. The purée may be smooth or, if you prefer a coarser texture, crush the fruit with a fork instead of pushing it through a nylon strainer. Use castor sugar except for rhubarb fool and, if you prefer it, use a custard instead of the cream.

Garnish rhubarb fool with toasted almonds or freshly grated lemon rind and serve it with plain crisp biscuits or sponge finger biscuits.

SERVES SIX

2 lb (900 g) rhubarb
2 tablespoons water
Grated rind of 1 small orange
Demerara sugar
½ pint (300 ml) double cream, lightly whipped

Wash the rhubarb and cut into pieces. Put it in a saucepan with the water and grated orange rind. Cover the pan and simmer gently for about 5 minutes or until the rhubarb is tender.

Drain the rhubarb and rub it through a sieve or put it in a liquidizer. If the purée is too stiff, add a little of the cooking liquid. Add sugar to taste and leave the purée to cool completely before folding in the cream. Taste the fool and add more sugar if necessary. Spoon into individual dishes and chill.

Fruit

Summer pudding
Blackcurrants, redcurrants, raspberries, blackberries and mulberries are all suitable for this pudding.

SERVES SIX

2 oz (50 g) sugar
½ pint (300 ml) water
2 apples, peeled, cored and sliced
1½ lb (700 g) mixed berries, washed
1 loaf stale white bread
Butter
1 teaspoon arrowroot

Put the sugar and water in a saucepan and stir over low heat until the sugar dissolves. Boil rapidly for 5 minutes. Add the fruit, cover the pan and simmer for about 10 minutes.

Strain the fruit, reserving the juice. Rub the fruit through a strainer to make a purée. Add half the reserved juice to the purée. Taste the purée, adding more sugar if necessary.

Slice the bread thinly, removing the crusts. Grease a 1-quart (1-litre) pudding bowl with a little butter. Line the bowl with overlapping slices of bread. Spoon over enough purée to cover the bottom of the bowl. Put a layer of bread on top. Repeat this layering of bread and purée until the bowl is full. Finish with a layer of bread. Cover the bowl with a plate and weigh it down with a heavy weight and leave overnight.

Mix the arrowroot with a little of the reserved juice. Put the rest of the juice in a saucepan and bring to the boil. Add the arrowroot mixture, stirring well, and continue stirring until the sauce has thickened. Remove the pan from the heat. Cool and then chill the sauce.

Turn the pudding out on to a serving dish. Pour some of the sauce over the pudding and serve the rest separately.

Danish apple cake

SERVES SIX

¼ lb (100 g) butter
1½ lb (700 g) apples, peeled, cored and sliced
Peel of ½ lemon
2 oz (50 g) sugar
½ lb (225 g) coarse fresh white breadcrumbs
½ pint (300 ml) cream

Melt ½ ounce (15 g) of the butter in a heavy saucepan and coat the bottom of the pan with it. Add the apples, lemon peel and sugar. Cover the pan and cook gently until the apples are transparent but still keep their shape. Remove the pan from the heat and discard the peel.

Melt the remaining butter in a frying-pan and fry the breadcrumbs until they are golden.

Arrange half the apples in a layer in a 1-quart (1-litre) soufflé dish. Use half the crumbs for the next layer, then the rest of the apples, and finally another layer of crumbs. Cover the dish with foil or cling wrap and put it in the refrigerator to chill.

Serve cold with the cream.

Pommes aux fruits glacés
This jellied apple sweet requires no gelatine as the pectin in the fruit sets naturally.

SERVES FOUR TO SIX

2 oz (50 g) candied orange and lemon peel, coarsely chopped
4 tablespoons rum
1 lb (450 g) sugar
¼ pint (150 ml) water
Rind and juice of 1 lemon
3 lb (1½ kg) tart cooking apples
2 oz (50 g) walnuts, coarsely chopped
¼ pint (150 ml) double cream, whipped

Put the candied orange and lemon peel in a cup with the rum to soak.

Dissolve the sugar in the water in a pan over very low heat. Add the lemon rind and juice.

Peel, core and thinly slice the apples. Add to the syrup. Increase the heat to high and boil rapidly, stirring constantly, for 20 minutes. If the mixture is still too liquid, boil it for 5 minutes longer. Be careful not to let the apples stick or burn. Remove the pan from the heat.

Sieve the apples. Stir in the walnuts and the candied peel and rum. Pour the apple mixture into a lightly oiled 1½-pint (900-ml) mould. Cover the mould and put it in the refrigerator for at least 6 hours or overnight.

Turn the jellied apple out on to a serving dish. Decorate with the whipped cream and serve.

Rødgrød med fløde
This traditional Danish dessert is made with any red berry or a combination of red berries.

SERVES SIX

½ lb (225 g) each redcurrants, raspberries, cranberries and strawberries
Sugar
Arrowroot
1 tablespoon slivered almonds
½ pint (300 ml) cream

Put the berries in a saucepan with 3 tablespoons of water. Bring to the simmer and cook until the skins burst and the juice runs out.

Push the fruit through a fine sieve, measure the purée and return it to the saucepan. Add sugar to taste.

To every pint (575 ml) of purée measure 1 tablespoon of arrowroot. Mix the arrowroot with 2 tablespoons of water and stir into the purée. Bring the mixture to the simmer and cook for 30 seconds or until the purée thickens. Remove the pan from the heat.

Pour the mixture into a serving dish. Scatter the almonds over the top. Cover the dish and put it into the refrigerator to chill well. Serve with the cream.

Blackcurrant mousse
Raspberries may be used instead of blackcurrants, or the two can be used in combination with excellent results.

SERVES SIX

1 lb (450 g) blackcurrants, stripped off their stalks and washed
3 to 4 oz (75 to 100 g) sugar
½ oz (15 g) gelatine
2 tablespoons orange juice
½ pint (300 ml) double cream, whipped until thick but not stiff
3 egg whites, stiffly beaten

Put the blackcurrants and the sugar—use the lesser amount adding more if necessary—in a saucepan and cook for a few minutes, stirring, until the juice runs from the fruit and the sugar dissolves. Press the fruit through a sieve to make a purée and set aside to cool completely.

Dissolve the gelatine in the orange juice over low heat and stir it into the blackcurrant purée. When the purée begins to thicken, gently fold in half of the whipped cream and then the stiffly beaten egg whites. Turn the mixture into an 8-inch (20-cm) bowl or soufflé dish, cover the top with cling wrap and put it in the refrigerator to set. Decorate the mousse with the remaining whipped cream and serve.

Strawberry mousse
Serve strawberry mousse with small macaroons.

SERVES SIX

½ oz (15 g) gelatine
2 lb (900 g) strawberries
½ pint (300 ml) double cream
4 tablespoons castor sugar
4 eggs, separated
2 tablespoons Kirsch

Dissolve the gelatine in 2 tablespoons of water over low heat.

Put the strawberries in a bowl and crush them with a fork.

Put the cream, sugar and egg yolks in the top of a double saucepan and whisk over barely simmering water until the custard is smooth and thick. Stir in the gelatine, strawberries and Kirsch. Taste the mixture and add more sugar if necessary. Set aside to cool, stirring occasionally.

Whip the egg whites until they are stiff and fold them into the strawberry mixture. Pour the mousse into a glass bowl and refrigerate until well chilled and set.

Blackcurrant kissel

SERVES FOUR

1 lb (450 g) blackcurrants
Grated rind of ½ lemon
¾ pint (450 ml) white wine
¼ lb (125 g) sugar
2 tablespoons arrowroot

Simmer the blackcurrants and lemon rind in half the wine for 20 minutes. Purée the fruit, stir in the sugar and return the mixture to the pan.

Mix the arrowroot with 3 tablespoons of the remaining wine. Stir it into the fruit purée with the rest of the wine and cook, stirring, until the kissel thickens. Serve warm or cold.

Cereals

Most of the rice that is available in the West is either long-grain or short-grain. Such long-grain varieties as basmati or Patna are served with curries or used to make pilaffs. Short-grain rice, for example Arborio, which comes from Italy, is used to make risottos. Although it is long-grained, Carolina rice is usually reserved for making desserts.

All rice, except Italian rice, should be rinsed under cold running water until the water runs clear. After washing, soak long-grain rice for about thirty minutes in cold water. The longer the rice soaks, the less time it will take to cook.

Processed rice should be prepared and cooked according to the instructions on the packet.

To boil long-grain rice use about one pint (575 ml) of water for every ten ounces (275 g) of rice. The juice of half a lemon added to the water will keep the rice perfectly white. Put the rice, the water and a teaspoon of salt into the saucepan and bring to a fast boil. Cover the pan, reduce the heat to very low and simmer for fifteen to twenty minutes or until the rice is cooked and all the water has been absorbed.

Pasta should be cooked in large quantities of boiling, salted water. Bring the water to a fast boil, add the pasta gradually so that the water does not go off the boil and cook for five to six minutes if the pasta is home made. Factory-made pasta should be cooked for about eleven minutes or the time recommended on the packet. When cooked, pasta should be tender and what the Italians call *al dente*, or resistant to the bite. Drain the cooked pasta, then toss it in butter and serve with a sauce or with plenty of freshly grated Parmesan cheese.

Spaghetti with pesto

Pesto is a famous Genovese sauce that is eaten with many kinds of pasta and is the traditional flavouring for Genovese minestrone. The dish may be served with grated Parmesan cheese.

SERVES FOUR

1 handful fresh basil, washed and chopped
2 oz (50 g) blanched pine nuts
2 garlic cloves
2 oz (50 g) Parmesan cheese
¼ pint (150 ml) olive oil
1 lb (450 g) spaghetti
2 oz (50 g) butter

Blend the basil, nuts and garlic in a liquidizer to form a smooth paste. Or use a pestle and mortar. Add the cheese and then, with the liquidizer at low speed, drip the oil in very slowly, making sure that it is binding with the paste before adding more.

Cook the spaghetti, drain it and transfer it to a hot serving dish. Toss the spaghetti with the butter and the pesto sauce and serve immediately.

Noodles Alfredo

SERVES FOUR

¼ lb (100 g) butter
1 lb (450 g) fresh noodles, cooked and kept hot
Freshly ground black pepper
¼ pint (150 ml) cream
2 oz (50 g) Prosciutto ham, cut into strips
¼ lb (100 g) Parmesan cheese, grated

Melt the butter in a saucepan over low heat. Add the noodles, black pepper, cream and ham and toss well over the heat until the mixture is heated through and well blended. Serve immediately with the grated cheese.

Ravioli

Both the fillings are enough for ½ pound (225 g) of pasta dough. Serve the ravioli with melted butter, grated Parmesan cheese, or with hot tomato sauce.

SERVES FOUR TO SIX

½ lb (225 g) pasta dough
Veal or cheese filling
1 oz (25 g) butter
¼ lb (100 g) Parmesan cheese, grated

Divide the dough in half (or in quarters if your board is not large enough). Roll out the dough on a floured board as thinly as possible. Put the rolled out dough on a clean cloth and cover it with another cloth while rolling out the remaining dough.

Using one sheet of dough as the base of the ravioli, put a teaspoonful of filling at regular intervals, about 1½ inches (3 cm) apart. Moisten with water around the filling. Lift the other (slightly larger) sheet of dough and put it on top—this should lie loosely over the filling. Using a wheel or sharp knife, cut between the rows of filling, separating each ravioli. Make sure that the edges are well pressed together so that no filling can escape. Put the prepared ravioli on a floured surface until ready for use—but do not stack them—and cover with a floured cloth if they are not to be cooked at once. They will keep for up to a day.

Bring plenty of salted water to a gentle boil in a large pan. Slip the ravioli in and cook for 6 to 8 minutes or until they rise in the pan. Using a slotted spoon, lift the ravioli out of the water and put into a heated dish. Serve with the butter and cheese.

VEAL FILLING

½ oz (15 g) butter
1 lb (450 g) minced veal
Salt and pepper
1 garlic clove, crushed
1 teaspoon mixed chopped sage and rosemary

Melt the butter in a saucepan. Add the veal and fry, stirring with a fork, until it is lightly browned. Season well and add the garlic and herbs. Reduce the heat, cover the pan and cook for about 40 minutes, stirring occasionally. Cool before using.

CHEESE FILLING

¼ lb (100 g) Parmesan cheese, grated
6 oz (175 g) Provolone cheese, grated
2 fl oz (50 ml) milk
3 eggs, beaten
Nutmeg
Marjoram
Salt and pepper

Mix all the ingredients together.

To make ravioli

Roll out two thin pasta sheets. Spoon filling over one sheet.

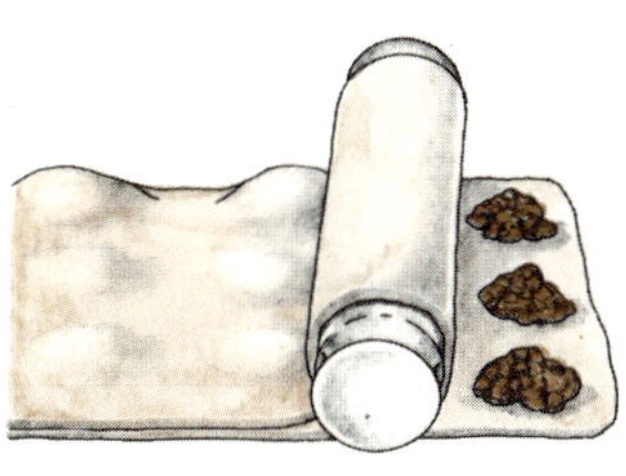

Lift the second sheet of dough over to cover the filling.

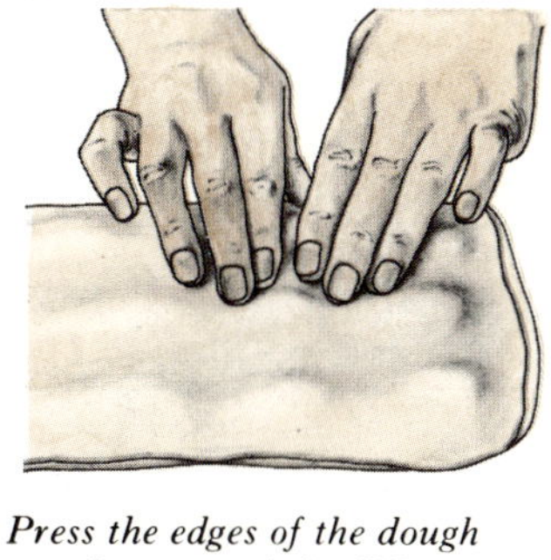

Press the edges of the dough together around the filling.

Using a wheel or sharp knife, cut the ravioli into squares.

Cereals

Gnocchi di semolina

SERVES FOUR

1 pint (575 ml) milk
¼ lb (100 g) semolina
Salt and pepper
Nutmeg
¼ lb (100 g) grated Parmesan
¼ lb (100 g) chopped ham
2 eggs, beaten
2 oz (50 g) butter

Pour the milk into the top part of a double saucepan and place over moderate heat. When the milk is almost boiling add the semolina and salt, pepper and nutmeg to taste. Reduce the heat to fairly low and cook, stirring, for about 40 minutes or until the mixture is very thick and stiff.

Remove the pan from the heat and stir in 3 ounces (75 g) of the cheese, the ham and eggs. Pour the mixture on to a shallow, greased tray. When the gnocchi is quite cold, cut it into rounds using a biscuit cutter.

Overlap the rounds in an ovenproof dish. Dot with butter and brown under a hot grill. Sprinkle with the remaining grated cheese and serve at once.

Polenta

Polenta can be bought either coarsely or finely ground. It may be used to make gnocchi, or it can be boiled, sliced, fried and served with tomato sauce.

SERVES SIX

½ lb (225 g) cornmeal (polenta)
Salt
2 oz (50 g) grated Parmesan
½ teaspoon paprika
2 oz (50 g) butter

Put ½ pint (300 ml) of cold salted water in a bowl and stir in the cornmeal.

Bring 1½ pints (900 ml) of water to the boil in a saucepan. Stir in the cornmeal and cook for about 10 minutes, stirring frequently. Pour the mixture into a loaf tin and set aside to cool. When it is cool put it in the refrigerator for 2 hours or until well chilled and firm.

Turn the polenta out and cut it into fairly thick slices. Arrange the slices, overlapping, in a buttered, shallow fireproof dish. Sprinkle the cheese and paprika over the top. Dot with the butter and grill until browned.

Christmas pudding

MAKES THREE PUDDINGS

1 tablespoon butter
1 lb (450 g) breadcrumbs from a home-made wholewheat loaf
14 oz (400 g) flour
¾ lb (350 g) sultanas
¾ lb (350 g) raisins
1 lb (450 g) currants
¾ lb (350 g) freshly grated suet
½ lb (225 g) candied peel
½ lb (225 g) glacé cherries
¾ lb (350 g) demerara sugar
2 cooking apples, grated
4 carrots, grated
¼ lb (100 g) blanched almonds, chopped
½ oz (15 g) grated nutmeg
1 tablespoon black treacle
7 eggs, beaten
1 pint (575 ml) ale
¼ pint (150 ml) brandy
1 teaspoon salt

Using the tablespoon of butter, grease three 2-pint (1-litre) pudding basins.

Mix all the ingredients together in a large mixing bowl, using a wooden spoon. Divide the mixture between the pudding basins and smooth the tops down with the back of the spoon. Cover each basin with greased paper and a floured pudding cloth with a 1-inch (2-cm) pleat in the centre. Tie the cloths firmly around the rims of the basins.

Use a steamer or put the pudding basins in a large saucepan (steam the puddings separately unless you have a very large pan) and pour in enough boiling water to come halfway up the sides of the basin. Put the pan over moderate heat. Cover tightly and steam for 6 hours, adding more boiling water to the pan from time to time. Repeat with the other two puddings.

When the puddings have been cooked store them for at least 6 months in a cool, damp-free place.

To serve the puddings, repeat the steaming process for 3 hours and turn them out of the basins.

From left to right: orange sponge pudding, spaghetti with pesto, and cooked, filled ravioli.

Boston steamed bread

MAKES ONE LOAF

¼ lb (100 g) wholewheat flour
¼ lb (100 g) rye flour
¼ lb (100 g) cornmeal
1 level teaspoon bicarbonate of soda
½ teaspoon salt
¼ lb (100 g) raisins
4 fl oz (125 ml) black treacle
½ pint (300 ml) buttermilk

Mix the dry ingredients together. Make a well in the centre and pour in the treacle and buttermilk. Using a wooden spoon mix the liquids together and gradually incorporate the flour mixture. Continue stirring until the mixture is well mixed.

Grease a 1-quart (1-litre) pudding basin. Pour in the mixture. Cover the basin with greased foil and tie it tightly under the rim.

Put the pudding basin in a saucepan containing 1 inch (2 cm) of boiling water. Cover the pan and cook for 3 hours, adding more water as it evaporates.

Serve the bread hot, or cool on a rack first.

Porridge

SERVES FOUR

1 pint (575 ml) water
1 rounded teaspoon salt
¼ lb (100 g) medium oatmeal

Bring the water to the boil and add the salt. Add the oatmeal gradually, keeping the water on the boil and stirring continuously with a wooden spoon to mix the oatmeal thoroughly. Simmer gently for 15 minutes, stirring occasionally.

Serve with salt, sugar or syrup, and milk or cream.

Creamed rice pudding

SERVES FOUR

3 tablespoons rice, washed and drained
1 pint (575 ml) milk
Vanilla pod
1 oz (25 g) castor sugar
¼ pint (150 ml) double cream

Put the rice in the top of a double saucepan with the milk and vanilla pod. Cook gently, stirring occasionally, for 1½ hours or until the rice is soft and creamy. Stir in the sugar. Remove the pan from the heat. Remove the vanilla pod and cool the rice. When the rice is cold fold in the whipped cream and chill for 1 hour before serving.

Orange sponge pudding

This sponge pudding can be made with other flavourings. Add 2 ounces (50 g) of chopped stem ginger and 1 teaspoon of ground ginger instead of the orange. Or put 4 tablespoons of syrup into the pudding basin before pouring in the sponge mixture.

SERVES FOUR TO SIX

¼ lb (100 g) butter
¼ lb (100 g) sugar
2 eggs
¼ lb (100 g) self-raising flour
Juice and finely grated rind of 1 large orange
Milk

Cream the butter and sugar together in a mixing bowl with a wooden spoon. Beat in the eggs one by one, adding 1 tablespoon of the flour with each egg. Fold in the remaining flour with the orange rind and juice. The batter should drop easily from the spoon, so stir in a little milk if necessary.

Pour the mixture into a greased 1½-pint (900-ml) pudding basin. Cover the top with a piece of foil with a 1-inch (2-cm) pleat in the centre. Tie down securely with string. Put the pudding in a large saucepan and pour in enough boiling water to come halfway up the sides of the basin. Cover the pan and steam the pudding for 1½ to 2 hours. Add more boiling water to the pan if necessary.

Eggs and dairy produce

Boiling eggs is not usually considered to be one of the more demanding kitchen tasks. Even this, however, can be done in more than one way. The most usual method is as follows:

Fill a saucepan with enough water to cover the eggs and bring to the boil. Lower the eggs into the water with a spoon; if they have been kept at room temperature for about an hour, they are less likely to crack. In three and a half to four minutes the eggs will be soft boiled—the yolks will be runny and the whites fairly soft. In about another minute the whites will firm up. At this stage they are what the French call *oeufs mollets*, which can be substituted, often with advantage, for poached eggs. In seven to ten minutes the eggs will be hard boiled. Very fresh eggs take about one minute longer to cook.

Another method is to put the eggs in a pan, cover with boiling water and leave them, away from the heat, for about ten minutes, when they will be lightly cooked. Alternatively, they may be put into a pan of cold water (a good method if you keep your eggs in the refrigerator) and brought to the boil slowly, by which time they will be lightly cooked. For a firm white, either continue simmering for half a minute, or turn off the heat and leave the eggs covered for another minute. For hard-boiled eggs cook for five minutes after the water has come to the simmer. Eggs cooked by either of these methods have more tender whites than those cooked by the first method.

If you are hard boiling eggs, put them into cold water as soon as they are cooked. This will prevent an unappetizing grey rim appearing between the yolk and the white, and also makes it easier to shell the eggs. If they are not to be used immediately keep them in a bowl of cold water until needed.

Technically, poached eggs are also cooked by immersion in boiling, or more usually barely simmering, water, but without their shells. Egg-poachers actually steam the eggs rather than poach them and the results are tougher and not so light as true poached eggs.

To poach an egg, bring a pan (preferably a frying-pan or sauté pan) of water to the boil. Add one tablespoon of vinegar—this helps to coagulate the whites. Some people also add a tablespoon of salt. Break each egg separately into a cup and slide it into the water. (It is difficult to poach more than two eggs at a time.) When the water comes back to the boil, remove the pan from the heat, cover it, and leave for three and a half to four minutes. Use a slotted spoon to lift the eggs out of the water, then drain them on kitchen paper. Trim off any straggly pieces of white. If the eggs are not needed immediately, they can be kept in a bowl of cold water for a few hours.

If the eggs are boiled for just one minute before being shelled, this will help to prevent the whites spreading out when the eggs are dropped into the poaching water. In this case they will be cooked in two and a half to three minutes after coming back to the boil.

Eggs in crispy rolls

These eggs may be served with béarnaise sauce.

SERVES FOUR

4 eggs
3 oz (75 g) butter, melted
1 garlic clove, crushed
Salt and pepper
2 teaspoons chopped fresh tarragon or chives
4 soft round rolls

Preheat the oven to 425°F (220°C, Gas Mark 7).

Bring a pan of water to the boil, lower the eggs into the water and cook for about 5 minutes from when the water comes back to the boil. Remove the eggs from the pan and plunge them into cold water. Leave for 10 minutes before removing the shells.

Meanwhile, mix the melted butter, garlic, salt, pepper and herbs together in a cup.

Cut the tops off the rolls and scoop out their centres. Brush the insides of the rolls generously with some of the butter mixture and then bake for about 5 minutes, or until the rolls are crisp.

Heat the eggs for 30 seconds in a pan of hot, salted water. Drain the eggs and put one into each roll. Spoon the remaining butter mixture over the eggs. Serve at once.

Eggs Florentine with ham

SERVES SIX

6 eggs
¾ pint (450 ml) béchamel sauce
2 oz (50 g) Gruyère cheese, grated
6 slices cooked ham
2 lb (900 g) fresh spinach, cooked, drained and kept warm in an ovenproof dish

Boil the eggs and shell them as in the preceding recipe. Heat the béchamel sauce in a saucepan and stir in half of the cheese. If necessary, reheat the eggs by immersing them in hot water for 30 seconds. Wrap each egg in a slice of ham, place them on the spinach and coat them with the sauce.

Sprinkle the remaining cheese on top of the sauce and brown under the grill.

Taramasalata eggs

Serve the eggs on a bed of wilted cucumber. To make wilted cucumber, slice the cucumber thinly, layer it in a bowl with salt. Put a weighted plate on top and leave it in the refrigerator for 2 hours. Drain, rinse and dry the cucumber.

SERVES SIX

6 eggs, hard boiled
¼ lb (100 g) smoked cod's roe
2 slices crustless white bread, soaked in milk
1 garlic clove, crushed
2 tablespoons olive oil
2 teaspoons lemon juice
Pepper

Cut the eggs in half lengthways, using a knife that has been dipped in water. Scoop out the yolks and rub them through a sieve.

Remove the skin from the cod's roe and squeeze out the milk from the bread. Beat the roe, bread and garlic together in a bowl, gradually mixing in the oil and lemon juice, until the paste is perfectly smooth. Or put the ingredients in a liquidizer. Season with pepper. Stir in the egg yolks. Pipe or spoon the mixture into the egg whites.

Eggs in aspic

Chopped ham or chopped smoked salmon may be used instead of the crab meat.

SERVES SIX

½ pint (300 ml) aspic
¼ lb (100 g) crab meat
6 eggs, poached, cooled and drained
2 to 3 spring onions
2 pieces canned pimiento

Cool the aspic slightly. Arrange the crab meat in 6 individual soufflé dishes or ramekins, spoon a thin layer of aspic over the crab meat and put the dishes in the refrigerator to set. When the aspic is firm, put an egg into each ramekin.

Cut the green tops of the spring onions into leaf shapes and the pieces of pimiento into flowers or other decorative shapes. Warm the aspic slightly and dip the leaves and flowers into it and arrange them on top of the eggs. Spoon over the remaining aspic carefully. Chill in the refrigerator before serving.

Swiss fondue

SERVES FOUR TO SIX

1 garlic clove
¾ pint (450 ml) white wine
¾ lb (350 g) Emmenthal cheese, grated
¾ lb (350 g) Gruyère cheese, grated
1 teaspoon cornflour
3 tablespoons Kirsch
French bread, cut into 1-inch (2-cm) cubes

Rub an earthenware or cast-iron casserole with the garlic. Pour in the wine and set the pan over low heat. As the wine begins to heat, stir in the cheese, a handful at a time. Continue stirring until all the cheese has been added and the mixture is creamy. Mix the cornflour with the Kirsch and add it to the fondue.

Put the casserole on a spirit stove (with the flame turned down to low) on the table. Serve with the bread. See page 218.

Curried eggs

SERVES FOUR

2 oz (50 g) clarified butter
1 large onion, peeled and sliced
1 to 2 tablespoons curry paste
1 tablespoon flour
¾ pint (450 ml) chicken stock
1 tablespoon mango chutney
1 tablespoon raisins or sultanas
2 teaspoons lemon juice
Salt and pepper
6 eggs, hard boiled
¾ lb (350 g) rice, cooked

Preheat the oven to 350°F (180°C, Gas Mark 4).

Melt the butter in a saucepan. Add the onion and fry until golden and transparent. Add the curry paste and fry, stirring constantly, for 1 minute. Stir in the flour. Gradually add the stock and bring to the boil, stirring to prevent lumps. Reduce the heat and simmer for 15 minutes. Stir in the chutney, raisins and lemon juice, and season to taste. Cover the pan and remove from the heat.

Cut the eggs in half lengthways. Put the rice in an ovenproof serving dish, and arrange the eggs on top. Pour the sauce over the eggs, cover the dish and put it in the oven for 15 minutes.

Charlotte russe

You can alter the flavour of the custard: for example try 4 tablespoons of sherry instead of the lemon juice and rind.

SERVES SIX

¼ pint (150 ml) lemon jelly
6 candied lemon slices
24 sponge fingers
½ pint (300 ml) milk
4 egg yolks
2½ to 4 oz (65 to 100 g) sugar
Salt
1 teaspoon cornflour
2 teaspoons gelatine
2 tablespoons hot water
2 fl oz (50 ml) lemon juice
Grated rind of 1 lemon
¾ pint (450 ml) double cream

Lightly oil the bottom of a 1-quart (1-litre) charlotte mould. Pour a thin layer of the lemon jelly into the mould. When the jelly is nearly set arrange the candied lemon slices attractively on top. Pour another thin layer of the lemon jelly on top. Arrange the sponge fingers upright around the sides of the mould, pushing the ends into the jelly. Trim them to fit and chill in the refrigerator.

Scald the milk by bringing it to just below boiling point. Mix the egg yolks, sugar to taste, pinch of salt and the cornflour in a bowl. Pour in a little hot milk and beat well. Gradually add the rest of the milk. Pour the egg and milk mixture into a heavy-bottomed pan or into the top half of a double saucepan and cook over low heat, stirring constantly, until the mixture is smooth and slightly thickened. Do not let the custard boil. Remove the pan from the heat.

Dissolve the gelatine in 2 tablespoons of hot water and pour it into the custard, stirring until it is well mixed. Set aside to cool. When the custard is cool stir in the lemon juice and grated lemon rind. Pour the custard into a bowl and put it in the refrigerator until it is quite cold and very nearly set.

Whip the cream until it is thick but not stiff and fold two-thirds of it into the custard. Pour the mixture into the lined mould. Chill the charlotte for 2 to 3 hours or until it has set. Unmould the charlotte on to a serving platter and decorate with the remaining whipped cream.

Charlotte russe

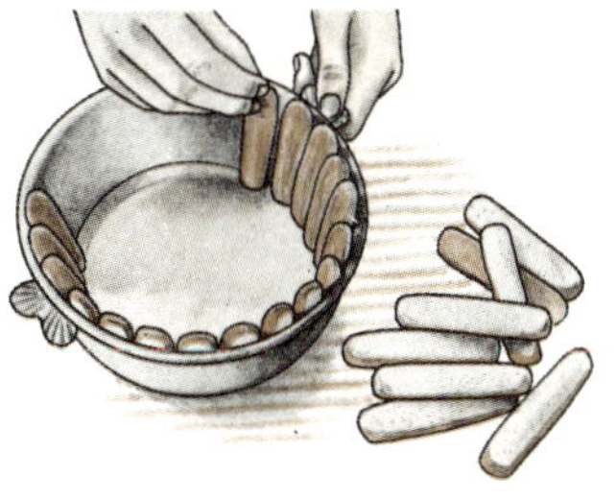

Arrange the sponge fingers around the sides of the mould.

Carefully trim the sponge fingers to fit the mould.

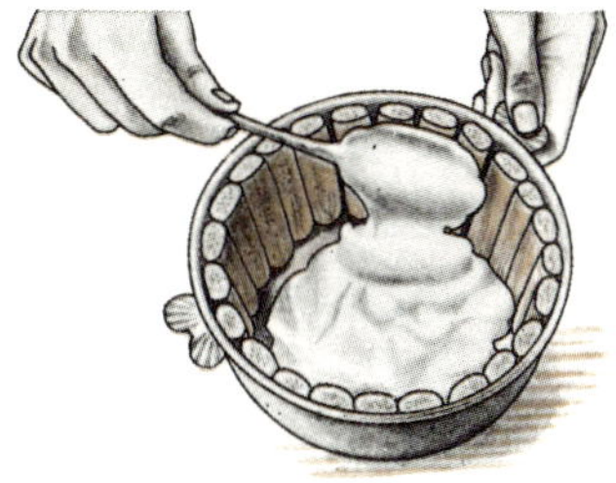

Spoon the nearly set custard into the lined mould.

Unmould the charlotte and decorate it with whipped cream.

Lemon mousse

SERVES FOUR

4 eggs, separated
3 oz (75 g) castor sugar
Grated rind and juice of 2 large lemons
2 teaspoons gelatine
¾ pint (450 ml) double cream, whipped
1 oz (25 g) almonds, blanched, toasted and finely chopped

Put the egg yolks, sugar, lemon rind and juice into a bowl and whisk over hot water until thick and mousse-like.

Put the gelatine in a cup with 2 tablespoons of cold water and stand the cup in hot water, off the heat, to dissolve the gelatine. Mix the gelatine into the egg and lemon mixture.

Put the bowl on ice and continue whisking from time to time, until the mixture is cold but not completely set.

Fold in most of the cream. Whisk the egg whites until stiff and fold them into the lemon mixture. Put the mousse into a serving bowl or into a 1-pint (575-ml) soufflé dish with a paper collar. Put the mousse into the refrigerator to chill thoroughly.

Before serving, remove the paper collar and decorate the mousse with the almonds and the remaining whipped cream.

Chocolate mousse

SERVES FOUR TO SIX

½ lb (225 g) bitter chocolate, broken into pieces
6 tablespoons water or coffee
1 oz (25 g) butter
2 tablespoons rum
4 eggs, separated

Melt the chocolate in the water over very low heat. Remove the pan from the heat and beat in the butter and the rum. Beat in the egg yolks one at a time.

Whisk the egg whites until they are stiff and mix them into the chocolate mixture. Spoon the mousse into small pots, cover the pots and refrigerate for up to 24 hours before serving.

Preparing a soufflé dish

Tie a band of greased paper around a soufflé dish to support a mousse until it sets or to make a raised soufflé.

Eggs and dairy produce

Crème brulée

SERVES FOUR

4 egg yolks, well beaten
Castor sugar
1 pint (575 ml) double cream
1-inch (2-cm) piece of vanilla pod

Combine the egg yolks with 1 tablespoon of sugar in a mixing bowl.

Put the cream and vanilla pod into a saucepan, bring slowly to boiling point and boil for one minute exactly. Remove the pan from the heat, lift out the vanilla pod and pour the cream on to the egg yolks and sugar, stirring all the time with a whisk. Strain the mixture into the top of a double saucepan and cook, stirring constantly, for 25 minutes or until the custard is thick enough to coat the back of a wooden spoon. Pour the custard into a buttered, heatproof serving dish, allow it to cool then chill in the refrigerator.

Sprinkle a layer of castor sugar to a depth of $\frac{1}{3}$ inch (1 cm) over the surface of the custard. Put the dish under a very hot grill until the sugar melts and turns golden brown. Return the custard to the refrigerator for 2 to 3 hours before serving.

Zabaglione

A richer variation of this classic dessert, called zabaglione à la créole, is made in the same way with 2 tablespoons of rum and $\frac{1}{4}$ pint (150 ml) of whipped double cream added when the mixture has cooled. The mixture must be whisked as it cools. The dessert is then chilled in glasses before serving.

SERVES FOUR TO SIX

6 egg yolks
6 tablespoons castor sugar
2 teaspoons very finely grated orange or lemon rind
6 tablespoons Marsala or white wine

Put the egg yolks, sugar and rind in a heatproof mixing bowl and whisk until the mixture becomes frothy. Stir in the Marsala or wine and set the bowl over a saucepan half-filled with barely simmering water. Whisk the mixture over low heat until it thickens and rises.

Remove the pan from the heat, divide the mixture between six glasses and serve immediately.

Bavarois

This classic dessert is a mixture of custard, gelatine, cream and flavouring. You can add any flavouring to the basic recipe. For example, for a coffee flavour add $\frac{1}{4}$ pint (150 ml) of strong black coffee, or 2 tablespoons of coffee essence. For a chocolate flavour dissolve $\frac{1}{4}$ pound (100 g) of bitter chocolate in the milk. For an orange flavour use the juice and finely grated rind or zest of 1 large orange. To extract the zest, rub the orange all over with 2 sugar lumps until they are completely impregnated with the oil in the skin. Then crush the sugar lumps and mix them in with the other sugar.

SERVES SIX

1 pint (575 ml) milk
1 vanilla pod
4 egg yolks
2 oz (50 g) castor sugar
1 tablespoon gelatine
2 tablespoons water
$\frac{1}{4}$ pint (150 ml) double cream, whipped

Put the milk and the vanilla pod in a saucepan and heat gently. Remove the pan from the heat and leave the milk to infuse.

Beat the egg yolks with the sugar in the top of a double saucepan. Remove the vanilla pod from the milk. Pour the milk on to the egg yolk and sugar mixture in a steady stream, beating all the time. Fit the top of the double saucepan over barely simmering water in the lower pan and cook the custard, stirring gently, until it is thick and coats the back of the spoon.

Dissolve the gelatine in the water over low heat and stir it into the custard. Strain the custard into a bowl. Set the bowl on ice and stir until the custard thickens. Fold in half the whipped cream and pour it into a lightly oiled $1\frac{1}{2}$-pint (900-ml) charlotte or jelly mould. Cover the mould and put it in the refrigerator for 4 hours.

Dip the bottom of the mould into hot water for 1 second then turn out the bavarois on to a serving dish. Decorate the bavarois with the remaining cream.

Three delicious dishes based on eggs and dairy produce: a luxurious, creamy dessert called bavarois, the traditional Swiss fondue, and a light supper snack, eggs florentine with ham.

Jamaican rum custard

SERVES FOUR

5 egg yolks plus 1 egg white
2 oz (50 g) soft brown sugar
1 oz (25 g) cornflour
1 pint (575 ml) milk
4 fl oz (125 ml) dark rum
¼ pint (150 ml) double cream, whipped

Combine the eggs, sugar and cornflour in a mixing bowl.

Scald the milk and stir a little of it into the egg mixture. Strain the mixture back into the pan of hot milk, beating constantly. Cook the custard, stirring continuously, until it is thick. Do not let the custard boil. Remove the pan from the heat and stir in the rum. Pour the custard into parfait glasses and serve chilled decorated with whipped cream.

Austrian chocolate pudding

SERVES SIX

6 oz (175 g) dark chocolate
½ pint (300 ml) milk
8 slices crustless fresh white bread, cubed
6 oz (175 g) butter, softened
6 oz (175 g) castor sugar
6 eggs, separated
2 oz (50 g) ground almonds
Grated rind of ½ orange
2 tablespoons crushed macaroons
½ pint (300 ml) double cream or chocolate sauce

Melt the chocolate in a little of the milk over low heat. Soak the bread in the remaining milk for 5 minutes.

Cream the butter and sugar together in a mixing bowl. Beat in the egg yolks one at a time. Beat in the melted chocolate. Beat the soaked bread with the milk to form a smooth mixture and stir it into the chocolate mixture with the ground almonds.

Beat the egg whites until they hold a stiff peak and fold them into the chocolate mixture carefully.

Generously butter a 2-quart (2-litre) pudding basin. Mix the orange rind and macaroons together and sprinkle the mixture over the bottom of the pudding basin. Pour in the chocolate mixture. Cover the bowl with aluminium foil with a 1-inch (2-cm) pleat down the centre, and tie down with string.

Fit a rack into a large saucepan. Put in the pudding basin. Pour in enough boiling water to come halfway up the side of the basin. Cover the pan and steam for 1 hour.

Unmould the pudding while hot. Serve with the cream or chocolate sauce.

Oeufs à la neige

SERVES FOUR

½ pint (300 ml) milk
½ pint (300 ml) cream
3 egg whites
Salt
3 oz (75 g) castor sugar
4 egg yolks
3 oz (75 g) vanilla sugar

Scald the milk and the cream together in a saucepan and draw the pan off the heat.

Beat the egg whites with a pinch of salt until they stand in peaks. Beat in the castor sugar, a little at a time, until the egg whites are stiff and glossy. Using a tablespoon, scoop out egg-shaped portions of the meringue mixture and drop a few of them at a time into the hot milk. Return the pan to low heat and poach the meringues gently (do not let the milk and cream mixture boil) for 2 or 3 minutes or until they are firm, turning them over once. Using a slotted spoon lift out the meringues and drain them on kitchen paper towels.

Beat the egg yolks with the vanilla sugar in the top of a double saucepan until well mixed. Add the hot milk and cream in a steady stream, stirring continually. Cook over very low heat, for about 15 minutes or until the custard is thick enough to coat the back of a wooden spoon.

Pour the custard into a serving bowl and leave to cool. When the custard is cool arrange the snow eggs on top. Put in the refrigerator to chill before serving.

Stewing and casseroling

Stewing and casseroling are methods of cooking meat, game, poultry, fish, vegetables or cereals very slowly, over a low heat or in an oven set at a low temperature. Bouillabaisse and other similar fish stews are the exceptions to the rule—they are cooked rapidly over high heat.

Basically there are two kinds of meat stews. White stews are made with veal, lamb, chicken or rabbit, which is sometimes soaked in cold, salted water for several hours or overnight to whiten the meat and to make the flavour more subtle. Rabbit and scrag end of lamb are the meats most commonly soaked.

Brown stews are made with beef, mutton, or such offal as oxtail, heart or kidney. Before the cooking liquid is added the meat is browned in hot fat or oil.

Stewed or casseroled meat or poultry is cut into pieces or joints before it is cooked. For pot roasting, however, the meat or poultry is left in one piece.

Pot roasting is a good way of cooking small joints or birds, which tend to become dry if cooked in the oven. Simply brown the meat or poultry in a little fat, reduce the heat, add a little more fat or a little wine or stock if necessary, then cover with a lid and cook until tender.

Braising is a method of cooking joints of meat, game, fish and vegetables first on top of the cooker and then in the oven. To braise meat, heat a little fat or oil in a flameproof casserole, then brown the meat over moderate heat. Remove the meat from the pan and keep it warm. In the hot fat cook about half to one pound (225 to 450 g) of diced or sliced root vegetables until they are tender. A couple of rashers of bacon, diced or left whole, may also be added to this mixture, which is called mirepoix.

When the vegetables are cooked, lay the meat on top, add a little liquid and some herbs and seasonings, then transfer the casserole to a preheated oven. Cook until tender. The mirepoix will have lost all its flavour by the end of the cooking time, so it is discarded. The cooking liquid, however, is strained and served with the meat.

Fish is braised in the same way as meat except that it is not browned before it is laid on the mirepoix. Such vegetables as celery and onions are excellent braised, but they should first be blanched to shorten the cooking time.

Pans used for stewing, pot roasting and braising should have thick bases and tight-fitting lids.

Fish and shellfish

- ***Lobster à l'americaine 108*** Green salad 213
- ***Matelote 109*** Garlic bread 189
- ***Cioppino 109*** Green salad 213, Garlic bread 189
- ***Mussel stew 109*** Boiled fennel 92, Grilled mushrooms 134
- ***Squid casserole 109*** Spinach and mushroom salad 212, Boiled rice 97
- ***Bouillabaisse 106***
- ***Fillets of haddock dieppoise 106*** Sauté potatoes 151, Spinach 92
- ***Zarzuela de pescado 106*** Aioli sauce 68
- ***Fish casserole with peppers 108*** Garlic bread 189
- ***Psari plaki 108*** Garlic mashed potatoes 180
- ***Belgian fish stew 108*** Boiled chicory 92, Soufflé potatoes 150
- ***Portuguese salt cod 108***
- ***Eels stewed in white wine 108*** Steamed broccoli 92, Mashed potatoes 93

Poultry and game birds

- ***Coq au vin 110*** Soufflé potatoes 150, Petits pois à la française 91
- ***Chicken in cider 110*** Crusty noodles 158, Deep-fried mushrooms 152, Marrow in caraway sauce 92
- ***Duck with olives 112*** Mushroom and herb casserole 121, Mashed potatoes 93
- ***Duck with cherries 112*** Potato croquettes 151, Boiled chicory 92
- ***Duck with turnips 112*** Garlic mashed potatoes 180
- ***Grouse casserole 112*** Garlic mashed potatoes 180 or Game chips 150, Red cabbage with apples 120
- ***Grouse en cocotte 112*** Potato straws 150, French beans 92
- ***Casseroled pheasant with cranberries and cream 113*** Game chips 150, Spinach purée 92
- ***Pheasant with Calvados 113***
- ***Guinea-fowl and celery casserole 113*** Butter beans with garlic, Mashed potatoes 93

Flemish pigeons with prunes and port 113
Potato croquettes 151, Green salad 213

Meat and game

Boeuf à la mode 114
Steamed broccoli 92, Boiled noodles 97

Kidneys braised in red wine 117
Sauté potatoes 151, Boiled peas 93, Deep-fried mushrooms 152

Carbonnade de boeuf à la flamande 114
Green salad 213, Garlic bread 189

Red-cooked hand of pork 117
Boiled rice 97, Stir-fried bean sprouts 153

Boeuf à la bourguignonne 114
Steamed cauliflower 92, Parisienne potatoes 151

Cassoulet 117
Green salad 213

Boeuf en daube 115
Boiled noodles 97, Steamed leeks 93

Lancashire hot-pot 117
Cabbage or spinach 92, Peas 93

Hungarian goulash 115
Green salad 213

Navarin printanier 118
Potato croquettes or Lyonnaise potatoes 151

Pot roast with prunes 116
Potato croquettes 151, Steamed broccoli 92

Jugged hare with forcemeat balls 118
Spinach 92

Beef olives 116
Garlic mashed potatoes 180, Chicory, orange and watercress salad 213

Rabbit stew 119
Leeks provençal 120, Mashed potatoes 93

Oxtail stew 116
Crusty noodles 158

Braised venison with juniper berries and soured cream 119
Carrot and parsnip purée 91, French beans 92

Osso bucco 116
Risotto alla Milanese 122 or Mashed potatoes, Boiled mange-tout peas 93

Blanquette de veau 116
Boiled new potatoes 93, Glazed carrots, Petits pois à la française 91

Vegetables

Ratatouille 121

Peperonata 121

Caponata 121

Braised lettuce 120

Chestnuts with Chinese cabbage 120
Boiled noodles or rice 97, Stir-fried bean sprouts 153

Red cabbage with apples 120

Casseroled celery 120

Buttered chicory 120

Braised onions 120

Leeks provençal 120

Sauerkraut 121

Mushroom and herb casserole 121
Boiled rice 97 or Crusty noodles 158

Stuffed peppers 121
Green salad 213, Peas 93

Cereals

Creole jambalaya 122
Green salad 213

Risotto alla Milanese 122
Green salad 213

Paella Valenciana 123

Biryani 123
Yoghurt, Cucumber

Barley and vegetable casserole 123

Burghul pilaff 122

Tomato rice 122
Avocado salad 213

First courses
Main courses
Light lunch-supper dishes
Accompaniments
Desserts
Miscellaneous

Fish and shellfish

The most famous fish stews come from around the Mediterranean. Bouillabaisse, for example, is so well loved in the south of France that poems have been written about it and its invention has been attributed to Venus. The secret of its success lies in boiling the stew over a high heat to amalgamate the oil and water.

Although in Marseilles bouillabaisse is made with such fish as the rascasse, or scorpion-fish, wonderful stews can be made in other parts of the world using many different salt-water fish—rock salmon, monkfish, cod, haddock, whiting and skate, for example—and such shellfish as cockles, mussels, prawns and scallops.

Bouillabaisse

It is always difficult to know whether to classify this dish as a soup or as a stew—really it is both, as the liquid is often served as a soup, separately from the fish itself. A true bouillabaisse, they say, cannot be made away from the Mediterranean, one possible reason being that one of the most traditional ingredients, the rascasse, or scorpion-fish, is not found elsewhere. For this version of bouillabaisse use a selection of available fish—the more varied the selection, the better the dish will be.

SERVES SIX

4 large tomatoes, peeled and chopped
2 onions, chopped
4 garlic cloves, chopped
6 fl oz (175 ml) olive oil
3 sprigs parsley
1 sprig fennel
1 bay leaf
Large pinch saffron
Salt and pepper
5 lb (2½ kg) fish—monkfish, conger eel, red snapper, John Dory, whiting, crawfish cut into chunks; scampi and prawns
12 slices French bread
½ pint (300 ml) aioli sauce

Put the tomatoes, onions and garlic into a large, heavy-bottomed pan with the oil. Add the herbs and the saffron and season well. Put the firmer fish (monkfish and conger eel) on top and cover with boiling water. Cook over high heat for 5 minutes. Then add the more tender fish (whiting, crawfish, John Dory, scampi and prawns) and continue boiling hard for another 10 minutes.

Meanwhile toast the bread in a hot oven (400°F/200°C, Gas Mark 6), without letting it brown.

Transfer the fish to a serving dish and keep hot. Continue to boil the broth for 2 minutes longer and check the seasoning. Strain the broth. Put two slices of toasted bread into each soup bowl and pour in just enough broth to moisten the bread well. Serve with the fish and the aioli.

Fillets of haddock dieppoise

SERVES FOUR

2 lb (900 g) haddock fillets
Small bay leaf
2 teaspoons lemon juice
Salt and pepper
¼ pint (150 ml) white wine
½ pint (300 ml) milk
1 oz (25 g) butter
1 oz (25 g) flour
6 oz (175 g) peeled shrimps
¼ pint (150 ml) cream

Preheat the oven to 350°F (180°C, Gas Mark 4).

Wash the fish and put it in a buttered ovenproof dish. Add the bay leaf and lemon juice, season well, pour over the wine and cover with foil. Bake in the centre of the oven for 20 minutes.

Meanwhile bring the milk to just below boiling point. Melt the butter in a small pan. Stir in the flour to make a roux. Cook for 30 seconds then pour in the milk gradually and bring to the boil, stirring briskly. Reduce the heat and simmer for 5 minutes. Draw the pan off the heat, and stir in half the shrimps, the cream and seasoning.

Remove the fish from the oven. Lift out the fish and arrange the fillets on a warm serving dish. Strain the cooking liquid and stir it into the sauce. Pour over the fish and garnish with the remaining shrimps.

Zarzuela de pescado (Spanish stewed fish)

SERVES SIX

2 quarts (4 lb/2 kg) mussels
8 fl oz (225 ml) dry white wine
¼ pint (150 ml) olive oil
2 large onions, chopped
1 lb (450 g) squid, sliced
6 large tomatoes, chopped
1 lb (450 g) hake or cod fillets, skinned and cut into large pieces
¾ lb (350 g) prawns, peeled, 6 reserved unpeeled
Salt and freshly ground black pepper
Large pinch saffron threads, soaked in 1 tablespoon boiling water for 5 minutes
2 large garlic cloves
1 oz (25 g) ground almonds
2 tablespoons chopped fresh parsley
12 slices French bread, fried

Put the mussels in a large sauté pan with half the wine. Cover the pan and cook for about 8 minutes over high heat, shaking the pan frequently. Drain the mussels and reserve the liquid. Shell the mussels, reserving a few in their shells and discarding any that have not opened.

Heat the olive oil in a large saucepan, add the onions and fry gently until they are golden. Add the squid, tomatoes and the remaining wine and cook for 2 to 3 minutes. Add the hake or cod and peeled prawns and season to taste. Pour in the reserved cooking liquid and the saffron mixture. Cover the pan and simmer for 7 to 10 minutes, or until the fish is cooked.

Put the garlic, almonds, parsley and 2 tablespoons of the cooking liquid into a small bowl and mix to a smooth paste. Stir the paste into the stew. Add the mussels. Ladle the stew into a large serving dish.

Garnish with the reserved prawns and mussels. Arrange the slices of fried bread around the dish.

Bouillabaisse, almost a religion in the south of France, is made with a variety of Mediterranean fish and flavoured with saffron, garlic and herbs.

Fish and shellfish

Fish casserole with peppers

SERVES FOUR

2 oz (50 g) butter
2 garlic cloves, chopped
1 lb (450 g) leeks, cut into chunks
1 green pepper, seeded and thinly sliced
¼ lb (100 g) mushrooms, whole or cut in half if large
4 ripe tomatoes, peeled and chopped
Salt and pepper
2 lb (900 g) cod or haddock steaks
1 tablespoon tomato purée
½ pint (300 ml) fish stock
Chopped parsley

Preheat the oven to 375°F (190°C, Gas Mark 5).

Melt the butter in a casserole. Add the garlic, leeks and green pepper and cook gently for 10 minutes or until soft. Add the mushrooms and tomatoes and season well. Put the fish on top. Blend the tomato purée with the fish stock and pour it over the fish. Cover the casserole and bake for 20 minutes.

Remove the casserole from the oven, sprinkle the parsley on top and serve at once.

Psari plaki (Greek fish stew)

SERVES FOUR TO SIX

4 lb (2 kg) bream, John Dory or turbot (a whole fish or large piece), cleaned
1 tablespoon lemon juice
Salt and pepper
2 tablespoons olive oil
3 large onions, sliced
2 garlic cloves, chopped
4 tablespoons chopped parsley
2 fl oz (50 ml) water
¼ pint (150 ml) white wine
1 lemon, thinly sliced
1 lb (450 g) tomatoes, peeled and sliced

Preheat the oven to 350°F (180°C, Gas Mark 4).

Arrange the fish in a buttered baking dish and sprinkle with the lemon juice and seasoning.

Heat the oil in a frying-pan and fry the onions, garlic and parsley gently until soft. Stir in the water and the wine and simmer for 1 minute. Pour this mixture over the fish. Arrange the lemon slices and tomatoes on top. Put the dish in the oven for 45 minutes or until the fish is cooked. Serve immediately.

Belgian fish stew

SERVES FOUR TO SIX

1 oz (25 g) butter
3 lb (1½ kg) carp or pike steaks
2 celery stalks, with the leaves
Salt and pepper
3 egg yolks
2 fl oz (50 ml) cream
1 tablespoon chopped parsley

Melt the butter in a large flameproof casserole. Put in the fish and the celery and enough water to cover. Season lightly, bring to the boil and cook over high heat for 10 minutes.

Lift out the fish and keep hot on a serving dish. Remove and discard the celery. Bring the cooking liquid to the boil again and boil hard until it is reduced to ¾ pint (450 ml).

Beat the egg yolks and cream together in a small bowl. Blend in a little of the hot liquid and add this mixture to the cooking liquid in the pan. Reduce the heat to very low and cook, stirring, until the sauce is thickened, but do not let it boil. Pour the sauce over the fish, sprinkle the parsley over the top and serve.

Portuguese salt cod

SERVES SIX

2 lb (900 g) dried salt cod
2 lb (900 g) potatoes, peeled and sliced
¼ pint (150 ml) olive oil
4 medium-sized onions, sliced
2 garlic cloves, crushed
4 tomatoes, peeled and sliced
12 black olives, pitted
4 hard-boiled eggs, sliced
1 tablespoon chopped parsley

Soak the cod overnight. Rinse well, drain and put the cod into a saucepan with just enough fresh cold water to cover. Bring to the boil, reduce the heat and simmer for 30 minutes. Add the potatoes and simmer for 20 minutes or until they are tender and the fish is cooked.

Preheat the oven to 350°F (180°C, Gas Mark 4).

Lift out the fish, remove the skin and bones and flake the flesh into 2-inch (5-cm) pieces. Drain the potatoes.

Heat 4 tablespoons of the olive oil in a frying-pan. Add the onions and garlic and fry gently until soft.

Arrange the potatoes, onions and garlic, tomatoes, cod and olives in layers in a deep casserole. Pour the remaining oil over the top. Cover the casserole and put it in the oven for 20 minutes or until it is thoroughly hot.

Remove the casserole from the oven. Arrange the hard-boiled eggs on top. Sprinkle the parsley over the eggs and serve.

Eels stewed in white wine

SERVES FOUR

2 tablespoons olive oil
1 tablespoon butter
2 lb (900 g) eels, skinned and cut into pieces
1 small onion, thinly sliced
2 garlic cloves, crushed
4 large tomatoes, peeled and chopped
1 tablespoon chopped basil
½ pint (300 ml) white wine
1 teaspoon salt
Freshly ground black pepper
Beurre manié

Heat the olive oil with the butter in a large flameproof casserole. When the fat is hot, add the eel pieces and the onion and fry, stirring constantly, for 5 minutes. Add the remaining ingredients, except the beurre manié, and bring to the boil, stirring.

Reduce the heat to very low, cover the casserole and simmer for 25 to 30 minutes, or until the eel is tender.

Remove the casserole from the heat. With a slotted spoon, lift out the eel pieces and put them in a warmed serving dish. Keep hot.

Return the casserole to the heat. Stir in the beurre manié, a few pieces at a time, until the sauce has thickened. Pour the sauce over the eel and serve.

Lobster à l'americaine

SERVES TWO

1 tablespoon olive oil
2 oz (50 g) butter
2-lb (900-g) uncooked lobster, cut into pieces (reserving the coral)
1 onion, peeled and chopped
1 garlic clove, finely chopped
Bouquet garni
2 tomatoes, peeled, quartered and seeded
2 tablespoons brandy
½ pint (300 ml) white wine
1 oz (25 g) flour
1 teaspoon lemon juice
Cayenne pepper
Salt and pepper
1 tablespoon chopped parsley (or parsley and tarragon)

Heat the oil and 1 ounce (25 g) of the butter together in a frying-pan. Add the lobster and fry over fairly high heat for 2 to 3 minutes on each side or until the shell turns red. Remove the lobster. Add the onion, garlic, bouquet garni and tomatoes to

the pan with a tablespoon of water and simmer gently for a few minutes. Put the lobster pieces on top, pour over the brandy and ignite. When the flames die down add the wine and, if necessary, enough water to just cover the lobster. Cover the pan and simmer for 15 to 20 minutes.

Meanwhile blend the coral with the remaining butter and the flour. Lift out the lobster, arrange the pieces on a heated serving dish and keep warm. Stir the butter and flour mixture into the sauce in the pan, add the lemon juice, a pinch of cayenne and season to taste. Strain the sauce over the lobster, sprinkle the herbs over the top and serve.

Matelote

In France, matelote usually refers to a stew of freshwater fish (eel, carp, pike or perch), but matelote à la normande, of which this is a version, uses salt-water fish.

SERVES SIX

1 quart (2 lb/900 g) mussels, scrubbed
½ pint (300 ml) court bouillon
2 lb (900 g) assorted fish (conger eel, gurnard, sole or plaice, whiting) cleaned and cut into 2-inch (5-cm) chunks
1 pint (575 ml) dry cider or white wine
Bouquet garni
Salt and pepper
2 oz (50 g) butter
1 oz (25 g) flour
½ lb (225 g) button mushrooms
12 slices French bread, fried until golden

Put the mussels in a large sauté pan. Pour in the court bouillon and bring to the boil, shaking the pan occasionally. Cover the pan, and cook for 5 minutes. Lift out the mussels, discarding any that have not opened, and keep warm. Strain and reserve the cooking liquid.

Put the fish into a flameproof casserole, pour in the cider or wine, together with the cooking liquid from the mussels, add the bouquet garni and seasoning. Cover the casserole and simmer for 15 minutes.

Remove the fish from the casserole and set it aside. Discard the bouquet garni, increase the heat and boil rapidly for 10 minutes. Reduce the heat to low. Mix 1 ounce (25 g) of the butter with the flour to make beurre manié. Divide the beurre manié into small pieces, and add them, one at a time, to the simmering liquid, stirring until the sauce thickens.

Return the fish to the casserole and cook until heated through.

Gently fry the mushrooms in the remaining butter.

Ladle the fish and sauce into a serving dish. Garnish with the mushrooms, mussels and bread.

Cioppino

This seafood stew is popular in San Francisco, where many of the early fishermen came originally from Italy.

SERVES EIGHT

4 tablespoons olive oil
1 onion, chopped
2 celery stalks, chopped
1 carrot, chopped
2 lb (900 g) tomatoes, peeled and chopped
3 garlic cloves, chopped
1 tablespoon tomato purée
8 fl oz (225 ml) dry white wine (or a mixture of wine and fish stock made from the trimmings of the fish)
2 lb (900 g) white fish (hake, haddock, cod)
1 quart (2 lb/900 g) clams or oysters in their shells, well scrubbed
2 lobsters, killed and chopped
1 lb (450 g) uncooked prawns, peeled
Salt and pepper

Put the olive oil in a large, heavy-bottomed saucepan with the chopped vegetables and garlic. Dilute the tomato purée in a little water and stir it into the pan. Cover the pan and simmer gently for 30 minutes.

Add the wine, the white fish, clams or oysters and lobsters and stir well. Cook, covered, for 10 minutes. Add the prawns and seasoning, and cook for a further 10 minutes. Discard any clams or oysters that have not opened and serve.

Mussel stew

SERVES FOUR

1 quart (2 lb/900 g) mussels, scrubbed
½ pint (300 ml) white wine
2 oz (50 g) butter
2 shallots, finely chopped
2 leeks, white part only, finely chopped
2 tomatoes, peeled and chopped
2 garlic cloves, chopped
1 oz (25 g) flour
¾ pint (450 ml) milk
1 tablespoon anise-flavoured liqueur
2 egg yolks
4 fl oz (125 ml) double cream
Salt and pepper

Put the mussels into a large sauté pan with the wine. Cover the pan and cook over high heat for 5 minutes. Transfer the mussels to a deep serving dish, discarding any that have not opened, and keep warm. Strain the cooking liquor.

Melt the butter in a saucepan. Add the shallots, leeks, tomatoes and garlic and fry gently, stirring, until soft. Stir in the flour. Pour in the mussel liquor and the milk gradually, stirring constantly to ensure there are no lumps. Continue cooking until the sauce thickens slightly. Add the liqueur and continue simmering gently for a few minutes.

Beat the egg yolks with the cream in a small bowl. Stir in a little of the hot sauce. Draw the pan off the heat and pour in the egg and cream mixture, stirring constantly. Adjust the seasoning, return the pan to a low heat for a few seconds. Pour the sauce over the mussels and serve.

Squid casserole

SERVES FOUR

4 fl oz (125 ml) olive oil
2 squid, cleaned and coarsely chopped
2 onions, thinly sliced
3 garlic cloves, crushed
1½ lb (700 g) tomatoes, chopped
1 tablespoon fresh rubbed thyme
Salt and freshly ground black pepper
4 fl oz (125 ml) dry white wine
10 black olives, pitted

Heat the olive oil in a flameproof casserole. Add the squid and onions and fry, stirring, until the onions are golden.

Stir in the remaining ingredients, except the olives, and bring to the boil. Reduce the heat to low and simmer, uncovered, for 30 minutes, stirring occasionally. Add the olives and cook for a further 5 minutes. Serve immediately, from the casserole.

Poultry and game birds

Stewing and casseroling are excellent methods of cooking poultry and game birds that are no longer young, for even a rather tough old bird, if it is cooked slowly in a well-flavoured liquid, can arrive at the table tender and tasting delicious.

Pot roasting, on the other hand, is a suitable method of cooking both young and old birds.

Use fresh poultry and game birds whenever possible. If you have to use a frozen bird see that it has thawed out completely before you start cooking.

Coq au vin

SERVES FOUR

¼ lb (100 g) streaky bacon, chopped
1½ oz (40 g) butter
12 pickling onions
4½- to 5-lb (2- to 2½-kg) roasting chicken, jointed
2 tablespoons brandy
¾ pint (450 ml) red wine (Burgundy or Beaujolais)
¼ pint (150 ml) chicken stock
Bouquet garni
2 garlic cloves, finely chopped
Salt and pepper
¼ lb (100 g) mushrooms
Beurre manié made from 1 oz (25 g) flour and 1 oz (25 g) butter

Put the bacon in a large flameproof casserole, set it over moderate heat and fry, stirring constantly, until it has rendered its fat.

Add ½ ounce (15 g) of the butter and fry the onions until they are golden. Transfer the onions and bacon to a plate and set aside.

Brown the chicken pieces on all sides in the fat, then pour the brandy over and ignite it. Shake the pan while the brandy is flaming. When the flames have subsided, pour in the wine and stock and add the bouquet garni, garlic and seasoning. Once the liquid is simmering, return the onions and bacon to the pan. Cover the pan, reduce the heat and simmer gently for at least 1 hour.

Meanwhile, melt the remaining butter in a small frying-pan and fry the mushrooms for 2 to 3 minutes. Add them to the casserole.

Add the beurre manié in small pieces, stirring constantly, until the sauce has thickened. Serve at once.

Chicken in cider

SERVES FOUR TO SIX

2 oz (50 g) butter
2 chickens, 2½ lb (1 kg) each, cut into quarters
Salt and pepper
2 onions, thinly sliced
3 apples, peeled, cored and sliced (reserve one apple in acidulated water for use as garnish)
8 small new carrots, scrubbed
1 bay leaf
Pinch thyme
8 fl oz (225 ml) dry cider
4 tablespoons double cream
1 egg yolk

Melt the butter in a flameproof casserole. Add the chicken pieces and brown them on all sides. Season well with salt and pepper. Add the onions, 2 apples, the carrots, bay leaf and thyme. Cook for one minute before adding the cider. Bring the cider to the boil, cover the pan and simmer gently for 35 minutes or until the chicken is tender. Transfer the chicken pieces to a serving dish, cover and keep warm in a very low oven.

Boil the cooking liquid until it has reduced by half. Remove and discard the bay leaf.

Combine the cream with the egg yolk in a small bowl. Stir in 2 to 3 spoonfuls of the hot liquid and pour it into the casserole, stirring until the sauce has thickened. Adjust the seasoning if necessary.

Pour the sauce over the chicken and garnish with the reserved apple slices.

Three superb dishes fit for any dinner party : braised duck with cherries, pheasant with Calvados, and the classic coq au vin.

Poultry and game birds

Duck with olives

SERVES FOUR

2 oz (50 g) butter
5-lb ($2\frac{1}{2}$-kg) duck, cut into quarters
4 fl oz (125 ml) dry vermouth
Salt and pepper
Bouquet garni
8 fl oz (225 ml) veal stock
2 tablespoons tomato purée
Beurre manié made from 1 oz (25 g) butter and 1 oz (25 g) flour
16 stuffed green olives
2 tablespoons olive oil
4 slices bread, cut into triangles

Preheat the oven to 350°F (180°C, Gas Mark 4). Melt the butter in a flameproof casserole. Add the duck quarters and fry them until they are well browned on all sides. Pour over the vermouth, season to taste and add the bouquet garni. Cover the casserole and put it in the oven for 40 minutes.

Remove the duck from the casserole and transfer it to a warmed serving dish. Keep hot.

Pour the stock into the casserole and bring it to the boil over moderate heat, scraping any sediment from the bottom of the pan. Remove and discard the bouquet garni. Reduce the heat to low, and when the sauce is barely simmering stir in the tomato purée, and then the beurre manié in small pieces, stirring constantly, until the sauce is thick. Add the olives and simmer for 3 minutes. Pour over the duck and keep hot.

Heat the olive oil in a large frying-pan over moderate heat. Add the bread triangles and fry them on both sides until they are golden-brown and crisp. Drain them well on kitchen paper towels and arrange them around the duck, serve immediately.

Duck with cherries

SERVES THREE TO FOUR

5-lb ($2\frac{1}{2}$-kg) duck
Salt and pepper
2 oz (50 g) butter
4 fl oz (125 ml) Madeira
1 tablespoon sugar
Juice and grated rind of 1 orange
$\frac{1}{4}$ pint (150 ml) chicken stock
24 red cherries, pitted
1 teaspoon cornflour

Rub the duck all over with the salt and pepper.

Melt the butter in a flameproof casserole and brown the duck on all sides. Pour in the Madeira. Cover the casserole, reduce the heat to low and cook for about 50 to 60 minutes or until the duck is cooked. Remove the duck from the casserole and transfer it to a warmed serving dish. Keep the duck hot in the oven.

Add the sugar, orange juice and rind and chicken stock to the casserole. Bring to the boil and simmer for 10 minutes. Skim off the fat and strain the liquid.

Return the liquid to the pan and add the cherries. Mix the cornflour with a tablespoon of water, stir in a little of the sauce and then pour the mixture into the pan. Cook for 3 minutes.

Taste and adjust seasoning if necessary. Pour a little sauce over the duck. Spoon some of the cherries into the dish and serve the rest of the sauce and cherries separately in a sauce boat.

Duck with turnips

SERVES THREE TO FOUR

1 large duck, trussed
$1\frac{1}{2}$ oz (40 g) seasoned flour
3 oz (75 g) butter
1 lb (450 g) small turnips, peeled and halved
2 tablespoons castor sugar
8 pickling onions, peeled
1 pint (575 ml) veal stock

Preheat the oven to 350°F (180°C, Gas Mark 4).

Coat the duck all over with half the seasoned flour. Melt the butter in a flameproof casserole and brown the duck on all sides.

Remove the duck and add the turnips. Sprinkle with the sugar. Cook over low heat until the turnips are golden brown. Add the onions and cook for a further 3 minutes. Remove the vegetables and set aside.

Stir in the rest of the flour and gradually add the stock, stirring constantly. Return the duck to the casserole, cover and put it in the oven for 40 minutes.

Add the turnips and onions and cook for 30 minutes.

Remove the duck from the casserole and put it on a hot serving dish. Remove the trussing string and arrange the turnips and onions around the duck.

Skim the fat off the sauce and boil over high heat for a few minutes. Strain the sauce over the duck and serve.

Grouse casserole

SERVES FOUR TO SIX

2 grouse, trussed
Salt and pepper
3 oz (75 g) butter
1 onion, chopped
$\frac{1}{4}$ lb (125 g) mushrooms, chopped
2 carrots, scrubbed and diced
1 celery stalk, diced
2 tablespoons whisky
$\frac{1}{2}$ pint (300 ml) chicken stock
1 tablespoon redcurrant jelly
6 bacon rolls, grilled and kept hot

Preheat the oven to 350°F (180°C, Gas Mark 4).

Season the grouse well with salt and pepper. Heat the butter in a flameproof casserole and brown the birds on all sides. Remove the grouse from the casserole. Add the onion, mushrooms, carrots and celery. Cook over low heat, stirring, until the vegetables are soft but not browned.

Return the grouse to the pan, pour over the whisky and ignite it. Shake the pan until the flames die down. Add the stock and cook, covered, in the oven for $1\frac{1}{4}$ hours.

When the grouse are cooked, cut them in half with poultry shears and place on a warmed serving dish.

Strain the sauce into another pan and boil until it has thickened slightly. Stir in the redcurrant jelly.

Spoon the sauce over the grouse and garnish with the bacon rolls.

Grouse en cocotte

SERVES FOUR

2 grouse, halved
2 tablespoons olive oil
3 fl oz (75 ml) red wine
1 tablespoon red wine vinegar
4 juniper berries
Strip lemon rind
1 teaspoon lemon juice
Salt and pepper
1 oz (25 g) butter
4 rashers streaky bacon
6 pickling onions
4 celery stalks, chopped
1 bay leaf
$\frac{1}{4}$ pint (150 ml) chicken stock
1 tablespoon redcurrant jelly
1 teaspoon arrowroot mixed with 1 tablespoon water

Prick the grouse all over with a fork. Mix the oil, wine, vinegar, berries, lemon rind and juice and seasoning together in

a large dish. Add the grouse and baste them well with the marinade. Leave for 24 hours in a cool place, turning the grouse from time to time. Lift out the grouse and dry them with kitchen paper towels. Reserve the marinade.

Preheat the oven to 325°F (170°C, Gas Mark 3).

Melt the butter in a flameproof casserole and gently fry the bacon and onions for 5 minutes. Add the grouse, celery, bay leaf, stock and reserved marinade. Cover the casserole and cook in the oven for 1¼ to 1½ hours or until the grouse is tender. Remove the casserole from the oven. Transfer the grouse and pickling onions to a warmed serving dish.

Stir the redcurrant jelly and arrowroot mixture into the casserole and set over moderate heat. Cook, stirring, for 1 to 2 minutes or until the liquid has thickened. Strain the sauce over the grouse and serve.

Casseroled pheasant with cranberries and cream

SERVES TWO

1 pheasant, trussed
Salt and pepper
¼ lb (100 g) bacon, chopped
1 oz (25 g) butter
2 fl oz (50 ml) brandy
Juice of 1 orange
¼ pint (150 ml) cream
2 teaspoons arrowroot
¼ pint (150 ml) cranberry sauce

Season the pheasant well with salt and pepper. Fry the bacon in a flameproof casserole over moderate heat until it has rendered its fat. Add the butter and brown the bird on all sides. Pour over the brandy and orange juice. Cover the casserole, reduce the heat and simmer gently for 1 hour or until the pheasant is tender.

Transfer the pheasant from the casserole to a warm dish and keep hot. Mix the cream with the arrowroot and stir it into the cooking liquid with the cranberry sauce. Cook over low heat until the sauce is thickened.

Carve the bird and arrange the meat on a warm serving dish, pour over some of the sauce and serve the rest separately.

Pheasant with Calvados

SERVES FOUR TO SIX

2 pheasants, trussed
Salt and pepper
¼ lb (100 g) butter
¼ lb (100 g) streaky bacon
1 teaspoon marjoram
3 cooking apples, peeled, cored and sliced (reserve a few slices in acidulated water for garnish)
Rind and juice of 1 lemon
3 tablespoons Calvados
½ pint (300 ml) chicken stock
¼ pint (150 ml) soured cream

Preheat the oven to 350°F (180°C, Gas Mark 4).

Rub the pheasants all over with salt and pepper.

Melt half the butter in a flameproof casserole and brown the birds on all sides. Add the bacon and marjoram and cook gently for 5 minutes. Remove the birds and bacon and set aside.

Melt the remaining butter in the pan and fry the apples until golden. Add the lemon juice and rind and the bacon. Place the pheasants on top of the apples, pour in the Calvados and ignite. When the flames die down, add the stock and bring to the boil. Cover the casserole and put it in the oven for 1 hour or until the pheasants are tender.

Stir in the soured cream and cook for a further 10 minutes. Garnish with the apple slices.

Guinea-fowl and celery casserole

SERVES FOUR TO SIX

2 guinea-fowl
Salt and pepper
2 oz (50 g) butter
1 Spanish onion, chopped
1 large head celery, cut into 1-inch (2-cm) lengths, blanched for 1 minute and drained
1 teaspoon thyme
1 teaspoon marjoram
6 rashers streaky bacon
8 fl oz (225 ml) dry white wine
2 teaspoons arrowroot mixed with 4 tablespoons cream

Preheat the oven to 325°F (170°C, Gas Mark 3).

Rub the guinea-fowl all over with the salt and pepper. Melt the butter in a large, heavy flameproof casserole. Put in the guinea-fowl and brown them all over. Lift out the birds and set aside. Add the onion to the pan and fry until it is soft but not browned. Add the celery and herbs. Put the guinea-fowl on top of the celery and lay the bacon on the birds' breasts. Pour in the wine and bring to the boil. Cover the casserole and put it in the oven for 50 to 60 minutes or until the birds are tender.

Remove the casserole from the oven. Transfer the guinea-fowl to a warmed serving dish and keep hot.

Strain the sauce into a saucepan and set over moderate heat. Stir in the arrowroot mixture and cook until the sauce has thickened. Pour the sauce over the guinea-fowl and serve.

Flemish pigeons with prunes and port

SERVES FOUR

1½ oz (40 g) butter
2 pigeons, trussed
8 pickling onions
2 fl oz (50 ml) port wine
¼ pint (150 ml) beef stock
Salt and pepper
12 dried prunes, soaked for 4 hours in lukewarm water and drained
1 teaspoon arrowroot mixed with 1 tablespoon stock

Preheat the oven to 325°F (170°C, Gas Mark 3).

Melt the butter in a flameproof casserole, add the pigeons and brown on all sides. Lift out the pigeons. Add the onions to the pan and cook until golden. Return the pigeons to the pan, pour in the wine and stock and add the seasoning. Cover the casserole and put it in the oven for 30 minutes.

Add the prunes and cook for another 30 minutes or until the pigeons are cooked.

Remove the casserole from the oven. Transfer the pigeons and prunes to a warmed serving dish and keep hot.

Strain the cooking liquid into a saucepan and set over moderate heat. Stir in the arrowroot mixture and cook the sauce until it has thickened. Pour the sauce over the pigeons and serve immediately.

Meat and game

Stewing, casseroling, braising and pot roasting are the best ways of dealing with the tougher cuts of meat, which become tender only if they are cooked very slowly over low heat. The long cooking time also enables the flavours of the meat and the herbs, spices and vegetables that are cooked with it to develop and blend. Stews improve in flavour by being kept for a day or two before eating.

Onions, tomatoes and such root vegetables as carrots and turnips are especially valuable for flavouring meat stews. Peppers are popular in Hungary and okra (ladies' fingers) are often used in Egypt.

Fruit can also complement meat. Apples and dried fruit go into a Danish pot roast of pork and also into the German *sauerbraten*, which is flavoured with cloves and allspice. Fruit and spices are also used in the North African *tajine* and in many Middle Eastern stews.

Tough cuts of meat, and game such as venison, also benefit from being soaked in a marinade for anything from two hours to two days. The marinade is usually made from a mixture of olive oil, wine or vinegar, herbs and spices, and in the Middle East yogurt is often used. Once the meat has been removed the marinade may be strained and added to the stock in which the meat is to be cooked.

Boeuf à la mode

This dish may also be served cold.

SERVES TEN

5 lb ($2\frac{1}{2}$ kg) beef (top rump, or topside), in one piece, boned, larded and tied
Salt and pepper
2 garlic cloves, crushed
3 tablespoons olive oil
3 onions, sliced
2 tablespoons brandy
$\frac{1}{2}$ pint (300 ml) wine
1 calf's foot, blanched
Piece of pork rind about the size of your hand, blanched
Beef stock or water
Bouquet garni
15 small onions
2 lb (900 g) carrots, sliced

Rub the meat with salt, pepper and garlic. Heat the oil in a large, heavy-based casserole and fry the onions until golden. Add the meat and brown it on all sides. Heat the brandy in a ladle, set it alight and pour it over the meat. When the flames die down add the wine, the calf's foot, pork rind and enough stock or water to cover. Season well, add the bouquet garni, cover and simmer over very low heat or in a very slow oven for at least 4 to 5 hours.

Drain the beef, remove and discard the calf's foot, pork rind and bouquet garni. Return the cooking liquid to the pan and carefully skim as much fat as possible off the top. The liquid should be fairly thick; if it is not, reduce it a little by boiling. Return the meat to the pan, add the onions and carrots and simmer for about 20 minutes.

Carbonnade de boeuf à la flamande

SERVES SIX TO EIGHT

3 lb ($1\frac{1}{2}$ kg) beef, chuck or topside
Salt and pepper
3 oz (75 g) dripping or lard
6 small onions, thinly sliced
1 oz (25 g) flour
1 pint (575 ml) dark beer
$\frac{1}{4}$ pint (150 ml) beef stock
1 tablespoon vinegar
1 teaspoon brown sugar
Bouquet garni

Cut the beef into thin slices and season well. Melt the dripping or lard in a large frying-pan. Add the beef, a few slices at a time, and fry quickly over high heat until browned on both sides. Lift out the meat and set aside.

Reduce the heat, add the onions to the frying-pan and fry, stirring, until browned. Using a slotted spoon lift out the onions. Layer the meat and onions in a flameproof casserole.

Stir the flour into the fat in the frying-pan. Pour in the beer and stock and stir and scrape to mix to a smooth sauce. Stir in the vinegar and sugar and season well. Pour the sauce over the meat and onions and put in the bouquet garni.

Cover the casserole and cook gently over low heat or in a 325°F (170°C, Gas Mark 3) oven for $1\frac{1}{2}$ to 2 hours or until the meat is tender. Skim off any excess fat and serve.

Boeuf à la bourguignonne

This is a good dish for the cheaper cuts of beef because the long marinating time makes the meat more tender.

SERVES SIX

3 lb ($1\frac{1}{2}$ kg) beef, topside or chuck
1 oz (25 g) beef dripping or butter
6 oz (175 g) fat bacon, cut into strips $\frac{1}{4}$ inch ($\frac{1}{2}$ cm) thick
12 small onions
1 oz (25 g) flour
$\frac{1}{2}$ pint (300 ml) beef stock
2 garlic cloves
Bouquet garni
1 oz (25 g) butter
12 button mushrooms
1 tablespoon chopped parsley

MARINADE

1 tablespoon olive oil
1 pint (575 ml) red wine or wine and water
1 onion, sliced
1 bay leaf
Salt and pepper

Cut the beef into $1\frac{1}{2}$-inch (3-cm) cubes and put them in a bowl. Mix the ingredients for the marinade together and pour it over the meat. Leave to marinate for at least 6 hours or overnight. Drain the beef and dry the cubes on kitchen paper towels. Strain and reserve the marinade.

Melt the dripping in a large, heavy saucepan. Add the bacon and fry, stirring, until the fat begins to run. Add the small onions and brown them over low heat. Using a slotted spoon remove the onions and bacon from the pan and set aside. Add the beef and brown quickly. Sprinkle the flour over the meat and cook for 2 minutes, stirring. Pour in the marinade and enough stock to cover the meat. Add the garlic and the bouquet garni. Cover the pan and simmer over low heat for 2 to $2\frac{1}{2}$ hours.

Remove the pan from the heat

Two French beef dishes, boeuf à la bourguignonne and boeuf à la mode.

and allow to cool. When the stew is cold skim off the fat.

Melt the butter in a small frying-pan. Add the mushrooms and fry, stirring, until they are lightly coloured. Add the reserved bacon and onions and the mushrooms to the beef. Return the pan to the heat and cook for a further 30 minutes.

Boeuf en daube

This is often served with noodles, boiled, drained and dressed with some of the sauce from the pot and grated cheese. If you are cooking the daube the day before, do not add the olives until the time comes to reheat it. Alternatively, a mixture of finely chopped garlic and parsley, sometimes with anchovies or capers added, is sprinkled on just before serving.

SERVES SIX

3 lb (1½ kg) braising beef
2 tablespoons olive oil
6 oz (175 g) salt pork, diced
4 onions, quartered
4 celery stalks, chopped into 1-inch (2-cm) pieces
4 carrots, sliced
2 garlic cloves, chopped
Bouquet garni
Salt and pepper
½ pint (300 ml) red wine
½ lb (225 g) black olives, pitted

Preheat the oven to 275°F (140°C, Gas Mark 1).

Cut the beef into cubes. Heat the oil in a heavy casserole. Add the salt pork and fry, stirring, until brown. Add the beef and fry, turning the pieces frequently until brown all over. Add the onions, celery, carrots, garlic and bouquet garni. Season, but remember the saltiness of the pork, and pour in the wine. Cover the casserole tightly and put it in the oven for 4 hours or until the meat is very tender.

Thirty minutes before the end of the cooking time skim any excess fat from the top of the daube and add the olives.

Hungarian goulash

SERVES FOUR

1 oz (25 g) butter
2 tablespoons olive oil
2 lb (900 g) stewing steak, cut into cubes
4 medium-sized onions, sliced
4 medium-sized potatoes, sliced
2 garlic cloves, crushed
1 large bay leaf
2 tablespoons paprika
Salt and freshly ground black pepper
4 tablespoons tomato purée
¼ pint (150 ml) beef stock
½ pint (300 ml) soured cream

Melt the butter with the olive oil in a large flameproof casserole. Add the beef and onions and fry them for 6 to 8 minutes, or until they are lightly browned.

Stir in the remaining ingredients and bring to the boil, stirring. Reduce the heat to very low, cover the casserole and cook for 2½ to 3 hours or until the meat is very tender and the onions and potatoes have almost melted away and thickened the liquid.

Meat and game

Pot roast with prunes

SERVES SIX TO EIGHT

4 lb (2 kg) rolled topside of beef
Salt and pepper
2 tablespoons oil
2 garlic cloves, chopped
Thinly pared rind of 1 lemon
$\frac{1}{4}$ pint (150 ml) port
$\frac{1}{2}$ pint (300 ml) beef stock
$\frac{1}{2}$ lb (225 g) prunes, stoned
$\frac{1}{2}$ lb (225 g) pickling onions
Beurre manié made with 1 oz (25 g) butter and 1 oz (25 g) flour

Rub the beef with the salt and pepper. Heat the oil in a casserole and brown the beef on all sides. Add the garlic, lemon rind, port and stock. Cover the casserole tightly and cook over very low heat or in a 300°F (150°C, Gas Mark 2) oven for 2 hours. Soak the prunes in water while the meat is cooking. At the end of the 2 hours, add the prunes and onions. Cover and cook for another 30 minutes or until the meat is tender when pierced with a fork. Transfer the meat to a warmed serving dish, surround with the prunes and onions and keep hot.

Skim as much fat as possible off the top of the cooking liquid and return the pan to the heat. Add the beurre manié a little at a time, stirring constantly until the sauce has thickened. Adjust the seasoning. Strain the sauce into a sauce boat.

Beef olives

Although olives are not included in this recipe they may be added both to the stuffing and to the sauce at the end of the cooking time. Serve beef olives with mashed potatoes.

SERVES FOUR

8 slices lean beef, beaten out thinly, approximately 3 by 4 inches (8 by 10 cm)
$\frac{1}{2}$ oz (15 g) butter
2 streaky bacon rashers, chopped
1 onion, finely chopped
1 carrot, finely diced
1 celery stalk, finely chopped
$\frac{1}{2}$ pint (300 ml) beef stock
1 tablespoon tomato purée
Salt and pepper
Bouquet garni
Beurre manié

STUFFING

$\frac{1}{2}$ oz (15 g) butter
1 bacon rasher, chopped
1 small onion, finely chopped
1 oz (25 g) fresh white breadcrumbs
$\frac{1}{2}$ lb (225 g) minced veal
1 tablespoon chopped mixed herbs
Salt and pepper
2 tablespoons beef stock

First make the stuffing. Melt the butter in a small frying-pan. Add the bacon and onion and fry, stirring, until softened. Combine the remaining ingredients in a bowl. Mix in the bacon and onion.

Lay the meat slices on a board. Spread the stuffing on the meat and roll up, tying the rolls with thread.

Heat the butter in a sauté pan. Add the meat rolls and brown them all over. Lift out the meat and set aside. Add the bacon and vegetables to the pan and fry, stirring, until they are lightly browned. Put the meat rolls on top of the vegetables. Mix the stock with the tomato purée and pour it over the meat. Season to taste, add the bouquet garni and bring to the boil. Cover the pan, reduce the heat to low and simmer the beef olives for $1\frac{1}{2}$ hours or until tender.

Lift out the beef olives, remove the thread, put them in a warm serving dish and keep hot.

Strain the sauce and return it to the pan. If the sauce is too thin add the beurre manié a little at a time, stirring over low heat until it has thickened. Pour the sauce over the beef olives and serve.

Oxtail stew

This is a good stew to make the day before you are going to serve it. Simmer the stew for about 3 hours, then leave it to cool until the next day. Remove all the fat from the top and simmer for another hour.

SERVES FOUR TO SIX

1 oxtail, jointed and soaked for 3 to 4 hours, or overnight, in cold water
2 tablespoons seasoned flour
2 oz (50 g) lard or dripping
2 onions, thinly sliced
2 carrots, thinly sliced
2 celery stalks, thinly sliced
Beef stock or water
Bouquet garni
Salt and pepper
Chopped parsley

Put the oxtail into a large pan of cold water, bring to the boil gradually and then simmer for about 10 minutes, skimming off the scum as it rises. Drain the oxtail pieces, dry well and roll in the seasoned flour.

Melt the lard or dripping in a heavy-bottomed pan and brown the oxtail on all sides. Remove the oxtail and put in the onions, carrots and celery and cook gently, stirring, for a few minutes, then put the oxtail back on top of them. Pour in enough stock or water to come half-way up the meat, add the bouquet garni and season well. Cover the pan tightly, reduce the heat to low and simmer very gently for $3\frac{1}{2}$ to 4 hours or until the meat is very tender. Sprinkle the parsley on top and serve.

Osso bucco (stewed shin of veal)

Traditionally a mixture of finely chopped garlic, parsley and grated lemon rind called a gremolata is sprinkled on top, and the dish is served with saffron-flavoured risotto milanese.

SERVES FOUR

2 oz (50 g) butter
4 pieces veal shin, about 2 inches (5 cm) thick
$\frac{1}{4}$ pint (150 ml) white wine or veal stock
1 lb (450 g) ripe tomatoes, peeled and coarsely chopped
1 garlic clove, crushed
Salt and pepper

GREMOLATA

1 garlic clove, finely chopped
2 tablespoons finely chopped parsley
Finely grated rind of $\frac{1}{2}$ lemon

Melt the butter in a large sauté pan. Add the veal and fry, turning occasionally, until browned. Pour in the wine or stock and simmer for 15 minutes. Add the tomatoes and garlic, season well and continue cooking, with the pan uncovered, until the cooking liquid is reduced a little.

Cover the pan and cook for 1 hour over low heat. Uncover and cook for a further hour. More liquid may be added if necessary.

About 10 minutes before serving, mix together the gremolata ingredients, sprinkle it over the meat and serve.

Blanquette de veau

Serve the blanquette with new potatoes, baby carrots and peas.

SERVES FOUR TO SIX

2-lb (900-g) shoulder or breast of veal, boned and cut into square pieces
Veal stock
1 carrot
1 onion, stuck with 2 cloves
1 celery stick
Bouquet garni
Salt and pepper
3 oz (75 g) butter
12 pickling onions
$\frac{1}{2}$ lb (225 g) mushrooms
1 oz (25 g) flour
2 egg yolks
4 fl oz (125 ml) cream
Grated nutmeg
Lemon juice

Put the veal in a large casserole. Pour in enough stock to cover the meat. Add the carrot, onion, celery and bouquet garni. Season well and bring to the boil. Reduce the heat to low, cover the pan and simmer gently for $1\frac{1}{2}$ hours.

Meanwhile, melt 1 ounce (25 g) of the butter in a small frying-pan. Add the pickling onions and fry them gently, stirring, for 5 minutes. Add the mushrooms and fry, stirring, for 2 minutes. Using a slotted spoon transfer the onions and mushrooms to the casserole 15 minutes before the end of the cooking time.

Lift out the meat, the pickling onions and the mushrooms. Strain and reserve the cooking liquid, discarding the carrot, onion, celery and bouquet garni. Return the meat, pickling onions and mushrooms to the casserole and keep warm and covered.

Melt the remaining butter in a saucepan. Stir in the flour to make a roux. Gradually pour in $\frac{3}{4}$ pint (450 ml) of the cooking liquid, stirring constantly to prevent lumps forming. Bring the sauce to the boil and cook until it thickens slightly. Draw the pan off the heat.

Combine the egg yolks with the cream in a small bowl. Stir in 2 to 3 spoonfuls of the hot sauce. Pour the egg mixture into the sauce, stirring. Add a pinch of nutmeg and a squeeze of lemon juice and adjust the seasoning. Pour the sauce over the meat and vegetables. Return the casserole to low heat. When the blanquette is heated through, serve immediately.

Kidneys braised in red wine

SERVES FOUR

1 oz (25 g) butter
1 tablespoon olive oil
3 veal kidneys
½ oz (15 g) flour
2 slices streaky bacon
2 carrots, diced
1 onion, diced
1 small turnip, diced
Salt and pepper
½ pint (300 ml) red wine
Bouquet garni
½ lb (225 g) mushrooms
2 tomatoes, peeled, seeded and coarsely chopped
1 tablespoon chopped fresh parsley

Preheat the oven to 325°F (170°C, Gas Mark 3).

Heat the butter and the oil in a sauté pan. Add the kidneys and sauté them, turning them over to cook on both sides. Add the flour and let it brown.

Put the bacon in an earthenware casserole, cover with the mixed vegetables and season well. Remove the kidneys from the sauté pan and put them on top of the vegetables. Add the wine to the sauté pan and bring it to the boil, stirring in any residue in the pan. Pour it over the kidneys, add the bouquet garni and bake for 30 minutes. Stir in the mushrooms and tomatoes. Cook for another 10 minutes.

Using a slotted spoon, lift out the kidneys and mushrooms. Strain the sauce, pushing the vegetables through the sieve into a saucepan, or blend in a liquidizer for a few minutes. Adjust the seasoning, return the kidneys and mushrooms to the sauce, reheat for 5 minutes and serve sprinkled with parsley.

Red-cooked hand of pork

This Chinese dish from the Shanghai area uses soy sauce to darken the food and give it its characteristic colour. Serve the pork with plain, boiled rice.

SERVES TWELVE

6-lb (3-kg) hand of pork, boned, rolled and tied
1 onion, sliced
8 tablespoons soy sauce
8 tablespoons red wine
1 tablespoon chopped root ginger
3 tablespoons sugar
2 tablespoons oil
2 teaspoons cornflour mixed with 2 tablespoons cold water

Preheat the oven to 350°F (180°C, Gas Mark 4).

Put the pork in a large casserole, pour in enough boiling water to cover the meat and bring back to the boil. Reduce the heat, cover the pan and simmer gently for about 20 minutes.

Remove the pan from the heat, lift out the meat and set aside. Pour away all but 1 pint (575 ml) of the cooking liquid and skim off all the fat and scum. Return the meat to the pan with all the remaining ingredients except the cornflour. Cover the casserole and put it in the oven for 3 to 4 hours, turning the meat every 30 minutes.

To serve, lift the pork out and cut it into serving pieces. Put it on a heated serving dish and keep warm. Stir the cornflour mixture into the sauce and simmer for 1 minute. Strain the sauce over the meat and serve at once.

Cassoulet

This excellent winter dish improves on reheating. There are many versions of it, depending on what is to hand; in the recipe given here, quantities and indeed ingredients (apart from the beans) are not critical. Preserved goose (*confit d'oie*) is sold, tinned, in many delicatessens.

SERVES EIGHT

2 lb (900 g) dried white haricot beans, soaked overnight and drained
2 onions, sliced
½ lb (225 g) salt pork, cubed
4 garlic cloves, crushed
Salt and pepper

Bouquet garni
1 quart (1 litre) veal stock or water
2 to 3 oz (450 g) dripping
Wing and leg of preserved goose (*confit d'oie*) or 1½-lb (700-g) boned shoulder of lamb, cubed
1-lb (450-g) boned shoulder of pork, cubed
1 lb (450 g) garlic sausage, thickly sliced
Toasted breadcrumbs

Place the beans in a large saucepan with the onions, salt pork, garlic, seasoning and bouquet garni. Pour in the stock or water, adding more if necessary to cover the ingredients, and bring to the boil. Cover the pan, reduce the heat and simmer gently for 1 hour. Remove the pan from the heat and drain. Discard the bouquet garni and reserve the liquid.

Preheat the oven to 300°F (150°C, Gas Mark 2).

Meanwhile, melt the dripping in a large pan and brown the goose or lamb and the pork. Put a layer of the beans in an earthenware casserole, then the goose or lamb, the pork and the garlic sausage. Cover with the rest of the beans. Pour in ½ pint (300 ml) of the reserved liquid, spread a layer of breadcrumbs on top and put the casserole into the oven for at least 1½ hours. More liquid can be added as necessary during the cooking time, and the crust that forms on top is usually pushed down and stirred into the mixture and more toasted breadcrumbs spread on top, a process which can be repeated several times. In the finished dish most of the liquid should have been absorbed, leaving the meat and beans succulent but not swimming in liquid.

Lancashire hot-pot

Irish stew is similar to this and uses the same ingredients, but Lancashire hot-pot is more succulent, with very little stewing liquid. Traditionally a deep, straight-sided pot is used. Mutton is the meat, which should be used for this dish, but if it is not available use lamb.

SERVES SIX

3 lb (1½ kg) best end of neck of mutton, cut into cubes
Salt and pepper
2 to 3 lb (900 g to 1½ kg) potatoes, sliced into rounds ⅛ inch (½ cm) thick
1 lb (450 g) onions, sliced
½ pint (300 ml) beef stock

Preheat the oven to 325°F (170°C, Gas Mark 3).

Fill an earthenware dish with well-seasoned layers of meat,

onion and potato in that order, finishing with a layer of potatoes neatly arranged in overlapping slices. Pour in the stock. Cover the dish and cook for 2½ to 3 hours.

Navarin printanier

This is a spring stew, made with fresh young vegetables. If you use mutton instead of lamb double the cooking time of the meat.

SERVES SIX

6 tablespoons dripping
3-lb (1½-kg) shoulder or breast of lamb, cut into 1½-inch (3-cm) cubes
2 tablespoons flour
1 garlic clove, crushed
1 pint (575 ml) veal stock or water
1 teaspoon tomato purée, mixed with 1 tablespoon water
Salt and pepper
Bouquet garni
20 pickling onions
1 lb (450 g) young carrots, cut into rounds
3 small turnips, cubed
Pinch of sugar
1 lb (450 g) new potatoes
2 lb (900 g) young French beans, sliced
1 lb (450 g) early peas, shelled
Chopped parsley

Melt 4 tablespoons of the dripping in a large sauté pan. When the fat is very hot add the meat and brown it, turning the pieces, over high heat. Pour off most of the fat, reduce the heat, sprinkle the flour over the meat and let it brown, stirring constantly. Stir in the garlic, stock or water, tomato purée, seasoning and bouquet garni. Cover the pan and simmer for 45 to 60 minutes.

Meanwhile, melt the remaining dripping in another pan. Add the onions, carrots, turnips and sugar and fry, turning the vegetables over frequently, until they are well browned.

Add the potatoes to the meat and cook for 10 minutes. Add the onions, carrots and turnips and simmer for 5 minutes. Add the beans and peas and simmer for a final 10 minutes or until all the vegetables are cooked and the meat meltingly tender.

If necessary skim the fat off the top of the stew. Sprinkle the parsley on top and serve.

Jugged hare with forcemeat balls

In this traditional English dish blood is used to thicken the sauce. If you prefer not to use the blood, a little extra beurre manié can be used instead. The stew takes a long time to make, but is well worth the effort. It improves with keeping and can be reheated the next day. Make the forcemeat balls on the day the stew is to be eaten.

SERVES SIX

1 hare, cut into serving pieces, the blood reserved
2 oz (50 g) seasoned flour
2 oz (50 g) dripping
2 large onions, chopped
2 carrots, sliced
2 celery stalks, sliced
Sprig rosemary
2 to 3 sprigs thyme
1 teaspoon allspice
Strip of lemon rind
Salt and pepper
1 to 2 oz (25 to 50 g) beurre manié
1 tablespoon redcurrant jelly
3 fl oz (75 ml) port or red wine

MARINADE

½ pint (300 ml) red wine
1 tablespoon oil
1 onion, coarsely chopped
1 bay leaf
1 thyme sprig
6 juniper berries, crushed
Salt and pepper

FORCEMEAT BALLS

2 oz (50 g) bacon, finely diced
1 onion, finely chopped
3 oz (75 g) fresh white breadcrumbs
2 tablespoons chopped suet
1 tablespoon chopped parsley
1 tablespoon fresh marjoram or 2 teaspoons dried marjoram
Salt and pepper
1 egg plus 1 egg yolk, beaten
Oil for frying

Mix together the marinade ingredients. Put the pieces of hare in a large, shallow dish, pour over the marinade and leave for at least 6 hours, turning from time to time.

Three warming meat stews: from left to right, Lancashire hot-pot, cassoulet and goulash.

Preheat the oven to 325°F (170°C, Gas Mark 3).

Remove the hare from the marinade. Strain and reserve the marinade. Dry the hare with a cloth and roll in the seasoned flour.

Melt the dripping in a heavy casserole and brown the pieces of hare on all sides. Add the onions, carrots and celery, cook for 1 to 2 minutes, then pour over the marinade and just enough water to cover the meat. Add the herbs, allspice and lemon rind, and season well. Cover the casserole tightly and put it in the oven for 3½ to 4 hours.

Remove the casserole from the oven. Lift out the pieces of hare. Strain the cooking liquid into a saucepan and return the hare to the casserole.

Remove and discard the herbs and rub the vegetables through a sieve into the saucepan. Add the beurre manié a little at a time, stirring constantly, and bring to the boil. Draw the pan off the heat and gradually add some of this hot gravy to the reserved blood, mixing well, then pour it back into the pan, still mixing. Stir in the redcurrant jelly and port or red wine. Strain the sauce on to the hare and reheat gently.

While the hare is reheating, make the forcemeat balls. Cook the bacon and the onion together in a saucepan until soft. Combine the breadcrumbs, suet, herbs and seasoning in a bowl. Add the bacon and onion and mix well. Add enough of the beaten egg to bind the ingredients together. Shape into balls the size of a walnut. Fry until golden. Serve with the hare.

Rabbit stew

This stew can also be made with hare; use red wine instead of white and cook gently for at least 3½ to 4 hours.

SERVES FOUR

4-lb (2-kg) rabbit, cut into pieces
2 tablespoons seasoned flour
2 oz (50 g) butter
½ pint (300 ml) chicken stock
¼ pint (150 ml) white wine
2 teaspoons tomato purée mixed with 1 tablespoon water
1 garlic clove, crushed
Bouquet garni
Salt and pepper
2 tablespoons double cream mixed with 2 teaspoons cornflour
1 tablespoon chopped parsley

Coat the rabbit pieces with the flour. Heat the butter in a heavy casserole. Add the rabbit pieces and fry until brown on all sides.

Pour in the stock, wine and tomato purée. Add the garlic, bouquet garni, season to taste and bring to the boil. Reduce the heat to low, cover the casserole and cook gently (or place in a 325°F/170°C, Gas Mark 3 oven) for 1½ to 2 hours, or until the rabbit is tender. Transfer the rabbit to a warmed serving dish and keep hot.

Stir the cream into the cooking liquid and simmer for a few seconds until the sauce thickens. Remove the bouquet garni. Pour the sauce over the rabbit. Sprinkle the parsley on top and serve.

Braised venison with juniper berries and soured cream

SERVES SIX

3 lb (1½ kg) boned shoulder of venison cut into 2-inch (5-cm) cubes
2 oz (50 g) seasoned flour
3 oz (75 g) butter
4 onions, sliced
2 tablespoons redcurrant jelly
12 chestnuts peeled and boiled until tender
2 teaspoons lemon juice
¼ pint (150 ml) soured cream, or single cream
Salt and pepper

MARINADE

¾ pint (450 ml) red wine
2 tablespoons olive oil
10 juniper berries, crushed
Salt and pepper
1 onion, sliced
Bouquet garni

Preheat the oven to 325°F (170°C, Gas Mark 3).

Put the ingredients for the marinade into a saucepan, bring to the boil, simmer for 20 minutes and allow to cool.

Put the venison into a deep earthenware bowl. When the marinade is quite cold pour it over the venison. Cover the bowl and leave the venison to marinate in a cool place for 2 days. Turn and baste the meat at least twice a day.

Preheat the oven to 325°F (170°C, Gas Mark 3).

Drain the meat, dry it, and roll in seasoned flour. Strain and reserve the marinade.

Melt the butter in a heavy casserole. Add the venison and fry, stirring, until browned on all sides. Add the onions and let them brown. Stir in any remaining seasoned flour, let it brown and gradually mix in the reserved marinade, stirring constantly. Cover the casserole and cook in the oven for 2 hours. Stir in the redcurrant jelly, chestnuts and lemon juice and cook for a further 15 minutes. Stir in the soured cream, adjust the seasoning and serve.

Vegetables

Stewing, braising and casseroling can improve and transform the flavour of many vegetables. Those that have a somewhat bland flavour when simply boiled or steamed are given additional taste and texture by combining them with other, contrasting vegetables. Such dishes as ratatouille, which is a superb stew made with tomatoes, aubergines, peppers and onions, or a mushroom and herb casserole can be served by themselves as a main course.

Strictly speaking, fruits should not be stewed as their qualities are most enhanced by gentle poaching. For the general treatment of fruits in liquid, and for purées, see the section on boiling and steaming.

Braised lettuce

This is a good dish to make in late summer when there is a glut of lettuces. Serve as an accompaniment to roast or grilled meat.

SERVES FOUR TO SIX

4 cos lettuces
½ oz (15 g) butter
¼ lb (125 g) streaky bacon, cut into strips
1 onion, chopped
1 carrot, chopped
¼ pint (150 ml) chicken or veal stock, hot
Salt and pepper
Bouquet garni

Preheat the oven to 350°F (180°C, Gas Mark 4).

Keep the lettuces whole, wash them well and trim the base as neatly as possible without detaching any leaves.

Blanch the lettuces in boiling salted water for 5 minutes. Drain them and put into a basin of cold water at once. Drain again, squeezing the lettuces to remove any excess moisture.

Rub the butter all round a large flameproof casserole. Line the bottom of the casserole with the bacon. Cover the bacon with the onion and carrot and lay the lettuces on top. Pour in the stock, season well and add the bouquet garni.

Lay a piece of buttered greaseproof paper on top of the lettuces, cover the casserole and put it in the oven for 45 minutes.

Lift out the lettuces, arrange them in a warmed serving dish and keep warm. Put the casserole over high heat and boil the cooking liquid for 5 to 10 minutes or until it is well reduced. Strain the liquid over the lettuces and serve.

Chestnuts with Chinese cabbage

SERVES FOUR TO SIX

5 tablespoons oil
2 tablespoons dried shrimps
½-inch (1-cm) piece fresh root ginger, peeled and finely chopped
1 lb (450 g) chestnuts, peeled, skinned and boiled for 25 minutes
4 medium-sized dried Chinese mushrooms, soaked for 30 minutes, drained, stalks removed and caps quartered
1½ lb (700 g) Chinese cabbage, washed, drained and coarsely chopped
¼ pint (150 ml) chicken stock
4 tablespoons soy sauce
2 tablespoons dry sherry
1½ tablespoons castor sugar

Heat the oil in a large sauté pan. Add the shrimps, ginger, chestnuts and mushrooms and stir over moderate heat for 2 minutes. Add the cabbage and cook, stirring, for 1 minute.

Pour in the stock, soy sauce and sherry. Add the sugar and cook over low heat for 20 to 25 minutes, stirring frequently.

Red cabbage with apples

SERVES FOUR

2 oz (50 g) salt pork, diced
2 onions, thinly sliced
2 lb (900 g) red cabbage, finely shredded
¼ pint (150 ml) cider
Salt and freshly ground black pepper
1 tablespoon soft brown sugar
3 cooking apples, peeled, cored and sliced

Sauté the salt pork in a large casserole until the fat runs. Add the onions and fry, stirring, until they are soft. Add the cabbage, cider, salt, pepper and sugar. Stir well, cover the pan and simmer for 1 hour. Stir in the apples and cook for another hour.

Casseroled celery

SERVES FOUR

2 heads celery, trimmed and cut into short lengths
2 oz (50 g) butter
¼ pint (150 ml) chicken or vegetable stock
Salt and pepper

Blanch the celery in boiling salted water for 5 minutes and drain.

Melt the butter in a heavy casserole, add the celery and cook, turning the pieces over, until they are lightly browned. Pour in the stock, season to taste and simmer for 1 to 1½ hours or until the celery is tender.

Buttered chicory

SERVES FOUR

1½ lb (700 g) chicory
Sugar
2 oz (50 g) butter
2 tablespoons water
Juice of ½ lemon
½ teaspoon salt

Drop the chicory into boiling water to which a little sugar has been added, blanch for 5 minutes and drain.

Melt the butter in a heavy pan and add the chicory. Cook for 3 minutes over low heat.

Add the water, lemon juice and salt and bring to a simmer. Cook, covered, over very low heat for 1 hour.

Braised onions

SERVES FOUR

2 lb (900 g) medium-sized onions, peeled
Salt
¼ lb (125 g) butter or 3 oz (75 g) bacon fat
2 oz (50 g) castor sugar
Pepper
Chicken or veal stock

Preheat the oven to 350°F (180°C, Gas Mark 4).

Parboil the onions in boiling salted water for 15 minutes.

Melt the butter or bacon fat in a heavy casserole. Add the onions and the sugar and cook over low heat, turning the onions occasionally, for 5 to 10 minutes. Season well and put the casserole in the oven for 1 hour or until the onions are tender and a rich gold colour. Baste from time to time, and if the onions get too dry pour in a little stock.

Leeks provençal

This dish may be served hot, or cold as a first course or salad.

SERVES FOUR TO SIX

4 tablespoons olive oil
2 lb (900 g) leeks, washed and cut into short lengths
1 green pepper, cored, seeded and thinly sliced
1 lb (450 g) tomatoes, skinned and quartered
12 large black olives, halved and pitted
Juice and rind of 1 lemon
Salt and pepper

Heat the oil in a large sauté pan. Add the leeks and stir well. Cover the pan, reduce the heat to low and cook gently for 10 minutes, stirring occasionally.

Add the pepper, tomatoes, olives, lemon rind and juice, salt and pepper. Cover the pan and cook for 15 minutes. Remove the lemon peel and serve.

Sauerkraut
You can make your own sauerkraut or buy it in jars or cans. If you buy it see that it is pickled in brine and not in vinegar.

SERVES FOUR

1 lb (450 g) sauerkraut
¼ lb (125 g) streaky bacon, chopped
1 carrot, quartered
1 onion, cut in half
Bouquet garni
Salt and pepper
Chicken or veal stock

Boil the sauerkraut in salted water for 10 minutes and drain well.

Heat the bacon in a heavy pan until the fat runs. Add the sauerkraut, carrot, onion, bouquet garni and season with salt and pepper. Pour in enough stock to cover the cabbage and bring to the boil. Reduce the heat, cover the pan and simmer gently on top of the stove or in a 300°F (150°C, Gas Mark 2) oven for 1 hour.

Remove the pan from the heat or oven and drain the sauerkraut. Discard the carrot, onion and bouquet garni and serve.

Mushroom and herb casserole
If fresh herbs are available use them in preference to dried ones, but double the quantities.

SERVES FOUR

1 oz (25 g) butter
¼ lb (100 g) streaky bacon, cut into pieces
1 garlic clove, crushed
¼ teaspoon thyme
¼ teaspoon oregano
¼ teaspoon basil
¼ teaspoon rosemary
¾ teaspoon paprika
1½ lb (700 g) mushrooms
Salt and black pepper
6 fl oz (175 ml) tomato sauce, hot
¼ lb (100 g) grated Parmesan cheese

Preheat the oven to 375°F (190°C, Gas Mark 5).

Melt the butter in a wide, heavy casserole. Add the bacon and fry, stirring, until the fat runs. Add the garlic, herbs and paprika, reduce the heat and cook for 2 minutes. Add the mushrooms and cook for 3 minutes, stirring. Season well.

Pour the tomato sauce over the mushrooms. Sprinkle the Parmesan cheese on top and cook on the top shelf of the oven for 10 minutes or until the top is slightly browned and bubbling.

Ratatouille
Ratatouille may be eaten either hot—as an accompaniment to other dishes—or cold, in smaller quantities, as an hors d'oeuvre.

SERVES FOUR

5 tablespoons olive oil
3 onions, thinly sliced
2 garlic cloves, chopped
2 green peppers, seeded and sliced into thin strips
1 red pepper, seeded and sliced into thin strips
3 medium-sized aubergines, degorged
4 courgettes, sliced
4 large tomatoes (or ½ lb/ 225 g canned tomatoes), skinned and chopped
Salt and freshly ground black pepper
¼ teaspoon each fresh or dried rosemary, thyme and basil

Heat the oil over low heat in a heavy casserole. Add the onions and garlic and cook for 5 minutes or until they are soft but not brown. Add the peppers, aubergines and courgettes, stir well and cook over very low heat for at least 30 minutes, stirring from time to time.

Add the tomatoes and season well with salt and black pepper. Add the herbs and cook for a further 30 minutes on low heat.

Stuffed peppers
Serve the peppers hot or cold, as an hors d'oeuvre or main dish.

SERVES FOUR

4 large or 8 small peppers
1 lb (450 g) lean minced beef
Grated rind and juice of 1 lemon
¼ lb (100 g) long-grain rice, washed and drained
1 teaspoon dried mint
1 teaspoon turmeric
1 teaspoon salt
1 teaspoon sugar
Cayenne pepper
2 tablespoons olive oil
2 tablespoons tomato purée, mixed in 8 fl oz (225 ml) water

Cut the tops off the peppers and remove the seeds and pith. Reserve the tops.

Put the minced beef, lemon rind and juice, rice, mint, turmeric, salt, sugar and a pinch of cayenne in a bowl and mix well. Stuff the peppers with the mixture.

Heat the oil in a saucepan just large enough to hold the peppers. Put the peppers in the pan, spoon a little of the tomato purée mixture on top of each pepper and cover them with the reserved tops. Pour the remaining tomato purée mixture around the peppers, reduce the heat, cover the pan and cook gently for 40 to 50 minutes or until the peppers are tender and the rice cooked.

Peperonata
This Italian dish may be served hot or cold, on its own or with meat and poultry.

SERVES SIX

4 tablespoons olive oil
1 large Spanish onion, thinly sliced
2 garlic cloves, crushed
1½ lb (700 g) red peppers, cored, seeded and cut into strips
2 lb (900 g) ripe tomatoes, skinned and chopped
Salt

Heat the oil in a sauté pan. Add the onion and garlic and fry until the onion is soft and lightly coloured. Add the peppers, cover the pan and cook gently for 20 minutes, stirring occasionally.

Add the tomatoes, season to taste with salt and cook, uncovered, for 30 minutes or until the tomatoes are cooked to a pulp.

Caponata
This Sicilian dish is traditionally served piled up on a platter with slices of crawfish or canned tuna fish arranged on top.

SERVES FOUR TO SIX

Olive oil
2 lb (900 g) aubergines, diced and degorged
1 head celery, stalks cut into small pieces
1 large onion, sliced
8 tablespoons tomato purée, mixed with 4 tablespoons water
1 tablespoon sugar
2 tablespoons capers
3 oz (75 g) black olives, pitted and quartered
6 anchovies, soaked in warm water for 15 minutes, drained and chopped
¼ pint (150 ml) wine vinegar
Salt and pepper

Heat some oil—the amount of oil is difficult to estimate as aubergine tends to absorb it rapidly—in a large frying-pan and fry the aubergines gently, turning them until they are browned all over. Using a slotted spoon lift them out and drain.

Put the celery in boiling water and blanch for 1 minute.

Heat 4 tablespoons of oil in a large saucepan. Add the onion and fry until soft. Stir in the tomato purée and sugar and cook, stirring, for 15 minutes or until the mixture is reduced and dark.

Add the celery, aubergines, capers, olives, anchovies and vinegar. Season if necessary, and simmer for 10 minutes.

Cereals

Cereals, because of their absorbent qualities and their relatively neutral flavour, are an ideal base for a stew or casserole containing several other more distinctive ingredients. The cereals most commonly used are rice, barley, cracked wheat, hominy (coarsely ground maize) and kasha (coarsely ground buckwheat, millet or barley).

There are several methods of casseroling cereals, but two in particular will serve for most purposes. Either add the cereal and the liquid after the other main ingredients and the flavourings have been cooked gently in butter or oil, or cook the cereal first in butter or oil with a little onion and garlic and a few spices before adding the rest of the ingredients and the cooking liquid.

Contrasting textures add interest to cereal-based stews and casseroles; for example, olives nuts, chopped peppers or dried fruit.

Creole jambalaya

This is an adaptation of a jambalaya from Louisiana. The dish was probably introduced to New Orleans by early Spanish explorers.

SERVES FOUR

6 tablespoons olive oil
1 large onion, chopped
2 garlic cloves, crushed
1 large green pepper, seeded and chopped
½ lb (225 g) long-grain rice, washed, soaked in cold water for 30 minutes and well drained
¾ lb (350 g) cooked ham, diced
1½ lb (700 g) tomatoes, skinned and chopped
½ pint (300 ml) water
½ teaspoon dried thyme
2 tablespoons chopped parsley
Salt and pepper
½ to 1 teaspoon cayenne pepper
¾ lb (350 g) peeled shrimps or prawns

Heat the oil in a large sauté pan. Add the onion, garlic and green pepper and fry, stirring, until the onion is golden. Add the rice and fry, stirring constantly, for 3 minutes. Stir in the ham, tomatoes, water, thyme, parsley, salt, pepper and cayenne and bring to the boil.

Cover the pan tightly, reduce the heat to low and simmer for 30 minutes or until the rice is tender and most of the liquid has been absorbed. Stir in the shrimps or prawns 5 minutes before the end of the cooking time.

Risotto alla Milanese

Good Italian rice such as Arborio or Vialone is the most suitable for making risotto. Risotto alla Milanese is served on its own or with Osso bucco.

SERVES FOUR

2 oz (50 g) butter
1 small onion, peeled and chopped
1 oz (25 g) beef marrow (optional)
¾ lb (350 g) Italian rice
¼ pint (150 ml) white wine
1 quart (1 litre) chicken stock, boiling
4 saffron threads, soaked in 2 tablespoons hot chicken stock for 10 minutes
1 oz (25 g) Parmesan cheese, grated

Melt half the butter in a large pan and cook the onion until it is golden. Stir in the bone marrow, if you are using it, and the rice and fry for 2 minutes. Add the wine, reduce the heat to low and cook until it has been absorbed. Add the hot stock, a cupful at a time, waiting until one cup has been absorbed before adding the next. After half the stock has been absorbed, check to see if the rice is cooked. If the rice is not tender, add another cupful of stock and check the rice again when it has been absorbed. It will take between 20 and 30 minutes for all the stock to be used. As the end of the cooking time is reached, stir the rice continuously with a fork to prevent sticking. When the rice is cooked mix in the saffron mixture, the remaining butter and the cheese and serve.

Burghul pilaff

SERVES FOUR

¼ lb (125 g) butter
1 onion, chopped
½ lb (225 g) cracked wheat (burghul), washed and drained
½ lb (225 g) mushrooms, cleaned and sliced
1 pint (575 ml) chicken stock
Salt and pepper

Melt the butter in a saucepan. Add the onion and cook gently until it is soft. Stir in the cracked wheat and the mushrooms, increase the heat and cook for about 5 minutes, stirring frequently. Add the chicken stock and seasoning and bring to the boil. Cook rapidly for about 5 minutes, then lower the heat and simmer for 10 minutes or until the liquid has been absorbed. Remove from the heat. Place a clean cloth over the pan, cover with a lid, then leave for about 15 minutes before serving.

Tomato rice

SERVES SIX TO EIGHT

1 onion, chopped
1 garlic clove, chopped
1 lb (450 g) tomatoes, blanched, peeled and chopped
2 fl oz (50 ml) vegetable oil
¾ lb (350 g) long-grain rice, washed, soaked in cold water for 30 minutes and drained
1½ pints (900 ml) chicken stock
Salt
Cayenne pepper

Put the onion, garlic and tomatoes in a liquidizer and reduce to a purée.

Heat the oil in a heavy pan. Add the rice and cook, stirring, over low heat until the oil has been absorbed, taking care that the rice does not burn. Add the tomato and onion purée and the stock. Season to taste with salt and a large pinch of cayenne and bring to the boil. Cover the pan and cook, over the lowest possible heat, for about 25 minutes or until the rice is tender.

Paella Valenciana

Paella may include both meat and seafood, seafood only, or simply vegetables.

Paella can be served with a green or mixed salad.

SERVES FOUR TO SIX

2 fl oz (50 g) olive oil
3 garlic cloves, halved
1 onion, chopped
3 tomatoes, blanched, peeled and chopped
1 sweet red pepper, seeded and sliced
1 chicken, cut into serving pieces
1 teaspoon paprika
¾ lb (350 g) rice
¼ teaspoon powdered saffron
1½ pints (900 ml) chicken stock
1 lb (450 g) peas, podded
½ lb (225 g) peeled shrimps
1 pint (575 ml) mussels, cleaned

Heat the oil in a large, shallow sauté pan. Add the garlic and cook gently for 2 to 3 minutes to flavour the oil. Remove and discard the garlic.

Add the onion, tomatoes, red pepper, chicken pieces and paprika. Cook for 10 minutes, stirring frequently.

Add the rice and cook for 2 to 3 minutes more, stirring constantly. Stir in the saffron, pour in the stock and bring to the boil. Add the peas and shrimps and cook, uncovered, over low heat for 15 minutes, or until almost all the liquid has been absorbed.

Place the mussels on top of the rice. Cover the pan and cook for 6 to 8 minutes until the mussels open. Discard any that remain closed. Serve hot.

Biryani

Of central Asian origin, Biryani is a favourite dish in Pakistan. Serve it with a yogurt and cucumber salad, various chutneys and relishes.

SERVES FOUR TO SIX

5 oz (150 g) butter
2 onions, finely chopped, plus 1 onion, finely sliced
1-inch (2-cm) piece fresh root ginger, peeled and finely chopped
4 garlic cloves, crushed
1 green chilli, finely chopped
2 teaspoons cumin seeds
2 lb (900 g) boned leg or shoulder of lamb, cut into cubes
1-inch (2-cm) piece cinnamon stick
6 cloves
6 whole cardamom pods
½ pint (300 ml) yogurt, mixed with ¼ pint (150 ml) water
Salt
¾ lb (350 g) basmati rice, washed and soaked in water for 30 minutes
½ teaspoon saffron threads, soaked in 3 tablespoons boiling water for 20 minutes
1 oz (25 g) flaked, blanched almonds
1 oz (25 g) raisins
2 hard-boiled eggs, quartered

Melt 2 ounces (50 g) of the butter in a large saucepan. Add the finely chopped onions, ginger, garlic, chilli and cumin seeds and fry, stirring frequently, over moderately low heat until the onions are soft.

Add the lamb, increase the heat and fry, turning the cubes over, for 10 minutes or until they are well browned. Add the cinnamon, cloves, cardamom, the yogurt and water mixture and 1 teaspoon of salt and bring to the boil. Cover the pan, reduce the heat to low and simmer for 30 minutes or until the lamb is nearly cooked.

Preheat the oven to 350°F (180°C, Gas Mark 4).

Meanwhile, cook the rice in plenty of boiling salted water for 2 minutes. Remove the pan from the heat and drain the rice.

Melt 2 ounces (50 g) of the remaining butter in a casserole.

Paella Valenciana and barley and vegetable casserole.

Spread one-third of the rice over the bottom of the casserole, sprinkle with 1 tablespoon of the saffron water and spoon half the lamb mixture over the rice. Repeat the layers ending with the rice and saffron.

Cover the casserole and put it in the oven for 40 minutes or until the rice is cooked.

Meanwhile, prepare the garnish. Heat the remaining butter in a small frying-pan and fry the sliced onion, stirring frequently, until it is golden brown. Using a slotted spoon, remove the onion and drain on kitchen paper towels.

Add the almonds and raisins to the frying-pan and fry, stirring, until lightly browned.

Remove the casserole from the oven and garnish with the fried onions, almonds, raisins and hard-boiled eggs.

Barley and vegetable casserole

Serve this dish with roast meat or poultry, or on its own.

SERVES FOUR

3 oz (75 g) butter
1 large onion, finely chopped
4 celery stalks, chopped
¼ lb (125 g) turnips, diced
½ lb (225 g) carrots, sliced
¼ lb (125 g) pearl barley
¾ pint (450 ml) chicken stock, boiling
1½ teaspoons salt
Black pepper
½ teaspoon thyme
1 tablespoon chopped parsley

Preheat the oven to 350°F (180°C, Gas Mark 4). Melt the butter in a large frying-pan. Add the onion and fry gently, stirring occasionally, until it is soft and golden. Add the celery, turnips and carrots and cook for 10 minutes, stirring to coat with the butter.

Stir in the barley. Remove the pan from the heat and spoon the mixture into a well-buttered casserole. Pour in the stock, season well with salt and black pepper and add the thyme.

Cover the casserole and put it in the oven for 45 to 60 minutes or until the barley is tender and all the stock has been absorbed.

Serve garnished with the parsley.

Grilling

Grilling is a quick, efficient way of cooking meat, poultry, young game birds, fish, cheese and some fruit and vegetables. One of the main advantages of this method is that little fat, and usually no liquid, is used, but the disadvantages are that only good-quality, and therefore expensive, cuts of meat are required, and the cooking must be done only minutes before the food is put on the table.

Barbecuing is closely related to grilling, so the food is usually prepared and cooked in exactly the same way, but with different utensils, and using a different source of heat (coals, charcoal or wood).

Preheat the grill before you start cooking. The grill rack or skewers on which the food is to be cooked should be brushed with fat or oil to prevent sticking, and if a rotisserie is to be used for meat, make sure that you put the spit through the centre of the joint or bird to ensure that it turns easily and cooks evenly.

The cuts of meat that are most suitable for grilling are steaks (including gammon steaks), chops, cutlets or bacon rashers. Shoulder or leg of lamb and leg and fillets of pork may be cut into cubes and used for kebabs, and whole legs may be spit-roasted. Sausages and such offal as kidney and liver are often included in a mixed grill. Large kidneys should be cut in half and skewered to keep them flat.

Game is hardly ever grilled or barbecued, but young, tender game birds or poultry can be cooked this way very successfully. Small birds, for example quail, may be cooked whole if they are split down the backbone and spread out flat. Larger birds may be cut in half or jointed.

All meat, poultry and game birds may be marinated in a mixture of oil, herbs and spices before being grilled. This not only ensures that the meat will be tender but adds to the flavour.

Fish and shellfish may also be marinated before being grilled. Shellfish and small fish, such as mackerel, whiting, sole, herring or mullet may be cooked whole, but cut larger fish into steaks or cutlets. Firm-fleshed fish are the most suitable for kebabs: use cod, halibut or haddock cut into cubes.

Mushrooms, tomatoes, aubergines, onions and peppers may all be grilled, and they are often added to meat or fish kebabs.

Grilled grapefruit is a popular first course, but there are other fruit that can be grilled—pear or peach halves, slices of pineapple or bananas, for example. They may be served as an accompaniment to meat, game or poultry, or by themselves as a first course or dessert. Bananas may also be cut into chunks and wrapped in slices of streaky bacon before being grilled.

Fish and shellfish

Mussels with parsley butter 128

Grilled oysters 128

Oyster on skewers 128

Haddock kebabs 127
Boiled fennel 92, Deep-fried parsley 153

Red mullet with dill butter 127
Asparagus 92, Sauté potatoes 151

Sea bass with herbs flambé 127
Chicory, orange and watercress salad 213, Potato croquettes 151

Grilled halibut steaks with orange sauce 127
Petits pois à la française 91, Soufflé potatoes 150

Grilled salmon steaks 127
Sauce hollandaise 67, Grilled mushrooms 134, Courgettes 93

Grilled lobster 127
Sauce hollandaise 67, Lyonnaise potatoes 151, Asparagus 92

Lobster thermidor 128
Avocado salad 213

Scallop brochettes 128
Green salad 213, Boiled rice 97

Seafood en brochettes 128
Boiled rice or noodles 97, Ratatouille 121

Herrings with mustard sauce 126
Potato croquettes 151, Steamed broccoli 92

Devilled herrings 126
Spinach purée 92, Green salad 213

Cod rarebit 127

Clams with Gruyère sauce 128
Green salad 213

Poultry and game birds

Grilled chicken livers 130

Chicken brochettes 130

Poussins with lemon butter 130
Boiled potatoes, peas 93

Spatchcock chicken 130 Mashed potatoes, Mange-tout peas 93, Sauté potatoes 151, Chestnuts with Chinese cabbage 120

Devilled turkey legs 130
Green salad 213, Boiled rice 97

Grilled partridge à la diable 130
Spinach purée 92, Courgettes 93, Potato straws 150

Grilled quail with orange and sage sauce 131
Green salad 213, Game chips 150

Meat and game

Pork saté 133

Lebanese kebabs 132

Minute steaks 132
Potato straws 150, Petit pois à la française 91

Tournedos Rossini 132
Green salad 213

Hamburgers 132
Tomato sauce 69, Potato chips 150,

Grilled pork chops 133
Sauté potatoes 151, Spinach purée 92

Gammon steaks with apricots 133
Mashed potatoes 93, Braised lettuce 120, Broad beans 92

Stuffed pork chops 133
Celery, apple and walnut salad 213, Potatoes à la dauphinoise 180

Mixed grill 132
Mashed potatoes 93

Vegetables, fruit and dairy produce

Grilled grapefruit 134

Grapefruit anisette 134

Welsh rabbit 135
Green salad 213

Grilled tomatoes 134

Grilled mushrooms 134

Peaches with wine 134
Sauce sabayon 69

Grilled pineapple with rum 134
Cream

Cheese toast 134

Cheese and walnut fingers 135

Grilled Roquefort toast 135

First courses

Main courses

Light lunch-supper dishes

Accompani-ments

Desserts

Miscellaneous

Fish and shellfish

All fish which is to be grilled should be brushed with oil or melted butter. Make two or three diagonal cuts in such round, oily fish as herring, mackerel or trout, to allow the heat to penetrate. Put the fish on a greased rack, skin side away from the heat if the fish has been filleted, and cook under or over a moderate heat until the flesh flakes easily when tested with a knife.

Cooking times depend on the thickness of the fish: a thin fillet may need only six to eight minutes, whereas a thick steak or a large whole mackerel may take fifteen or sixteen minutes. Baste when necessary with melted butter or oil, and season just before bringing the fish to the table or serve with savoury butter.

Such shellfish as lobster and crawfish must be killed just before grilling, and then coated with a sauce or brushed with melted butter and sprinkled with grated cheese. A $1\frac{1}{4}$- to $1\frac{1}{2}$-pound (550- to 700-g) lobster will take about ten minutes to cook through.

Herrings with mustard sauce

SERVES FOUR

2 tablespoons French mustard
1 tablespoon cream
$\frac{1}{2}$ pint (300 ml) béchamel sauce
4 herrings, gutted
1 tablespoon oil or melted butter

First make the sauce. Stir the mustard and cream into the béchamel sauce and keep hot. Preheat the grill to moderate. Brush the herrings all over with the oil or butter and place them on the grill rack. Grill for 3 to 4 minutes on each side and serve immediately with the mustard sauce.

Devilled herrings

SERVES FOUR

4 herrings, cleaned and gutted
4 tablespoons French mustard
4 tablespoons white breadcrumbs, mixed with $\frac{1}{2}$ teaspoon salt and black pepper and $\frac{1}{4}$ teaspoon cayenne pepper
2 tablespoons melted butter
1 lemon, quartered

Preheat the grill to fairly low.

Score the skin of the herrings on both sides. Coat them with mustard and then roll in the seasoned breadcrumbs. Sprinkle over the melted butter. Grill for about 8 minutes, turning once. Serve with lemon wedges.

Haddock kebabs

Serve haddock kebabs with a green salad or savoury rice.

SERVES FOUR

8 rashers streaky bacon
2 lb (900 g) haddock steaks, 1 inch (2 cm) thick
1 oz (25 g) seasoned flour
16 small pickling onions or 4 medium onions, quartered
16 tiny tomatoes or 8 medium-sized tomatoes, halved
2 oz (50 g) melted butter, seasoned with salt and black pepper

LEMON SAUCE

Juice of 1 lemon
1 tablespoon chopped fresh parsley
½ pint (300 ml) hot béchamel sauce made with milk in which the rind of 1 lemon has infused for 15 minutes

First make the sauce. Stir the lemon juice and parsley into the prepared béchamel. Keep hot.

Divide each bacon rasher in half. Cut the fish into 16 cubes, roll them in seasoned flour and wrap a piece of bacon round each cube.

Blanch the onions for 5 minutes and drain them.

Preheat the grill to high. Thread 4 skewers with pieces of fish, onion and tomato. Brush all over with seasoned butter and grill until cooked through, turning the skewers frequently to ensure that the kebabs are cooked on all sides.

Serve with the lemon sauce.

Sea bass with herbs flambé is a spectacular dinner party dish.

Red mullet with dill butter

SERVES TWO

4 medium-sized red mullet, cleaned and gutted
2 tablespoons olive oil
1 lemon, cut into quarters

DILL BUTTER

1½ oz (40 g) butter, softened
1 tablespoon finely chopped fresh or 2 teaspoons dried dill weed
1 teaspoon lemon juice
1 garlic clove, crushed
Salt and black pepper

Make the dill butter first. Mix the softened butter with the dill, lemon juice, garlic and seasoning. Set aside.

Preheat the grill to moderate. Brush the fish with the oil and grill for about 5 minutes on each side. Transfer the mullet to a warm platter and spread with the dill butter. Serve with lemon wedges.

Cod rarebit

SERVES FOUR

1½ lb (700 g) cod fillets or 4 cod steaks
1 oz (25 g) melted butter
2 oz (50 g) Cheddar cheese, grated
2 tablespoons cream
Salt and black pepper
4 slices hot toast

Preheat the grill to fairly low.

Brush the fish with melted butter and grill for about 15 minutes, turning once.

Mix the grated cheese with the cream and seasoning and place spoonfuls of the mixture evenly over the fish. Continue to grill until the cheese has melted and browned.

Serve on the hot toast.

Sea bass with herbs flambé

SERVES FOUR

3-lb (1½-kg) sea bass, cleaned and gutted
2 to 3 tablespoons oil
Salt and black pepper
2 or 3 sprigs each of thyme, rosemary and fennel, and additional sprigs for garnish
3 tablespoons Pernod

Preheat the grill to moderate.

Make two or three slits on either side of the fish. Brush the fish all over with the oil and season with salt and pepper. Put sprigs of herbs into the incisions and into the gut cavity. Grill the fish for about 20 minutes, turning once.

Place the fish on a heatproof serving dish that has been lined with sprigs of herbs. Warm the Pernod, ignite it and pour over the fish.

Grilled halibut steaks with orange sauce

This method of grilling white fish keeps it moist. It is also suitable for skinned whole plaice and sole.

SERVES FOUR

Grated rind of 1 orange
1 tablespoon chopped fresh chives
½ pint (300 ml) béchamel sauce, hot
4 halibut steaks
1 oz (25 g) seasoned flour
2 oz (50 g) butter
Juice of ½ orange

First prepare the sauce. Stir the grated orange rind and chives into the béchamel. Keep the sauce hot until the fish is ready.

Before heating the grill, remove the wire rack from the grill pan and grease the bottom of the pan.

Coat the steaks in the seasoned flour and lay them in the grill pan. Dot them with butter and cook under medium heat for 5 minutes on each side, basting frequently with butter to keep the fish moist.

Transfer the fish to a warmed serving dish, sprinkle with the orange juice and serve the sauce separately.

Grilled salmon steaks

A hollandaise sauce may be served with the salmon instead of the maître d'hôtel butter.

SERVES FOUR

4 large salmon steaks
2 oz (50 g) butter, melted
Salt and black pepper
2 oz (50 g) maître d'hôtel butter
Lemon wedges

Preheat the grill to moderate.

Brush the fish with melted butter and grill for 3 to 5 minutes on each side, or until the fish is cooked.

Transfer the fish to a warmed serving dish and season lightly. Divide the maître d'hôtel butter between the salmon steaks and serve with lemon wedges.

Grilled lobster

SERVES TWO

¼ lb (100 g) melted butter
2 uncooked lobsters (about 1 lb/450 g each) split in half and prepared, claws cracked
Salt and black pepper
4 tablespoons fresh white breadcrumbs
Parsley

Preheat the grill to moderate.

Pour half the melted butter over the flesh of the lobsters and place them, shell-sides down, with the claws, under a medium grill. Cook for 15 minutes or until the lobsters are cooked and the shells bright red. Season well.

Meanwhile, heat the remaining butter in a small pan, add the breadcrumbs and fry until they are golden. Sprinkle the breadcrumbs on the lobsters and grill until the crumbs are lightly browned. Garnish with parsley.

Fish and shellfish

Lobster thermidor

This dish is best served with a mixed green salad.

SERVES FOUR

4 uncooked lobsters (about 1 lb/450 g each), split in half and prepared, claws cracked
Olive oil
3 tablespoons finely chopped shallots
1 tablespoon chopped fresh tarragon
1 tablespoon chopped fresh parsley
¼ pint (150 ml) white wine
1 oz (25 g) butter
1 oz (25 g) flour
½ pint (300 ml) milk
½ pint (300 ml) double cream
Pinch cayenne pepper
Salt and black pepper
1 egg yolk, beaten
2 teaspoons French mustard
3 tablespoons grated Parmesan cheese

Preheat the grill to fairly low.

Place the lobsters, shell-sides down, with the claws, on an oiled grill pan. Brush them with oil and cook under a gentle heat for about 15 minutes, or until the lobsters are cooked and the shells bright red.

Meanwhile, put the shallots, herbs and wine in a small saucepan and bring to the boil. Simmer until all but 2 tablespoons of the liquid has evaporated. Strain the liquid and set aside.

Melt the butter in another pan and stir in the flour. Gradually add the milk and cream, stirring constantly. Add the cayenne and seasoning to taste. Pour in the reduced wine and cook until the sauce thickens. Remove the pan from the heat and stir in the egg yolk and mustard. Keep the sauce warm in a bain-marie, stirring frequently to prevent a skin forming.

When the lobsters are cooked, remove them from the grill. Increase the grill heat to hot.

Remove the tail meat and meat from the cracked claws and cut it into small cubes. Add half the sauce to the lobster meat, mix well and fill the tail shells of the lobsters with this mixture. Pour the rest of the sauce over the lobsters, coating the meat. Sprinkle with the cheese and grill for about 5 minutes, or until the tops are golden.

Scallop brochettes

Serve these brochettes on a bed of rice with a green salad, or by themselves as a first course.

SERVES FOUR

16 small scallops, removed from their shells
16 button mushrooms, wiped clean
1 large orange, cut into 16 pieces
8 mint leaves, cut in half

MARINADE
2 fl oz (50 ml) olive oil
2 fl oz (50 ml) white wine
1 garlic clove, crushed
Salt and freshly ground black pepper
Juice of 1 lemon

Mix the marinade ingredients in a shallow dish and add the scallops, stirring to coat them well. Set aside in a cool place for 1 hour.

Preheat the grill to moderate.

Drain the scallops and reserve the marinade. Thread the scallops alternately with the remaining ingredients on four long skewers. Line the grill pan with foil and lay the skewers in the pan. Grill for 20 minutes, basting with the marinade and turning them over frequently. Transfer the brochettes to warmed plates and serve immediately.

Seafood en brochettes

SERVES FOUR

12 large mussels, steamed and removed from their shells
4 slices streaky bacon, stretched and each cut into 3 and rolled up
12 Dublin Bay prawns, shelled
12 button mushrooms
1 green pepper, cored, seeded and cut into 12 pieces
1 garlic clove, crushed
2 oz (50 g) butter
Salt and black pepper
Parsley sprigs

Preheat the grill to moderate.

Thread the mussels, bacon rolls, prawns, mushrooms and green pepper alternately on to 4 long skewers.

Put the garlic, butter, salt and pepper into a saucepan, and heat very gently until the butter has melted. Brush the brochettes with the melted butter and grill for about 8 minutes, turning them over frequently, until they are cooked.

Garnish with parsley sprigs.

Mussels with parsley butter

This dish makes an excellent first course served with French bread.

SERVES FOUR

24 large mussels, cooked
¼ lb (125 g) butter, softened
2 garlic cloves, crushed
1½ tablespoons finely chopped fresh parsley
6 tablespoons fine white breadcrumbs

Preheat the grill to hot.

Remove the mussels from their shells and place each one in a half shell.

Mix together the butter, garlic and parsley. Spread it equally over the mussels. Sprinkle with the breadcrumbs.

Place the mussels in a shallow flameproof dish and grill for about 3 minutes, or until the butter has melted and the crumbs are golden.

Oysters on skewers

This dish is served as a first course.

SERVES FOUR

12 oysters, removed from their shells with the liquor reserved
12 button mushrooms
2 oz (50 g) melted butter
1 teaspoon lemon juice
3 tablespoons dried white breadcrumbs
Freshly ground black pepper
4 large lemon slices

Preheat the grill to low.

In a shallow pan, poach the oysters for 1 minute in their own liquor. Arrange them alternately with mushrooms on small skewers.

Mix the melted butter and lemon juice and dip the skewers in this mixture before rolling them in the breadcrumbs.

Place on an oiled grill rack and grill for about 4 minutes, sprinkling with the butter and turning them over frequently.

Season with the pepper and serve at once with lemon slices.

Clams with Gruyère sauce

SERVES FOUR

24 clams
1 oz (25 g) butter
1 shallot, finely chopped
2 teaspoons chopped fresh parsley
¼ pint (150 ml) double cream
2 tablespoons grated Gruyère cheese
Salt and pepper
1 tablespoon dried breadcrumbs

Open the clams, wash off any grit and return them to their half-shells.

Melt the butter in a small saucepan and cook the shallot until soft. Add the parsley, cook for another minute and then add the cream. Simmer for 1 minute before adding the cheese, salt and freshly ground pepper.

Preheat the grill to moderate.

Place the clams in a heatproof dish and pour the sauce over them. Sprinkle with the breadcrumbs. Grill for about 5 minutes and serve at once.

Grilled oysters

Serve these grilled oysters as a first course.

SERVES TWO

1 bunch watercress, stalks trimmed off and leaves finely chopped
4 tablespoons cream
1 teaspoon lemon juice
Pinch cayenne pepper
Salt
2 tablespoons grated Parmesan cheese
12 oysters, cleaned and top shells removed
2 tablespoons dried white breadcrumbs

Preheat the grill to moderate.

Put the watercress, cream, lemon juice, cayenne pepper and salt in a small saucepan and cook over low heat until the watercress is cooked. Rub the mixture through a fine sieve into a small bowl and stir in the cheese.

Lay the oysters on a heatproof serving dish. Spoon the sauce equally over each oyster and sprinkle the surface with the breadcrumbs.

Place the dish under the grill for 5 minutes, or until the top is golden and bubbling. Serve hot.

Compound butters

Compound butters can be made with almost any savoury flavourings, providing the flavourings are not too liquid.

Compound butters are always chilled before being used, and can either be served in small pots or cut into fancy shapes. They are always served with hot food unless spread on toast.

Maître d'hôtel butter

2 oz (50 g) butter
2 teaspoons lemon juice
2 teaspoons finely chopped fresh parsley
Salt and black pepper

Cream the butter and add the lemon juice very gradually, a few drops at a time. Mix in the parsley and seasoning.

Egg and chive butter

2 oz (50 g) butter, softened
2 yolks of hard-boiled eggs
Salt and freshly ground black pepper
1 tablespoon chopped fresh chives
1 teaspoon French mustard

Put the butter and egg yolks in a small bowl and mash the yolks into the butter until the mixture is smooth and evenly combined. Beat in the remaining ingredients.

Orange butter

Lemon can be substituted for orange, in the same quantities, to make a lemon butter.

2 oz (50 g) butter
Grated rind of ½ orange
2 teaspoons orange juice
Salt and black pepper

Soften the butter, mix in the orange rind and juice and season to taste.

Shallot butter

2 oz (50 g) butter
2 shallots, peeled, chopped and pounded

Soften the butter and mix well with the pounded shallots. Rub the butter mixture through a fine sieve.

Shrimp butter

2 oz (50 g) shrimps, cooked and peeled
2 oz (50 g) butter, softened
¼ teaspoon salt

Pound the shrimps in a mortar to make a smooth paste. Place the butter and salt in a small mixing bowl and gradually beat in the shrimps. Rub the butter mixture through a fine sieve.

Garlic butter

2 garlic cloves, peeled and crushed
2 oz (50 g) butter

Pound the garlic and beat into the butter. Rub the butter mixture through a fine sieve.

Mustard butter

2 oz (50 g) butter
1 tablespoon French mustard

Soften the butter and mix in the mustard slowly, blending well.

Herb butter

Tarragon, chives, or chervil and chives may be used to make a herb butter. Use approximately 1½ tablespoons of herbs to 2 oz (50 g) of butter. Blanch the herbs in boiling water before pounding them. Add them to the softened butter and season well. Rub the butter mixture through a fine sieve.

Tomato butter

1 tablespoon tomato purée
2 oz (50 g) butter

Beat the tomato purée into the softened butter.

Anchovy butter

4 anchovy fillets
2 oz (50 g) butter
1 teaspoon lemon juice
Black pepper

Pound the anchovy fillets to a paste and work them into the softened butter with the lemon juice and freshly ground black pepper. Rub the butter mixture through a fine sieve.

Delicately flavoured compound butters are the perfect accompaniment to grilled fish or meat—or spread them on melba toast to eat with salads.

Poultry and game birds

To grill poultry or game birds brush the whole, halved or jointed birds with plenty of melted butter, oil or marinade as the flesh tends to become dry. Grill under a moderate heat until the juices run clear when the flesh is pierced: about twelve to fourteen minutes for small joints, or a small bird such as quail, and twenty to thirty minutes for a spring chicken skewered flat, or large joints.

Poussins with lemon butter

A poussin is a 4- to 6-week-old chicken weighing between ½ and 1 pound (225 and 450 g), and is only sufficient for 1 portion. A larger bird, up to 2 pounds (900 g), is called a double poussin.

SERVES FOUR

4 poussins
Salt and pepper
3 oz (75 g) lemon butter

Preheat the grill to moderate.

Using a sharp knife cut the poussins through the breastbone and, with your hands, bend the two halves until they crack and lie flat.

Grease the rack in the grill pan and lay the birds on it, bone-side up. Season well with salt and pepper. Brush lavishly with the lemon butter.

Grill—the birds must be at least 3 inches (8 cm) below the heat—for 8 minutes, baste well with more butter and grill for a further 7 minutes. Turn the birds over and grill, basting once, for a further 15 minutes. Test by piercing the thighs with the point of a sharp knife—if the juices run clear the birds are cooked. Serve immediately.

Chicken brochettes

Serve chicken brochettes with fried rice and a variety of salads.

SERVES FOUR

4 chicken breasts, boned
32 small onions
32 cherry tomatoes, or 8 medium tomatoes, quartered
2 green peppers, cut into pieces

MARINADE

4 tablespoons olive oil
4 tablespoons lemon juice
2 garlic cloves, crushed
1 teaspoon salt
¼ teaspoon cayenne pepper

Mix the marinade ingredients in a bowl. Cut the chicken breasts into 1-inch (2-cm) cubes and add them to the marinade. Set aside for at least 2 hours, turning the chicken occasionally.

Preheat the grill to hot.

Thread 8 skewers with the chicken and vegetables.

Grill the brochettes on one side for about 4 minutes, turn and grill for a further 4 minutes or until the meat is cooked. Serve at once.

Spatchcock chicken

Spatchcock means a bird killed and cooked immediately. This rarely happens today, but the name lives on to denote a simple dish of grilled spring chicken. Spring chickens, also known as broilers, are 3 months old and weigh between 2 and 2½ pounds (900 g and 1 kg). Two birds will feed 4 people.

SERVES FOUR

2 spring chickens
Salt and pepper
Juice of 1 lemon
¼ lb (100 g) butter, melted
1 garlic clove, crushed
2 teaspoons flour
¼ pint (150 ml) white wine
8 bacon rolls, grilled
Lemon wedges

Split the chickens in half down the back. Cut out the backbone. Season well, sprinkle with lemon juice and set aside for 10 minutes.

Preheat the grill to moderate.

Brush the birds lavishly with the butter and place them bone-side up on a greased rack under the grill—they should be at least 3 inches (8 cm) from the heat. Grill for about 30 minutes on each side, basting regularly.

Pierce the thighs with a skewer or the point of a sharp knife—if the juices run clear the birds are cooked.

Put the grilled chickens on a heated serving dish, cover and keep hot in a low oven.

Pour the butter from the grill pan into a saucepan, adding any left over from basting. Add the garlic and fry over gentle heat for a few seconds. Stir in the flour. Pour in the wine and cook, stirring, until the sauce comes to the boil. Adjust the seasoning and add a little lemon juice.

Serve the chicken garnished with the bacon rolls and lemon wedges, and with the sauce served separately.

Grilled chicken livers

SERVES SIX

6 rashers streaky bacon
6 (approximately ½ lb/450 g) chicken livers, cleaned and halved
12 wooden cocktail sticks soaked in cold water

Preheat the grill to high.

Flatten the bacon rashers and cut them in half. Wrap each chicken liver half in a strip of the bacon and secure with a cocktail stick.

Put the rolls under the grill and cook, turning, for 10 minutes, or until the bacon is crisp on all sides—the liver should be slightly pink on the inside.

Devilled turkey legs

SERVES FOUR

4 turkey legs
Salt and black pepper
1 tablespoon French mustard
1 tablespoon lemon juice
3 oz (75 g) melted butter

Skin the turkey legs and make two or three deep incisions in the flesh of each leg. Season well, coat with the mustard and lemon juice and rub into the flesh. Set aside for 1 hour.

Preheat the grill to moderate.

Brush the turkey legs with melted butter. Put them in the grilling pan and place 4 inches (10 cm) below the heat for 15 minutes, or until cooked.

Transfer to a warmed dish and serve at once.

Grilled partridge à la diable

SERVES FOUR

2 young partridges
¼ lb (125 g) melted butter
Salt and pepper
2 oz (50 g) fresh white breadcrumbs
1 lemon, thinly sliced
2 oz (50 g) black olives, pitted
1 bunch watercress, washed

SAUCE À LA DIABLE

¼ oz (10 g) butter
1 shallot, finely chopped
6 fl oz (175 ml) wine vinegar
½ pint (300 ml) espagnole sauce
2 tablespoons tomato purée
Worcestershire sauce
Salt and pepper
Cayenne pepper

Three grilled poultry dishes to serve with salads or savoury rice: devilled turkey legs, chicken brochettes and poussins with lemon butter.

First prepare the sauce. Heat the butter in a small saucepan, add the shallot and fry gently until soft. Pour in the vinegar and boil until it is reduced by half.

Stir in the espagnole sauce and tomato purée and cook, covered, for 5 minutes. Season to taste with Worcestershire sauce, salt, pepper and cayenne. Keep hot until the partridges are ready.

Preheat the grill to moderate.

Split the partridges down the back, open them out and flatten. Keep them flat by threading them on 2 skewers. Brush with the melted butter and season with salt and freshly ground pepper.

Cook under the grill for about 10 minutes each side, brushing frequently with the butter. Remove the partridges from under the grill and coat with the breadcrumbs. Return to the grill and cook gently for another 5 minutes, basting frequently with the butter until the crumbs are golden. Test the birds by piercing the thighs with the point of a sharp knife—if the juices run clear the birds are cooked. Remove from under the grill.

Arrange the birds on a warmed serving dish, garnish with slices of lemon, the olives and watercress. Serve with the sauce in a sauce boat.

Grilled quail with orange and sage sauce

Quail can be grilled with almost any herb, providing that the flavour is not too aggressive.

SERVES TWO

¼ lb (100 g) butter
Juice and grated rind of 1 orange
2 teaspoons finely chopped fresh sage
1 small garlic clove, crushed
½ teaspoon German mustard
4 quail, cleaned and split through the backbones
4 sprigs watercress
½ pint (300 ml) apple sauce

Preheat the grill to moderate.

Put the butter, orange juice and rind, sage, garlic and mustard in a small saucepan and place over low heat until the butter has melted.

Place the quail, skin-sides uppermost, on a flameproof dish. Pour over the butter sauce and place the dish under the grill. Grill for about 7 minutes on each side, basting with the butter sauce, until the quail are cooked. Test by piercing the thighs with the point of a sharp knife—if the juices run clear the birds are cooked. Serve immediately, garnished with the watercress, and with the apple sauce served separately in a sauce boat.

Meat and game

Use only tender cuts of meat for grilling—beef steaks and lamb chops are ideal. Pork chops must be marinated, covered with glaze or well basted during cooking because the meat tends to be dry. Pork is never eaten underdone so be careful to grill it until it is cooked through.

Nick the fat on the meat to prevent it curling during cooking. If you have an adjustable grill the meat should be about three inches (8 cm) from the heat source.

Always preheat the grill and grease the rack or skewers.

Season with salt after cooking because salt draws out the juices and tends to make the meat tougher.

Prick sausages before grilling to release the fat and to prevent them bursting during cooking.

Mixed grill

SERVES FOUR

4 lamb cutlets
4 lambs' kidneys, split, cores removed and secured open with wooden cocktail sticks
2 tomatoes, halved
¼ lb (100 g) mushrooms
5 tablespoons melted butter
8 chipolata sausages
4 bacon rashers
1 bunch watercress, washed

Preheat the grill to moderate. Line the grill pan with foil. Brush the cutlets, kidneys, tomato halves and mushrooms with the butter.

Place the cutlets and sausages in the grill pan and cook for 2 to 3 minutes. Add the lambs' kidneys and continue to cook for a further 5 minutes. Turn all the meat over and add the bacon, tomatoes and mushrooms. Cook for another 3 minutes, then turn the bacon and mushrooms and cook for 2 to 3 minutes longer until they are ready.

Lower the pan away from the heat if the meat is browning too fast.

Remove the cocktail sticks from the kidneys. Transfer everything to a hot platter, pour over the pan juices and garnish with watercress.

Minute steaks

SERVES FOUR

4 entrecôte steaks, ¼ inch (½ cm) thick
1 tablespoon olive oil
Salt and black pepper
½ pint (300 ml) béarnaise sauce

Preheat the grill to high.

Brush the steaks with oil and cook for 1 minute on each side. Transfer them to a warm dish, pour over the pan juices, season and serve at once with the béarnaise sauce.

Tournedos Rossini

SERVES FOUR

¼ lb (125 g) butter
4 slices French bread
4 slices pâté de foie gras
½ lb (225 g) mushrooms
4 tournedos, 1½ inch (3 cm) thick
2 fl oz (50 ml) Madeira
½ pint (300 ml) demi-glace sauce

Pre-heat the grill to high.

Melt 2 ounces (50 g) of the butter in a large frying-pan. Add the bread and fry on both sides over moderate heat until golden and crisp. Drain the croûtons on kitchen paper and keep warm on a serving dish.

Add another 1 ounce (25 g) of butter to the frying-pan and cook the slices of foie gras very quickly over high heat, turning once, until they are golden. Remove from the pan and keep warm in another dish.

Add the mushrooms to the pan and cook gently while the steaks are being grilled.

Melt the remaining butter and brush it over the steaks. Cook under the grill for about 3 minutes on each side. Pour any juices from the grill pan over the mushrooms in the frying-pan.

Put one tournedos on top of each croûton on the serving dish, lay a slice of foie gras on each steak and top with a cooked mushroom. Arrange the remaining mushrooms around the tournedos. Reserve the liquid in the frying-pan and keep the serving dish warm while the sauce is prepared.

Stir the Madeira and the demi-glace into the juices in the frying-pan. Bring to the boil. Pour some of the sauce into the serving dish and serve the rest separately.

Grilling Times	MODERATE HEAT
Rump steak 1 in (2 cm) thick	
High heat for 1 min each side then	about 6 mins (rare)
	about 12 mins (well done)
Fillet steak 1½–2 in (3–5 cm) thick	
High heat for 1 min each side then	8–10 mins (rare)
	12–16 mins (well done)
Lamb chops 1½ in (3 cm) thick	16–20 mins
Pork cutlets 1½ in (3 cm) thick	20–25 mins
Gammon steak	10–15 mins
Bacon rashers	about 5 mins
Liver	4–8 mins
Kidneys	5–10 mins
Sausages	15–20 mins

Lebanese kebabs

Serve Lebanese kebabs with pitta and a tomato and olive salad.

SERVES FOUR

1½ lb (700 g) boned leg or shoulder of lamb cut into ½-inch (1-cm) cubes
1 onion, finely chopped
¼ pint (150 ml) natural yogurt
2 tablespoons chopped mint
Salt and pepper
1 tablespoon olive oil
1 garlic clove, crushed

Put the meat in a large bowl. Mix all the remaining ingredients together and pour over the meat. Cover the bowl and refrigerate for 8 hours, or overnight, stirring occasionally.

Preheat the grill to high.

Drain the meat and thread on to 4 skewers. Grill for 8 to 10 minutes, basting frequently with the marinade and turning the skewers, until the meat is cooked.

Hamburgers

Additions can include fresh or dried herbs, finely chopped onion and crushed garlic. Grated carrot will make the hamburger more juicy and a slice of bread crumbled into the meat will both lighten and "stretch" it. The yolk of an egg will help to bind the mixture. Serve with chips, sliced raw onion and sliced tomatoes.

SERVES FOUR

1 lb (450 g) minced steak
Salt and black pepper
4 soft rolls, split and toasted

Preheat the grill to high.

Mix the meat and seasoning together and shape the mixture into 4 hamburgers about 1 inch (2 cm) thick. Grill for 3 minutes on each side if you like your hamburgers rare, 4 to 5 minutes each side for medium and 6 minutes each side for well done.

Serve inside the rolls.

Pork saté

Serve as a starter or main course.

SERVES FOUR TO EIGHT

2 lb (900 g) pork fillet, cut into 1-inch (2-cm) cubes

MARINADE

Juice of 1 lemon
½ to 1 teaspoon cayenne pepper
3 garlic cloves, crushed
1 tablespoon oil
2 tablespoons soft brown sugar
2 tablespoons molasses
8 tablespoons soy sauce

PEANUT SAUCE

3 tablespoons oil
1 onion, finely chopped
2 garlic cloves, crushed
½ to 1 teaspoon cayenne pepper
½ teaspoon turmeric
2 teaspoons ground coriander
3 tablespoons smooth peanut butter
Coconut milk made from ¾-inch (2-cm) slice creamed coconut dissolved in ¾ pint (450 ml) boiling water
Salt

Thread the pork cubes on to skewers. Mix all the marinade ingredients together in a shallow dish. Put the skewers into the marinade and set aside for 3 to 4 hours, turning the skewers and basting the meat occasionally.

Meanwhile prepare the sauce. Heat the oil in a saucepan. Add the onion and garlic and fry, stirring, until golden. Add the cayenne, turmeric and coriander and fry for 1 minute. Stir in the peanut butter and pour in the coconut milk. Bring to the boil, stirring. Reduce the heat to low, cover the pan and simmer for 20 minutes. Stir in 5 tablespoons of the marinade. Taste the sauce and add salt if necessary.

Preheat the grill to moderate. Grease the grill rack. Grill the pork, basting with the marinade, for 5 minutes on each side, or until the pork is cooked through.

Pour the peanut sauce into individual bowls or saucers and serve with the saté.

Grilled pork chops

SERVES FOUR

4 pork loin chops
1 orange, thinly sliced

GLAZE

2 tablespoons honey
Rind and juice of 1 orange
1 teaspoon lemon juice
1 teaspoon soy sauce
Salt and black pepper

Preheat the grill to moderate.

Mix the ingredients for the glaze in a saucepan and bring to the boil. Simmer for 3 minutes.

Nick the fat on the chops. Grease the grill rack. Put the chops on the rack and brush them with the glaze. Grill, basting frequently, for about 10 minutes. Turn the chops, brush with the glaze and grill, basting occasionally, for 10 minutes or until the chops are cooked.

Serve immediately, garnished with the orange slices.

Stuffed pork chops

SERVES FOUR

2 oz (50 g) prunes, simmered until tender in ¼ pint (150 ml) sweet cider, then stoned and chopped
2 oz (50 g) fresh white breadcrumbs
1 teaspoon rubbed sage
Salt and pepper
½ small onion, grated
½ oz (15 g) butter, melted
1 small egg yolk, beaten
4 pork chops
1 tablespoon oil

Preheat the grill to hot.

Mix all the ingredients except the pork chops and oil.

With a sharp, pointed knife, cut the meat away from the bone of the chops. Cut an incision in the meat at the leanest part, making a pocket for the stuffing. Fill the pockets with the stuffing mixture and sew them up with trussing thread.

Brush with oil and grill for about 15 minutes on each side.

Gammon steaks with apricots

Pineapple rings may be used instead of the apricots. Serve with garlic mashed potatoes and boiled peas or broccoli.

SERVES FOUR

4 gammon steaks, ½ inch (1 cm) thick
1 lb (450 g) canned apricots, drained
1 oz (25 g) butter, cut into pieces
2 oz (50 g) soft brown sugar
Sage leaves to garnish

Preheat the grill to moderate.

Nick the fat on the steaks. Grill the gammon for 5 minutes on each side.

Arrange the apricots on top of the steaks, dot with the butter and sprinkle the sugar on top. Return the steaks to the heat and grill until the apricots are browned.

Serve garnished with the sage leaves.

Vegetables, fruit and dairy produce

The vegetables that are most commonly grilled are mushrooms (the large, open ones) and tomatoes.

Tomatoes may be grilled whole or cut across in half. Brush with oil and cook for about ten to fifteen minutes. Grill the rounded sides of tomato halves first to prevent the soft, uncooked pulp from slipping out of the skin. Serve grilled mushrooms or tomatoes on toast or as an accompaniment to fish, meat or poultry.

Slices of degorged aubergine may also be grilled. Brush them with oil and cook until they are brown on both sides.

In the south of France a delectable first course is made with grilled green peppers. Put the whole peppers under high heat until their skins blister and can be rubbed off easily under cold running water. Core and seed the peppers, cut them into strips and marinate in a herb-flavoured vinaigrette for at least thirty minutes.

With very few exceptions (for example grapefruit, peaches and pineapple), fruit are never grilled.

Dairy produce and cereals, with the exception of cheese and bread, are never cooked under a grill. The best cheeses for grilling are hard cheeses, such as Cheddar, Edam, Gruyère, Parmesan and Cheshire cheese.

Grilled tomatoes

SERVES FOUR

4 large tomatoes
6 tablespoons dry breadcrumbs
1 garlic clove, crushed
1 tablespoon chopped fresh basil
1 tablespoon chopped parsley
1 tablespoon grated Parmesan cheese
Salt and pepper
Melted butter or olive oil

Preheat the grill to moderate.

Cut the tops off the tomatoes and scoop the flesh into a bowl. Turn the tomatoes upside down on kitchen paper towels to drain.

Mix the chopped tomato pulp with the breadcrumbs, garlic, herbs, cheese and seasoning. Mix in a little melted butter or oil. Fill the tomatoes with this mixture, sprinkle with butter or oil and grill for about 10 minutes or until they are heated through.

Grilled mushrooms

For plain grilled mushrooms brush the mushroom caps with melted butter, season to taste and grill them cap-sides up for about 3 minutes. Turn them over and grill for a further 3 minutes. Serve the mushrooms on toast.

SERVES FOUR

12 large mushrooms
1½ oz (40 g) butter
1 garlic clove, crushed
1 small onion, chopped
6 tablespoons dry breadcrumbs
Salt and pepper
2 teaspoons chopped parsley
1 tablespoon melted butter

Preheat the grill to moderate.

Wipe the mushrooms. Remove the stalks and chop them finely.

Melt the butter in a small saucepan and gently fry the mushroom stalks, garlic and onion for 3 to 4 minutes. Add the breadcrumbs, seasoning and parsley and cook for a further 2 minutes. Fill the caps with the mixture. Put them in a grilling pan that has been lightly greased. Sprinkle the tops with the melted butter and grill for 5 minutes. Serve immediately.

Grilled grapefruit

SERVES FOUR

2 grapefruit, halved
4 tablespoons sherry
4 teaspoons demerara sugar

Preheat the grill to hot.

Sprinkle the grapefruit halves with sherry and spread with the sugar. Cook under the grill for a few minutes until glazed.

Grapefruit anisette

SERVES FOUR

2 pink-fleshed grapefruit, halved
4 teaspoons Pernod
2 tablespoons castor sugar
8 mint leaves, washed

Preheat the grill to hot.

Sprinkle the grapefruit with the Pernod and leave to soak in for 5 minutes. Sprinkle with the sugar and cook under the grill, 5 to 6 inches (13 to 15 cm) from the heat, for about 8 minutes, or until glazed.

Garnish with mint leaves and serve at once or leave to cool.

Peaches with wine

SERVES FOUR

4 large, ripe peaches, halved and stoned
4 tablespoons white wine or dry sherry
4 tablespoons soft brown sugar
1 oz (25 g) butter, cut into small pieces
¼ pint (150 ml) whipped cream

Preheat the grill to hot.

Put the peaches, cut-sides up, in a grill pan. Fill the centres with the wine or sherry, sprinkle with the sugar and dot with the butter. Cook under the grill until the sugar has melted and the wine is hot.

Serve with the whipped cream.

Grilled pineapple with rum

Kirsch may be used instead of rum.

SERVES FOUR TO SIX

1 ripe pineapple
4 to 6 tablespoons Jamaican rum
4 tablespoons soft brown sugar
1 pint (575 ml) good-quality vanilla ice-cream

Preheat the grill to moderate.

Cut the pineapple in half lengthways. Scoop out the flesh and cut into small cubes. Toss the flesh with the rum and return to the shells. Cover the leaves with foil.

Put the pineapple halves in the grill pan, sprinkle with the sugar and cook under the grill until the sugar has melted.

If the pineapple is too near the heat, the rum may ignite, but the flames will soon subside if the grill pan is lowered.

Remove the foil and serve at once with the ice-cream.

Cheese toast

MAKES SIXTEEN PIECES

4 slices bread
1 oz (25 g) butter
¼ lb (125 g) Cheddar cheese, grated
¼ teaspoon baking powder
1 egg, separated
Salt and pepper

Preheat the grill to hot.

Remove the crusts from the bread and cut each slice into 4 triangles. Toast lightly and butter on one side. Keep warm.

Mix the cheese, baking powder, egg yolk and seasoning. Beat the egg white until it is stiff and fold it in. Spread the mixture thickly on the toast and place under the grill until brown and puffed.

Welsh rabbit

To make a buck rabbit put a poached egg on a Welsh rabbit.

SERVES FOUR

½ lb (225 g) Cheddar cheese, grated
1 oz (25 g) butter
1 teaspoon prepared mustard
3 tablespoons beer
Salt and pepper
Cayenne pepper
4 slices bread, toasted and kept warm

Preheat the grill to hot.

Mix the cheese, butter, mustard, beer and seasoning in a small saucepan over low heat. Stir until completely blended.

Pour over the toast and grill until brown.

Cheese and walnut fingers

MAKES TWENTY-FOUR FINGERS

8 slices brown bread, toasted and kept warm
6 oz (175 g) cream cheese
2 oz (50 g) chopped walnuts
Salt and pepper

Preheat the grill to hot.

Mix the cheese, nuts and seasoning and spread on to the toast. Cut each slice into three. Grill until lightly browned.

Cooked under the grill: cheese toast, grapefruit and tomatoes.

Grilled Roquefort

SERVES TWO TO FOUR

4 slices bread
1 oz (25 g) butter
4 slices chicken or ham
¼ lb (125 g) Roquefort cheese, creamed

Preheat the grill to hot.

Toast the bread slightly and butter it. Place a slice of meat on each piece of toast and spread with the cheese—grill until bubbling and golden.

Frying and sautéing

Shallow frying, sautéing, deep-fat frying and stir-frying are all ways of cooking food in hot fat.

For shallow frying use a good-quality heavy frying-pan and only a small amount of dripping, lard, polyunsaturated margarine, butter or oil, or a mixture of butter and oil.

Sautéing is closely related to shallow frying, but only butter or oil or a mixture of both is used. Heat the pan well and add just enough fat to grease the pan. When it is hot, add the food. Cook briskly, shaking the pan frequently to keep the food moving so that it browns on all sides equally and does not stick.

Often after a preliminary sautéing a little liquid is added, the pan covered and the food cooked over gentle heat until done. A straight-sided sauté pan with a lid is useful, particularly for poultry and meat.

For deep-fat frying you need a deep, heavy saucepan fitted with a frying basket. The saucepan must never be more than two-thirds full of oil because if it bubbles over on to the stove the fat might catch fire. On the other hand, there must be enough fat to cover the food.

A deep-frying thermometer is the most accurate way of judging the temperature of the fat. Keep it in a jug of hot water and wipe it dry before putting it in the hot oil. If a thermometer is not available use a one-inch (2-cm) cube of day-old bread to estimate the temperature. When the oil is hot drop in the cube and check the time it takes to brown with a kitchen timer. If it takes thirty-five seconds to brown the temperature will be approximately 400°F (204°C); if it takes forty seconds it will be approximately 375°F (190°C); if it takes fifty seconds it will be approximately 360°F (182°C) and if it takes fifty-five seconds it will be approximately 350°F (176°C).

Most foods require a temperature of about 375°F (190°C), but some, such as potato chips, whitebait, croûtons and precooked foods, require a second frying at a temperature of about 400°F (204°C).

Stir-frying is a method of frying practised by the Chinese, who use a large pan with a rounded base called a wok. (As an alternative use a large, heavy frying-pan.) Cut the food into small pieces and fry it quickly in a little hot oil, stirring constantly. It may take only fifteen seconds to cook and rarely takes more than five minutes.

Fish and shellfish

- ***Fried whitebait 138*** Sauce tartare 68, Brown bread 198
- ***Sautéed soft roes 138***
- ***Clam fritters 140***
- ***New England fried scallops 140*** Deep-fried parsley 153
- ***Fried fish 138*** Sauce tartare 68, Potato chips 150
- ***Fish cakes 138*** Tomato sauce 69, Mashed potatoes 93, Green beans 92
- ***Fritto misto di mare 138*** Sauce tartare 68
- ***Bass à la provençale 138*** Garlic bread 189, Boiled fennel 92
- ***Filets de sole meunière 140*** Lemon butter 129, Boiled potatoes 93, Casseroled celery 120
- ***Herrings in oatmeal 140*** Tomato sauce 69, Leeks 93
- ***Trout with almonds 140*** Sauté potatoes 151
- ***Fillets of sole à la panetière 140*** Green salad 213
- ***Fried eels 140*** Sauce hollandaise 67, Spinach purée 92
- ***Kedgeree 140*** Green salad 213
- ***Stir-fried giant prawns 140*** Stir-fried bean sprouts 153
- ***Sautéed frogs' legs à la niçoise 141*** Potato croquettes 151, French beans 92
- ***Fried scampi 141*** Sauce tartare 68, Brown bread 198
- ***Squirrel fish 141*** Stir-fried bean sprouts 153
- ***Bean sprouts and prawns Chinese style 141***

Poultry and game birds

- ***Chicken Maryland 142*** Potato croquettes 151, Corn fritters 153, Sautéed bananas 154
- ***Chicken sauté à la bordelaise 142***
- ***Chicken sauté à l'italienne 142*** Sauté potatoes 151, Spinach 92
- ***Chicken Kiev 144*** Steamed broccoli 92, Mashed potatoes, Courgettes 93
- ***Deep-fried chicken 144*** Sauce tartare 68, Potato chips 150
- ***Chicken lemon sauté 144*** Soufflé potatoes 150, Mange-tout peas 93
- ***Poulet sauté chasseur 144*** Large croûtons 158, Runner beans 92
- ***Chicken sauté paprika 145*** Rösti 151, Spinach 92
- ***Guinea-fowl sautéed with juniper berries 145*** Green bean salad 212, Garlic mashed potatoes 180
- ***Sautéed partridge jubilee 145*** Green salad 213, Sauté potatoes 151

Wild duck à la seville 145
Chicory, orange and watercress salad 213, Game chips 150

Chicken kromeski 144
Green salad 213, Broccoli, Spinach 92

Chicken with almonds 145
Stir-fried bean sprouts 153

Stir-fried chicken and mushrooms 145

Chicken liver sauté 145
Large croûtons 158

Meat and game

Steak au poivre 146
Grilled tomatoes 134, Baked potatoes 180

Steak Diane 146
Braised onions 120, Broccoli 92, Sauté potatoes 151

Beef stroganoff 146
Green salad 213, Steamed rice 97

Entrecôte à la viennoise 146
Sauce béarnaise 67, Fried mushrooms 152

Veal Zurich style 147
Rösti 151, Petit pois à la française 91

Veal cutlets Milanese style 147
Green salad 213, Sauté potatoes 151

Fondue bourguignonne 148

Veal marsala 148
Courgettes 93, Fried mushrooms 152

Noisettes of lamb with stuffed tomatoes 148
Leeks provençale 120, Sauté potatoes 151

Saltimbocca 148
Large croûtons 158

Sautéed venison steaks 148
Brussels sprouts with chestnuts 91, Celeriac 93

Veal chops en papillote 148
New potatoes 93, French beans 92

Sautéed sweetbreads Saint Médard 149
Celery, apple and walnut salad 213, Braised onions 120

Meatballs with sweet and sour sauce 149
Fried rice 158

Entrecôte au poivre vert 149
French beans 92, Carrot and parsnip purée 91

Tournedos au vin rouge 149
New potatoes, Peas 93

Wiener schnitzel 149
Broccoli 92, Sauté potatoes 151

Sautéed liver and bacon 149
Fried mushrooms 152, Mashed potatoes 93

Fruit and Vegetables

Bubble and squeak 152
Grilled bacon 132

Pipérade 153
Large croûtons 158

Fried apples and bacon 155

Pakoras with mint chutney 152

Potatoes
chips 150
straws 150
soufflé 150
sauté 151
Lyonnaise 151
Parisienne 151
croquettes 151
rösti 151
scones 152

Onions 152

Mushrooms 152
Duxelles 152

Fritters
aubergine 153
corn 153
cauliflower cheese 152
banana and bacon 154
apple 154
special apple 154
apricot 154
winter 154

Sautéed aubergines 152
Stir-fried bean sprouts 153
Deep-fried parsley 153

Sautéed bananas 154

Apples with Calvados 155

Caramelized pineapple 155

Salted almonds 155

Cereals

Fried bread 158
Croûtons 158
Fried rice 158
Crusty noodles 158

Crêpes Suzette 157

Beignets soufflés 158

Pancakes 156
Drop scones 157
Blini 157
Crumpets 157
Muffins 157
Waffles 157
English doughnuts 157
American doughnuts 158
French toast 158
Fritter batter 156

- First courses
- Main courses
- Light lunch-supper dishes
- Accompaniments
- Desserts
- Miscellaneous

Eggs and dairy produce

Fried mozzarella cheese 162

Mozzarella in carrozza 162

Fried eggs 160
Beurre noir 68

Scrambled eggs 160

Scrambled eggs with mushrooms 160

Scrambled eggs with cheese 160

Scotch woodcock 160

French omelette 160
Green salad 213

Omelette fines herbes 160
Green salad 213

Mushroom omelette 160
Green salad 213

Cheese omelette 160
Green salad 213

Omelette Arnold Bennett 160
Green salad 213

Spanish omelette 161
Green salad 213

Egg fu-yung 161

Scotch eggs 161
Salads: Potato 93, Tomato 213

Scrambled eggs with chicken 162

Scrambled eggs with chicken livers 162

Scrambled eggs with smoked salmon 162
Green salad 213

Bean sprouts with omelette shreds 162

Huevos rancheros 162

Kuku sabsi 161

Ajja 162

Omelette au Grand Marnier 161

Omelette flambée 161

Fish and shellfish

The nicest way to shallow-fry fish is in butter, which is then poured over the fish when it is served. A milk and flour or egg and breadcrumb coating may be used for all types of fish, but the Scottish way of frying herrings in coarse oatmeal adds an even more interesting flavour and crunchy texture.

For deep frying, fish is usually coated with batter. Heat the oil to a temperature of 375°F (190°C) and fry the fish until it is golden brown. Fillets and small whole fish will take from five to eight minutes.

Scallops, scampi and precooked mussels may also be coated with batter and deep fried and take about three to four minutes.

Fried fish

SERVES FOUR

2 lb (900 g) white fish fillets, skinned
Oil for deep frying
$\frac{3}{4}$ pint (450 ml) fritter batter

Dry the fish well on kitchen paper towels. Heat the oil to 375°F (190°C).

Coat the fish with the batter and lower it into the hot fat. Fry for 5 minutes or until the fish is crisp and golden.

Fish cakes

SERVES FOUR

1 lb (450 g) fish, steamed or boiled
$\frac{1}{2}$ lb (225 g) potatoes, boiled
3 tablespoons cream
1 oz (25 g) butter
$\frac{1}{4}$ lemon
2 tablespoons chopped parsley
Salt and pepper
1 egg, beaten
Toasted breadcrumbs
Oil for frying
1 lemon, cut into wedges

Flake the fish and remove any skin or bones. Mash the potatoes with the cream and butter until smooth. Add a squeeze of lemon juice and blend with the fish, parsley and seasoning. With floured hands shape the mixture into eight round, flat patties. Chill for at least 1 hour to make the patties firm.

Dip the patties in the beaten egg, then in the breadcrumbs, and either deep fry at 375°F (190°C) for about 6 minutes or shallow fry for 10 to 12 minutes. Drain on kitchen paper towels. Garnish with the lemon wedges and serve.

Fried whitebait

SERVES FOUR

1 lb (450 g) whitebait
2 tablespoons seasoned flour
Oil for deep frying
Cayenne pepper
2 lemons, cut into quarters

Put the whitebait and the flour in a plastic or paper bag and shake gently until the whitebait are well coated.

Heat the oil to 375°F (190°C). Using a frying basket lower a few whitebait at a time into the oil and fry for about 2 minutes. Drain well on kitchen paper towels. When all the whitebait are fried and drained put them all together in the frying basket. Reheat the oil until it reaches 400°F (204°C) and plunge the basket in the oil for 1 minute to crisp the whitebait. Drain well, sprinkle with cayenne pepper and serve with the lemon quarters.

Fritto misto di mare

SERVES FOUR TO SIX

1 lb (450 g) calamari (squid or inkfish), ink sac and cuttle bone removed
Salt
4 to 8 red mullet (smaller ones are best), cleaned
2 lb (900 g) prawns, unshelled
$\frac{1}{4}$ lb (100 g) seasoned flour
Oil for deep frying

Cut the body and tentacles of the calamari into $\frac{1}{4}$-inch ($\frac{1}{2}$-cm) rings. Bring some well-salted water to the boil in a saucepan. Add the calamari and boil for about 25 minutes or until tender. (Large calamari will take longer to cook.) Drain the calamari.

Roll all the fish in the flour until lightly coated. Heat the oil to 375°F (190°C). Add the fish a few at a time. Fry the larger fish for 10 to 15 minutes and the smaller pieces for 5 to 8 minutes or until they are golden. Serve immediately.

Sautéed soft roes

SERVES TWO

2 oz (50 g) butter
1 small onion, finely chopped
$\frac{1}{2}$ lb (225 g) soft herring roes, cut into pieces
1 oz (25 g) seasoned flour
2 tablespoons sherry
4 toast triangles
1 tablespoon chopped parsley

Melt the butter in a sauté pan and fry the onion gently until soft. Coat the roes lightly with the seasoned flour and add them to the pan. Fry gently for 2 to 3 minutes, stirring to prevent them sticking. Add the sherry and continue to cook for 1 to 2 minutes. Serve on hot toast, sprinkled with parsley.

Bass à la provençale

SERVES FOUR

2 sea bass, about $1\frac{1}{2}$ lb (700 g)
Oil for frying
2 tablespoons seasoned flour
1 pint (575 ml) tomato sauce
2 garlic cloves, finely chopped
3 tablespoons breadcrumbs

Preheat the grill to moderate.

Scale the bass and make shallow diagonal cuts in the skin. Heat plenty of oil—enough to come half-way up the fish—in the frying-pan.

Roll the fish in the flour and fry on both sides until cooked through. Transfer the fish to a flameproof dish and cover with the sauce.

Heat 1 tablespoon of oil in a small frying-pan and fry the garlic gently for a few seconds. Sprinkle the garlic and the breadcrumbs over the sauce and put the dish under the grill. Cook until the crumbs are browned.

Delicious fritto misto di mare is made from a selection of deep-fried fish and shellfish.

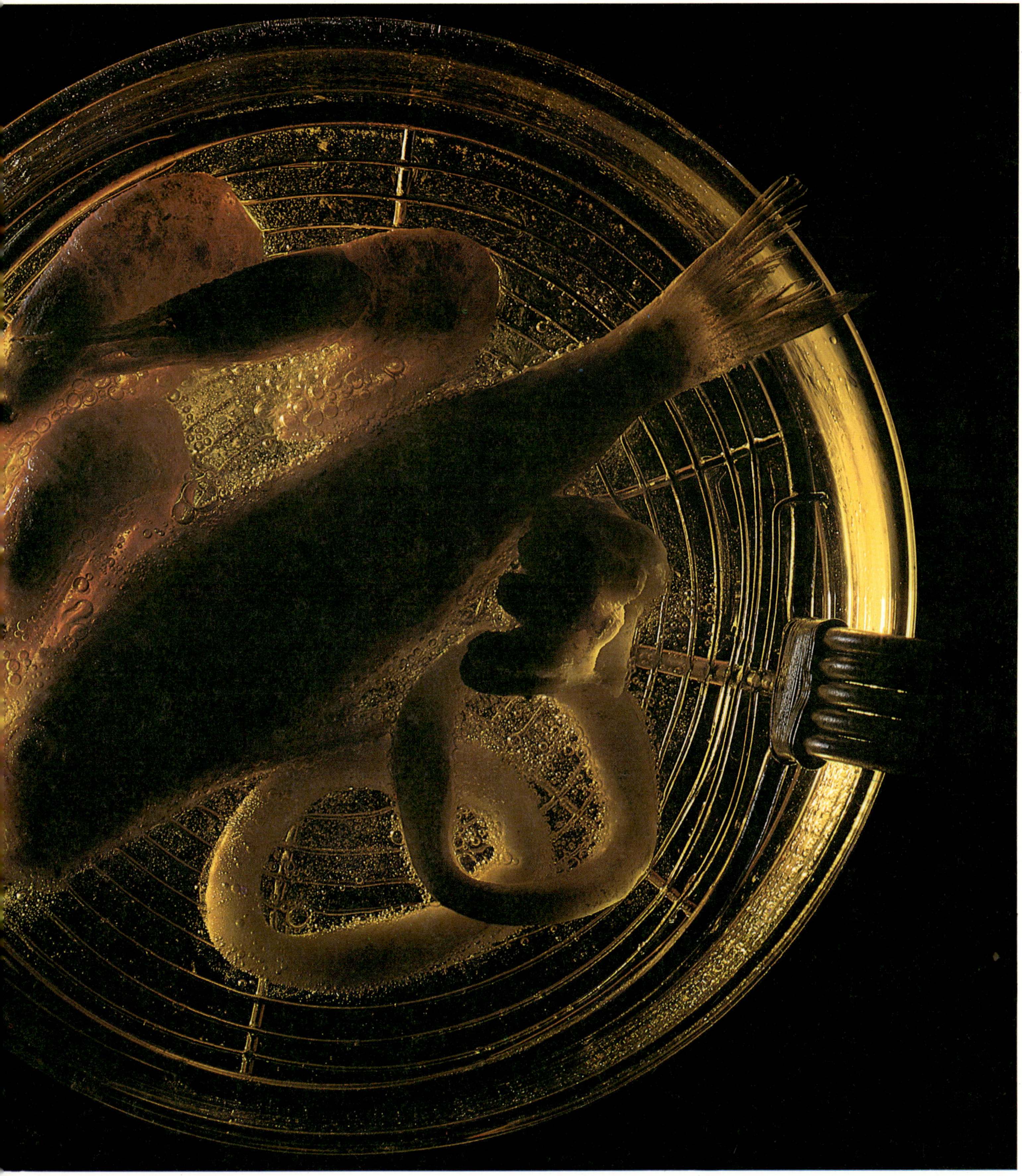

Fish and shellfish

Filets de sole meunière

SERVES FOUR

2 sole, about $1\frac{1}{2}$ lb (700 g) each, filleted
1 oz (25 g) seasoned flour
2 oz (50 g) butter
2 teaspoons lemon juice
1 lemon, quartered
1 tablespoon chopped fresh parsley

Skin the sole fillets carefully and pat them dry with kitchen paper towels. Roll the fillets in the flour.

Melt half the butter in a frying-pan. Add the fillets and fry for 2 to 3 minutes over moderate heat, shaking the pan to prevent the fish sticking. When brown turn the fillets over and fry for a further 2 to 3 minutes on the other side or until the fish are cooked. Transfer the fish to a warm dish and keep hot.

Wipe out the pan with kitchen paper towels and return to the heat. Add the remaining butter, and when it has turned golden stir in the lemon juice. Pour the butter over the fish, garnish with the lemon wedges, sprinkle with parsley and serve immediately.

Herrings in oatmeal

SERVES FOUR

4 herrings, cleaned
1 tablespoon lemon juice
Salt and pepper
4 tablespoons medium-ground oatmeal
2 oz (50 g) butter or dripping

Split the fish down the back and remove the backbones. Score the skin. Brush with the lemon juice and season well. Roll the herrings in the oatmeal until they are completely coated.

Heat the butter or dripping in a frying-pan and add the herrings, skin side uppermost. Fry for about 5 minutes on each side or until browned and cooked. Drain on kitchen paper towels and serve at once.

Trout with almonds

SERVES FOUR

4 trout, washed, scaled and cleaned
2 tablespoons seasoned flour
3 oz (75 g) butter
2 lemons
2 oz (50 g) slivered almonds

Roll the trout in the seasoned flour. Melt 2 ounces (50 g) of the butter in a large sauté or frying-pan. Fry the trout for about 5 minutes on each side or until well browned and cooked. Transfer the fish to a serving dish and keep hot.

Add the remaining butter and when it has melted add the juice of $\frac{1}{2}$ lemon. Add the almonds and fry, shaking the pan occasionally, until golden. Pour the almonds and butter over the trout. Garnish with the remaining lemons cut into quarters.

Fillets of sole à la panetière

A la panetière originally meant that the dish was presented in a hollowed-out loaf, or in croustades. A pastry case is lighter and more suited to modern tastes. A variation would be to serve each portion in an individual vol-au-vent case.

SERVES FOUR

2 sole, filleted
2 tablespoons seasoned flour
$\frac{1}{4}$ lb (100 g) butter
1 lb (450 g) mushrooms, chopped
$\frac{1}{4}$ pint (150 ml) cream
Salt and pepper
Nutmeg
1 10-inch (25-cm) vol-au-vent case, baked and kept warm

Trim the sole fillets, flatten, fold over once and dip in seasoned flour.

Melt half the butter in a frying-pan. Add the mushrooms and fry until soft. Draw the pan off the heat and stir in the cream. Return to very low heat and cook for a few minutes longer, but do not allow the cream to boil or it will curdle. Season with salt, pepper and a pinch of grated nutmeg and keep hot.

Heat the remaining butter in a sauté pan. Sauté the fillets for about 5 minutes on each side or until cooked through. Arrange the fish around the inside of the vol-au-vent case and fill the centre with the mushrooms.

Fried eels

SERVES FOUR

2 lb (900 g) small eels, skinned
$\frac{1}{4}$ pint (150 ml) milk
2 oz (50 g) seasoned flour
Oil for deep frying
1 lemon, quartered
Parsley sprigs

Score the eels. Twist them into figure-of-eight shapes and secure them with skewers. Put the milk in a dish. Put the eels in the milk and leave for a few minutes and then roll them in the flour.

Heat the oil to 375°F (190°C). Add the eels and fry until crisp, golden and cooked. Drain on kitchen paper towels and serve on a folded napkin. Garnish with lemon quarters and parsley.

Kedgeree

In the nineteenth century, the British in India developed kedgeree from a local dish of rice cooked with lentils called kicheri. Bearing little resemblance to the original dish, kedgeree is most often made from left-over fish and rice. Although it is traditionally served at breakfast, try it as a supper dish accompanied by a crisp green salad.

SERVES FOUR

3 oz (75 g) butter
1 lb (450 g) smoked haddock, cooked, skin and bones removed, and flaked
$\frac{1}{2}$ lb (225 g) long-grain rice, boiled
2 hard-boiled eggs, chopped
Salt and pepper
Milk
Chopped parsley

Melt the butter in a large saucepan. Add the flaked fish and rice and stir over moderate heat until heated through. Stir in the eggs and seasoning. If the mixture looks too dry add 1 to 2 tablespoons of milk. Garnish with parsley and serve.

Clam fritters

Serve clam fritters as an hors d'oeuvre.

SERVES FOUR

24 small clams
$\frac{1}{2}$ pint (300 ml) fritter batter
Oil for deep frying
Lemon wedges
Parsley sprigs
$\frac{1}{2}$ pint (300 ml) tartare sauce

Put the clams in a saucepan with a little water and set over moderate heat for about 7 minutes. Remove the clams from the shells and pat them dry, discarding any that have not opened.

Heat the oil to 375°F (190°C). Dip the clams in the batter and deep fry for about 4 minutes or until golden. Arrange the clams in a basket lined with a napkin and garnish with lemon and parsley. Serve with tartare sauce.

New England fried scallops

Scallops can be deep fried, but their flavour is better enhanced by shallow frying in butter.

SERVES FOUR

12 scallops
White wine
2 tablespoons oil
1 tablespoon lemon juice
Salt and pepper
1 teaspoon chopped parsley
1 egg, beaten
Browned breadcrumbs
2 oz (50 g) butter
2 oz (50 g) tarragon butter
1 lemon, cut into quarters

Prepare the scallops and put them in a saucepan with enough white wine to cover. Simmer for 3 to 4 minutes. Set them aside to cool, then cut them in half across.

Mix together the oil, lemon juice, seasoning and parsley in a bowl. Toss the scallops in this mixture and leave to marinate for 30 minutes. Drain well and dip them in the beaten egg and coat with breadcrumbs.

Melt the butter in a frying-pan. Add the scallops and fry until browned on all sides. Serve with the tarragon butter and the lemon quarters.

Stir-fried giant prawns

For this adaptation of a Chinese dish use any large prawn about 5 inches (13 cm) in length. Serve the prawns as a first course or as part of a Chinese meal.

SERVES FOUR

8 large prawns, peeled, uncooked
Salt
$2\frac{1}{2}$ tablespoons soy sauce
$2\frac{1}{2}$ tablespoons dry sherry
1 tablespoon tomato purée
1 tablespoon vinegar
1 teaspoon Chinese chilli sauce
3 tablespoons oil

1 small onion, finely chopped
½-inch (1-cm) piece fresh root ginger, peeled and sliced
1 garlic clove, crushed
1 teaspoon sugar

Rub the prawns all over with salt. Mix the soy sauce, sherry, tomato purée, vinegar and chilli sauce in a small bowl. Set aside.

Heat the oil in a large frying-pan. Add the onion, ginger and garlic and stir-fry for 30 seconds. Add the prawns and stir-fry for 1 minute. Sprinkle the sugar over the prawns and pour in the soy and sherry mixture. Cook, stirring constantly, for 5 minutes. Serve immediately.

Bean sprouts and prawns Chinese style

SERVES FOUR

4 tablespoons oil
1 piece crystallized ginger, cut into fine strips
½ lb (225 g) mange-tout, washed
3 celery stalks, cut into fine strips
¼ lb (125 g) dried Chinese mushrooms, soaked in water for 20 minutes, drained and chopped
1 lb (450 g) bean sprouts, washed
1 teaspoon salt
1 garlic clove, finely chopped
1-inch (2-cm) piece fresh root ginger, finely chopped
½ lb (225 g) peeled prawns
Pepper
1 tablespoon soy sauce
2 teaspoons cornflour mixed with 2 tablespoons cold water
1 tablespoon dry sherry

Heat half the oil in a wok or large frying-pan and fry the ginger, mange-tout and celery for 3 minutes. Add the mushrooms and bean sprouts and fry, stirring constantly, for about 3 minutes. Stir in the salt. Using a slotted spoon, lift out the vegetables and set aside.

Add more oil to the pan, if necessary, and fry the garlic and the root ginger until golden. Add the prawns and cook, stirring, for 1 minute. Season with pepper. Return the vegetables to the pan. Mix the soy sauce with the cornflour mixture and sherry, add it to the pan and continue to stir-fry over gentle heat for about 4 minutes.

Sautéed frogs' legs à la niçoise

SERVES FOUR

12 pairs frogs' legs
½ pint (300 ml) milk
¼ lb (100 g) seasoned flour
2½ tablespoons oil
6 tomatoes, peeled and coarsely chopped
1 onion, finely chopped
1 garlic clove, crushed
Salt and pepper
2 oz (50 g) clarified butter
1 tablespoon chopped fresh parsley

Dip the frogs' legs in the milk and coat with the seasoned flour. Heat ½ a tablespoon of the oil in a saucepan. Add the tomatoes, onion and garlic, season well and cook over a medium heat. Heat the remaining oil with the clarified butter in a frying-pan and sauté the frogs' legs for about 10 minutes, turning once, or until browned on both sides.

Arrange the frogs' legs on a serving dish. Put a spoonful of tomato mixture on top of each pair of legs and sprinkle with parsley before serving.

Fried scampi

A single coating of egg and breadcrumbs can be used, but the double coating gives the fish a much crisper exterior. This recipe will serve two people as a main course and four as a first course.

SERVES TWO TO FOUR

2 egg yolks, mixed with 3 tablespoons milk
6 oz (175 g) dried white breadcrumbs
1 lb (450 g) large Dublin Bay prawns, peeled
Vegetable oil for deep frying
½ pint (300 ml) tartare sauce

Put the egg yolk mixture on one plate and the breadcrumbs on another. Dip each prawn first in the egg yolk mixture and then in the breadcrumbs, coating them all over. Repeat the process to give them a double coating.

Heat the oil to 375°F (190°C). Put all the coated prawns into a deep-frying basket and lower it into the oil. Fry the prawns for about 3 minutes, or until they are cooked through and a deep golden colour.

Line a warmed serving dish with a cloth or paper napkin. Place the prawns in the dish and serve immediately, with the tartare sauce in a separate bowl.

Squirrel fish

SERVES FOUR

2-lb (900-g) sea bass, cleaned and head removed
2 oz (50 g) flour
Oil for deep frying
2 tablespoons oil
1 onion, thinly sliced
4 dried Chinese mushrooms, soaked for 20 minutes in cold water, drained, and caps chopped
2 tomatoes, skinned and chopped
2 oz (50 g) bamboo shoots, thinly sliced
3 tablespoons chicken stock
3 tablespoons wine vinegar
2 tablespoons castor sugar
1 tablespoon soy sauce
1 tablespoon tomato purée
1 tablespoon cornflour, mixed with 4 tablespoons water

Split the fish but leave the tail intact. Cut out the backbone. Open out the fish and score the flesh with criss-cross cuts to within ¼ inch (½ cm) of the skin. Dredge with flour.

Heat the oil to 350°F (176°C). Fry the fish for 5 minutes. Lift out the fish and drain.

Heat the 2 tablespoons of oil in a frying-pan. Add the onion and stir-fry for 1 minute. Add the mushrooms, tomatoes and bamboo shoots and stir-fry for 2 minutes.

Combine the stock, vinegar, sugar, soy sauce, tomato purée and cornflour. Pour the mixture into the pan and cook, stirring constantly, until the sauce is thick. Remove from the heat.

Reheat the oil in the deep-frying pan to 375°F (190°C) and fry the fish again for 2 minutes or until it curls up.

Drain the fish and put it on a serving dish. Pour the sauce over the top and serve.

Coating fish for frying

To fry fish in breadcrumbs, dip them first in egg and milk.

Coat the fish all over in fresh or dried breadcrumbs.

To deep fry fish, dip them in a bowl of batter.

Drop the coated fish into hot oil and fry until golden.

Poultry and game birds

In the West the poultry that is most commonly cut into joints or small pieces and fried is chicken and turkey, but in the Middle East many very small birds are fried in butter, sprinkled with lemon juice and served between pieces of hot pitta.

For shallow frying, coat chicken or turkey pieces with seasoned flour or egg and breadcrumbs. After the initial browning reduce the heat and cook for fifteen to twenty minutes or until tender. Test by piercing the flesh with the point of a sharp knife—if the juices run clear the meat is cooked.

The length of time it takes to sauté chicken or turkey depends on the size of the pieces and whether or not liquid is to be added after the initial browning. The leg or thigh takes longer to cook than the breast or a wing, but should not take longer than about twenty-five to thirty minutes.

Game birds and small chickens may be cut in half and cooked slowly and gently in plenty of butter—a little wine, water or stock may be added after browning.

Chicken Maryland

This traditional American dish may be served with corn fritters and crisp bacon rolls.

SERVES FOUR

4-lb (2-kg) chicken, cut into serving pieces
3 oz (75 g) seasoned flour
Bacon fat or oil for frying
$1\frac{1}{2}$ tablespoons flour
8 fl oz (225 ml) cream
8 fl oz (225 ml) milk
Salt and pepper

Coat the chicken pieces thoroughly in the seasoned flour.

In a large sauté pan, heat 1 to $1\frac{1}{2}$ inches (2 to 3 cm) of bacon fat or oil. When the oil or fat is very hot add the chicken pieces and fry, turning occasionally, until browned on all sides. Reduce the heat to low, cover the pan and cook for 25 minutes or until the chicken is cooked. Alternatively, after the initial browning, transfer the chicken pieces to a covered ovenproof dish and cook in a 375°F (190°C, Gas Mark 5) oven for 30 minutes.

Test by piercing the flesh with the point of a sharp knife—if the juices run clear the chicken is cooked. Transfer the chicken pieces to a warmed serving dish and keep hot.

Pour away all but 4 tablespoons of the fat or oil in the pan. Stir in the flour and cook, stirring, for 2 minutes. Add the milk and cream gradually, stirring constantly to prevent lumps forming. Bring the sauce to the simmer and cook slowly until it is thick and smooth. Season to taste.

Pour the sauce into a sauce boat and serve with the chicken.

Chicken sauté à la bordelaise

SERVES FOUR

2 oz (50 g) butter
1 fl oz (25 ml) olive oil
4-lb (2-kg) chicken, jointed
1 garlic clove, crushed
$\frac{1}{4}$ pint (150 ml) chicken stock
5 tablespoons white wine
1 teaspoon meat glaze
1 tablespoon tomato purée
Salt
Black pepper
3 artichoke hearts, cooked, cut in quarters and fried in butter
1 lb (450 g) potatoes, sautéed
Deep-fried onion rings
Deep-fried parsley sprigs

Heat the butter with the oil in a sauté pan and sauté the chicken pieces until they are brown on all sides. Reduce the heat, cover and cook for about 30 minutes or until the chicken is tender. Test by inserting the point of a sharp knife into the flesh—if the juices run clear the chicken is cooked. Transfer the chicken to the centre of a large, warmed serving dish and keep hot.

Add the garlic to the sauté pan and fry for 1 minute. Stir in the stock, wine, meat glaze, purée and seasoning. Bring to the boil and cook, stirring constantly, until the sauce is reduced and slightly thickened. Strain the sauce over the chicken. Surround the chicken with the remaining ingredients and serve.

Chicken sauté a l'italienne

SERVES FOUR

4-lb (2-kg) chicken, jointed
Salt and pepper
$1\frac{1}{2}$ oz (40 g) butter
1 tablespoon olive oil

ITALIAN SAUCE

$\frac{1}{4}$ pint (150 ml) white wine
3 tablespoons duxelles
$\frac{1}{2}$ pint (300 m) demi-glace sauce
2 tablespoons tomato purée
Salt and pepper
1 tablespoon chopped ham
1 teaspoon chopped tarragon
1 teaspoon chopped chervil
1 tablespoon chopped parsley

Rub the chicken pieces with salt and pepper.

Heat the butter and oil in a sauté pan and cook the chicken pieces gently, turning them occasionally, for 30 to 40 minutes or until they are cooked. Test by inserting the point of a sharp knife into the flesh—if the juices run clear, the chicken is cooked.

While the chicken is cooking prepare the sauce. Mix the wine and the duxelles in a saucepan and bring to the boil. Boil rapidly until the wine is reduced by half. Stir in the demi-glace sauce and the tomato purée. Taste the sauce and add seasoning if necessary. Stir in the ham, tarragon, chervil and 1 teaspoon of the parsley.

Transfer the chicken to a warmed serving dish. Keep hot.

Pour the Italian sauce into the sauté pan. Bring to the boil, stirring and scraping the bottom of the pan.

Pour the sauce over the chicken, garnish with the remaining parsley and serve.

From left to right: chicken Kiev, chicken sauté à la bordelaise, and chicken Maryland.

Poultry and game birds

Chicken Kiev

Flatten the chicken breasts between sheets of cellophane.

Make the butter filling, shape it into a rectangle and chill.

Enclose one-quarter of the butter in each chicken breast.

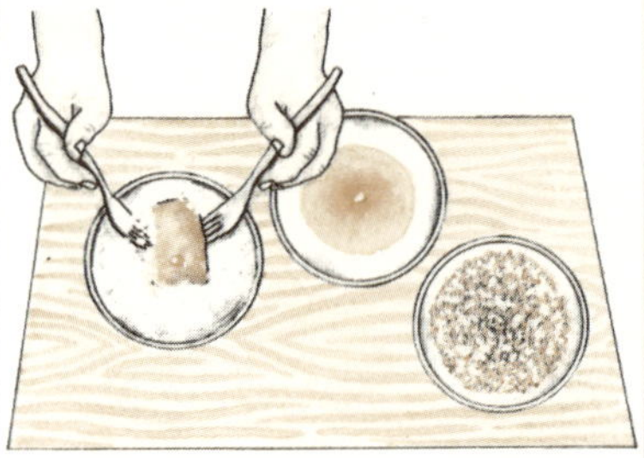

Fasten with cocktail sticks and coat in flour, egg and breadcrumbs.

Fry the chicken rolls in hot oil until crisp and golden brown.

Chicken Kiev

SERVES FOUR

4 chicken breasts, skinned and boned
2 oz (50 g) butter
1 tablespoon chopped fresh parsley
1 teaspoon chopped fresh tarragon
2 garlic cloves, crushed
Grated rind and juice of ½ lemon
Salt and pepper
Seasoned flour
1 egg, beaten
¼ lb (125 g) dry breadcrumbs
Oil for deep frying
1 lemon, quartered
1 bunch watercress, washed

Place the chicken breasts between 2 pieces of cellophane and flatten with a mallet or rolling pin.

Cream the butter in a mixing bowl. Beat in the herbs, garlic, lemon rind and seasoning and moisten with a teaspoon of the lemon juice. Shape the butter into a rectangle and chill in the refrigerator until firm.

Cut the chilled butter in 4 equal pieces and put 1 piece in the centre of each flattened chicken breast. Roll up tightly, folding in the edges so that the butter is completely encased, and secure each roll with a cocktail stick. Coat the chicken rolls first with flour, then with egg and lastly with the breadcrumbs. Put them on a plate and chill in the refrigerator for at least 1 hour.

Heat the oil to 375°F (190°C). Fry the chicken rolls for about 7 minutes or until they are golden. Drain well, transfer to a warmed platter, garnish with the lemon wedges and watercress and serve.

Deep-fried chicken

SERVES FOUR

2 tablespoons soy sauce
4 tablespoons lemon juice
½-inch (1-cm) piece fresh root ginger, peeled and grated
1 lb (450 g) cooked chicken, cut into 1½-inch (3-cm) cubes
Oil for deep frying
½ pint (300 ml) fritter batter
1 lemon, quartered

Mix the soy sauce, lemon juice and ginger in a large bowl for the marinade. Put the chicken in the marinade and leave, turning occasionally, for at least 1 hour.

Remove the chicken from the marinade and dry well on kitchen paper towels.

Heat the oil to 375°F (190°C). Coat the chicken cubes in the batter. Lower them into the oil in small batches and fry until golden. Using a slotted spoon, remove the chicken pieces and drain on kitchen paper towels. When all the chicken pieces have been fried increase the heat of the oil and return the whole batch in a frying-basket to the hot oil for a few seconds to crisp.

Drain and transfer the chicken pieces to a warmed serving dish and serve with lemon quarters.

Chicken lemon sauté

SERVES FOUR

4-lb (2-kg) chicken, cut into pieces
Salt and pepper
1 tablespoon oil
2 oz (50 g) butter
½ oz (15 g) flour
Rind and juice of 1 lemon
¼ pint (150 ml) chicken stock
2 tablespoons dry vermouth
2 teaspoons chopped fresh tarragon
4 tarragon sprigs, blanched

Season the chicken pieces.

Heat the oil and butter in a large sauté pan and sauté the chicken pieces for 8 to 12 minutes until they are evenly browned.

Transfer the chicken to a warmed dish and keep hot.

Pour off all but 1 tablespoon of the fat. Stir in the flour and cook for 2 minutes. Add the lemon juice and rind, stock, vermouth and chopped tarragon. Stir over moderate heat until the sauce has thickened.

Return the chicken pieces to the sauté pan. Cover the pan and simmer the chicken pieces very gently for 25 to 30 minutes or until they are cooked. Test by piercing the flesh with the point of a sharp knife—if the juices run clear the chicken is cooked. Transfer the chicken pieces to a warmed serving dish, strain the sauce over the chicken and garnish with the tarragon sprigs.

Poulet sauté chasseur

SERVES FOUR

1½ oz (40 g) butter
1 tablespoon oil
4-lb (2-kg) chicken, cut into serving pieces
6 oz (175 g) mushrooms, sliced
1 shallot, chopped
¼ pint (150 ml) white wine
½ pint (300 ml) chicken stock
1 tablespoon tomato purée
1 tablespoon brandy
Salt and pepper
1 teaspoon finely chopped fresh tarragon
1 teaspoon finely chopped fresh chervil
1 tablespoon finely chopped fresh parsley
Beurre manié

Heat the butter and oil in a large sauté pan and sauté the chicken pieces for 15 minutes or until they are well browned on all sides.

Reduce the heat and continue frying for 15 minutes. Add the mushrooms and shallot and fry, stirring, for 3 to 4 minutes or until the chicken is cooked. Test by inserting the point of a sharp knife into the flesh—if the juices run clear the chicken is cooked. Transfer the chicken to a warmed dish and keep hot.

Pour the wine into the pan and bring to the boil for 1 minute. Stir in the stock, tomato purée, brandy, seasoning, tarragon, chervil and 1 teaspoon of the parsley. If the sauce is too thin, stir in a little beurre manié, until slightly thickened.

Pour the sauce over the chicken, sprinkle the remaining parsley on top and serve.

Chicken kromeski

SERVES FOUR

¾ lb (350 g) cooked chicken, minced
1 teaspoon dried dill weed
2 oz (50 g) mushrooms, cooked and finely chopped
Salt and pepper
1 egg yolk
3 fl oz (75 ml) very thick béchamel sauce, made with ½ oz (15 g) butter and flour to 3 fl oz (75 ml) milk
8 bacon rashers
Oil for deep frying
½ pint (300 ml) fritter batter 1
½ pint (300 ml) tomato sauce

Mix the chicken, dill weed, mushrooms, seasoning, egg yolk and béchamel together. With well-floured hands shape the mixture into 8 croquettes.

Lay the bacon flat on a board, put 1 croquette on each rasher and roll up. Chill for 1 hour.

Heat the oil to 375°F (190°C). Dip the rolls in the batter and fry for 3 to 4 minutes or until golden brown. Drain on kitchen paper towels and serve hot with the tomato sauce.

Chicken with almonds

SERVES TWO TO FOUR

1 lb (450 g) boned chicken breasts, diced
1 tablespoon cornflour
2 tablespoons light soy sauce
2 tablespoons dry sherry
1 teaspoon sugar
2 tablespoons oil
½-inch (1-cm) piece fresh root ginger, peeled and finely chopped
6 spring onions, sliced
2 garlic cloves, crushed
¼ lb (125 g) almonds, blanched and split
Pepper

Rub the chicken cubes all over with the cornflour. Set aside.

Combine the soy sauce, sherry and sugar in a bowl.

Heat the oil in a large frying-pan. Add the ginger, spring onions and garlic and stir-fry for 30 seconds. Add the chicken and stir-fry for 2 minutes. Add the almonds and fry for 1 minute. Pour in the soy sauce mixture and some pepper and cook for 1½ minutes. Serve immediately.

Chicken sauté paprika

SERVES FOUR

4-lb (2-kg) chicken, jointed
Salt and pepper
2 oz (50 g) butter
2 tablespoons paprika
½ pint (300 ml) cream

Rub the chicken pieces all over with salt and pepper.

Melt the butter in a large sauté pan and fry the chicken pieces gently on all sides without browning. Stir in the paprika. Cover the pan and cook gently for about 30 to 35 minutes or until the chicken is tender. Test by piercing the flesh with the point of a sharp knife—if the juices run clear the chicken is cooked.

Transfer the chicken pieces to a warmed serving dish and keep hot.

Pour the cream into the sauté pan. Stir and scrape the pan to mix and bring to the boil. Boil until the cream is reduced by half.

Taste the sauce and add more salt and pepper if necessary. Pour the sauce over the chicken and serve.

Stir-fried chicken and mushrooms

SERVES FOUR

1 lb (450 g) boned chicken breasts, cut into ½-inch (1-cm) cubes
Salt
1 tablespoon cornflour
2 tablespoons sherry
2 tablespoons light soy sauce
4 tablespoons oil
1 garlic clove, crushed
½-inch (1-cm) piece fresh root ginger, peeled and grated
2 oz (50 g) dried mushrooms, soaked in water for 20 minutes and chopped
2 oz (50 g) water chestnuts, cut into small cubes

Rub the chicken all over with salt and cornflour. Set aside.

Mix the sherry and soy sauce in a small bowl. Set aside.

Heat 3 tablespoons of the oil in a wok or a large sauté pan over high heat. Stir in the garlic, ginger and mushrooms and stir-fry for 15 seconds. Add the chicken pieces. Stir-fry for 4 minutes. Pour in the sherry and soy sauce, reduce the heat and cook for 30 seconds. Add the water chestnuts and cook for a further 30 seconds. Serve immediately.

Guinea-fowl with juniper berries

Guinea-fowl has dry flesh so cook it very gently.

SERVES FOUR

3 oz (75 g) butter
2 guinea-fowl, cut in half
Juice and thinly pared rind of 1 orange
6 juniper berries, bruised
Salt and pepper
¼ pint (150 ml) Dubonnet

Melt the butter in a large sauté pan over low heat. Add the guinea-fowl and cook them gently, turning occasionally, for 15 minutes. Add the orange rind, juniper berries and seasoning and continue frying gently for another 15 minutes until the birds are browned.

Pour in the orange juice, scrape and stir to mix and bring to the simmer. Cover the pan and simmer very gently for a further 20 to 30 minutes or until the birds are cooked. Test by piercing the thighs with a skewer or the point of a knife. If the juices run clear the birds are cooked.

Lift out the birds and set aside on a plate. Remove the orange peel and juniper berries if you like. Pour the Dubonnet into the pan. Increase the heat and stir, scraping the bottom of the pan. Simmer the sauce for 30 seconds. Return the birds to the pan, baste with the sauce and simmer for 30 seconds or until hot. Serve immediately.

Wild duck à la Seville

Sweet oranges may be substituted for the Sevilles, but the flavour is less interesting.

SERVES FOUR

2 oz (50 g) butter
1 tablespoon oil
2 small wild ducks or 1 large mallard, jointed
¼ pint (150 ml) stock
2 Seville oranges
4 sugar lumps
2 tablespoons wine vinegar
Juice of ½ lemon
Salt and black pepper

Heat the butter and oil in a large sauté pan and sauté the duck pieces until they are well browned on all sides. Pour on the stock, cover the pan and cook for about 20 minutes or until the duck is cooked. Test by inserting the point of a sharp knife into the flesh—if the juices run clear the duck is cooked. Remove the duck pieces to a warmed serving dish and keep hot.

Meanwhile, pare the rind from one orange, cut into julienne strips and blanch. Remove the zest from the other orange by rubbing the skin with the sugar lumps.

Crush the sugar and stir into the pan with the vinegar, juice of 1 orange, lemon juice and seasoning. Bring to the boil and cook until syrupy. Taste and add more sugar or seasoning if necessary.

Strain the sauce over the duck, garnish with the orange rind and serve at once.

Sautéed partridge jubilee

SERVES FOUR

2 oz (50 g) butter
2 tablespoons olive oil
2 young patridges, halved
4 slices brown bread, cut in half diagonally
1½ oz (40 g) bacon fat
¼ lb (100 g) pâté de foie
½ lb (225 g) ripe black cherries, pitted
1 teaspoon sugar
1 teaspoon lemon juice
Salt and pepper
8 tablespoons Madeira
1 bunch watercress, washed

Heat the butter with the oil and sauté the partridges until browned on all sides. Continue cooking for about 25 minutes, until the birds are tender.

Meanwhile, fry the bread in the bacon fat, drain and spread with the pâté. Put the fried bread on a warm serving dish and put the partridges on top.

Return the sauté pan to the heat and stir in the cherries, sugar, lemon juice, seasoning and Madeira. Bring to the boil. Pour the sauce over the partridges and serve at once, garnished with watercress.

Chicken liver sauté

SERVES FOUR

1½ lb (700 g) chicken livers
2 oz (50 g) butter
1 Spanish onion, finely chopped
¼ pint (150 ml) red wine
½ teaspoon dried thyme
¼ bay leaf
Salt and pepper

Remove any skin or membrane from the chicken livers and cut each liver into quarters.

Melt the butter and fry the onion until it begins to colour. Add the chicken livers and fry quickly for 2 minutes.

Stir in the wine, herbs and seasoning. Cover and simmer for 3 to 4 minutes. Remove the bay leaf and serve at once.

Meat and game

The most suitable cuts of meat for shallow frying are beef fillet, rump or sirloin steak, lamb cutlets, lamb, veal or pork chops and such offal as liver and kidneys. Sausages, hamburgers and bacon may also be cooked in this way.

To fry steak, nick the fat around the outside to prevent the meat from curling up during cooking. Put the pan over high heat. Add just enough fat to grease the bottom of the pan. Fry the steak quickly on both sides to seal in the juices. Reduce the heat to moderate and cook, turning the meat occasionally, until the steak is cooked—a one-inch (2-cm) fillet steak will cook rare in four minutes. A one-and-a-half-inch (3-cm) steak will take about eight minutes. Season only when cooking is completed. Serve the steak with the deglazed pan juices poured over it.

Cook chops and cutlets in the same way but after the initial browning turn the heat down to fairly low and cook for a longer period—about sixteen to twenty minutes. Well-flattened veal escalopes, fried either plain or coated with flour or egg and breadcrumbs are ready as soon as they are browned on both sides. Coat thinly sliced liver with seasoned flour and fry for about six to eight minutes. Slit kidneys, skin and fry, flat side first, for about three to four minutes on each side over gentle heat. Prick sausages before frying to stop them bursting and fry for fifteen to twenty minutes or until they are well browned all over and cooked through. To fry bacon rashers, snip the rinds and cook for about five minutes.

Steak au poivre

The best steaks for this dish are fillet steaks. If rump steaks are used, score any fat to prevent the steaks curling up.

SERVES FOUR

1 to 3 tablespoons peppercorns, depending on taste
4 steaks, about 1 inch (2 cm) thick, weighing at least ½ lb (225 g) each
1 oz (25 g) butter
1 tablespoon olive oil
Salt
2 tablespoons brandy
4 tablespoons demi-glace sauce

Crush the peppercorns with a pestle or rolling-pin. Wipe the steaks dry and press the crushed peppercorns into both sides of the meat using the heel of your hand.

Heat the butter and oil together in a heavy frying-pan until very hot. Put in the steaks and fry for 3 to 4 minutes on each side for medium-rare, less for rare. Transfer the steaks to a hot dish and sprinkle with salt. Pour the brandy and demi-glace into the hot pan and boil rapidly for 30 seconds, scraping in all the sediment sticking to the pan. Pour the sauce over the steaks and serve at once.

Steak Diane

SERVES FOUR

4 fillet steaks, ¾ inch (2 cm) thick
1 oz (25 g) butter
1 tablespoon olive oil
1 tablespoon lemon juice
1 tablespoon Worcestershire sauce
1 teaspoon Dijon mustard
1 shallot, finely chopped
2 tablespoons chopped parsley

Flatten the steaks between greaseproof paper to about ¼ inch (½ cm) thick with a mallet or rolling pin.

Heat the butter and oil together in a heavy frying-pan until they are very hot. Put in the steaks and fry for 1 minute on each side if you like them medium-rare, longer if you like them well done. Transfer the steaks to a warmed serving dish and keep hot.

Add the lemon juice, Worcestershire sauce, mustard and shallot to the pan. Cook for one minute over medium heat, stirring all the time. Stir in the parsley. Pour the sauce over the steaks and serve.

Beef stroganoff

The success of this dish lies in the quick frying of the meat in very hot butter until brown all over. If the butter is not hot enough the meat will stew and the dish will not be as good.

SERVES FOUR

1½ to 2 lb (700 to 900 g) fillet steak
2 oz (50 g) clarified butter
2 medium-sized onions, thinly sliced
½ lb (225 g) button mushrooms, sliced
Salt and pepper
¼ pint (150 ml) soured cream

Cut the steak into thin strips, slightly on the diagonal, about ½ inch (1 cm) wide and 2 inches (5 cm) long.

Melt the butter in a large sauté pan and fry the onions until soft. Add the mushrooms and cook gently for 2 to 3 minutes.

Using a slotted spoon transfer the onions and mushrooms to a plate and keep hot. Increase the heat, adding more butter to the pan if necessary. When the butter is very hot put in the beef and fry quickly for 4 to 5 minutes. Return the onions and mushrooms to the pan and season well. Cook for another minute or two. Pour in the cream, let it come to just under boiling point and serve immediately.

Entrecôte à la viennoise

SERVES FOUR

4 entrecôte steaks, ¾ inch (2 cm) thick
Salt
1 teaspoon paprika
2 tablespoons plain plus 2 tablespoons seasoned flour
2 oz (50 g) butter or lard
2 onions, sliced into rings

Put the steaks between 2 sheets of greaseproof paper and beat with a rolling pin or mallet to flatten them. Season with salt and paprika and coat the steaks with the plain flour. Melt the

Three easy-to-make meat dishes: from top to bottom, sweet and sour meatballs, Wiener schnitzel and entrecôte au poivre vert.

butter or lard in a frying-pan over high heat and fry the steaks on both sides for 4 minutes until brown. Transfer to a warmed serving dish and keep hot.

Dip the onion rings in the seasoned flour and fry in the hot fat. Drain well on kitchen paper towels and arrange on top of the steaks. Serve at once.

Veal Zurich style

SERVES FOUR

1½ lb (700 g) boned leg of veal
3 tablespoons seasoned flour
2 oz (50 g) butter
1 tablespoon finely chopped shallots or spring onions
½ teaspoon paprika (optional)
¼ pint (150 ml) dry white wine
¼ pint (150 ml) cream
Salt and pepper

Slice the veal as thinly as possible across the grain and cut these slices into thin strips. Toss in seasoned flour.

Heat the butter in a sauté pan. Add the shallots or spring onions and fry for 1 to 2 minutes. Add the veal and sauté over high heat for 2 minutes or until well browned. Sprinkle with paprika, if you are using it. Reduce the heat, pour in the wine and bring to simmering point. Stir in the cream and reheat, but do not boil. Adjust the seasoning and serve at once.

Veal cutlets Milanese style

SERVES FOUR

4 veal cutlets
Salt and pepper
1 egg, beaten
2 oz (50 g) dried fine breadcrumbs
2 oz (50 g) butter
1 tablespoon olive oil

Flatten the cutlets. Season well, then dip in beaten egg and coat with the breadcrumbs.

Heat the butter and oil together and when hot fry the cutlets for 3 to 4 minutes on each side or until cooked through.

Meat and game

Fondue bourguignonne

The cooking is done by each guest at table, where the oil is kept hot over a spirit burner. Long skewers or fondue forks are a necessity.

SERVES FOUR TO SIX

2 lb (900 g) fillet or rump steak
1 pint (575 ml) corn oil
4 bowls of sauces such as béarnaise, horseradish, mayonnaise, aioli or chilli

Cut the steak into $\frac{1}{2}$-inch (1-cm) cubes, trimming off any fat or gristle. Heat the oil in the fondue pan until it is bubbling and very hot. Divide the meat between the guests and let each one in turn skewer a piece of meat and fry it in the hot oil. The meat is then dipped in the selected sauce before being eaten.

Veal Marsala

SERVES FOUR

8 small, thin veal escalopes
Salt and pepper
1 oz (25 g) flour
2 oz (50 g) butter
1 teaspoon lemon juice
2 to 3 tablespoons Marsala
2 tablespoons finely chopped parsley

Flatten the pieces of veal. Season with salt and pepper and roll in the flour. Melt the butter in a heavy sauté pan and sauté the veal for 3 to 4 minutes on each side or until golden.

Add the lemon juice and Marsala, stir well to amalgamate with all the pan juices, and simmer for 1 to 2 minutes. Serve sprinkled with parsley.

Noisettes of lamb with stuffed tomatoes

SERVES FOUR

8 lamb noisettes
Salt and pepper
3 oz (75 g) butter
1 small onion, finely chopped
$\frac{1}{4}$ lb (100 g) mushrooms, chopped
2 oz (50 g) cooked ham, chopped
2 teaspoons chopped mint
1 garlic clove, crushed
3 tablespoons yogurt
8 small tomatoes
8 round croûtons, hot
$\frac{1}{4}$ pint (150 ml) veal stock
2 teaspoons tomato purée
Fresh mint sprigs
1 lemon, sliced

Season the noisettes and set aside.

Preheat the oven to 350°F (180°C, Gas Mark 4). Melt half the butter in a saucepan and fry the onion until transparent. Add the mushrooms, ham, mint and garlic. Stir over moderate heat until the mushrooms are tender. Remove the pan from the heat and stir in the yogurt.

Cut the tops off the tomatoes and scoop out the centres. Fill the tomatoes with the mushroom and ham mixture and put them in a baking dish. Bake for 20 minutes.

Meanwhile, melt the rest of the butter in a frying-pan and fry the noisettes for 5 to 8 minutes on each side or until cooked and brown. Arrange the croûtons on a serving dish, put a noisette on each croûton and keep hot. Deglaze the pan with the stock. Boil until reduced by about half and stir in the tomato purée. Spoon the sauce over the noisettes, arrange the tomatoes in the centre of the dish and garnish with the mint sprigs and lemon slices.

Saltimbocca

SERVES FOUR

8 thin veal escalopes about 3 inches (8 cm) across
Salt and pepper
8 slices Parma ham the same size as the veal
8 sage leaves
2 oz (50 g) butter
4 tablespoons white wine

Flatten the veal well. Season lightly with salt and pepper. Put a sage leaf and then a slice of ham on top of each piece of veal. Roll and secure with a cocktail stick.

Heat the butter in a large frying-pan. When the butter is foaming add the rolls and fry briskly on all sides for 6 to 8 minutes or until they are cooked through and golden.

Transfer the escalopes to a warmed dish and keep hot.

Stir the wine into the juices in the pan and bring to the boil, scraping and stirring. Pour over the escalopes and serve.

Sautéed venison steaks

SERVES FOUR

4 venison steaks, $\frac{3}{4}$ inch (2 cm) thick
Salt and black pepper
1 onion, sliced
Rind and juice of $\frac{1}{2}$ lemon
8 juniper berries, crushed
$\frac{1}{2}$ teaspoon dried thyme
$\frac{1}{4}$ pint (150 ml) vermouth
2 tablespoons olive oil
2 oz (50 g) butter
2 tablespoons redcurrant jelly
1 lemon, sliced
Watercress

Season the steaks well on both sides and put them in a dish.

Mix together the onion, the lemon rind and juice, the juniper berries, thyme, vermouth and oil. Rub this into the steaks, cover the dish and refrigerate for at least one day.

Drain the meat and dry on kitchen paper towels. Reserve the marinade. Heat the butter in a heavy frying-pan. Fry the venison over low heat for about 10 to 12 minutes on each side. Cover the pan and cook for a further 20 minutes, turning once. Transfer the steaks to a warmed serving dish and keep hot.

Strain the marinade into the pan, add the redcurrant jelly and bring to the boil, stirring. Adjust the seasoning and pour the sauce over the steaks. Garnish with the lemon and watercress.

Veal chops en papillotes

The chops are brought to table in their paper wrappings.

SERVES FOUR

1 oz (25 g) butter
4 veal chops
Greaseproof paper or vegetable parchment
Oil
8 slices ham, the same size as the veal chops
8 tablespoons duxelles
Salt and pepper

Melt the butter in a frying-pan and fry the chops for 10 minutes on each side or until they are cooked through.

Preheat the oven to 400°F (200°C, Gas Mark 6).

Cut the greaseproof paper into 4 heart-shaped pieces. Lightly oil the paper. Lay 1 slice of ham on one half of each heart. Spread 1 tablespoon of duxelles on each slice and cover with the veal chops. Spread another tablespoon of duxelles on each chop and cover with another slice of ham. Season to taste.

Fold the other half of the paper hearts over and fold the edges like a hem. Put the papillotes on a baking tray and bake for 15 minutes or until the paper is puffed up and beginning to colour.

Remove the papillotes from the oven and serve immediately.

Making papillotes

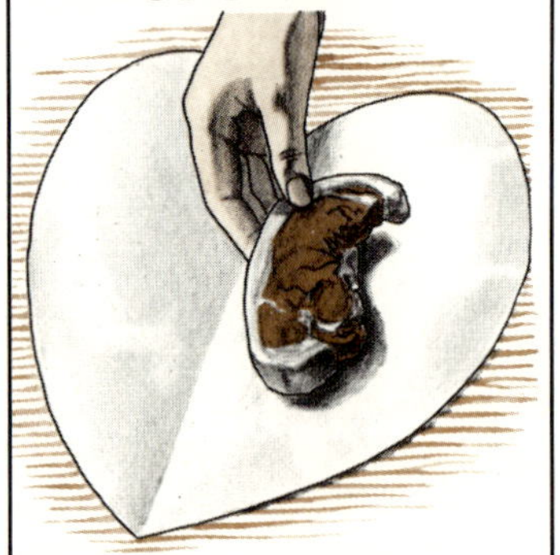

Put the ham and veal chop on a heart-shaped piece of paper.

Cover with duxelles and another slice of ham.

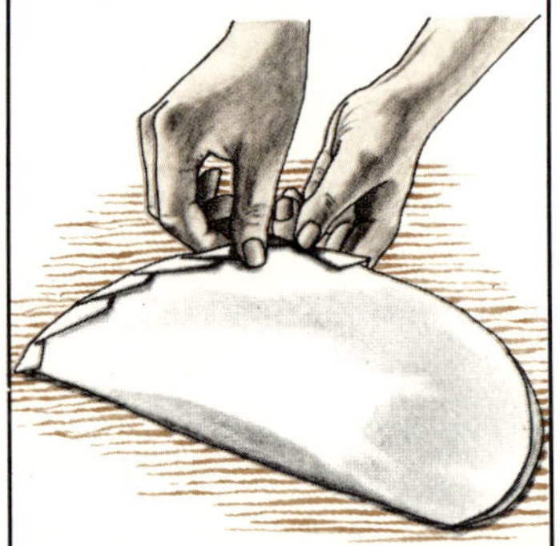

Fold the paper heart in half and pleat the edges to seal it.

Sautéed sweetbreads Saint Medard

Calves' sweetbreads are considered to be the most delicately flavoured of all offal. If you are using lambs' sweetbreads you will need ¼ pound (100 g) per person.

SERVES TWO

1 pair calf's sweetbreads, soaked, blanched and trimmed
1 oz (25 g) seasoned flour
2 oz (50 g) butter
1 tablespoon oil
1 tablespoon brandy
Salt and pepper
Nutmeg
¼ lb (100 g) mushrooms, sliced
2 oz (50 g) black olives, pitted and sliced
4 tablespoons Madeira
Juice of ½ lemon
¼ pint (150 ml) soured cream
4 slices bread cut into triangles and fried in butter

If you have time, press the sweetbreads between two pieces of greaseproof paper with a weight on top for at least 2 hours or overnight. This improves the texture and makes the sweetbreads an even thickness.

Slice the sweetbreads in half horizontally and toss them in the flour. Heat the butter and oil in a frying-pan and sauté the sweetbreads until golden on both sides. Heat the brandy in a ladle or small saucepan, ignite it, pour it over the sweetbreads and shake the pan gently until the flames die down. Season with salt, pepper and a little grated nutmeg.

Add the sliced mushrooms and olives and cook for a further 1 to 2 minutes. Stir in the Madeira and simmer for 5 minutes. Add the lemon juice and the soured cream. Reheat but do not boil. Garnish with the fried bread and serve at once.

Sautéed liver and bacon

SERVES FOUR

8 rashers streaky bacon
2 onions, cut into rings
1 lb (450 g) lambs' liver, thinly sliced
1 oz (25 g) well-seasoned flour
12 tablespoons stock
1 tablespoon chopped fresh tarragon (optional)
1 tablespoon butter
4 tomatoes, cut in half crossways and grilled

Fry the bacon and onions in a heavy frying-pan. Transfer the bacon and onions to a warmed serving dish and keep hot. Toss the liver in the seasoned flour and cook for about 2 minutes on each side. Transfer to the serving dish and keep hot.

Deglaze the frying-pan with the stock, add the chopped tarragon, if you are using it, and the butter.

Pour the sauce over the liver and serve at once, garnished with the grilled tomatoes.

Meatballs with sweet and sour sauce

These meatballs may be served with other sauces or with yogurt or soured cream. If you prefer a more spicy flavour add finely chopped root ginger, green chilli and garlic to the meat mixture and leave out the mushrooms.

SERVES FOUR

1½ lb (700 g) minced meat (pork or beef)
1 small onion, finely chopped
2 oz (50 g) mushrooms, finely chopped
1 teaspoon salt
1 teaspoon sugar
¼ teaspoon cayenne pepper
1 oz (25 g) fresh white breadcrumbs
1 egg yolk
3 tablespoons soy sauce
4 to 6 tablespoons oil

SAUCE

2 tablespoons oil
1 oz (25 g) dark brown sugar
1 teaspoon soy sauce
1 lb (450 g) canned pineapple chunks, drained and the liquid reserved
2 tablespoons wine vinegar
3 carrots, thinly sliced on the diagonal
2 green peppers, thinly sliced
1 tablespoon cornflour
3 tomatoes, quartered

Combine all the ingredients for the meatballs except the oil. With floured hands form the mixture into small balls.

Heat the oil in a large frying-pan and fry the meatballs for about 5 minutes or until they are cooked through and well browned.

Using a slotted spoon transfer the meatballs to a plate and set aside.

To make the sauce, rinse out the pan and return it to the heat. Pour in the oil, stir in the sugar, soy sauce, all but 3 tablespoons of the reserved pineapple liquid and the vinegar. Bring to the boil. Add the carrots and green pepper, reduce the heat and simmer for 2 minutes.

Mix the cornflour with the reserved 3 tablespoons of pineapple liquid and stir it into the pan. Cook for 1 minute and add the pineapple chunks, meatballs and tomatoes. Simmer for a few minutes until the meatballs are heated through. Serve immediately.

Entrecôte au poivre vert

SERVES FOUR

1 oz (25 g) butter
4 entrecôte steaks
Salt
2 tablespoons brandy
4 fl oz (125 ml) cream
1 to 2 tablespoons canned green peppercorns

Melt the butter in a large, heavy frying-pan over moderate heat. Add the steaks and fry them for 1 minute on each side. Reduce the heat to moderate and cook for a further 1 to 2 minutes on each side. Remove the steaks, season with salt and keep them hot on a warmed serving dish.

Add the brandy to the pan and stir, scraping the bottom of the pan to dislodge the sediments. Stir in the cream and peppercorns and, when the sauce is hot but not boiling, remove the pan from the heat and pour it over the steaks. Serve immediately.

Tournedos au vin rouge

Tournedos are cut from the heart of the fillet and should be at least 1 to 1½ inches (2 to 3 cm) thick. Serve the tournedos with new potatoes and young peas.

SERVES FOUR

2 oz (50 g) butter
1 tablespoon olive oil
4 tournedos
¼ pint (150 ml) red wine
4 round croûtons, hot
2 tablespoons meat glaze
Salt and pepper
2 teaspoons chopped fresh tarragon

Melt ½ oz (15 g) of the butter with the oil in a heavy frying-pan. When the fat is very hot add the tournedos and fry for 1 minute on each side to brown.

Pour in the wine, cook for a few seconds then reduce the heat to low and cook gently for about 3 to 4 minutes.

Arrange the croûtons on a warmed serving dish. Put the steaks on top of the croûtons and keep hot.

Increase the heat, stir the meat glaze into the wine and boil until reduced and syrupy. Remove the pan from the heat. Cut the remaining butter into small pieces and stir into the sauce one piece at a time. Season to taste and stir in the tarragon. Pour the sauce over the steaks and serve.

Wiener schnitzel

The escalopes for this dish should be large, round and paper thin. They are best served crisp, dry and straight from the frying-pan. Serve with a mixed salad.

SERVES FOUR

4 large veal escalopes
2 tablespoons seasoned flour
1 egg, beaten
Dried white breadcrumbs
2 to 3 oz (50 to 75 g) butter
1 to 2 tablespoons olive oil
1 lemon, peeled and cut into slices
2 hard-boiled eggs, the whites and yolks separated and finely chopped
4 to 8 green olives, pitted and halved
8 anchovy fillets
1 to 2 tablespoons chopped capers

Flatten the escalopes well. Dip in seasoned flour, then in the egg and coat with breadcrumbs.

Heat the butter and oil in a heavy pan and sauté the escalopes for 3 to 4 minutes on each side until golden brown. Drain well on kitchen paper towels and serve garnished with the lemon slices and eggs, olives, anchovies and capers.

Vegetables

A very wide variety of vegetables may be fried or sautéed.

For shallow frying very little fat is required—about one tablespoon of oil or butter for one pound (450 g) of vegetables. Cut or slice the vegetables evenly. Heat the fat in a frying or sauté pan and when it is very hot add the vegetables. Reduce the heat to low, cover the pan and cook, stirring occasionally, until the vegetables are tender.

To stir-fry, cut root vegetables into small, even-sized pieces, shred cabbage finely or cut into pieces and leave such vegetables as mange-tout whole. Cooked uncovered throughout, the vegetables are stirred constantly over high or moderately high heat and rarely take longer than five minutes to cook. About two tablespoons of oil will be required for one pound (450 g) of vegetables.

Many vegetables are suitable for deep frying, but with a few exceptions—potatoes, sweet potatoes and parsley, for example—they must be dipped in batter first. Heat the oil for deep frying vegetables (except potatoes) to 350° to 375°F (176° to 190°C). Potato chips and soufflé potatoes are fried twice; chips at 330°F (165°C) and then again at 375° to 400°F (190° to 204°C) and soufflé potatoes at 250°F (121°C) and 400°F (204°C). Soak potatoes in ice-cold water for thirty minutes before frying to remove excess starch.

Potato chips

SERVES FOUR

4 large old potatoes
Oil for deep frying
Salt

Peel the potatoes and cut them into ½-inch (1-cm) thick sticks using either a chip-cutter or a sharp knife.

As the chips are cut, put them in enough cold water to cover. Put all the chips in a colander and rinse them under cold running water. Alternatively, soak in iced water for 30 minutes. Drain and dry them with a clean towel.

Heat the oil to 330°F (165°C).

Put small batches of chips at a time in the frying basket and fry, shaking the basket gently, for about 2 to 3 minutes. Remove the chips and drain on kitchen paper towels.

When all the chips have been fried once, heat the oil to 375°F (190°C) and fry them again for a further 3 to 4 minutes or until they are crisp and golden brown. Remove and drain well on kitchen paper towels. Keep warm in an uncovered serving dish in the oven. Sprinkle the chips with plenty of salt and serve immediately.

Potato straws

Potato straws are prepared like chips except that they are cut into matchstick shapes and fried for a shorter period.

Game chips

Game chips are made from wafer-thin slices of potato (a mandolin cutter gives the best results) and fried for 2 to 4 minutes at 375°F (190°C).

Soufflé potatoes

Soufflé potatoes are difficult to make. They do not always puff up. Use old starchy potatoes cut very thinly lengthways (cut the slices in half if they are too big). Soak in iced water for 30 minutes, drain and dry well.

Heat the oil to 250°F (121°C) and fry the potatoes for 4 minutes. Lift out and drain. Increase the temperature of the oil to 400°F (204°C) and fry the potatoes again until they puff up.

Sprinkle with salt before serving.

Deliciously crisp vegetable fritters made with aubergines, mushrooms and courgettes.

Sauté potatoes

The provençal version of sauté potatoes has chopped garlic and parsley added just before the potatoes are ready.

SERVES FOUR

2 lb (900 g) old potatoes, peeled
3 oz (75 g) butter, or 2 tablespoons oil and 1 oz (25 g) butter
Salt and pepper

Boil the potatoes until they are just tender. Drain and leave to cool. Cut into $\frac{1}{4}$-inch ($\frac{1}{2}$-cm) thick slices.

Melt the butter or butter and oil in a large sauté or frying-pan and when it is hot add the potato slices and seasoning.

Sauté for about 5 minutes, shaking the pan occasionally, or until the undersides are well browned. Turn the whole batch of potatoes over and continue cooking, shaking the pan occasionally, until the potatoes are lightly browned.

Arrange in a warmed dish, season and serve at once.

Lyonnaise potatoes

Prepare as above, adding 4 thinly sliced onions with the potatoes.

Parisienne potatoes

Using a metal scoop, cut potatoes into balls and boil until nearly tender. Drain and sauté in butter in a frying-pan until cooked through and golden brown.

Potato croquettes

The croquettes may be varied by mixing the mashed potatoes with chopped herbs, grated onion, cheese or a little chutney.

Croquettes may also be shallow fried in $1\frac{1}{2}$ oz (40 g) butter and 4 tablespoons oil.

SERVES FOUR

2 lb (900 g) old potatoes, boiled and mashed
4 egg yolks
1 oz (25 g) butter
$1\frac{1}{2}$ teaspoons salt
$\frac{1}{2}$ teaspoon black pepper
About $\frac{1}{4}$ pint (150 ml) hot milk
1 egg, beaten
$\frac{1}{4}$ lb (125 g) dry white breadcrumbs
Oil for deep frying

Mix the potatoes, egg yolks, butter and seasoning in a large bowl. Add enough hot milk to make a firm paste and beat well until it is quite smooth.

With floured hands, divide the mixture into even-sized pieces made from about 2 tablespoons of potato. Set aside in the refrigerator on a lightly floured tray, in a single layer, and chill for 30 minutes or until firm.

Roll the pieces into cork shapes and dip them first in the beaten egg, then in the breadcrumbs, coating them all over.

Heat the oil to 375°F (190°C). Put a few of the croquettes in a single layer in a frying basket and lower into the hot oil. Fry for 3 to 5 minutes, or until they are golden brown on all sides. Drain well on kitchen paper towels and keep hot while you fry the remaining croquettes.

Rösti

A Swiss specialty, rösti is often served as a breakfast dish. Chopped onion, ham or grated cheese can be added to the potatoes before frying.

SERVES FOUR

2 lb (900 g) potatoes
Salt and pepper
3 oz (75 g) butter

Cook the potatoes in their skins in boiling water for 10 minutes. Drain and leave them to cool. When they are cold, peel them and grate the flesh coarsely into a bowl. Mix with salt and pepper to taste.

Melt half the butter in a large, heavy frying-pan and when it is sizzling add the potatoes, smoothing the top down lightly. Fry over moderate heat, loosening the base occasionally with a wooden spatula to prevent sticking.

After about 10 minutes, press the potatoes down with the spatula to form a cake. Invert a plate over the frying-pan and turn the rösti out on to it.

Melt the remaining butter in the pan. Slide the rösti back into the frying-pan and cook the other side, shaking the pan occasionally, for a further 10 to 15 minutes or until the underside is golden and crisp.

Turn the rösti out on to a warmed plate and serve at once.

Vegetables

Bubble and squeak

The quantities of potato and greens can be varied according to what is available, but the traditional proportions are half and half.

The mixture may be cooked as one large pancake or formed into individual cakes. Serve with grilled sausages or bacon.

SERVES FOUR

½ lb (225 g) mashed potatoes
½ lb (225 g) cooked green or white cabbage, greens or Brussels sprouts, coarsely chopped
Salt and freshly ground black pepper
2 oz (50 g) bacon fat, dripping or butter

Mix the potatoes, cabbage and seasoning in a bowl.

Melt the fat in a large frying-pan. Put the potato mixture into the pan and press it down well. Fry for about 4 minutes on each side until it is lightly browned and heated through. Slide on to a warmed serving plate and serve immediately.

Potato scones

This Irish/Scottish dish is not really a scone at all—it is more like a thick crêpe.

Potato scones may be eaten hot with plenty of butter and syrup or honey, or served with bacon or sausages.

MAKES ABOUT TWELVE

½ lb (225 g) freshly boiled potatoes, mashed
1½ oz (40 g) butter, melted
½ teaspoon salt
2 oz (50 g) flour

Mix the potatoes, butter and salt in a bowl. Add the flour gradually (the quantity required will depend upon the flouriness of the potatoes) until a soft dough forms. The dough must not be too dry.

On a lightly floured board, roll out the dough to about ¼ inch (½ cm) thick. Cut into large circles, about 6 to 8 inches (15 to 20 cm) in diameter, and cut each circle into quarters.

Cook either on an ungreased hot griddle or in a lightly greased heavy frying-pan for about 4 minutes on each side, or until the scones are lightly browned. Serve immediately.

Fried onions

Shallow-fried onions are cooked gently to produce a soft, almost creamy texture. The addition of cream and egg yolks makes this an excellent filling for a quiche.

SERVES FOUR

1½ oz (40 g) butter
1 lb (450 g) onions, thinly sliced
Salt and pepper

Melt the butter in a heavy frying-pan and stir in the onions, coating well with butter. Season to taste. Cover and fry very gently over very low heat, stirring frequently, for 15 minutes. Uncover the pan and fry for a further 20 minutes or until the onions are golden and tender.

Deep-fried onions

SERVES FOUR

1 lb (450 g) large onions, cut into ¼-inch (½-cm) slices
¼ pint (150 ml) fritter batter 1
Oil for deep frying

Heat the oil to 375°F (190°C). Separate the onion slices into rings. Dip the rings in the batter and fry them for 2 to 4 minutes or until golden brown. Remove with a slotted spoon and drain well on kitchen paper towels. Serve hot.

Fried mushrooms

SERVES FOUR

2 oz (50 g) butter
1 lb (450 g) mushrooms, wiped clean and sliced or halved or left whole, depending on size
Salt and pepper

Melt the butter in a large, heavy frying-pan. Add the mushrooms, season well and fry, stirring, for about 5 minutes.

Serve the pan juices with the mushrooms.

Deep-fried mushrooms

Serve hot as a first course with tartare sauce.

SERVES FOUR TO SIX

1 egg, well beaten
2 oz (50 g) fresh white breadcrumbs
1 lb (450 g) mushrooms, wiped clean
Oil for deep frying

Put the egg on one plate and the breadcrumbs on another and coat the mushrooms first with the egg and then the breadcrumbs.

Heat the oil to 375°F (190°C). Drop in the mushrooms and fry for about 3 minutes, or until they are lightly browned. Drain well and serve hot.

Duxelles

A useful flavouring for soups, sauces, stuffings and stews.

MAKES EIGHT TABLESPOONFULS

1 lb (450 g) mushrooms, wiped clean
¼ lb (125 g) butter
2 shallots, chopped
Salt and black pepper
Nutmeg

Chop the mushrooms finely, including the stalks. Put them on a clean cloth or on a kitchen paper towel, twist the towel and squeeze out any moisture.

Melt the butter in a frying-pan and fry the shallots gently for about 5 minutes.

Stir in the mushrooms and seasoning and cook over moderate heat, stirring constantly, for 40 to 50 minutes or until almost all the moisture has evaporated and the mixture is thick and rich.

Remove the pan from the heat and use immediately or store in the refrigerator.

Cauliflower cheese fritters

Broccoli may be prepared in the same way, but the cheese should be omitted from the batter.

SERVES FOUR TO SIX

1 cauliflower, washed
Oil for deep frying
2 tablespoons grated Parmesan cheese
½ pint (300 ml) fritter batter 1

Separate the cauliflower into florets and cook in boiling salted water for 5 minutes. Drain well and dry on kitchen paper towels. Set aside.

Heat the oil to 375°F (190°C).

Mix the cheese into the batter. Dip each floret in the batter and drop it into the oil. Fry for 4 to 5 minutes or until the fritters are golden brown.

Remove the fritters from the oil with a slotted spoon, drain well on kitchen paper towels and serve hot.

Pakoras with mint chutney

Pakoras are Indian fritters. They are spicy and salty and usually served with a chutney. Use any vegetable: whole spinach leaves, partially cooked cauliflower florets or thinly sliced potatoes. Gram (chick-pea) flour, or *besan* as it is called, is available at Indian or Pakistani food shops.

SERVES FOUR

¼ lb (125 g) gram flour
1 to 2 teaspoons chilli powder
1 teaspoon salt
½ teaspoon baking powder
Oil for deep frying
4 onions

MINT CHUTNEY

1 handful mint leaves, stalks removed
¼ pint (150 ml) yogurt
Juice of 1 lemon
2 green chillies, cores and seeds removed
4 tablespoons desiccated coconut
1 teaspoon salt
½ teaspoon sugar

First make the chutney. Put all the ingredients in a liquidizer and blend until smooth. Taste and adjust the seasoning. Put in a bowl and refrigerate for 3 hours.

To make the fritters, sift the flour, chilli powder, salt and baking powder into a bowl. Beat in enough water to make a light batter.

Heat the oil to 375°F (190°C).

Slice the onions and push into rings. Dip the rings into the batter and fry them singly. Alternatively, slice the onions thinly, mix with the batter and fry spoonfuls at a time.

Fry the onions until brown and crisp. Drain on kitchen paper towels and serve immediately with the chutney.

Sautéed aubergines

Other vegetables may be sautéed in the same way, but parsnips, Jerusalem artichokes, celeriac, salsify and sweet potatoes should be boiled until just tender, sliced and then sautéed.

SERVES FOUR

2 oz (50 g) butter
2 medium-sized aubergines, cut in ¼-inch (½-cm) slices, degorged, rinsed and patted dry

$\frac{1}{4}$ pint (150 ml) tomato sauce, kept hot
Chopped fresh parsley

Melt the butter in a large, heavy frying-pan and sauté the aubergines, turning occasionally, until golden brown on both sides. Lift from the pan with a slotted spoon, allowing any excess butter to drip back into the pan.

Transfer to a warm dish, pour over the tomato sauce, garnish with parsley and serve at once.

Aubergine fritters

Courgettes and marrow may be prepared in the same way.

SERVES FOUR

2 medium-sized aubergines, cut into $\frac{1}{4}$-inch ($\frac{1}{2}$-cm) slices or sticks, degorged, rinsed and thoroughly dried
$\frac{1}{4}$ pint (150 ml) fritter batter 1
Oil for deep frying

Heat the oil to 375°F (190°C).

Coat the aubergines in batter and fry for 3 to 4 minutes or until golden brown.

Remove the aubergines from the oil with a slotted spoon, drain well on kitchen paper towels and serve at once.

Corn fritters

Serve as an accompaniment to Chicken Maryland.

SERVES FOUR

$\frac{1}{4}$ lb (125 g) self-raising flour
1 egg, beaten
$\frac{1}{4}$ pint (150 ml) milk
Salt and freshly ground black pepper
One 11-oz (300-g) tin sweetcorn, drained, or 2 to 3 cobs of corn, cooked and stripped of kernels
2 oz (50 g) butter

Sift the flour into a bowl. Make a well in the centre and pour in the egg and milk. Add seasoning to taste and stir to draw the flour gradually into the liquid. When all the flour is incorporated, beat well until the batter is smooth. Stir in the sweetcorn.

Melt the butter in a large frying-pan and when it is hot drop in large spoonfuls of batter and fry for 2 to 3 minutes on each side or until the fritters are crisp and golden.

Pipérade

Pipérade can be served as a first course by itself, or as a light main dish on croûtons or slices of fried ham or gammon.

SERVES TWO

2 tablespoons olive oil
2 shallots, finely sliced
1 garlic clove, crushed
4 green peppers, cored, seeded and cut into strips
1 red pepper, cored, seeded and cut into strips
$1\frac{1}{2}$ lb (700 g) ripe tomatoes, skinned and chopped
1 tablespoon chopped fresh herbs
4 eggs, lightly beaten with plenty of salt and freshly ground pepper

Heat the oil in a large frying-pan over moderate heat. When the oil is hot, add the shallots and fry them until they are golden. Add the garlic and peppers and fry until the peppers are nearly tender. Stir in the tomatoes and herbs and cook until the tomatoes have formed a pulp.

Pour in the eggs and cook, stirring once or twice, until the mixture sets lightly. Serve immediately.

Deep-fried parsley

Fried parsley is used as a garnish for a variety of dishes, particularly grilled or fried fish.

SERVES FOUR

1 large handful fresh parsley, washed if necessary, and thoroughly dried
Oil for deep frying

Cut off the parsley stems, leaving only the leaves.

Heat the oil to 375°F (190°C) and lower the parsley into the oil in a frying basket. The oil will hiss and bubble vigorously for 1 to 2 minutes. As soon as the hissing stops, remove the basket. The parsley should be very crisp and green. Drain well and serve at once.

Stir-fried bean sprouts

Almost any vegetable may be used—whole mange-tout, shredded Chinese cabbage, sliced green beans or diced bamboo shoots. Small pieces of raw or cooked meat, fish or shellfish may be added.

SERVES FOUR

2 tablespoons vegetable oil
1 onion, thinly sliced
2 teaspoons finely shredded root ginger
1 lb (450 g) bean sprouts, washed
Salt

Heat the oil in a large frying-pan or wok and fry the onion and ginger, stirring constantly, for 2 minutes.

Add the bean sprouts and salt to taste and stir-fry for a further 2 minutes. Serve immediately.

Fruit

Fruit for shallow frying or sautéing should be quite ripe but not mushy. Those most successfully cooked in this way are apples, pineapples, bananas, peaches and apricots. Serve them as an accompaniment to meat, game and poultry dishes—apples, for example, go well with bacon, and peaches complement pork or goose.

Shallow-fried fruits may also be served for dessert, and they taste especially good if they are marinated in wine or liqueur for an hour or so before cooking. Add a little sugar and such spices as cinnamon, nutmeg, allspice or ginger and a few drops of lemon juice half-way through the cooking time when the fruit has been turned.

All the fruits suitable for shallow frying may also be dipped in fritter batter and deep fried.

Special apple fritters

SERVES FOUR

4 tart, crisp apples, peeled and cored
1 tablespoon lemon juice
Grated rind of 1 lemon
1 tablespoon apricot brandy
4 tablespoons icing sugar, sifted
6 tablespoons apricot jam
4 tablespoons water
$\frac{1}{4}$ lb (125 g) macaroons, finely crushed
$\frac{1}{4}$ pint (150 ml) fritter batter 1
Oil for deep frying
$\frac{1}{4}$ pint (150 ml) double cream, lightly whipped

Cut the apples into thick rings. Put them on a plate and sprinkle with the lemon juice, lemon rind, apricot brandy and 3 tablespoons of the icing sugar. Turn the apple rings in the mixture to coat them evenly.

Put the jam and water into a saucepan. Bring to the boil, then simmer for 5 minutes. Sieve the glaze, and if it is not thick enough, return it to the pan and cook for a little longer.

Coat each apple ring with the glaze. Put the macaroon crumbs on a plate. Dip the apple rings in the crumbs to coat well on both sides. Put the apple rings on a plate and set aside for 15 minutes.

Heat the oil to 375°F (190°C). Have the batter ready in a bowl. Using a skewer or fork dip the apple rings in the batter and then drop them into the oil. Fry, turning once or twice, until the apple rings are crisp and golden brown.

Drain on kitchen paper towels. Dust with the remaining icing sugar and serve hot with the cream.

Apple fritters

The prepared fruit may be marinated in liqueur and then drained before being dipped in the batter.

Other fruits that may be used are banana or pear halves, pineapple or orange slices and pitted cherries. Prunes should be marinated in tea or port for a few hours or overnight. Stone them and stuff each one with a blanched almond.

SERVES FOUR

4 large apples, peeled, cored and cut into $\frac{1}{4}$-inch ($\frac{1}{2}$-cm) thick rings
$\frac{1}{4}$ lb (125 g) vanilla sugar
$\frac{3}{4}$ pint (450 ml) fritter batter 1
Oil for deep frying
Icing sugar

Dip the apple rings in the vanilla sugar and then coat them in the batter. Heat the fat to 375°F (190°C) and fry the apple rings for about 4 minutes or until they are golden. Drain well, sprinkle over the icing sugar and serve.

Apricot fritters

Peach halves or whole strawberries may also be used. Marinate the apricots in the juice of freshly squeezed oranges. Drain before coating in batter.

Winter fritters

Soak mixed dried fruit in sherry for several hours. Drain, mix into the batter and fry spoonfuls at a time. Drain well and dredge with icing sugar.

Sautéed bananas, caramelized pineapple and apple fritters.

Banana and bacon fritters

SERVES FOUR

2 large bananas, peeled and cut in half lengthways
8 bacon rashers, cut across in half
$\frac{1}{4}$ pint (150 ml) fritter batter 1
Oil for deep frying

Cut the banana halves into 4 pieces, making 16 in all. Wrap each piece in bacon and secure with a cocktail stick.

Heat the oil to 375°F (190°C). Dip the bacon rolls into the batter and drop into the oil. Fry until golden brown and crisp.

Sautéed bananas

SERVES FOUR

2 oz (50 g) butter
4 bananas, peeled and sliced lengthways

1 tablespoon soft brown sugar
Juice and grated rind of 1 orange
1 tablespoon flaked almonds, toasted

Melt the butter in a large sauté pan and, when it is hot, add the bananas. Cook for 3 minutes, then turn the bananas carefully. Sprinkle over the sugar, orange juice and rind and cook for a further 3 minutes. Transfer the bananas to a warm serving platter, pour over the juices, and scatter the almonds on top. Serve at once.

Fried apples and bacon

SERVES THREE TO FOUR

1 oz (25 g) butter
½ lb (225 g) bacon rashers
2 tablespoons brown sugar
1 lb (450 g) cooking apples, peeled, cored and sliced

Melt the butter in a frying-pan, add the bacon and fry until crisp. Remove the bacon from the pan, put it in a warmed serving dish and keep hot.

Add the sugar to the pan and stir well. Add the apple slices and cook for about 5 minutes or until they are quite soft and well caramelized.

Transfer the apples to the serving dish and serve at once.

Apples with Calvados

SERVES FOUR

2 oz (50 g) butter
2 lb (900 g) dessert apples, peeled, cored and sliced
2 oz (50 g) castor sugar
Grated rind of ½ lemon
2 tablespoons Calvados

Melt the butter in a large sauté pan. Add the apples, sugar and lemon rind and cook for about 4 minutes, shaking the pan once or twice, until the apples begin to change colour. Pour on the Calvados, cook for another 2 minutes and serve at once.

Caramelized pineapple

SERVES FOUR

2 oz (50 g) butter
2 tablespoons honey
1 pineapple, peeled, cut in ½-inch (1-cm) slices and cored
1 tablespoon brown sugar
Juice of ½ lemon
2 oz (50 g) toasted almonds

Melt the butter in a large frying-pan. Stir in the honey, and when the mixture bubbles add the pineapple rings. Sprinkle with the sugar and cook quickly for 1 minute. Turn, baste with the syrup and sprinkle with the lemon juice.

Overlap the pineapple rings on a warmed serving platter, sprinkle the almonds on top and serve at once.

Salted almonds

For devilled almonds add ¼ to ½ teaspoon cayenne pepper while frying.

SERVES FOUR

1 tablespoon oil
½ lb (225 g) almonds, blanched
Salt

Heat the oil in a large frying-pan. Add the almonds and fry, turning them over frequently, until golden brown. Remove and spread on kitchen paper towels. Toss the almonds in salt while they are still warm.

Cereals

Pancakes, fritters, waffles, crumpets—so many of the foods made with batter are easy to cook, inexpensive and delicious.

For pancakes, use a special straight-sided pancake pan or a heavy frying-pan about six inches (15 cm) in diameter. Ideally it should be made of cast-iron and seasoned when newly bought (see page 8). Any pan kept exclusively for pancakes should never be washed, just lightly oiled and wiped clean.

Waffles can only be cooked in a special waffle iron, which should be seasoned in a similar way to a pancake or omelette pan. It should not need further greasing as waffle batter is fairly buttery.

Crumpets and muffins are best cooked on a lightly greased griddle or on a heavy baking sheet.

The other cereals that can be fried are rice, noodles and bread, which can be served as accompaniments to a wide variety of dishes.

Fritter batter 1

For a sweet batter add 2 teaspoons of castor sugar to the flour.

MAKES ABOUT EIGHT FLUID OUNCES (225 ML)

¼ lb (100 g) flour
¼ teaspoon salt
1 tablespoon cooking oil
1 egg, separated
¼ pint (150 ml) tepid beer, milk or water, or a combination of these

Sift the flour and salt into a mixing bowl. Make a well in the centre and pour in the oil and egg yolk. Using a wire whisk mix the oil and egg yolk together, gradually drawing in the flour and adding the liquid a little at a time. Whisk the batter until smooth and creamy. If beer is used, set aside, covered, for at least 2 hours.

Beat the egg white until stiff and fold into the batter. Use immediately.

Fritter batter 2

MAKES ABOUT EIGHT FLUID OUNCES (225 ML)

¼ oz (10 g) fresh yeast
¼ pint (150 ml) warm water
¼ lb (100 g) plain flour
¼ teaspoon salt
1 tablespoon cooking oil or melted butter
1 egg white, stiffly beaten (optional)

Dissolve the yeast in half the water. Set aside in a warm place for 10 minutes or until puffed up and frothy.

Sift the flour and salt into a mixing bowl. Make a well in the centre and pour in the yeast. Using a wire whisk gradually incorporate the flour, adding the remaining water and the oil or butter a little at a time. Whisk the batter until smooth and creamy. Leave, covered, in a warm place for about 1 hour.

If a crisper fritter is required fold in the stiffly beaten egg white just before the batter is used.

Pancakes (crêpes)

If the first pancakes are to be kept warm while the remainder are being cooked, overlap them on a lightly buttered ovenproof dish and keep covered in a moderate oven. Alternatively, a large plate can be placed over a saucepan of hot water, the pancakes stacked on the plate and covered with a second plate.

Pancakes can be cooked in advance, cooled and stored for later use. They may be stacked, with a piece of greaseproof paper between each one, and stored in an airtight container in the refrigerator for 2 to 3 days or in the deep-freeze for 3 months.

Serve pancakes in the traditional Shrove Tuesday fashion with just a squeeze of lemon juice and some castor sugar. Or fill with jam or ice-cream, roll and dust with icing sugar.

MAKES ABOUT TWELVE

¼ lb (100 g) flour
Pinch salt
1 whole egg plus 1 egg yolk, beaten
1 oz (25 g) butter, melted
½ pint (300 ml) milk, or half milk and half water
Butter for frying

Sift the flour and salt into a mixing bowl. Make a well in the centre and put in the eggs and melted butter. Using a wire whisk beat the eggs and melted butter together, incorporating the flour gradually and adding the milk a little at a time. Beat until smooth.

Heat a frying-pan and melt a scant ¼ ounce (10 g) of butter, rolling it around the base and sides of the pan. When it is very hot (if a few drops of water flicked into the pan spit and jump, the pan is hot enough) pour in a tablespoon of batter and tip the pan so that it runs all over the base. If the first pancake is too thick add a little more liquid to the batter.

After about 30 seconds the underside of the pancake will be golden and cooked. Either toss the pancake by flicking the pan sharply upwards with a firm movement of the wrists, or turn carefully with a large fish-slice.

If the pan should become very dry, melt another small nut of butter before cooking the remaining batter.

Pancakes

Melt some butter in a pancake pan and when it is very hot pour in the pancake batter.

Swirl the batter around the pan and cook one side. Flip the pancake over carefully.

Crêpes Suzette

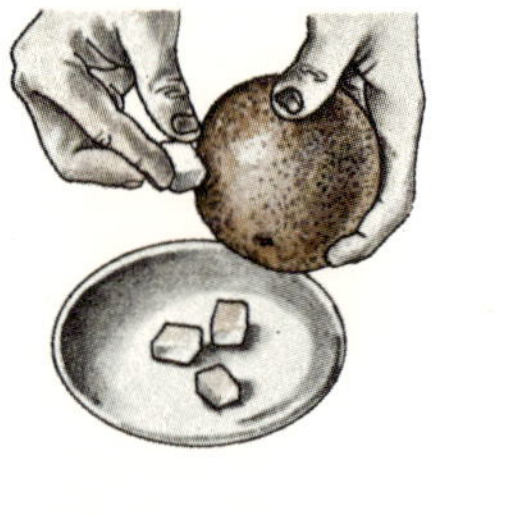

To make the filling, rub sugar lumps over the orange skins to extract the zest.

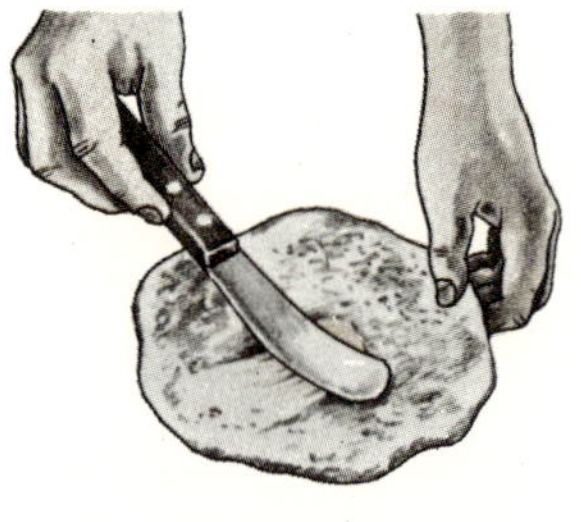

Using a palette knife, spread a little of the orange butter evenly over each pancake.

Fold the pancakes into quarters and lay them, overlapping, in an ovenproof serving dish.

Warm the brandy and Cointreau slightly, ignite them and pour over the crêpes. Serve hot.

Crêpes Suzette

SERVES SIX

6 sugar lumps
2 oranges
¼ lb (125 g) unsalted butter
1 tablespoon orange juice
5 tablespoons Cointreau
12 paper-thin crêpes
4 tablespoons brandy

Preheat the oven to 425°F (220°C, Gas Mark 7).

Rub the sugar lumps all over the rind of the oranges until they are completely impregnated with the oil. Put the sugar in a bowl and crush the lumps.

Cream the butter. Add the crushed sugar and beat until smooth. Beat in the orange juice and 1 tablespoon of the Cointreau.

Spread the crêpes with the orange butter. Fold the crêpes in quarters like a handkerchief and lay them overlapping in an ovenproof dish. Cover and put in the oven for 5 minutes.

Put the remaining Cointreau and brandy in a small saucepan, warm slightly, set alight and pour flaming on to the crêpes. Serve immediately.

Drop scones

These small, thick pancakes may be eaten hot with butter, jam, honey or syrup or can be cooled and stored for several days in an airtight container. They can then be eaten cold or toasted.

MAKES ABOUT TWELVE

½ lb (225 g) self-raising flour
Pinch salt
1 oz (25 g) castor sugar
2 eggs, beaten
1 tablespoon golden syrup
½ pint (300 ml) milk
Oil or butter

Sift the flour and salt into a mixing bowl and add the sugar.

Make a well in the centre and pour in the eggs and syrup. Using a wooden spoon beat the eggs and syrup, gradually drawing in the flour and adding the milk by degrees. When the batter has the consistency of thick cream stop adding the milk.

Lightly grease a griddle or heavy frying-pan with oil or butter and put it over moderate heat. Drop spoonfuls of the batter on to the griddle. After 2 to 3 minutes bubbles will appear on the surface and the underside will be golden. Turn the scones using a fish-slice. Cook the second side for 2 to 3 minutes or until golden.

Blini

These light yeast pancakes are a Russian speciality traditionally served with caviar and soured cream. They may also be served with smoked roe, chopped hard-boiled egg and melted butter.

Blini should be no larger than 2 to 3 inches (5 to 8 cm) in diameter.

MAKES ABOUT FORTY

¼ oz (10 g) fresh yeast
¼ teaspoon sugar
¼ pint (150 ml) warm water
6 oz (175 g) buckwheat flour
¾ pint (450 ml) milk, warm
6 oz (175 g) flour, sifted
3 eggs, separated
½ teaspoon salt
2 tablespoons melted butter
¼ lb (100 g) butter

Mash the yeast with the sugar in a small bowl. Mix in the water and set aside in a warm place for about 10 to 15 minutes or until the yeast is puffed up.

Put the buckwheat flour in a large mixing bowl, beat in the yeast mixture and enough of the milk to make a smooth batter the consistency of thick cream. Cover the bowl with a cloth and leave in a warm place for 2 hours or until the batter has risen and doubled in bulk.

Meanwhile, make a second batter. Put the flour into another bowl and beat in the egg yolks, salt, melted butter and the remaining milk. Combine the two batters, cover the bowl and leave in a warm place for 30 minutes.

Whisk the egg whites until stiff, fold into the batter, cover again and leave in a warm place for a further 20 minutes.

Heat a large, heavy frying-pan or griddle. Add ½ ounce (15 g) of the butter and when it is sizzling pour in 4 separate tablespoons of the batter, to make 4 blini. Cook for about 1 minute or until golden. Turn the pancakes and if necessary add more butter. Cook for 1 minute. Remove from the pan and keep warm while you cook the remaining blini. Serve at once.

Crumpets

Crumpet rings and a griddle or a heavy baking sheet are needed for making crumpets.

MAKES TEN

¼ oz (10 g) yeast
¼ teaspoon sugar
½ pint (300 ml) milk, lukewarm
½ lb (225 g) flour
¼ teaspoon salt

Mash the yeast with the sugar in a small bowl. Beat in 2 tablespoons of the milk and set aside in a warm place for 15 minutes or until puffed up and frothy.

Put the flour and salt in a large, warm mixing bowl, make a well in the centre and pour in the yeast and the rest of the milk. Mix thoroughly, gradually drawing in the flour, until the batter has the consistency of thin cream. Add more warm milk if necessary. Cover the bowl with a cloth and put in a warm place for 45 minutes or until the batter has doubled in bulk.

Lightly grease a griddle or heavy baking sheet. Use as many rings as the griddle or baking sheet will take and heat.

Pour about 2 tablespoons of the batter into each ring; the batter must fill the ring to a depth of about ¼ inch (½ cm). Cook for about 5 minutes or until bubbles appear and the batter is slightly set and golden brown underneath. Remove the rings, turn the crumpets and cook on the second side until golden. Toast before eating.

Muffins

Serve muffins toasted and buttered, on their own or with scrambled or poached eggs.

MAKES EIGHT

½ lb (225 g) flour
½ teaspoon salt
2 teaspoons baking powder
2 tablespoons sugar
1 egg
2 oz (50 g) butter, melted
¼ pint (150 ml) buttermilk

Sift the flour, salt and baking powder into a large bowl and mix in the sugar.

Beat the egg lightly in another bowl. Mix in the butter and the buttermilk.

Mix the buttermilk mixture into the dry ingredients quickly and lightly to make a soft dough. Ignore any lumps, and do not overmix the dough.

Using floured hands, divide the dough into 8 pieces. Roll each piece into a ball, then flatten it with your hand or with a rolling-pin until it is about ½ inch (1 cm) thick. Use crumpet rings if you want to make quite sure that the muffins keep their shape. Cook on both sides on a greased griddle until they are lightly browned.

Waffles

Waffles can be eaten plain, with maple syrup, jam or honey, or the batter can be prepared with pieces of finely chopped bacon, fruit or grated cheese.

MAKES ABOUT TWENTY

6 oz (175 g) flour
¼ teaspoon salt
2 teaspoons baking powder
1 tablespoon castor sugar
2 large eggs, separated
½ pint (300 ml) milk
4 tablespoons melted butter

Sift the flour, salt, baking powder and sugar into a large mixing bowl. Make a well in the centre and pour in the egg yolks. Add the milk and butter and mix quickly and lightly—it does not matter if the batter is not smooth.

Whisk the egg whites until stiff and fold into the batter.

Have the waffle iron heated, pour in enough batter to completely cover the base of the iron, close the lid and cook until no more steam escapes from the iron—about 2 to 4 minutes. Serve at once, very hot.

English doughnuts

These doughnuts may be slit with the point of a sharp knife and stuffed with 1 teaspoon of jam.

MAKES TWELVE

½ oz (15 g) fresh yeast
¼ teaspoon plus 3½ oz (90 g) sugar
¼ pint (150 ml) milk, warmed
½ lb (225 g) flour
¼ teaspoon salt
2 oz (50 g) butter
1 egg, beaten
Oil for deep frying

Cereals

Mix the yeast with the ¼ teaspoon of sugar in a small bowl. Add 2 tablespoons of the warm milk and mix until smooth. Set aside in a warm place for 15 minutes or until it is puffed up and frothy.

Sift the flour and salt into a warmed bowl. Rub the butter into the flour. Stir in 1 ounce (25 g) of the sugar.

Make a well in the flour mixture and pour in the yeast, the remaining milk and the egg. Mix well to make a dough and knead until smooth. Cover the bowl with a cloth and leave to stand in a warm place for 45 minutes or until the dough has risen and doubled in bulk.

Turn out the dough and knead for 5 minutes. Roll the dough out on a floured board to about ¼ inch (½ cm) thick. Using a well-floured, plain 2-inch (5-cm) cutter, cut the dough into circles.

Put the doughnuts on a lightly floured baking tray in a warm place for 30 minutes or until they have doubled in size.

Heat the oil to 375°F (190°C) in a deep-frying pan. Fry 4 to 5 doughnuts at a time for about 3 to 5 minutes until they are golden brown, turning them once.

Using a slotted spoon lift them out and drain well on kitchen paper towels. Leave to cool a little and sprinkle with the remaining sugar. Eat hot.

American doughnuts

MAKES TWELVE

1 egg
2 fl oz (50 ml) milk
2 oz (50 g) butter, melted
½ lb (225 g) flour
2 teaspoons baking powder
Salt
Grated nutmeg
Ground cinnamon
3 oz (75 g) castor sugar
Oil for deep frying

Beat the egg in a small bowl. Beat in the milk and melted butter.

Sift the flour, baking powder and a pinch each of salt, nutmeg and cinnamon into a large bowl. Stir in 2 ounces (50 g) of the sugar. Make a well in the centre and pour in the egg and milk mixture. Mix it in well to make a dough. Add more milk if the dough is too firm.

Cover the dough and put it in the refrigerator for 30 minutes.

Roll out the dough on a lightly floured board until it is ½ inch (1 cm) thick. Using a 2½-inch (6-cm) biscuit cutter cut out rounds. Use a 1½-inch (3-cm) cutter to cut out the centres. Leave the doughnuts to rest for 10 minutes.

Heat the oil to 375°F (190°C) in a deep-frying pan. Add the doughnuts and fry for 5 minutes or until they are golden brown. Using a slotted spoon, lift out the doughnuts and drain well.

Dust the doughnuts with the remaining sugar.

Beignets soufflés

These French fritters may be served just sprinkled with castor sugar or with a sauce—a tart fruit sauce is best.

SERVES SIX

Oil for deep frying
5 oz (150 g) choux pastry
Castor sugar

LEMON SAUCE

3 oz (75 g) sugar
1 level teaspoon cornflour
½ pint (300 ml) water
1 oz (25 g) butter
Rind and juice of 1 lemon

First make the sauce. Mix the sugar and cornflour together in a saucepan. Pour in the water gradually and stir to mix until the sauce begins to bubble. Simmer for 1 minute, then remove from the heat. Stir in the butter and the lemon rind and juice.

Heat the oil to 370°F (180°C). Drop teaspoonfuls of the choux pastry into the hot oil and fry until golden brown. Drain, dust with sugar and serve with the sauce.

French toast

French toast may be served with jam or a fruit purée.

SERVES FOUR

3 fl oz (75 ml) milk
1 egg, beaten
Pinch salt
1 oz (25 g) vanilla sugar
4 slices day-old white bread, crusts removed
2 oz (50 g) butter

Whisk the milk, egg, salt and sugar and put it in a dish.

Put the bread in the egg and milk mixture and set aside for 5 minutes, turning once.

Heat the butter in a frying-pan and when it is sizzling put in the bread and fry for 2 to 3 minutes on each side or until golden.

Using a fish-slice, lift out the French toast, hold over the pan for a few seconds to drain and serve immediately.

Fried bread

Serve with fried egg and bacon or as an accompaniment to meat or poultry dishes.

SERVES TWO

1½ oz (40 g) bacon fat or dripping
2 slices day-old bread, halved

Heat the fat in a frying-pan and when it is very hot put in the bread and fry quickly on both sides until lightly browned.

Lift with a fish-slice, hold over the pan for a few seconds to drain and serve at once.

Croûtons

Croûtons can be made in all sizes and shapes. Large croûtons are used as a base on which to put steaks and noisettes. Small croûtons are used as garnishes for soups.

They may be shallow fried in butter or deep fried in oil and are prepared from thick slices of day-old white bread cut into squares, rounds or heart-shapes.

If the croûtons are shallow fried, the butter should not be too hot. Turn them after 2 to 3 minutes or when golden brown. To deep fry heat the oil to 375°F (190°C). Use a frying-basket and drain well on kitchen paper towels. Sprinkle over soup at the last minute.

Fried rice

This dish must be planned ahead of time, because the rice must be boiled the day before you intend to serve it. Let the rice cool then refrigerate for 24 hours.

SERVES FOUR TO SIX

½ lb (225 g) rice, cooked and drained
2 fl oz (50 ml) oil
2 garlic cloves, peeled and finely chopped
½ lb (225 g) lean pork or chicken, cut into thin strips
3 tablespoons soy sauce
Freshly ground black pepper
2 eggs
6 spring onions, sliced (including the green part)

Heat the oil in a heavy sauté pan until it is very hot. Add the garlic and pork or chicken and fry for 5 minutes, stirring occasionally. Add the cooked rice, soy sauce and pepper to taste. Fry, stirring constantly, until the rice is heated through and the meat is cooked. This should take no more than five minutes. Taste and add more soy sauce if necessary.

Beat the eggs and stir them quickly into the meat and rice. Cook for 1 to 2 minutes or until the eggs just begin to set.

Remove the pan from the heat, mix in the spring onions and serve.

Crusty noodles

These noodles make a good accompaniment for roast beef.

SERVES FOUR

1 lb (450 g) fine noodles
1 teaspoon salt
2 oz (50 g) butter
Pepper

Thirty minutes before you want to fry the noodles, cook them in plenty of boiling salted water for about 2 minutes—timed after the water has returned to the boil. Empty the noodles into a strainer and wash thoroughly in hot water to remove the starch. Drain and leave to cool.

Heat a 7-inch (18-cm) heavy frying-pan. Add the butter and when it sizzles put in the noodles and stir them around. Sprinkle with pepper and more salt, if necessary. Reduce the heat to low and let the noodles cook very slowly for 10 to 15 minutes or until there is a light brown crust on the bottom. Using a spatula lift up the edge of the noodles—if the bottom is not set in a brown crust continue frying for a few more minutes.

Clockwise : muffins and waffles for tea and Crêpes Suzette for a special dinner-party dessert.

Eggs and dairy produce

Frying brings out the best in eggs; methods include scrambling, making omelettes, and of course frying them whole as in eggs and bacon.

Scrambling is one of the most delicate ways of cooking eggs. The heat should be gentle and the moment the eggs begin to set well the pan should be drawn off the heat—the heat of the pan being sufficient to finish cooking the eggs. Use a heavy pan, preferably with a non-stick coating—unlined pans are difficult to clean after scrambling eggs.

A little milk or cream—one tablespoon for two eggs—may be stirred in at the end of the cooking time. In that case reduce the amount of butter used.

There are three different types of omelette: the French omelette, which is slightly liquid in the middle, the fluffy soufflé omelette, which is more often served as a dessert, and the Spanish omelette, a more solid dish, which is made in an entirely different way—a way also used to make Egyptian and Chinese omelettes.

Ideally an omelette pan should be made of iron, and seasoned before it is used (see page 8). If possible it should only be used for making omelettes and it should never be washed—just oil it lightly and wipe it with a clean cloth. The size of the pan is important. If the base of the pan is five inches (13 cm) in diameter it will make a two- to three-egg omelette; if it is seven inches (18 cm) it will make a four-egg omelette and if it is nine inches (23 cm) it will make a six-egg omelette.

Fillings for omelettes are spread off centre just before the omelette is folded and turned out.

Fried eggs

These are the traditional eggs of bacon and eggs. If bacon has been cooked in the frying-pan before the eggs, use the bacon fat to fry them.

Fried eggs are also delicious served with beurre noir.

SERVES TWO TO FOUR

1 oz (25 g) bacon fat, dripping or butter
4 eggs
Salt and pepper

Heat the fat in a frying-pan over low heat and break in the eggs. Tip the pan slightly so that the eggs may be basted with the fat. (Some people prefer the egg cooked without basting—in this case, cover immediately with a lid.)

Cook the eggs for about 3 minutes, basting several times until the whites set. Season with salt and pepper. Using a fish-slice, lift the eggs out of the fat, hold over the pan until any excess fat has run off and transfer to hot plates. Serve at once.

If desired, the eggs may be turned over carefully during the frying, but do not attempt this until the eggs have begun to set.

Scrambled eggs

Scrambled eggs are very versatile and can be combined successfully with many vegetables, cheeses, smoked meats and fish. They may be served hot or cold by themselves, or in small vol-au-vent or tomato cases.

SERVES TWO

4 eggs
Salt and freshly ground black pepper
1½ oz (40 g) butter
2 slices buttered toast, kept hot

Break the eggs into a bowl and season well. Using a fork, lightly beat the eggs until the whites and yolks are blended.

Melt half the butter over low heat and pour in the eggs. Using a wooden spoon, and keeping the heat low, stir the eggs, pulling large curds from the base of the pan. At the same time add the remaining butter a little at a time.

When almost all the egg has formed moist curds, remove the pan from the heat. Stir until cooked and creamy. Spoon on to the hot toast. Serve immediately.

Scrambled eggs with mushrooms

Allow 2 oz (50 g) of sliced mushrooms for each person. Sauté the mushrooms in butter in a separate pan.

Put the eggs on hot buttered toast and pour over the mushrooms and juices.

Scrambled eggs with cheese

Allow 1 oz (25 g) of grated hard cheese or creamed soft cheese for each person. Just before the eggs are removed from the heat, stir in the cheese. Serve at once with grilled tomatoes.

Scotch woodcock

Have ready one slice of hot toast spread with anchovy paste for each person. Season the eggs with salt and cayenne and scramble as usual. Just before the eggs are ready, stir in 1 tablespoon of cream per portion. Spoon the eggs on to the toast and serve at once.

French omelette

SERVES ONE TO TWO

2 to 3 eggs
Salt and freshly ground black pepper
½ oz (15 g) butter

Break the eggs into a bowl, season well and beat lightly with a fork.

Heat the omelette pan until it is very hot over moderate heat. Add the butter and swirl it round the pan. It will melt instantly. When it foams, pour in the eggs and shake the pan gently backwards and forwards. The eggs will begin to set at once, so stir with a fork, drawing in large flakes of cooked eggs from the sides of the pan. In 1 to 2 minutes the omelette will be nearly cooked. Tilt the pan away from you and, using a palette knife, lift up the edge of the omelette so that some of the uncooked egg will run from the middle of the omelette on to the base of the pan. Leave on the heat for a few seconds more so that the underneath can take on a golden colour.

Tilt the pan and flip half the omelette over. Turn on to a warmed plate and serve at once.

Omelette fines herbes

For each serving add 1 tablespoon of mixed chopped fresh herbs to the eggs while they are being beaten.

Mushroom omelette

Allow 2 ounces (50 g) of mushrooms for each serving. Chop the mushrooms and sauté them in a little butter. Fill the omelette, fold over and serve.

Cheese omelette

Allow 2 oz (50 g) of grated Parmesan, Cheddar and Parmesan or Gruyère and Parmesan per person. Beat the cheese with the eggs or sprinkle it on the omelette just before folding and serving.

Omelette Arnold Bennett

SERVES TWO

2 oz (50 g) butter
6 oz (175 g) smoked haddock, cooked, skinned, boned and flaked
4 eggs, separated
¼ pint (150 ml) cream
Salt
2 tablespoons grated Parmesan cheese

Melt half the butter in a small saucepan, stir in the smoked haddock and heat through.

Preheat the grill to high.

Beat the egg yolks with half the cream and season to taste. Stir in the haddock.

Whisk the egg whites until they form soft peaks and fold into the egg yolk and haddock mixture.

Melt the remaining butter in a large omelette pan. Pour in the egg mixture, shake the pan once or twice and cook until just set.

Slide the unfolded omelette on to a heatproof serving dish, pour over the remaining cream, sprinkle the cheese on top and put under the grill for a few seconds to brown. Serve immediately.

Spanish omelette

Eaten hot or cold, a Spanish omelette may include such ingredients as sweet peppers, spinach, peas, mushrooms, parsley, ham, anchovies or slices of chorizo sausage.

SERVES FOUR

3 tablespoons olive oil
1 garlic clove, crushed
2 large onions, sliced
2 large potatoes, peeled and cut into ¼-inch (½-cm) cubes
Salt
6 eggs

Heat the oil in a frying-pan. Add the garlic, onions, potatoes and salt to taste. Cover the pan and cook gently, stirring occasionally, for 15 to 20 minutes or until the potatoes are cooked through. Using a slotted spoon lift out the vegetables.

Break the eggs into a bowl and beat lightly with a fork to mix the whites and yolks. Stir in the cooked vegetables. Reheat the oil in the pan and when it is very hot pour in the egg and vegetable mixture, spreading it to fill the pan evenly. Cook for 5 minutes, shaking the pan occasionally. When the bottom has set, put a plate over the pan and invert the omelette on to the plate, then slide it back into the pan and brown the other side. Alternatively, brown the top of the omelette under a hot grill.

Cut into wedges and serve.

Omelette au Grand Marnier

SERVES TWO

3 eggs
Grated rind and segments of 1 orange
1 oz (25 g) castor sugar
2 tablespoons Grand Marnier
½ oz (15 g) butter

Beat the eggs with the orange rind, half the sugar and the Grand Marnier.

Preheat the grill to high.

Melt the butter in an omelette pan, and when it is hot pour in the egg mixture and cook as for a French omelette. When it is almost ready, put the orange segments on one half of the omelette, leave for 30 seconds, fold in half and turn on to a warm serving dish.

Sprinkle the omelette with the remaining sugar and glaze under the grill for 30 seconds. Serve at once.

Omelette flambée

Make sure you have one end of the skewer wrapped in a cloth when you are heating it.

SERVES TWO

4 eggs
Salt
1 oz (25 g) castor sugar
½ oz (15 g) butter
4 tablespoons Jamaican rum, cognac, whisky or Calvados

Beat the eggs, a pinch of salt and half the sugar together with a fork. Melt the butter in an omelette pan. Pour in the egg mixture and cook as for a French omelette. Fold and slide on to a heatproof dish. Sprinkle the rest of the sugar on top of the omelette. Heat a skewer until it is red-hot and mark the top of the omelette with a criss-cross pattern. Warm the rum, pour over the omelette and ignite. Serve immediately.

Egg fu-yung

A traditional Chinese omelette, egg fu-yung may include a variety of ingredients such as mushrooms, prawns, chicken and ham.

SERVES TWO

2 tablespoons cooking oil
2 spring onions, chopped
¼ lb (125 g) bean sprouts, washed
4 eggs
1 teaspoon soy sauce
Salt and pepper
2 oz (50 g) cooked crab meat, flaked

Heat 1 tablespoon of oil in a frying-pan and stir-fry the spring onions and the bean sprouts for 2 minutes. Using a slotted spoon lift out the onions and bean sprouts and set aside on a plate.

Lightly beat the eggs with the soy sauce and seasoning. Heat the remaining oil in the frying-pan. Pour in the egg mixture. Quickly stir in the crab meat, spring onions and bean sprouts. When the bottom sets, turn the omelette over using a fish-slice. Cook for 1 minute and serve.

Scotch eggs

Scotch eggs may be served hot or cold and will keep for several days in a refrigerator.

SERVES FOUR

¾ lb (350 g) pork sausage meat
Salt and pepper
Pinch mace
4 hard-boiled eggs, shelled
1 egg, beaten
2 oz (50 g) dry breadcrumbs
Oil for deep frying

In a large bowl mix the sausage meat, seasoning and mace. Divide the mixture into four pieces. Flatten each piece between the palms of your hands. Put an egg in the centre of each piece and bring the sides up to enclose the egg completely.

Dip the coated eggs in beaten egg and then in breadcrumbs; press the crumbs on firmly.

Heat the oil to 375°F (190°C). Fry the scotch eggs until the coating is well browned. Drain well.

Kuku sabsi

This omelette from Iran can be made from any green leaf vegetable.

SERVES FOUR

1½ oz (40 g) butter
1 onion, sliced
½ lb (225 g) spinach, washed, drained and finely chopped
2 tablespoons chopped fresh herbs
1 tablespoon chopped walnuts
Salt and pepper
6 eggs, lightly beaten

Melt the butter in a frying-pan and fry the onion until soft. Add the spinach, herbs and walnuts and fry, stirring, for 2 to 3 minutes. Season well and pour in the eggs. Stir with a fork for a few seconds. Reduce the heat and cook until the eggs have almost set.

Preheat the grill to hot. Put the pan under the grill until the omelette is lightly browned. Cut into wedges and serve.

Making an omelette

As the eggs begin to set, stir the bottom with a fork.

Tilt the pan and, with a spatula, lift up the edge of the omelette.

When the omelette is cooked, fold one half over the other.

Slide the folded omelette on to a heated plate and serve at once.

Eggs and dairy produce

Huevos rancheros

SERVES TWO

2 tablespoons olive oil
1 garlic clove, crushed
1 onion, finely chopped
1 green pepper, cored, seeded and finely chopped
1 lb (450 g) tomatoes, peeled and chopped
½ teaspoon cayenne pepper
Salt and pepper
¼ lb (125 g) ham, cut into strips
4 eggs, fried and kept hot

Heat the oil in a frying-pan. Add the garlic, onion and pepper and fry for 5 minutes. Add the tomatoes, cayenne pepper and salt and pepper to taste. Simmer the mixture uncovered, stirring occasionally, until it is thick.

Stir in the ham. Spoon the mixture on to a heated serving plate. Arrange the fried eggs on top and serve.

Scrambled eggs with chicken livers

SERVES FOUR

1 oz (25 g) butter
2 bacon rashers, diced
½ lb (225 g) chicken livers, cut into quarters
Salt and pepper
6 eggs, lightly beaten
4 slices hot buttered toast
1 tablespoon chopped parsley

Melt the butter in a frying-pan and fry the bacon for 1 minute. Add the chicken livers and fry, stirring, for 1 to 2 minutes or until lightly cooked. Season well and pour in the eggs. Reduce the heat and cook gently, stirring, until the eggs are just set.

Pile the eggs on to the toast, sprinkle with parsley and serve.

Scrambled eggs with smoked salmon

SERVES FOUR

2 oz (50 g) butter
4 slices smoked salmon, chopped
8 eggs, lightly beaten
2 teaspoons chopped chives
Salt and pepper
4 slices hot buttered toast

Melt the butter in a saucepan, add the salmon and heat very gently. Pour in the eggs and cook, stirring, until lightly set. Stir in the chives. Taste the mixture and season if necessary. Spoon the mixture on to the toast and serve immediately.

Bean sprouts with omelette shreds

SERVES TWO

4 eggs
2 teaspoons soy sauce
3 tablespoons oil
½-inch (1-cm) piece fresh root ginger, peeled and finely chopped
3 spring onions, finely sliced
½ lb (225 g) bean sprouts

Lightly beat the eggs with the soy sauce. Heat half the oil in a frying-pan and pour in the eggs. Let the eggs set in a thin omelette. When the omelette is browned underneath lift it out and cut it into large shreds.

Add the remaining oil to the pan and stir-fry the ginger and spring onions for 1 minute. Add the bean sprouts and stir-fry for 2 minutes. Add the omelette shreds and fry for 1 minute more. Serve immediately.

Ajja

Omit or halve the amount of green chillies in this spicy Tunisian dish if you are not used to the taste of hot food.

SERVES FOUR

2 tablespoons olive oil
1 lb (450 g) Spanish chorizo sausage, cut into ½-inch (1-cm) slices
2 onions, sliced
2 garlic cloves, crushed
1 to 2 green chillies, chopped
1 lb (450 g) tomatoes, peeled and chopped
3 green peppers, sliced
Salt and pepper
6 eggs, lightly beaten

Heat the oil in a large sauté pan. Add the sausage and fry, stirring, until browned. Add the onions, garlic and green chillies and fry for 2 to 3 minutes. Add the tomatoes and peppers and cook, stirring, for 10 minutes. Add salt and pepper to taste.

Pour in the eggs, reduce the heat to low and cook, stirring, until the eggs have just set. Serve immediately.

Scrambled eggs with chicken

SERVES FOUR

1 oz (25 g) butter
½ lb (225 g) cooked chicken, cut into strips
4 spring onions, chopped
Pinch cayenne pepper
Salt and black pepper
6 eggs
2 tablespoons soured cream

Melt the butter in a saucepan over moderate heat.

Mix all the ingredients together in a bowl. Pour into the saucepan and cook, stirring, until lightly set. Serve hot.

Mozzarella in carrozza

Fried cheese sandwiches are a popular dish in southern Italy. The name literally means mozzarella in a carriage.

SERVES FOUR

16 thin slices of bread from a small sandwich loaf
1 lb (450 g) mozzarella cheese, cut into thin slices
2 eggs
2 tablespoons milk
Salt
Oil for deep frying

Trim the crusts off the bread The name literally means mozzarella in a carriage.

Beat the eggs, milk and a little salt together on a plate. Dip the sandwiches in the egg mixture, turning to coat them well. Set aside for 30 minutes.

Heat the oil to 375°F (190°C). Fry the sandwiches until they are golden brown on both sides. Drain on kitchen paper towels. Serve immediately.

Fried mozzarella cheese

SERVES FOUR

1 lb (450 g) mozzarella cheese, thinly sliced
Flour
2 eggs, lightly beaten
Dry breadcrumbs
Oil for deep frying

Dust the cheese slices with flour. Dip them in the egg and then in the breadcrumbs to coat them well.

Heat the oil to 375°F (190°C) and fry the cheese until golden brown on both sides. Drain on kitchen paper towels. Serve immediately.

Roasting and baking

True roasting—one of the most primitive methods of cooking known to man—has, along with the spit, jack and the servant to turn it, long since disappeared from Western kitchens. It still survives, however, almost unchanged in parts of Greece, Spain, Italy and in many countries of the Middle East where suckling pigs, lamb or kid are roasted whole, flavoured with garlic and sprigs of rosemary, marjoram or fennel.

What we now call roasting is really baking and this too is a time-honoured method of cooking. The nomads of Central Asia still use their age-old clay ovens and in the remoter parts of some European countries the old "robber-style" cooking in underground ovens continues to this day.

Only good-quality meat and poultry should be used for roasting. The poorer cuts and older birds may be baked in pies or turned into meat loaves and pâtés. Almost any kind of fish and some shellfish are suitable for baking. Many vegetables, plain or stuffed, fruit, dairy produce and cereals are transformed by baking into delicious desserts, pies, pasties, soufflés, cakes and breads.

Fish and shellfish		*Poultry and game birds*
Crab au gratin 168 Melba toast 81 ***Crab soufflé 168*** Green salad 213	***Roast carp with julienne vegetables 168***	***English roast chicken 170*** Bread sauce 69, Peas 93, Roast potatoes 180
Baked scallops 169 ***Smoked haddock flan 169*** Green salad 213	***Kulibyaka 169*** Green salad 213	***French roast chicken 170*** Green salad 213, Glazed carrots 91, Garlic mashed potatoes 180
Salmon baked in foil 166 Sauces: Hollandaise, Mousseline 67 New potatoes 93, Broccoli 92	***Fish pie 169*** Tomato salad 213	***Roast duck with apricots 170*** Casseroled celery 120, Potato croquettes 151, Peas 93
Baked mackerel 166 Sauté potatoes 151, Chicory, orange and watercress salad 213	***Eel pie 169*** Broccoli 92	***Roast turkey 172*** Bread sauce 69, Brussels sprouts 92, Potato croquettes 151
Baked fish with olives 166 Fennel 92, Boiled potatoes 93		***Guinea-fowl with apples 172*** Large croûtons 158, French beans 92
Roast stuffed bass 167 Sauté potatoes 151		***Goose with sauerkraut 172*** Purple broccoli 92, Boiled potatoes, Courgettes 93
Truites en papillotes 167 Green salad 213		***Pheasant with celery 172*** Game chips 150
Sole Ormondville 167 Green salad 213		***Roast partridge with vine leaves 173*** Large croûtons 158, Spinach purée 92
Indonesian baked fish 168		***Country chicken pie 173*** Peas 93
Halibut with lemon sauce 168 Sauté potatoes 151		***Game pie 173*** Chicory, orange and watercress salad 213

Meat and game

Roast ribs of beef with Yorkshire pudding 174
Horseradish sauce 89
Glazed carrots 91
Broccoli 92

Stuffed loin of pork 177
Brussels sprouts 92,
New potatoes 93

Beef Wellington 174
Green salad 213,
Courgettes 93

Haunch of venison 178
Casseroled celery 120,
Garlic mashed potatoes 180

Roast breast of veal with soured cream and tarragon 174
Spinach purée 92,
Braised onions 120,
Roast potatoes 180

Pork pie 178
Salads:
Carrot and apple 213,
Potato 93

Roast shoulder of lamb with herb stuffing 176
Mint sauce 69,
Broad beans 92,
Roast potatoes 180

Cornish pasty 179
Green salad 213

Crown roast 176
Mint sauce 69,
French beans 92,
Garlic mashed potatoes 180

Steak and kidney pie 179
Glazed carrots 91,
New potatoes 93

Baked ham 178
Cumberland sauce 69
Chicory, orange and watercress salad 213
New potatoes 93

Honey-glazed ham 178
Celery, apple and walnut salad 213,
Sweet potato soufflé 180

Roast suckling pig 178
Apple sauce 69,
Peas 93,
Roast potatoes 180

Roast pork 176
Baked apples,
French beans 92,
Mashed potatoes 93

Pork spareribs 177
Green salad 213

Vegetables

Stuffed vine leaves 182

Baked spiced avocados 183

Mushroom vol-au-vents 181

Aubergine à la nîmoise 180

Ham-stuffed potatoes 180
Tomato salad 213

Haddock-stuffed potatoes 180
Steamed fennel 92

Stuffed baked marrow 181
Garlic mashed potatoes 180

Moussaka 181
Green salad 213

Boston baked beans 180
Boston steamed bread 99

Baked tomatoes 182

Baked stuffed onions 183

Chicorée au gratin 181

Baked potatoes 180

Garlic mashed potatoes 180

Potatoes à la dauphinoise 180

Sweet potato soufflé 180

Fruit

Mince pies 184
Brandy butter 69

Apple pie 184
Whipped cream

Apple dumplings 184
Custard sauce 69

French apple flan 184
Whipped cream

Apple strudel 184
Whipped cream

Rhubarb crumble 185

Cherry flan 185

Lemon meringue pie 185

Pear tart 186

Date bars 186

Clafoutis 186

Pineapple upside-down cake 186
Whipped cream

Cereals

Macaroni cheese 188
Green salad 213

Baked pasta with seafood 188

Cannelloni di spinace 188
Green salad 213

Lasagne 189
Green salad 213

Pizza Napoletana 188
Pizza con cozze 188
Pizza alla francescana 188
Green salad 213

Baked chicken pancakes 189

Garlic bread 189

Rice pudding 189
Fruit sauce 69

Oatmeal and apple pudding 189
Whipped cream

Bread and butter pudding 189

Cakes, pastries and biscuits 190-7

Breads 198-201

Eggs and dairy produce

Quiche Lorraine 203
Green salad 213

Tarte au gruyère 203
Green salad 213

Oeufs sur le plat 203
Brown bread 198

Cheese soufflé 203

Chocolate soufflé 204

Baked custard 204

Caramel custard 204

Petit pots de crème au chocolat 204

Meringue hazelnut gâteau 205

Meringues 204

Meringue baskets 205

Pavlova 205

Baked Alaska 205

Queen of Puddings 205

Raspberry tart 205

First courses
Main courses
Light lunch-supper dishes
Accompaniments
Desserts
Miscellaneous

Fish and shellfish

Whole fish, steaks or fillets may be baked in the oven with a little butter and seasoning. Preheat the oven to about 375°F (190°C, Gas Mark 5) and cook until the flesh is opaque and comes away from the bone easily.

Whole fish can be stuffed with all sorts of different mixtures. Sometimes the stuffing mixture is spread over fish fillets, which are then rolled up before being baked. Alternatively the stuffing mixture may be used as a bed on which whole fish, steaks or fillets are cooked. A very little liquid may also be added—use fish stock, white wine, cider or lemon juice.

A topping of grated cheese and breadcrumbs gives baked fish a pleasantly crisp crust. Alternatively, bake the fish in a cheese, béchamel or velouté sauce with breadcrumbs and a few small pieces of butter sprinkled on top.

When shellfish are cooked in the oven they are usually coated in a sauce or made into soufflés or gratins.

Salmon baked in foil

This is an excellent way of dealing with large fish when you have no fish kettle to steam them in; the foil keeps all the flavour and juices in. An hour will be enough to cook a fish, or piece of fish, weighing up to 6 pounds (3 kg); allow 10 minutes per pound for fish larger than this.

Smaller fish can be cooked in the same way. Trout, for instance, will cook in 20 to 30 minutes. Salmon steaks can be sprinkled with lemon juice, seasoning, butter and herbs and individually wrapped in foil; they will cook in about 20 minutes.

Serve hot salmon with hollandaise or mousseline sauce, boiled new potatoes and a lettuce and cucumber salad. Cold salmon is traditionally served with mayonnaise or a sauce verte, boiled potatoes and a cucumber salad.

SERVES SIX TO EIGHT

Butter or oil
4-lb (2-kg) salmon (or salmon trout, turbot or other firm fish), cleaned
Lemon juice
Parsley, rosemary, thyme or dill sprigs
Salt and pepper
½ pint (300 ml) sauce mousseline

Preheat the oven to 325°F (170°C, Gas Mark 3).

Tear off a piece of foil large enough to totally enclose and seal in the fish. If the fish is to be served hot, grease the foil with butter; if it is to be served cold, grease the foil with oil. Sprinkle the inside of the fish with lemon juice, seasoning, a little butter and some sprigs of fresh herbs. Wrap the foil round securely and seal the edges well so that no juices or steam can escape. Bake for 1 hour.

If the salmon is to be served hot, remove the foil and skin the fish. Leave it to rest for 10 to 15 minutes before serving (5 minutes in the case of salmon steaks or smaller fish). Serve with the sauce handed round separately.

Baked mackerel

SERVES FOUR

4 small mackerel, filleted
Salt and pepper
2 tablespoons oil
2 large onions, chopped
1 garlic clove, chopped
2 tomatoes, peeled and chopped
1 green and 1 red pepper, seeded and sliced
2 teaspoons lemon juice
¼ pint (150 ml) tomato juice
1 oz (25 g) butter

Preheat the oven to 350°F (180°C, Gas Mark 4).

Season the mackerel fillets. Heat the oil in a large frying-pan. Fry the onions and garlic until soft. Add the tomatoes, peppers and seasoning and cook for 1 minute. Put the vegetables in an ovenproof dish. Arrange the mackerel fillets on top of the vegetables, sprinkle the fish with lemon juice and pour the tomato juice over the top. Dot with the butter, cover the dish and bake for 30 minutes.

Baked fish with olives

Freshly caught fish are usually best when cooked quite simply. This recipe from southern Italy can be used for bream, bass, red mullet or other firm fish.

SERVES FOUR

2-lb (900-g) fresh bream or large red mullet, scaled and cleaned
Salt
Olive oil
Vinegar
¼ lb (125 g) green olives, pitted

Preheat the oven to 350°F (180°C, Gas Mark 4).

Dry the fish with kitchen paper towels. Lightly salt the insides. Put a little olive oil in a baking dish and lay the fish on top. Sprinkle lightly with vinegar and a little more salt, cover with the olives and bake for 20 to 30 minutes.

Fish baked in foil retains its natural flavour and juices.

Roast stuffed bass

SERVES FOUR

3- to 4-lb (1½- to 2-kg) bass or 4 small bass, cleaned
4 tomatoes, peeled and diced
2 onions, diced
3 fl oz (75 ml) white wine

STUFFING
¼ lb (100 g) soft breadcrumbs
Milk
3 tablespoons olive oil
1 large onion, diced
1 shallot, diced
¼ lb (100 g) mushrooms, chopped
1 tablespoon chopped chives
1 tablespoon chopped parsley
1 tablespoon chopped chervil
Salt and pepper
1 egg, beaten

First make the stuffing: soak the breadcrumbs in a little milk and squeeze them dry.

Heat the oil in a frying-pan. Add the onion and shallot and fry for about 5 minutes. Add the mushrooms and herbs and continue cooking for another 3 to 4 minutes. Remove the pan from the heat. Stir in the breadcrumbs, season well and bind together with the beaten egg. Stuff the fish with this mixture and sew up or secure with wooden cocktail sticks.

Preheat the oven to 325°F (170°C, Gas Mark 3).

Put the tomatoes and onions in a baking dish, add the wine and lay the fish on top. Cover with foil and bake for 1 hour (or 30 minutes if using small bass). Remove the string or cocktail sticks and serve.

Truites en papillotes

SERVES FOUR

1 oz (25 g) butter
4 trout, filleted
1 tablespoon double cream
1 teaspoon Pernod
8 tablespoons duxelles
Oil
Salt and pepper
1 tablespoon finely chopped parsley

Preheat the oven to 350°F (180°C, Gas Mark 4). Melt the butter in a frying-pan. Fry the trout fillets gently for 2 to 3 minutes or until they are half-cooked.

Stir the cream and Pernod into the duxelles.

Cut 4 hearts out of foil or greaseproof paper large enough to enclose 2 fillets with space to spare around the edge. Brush with oil. Spread a little of the duxelles on one half of each heart and put 2 fillets on it. Season to taste. Cover with more of the duxelles and sprinkle a little parsley on top. Fold over the other half of the heart and secure by folding the edges like a hem. Cook on a baking sheet for 20 minutes or until the packets are puffed up. Serve in the packets.

Sole Ormondville

SERVES FOUR

4 sole, filleted
Salt and pepper
1½ oz (40 g) butter
1 teaspoon lemon juice
¼ pint (150 ml) dry white wine or cider
1 pint (1 lb/450 g) mussels, scrubbed
4 tablespoons court bouillon
¼ lb (100 g) peeled cooked prawns
½ lb (225 g) button mushrooms
1 teaspoon flour
Cayenne pepper
¼ pint (150 ml) cream
1 egg yolk, beaten
8 small triangles fried bread

Preheat the oven to 350°F (180°C, Gas Mark 4).

Season the fillets and fold them over. Butter a baking dish with ½ ounce (15 g) of the butter and arrange the fillets in it. Sprinkle the fish with the lemon juice and pour over the wine or cider. Cover the dish with foil and bake for 10 to 15 minutes or until cooked.

Meanwhile put the mussels in a saucepan with the court bouillon and bring to the boil. Cover the pan, reduce the heat and simmer for 5 minutes. Remove the mussels from their shells, discarding any that have not opened.

Melt the remaining butter in a frying-pan and sauté the prawns and mushrooms for 2 minutes.

Arrange the fish on a serving dish, surrounded by the mussels, prawns and mushrooms. Strain the liquor from the baking dish into a saucepan. Heat until boiling. Remove the pan from the heat. Mix the flour and a pinch of cayenne with the cream and stir it into the pan. Return the pan to low heat and cook at just below simmering point until thickened. Pour the sauce on to the egg yolk, whisking well. Season to taste, pour the sauce over the fish and serve garnished with triangles of fried bread.

Fish and shellfish

Indonesian baked fish
This recipe is suitable for such fish as herring or mackerel, haddock, shad or whiting.

SERVES FOUR

2 lb (900 g) fish fillets
1 garlic clove, finely chopped
Salt and pepper
2 oz (50 g) butter
2 tablespoons soy sauce
2 tablespoons lemon juice
Chilli powder

Preheat the oven to 375°F (190°C, Gas Mark 5).

Sprinkle the fish with the chopped garlic, salt and pepper. Put into a buttered baking dish and bake for 15 minutes.

Melt the butter in a small pan and stir in the soy sauce, lemon juice and a pinch of chilli powder. Pour this over the fish and cook for another 15 to 20 minutes.

Halibut with lemon sauce

SERVES FOUR

2 oz (50 g) butter
4 halibut steaks
Salt and pepper
1 onion, finely chopped
2 celery stalks, finely chopped
¼ lb (100 g) mushrooms, finely chopped
2 tomatoes, peeled and chopped
1 tablespoon mixed chopped herbs (parsley, dill, thyme or rosemary)
1 lemon, sliced

SAUCE
Juice of 1 lemon
2 teaspoons cornflour
¼ pint (150 ml) fish stock
1 egg, beaten
Salt and pepper

Preheat the oven to 375°F (190°C, Gas Mark 5).

Grease a baking dish with a little of the butter. Remove the bone from the centre of each halibut steak. Sprinkle the fish steaks with salt and pepper and arrange them in the baking dish. Melt the remaining butter in a frying-pan and fry the onion and celery until soft. Add the mushrooms and fry, stirring, until soft. Add the tomatoes, seasoning and herbs.

Spoon the mixture into the centre of each steak. Cover with greased paper and then with foil and bake for 20 to 25 minutes or until the fish is cooked.

Meanwhile make the sauce. In a small bowl mix the lemon juice with the cornflour. Heat the stock in a pan, add a little to the cornflour mixture, mix thoroughly and return to the pan and cook, stirring, for 1 minute. Remove the pan from the heat, allow the sauce to cool for 1 minute and pour over the egg, beating constantly. Season to taste.

Remove the fish from the oven and take off the foil and paper. Pour the sauce over the fish and garnish with the lemon slices. Serve immediately.

Roast carp with julienne vegetables

SERVES SIX

3-lb (1½-kg) carp, cleaned
Salt and pepper
Vinegar
Rosemary, thyme and parsley sprigs
2 tablespoons soy sauce
2 oz (50 g) butter, cut into pieces
1 garlic clove, finely sliced
½-inch (1-cm) piece fresh root ginger, finely sliced
2 carrots
½ cucumber
4 spring onions
2 tablespoons chicken stock

Soak the carp in cold salted water for 30 minutes.

Preheat the oven to 375°F (190°C, Gas Mark 5).

Rinse the fish in vinegar and water and dry on kitchen paper towels.

Rub the fish with plenty of salt and pepper. Arrange a bed of herbs in a roasting tin and lay the carp on the herbs. Sprinkle the soy sauce over the fish and cover with the butter, garlic and ginger. Place a piece of greased paper or foil over the fish to prevent it burning. Roast for 30 to 40 minutes.

Meanwhile cut the carrots, cucumber and spring onions into 2-inch (5-cm) julienne strips. Put the vegetables in a saucepan, cover with salted water and simmer for 5 minutes. Drain and set aside. Arrange the fish on a serving dish and garnish with the vegetables. Pour the stock into the roasting tin and bring to the boil. Strain the sauce over the fish.

Crab au gratin

SERVES FOUR

1 teaspoon anchovy essence
½ pint (300 ml) mornay sauce
1 large crab about 2 lb (900 g), cooked, the meat removed and the small claws reserved
Juice of 1 lemon
2 oz (50 g) grated Parmesan cheese
1 oz (25 g) fresh white breadcrumbs
1 oz (25 g) butter
1 lemon, cut into wedges

Preheat the oven to 350°F (180°C, Gas Mark 4).

Mix the anchovy essence into the mornay sauce. Scrub the shell of the crab and dry thoroughly. Mix the dark crab meat with 4 tablespoons of the sauce and 1 tablespoon of the lemon juice. Spread this mixture in the bottom of the shell. Mash the rest of the crab meat with the remaining lemon juice and pile it into the shell. Mask with the remaining sauce.

Toss the cheese and breadcrumbs together, sprinkle them over the crab meat, dot with butter and bake for 20 minutes or until the top is golden brown. Serve garnished with the small claws and the lemon wedges.

Crab soufflé
Serve with a green salad.

SERVES TWO TO THREE

1 oz (25 g) plus 1 teaspoon butter
3 tablespoons grated Parmesan cheese
½ lb (225 g) cooked crab meat
½ pint (300 ml) milk
1 oz (25 g) flour
1 teaspoon tomato purée
Tabasco sauce
1 teaspoon dry mustard
Salt and pepper
3 egg yolks
4 egg whites

Preheat the oven to 350°F (180°C, Gas Mark 4).

Grease an 8-inch (20-cm) soufflé dish with a teaspoon of the butter and sprinkle 1 tablespoon of the cheese over the bottom and sides. Put a greaseproof paper collar around the soufflé dish. Flake the crab meat and set it aside in a small bowl.

Heat the milk to just under boiling point and set aside. Melt the remaining butter in a saucepan. Stir in the flour and cook for 1 to 2 minutes. Gradually add the hot milk, stirring constantly until smooth. Blend in the tomato purée, Tabasco to taste, the mustard and seasoning.

Beat the egg yolks in a bowl. Stir in a little of the hot sauce then add the mixture to the pan with the crab meat. Cool the sauce. Beat the whites until stiff and fold them into the sauce. Pour the mixture into the soufflé dish. Sprinkle with the remaining cheese and bake for 35 minutes or until the soufflé has risen and is firm to the touch on the outside but creamy inside. Remove the paper collar and serve immediately.

Baked scallops

SERVES FOUR

8 large scallops, cleaned
6 fl oz (175 ml) white wine
4 fl oz (125 ml) water
½ lemon
1¾ oz (45 g) butter
½ lb (225 g) mushrooms, sliced
¾ oz (20 g) flour
¼ pint (150 ml) cream
Salt and pepper
Cayenne pepper
2 oz (50 g) Gruyère cheese, grated

Preheat the oven to 375°F (190°C, Gas Mark 5).

Put the scallops in a saucepan with the wine, water and a squeeze of lemon juice and simmer for 5 minutes. Drain the scallops; strain and reserve the cooking liquid. Cut each scallop into quarters.

Melt 1 ounce (25 g) of the butter in a frying-pan and fry the mushrooms for 2 to 3 minutes.

Melt the remaining butter in a saucepan. Stir in the flour to make a roux. Remove the pan from the heat and gradually pour in the cooking liquid, stirring constantly. Bring to the boil and cook for 5 minutes. Stir in the cream and boil until the sauce is thick and syrupy. Season to taste with salt, pepper and cayenne.

Mix the scallops and mushrooms into the sauce. Divide the mixture between 4 scallop shells. Sprinkle the cheese on top. Put the shells on a baking tray and bake on the top shelf of the oven for 10 to 15 minutes or until golden brown and bubbling.

Kulibyaka

This Russian fish pie can be made with any fine-flavoured fish. There are many versions, including one using meat and vegetables, but the classic one is with salmon and rice (or *kasha*, buckwheat groats). Brioche dough may be used instead of pastry.

SERVES FOUR

½ lb (225 g) puff pastry
¾ lb (350 g) salmon
Salt and pepper
Lemon juice
3 oz (75 g) cooked rice
2 tablespoons chopped parsley
1 tablespoon chopped dill
3½ oz (90 g) butter
2 oz (50 g) mushrooms, chopped
1 onion, finely chopped
2 hard-boiled eggs, chopped
Nutmeg

Preheat the oven to 450°F (230°C, Gas Mark 8).

Roll out the pastry to a rectangle 16 by 8 inches (40 by 20 cm), lift it on to a greased baking sheet and set aside to rest.

Put the fish in a saucepan with a little salt, lemon juice and water to cover. Bring to the simmer and cook for 10 minutes. Remove the salmon from the pan and leave to cool. Flake the fish in a bowl and mix in the rice, herbs and seasoning.

Melt 1½ oz (40 g) of the butter in a frying-pan and fry the vegetables until soft. Put half the fish and rice mixture on one half of the pastry. Spread with chopped egg and the mushroom and onion. Season, add a pinch of nutmeg, and cover with the rest of the fish. Dampen the edges of the pastry, fold over and seal. Make diagonal cuts across the top of the pastry and bake for 40 minutes.

Remove the pie from the oven. Melt the remaining butter and brush the pastry, pouring the excess into the pie through the cuts. Serve hot.

Fish pie

SERVES FOUR

1½ lb (700 g) cooked white fish
¾ pint (450 ml) béchamel sauce
Salt and pepper
Cayenne pepper
1 tablespoon anchovy essence (optional)
2 hard-boiled eggs, sliced
1½ lb (700 g) mashed potatoes
1 egg, beaten
2 tablespoons cream
Nutmeg
1 oz (25 g) butter, melted

Preheat the oven to 375°F (190°C, Gas Mark 5).

Flake the fish and mix it with the béchamel sauce. Season well, adding a pinch of cayenne pepper and the anchovy essence if you are using it. Turn the mixture into a deep pie dish and cover with the sliced eggs.

Beat the potatoes with the egg, cream and a little grated nutmeg. Pile it over the fish mixture or pipe it over using a large star nozzle. Sprinkle with melted butter and bake for 20 to 25 minutes or until heated through and golden brown on top.

Eel pie

SERVES FOUR

½ lb (225 g) puff pastry
2 lb (900 g) eel fillets, cut into 2-inch (5-cm) pieces
1 oz (25 g) butter
¼ lb (100 g) stuffed olives, chopped
4 hard-boiled eggs, sliced
Salt and pepper
Nutmeg
2 tablespoons chopped parsley
¼ pint (150 ml) dry white wine
Milk or beaten egg to glaze
2 tablespoons demi-glace sauce

Preheat the oven to 350°F (180°C, Gas Mark 4).

Roll out the pastry to fit the top of a deep pie dish and leave to rest. Blanch the eel pieces in boiling salted water for 2 minutes, drain and cool.

Grease the pie dish with a little of the butter. Layer the eel pieces with the olives and hard-boiled egg slices, sprinkling each layer with salt, pepper, grated nutmeg and parsley.

Pour in the wine and dot the top with the remaining butter cut into flakes. Dampen the edge of the pie dish and cover with the pastry. Crimp the edges, brush the pastry with milk or beaten egg, decorate with pastry leaves and make a cut in the middle to allow the steam to escape. Bake for 1 hour, or until the pastry is golden brown. When ready to serve pour the demi-glace through the cut in the pastry. Serve hot or cold.

Smoked haddock flan

SERVES SIX

1½ oz (40 g) butter
2 onions, chopped
¼ lb (125 g) mushrooms, sliced
2 tomatoes, peeled and diced
1 lb (450 g) smoked haddock
¼ pint (150 ml) milk
Pepper
Mace
Bay leaf
¼ pint (150 ml) cream
3 eggs
Grated rind of 1 lemon
Salt
10-inch (25-cm) shortcrust flan case, baked blind

Preheat the oven to 350°F (180°C, Gas Mark 4).

Melt the butter in a frying-pan and fry the onions until soft. Add the mushrooms and cook for 2 to 3 minutes until the juices run. Add the tomatoes and cook for 1 minute. Remove the pan from the heat. Allow to cool.

Put the haddock in a sauté pan with the milk, pepper, mace and bay leaf to taste, and simmer very gently for 10 minutes. Remove the fish, discard the skin and bones and flake the flesh. Reserve the cooking liquid.

Beat the cream and eggs together, add the lemon rind, and strain in the reserved cooking liquid. Season if necessary taking into account the saltiness of the smoked haddock.

Put the vegetable mixture into the flan case, spreading it over the bottom. Put the fish on top and pour over the egg and cream mixture. Bake for 30 to 40 minutes or until the top is puffed up and golden brown.

Poultry and game birds

Roasting is the traditional method of cooking young poultry and game birds. A lean bird should be larded with streaky bacon rashers or pork fat and well basted during cooking. You can also put a little butter inside the bird or stuff it with a variety of fruits or vegetables—sautéed mushrooms and onions, for example—or just a few herbs and a little garlic.

A very fatty bird like a goose or a duck should be roasted on a rack placed over a baking tin. The tin may need to be emptied of fat during the cooking time.

Most birds are roasted until they are cooked through. Test by inserting the tip of a knife into the bird's thigh, which is the part that takes longest to cook: if the juices run clear, the bird is cooked.

English roast chicken

The traditional accompaniments are crisply grilled bacon rolls and bread sauce.

Chipolata sausages are often baked separately in the oven—they take 45 to 60 minutes to brown and cook through—and served with the chicken.

SERVES FOUR

4-lb (2-kg) chicken, giblets reserved
1 oz (25 g) dripping or bacon fat
Salt and pepper
1 onion, sliced
1 carrot, sliced
Thyme or marjoram
½ pint (300 ml) bread sauce, kept hot

Preheat the oven to 375°F (190°C, Gas Mark 5).

Rub the chicken with the dripping or bacon fat and put it in a roasting tin. Roast for 25 minutes on each side, basting every 15 minutes. Season the bird well and turn it on to its back for the last 30 minutes or until done. Insert a skewer into one leg—if the juices run clear the chicken is cooked.

While the chicken is roasting put the giblets, onion, carrot and a pinch of thyme or marjoram in a saucepan with 1 pint (575 ml) of water and bring to the boil. Reduce the heat and simmer. When the chicken is cooked transfer it to a serving dish and keep hot. Pour off most of the fat from the roasting tin and strain in the giblet stock. Set the roasting tin over heat and boil, stirring in all the sediment, until the gravy is reduced and well flavoured. Strain the gravy into a heated sauce boat. If you prefer a thickened gravy, mix 1 teaspoon of arrowroot (or cornflour) with a little cold water and mix it into the roasting pan. Cook, stirring constantly, until the gravy has thickened.

Serve the chicken with the gravy and bread sauce.

French roast chicken

SERVES FOUR

4-lb (2-kg) chicken, with giblets
1 onion, sliced
1 carrot, sliced
Thyme or marjoram
2 oz (50 g) butter
Salt and pepper
4 slices streaky bacon
Fresh tarragon or parsley sprigs
1 lemon slice

First make the stock. Put the giblets, onion, carrot and a pinch of thyme or marjoram in a saucepan with 1 pint (575 ml) of water and bring to the boil. Reduce the heat and simmer for 1½ hours. Remove the pan from the heat and strain the stock into a bowl. Set aside.

Preheat the oven to 375°F (190°C, Gas Mark 5). Spread the chicken with 1 ounce (25 g) of the butter. Season well and cover the breast with the bacon slices. Put a few sprigs of tarragon or parsley inside the chicken with the remaining butter, salt, pepper and the lemon slice.

Roast the bird as for English roast chicken, but use the stock for basting. Remove the bacon for the last 15 minutes to allow the breast to brown.

Make the gravy as for English roast chicken, but without the arrowroot or cornflour, and reduce the quantity of gravy by boiling it down to no more than ¼ pint (150 ml).

Roast duck with apricots

Serve with potato croquettes.

SERVES THREE TO FOUR

5-lb (2½-kg) duck, trussed
Salt and pepper
Rind and juice of 1 orange
1 lb (450 g) apricots, blanched, peeled and halved
¼ pint (150 ml) Madeira
2 fl oz (50 ml) veal stock
1 teaspoon sugar
1 teaspoon cornflour

Preheat the oven to 425°F (220°C, Gas Mark 7).

Rub the duck with salt and pepper. Put the orange rind inside the cavity. Prick the duck all over with a fork. Put the duck on its back on a rack in a roasting tin and bake for 20 minutes.

Reduce the oven temperature to 350°F (180°C, Gas Mark 4). Put the orange juice in a small pan and bring to just under boiling point. Turn the duck on its side, baste with the orange juice and cook for 20 minutes. Turn it on its other side, baste with the orange juice and cook for a further 20 minutes.

Remove the duck from the oven and put it in an earthenware baking dish. Arrange the apricot halves around the duck. Pour off all the fat from the roasting tin. Put the roasting tin over heat and pour in the Madeira and stock. Stir and scrape the bottom of the tin to amalgamate the sediments with the wine. Season to taste and stir in the sugar. Mix the cornflour with a tablespoon of water and mix it into the sauce. Bring the sauce to the boil and boil for 1 minute. Pour the sauce over the duck.

Return the baking dish to the oven and bake for 30 minutes or until the duck is cooked.

Two traditional English dishes: a raised game pie and roast chicken garnished with grilled bacon rolls and sausages.

Poultry and game birds

Roast turkey

There are several ways of roasting turkeys. Very large birds can be wrapped in foil and cooked at 250°F (130°C, Gas Mark ½) overnight, the heat being increased only in the last 30 minutes when the foil is removed, to brown the bird. Or roast the turkey at 300°F (150°C, Gas Mark 2) allowing 15 minutes per pound plus 1 hour.

SERVES TEN

10-lb (4½-kg) turkey
¼ lb (125 g) butter
Salt and pepper
Dripping
1 oz (25 g) flour
1 pint (575 ml) giblet stock

CHESTNUT STUFFING

1 lb (450 g) chestnuts, peeled
1 pint (575 ml) chicken stock
1 lb (450 g) sausage meat
2 tablespoons chopped parsley
1 oz (25 g) butter
1 onion, finely chopped
Salt and pepper

Preheat the oven to 375°F (190°C, Gas Mark 5).

First make the stuffing. Put the chestnuts in a saucepan with the stock and bring to the boil. Reduce the heat, cover the pan and simmer for 40 minutes or until the chestnuts are tender.

Purée the chestnuts in a food mill or in a liquidizer. Mix the purée with the sausage meat and parsley in a bowl.

Heat the butter in a frying-pan and fry the onion until soft. Add the onion to the other ingredients, season to taste and mix well. Put the stuffing into the cavity and crop of the bird. Secure with a skewer or sew up with strong thread.

Mash the butter with the salt and pepper and smear all over the turkey. Heat plenty of dripping—at least 1 inch (2 cm) in depth—in the roasting tin. Put in the bird on its side, cover with foil and roast for 1¼ hours. Turn the bird on its other side and roast for 1¼ hours. Turn the bird on its back and roast for a further 70 minutes. Baste regularly every 20 minutes. Take the foil off for the last 30 minutes for the breast to brown. Test by piercing the thigh with a skewer—if the juices run clear the turkey is cooked.

When the turkey is cooked lift it out of the tin on to a carving board or large dish. Pour most of the fat out of the roasting tin. Stir in the flour. Scrape in all the bits from the sides and cook, stirring, over heat until the flour is golden. Add the giblet stock. Boil for 1 to 2 minutes and strain into a gravy boat and serve with the turkey.

Roasting poultry and game birds

Chicken	
20 mins per lb	375°F (190°C, Gas Mark 5)
(2 lb dressed weight minimum cooking time 50 to 60 minutes)	
Duck	
20 mins per lb	425°F (220°C, Gas Mark 7) for first 20 mins then 350°F (180°C, Gas Mark 4)
Goose (stuffed)	
20 mins per lb	425°F (220°C, Gas Mark 7) for first 20 mins then 325°F (170°C, Gas Mark 3)
Turkey (stuffed)	
20 mins per lb plus 20 mins (unstuffed)	375°F (190°C, Gas Mark 5)
15 mins per lb plus 15 mins	
Guinea-fowl	
45 to 60 mins	375°F (190°C, Gas Mark 5)
Pheasant	
50 or 60 mins	425°F (220°C, Gas Mark 7) or 375°F (190°C, Gas Mark 5)
Pigeon	
25 to 30 mins	425°F (220°C, Gas Mark 7)
Wild duck	
30 mins	425°F (220°C, Gas Mark 7)
Grouse and partridge	
30 to 40 mins	425°F (220°C, Gas Mark 7)
Woodcock, snipe and quail	
15 to 20 mins	425°F (220°C, Gas Mark 7)

Guinea-fowl with apples

SERVES TWO

1 guinea-fowl
Salt and pepper
Streaky bacon
3 oz (75 g) butter
3 firm dessert apples, thinly sliced
6 fl oz (175 ml) double cream
3 fl oz (75 ml) Calvados (optional)

Preheat the oven to 375°F (190°C, Gas Mark 5).

Season the bird well and cover with the bacon. Heat 2 ounces (50 g) of the butter in a frying-pan and gently fry the apples for 2 to 3 minutes. Melt the remaining butter in a baking dish and put in the guinea-fowl. Arrange the apple slices around it and pour over half of the cream. Roast, basting from time to time, for about 45 minutes or until the bird is done. Test by inserting a skewer into the thigh—if the juices run clear the bird is cooked.

Remove the bird to a serving dish and keep warm. Stir the rest of the cream into the apples, reheat gently, add the Calvados if liked, adjust the seasoning and serve with the guinea-fowl.

Goose with sauerkraut

SERVES EIGHT

10-lb (4½-kg) goose
Salt and pepper
2 lb (900 g) sauerkraut, braised and kept hot
8 frankfurters, hot
½ pint (300 ml) white wine
½ pint (300 ml) giblet stock

STUFFING

1 oz (25 g) butter
2 Spanish onions, sliced
2 lb (900 g) sausage meat
6 oz (175 g) soft bread-crumbs
1 teaspoon caraway seeds
Salt and pepper

Preheat the oven to 425°F (220°C, Gas Mark 7).

First make the stuffing. Melt the butter in a frying-pan and fry the onions until soft. Put them in a bowl and mix in the sausage meat, breadcrumbs, caraway seeds and seasoning. Put the stuffing into the goose and sew it up with strong thread.

Prick the goose all over with a fork and rub with salt and pepper. Put the bird on its side on a rack in the roasting tin and roast for 20 minutes.

Lift out the bird and pour off the fat from the roasting tin. Reduce the oven temperature to 325°F (170°C, Gas Mark 3) and roast, turning the bird, for a further 3 hours or until the goose is tender and the juices run clear when the thigh is pierced with the point of a sharp knife.

Put the goose on a large serving dish. Surround it with the sauerkraut and frankfurters and keep hot

Pour away all the fat from the roasting tin. Pour in the wine and stock and bring to the boil, stirring. Boil rapidly until the gravy is reduced by half. Pour the gravy into a sauce boat and serve with the goose.

Pheasant with celery

SERVES TWO TO THREE

1 pheasant, trussed
Salt and pepper
¼ lb (100 g) butter
1 carrot, quartered
1 onion, quartered
2 slices streaky bacon
4 celery hearts
Juice of ½ lemon
½ tablespoon flour
¼ pint (150 ml) stock or white wine
¼ pint (150 ml) cream

Preheat the oven to 375°F (190°C, Gas Mark 5).

Season the pheasant well. Melt 1 ounce (25 g) of the butter in a heavy fireproof casserole. Put in the pheasant and brown the bird on all sides over moderate heat. Put in the carrot and onion. Lay the bacon over the bird's breast and roast for about 50 minutes. Baste frequently.

Meanwhile quarter the celery hearts. Put them into a saucepan with a little salted water and the lemon juice and bring to the boil. Reduce the heat to low, cover the pan and cook for 20 minutes.

When the pheasant is cooked lift it out and keep it warm. Discard the bacon, onion and carrot. Sprinkle the flour into the casserole and cook on top of the stove, stirring, until smooth. Gradually blend in the stock or wine. Bring to the boil stirring. Stir in the cream. Season to taste.

Drain the celery and put in the dish with the sauce. Put the pheasant on top. Reheat in the oven for about 8 minutes and serve.

Roast partridge (or quail) with vine leaves

It is traditional in many countries to enclose small game birds in vine leaves. All the juices and flavour are retained, just as in modern cooking with foil. Serve the birds on croûtons of bread fried in butter, if liked. One partridge is usually enough for 2 people, but allow one quail per person.

SERVES FOUR

2 partridge (or 4 quail)
Salt and pepper
3 oz (75 g) butter
Streaky bacon
Vine leaves

Preheat the oven to 425°F (220°C, Gas Mark 7). Season the insides of the birds with salt and pepper and put a little butter inside each one. Cover the breasts with bacon and enclose the birds in vine leaves. Put them into a well-buttered baking dish in which they will fit nicely and roast for 30 minutes, or until the juices run clear when the thighs are pierced with a skewer.

Country chicken pie

SERVES FOUR

1 lb (450 g) cooked chicken meat, cut into 1-inch (2-cm) pieces
$\frac{1}{4}$ lb (100 g) cooked ham, cut into $\frac{1}{2}$-inch (1-cm) cubes
$\frac{3}{4}$ pint (450 ml) béchamel sauce
$\frac{1}{2}$ oz (15 g) butter
$\frac{1}{4}$ lb (100 g) mushrooms, sliced
Salt and pepper
6 oz (175 g) shortcrust pastry
Beaten egg to glaze

Preheat the oven to 425°F (220°C, Gas Mark 7).

Mix the chicken and ham with the béchamel sauce.

Melt the butter in a small frying-pan. Add the mushrooms and fry for 2 to 3 minutes. Mix the mushrooms into the chicken mixture. Season and spoon the mixture into a pie dish.

Roll out the dough. Dampen the rim of the pie dish with water. Lift the dough and lay it on the pie dish and crimp the edges. Brush the dough with beaten egg and prick with a fork. Bake for 25 minutes or until the pastry is golden brown.

Game pie

SERVES EIGHT

2 lb (900 g) mixed game
$\frac{3}{4}$ lb (350 g) hot-water crust pastry
$\frac{1}{4}$ lb (100 g) streaky bacon
1 lb (450 g) sausage meat
$\frac{1}{4}$ lb (100 g) mushrooms, sliced
Salt and pepper
2 tablespoons chopped fresh thyme, sage and marjoram
Beaten egg to glaze
$\frac{1}{4}$ pint (150 ml) well-flavoured aspic

Preheat the oven to 400°F (200°C, Gas Mark 6).

Remove the flesh from the game and cut into strips. Line a greased pie mould with the hot-water crust dough, saving a third of the dough for the lid. Put the bacon in a layer at the bottom of the pie case. Cover with a layer of sausage meat then layer the game, the rest of the sausage meat and the mushrooms. Season well between each layer and sprinkle with the herbs.

Roll out the remaining dough to make the lid. Dampen the edges of the dough and cover the pie. Press to seal, trim and decorate. Brush with the beaten egg. Make a hole in the centre of the lid for the steam to escape. Bake for 30 minutes. Reduce the temperature of the oven to 300°F (150°C, Gas Mark 2) and bake for another $1\frac{1}{2}$ hours. Remove the pie from the oven and allow to cool.

Heat the aspic just enough to melt it and pour it into the pie through a funnel placed in the steam vent. Chill the pie for at least 6 hours before serving.

Carving a turkey

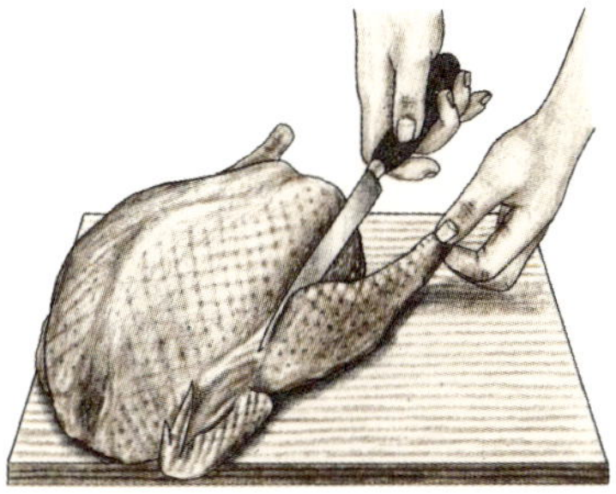

Holding the drumstick, cut off the leg including the thigh. Then cut off the wing.

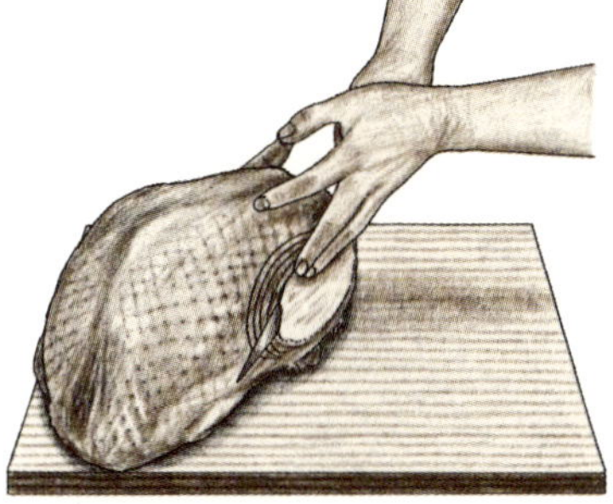

Hold the knife parallel to the body. Carve downwards cutting the white meat in thin slices.

Separate the drumstick from the thigh by cutting through the joint. Slice the thigh thinly.

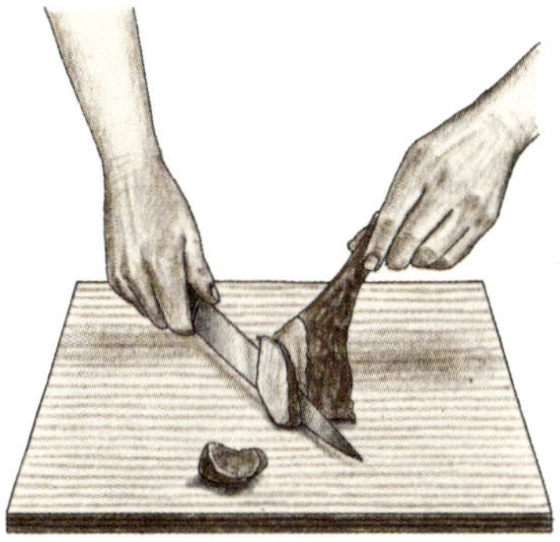

Hold the drumstick upright and carve the meat in thin slices, or serve the drumstick whole.

Carving a chicken

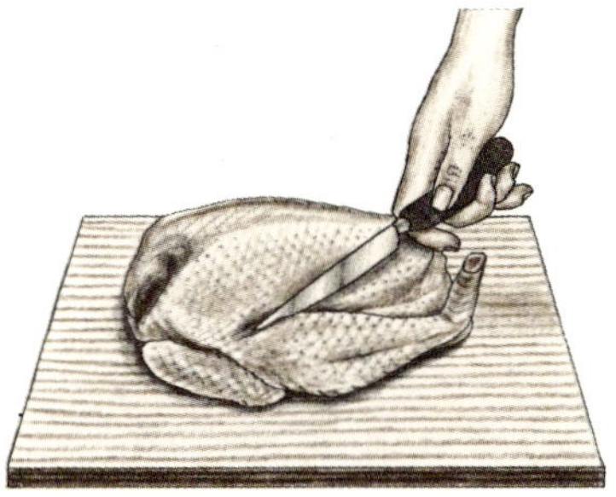

Cut off the legs. Separate the thighs from the drumsticks. Cut off the wings.

Cutting downwards, carve the breast in neat slices from either side of the breast bone.

Carving a duck

Using a knife or poultry shears cut the wings and legs from either side of the body.

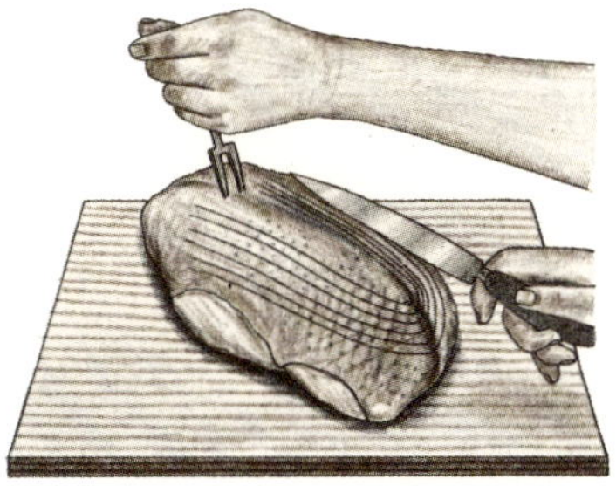

Make a downward cut on each side of the breastbone. Cut thick parallel slices from both sides.

Meat and game

Large joints of meat or game are the best for roasting because small joints tend to dry up during cooking. Very lean meat should be larded or barded and basted frequently during cooking.

Put beef into a very hot oven for the first fifteen minutes to brown the outsides and seal in the juices, then lower the heat a little for the rest of the cooking time. With the exception of beef, most meat and game is usually well cooked, but in France lamb is often served still slightly pink at the centre of the joint.

Raised meat pies should be made a day in advance to allow time for the inside of the pastry to absorb some of the meat juices.

Roast ribs of beef with Yorkshire pudding

Serve the beef with horseradish sauce or mustard.

SERVES SIX

Dripping
2 short fore ribs of beef, chined and trimmed at the end (about 6 to 7 lb/ 3 kg)
1 teaspoon Dijon mustard
Salt and pepper
2 lb (900 g) peeled potatoes, cut into even-sized pieces
½ pint (300 ml) stock or water

YORKSHIRE PUDDING

¼ lb (100 g) flour
Salt
1 egg
½ pint (300 ml) milk

Preheat the oven to 450°F (230°C, Gas Mark 8).

Heat 4 tablespoons of dripping in a roasting tin. Rub the beef fat with the mustard, salt and pepper and stand with the fat uppermost in the roasting tin. Roast for 1¾ to 2 hours, reducing the oven temperature after 15 minutes to 375°F (190°C, Gas Mark 5).

After 15 minutes add the potatoes and turn them in the fat. Turn the potatoes once or twice during the rest of the cooking time to brown on all sides.

Meanwhile make the batter for the Yorkshire pudding. Sift the flour and a pinch of salt into a bowl. Make a well in the centre and break in the egg. Add half the milk and mix with the egg. Stirring slowly incorporate the flour to make a batter. Gradually add the remaining milk. Thirty minutes before the beef is cooked pour a teaspoon of the hot dripping into 6 individual Yorkshire pudding tins and put them on the top rack of the oven to heat. After 5 minutes pour the batter into the tins and leave to cook for about 20 minutes. If one large tin is used, the cooking time will be about 30 minutes.

Transfer the meat to a carving board and the potatoes and Yorkshire puddings to a heated dish. Keep hot. Carefully pour off the fat from the roasting tin, leaving the meat juices behind. Add the stock or water. Bring to the boil and stir, scraping the sides of the pan. Strain the gravy into a heated sauce boat.

Roasting meat and game

Beef (on the bone)	
15 mins per lb plus 15 mins (boned)	450°F (230°C, Gas Mark 8) for first 15 mins then 375°F (190°C, Gas Mark 5)
20 mins per lb plus 10 mins	
Mutton (on the bone)	
25 mins per lb plus 25 mins	400°F (200°C, Gas Mark 6) for first 15 mins then 375°F (190°C, Gas Mark 5)
Lamb (on the bone)	
20 mins per lb plus 20 mins (boned)	375°F (190°C, Gas Mark 5)
30 mins per lb plus 20 mins	
Pork (on the bone)	
35 mins per lb (boned)	425°F (220°C, Gas Mark 7) for first 20 mins then 325°F (170°C, Gas Mark 3)
45 mins per lb	
Veal	
25 mins per lb plus 25 mins	375°F (190°C, Gas Mark 5)
Venison	
25 mins per lb plus 30 mins	350°F (180°C, Gas Mark 4) then 475°F (240°C, Gas Mark 9) for last 30 mins

Beef Wellington

If you prefer, wrap the beef in a rich shortcrust instead of using puff pastry.

Serve beef Wellington with green beans, courgettes or ratatouille.

SERVES SIX TO EIGHT

1 beef fillet about 3 lb (1½ kg)
1 tablespoon oil
Salt and pepper
Duxelles made from 1 lb (450 g) mushrooms, cooled
¼ lb (100 g) pâté de foie gras
1 lb (450 g) puff pastry
Beaten egg to glaze
½ pint (300 ml) Madeira sauce

Preheat the oven to 425°F (230°C, Gas Mark 8).

Rub the beef all over with the oil and salt and pepper. Put the meat on a rack and roast for 40 minutes.

Take the meat out of the oven and set aside to cool completely.

Meanwhile mix the duxelles with the foie gras. When the meat has cooled spread the top and sides with the duxelles mixture.

Roll out the pastry dough into a rectangle ¼ inch (½ cm) thick and large enough to enclose the fillet. Put the fillet, top side down, on to the pastry dough. Enclose the meat in the dough to make a neat parcel. Dampen and seal the ends. Reserve the trimmings.

Put the meat on a baking sheet with the seam side down.

Roll out the trimmings and cut out pastry leaves. Brush the top of the pastry with the beaten egg and arrange the pastry leaves on top in a decorative pattern. Brush with more egg. Pierce the pastry in 3 places.

Bake for 40 minutes or until the pastry is puffed up and golden brown. Serve with the Madeira sauce.

Roast breast of veal with soured cream and tarragon

Instead of tarragon use a few sprigs of rosemary or marjoram. Serve the veal with mashed potatoes, purple or green sprouting broccoli and glazed carrots or sautéed courgettes.

SERVES SIX

1 boned breast of veal, weighing about 3 lb (1½ kg) when boned
Salt and pepper
2½ oz (75 g) butter
2 medium-sized onions, chopped
¼ lb (100 g) soft brown breadcrumbs
1 tablespoon chopped tarragon
Grated rind of 1 lemon
1 tablespoon lemon juice
Salt and freshly ground black pepper
2 eggs, beaten
½ pint (300 ml) veal stock (made from the bones)
¼ pint (150 ml) soured cream
Few tarragon sprigs

Preheat the oven to 375°F (190°C, Gas Mark 5).

Lay the veal flat on a board, skin-side down. Season with salt and pepper.

Melt 1½ ounces (40 g) of the butter in a frying-pan and fry the onions until soft. Remove the pan from the heat and mix in the breadcrumbs, tarragon, lemon rind and juice. Season to taste and bind with the egg. Spread the stuffing over the veal and roll up like a Swiss roll. Secure with string. Melt the remaining butter in a roasting tin. Put in the meat and roast for about 1¾ hours, basting frequently with the juices.

Transfer the meat to a heated serving dish. Pour the stock into the tin and bring to the boil on top of the cooker, scraping in the bits. Boil until reduced by half. Remove the pan from the heat, allow to cool a little and stir in the soured cream and the tarragon sprigs. Reheat but do not boil. Adjust the seasoning.

Remove the string and carve the meat into slices. Pour over a little of the sauce, serving the rest in a sauce boat.

A classic dish : roast ribs of beef with Yorkshire pudding.

Meat and game

Roast shoulder of lamb with herb stuffing

Use other herbs, such as rosemary, chervil, basil, marjoram or mint, in the stuffing. Serve the lamb with roast potatoes and broad beans.

SERVES SIX

1 boned shoulder of lamb weighing 3½ lb (1½ kg)
3 tablespoons dripping
Salt and pepper
½ pint (300 ml) stock made from the lamb bones

STUFFING
1½ oz (40 g) butter
1 onion, chopped
1 garlic clove, chopped
¼ lb (100 g) breadcrumbs
6 tablespoons chopped fresh parsley
1 teaspoon chopped fresh thyme
Salt and pepper
2 eggs, beaten

Preheat the oven to 375°F (190°C, Gas Mark 5).

To make the stuffing, melt the butter in a frying-pan and fry the onion and garlic until soft. Remove the pan from the heat and stir in the rest of the stuffing ingredients. Open up the meat and put the mixture in the centre. Roll and tie securely. Put the dripping and meat in a roasting tin, sprinkle with salt and pepper and roast for about 2 hours, basting frequently. Lift out the meat and keep warm.

Pour off most of the fat from the tin. Put the roasting tin over heat and pour in the stock. Bring to the boil, stirring and scraping the bottom of the tin. Boil for 12 to 13 minutes. Adjust the seasoning. Pour the gravy into a sauce boat and serve with the meat.

Crown roast

The stuffing for a crown roast is a matter of taste—use the herb stuffing for the roast shoulder of lamb or combine ¼ pound (125 g) of rice, cooked, 1 lightly fried chopped onion and 2 chopped garlic cloves, 1 ounce (25 g) each of sultanas, chopped almonds and walnuts, seasoning to taste, and the juice of ½ lemon.

SERVES SIX

1 crown roast (approximately 12 chops)
Approximately 1 to 1½ lb (450 to 700 g) stuffing
Dripping
½ pint (300 ml) strong stock
Salt and pepper

Preheat the oven to 375°F (190°C, Gas Mark 5).

Fill the crown roast with the stuffing. If you are using the rice stuffing dot the top with a little butter.

Heat the dripping in a roasting tin. Put the crown roast in the tin. Cover each bone with a piece of foil to stop it burning. Roast for 1¼ to 1½ hours, basting occasionally.

Transfer the meat to a serving dish and keep warm. Remove the pieces of foil and replace them with cutlet frills if you like.

Pour off most of the fat from the tin. Add the stock and bring to the boil on top of the stove, scraping and stirring. Season to taste and strain into a heated gravy boat.

Serve immediately.

Roast pork

The choicest cut for roasting is the loin, but other common roasting cuts are the shoulder or leg. There is a basic difference between the French and English methods of roasting: the French remove the skin first, whereas the English leave it on to become crisp, delicious crackling. If roasting pork in the French style, rub the meat with crushed thyme (or marjoram) and bay leaf about an hour before cooking.

To roast pork in the English style score the skin and rub it with fat and salt. Roast according to the chart—the crackling should be crisp at the end of the cooking time. Serve with apple sauce or baked apples and gravy.

SERVES FOUR TO SIX

3 lb (1½ kg) boned loin of pork, skinned and rolled
2 garlic cloves, slivered
Sage
1 teaspoon black peppercorns, coarsely crushed
Rind and juice of 1 lemon
½ teaspoon salt
1 tablespoon olive oil
8 fl oz (225 ml) white wine

Carving a shoulder of lamb

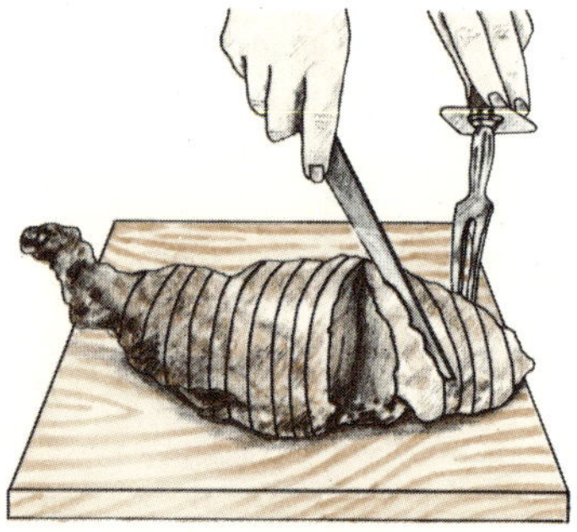

First cut a thick wedge-shaped slice. Then carve to your left.

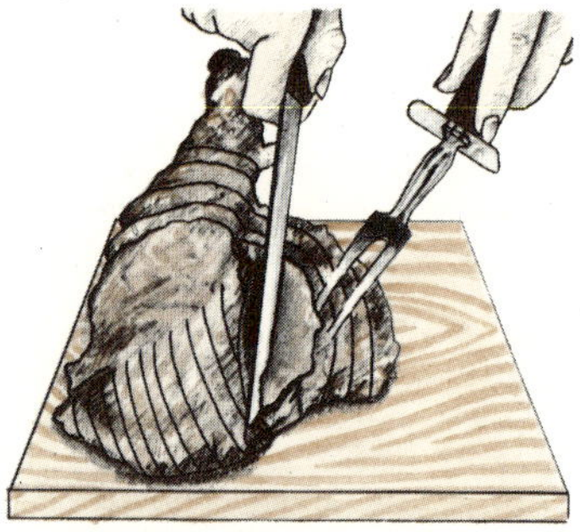

Turn the meat and continue slicing down to the bone.

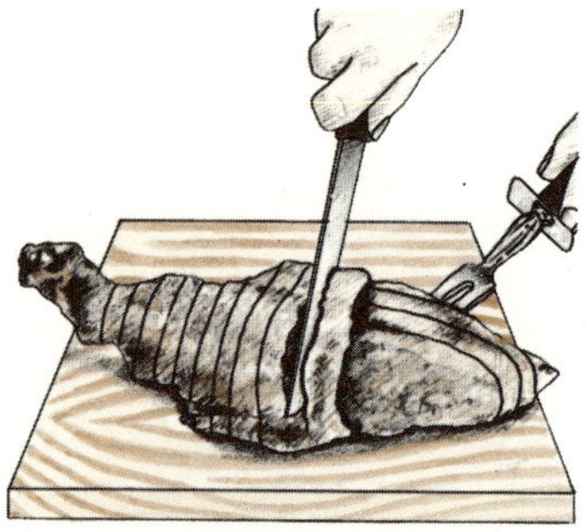

Now carve from the first cut down to the shank bone.

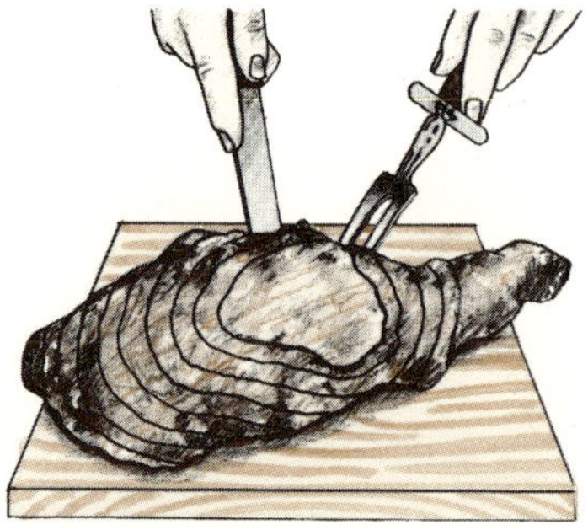

Turn the meat over, cut away the fat and slice across.

Carving a leg of lamb

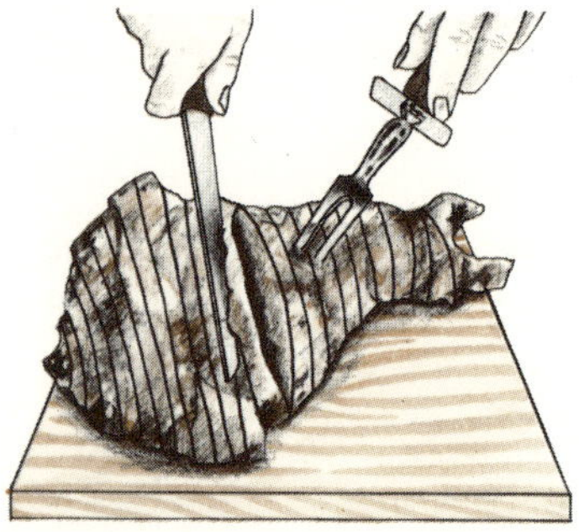

First cut a thick wedge-shaped slice then carve on either side.

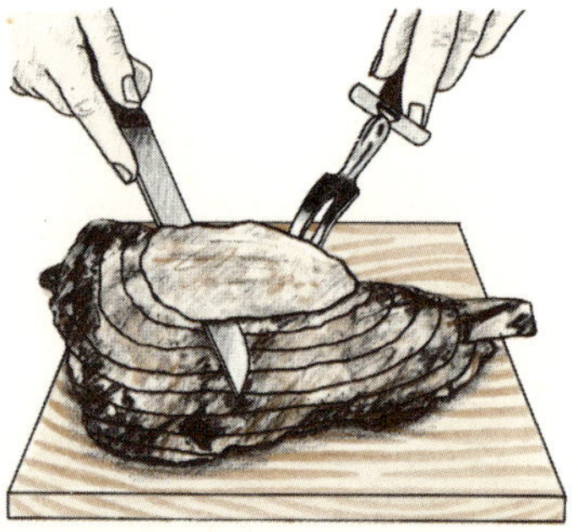

Turn the leg over, cut away the fat and carve across.

Carving ribs of beef

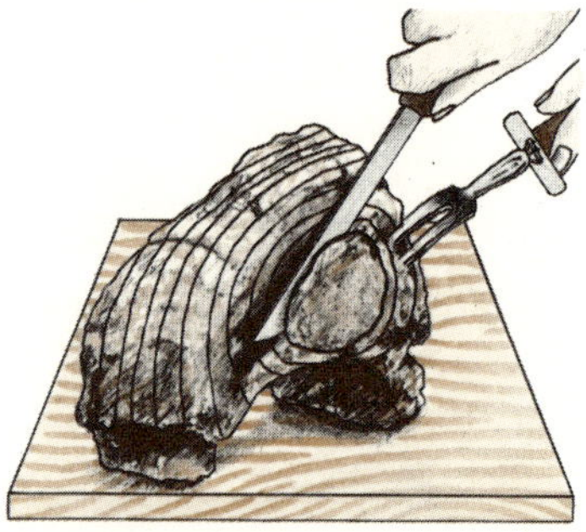

Remove the chine bone, loosen the meat from the ribs and slice.

Make downward cuts, slanting the knife to get larger slices.

Preheat the oven to 375°F (190°C, Gas Mark 5).

Trim the pork of any excess fat. Using a sharp knife make a number of incisions in the meat and insert the garlic slivers and a little sage. Mix the peppercorns, lemon rind and juice, salt and olive oil together and rub over the pork.

Put the pork on a rack in a roasting tin and roast for 2 to $2\frac{1}{4}$ hours or until the meat is thoroughly cooked. Test the meat by piercing it to the centre with a skewer—if the juices run clear it is done.

Lift out the meat and put it on a carving board and keep warm. Pour away the fat in the roasting tin and put in the wine. Put the tin over heat and bring the wine to the boil, stirring and scraping. Boil rapidly to reduce the gravy. Adjust the seasoning and serve.

Stuffed loin of pork

SERVES SIX TO EIGHT

$\frac{1}{2}$ lb (225 g) prunes, soaked for 3 hours in cold water and drained
2 medium-sized cooking apples, peeled, cored and finely chopped
2 teaspoons brown sugar
Finely grated rind of 1 lemon
5 lb ($2\frac{1}{2}$ kg) boned loin of pork
2 oz (50 g) butter
2 tablespoons white wine
8 fl oz (225 ml) soured cream

Put the prunes in a saucepan with enough cold water to cover. Bring to the boil over moderate heat and simmer for 15 minutes, or until the prunes are tender.

Drain the prunes, and when they are cold enough to handle, remove the stones and chop the flesh. Mix with the apples, sugar and lemon rind.

Lay the pork, fat-side down, on the work surface. Cover the meat, to within 1 inch (2 cm) of the short ends, with the prune stuffing and roll it up tightly. Tie the roll at $\frac{1}{2}$-inch (1-cm) intervals with trussing string.

Preheat the oven to 350°F (180°C, Gas Mark 4).

Melt the butter in a roasting tin over moderate heat. Add the pork roll and brown it well on all sides.

Roast the meat for about $3\frac{1}{2}$ hours, or until it is cooked and the juices run clear when it is pierced with the point of a sharp knife.

Remove the meat from the oven and carve it into thick slices. Put the slices on a warmed serving dish and keep hot.

Pour off all the fat from the roasting tin. Put the tin over moderate heat and add the wine. Scrape the bottom of the pan to dislodge any sediments. Add the cream and cook gently until the sauce is hot and smooth. Pour the sauce over the pork and serve immediately.

Pork spareribs

SERVES FOUR

$3\frac{1}{2}$ to 4 lb ($1\frac{1}{2}$ to 2 kg) pork spareribs, trimmed and cut into 2-rib pieces

MARINADE

4 tablespoons clear honey
Juice of 1 lemon
1 tablespoon Dijon mustard
2 tablespoons tomato purée
3 tablespoons soy sauce
$\frac{1}{4}$ teaspoon cayenne pepper
Salt
1 teaspoon grated root ginger
2 garlic cloves, crushed

Combine the marinade ingredients in a saucepan, and simmer for 2 minutes. Set aside to cool.

Put the spareribs in a large dish. Pour over the marinade and set aside for at least 12 hours, turning once.

Preheat the oven to 350°F (180°C, Gas Mark 4).

Drain the spareribs and put them in a roasting tin. Reserve the marinade.

Roast the spareribs for 1 hour. Lift out the ribs and pour away the fat. Increase the oven temperature to 425°F (220°C, Gas Mark 7) and put the ribs back into the roasting tin, brush with the marinade and return to the oven for 15 minutes or until crisp. Brush once again with the marinade to glaze during the last five minutes.

Raised pork pie

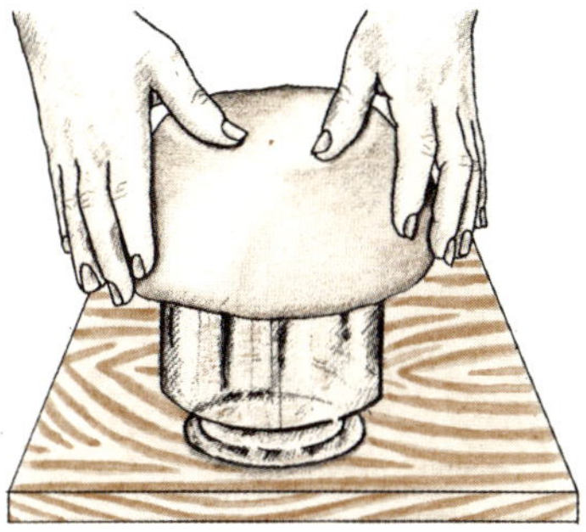

Press the dough over an upturned, lightly greased jar.

Turn right side up, remove the jar, put in the filling and cover

Put a double thickness of paper around the pie and tie to secure.

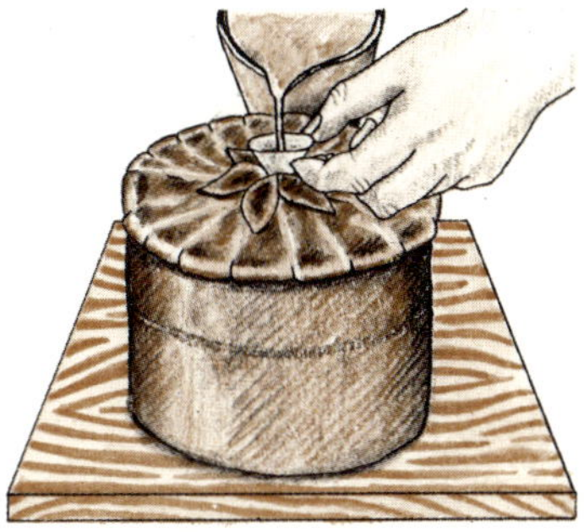

After baking pour the stock through a funnel into the pie.

Beef Wellington

Spread the top and sides of the fillet with pâté and duxelles.

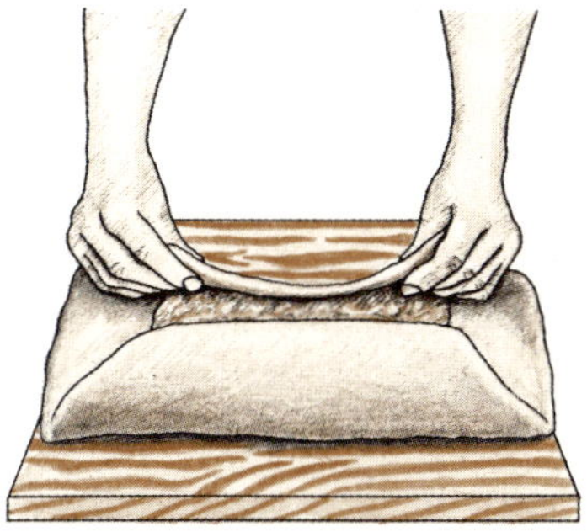

Roll out the pastry and put the fillet in the centre.

Enclose the meat in the pastry, dampen well and seal the ends.

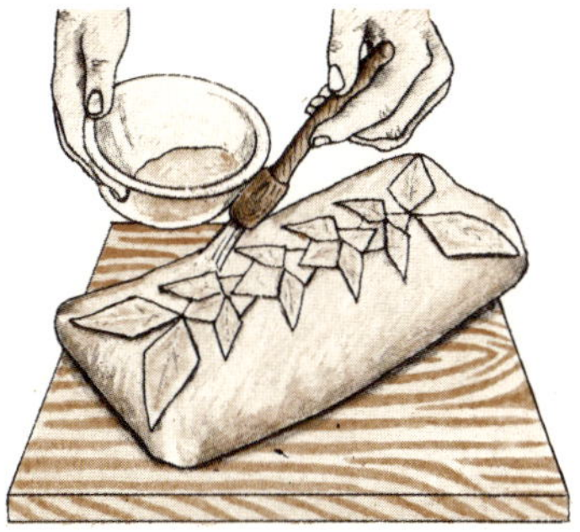

Decorate the top with pastry leaves and brush with beaten egg.

Meat and game

Roast suckling pig

SERVES ABOUT FIFTEEN

1 suckling pig weighing about 12 lb (6 kg)
2 oz (50 g) seasoned flour
2 oz (50 g) butter
1 lb (450 g) mushrooms, chopped
½ lb (225 g) pig's liver, chopped
4 lb (2 kg) minced veal
2 teaspoons salt
½ teaspoon pepper
1 teaspoon allspice
2 tablespoons each parsley and thyme
1 teaspoon sage
¼ pint (150 ml) sherry
2 eggs, beaten
1 lb (450 g) chestnuts, peeled
1 pint (575 ml) chicken stock
1 stuffed green olive
16 small red apples, baked
¾ pint (450 ml) cranberry sauce

Preheat the oven to 450°F (220°C, Gas Mark 8).

Rub the suckling pig with the seasoned flour. Cover the feet, ears and tail with foil.

Melt the butter in a frying-pan and fry the mushrooms until soft. Tip the mushrooms into a large mixing bowl. Add the liver, veal, salt, pepper, allspice, herbs, sherry and eggs and mix well.

Stuff the pig with the mixture and sew up. Put a block in its mouth and arrange it, kneeling, on a rack in the oven with a roasting tin underneath. Roast for 15 minutes, then reduce the oven temperature to 325°F (170°C, Gas Mark 3) and continue roasting for about 9 hours or for 35 minutes per pound (weighed with stuffing), until thoroughly cooked. Baste frequently with the dripping.

Meanwhile, put the chestnuts in a saucepan, cover with the stock and simmer for 40 minutes or until they are tender. Drain the chestnuts. Empty the roasting tin of almost all the dripping, put in the chestnuts and roast for the last 30 minutes.

Cover the pig with foil if it is browning too much. When cooked transfer the pig to a wooden board, put a slice of olive in each eye socket and replace the block in its mouth with a red apple.

Garnish with the chestnuts and the baked apples, filled with the cranberry sauce.

To carve, first separate the shoulders and legs from the carcass. Then cut the ribs into chops.

Baked ham

This method of cooking is ideal for whole hams which may be too large to fit into a saucepan.

SERVES TEN

1 ham, about 15 lb (7 kg), soaked in cold water overnight
2 lb (900 g) flour
1 pint (575 ml) water

Preheat the oven to 300°F (160°C, Gas Mark 2).

Rinse and dry the ham. Remove the skin. Put the flour in a large bowl and mix in the water to make a dough. Roll out the dough large enough to enclose the ham completely. There must be no gaps or holes in the dough. Dampen the edges and seal. Put in a large roasting tin and bake for 6 hours or for 25 minutes per pound plus 30 minutes.

Take the ham out of the oven and remove and discard the pastry covering. The ham is now ready to be served, glazed in the oven or covered in browned breadcrumbs.

Honey-glazed ham

SERVES TEN

1 baked or boiled ham, about 15 lb (7 kg)

GLAZE

¼ lb (100 g) honey
Grated rind and juice of 1 orange
1 tablespoon prepared mustard
About 24 whole cloves

Preheat the oven to 425°F (210°C, Gas Mark 7).

Score the ham fat diagonally at 1-inch (2-cm) intervals, first in one direction, then in the other, to make a diamond pattern.

Mix the honey with the orange rind, mustard and enough orange juice to make a spreadable mixture. Spread the ham with the glaze. Stud the corners of each diamond with the cloves. Put the ham in a roasting tin and bake for 30 minutes.

Remove from the oven. Cool completely before serving.

Haunch of venison

Serve with braised celery and garlic mashed potatoes.

SERVES EIGHT TO TEN

5 lb (2½ kg) haunch of venison
½ lb (225 g) salt pork cut into strips
Salt
2 tablespoons whisky
¼ pint (150 ml) double cream
16 to 20 prunes, soaked and simmered for 10 minutes
12 chestnuts, peeled and simmered in stock for 40 minutes
2 lemons, cut into wedges
¾ pint (450 ml) cranberry sauce

MARINADE

1 pint (575 ml) red wine
4 tablespoons wine vinegar
8 tablespoons olive oil
Bouquet garni
12 peppercorns, bruised
6 juniper berries, bruised
3 cloves
2 carrots, sliced
2 celery stalks, sliced
2 onions, sliced

Lard the venison with the salt pork. Combine all the marinade ingredients in a large bowl. Put the venison into the marinade and leave for 2 days, turning occasionally.

Preheat the oven to 350°F (180°C, Gas Mark 4).

Lift out and dry the venison. Strain and reserve the marinade. Put the herbs, celery, carrots and onions from the marinade into a roasting tin. Rub the venison with a little salt and put it on top of the herbs and vegetables. Roast for 2 hours basting occasionally with the reserved marinade.

Increase the oven temperature to 400°F (200°C, Gas Mark 9) and cook for 30 minutes. Lift out the venison and put it on a heated serving dish. Warm the whisky in a ladle, ignite it and pour it over the meat. Keep the venison warm while you make the gravy.

Pour off the fat from the roasting tin. Pour in the remaining marinade and bring to the boil on top of the stove, stirring and scraping the bottom of the tin. Boil until the liquid is reduced by one-third. Remove the roasting tin from the heat and stir in the cream, adjust the seasoning and strain the gravy into a sauce boat.

Arrange the prunes and chestnuts around the venison together with the lemon wedges. Serve with the cranberry sauce and gravy.

Pork pie

SERVES FOUR

¾ lb (350 g) hot water crust pastry
¾ lb (350 g) lean pork, cut into ¾-inch (2-cm) cubes
½ lb (225 g) unsmoked bacon, thinly sliced and cut into pieces
1 teaspoon sage
½ teaspoon allspice
¼ teaspoon salt
Pepper
Beaten egg
½ pint (300 ml) degreased jellied stock, made from pig's trotters

Preheat the oven to 350°F (180°C, Gas Mark 4).

Lightly grease the outer base and sides of a 2-pound (900 g) jam jar, and grease a baking sheet.

Set aside one-quarter of the pastry dough for the lid and keep warm. Spread the remaining dough into a circle and put it over the base of the upturned jam jar. Press the dough down evenly over the jar with your hands until it reaches the shoulder of the jar and is about ½ inch (1 cm) thick all round. Set aside to cool.

Cut a double thickness of brown paper or greaseproof paper the same depth as the dough case and long enough to go round its circumference. Wrap the paper round the dough and secure it in place with paper clips or string.

Turn the jam jar right side up on to the baking sheet and gently lift out the jar leaving the dough case.

Mix the pork, bacon, sage, allspice and salt and pepper in a bowl. Carefully fill the dough case with the meat and trim the top to come level with the meat.

Press the remaining dough into a round to make the lid. Put it on top of the pie, dampen the edges and pinch to seal.

Use any trimming to make leaves or flowers. Dampen them and arrange on top of the pie.

Brush with the beaten egg. Pierce a hole in the centre of the pie to allow the steam to escape. Bake the pie for 2¼ hours, removing the paper collar half way through the cooking time.

Remove the pie from the oven and leave it to cool.

Heat the jellied stock until it has melted. Using a funnel placed in the steam vent pour in the cooled stock until it comes to just below the pie lid.

Chill the pie in the refrigerator for at least 4 hours.

Three ways of baking meat in pastry: beef Wellington, top left; Cornish pasty, top right and pork pie.

Steak and kidney pie

SERVES FOUR

1½ lb (700 g) stewing steak, trimmed of all fat and cut into 1-inch (2-cm) cubes
½ lb (225 g) ox kidney, cut into 1-inch (2-cm) cubes
2 oz (50 g) seasoned flour
1½ oz (40 g) dripping
2 medium-sized onions, chopped
½ lb (225 g) mushrooms, quartered
Bouquet garni
½ pint (300 ml) beef stock
Salt and pepper
6 oz (175 g) flaky pastry
1 egg, beaten

Roll the meat in the seasoned flour, coating it well.

Melt the dripping in a sauté pan. Add the meat, a few pieces at a time and fry quickly until browned all over. Transfer the meat as it browns to a saucepan.

Add the onions to the sauté pan, fry until lightly browned and add to the meat. Fry the mushrooms for 2 to 3 minutes and put them in the saucepan. Put in the bouquet garni. Pour the stock into the sauté pan and bring to the boil stirring and scraping the bottom of the pan. Season to taste and pour the stock over the meat and vegetables. Cover the pan and simmer over very low heat for 1½ hours or until the meat is tender. Discard the bouquet garni.

Preheat the oven to 375°F (190°C, Gas Mark 5).

Using a slotted spoon transfer the meat and vegetables to a deep pie dish. If the cooking liquid is too thin thicken it by boiling it down or by adding a little beurre manié, or a spoonful of flour mixed in cold water. Pour the boiling liquid into the pie dish.

Roll out the pastry dough to make a lid. Dampen the edges of the pie dish and put the dough on top. Trim and press down to seal. Crimp the edges. Use the trimmings to make flowers and leaves and decorate the top of the pie. Make a hole in the centre for the steam to escape and brush all over with the egg.

Bake for 40 minutes or until the top is puffed up and golden.

Cornish pasty

SERVES TWO TO FOUR

½ lb (225 g) shortcrust pastry made with lard
1 egg, lightly beaten

FILLING

½ lb (225 g) rump steak or topside of beef, finely chopped
2 oz (50 g) onions, finely chopped
¼ lb (100 g) potatoes, thinly sliced
2 oz (50 g) turnip, chopped
Salt and pepper
Thyme

Preheat the oven to 350°F (180°C, Gas Mark 4). Lightly grease two baking sheets.

First make the filling. Mix the meat with the vegetables. Season well with the salt, pepper and a large pinch of thyme.

Divide the dough in half and roll each half into a round about 8 inches (20 cm) in diameter.

Divide the filling between the two rounds, laying it down the middle. Brush round the edges of the dough with the beaten egg. Lift the dough on either side of the filling to meet on top and pinch to seal all along the edge.

Pierce the pasties with a skewer to make 2 vents for the steam to escape.

Put the pasties on the baking sheets, brush all over with the egg and bake for 1 hour.

Vegetables

Most root vegetables and vegetable fruits can be cooked in the oven. Small new potatoes can be baked in foil with a little butter, salt and pepper and a sprinkling of mint or parsley. Larger potatoes may be baked in their jackets, or peeled and quartered, parboiled for five minutes and roasted round a joint of meat—they will take about forty minutes. Alternatively, potatoes can be cooked au gratin with cheese and cream.

For a main course there is a wide range of recipes for stuffed vegetable fruits. Aubergines, tomatoes, courgettes and peppers make excellent cases for such ingredients as rice and minced meat, flaked fish and shellfish, grated cheese, dried fruit, herbs and nuts.

Baked potatoes

Baked potatoes are delicious with just a knob of butter, but they can also be scooped out, mixed with other ingredients and baked again for 10 minutes.

SERVES FOUR

4 fairly large potatoes, scrubbed clean and dried
1 oz (25 g) butter

Preheat the oven to 375°F (190°C, Gas Mark 5).

Prick the potatoes all over with a fork and then rub them with the butter. Place them on the oven rack, or on a baking sheet, and bake for 1 to 1½ hours, or until the skin is very crisp and the potatoes are tender in the centre—test them with a long, thin skewer. Serve hot.

Ham-stuffed potatoes

SERVES FOUR

4 hot baked potatoes
1 oz (25 g) butter
¼ lb (125 g) smoked ham, diced
2 teaspoons chopped fresh chives
2 tablespoons double cream
Salt and freshly ground black pepper

Preheat the oven to 375°F (190°C, Gas Mark 5).

Cut a thin slice off the top of each potato and set it aside. Using a teaspoon, scoop the flesh out into a bowl, taking care to keep the skins intact. Add the remaining ingredients and mash them together with a fork. Spoon the mixture into the skins and place them upright in a baking dish small enough to prevent the potatoes from falling over. Replace the lids if you like, or replace them just before serving if you want the top to brown. Bake for 10 to 15 minutes, or until very hot. Serve immediately.

Haddock-stuffed potatoes

SERVES FOUR

Scoop out the flesh of 4 baked potatoes and mix it with ½ pound (225 g) flaked cooked haddock and 2 tablespoons soured cream.

Garlic mashed potatoes

SERVES FOUR

2 lb (900 g) potatoes, mashed
2 fl oz (50 ml) cream
2 oz (50 g) butter
2 large egg yolks
4 garlic cloves, crushed
Salt and pepper
Small pinch nutmeg

Preheat the oven to 375°F (190°C, Gas Mark 5).

Put all the ingredients in a mixing bowl and beat well with a wooden spoon to mix the ingredients together thoroughly. Spoon the mixture into a forcing bag fitted with a large star nozzle and either pipe the mixture into a baking dish, or pipe individual rounds on a greased baking sheet.

Place the dish or baking sheet in the oven and bake for 20 minutes, or until the top is lightly browned.

Potatoes à la dauphinoise

SERVES FOUR

2 oz (50 g) butter
1 garlic clove, crushed
2 lb (900 g) potatoes, peeled, thinly sliced and washed
¼ lb (125 g) Gruyère cheese, grated
Salt and pepper
Grated nutmeg
½ pint (300 ml) scalded milk or cream
1 egg, beaten

Preheat the oven to 350°F (180°C, Gas Mark 4).

Mash half the butter with the garlic clove and use it to grease a shallow baking dish. Place a layer of potatoes in the bottom of the dish and sprinkle with a little of the cheese, salt, pepper and nutmeg. Repeat the layers until you have used all the potatoes and nearly all the cheese. Beat the milk or cream and egg together, and strain the mixture over the potatoes. Sprinkle over the remaining cheese. Cut the remaining butter into small pieces and dot it over the top. Bake for about 1¼ hours or until the potatoes are tender and the top is golden. Serve at once.

Sweet potato soufflé

SERVES FOUR

1 teaspoon olive oil
1 lb (450 g) sweet potatoes, boiled and mashed
4 tablespoons cream
1 tablespoon sugar
Salt
1 oz (25 g) butter
1 orange
3 egg yolks
½ teaspoon ground cinnamon
Pinch grated nutmeg
4 egg whites, stiffly beaten

Preheat the oven to 375°F (190°C, Gas Mark 5).

Using the teaspoon of oil, grease a medium-sized soufflé dish and set it aside.

Put the potato in a bowl and add the cream, sugar, salt and butter. Beat the mixture with a wooden spoon until smooth.

Grate the orange rind and add it to the purée, with the chopped orange flesh. Beat in the egg yolks, with the cinnamon and nutmeg. Fold in the stiffly beaten egg whites. Pour the mixture into the soufflé dish and bake for 45 minutes, or until the soufflé is well risen and golden brown on the top. Serve immediately.

Boston baked beans

This is traditionally served with Boston steamed bread.

SERVES SIX

2 lb (900 g) dried haricot beans, soaked overnight in cold water and drained
2 oz (50 g) dark brown sugar
4 tablespoons molasses
Salt and freshly ground black pepper
1 tablespoon dry mustard
1 lb (450 g) salt pork, cut into 2-inch (5-cm) cubes, blanched for 5 minutes in boiling water and drained
1 onion, peeled

Put the beans in a large saucepan and add enough cold salted water to cover. Bring to the boil over high heat, skimming off the scum as it rises. Reduce the heat to low, cover the pan and simmer for 1 hour, adding more boiling water if necessary. Drain the beans in a colander.

Preheat the oven to 250°F (130°C, Gas Mark ½).

Mix the sugar, molasses, salt, pepper and mustard together. Layer the beans, molasses mixture and salt pork in a deep, ovenproof pot and bury the onion in the middle. Add enough boiling water to cover and put the lid on the pot. Bake for 6 to 8 hours or until the beans are very tender. As the water evaporates, add more because the beans must be kept moist. Remove the lid for the last hour of baking to let the top brown. Serve hot.

Aubergines à la nîmoise

SERVES TWO

3 tablespoons olive oil
1 large aubergine, cut in half, degorged, rinsed and dried
¼ lb (100 g) cooked rice
3 tomatoes, peeled, seeded and chopped
1 tablespoon tomato purée
1 garlic clove, crushed
1 tablespoon chopped fresh basil
1 teaspoon chopped fresh chives
Salt and pepper

Preheat the oven to 350°F (180°C, Gas Mark 4).

Heat the oil in a frying-pan and add the aubergine, skin-side uppermost. Reduce the heat to low, cover the pan and cook for about 10 minutes. Remove the aubergine halves from the pan and drain them well. Scoop out the pulp with a teaspoon, leaving the skin intact. Chop the pulp and mix with the rice, tomatoes, tomato purée, garlic, basil and chives. Season to taste. Fill the skins with the stuffing and place them in a baking dish. Sprinkle with a little oil from the frying-pan and bake for about 35 minutes. Serve at once.

Moussaka

SERVES FOUR

Olive oil
$1\frac{1}{2}$ lb (700 g) aubergines, thinly sliced, degorged, rinsed and patted dry
1 oz (25 g) butter
1 onion, finely chopped
3 large garlic cloves, crushed
$1\frac{1}{2}$ lb (700 g) minced lamb
$1\frac{1}{2}$ lb (700 g) tomatoes, chopped
2 tablespoons tomato purée
1 teaspoon dried thyme
1 teaspoon dried rosemary
Salt and freshly ground black pepper
12 fl oz (350 ml) mornay sauce
2 large egg yolks
2 tablespoons Parmesan cheese

Pour a very little olive oil into a large frying-pan—it should be just enough to make a thin film over the bottom. Heat the frying-pan over fairly high heat and, when hot, add enough aubergine slices to cover the base in a single layer. Press the slices down so they are coated with some of the oil and turn them over quickly. Fry for $1\frac{1}{2}$ minutes on each side, or until they are lightly browned.

Set the fried slices aside on a plate and continue frying the remaining slices in the same way, adding more oil to the pan.

When all the aubergines have been fried, set them aside and make the meat sauce. Melt the butter in a saucepan and add the onion. Fry, stirring, for 5 minutes then add the garlic and lamb and fry for about 8 minutes, or until the lamb is browned. Stir in the tomatoes, tomato purée, thyme, rosemary and plenty of salt and pepper. Reduce the heat to low, cover the pan and simmer, stirring occasionally, for 15 minutes. Remove the pan from the heat and set aside.

Preheat the oven to 375°F (190°C, Gas Mark 5).

Mix the mornay sauce with the egg yolks and set aside.

Layer the aubergine slices and meat sauce in a large, round baking dish, beginning and ending with the aubergine. Spoon the mornay sauce over the last layer of aubergine slices to cover them completely, and sprinkle over the Parmesan cheese. Bake in the oven for about 1 hour, or until the top is well browned. Serve immediately.

Mushroom vol-au-vents

SERVES FOUR

1 oz (25 g) butter
$\frac{1}{2}$ lb (225 g) button mushrooms, sliced
$\frac{1}{4}$ lb (125 g) cooked ham, cubed
$\frac{1}{2}$ pint (300 ml) velouté sauce
3 tablespoons cream
2 oz (50 g) Gruyère cheese, grated
Salt and pepper
4 vol-au-vent cases

Preheat the oven to 375°F (190°C, Gas Mark 5).

Melt the butter in a saucepan. Add the mushrooms and fry, stirring, for 3 to 4 minutes.

Stir in the ham, velouté sauce, cream, Gruyère cheese and salt and pepper to taste.

Pile the mixture into the vol-au-vent cases and bake for 10 to 15 minutes or until bubbling on top and heated through.

Chicorée au gratin

This is a very popular dish in Belgium; it can also be made with broccoli, celery and fennel.

SERVES FOUR

1 teaspoon butter
1 tablespoon sugar
1 teaspoon lemon juice
4 large heads chicory, washed and trimmed
4 large slices lean ham
$\frac{1}{2}$ pint (300 ml) mornay sauce
2 tablespoons double cream
1 tablespoon grated Parmesan cheese

Preheat the oven to 375°F (190°C, Gas Mark 5). Using the teaspoon of butter, grease a medium-sized baking dish and set it aside.

Fill a medium-sized saucepan with salted water and add the sugar and lemon juice. Bring to the boil over moderate heat and add the chicory. When the water has come back to the boil reduce the heat to low and simmer for 10 minutes. Drain the chicory and reserve 2 tablespoons of the cooking liquid.

Wrap one chicory in each ham slice and place the rolls in a baking dish. Mix the mornay sauce with the reserved cooking liquid and the cream and pour over the rolls to cover them completely. Sprinkle with the Parmesan cheese and bake for 30 minutes. Serve hot.

Stuffed baked marrow

This needs no vegetable accompaniment other than garlic mashed potatoes or croquette potatoes.

SERVES FOUR

3 lb ($1\frac{1}{2}$ kg) marrow
1 tablespoon oil
2 onions, chopped
10 oz (275 g) sausage meat
2 tomatoes, skinned and chopped
2 tablespoons tomato purée
2 oz (50 g) cooked rice
Salt and pepper
$\frac{1}{2}$ teaspoon dried sage
1 tablespoon butter
$\frac{1}{2}$ pint (300 ml) tomato sauce, hot

Preheat the oven to 375°F (190°C, Gas Mark 5).

Cut the stalk end off the marrow and set it aside. Scoop the seeds out of the marrow with a metal spoon and discard them. Bring a large saucepan of salted water to the boil. Add the marrow and blanch it for 5 minutes. Drain well and set aside.

Heat the oil in a small frying-pan and fry the onions, stirring, for 6 minutes or until soft. Stir in the sausage meat and cook, stirring, for 15 minutes. Stir in the tomatoes, tomato purée, rice, seasoning and sage. Remove the pan from the heat and stuff the mixture into the marrow. Replace the stalk end, securing it with skewers or cocktail sticks.

Using the butter, grease a piece of foil large enough to enclose the marrow. Wrap the marrow in the foil and place it in a baking tin. Put in the oven and bake for 1 hour, or until tender. Remove the marrow from the oven and unwrap it. Cut it into thick slices and serve with the tomato sauce.

Vol-au-vent cases

To make a large vol-au-vent, cut out a circle of puff pastry.

Lightly score a smaller circle and a pattern on the dough.

Small cases are made with two sizes of pastry cutters.

Once baked, the insides are scooped out. Retain the lids.

Stuffed vine leaves

Prepacked vine leaves can be bought from some delicatessens. Blanch fresh leaves in boiling water for 2 minutes.

SERVES FOUR

½ lb (225 g) minced lamb
¼ lb (125 g) long-grain rice, washed, soaked in cold water for 30 minutes, blanched for 2 minutes and drained
3 tablespoons tomato purée
2 tablespoons chopped mint
Salt and pepper
2 garlic cloves, crushed, plus 1 garlic clove, sliced
2 tablespoons lemon juice
16 vine leaves
½ pint (300 ml) chicken stock, hot

Preheat the oven to 325°F (170°C, Gas Mark 3).

Put the lamb, rice, 1 tablespoon of the tomato purée, half the mint, salt, pepper, crushed garlic and lemon juice in a bowl and beat well to mix.

Lay a vine leaf out flat on your work surface. Put a little filling on the stem end of the leaf and fold the stem end over. Fold the sides inwards, and roll up the leaf, from the stem end, to make a tight, cigar-shaped parcel.

Lay the vine leaves in a greased, shallow baking dish in a single layer, packing them in tightly so they do not open out during cooking. Pack the garlic slices and remaining mint between the parcels.

Mix the chicken stock with the remaining tomato purée and pour the mixture over the rolls. Place the dish in the oven and bake for 1 hour, or until the rice inside the vine leaves is tender.

Baked tomatoes

SERVES FOUR

8 large tomatoes, washed
Salt and pepper
Dried basil
½ oz (15 g) butter
1 shallot, finely chopped
¾ lb (350 g) mushrooms, sliced
1 lb (450 g) cooked chicken, boned and diced
2 tablespoons cream
2 oz (50 g) fine breadcrumbs
2 oz (50 g) Gruyère cheese, grated
1 oz (25 g) Parmesan cheese, grated
Nutmeg
4 tablespoons melted butter

Preheat the oven to 375°F (190°C, Gas Mark 5).

Cut the tops off the tomatoes and scoop out the flesh. Sprinkle the insides with a little salt, pepper and basil. Put the tomatoes in a greased baking dish.

Melt the butter in a saucepan. Add the shallot and fry gently, stirring, until it is soft. Add the mushrooms and fry for 2 minutes. Stir in the chicken and cream and season to taste. Stuff the tomatoes with this mixture.

From left to right: stuffed vine leaves, baked tomatoes, baked stuffed onions and baked spiced avocados.

Mix the breadcrumbs, Gruyère and Parmesan together and season lightly. Spoon this over the chicken mixture. Grate a little nutmeg over the filling and sprinkle liberally with the butter.

Bake for 15 minutes or until the tomatoes are heated through and brown and bubbling on top.

Baked stuffed onions

SERVES FOUR

3 large onions, boiled
1 oz (25 g) butter
2 tablespoons fresh white breadcrumbs
½ lb (225 g) lean minced beef
1 tablespoon chopped fresh parsley
Salt and pepper
2 tablespoons double cream
2 tablespoons melted butter

Preheat the oven to 375°F (190°C, Gas Mark 5).

When the onions are cool enough to handle, slit each one on one side down to the centre and carefully slip off about 8 of the largest layers. Chop up what remains of one of the onions and reserve what is left of the other two for future use.

Melt the butter in a frying-pan and add the chopped onion. Fry, stirring, until it is golden.

Put the fried onion in a mixing bowl and add the breadcrumbs, beef, parsley, salt and pepper and cream. Beat well with a wooden spoon to mix. Put 2 teaspoons of the filling on each onion layer and roll up.

Place the rolls upright in a greased baking dish, sprinkle over the melted butter and bake for 30 minutes, or until browned.

Baked spiced avocados

SERVES FOUR

2 large, ripe avocados
2 garlic cloves, crushed
1 teaspoon salt
Few drops Tabasco sauce
1 tablespoon ground coriander
1 teaspoon cumin seeds
¼ teaspoon ground ginger
2 teaspoons garam masala
½ lb (225 g) cooked prawns
2 tablespoons soured cream
1 teaspoon lemon juice
4 lemon wedges

Preheat the oven to 350°F (180°C, Gas Mark 4).

Cut the avocados in half and remove the stones. Using a teaspoon, scoop all the flesh out into a bowl, being careful not to damage the skins.

Mash the avocado flesh with a fork until it is smooth. Stir in the remaining ingredients, except the lemon wedges. Pile the mixture into the reserved skins and carefully transfer them to a baking dish. Place the dish in the oven and bake for 20 minutes. Transfer the avocados to individual plates and serve with the lemon wedges.

Fruit

Simple but delicious desserts can be made by baking such fruit as apples, pears or bananas: for example, stuff the cores of apples or pears with a mixture of raisins, honey, cloves and cinnamon, brush the skins with melted butter and bake in a fairly hot oven until tender. Bananas are much improved by being baked with a little butter, rum, brown sugar and lemon juice and even the hardest pears are delicious cooked in red wine.

Fruit pies are usually covered with shortcrust pastry, pâte sucrée or flaky pastry. A one-quart (1-litre) pie dish will take about two pounds (900 g) of fruit. Although the traditional fillings such as apple and gooseberry are always popular, try mixing such fruit as cherries and rhubarb, prunes and apricots or peaches and oranges.

Apple strudel

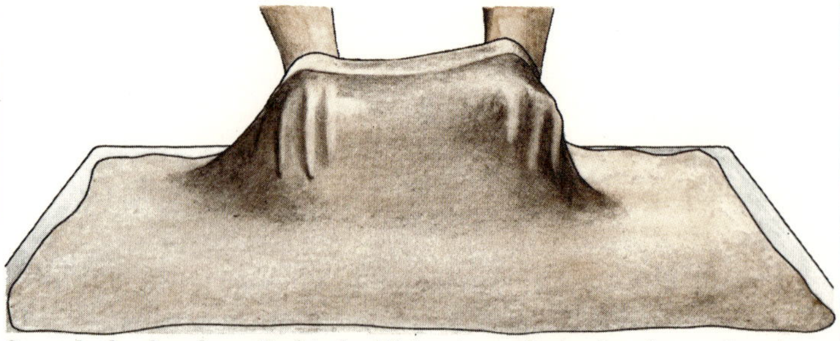

Stretch the dough until thin by lifting it on the backs of your hands.

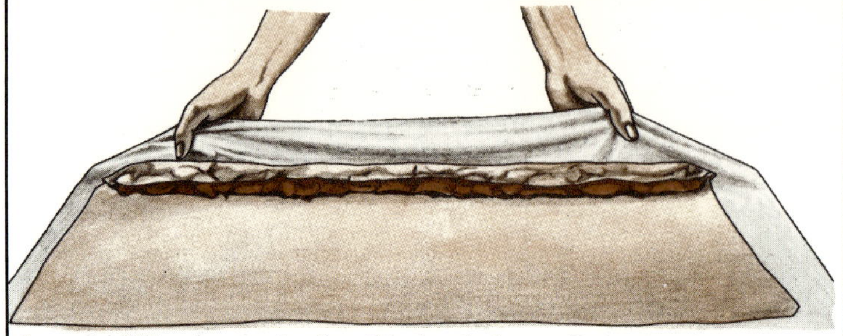

Lay the filling in a strip then lift the cloth to roll the dough over.

Mince pies

MAKES ONE 8-INCH (20-CM) PIE OR TWELVE INDIVIDUAL PIES

$\frac{1}{2}$ lb (225 g) shortcrust pastry
$1\frac{1}{2}$ lb (700 g) mincemeat
Castor sugar

Preheat the oven to 425°F (220°C, Gas Mark 7).

Roll out two-thirds of the pastry dough and line an 8-inch (20-cm) pie plate. Spoon in the mincemeat. Roll out the remaining dough and cover the pie, pressing the edges together.

Bake for 40 to 45 minutes. Individual pies will take 20 to 25 minutes.

Mincemeat

Mincemeat will keep for up to 1 year in a cool place.

MAKES ABOUT SEVEN POUNDS (3 KG)

1 lb (450 g) currants, coarsely chopped
1 lb (450 g) seedless raisins, coarsely chopped
1 lb (450 g) sultanas, coarsely chopped
$\frac{1}{2}$ lb (225 g) mixed peel, chopped
3 large apples, grated
1 lb (450 g) suet, grated
$\frac{1}{4}$ lb (100 g) almonds, chopped
1 lb (450 g) soft brown sugar
Rind and juice of 2 lemons
1 teaspoon mixed spice
1 teaspoon ground nutmeg
$\frac{1}{4}$ pint (150 ml) brandy

Wash and dry the fruit. Mix all the ingredients together moistening with the brandy. Spoon the mixture into jars. Cover tightly and keep for at least 1 month before using.

Apple pie

SERVES FOUR TO SIX

2 lb (900 g) apples, peeled, cored and thinly sliced
1 quince, peeled, cored and thinly sliced
3 oz (75 g) granulated sugar
6 oz (175 g) shortcrust pastry
Castor sugar

Preheat the oven to 400°F (200°C, Gas Mark 6).

Layer the apple and quince in a baking dish. Sprinkle each layer with the granulated sugar. Shape the top layer of apples in a dome to come above the top of the dish. Pour in 4 tablespoons of water.

Roll out the pastry dough $\frac{1}{4}$ inch ($\frac{1}{2}$ cm) thick. Cut a strip of dough to go round the top of the pie dish. Dampen the strip and press it down on the rim of the dish. Lay the rest of the dough on top to form a lid. Trim the dough and crimp the edges. Brush the top with water and dredge with castor sugar.

Bake for 15 minutes. Reduce the oven temperature to 375°F (190°C, Gas Mark 5) and continue baking for 25 minutes.

Apple dumplings

SERVES SIX

$\frac{3}{4}$ lb (350 g) shortcrust pastry
6 cooking apples, peeled and cored
$\frac{1}{4}$ lb (125 g) brown sugar
1 teaspoon ground cinnamon
12 cloves
Milk
Castor sugar
$\frac{3}{4}$ pint (450 ml) custard sauce

Preheat the oven to 400°F (200°C, Gas Mark 6). Lightly grease a large baking sheet.

Divide the pastry dough into 6 equal pieces, reserving a little for decoration. Pat each piece into a round. Put an apple on each round and work the dough up the sides of the apple, leaving the top open. Mix the sugar and cinnamon together. Spoon the mixture into the centres of the apples putting 2 cloves in each cavity. Seal the pastry over the tops of the apples, using a little water to dampen the edges.

Put the apples upside down on the baking sheet. Roll out the reserved pastry dough, and cut out leaves. Decorate the apple dumplings, brush with milk, and dust with castor sugar. Bake for 30 minutes.

Serve hot with the custard.

French apple flan

SERVES FOUR TO SIX

6 oz (175 g) pâte sucrée
$1\frac{1}{2}$ lb (700 g) cooking apples, peeled, cored and sliced
2 oz (50 g) sugar
Grated rind of 1 lemon
4 green dessert apples, cored and thinly sliced
$1\frac{1}{2}$ oz (40 g) melted butter
4 tablespoons sieved marmalade, warm

Preheat the oven to 425°F (220°C, Gas Mark 7).

Roll out the pastry dough and line a 10-inch (25-cm) loose-bottomed, fluted flan tin with it and bake blind. Reset the oven to 400°F (200°C, Gas Mark 6).

Meanwhile simmer the cooking apples with a tablespoon of water until soft. Mash with a wooden spoon to make a purée. Stir in the sugar and lemon rind. Set aside to cool slightly.

Fill the flan case with the apple purée. Arrange the sliced apples in overlapping circles on top of the purée. Brush with the butter. Bake for 25 minutes or until the apples are lightly browned. Remove from the oven and brush the top with the marmalade. Serve hot or cold.

Apple strudel

Serve apple strudel warm or cold with whipped cream.

SERVES TEN TO TWELVE

10 oz (275 g) strudel pastry dough
$\frac{1}{2}$ lb (225 g) butter, melted
Sifted icing sugar

STRUDEL FILLING

1 oz (25 g) toasted breadcrumbs
$\frac{1}{4}$ lb (100 g) raisins
3 lb ($1\frac{1}{2}$ kg) cooking apples, peeled, cored and finely sliced
Grated rind of 1 lemon

1 tablespoon lemon juice
2 oz (50 g) ground almonds
3 oz (75 g) blanched, toasted almonds, chopped
¼ lb (100 g) sugar
2 teaspoons ground cinnamon

First prepare the filling. Lightly mix all the ingredients together in a bowl.

To shape the strudel, cover a large table with a cloth or sheet. Dust the cloth lightly with flour. Put the dough in the centre of the cloth and roll it out as thinly as possible.

Put your hands, palms downwards, under the dough. Gradually stretch the dough by lifting it on the backs of your hands until it is paper thin. Work your way round the table stretching the dough to a uniform thickness.

If a few small holes appear in the dough do not worry. When the dough is as thin as paper, straighten the edges with a pair of scissors.

Preheat the oven to 425°F (220°C, Gas Mark 7). Grease 2 or 3 baking sheets.

Brush the dough with two-thirds of the butter. Starting at one of the shorter ends lay the filling in a long strip on the dough. Leave a clear 2-inch (5-cm) margin on each side and in front of you. Fold the margins of the two longer sides over the filling and brush the folds with butter.

Now lift up the cloth in front of you and roll the dough over the filling. Continue rolling until the filling is completely rolled up in the dough.

Using a sharp knife cut the strudel into lengths to fit on the baking sheets. Put the strudel on the baking sheets with the seams underneath. Brush generously with butter and put in the oven. Reduce the oven temperature to 350°F (180°C, Gas Mark 4) and bake for 45 minutes or until the strudel is golden brown on top.

Serve the strudel warm or cold, dusted with icing sugar.

Rhubarb crumble

Use other fruit—apples, apples and blackcurrants, redcurrants or gooseberries—to make crumble. Serve with cream or with a custard sauce.

SERVES FOUR

2 lb (900 g) rhubarb, cut into chunks
Grated rind of 1 large orange
¼ lb (125 g) sugar

CRUMBLE TOPPING

¼ lb (125 g) flour
1 teaspoon ground cinnamon
3 oz (75 g) butter
2 oz (50 g) granulated sugar

Preheat the oven to 375°F (190°C, Gas Mark 5). Lightly butter a 2½-pint (1¼-litre) soufflé or deep baking dish.

Put the rhubarb, orange rind and sugar into the baking dish and mix well.

To make the crumble mix the flour and cinnamon in a bowl. Rub in the butter and mix in the sugar. Pile the crumble mixture on top of the fruit. Do not worry if the topping is higher than the top of the dish, it will sink when the fruit cooks and softens.

Bake the crumble for 45 to 60 minutes or until the top is browned and well settled.

Serve hot or cold.

Cherry flan

When morello cherries are in season use 1½ pounds (700 g) of fresh cherries, remove the pits and poach in a syrup made of ½ pint (300 ml) of water and 5 oz (150 g) of sugar for 5 minutes. Drain the cherries, return the syrup to the pan and boil it until it thickens. Serve the flan with whipped cream.

SERVES SIX

6 oz (175 g) almond pastry
1 lb (450 g) canned, pitted morello cherries
1 tablespoon arrowroot
Grated rind of 1 large lemon
1 oz (25 g) castor sugar
1 egg
2 fl oz (50 ml) double cream

Preheat the oven to 425°F (220°C, Gas Mark 7).

Roll out the pastry dough and with it line a 9-inch (23-cm) flan dish. Bake blind. Remove the pastry case from the oven and reduce the temperature to 375°F (190°C, Gas Mark 5).

Drain the cherries. Measure out ¼ pint (150 ml) of the syrup into a saucepan and mix in the arrowroot. Bring the mixture to the boil stirring and cook for 1 minute or until the syrup is thick and smooth.

Arrange the cherries in the pastry case and spoon the thickened syrup over the top.

Mix the lemon rind with the castor sugar in a bowl. Add the egg. Put the bowl over barely simmering water and whisk until the mixture is thick and pale and leaves a trail when the whisk is lifted.

Remove the bowl from the heat and gently fold in the cream. Pour the mixture over the cherries. Bake for 30 minutes or until the top is lightly browned.

Remove the tart from the oven and cool.

Lemon meringue pie

SERVES FOUR TO FIVE

6 oz (175 g) rich shortcrust pastry
3 tablespoons cornflour
½ pint (300 ml) water
2 oz (50 g) sugar
Pinch salt
3 egg yolks
Rind and juice of 2 lemons
2 egg whites
¼ teaspoon cream of tartar
¼ lb (125 g) castor sugar

Preheat the oven to 425°F (220°C, Gas Mark 7).

Roll out the pastry dough, line an 8-inch (20-cm) fluted flan ring and bake blind. Reset the oven to 325°F (170°C, Gas Mark 3).

Mix the cornflour with the water, sugar and salt in a saucepan. Stir over low heat until the mixture is thick and bubbling. Remove the pan from the heat. Lightly beat the egg yolks in a bowl. Stir in a little of the hot cornflour mixture then pour into the saucepan, whisking all the time. Stir in the lemon rind and juice. Cool the mixture for 15 minutes, stirring occasionally, then pour it into the pie shell. Set aside to cool.

Meanwhile beat the egg whites with the cream of tartar until stiff. Gradually beat in the sugar, saving a spoonful to sprinkle on the top. Pile the meringue on to the pie to cover the filling completely. Sprinkle the sugar over the top. Bake for 20 to 25 minutes or until the meringue is crisp and golden. Serve cool.

Baking blind

Baking blind is a method of baking pastry cases without a filling. To prevent the dough in the base of the case from rising, the bottom and sides are lined with foil and weighed down with dried beans or rice. The pastry is baked at 425°F (220°C, Gas Mark 7). The foil and beans or rice are removed after 15 minutes and the pastry case is baked for a further 5 minutes to brown. Store the beans or rice and use again.

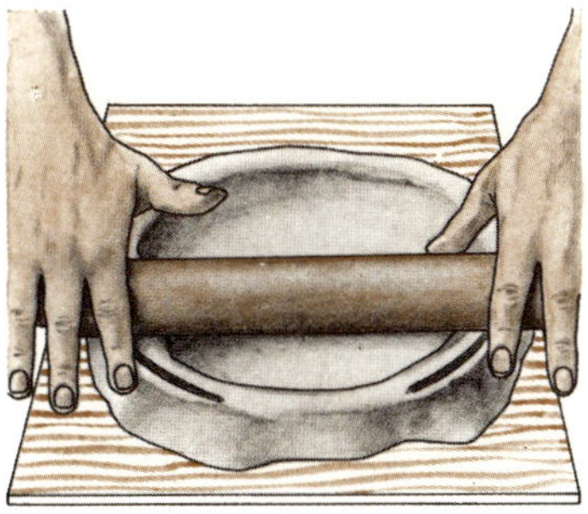

Line the tin with pastry dough.

Trim and crimp the edges.

Line with foil and beans or rice.

Fruit

Pear tart

SERVES FOUR TO SIX

6 oz (175 g) rich shortcrust pastry
1½ oz (40 g) sugar
½ pint (300 ml) water
1½ lb (700 g) pears, peeled, quartered and cored
½ pint (300 ml) cream
1 vanilla pod
2 egg yolks
2 teaspoons cornflour
2 oz (50 g) stem ginger, chopped
1 oz (25 g) split blanched almonds, toasted

Preheat the oven to 425°F (220°C, Gas Mark 7).

Roll out the pastry dough, line a 9-inch (23-cm) tart tin with it and bake blind.

Reset the oven to 325°F (170°C, Gas Mark 3).

Dissolve 1 tablespoon of the sugar in the water in a saucepan. Add the pears and poach them gently for 12 minutes or until just tender. Remove the pan from the heat and let the pears cool in the syrup.

Scald the cream and the vanilla pod and set aside for 10 minutes. Remove the vanilla pod. Beat the egg yolks with the cornflour and the remaining sugar. Stir in the hot cream.

Drain the pears and arrange them in the pastry case. Sprinkle the chopped ginger over them. Strain the custard over the pears. Bake the tart for 45 minutes or until the custard is lightly set.

Sprinkle the almonds over the top and serve warm.

Date bars

MAKES 12

½ lb (225 g) stoned cooking dates
¼ pint (150 ml) water
¼ lb (125 g) rolled oats
¼ lb (125 g) wholewheat flour
2 tablespoons brown sugar
½ teaspoon ground allspice
¼ lb (100 g) butter, softened

Preheat the oven to 350°F (180°C, Gas Mark 4).

Put the dates and water in a small saucepan and simmer for 15 minutes or until the dates are soft. Mash the dates into a pulp. Set aside to cool.

Mix the oats, flour, sugar and allspice together. Rub in the butter and mix well together.

Lightly butter a 1½-inch (3-cm) deep, 8-inch (20-cm) square tin. Spread half the flour and butter mixture over the bottom of the tin, pressing it down evenly. Spread the date pulp over the top and the remaining flour and butter mixture over the dates with your fingertips. This is difficult to do smoothly and requires a little patience.

Bake for 30 minutes. Remove the tin from the oven. Cut the mixture into bars in the tin. Leave to cool completely before removing from the tin.

Clafoutis

Although the traditional fruit used in a clafoutis is cherries, other fruit may also be used.

SERVES FOUR TO SIX

3 eggs
3 oz (75 g) sugar
¼ lb (100 g) flour
Pinch salt
2 tablespoons melted butter
½ pint (300 ml) milk
1 lb (450 g) pitted black cherries
1 oz (25 g) butter, cut into pieces
1 tablespoon icing sugar
½ pint (300 ml) custard sauce

Preheat the oven to 400°F (200°C, Gas Mark 6). Butter a 9-inch (23-cm) flan dish.

Whisk the eggs and sugar in a large bowl until foamy and pale. Gradually whisk in the flour, salt, the melted butter and milk. Put the cherries in the flan dish. Pour over the batter, dot with the butter and bake for 30 minutes, or until the top is firm to the touch. If the top begins to brown too much, cover with foil. Sprinkle with icing sugar and serve warm with the custard.

Pineapple upside-down cake

Serve this cake as a dessert with whipped cream.

SERVES FOUR TO SIX

¼ lb (100 g) soft dark-brown sugar
2 oz (50 g) plus ¼ lb (100 g) butter
1 lb (450 g) canned pineapple slices, drained
5 to 6 glacé cherries
¼ lb (100 g) castor sugar
2 eggs
¼ lb (100 g) self-raising flour
¼ teaspoon vanilla essence

Preheat the oven to 350°F (180°C, Gas Mark 4).

Put the brown sugar and 2 ounces (50 g) of the butter in a 10-inch (25-cm) oval dish about 2 inches (5 cm) deep. Put the dish in the oven for a few minutes until the sugar and butter have melted.

Remove the dish from the oven

and spread the sugar and butter mixture evenly. Arrange the pineapple slices on top. Put the glacé cherries in the centres of the pineapple slices. Set aside.

Cream the castor sugar with the remaining $\frac{1}{4}$ pound (100 g) of butter in a bowl until the mixture is pale and fluffy.

Beat in the eggs one by one with a tablespoon of flour. Mix in the vanilla essence and fold in the remaining flour. Pour the cake mixture over the pineapple slices and bake for 30 to 40 minutes or until a skewer inserted into the sponge comes out clean.

Remove the cake from the oven and cool for 20 minutes. Turn out on to a serving dish. Serve cool.

Three delightful fruit puddings to serve hot or cold: lemon meringue pie, apple dumplings and rhubarb crumble.

Cereals

Macaroni cheese

SERVES FOUR

2 oz (50 g) plus 1 teaspoon butter
½ lb (225 g) macaroni, cooked and drained
Salt and pepper
1 pint (575 ml) mornay sauce
2 oz (50 g) lean ham, diced
2 oz (50 g) grated Cheddar cheese
2 oz (50 g) soft white breadcrumbs

Preheat the oven to 425°F (220°C, Gas Mark 7). Grease a medium-sized baking dish with the teaspoon of butter.

Put the macaroni in a mixing bowl with half the butter, the salt, pepper, mornay sauce and ham. Mix gently then pour into the baking dish. Sprinkle with the cheese and breadcrumbs and dot with the remaining butter. Put into the oven for 10 to 15 minutes, or until the top is lightly browned. Serve at once.

Baked pasta with seafood

SERVES FOUR

1 teaspoon vegetable oil
½ lb (225 g) pasta shells, cooked and drained
½ lb (225 g) cooked shelled mussels
¼ lb (125 g) cooked peeled prawns
1 pint (575 ml) béchamel sauce
1 teaspoon anchovy essence
2 oz (50 g) Parmesan cheese, grated
1 oz (25 g) butter

Preheat the oven to 425°F (220°C, Gas Mark 7). Grease a large baking dish with the teaspoon of oil.

Mix all the ingredients except the cheese and butter together and spoon into the baking dish. Sprinkle with the cheese and dot with the butter. Bake for 10 to 15 minutes, or until the top is well browned and bubbling. Serve immediately.

Pizza dough

MAKES HALF POUND (225 G)

½ oz (15 g) fresh yeast
¼ teaspoon sugar
4 fl oz (125 ml) lukewarm water
½ lb (225 g) strong white flour
½ teaspoon salt
1 tablespoon plus 2 teaspoons olive oil

Put the yeast, sugar and 2 tablespoons of the water into a small bowl and mash the mixture with a fork to make a smooth paste. Set the bowl aside in a warm draught-free place for about 15 minutes, or until the mixture is puffed up and frothy.

Sift the flour and salt into a bowl and make a well in the centre. Pour in the yeast mixture, the remaining water and the tablespoon of oil. Mix the liquids together, gradually incorporating the flour. Mix the dough with your hands until it begins to leave the sides of the bowl. Turn the dough out on to a lightly floured surface and knead it for about 10 minutes, or until it is smooth and elastic.

Rinse, dry and lightly grease the mixing bowl. Shape the dough into a ball and place it in the bowl. Cover the bowl with a damp cloth and set aside in a warm, draught-free place for about 1 hour, or until the dough has doubled in bulk.

Turn the dough out on to the work surface again and knead it for 3 minutes. Divide the dough in half and shape each half into a ball. Flatten each ball by pressing down with the heel of your hand until it forms a circle about ¼ inch (½ cm) thick. Brush the top of the dough with the remaining olive oil.

The pizza base is now ready to be covered with whichever savoury mixture you are using and baked in the oven.

Pizza Napoletana

This is the classic Neapolitan pizza—simple but delicious.

MAKES TWO PIZZAS

½ lb (225 g) pizza dough shaped into 2 circles
8 medium-sized tomatoes, blanched, skinned and chopped
Salt and freshly ground black pepper
8 thin slices mozzarella cheese
8 anchovy fillets
6 black olives, halved and pitted
1 teaspoon chopped fresh oregano
1 teaspoon chopped fresh basil
2 teaspoons olive oil

Preheat the oven to 450°F (230°C, Gas Mark 8).

Lightly grease a large baking sheet. Put the two pizza dough circles on the sheet.

Put half the tomatoes on each pizza and sprinkle with a little salt and lots of black pepper. Put 4 slices of mozzarella cheese on each pizza and garnish with the anchovies and olives. Sprinkle over the herbs and moisten with the olive oil.

Bake the pizzas for about 20 minutes, or until the cheese has melted and is bubbling. Serve hot or cold.

Pizza con cozze

Make in exactly the same way as pizza napoletana, but substitute 16 cooked and shelled mussels for the anchovies, adding them in the last 5 minutes of baking time. Sprinkle the top liberally with coarsely ground black pepper.

Pizza alla Francescana

MAKES TWO PIZZAS

½ lb (225 g) pizza dough shaped into 2 circles
1 tablespoon olive oil
¼ lb (125 g) mushrooms, thinly sliced
4 medium-sized tomatoes, skinned and chopped
¼ lb (125 g) prosciutto ham, cut into thin strips
1 teaspoon chopped fresh basil
Salt and pepper
8 thin slices mozzarella cheese

Preheat the oven to 450°F (230°C, Gas Mark 8).

Lightly grease a baking sheet. Put the two pizza circles on the baking sheet.

Heat the oil in a small saucepan and add the mushrooms. Fry for 2 minutes, stirring constantly. Add the tomatoes and cook for 5 minutes, stirring occasionally.

Remove the pan from the heat and spread half the mixture over each pizza. Cover the mixture with the ham strips and sprinkle over the basil and plenty of salt and pepper. Lay the cheese slices over the top.

Place the baking sheet in the oven and bake for about 15 to 20 minutes, or until the cheese has melted and is bubbling.

Cannelloni di spinace

If you are using fresh pasta, cut two large sheets of thinly rolled-out pasta into oblongs about 3 by 4 inches (8 by 10 cm). Cook the pasta as usual, drain it and cool. Put about 1 tablespoon of filling along one edge of each oblong and roll them up, placing them join-sides down in the baking dish.

SERVES FOUR

1 oz (25 g) butter
1 onion, finely chopped
2 garlic cloves, crushed

½ lb (225 g) minced veal
5 oz (150 g) frozen chopped spinach, thawed and drained
2 teaspoons chopped fresh basil
Salt and freshly ground black pepper
1 egg yolk beaten with 2 tablespoons double cream
½ lb (225 g) cannelloni squares or tubes, cooked and drained
½ pint (300 ml) béchamel sauce, made with 1 oz (25 g) butter and flour, ½ pint (300 ml) milk and 3 tablespoons double cream
½ pint (300 ml) tomato sauce
2 tablespoons grated Parmesan cheese

Melt the butter in a saucepan and add the onion. Fry for 6 minutes, stirring. Add the garlic, veal, spinach, basil, salt and pepper and cook, stirring, for 5 minutes. Remove the pan from the heat and stir in the egg yolk and cream mixture. Set the mixture aside to cool.

Preheat the oven to 375°F (190°C, Gas Mark 5). Lightly grease an oblong baking dish and set it aside.

Stuff the mixture into the cannelloni tubes and put them in the baking dish. Pour over the béchamel sauce and then the tomato sauce. Sprinkle over the Parmesan cheese and bake in the oven for about 30 to 40 minutes, or until the top is well browned and bubbling. Serve immediately.

Lasagne

SERVES SIX

2 oz (50 g) butter
2 onions, finely chopped
2 garlic cloves, crushed
1½ lb (700 g) lean minced beef
1 teaspoon dried rosemary
1 tablespoon chopped fresh basil
1 teaspoon dried oregano
1 lb (450 g) tomatoes, skinned and chopped
2 tablespoons tomato purée
Salt and freshly ground black pepper
4 tablespoons beef stock
1 pint (575 ml) béchamel sauce
4 tablespoons double cream
1 egg yolk
4 tablespoons grated Parmesan cheese
1 lb (450 g) lasagne sheets (plain or verde), cooked and drained

Melt the butter in a saucepan and add the onions. Fry, stirring, for 6 to 8 minutes or until they are golden brown. Add the garlic and beef and fry for a further 8 minutes. Stir in the rosemary, basil, oregano, tomatoes, tomato purée, salt, pepper and stock and reduce the heat to fairly low. Cover the pan and cook, stirring occasionally, for 20 minutes.

Preheat the oven to 400°F (200°C, Gas Mark 6).

Mix the béchamel sauce with the cream, egg yolk and half the cheese. Layer the lasagne, meat sauce and béchamel in a large ovenproof dish in that order, ending with a layer of béchamel. Sprinkle over the remaining cheese and bake in the oven for 40 minutes, or until the top is well browned.

Baked chicken pancakes

SERVES FOUR

1 oz (25 g) butter
1 green pepper, cored, seeded and diced
1 onion, finely chopped
1 garlic clove, crushed
½ lb (225 g) mushrooms, thinly sliced
3 tablespoons double cream mixed with 1 teaspoon cornflour
Salt and pepper
1 teaspoon paprika
1 lb (450 g) cooked chicken meat, diced
¼ lb (125 g) peeled cooked prawns
6 large pancakes
½ pint (300 ml) mornay sauce
2 tablespoons grated Parmesan cheese

Preheat the oven to 375°F (190°C, Gas Mark 5).

Melt the butter in a saucepan and add the pepper and onion. Fry, stirring constantly, for 6 to 8 minutes or until the onion is golden. Add the garlic and mushrooms and fry for 4 minutes, stirring. Stir in the cream mixture, the salt and pepper, paprika, chicken and prawns. Cook, stirring constantly, until the mixture has thickened. Remove the pan from the heat.

Put one pancake into a round baking dish and spread over one-fifth of the mixture. Top with another pancake and continue making layers, ending with a pancake. Pour the mornay sauce over the top and sprinkle with the Parmesan cheese. Bake in the oven for 30 minutes, or until the top is well browned. Serve immediately.

Garlic bread

SERVES FOUR TO SIX

1 medium-sized French bread
6 oz (175 g) butter, softened
2 to 3 large garlic cloves, crushed

Preheat the oven to 425°F (220°C, Gas Mark 7).

Cut the bread into slices approximately 1½ inches (3 cm) thick. Put the butter and garlic into a small bowl and mash them together with a fork. Spread the butter on one side of the bread slices and put the loaf back together again. Wrap it completely in foil and bake in the oven for 20 minutes.

Line a bread basket with a paper napkin. Remove the bread from the oven and discard the foil. Arrange the bread slices in the basket and serve immediately.

Rice pudding

SERVES FOUR

2 oz (50 g) Carolina rice, washed and drained
2 tablespoons castor sugar
¼ teaspoon vanilla essence
½ pint (300 ml) milk
½ pint (300 ml) cream
1 oz (25 g) butter, cut into small pieces
¼ teaspoon grated nutmeg

Preheat the oven to 300°F (150°C, Gas Mark 2).

Put the rice into a 1½-pint (900-ml) greased pie dish with the sugar, vanilla essence, milk, cream and the butter. Stand on a baking sheet and put into the oven for 25 minutes. Stir well, sprinkle with nutmeg and cook for a further 2 hours, or until well browned on the outside and creamy inside.

Oatmeal and apple pudding

SERVES FOUR

1 teaspoon butter
4 tablespoons soft brown sugar
8 tablespoons medium oatmeal
Pinch of salt
4 cooking apples, peeled, cored and thinly sliced
4 tablespoons melted butter

Preheat the oven to 375°F (190°C, Gas Mark 5). Lightly grease a medium-sized baking dish with the teaspoon of butter.

Mix the sugar, oatmeal and salt together. Put some of the apple slices in the base of the dish and sprinkle over some of the oatmeal mixture, then some of the melted butter. Repeat the layers until all the ingredients have been used up, ending with some butter.

Put the dish in the oven and bake for about 40 minutes, or until the apples are tender and the top of the dish is golden brown.

Serve immediately.

Bread and butter pudding

SERVES FOUR

2 oz (50 g) butter
6 slices fresh white bread, cut into triangles, crusts removed
1 oz (25 g) chopped peel
1 oz (25 g) sultanas
1 oz (25 g) raisins or currants
2 tablespoons castor sugar
½ teaspoon mixed spice
3 eggs
¼ teaspoon vanilla essence
¾ pint (450 ml) milk
½ pint (300 ml) cream

Lightly grease a 1-quart (1-litre) baking dish with a teaspoon of the butter. Butter the bread triangles with the remaining butter and layer them in the dish with the chopped peel, sultanas, raisins or currants, sugar and mixed spice.

Beat the eggs with the vanilla essence, milk and cream and pour the mixture over the bread. Set aside to soak for 30 minutes.

Meanwhile, preheat the oven to 350°F (180°C, Gas Mark 4).

Put the pudding in the oven and bake for about 1 hour, or until the custard has set and the top is lightly browned. Serve hot.

Cereals/biscuits and small cakes

To prepare a cake tin, grease the entire inside surface with a thin layer of butter, lard or oil, then sprinkle in a small amount of flour and tap the tin lightly until the flour is evenly distributed all over the greased area. Add a little castor sugar to the flour if you are making a sponge cake.

For cakes that take a long time to cook, grease the tin and line it with two layers of greased greaseproof paper.

All ingredients for cake-making should be at room temperature. Fruit and nuts should be prepared in advance, and glacé cherries should be rinsed and patted dry with absorbent kitchen paper towels.

Preheat the oven to the temperature stated in the recipe. To test that the cake is cooked, insert a thin skewer or sharp-pointed knife into the centre. If it comes out quite clean the cake is ready.

Let the cake cool in the tin for a few minutes, then run a knife round the edge and turn it out on to a wire rack.

Brownies

MAKES TWENTY-FOUR

9 oz (250 g) plain chocolate, broken into pieces
6 oz (175 g) sugar
3 tablespoons water
¼ lb (125 g) butter
½ teaspoon vanilla essence
3 eggs
6 oz (175 g) flour
1 teaspoon baking powder
¼ lb (125 g) walnuts, chopped

Preheat the oven to 350°F (180°C, Gas Mark 4).

Lightly grease a 1-inch (2-cm) deep, 11- by 7-inch (28- by 18-cm) baking tin.

Put the chocolate, sugar, water, butter and vanilla essence in a saucepan and stir to melt. Remove the pan from the heat and cool slightly.

Beat in the eggs. Sift the flour and baking powder on to the mixture and mix in. Fold in the walnuts. Pour the mixture into the baking tin and bake for 30 minutes or until a thin skewer inserted into the centre comes out clean. Cool before cutting.

Scones

If using milk instead of buttermilk, use self-raising flour and omit the bicarbonate of soda.

MAKES ABOUT TEN

½ lb (225 g) flour
½ level teaspoon bicarbonate of soda
Salt
1 oz (25 g) butter
¼ pint (150 ml) buttermilk
Milk

Preheat the oven to 400°F (200°C, Gas Mark 6).

Mix the flour, bicarbonate of soda and a pinch of salt in a bowl. Rub in the butter, and mix to a soft dough with the buttermilk, adding more if necessary.

Turn the dough out on to a lightly floured board and knead lightly. Pat the dough out until it is 1 inch (2 cm) thick, cut into 1½-inch (3-cm) rounds and brush with a little milk.

Bake for 10 to 12 minutes or until the scones are lightly browned. Serve hot.

Shortbread

MAKES TWO 6-INCH (15-CM) ROUNDS

6 oz (175 g) flour
3 oz (75 g) rice flour
¼ lb (100 g) plus 1 tablespoon castor sugar
6 oz (175 g) butter

Preheat the oven to 350°F (180°C, Gas Mark 4). Lightly grease a baking sheet.

Put the flours and ¼ pound (100 g) of castor sugar in a bowl. Add the butter and cut it into small pieces, then rub it into the flour and sugar with your fingertips. Keep rubbing until the mixture is soft enough to form a smooth dough. Divide the dough in half. Pat into circles about 6 inches (15 cm) in diameter. Put on the baking sheet. Pinch the edges of the dough to make a pattern, and prick the surface with a fork. Mark each round into sixths with a knife.

Bake for 10 minutes then turn down the heat to 300°F (150°C, Gas Mark 2), and continue baking for about 35 to 40 minutes or until the shortbread is crisp and pale gold on the outside.

Remove the shortbread from the oven and sprinkle over the remaining sugar. When the shortbread is cool, break it into pieces and serve.

Almond biscuits

MAKES ABOUT TWENTY

6 oz (175 g) flour
1 teaspoon baking powder
3 oz (75 g) butter, cut into small pieces
2 oz (50 g) ground almonds
½ lb (225 g) sugar
1 egg, beaten
1 teaspoon almond essence
Flaked blanched almonds

Preheat the oven to 350°F (180°C, Gas Mark 4). Lightly grease a baking sheet and dust with flour.

Sift the flour and baking powder into a bowl. Rub in the butter then stir in the ground almonds and sugar. Make into a stiff dough with the egg and almond essence. Break off walnut-sized pieces of the dough and roll them into balls. Flatten the balls between the palms of your hands and place them on the baking sheet. Brush with cold water and place a flaked almond on each biscuit. Bake for 10 to 15 minutes or until the biscuits are firm. Cool on a wire rack.

Brandy snaps

MAKES ABOUT EIGHTEEN

2 oz (50 g) butter
2 oz (50 g) treacle or golden syrup
2 oz (50 g) castor sugar
1 teaspoon lemon juice
2 oz (50 g) plain flour
1 teaspoon ground ginger
1 teaspoon brandy (optional)
¼ pint (150 ml) double cream

Preheat the oven to 375°F (180°C, Gas Mark 4). Grease 2 baking trays.

Heat the butter, treacle or syrup and sugar in a saucepan over moderate heat, stirring occasionally until the sugar has melted. Add the lemon juice and remove from the heat.

Stir in the flour and ginger and mix to a smooth dough. Add the brandy, if used.

Put teaspoonfuls of the mixture on the trays several inches apart. Bake until the biscuits are rich brown and lacy. Cool them

Faulty

BKTO

BKTO 0118

4-99.

Lost page cover torn

FOR LIZ IF POSS

TA.

A delectable choice of cakes and pastries to serve with coffee or for dessert. From left to right: florentine, brownies, crostata di ricotta, Danish pastries and date and walnut loaf.

for a moment then, while they are still warm, wrap each one around a wooden spoon handle. Allow to become firm before removing from the handle.

If not required immediately, cool and store in a tin. When ready to serve whip the cream and, using a forcing bag, pipe it into the brandy snaps.

Florentines

MAKES ABOUT TEN

2 oz (50 g) butter
2 oz (50 g) sugar
1 tablespoon honey
1 oz (25 g) blanched slivered almonds
1 tablespoon chopped hazelnuts
2 tablespoons chopped glacé cherries
2 tablespoons chopped mixed peel
1 tablespoon chopped angelica
2 oz (50 g) flour
½ lb (225 g) plain chocolate

Preheat the oven to 350°F (180°C, Gas Mark 4).

Line a large baking sheet with greased greaseproof paper and set it aside.

Melt the butter, sugar and honey in a medium-sized saucepan over moderate heat, stirring until the sugar has dissolved. Bring to the boil and remove the pan from the heat. Stir in the remaining ingredients, except the chocolate.

Drop heaped teaspoonfuls of the mixture, spaced well apart, on to the baking sheet. Bake for 10 minutes, or until the florentines have spread out and are golden brown.

Remove the baking sheet from the oven and let the florentines cool slightly before lifting them off the baking sheet with a palette knife and cooling them on a wire rack.

While the florentines are cooling, melt the chocolate in a bowl over a pan of simmering water.

Using the palette knife, spread the chocolate thickly over the back of each florentine, and run a fork over the chocolate to make an attractive pattern. Place the florentines, chocolate side uppermost, on the wire rack and set aside until the chocolate has hardened.

Chocolate chip biscuits

MAKES ABOUT TWENTY

2 oz (50 g) butter
¼ lb (100 g) light brown sugar
1 egg yolk
1 tablespoon milk
2 drops vanilla essence
¼ lb (100 g) self-raising flour
3 oz (75 g) chocolate chips

Preheat the oven to 375°F (190°C, Gas Mark 5).

Lightly grease a baking sheet and set it aside.

Cream the butter and sugar in a bowl. Beat in the egg yolk, milk and vanilla essence. Fold in the flour and chocolate chips.

Drop teaspoonfuls of the batter, spaced well apart, on the baking sheet and bake for about 12 minutes, or until the biscuits are golden brown. Cool on a wire rack before serving.

Butter biscuits

Serve plain or sandwiched together with a buttercream filling flavoured with chocolate or orange. The biscuits can be piped in long shapes and both ends can be dipped in melted chocolate after they have cooked.

MAKES THIRTY

½ lb (225 g) salted butter
2 oz (50 g) castor sugar
½ teaspoon vanilla essence
½ lb (225 g) flour

Preheat the oven to 375°F (190°C, Gas Mark 5). Lightly grease a baking sheet.

Put the butter in a mixing bowl and cream it with the sugar. Add the vanilla essence and the flour and mix lightly to form a smooth dough. Put the dough into a forcing bag and pipe it on to the baking sheet in various shapes.

Bake for 10 to 15 minutes, or until the biscuits are golden but not browned. Cool on the baking tray.

Cereals/pastries and cakes

Macaroons

The baking sheet may be lined with edible rice paper if you like. The paper is trimmed to the shape of the biscuits after baking.

The flavour can be varied by using other nuts—for example walnuts or hazelnuts.

MAKES ABOUT TWELVE

1 egg white, beaten until stiff
2 oz (50 g) ground almonds
3 oz (75 g) castor sugar
1 tablespoon ground rice
2 drops almond essence
1 teaspoon water
Split blanched almonds

Preheat the oven to 325°F (170°C, Gas Mark 3).

Using a metal spoon, gently blend all the ingredients except the split almonds together in a mixing bowl.

Line a baking sheet with vegetable parchment or rice paper and drop teaspoonfuls of the mixture, spaced well apart, on the sheet. Put 1 split almond on top of each spoonful.

Place in the oven and bake for about 20 minutes, or until the macaroons are pale gold and firm on top. Cool on a wire rack before serving.

Coffee éclairs

These can also be made with a chocolate-flavoured icing and filling, or just filled with sweetened whipped cream flavoured with vanilla essence.

MAKES EIGHTEEN

1 teaspoon butter
5 oz (150 g) choux pastry dough
½ pint (300 ml) crème pâtissière
2 tablespoons black coffee
½ lb (225 g) icing sugar
2 tablespoons warm water

Preheat the oven to 425°F (220°C, Gas Mark 7). Using the teaspoon of butter, grease a large baking sheet and set it aside.

Put the dough into a forcing bag fitted with a plain nozzle. Pipe 2- to 3-inch (5- to 8-cm) lengths of the dough, well spaced out, on to the baking sheet and bake for 15 to 20 minutes, or until they are cooked and golden.

Remove the éclairs from the oven and put them on a wire rack. Slit them down one side to let the steam escape and cool thoroughly.

When the éclairs are completely cold, mix the crème pâtissière with 1 tablespoon of the coffee and pipe or spoon the mixture into the éclairs.

Sift the icing sugar into a small bowl and add the remaining tablespoon of coffee and 1 tablespoon of the warm water. Beat the icing, adding more water if necessary, until it is smooth and glossy. Spread the icing over the tops of the éclairs with a palette knife and set them aside for 1 hour before serving.

Danish pastries

MAKES EIGHT

½ oz (15 g) fresh yeast
¼ teaspoon plus 1 tablespoon castor sugar
5 tablespoons warm water
½ lb (225 g) flour
Salt
1 egg, beaten
6 oz (175 g) butter
4 glacé cherries, halved

Danish pastries

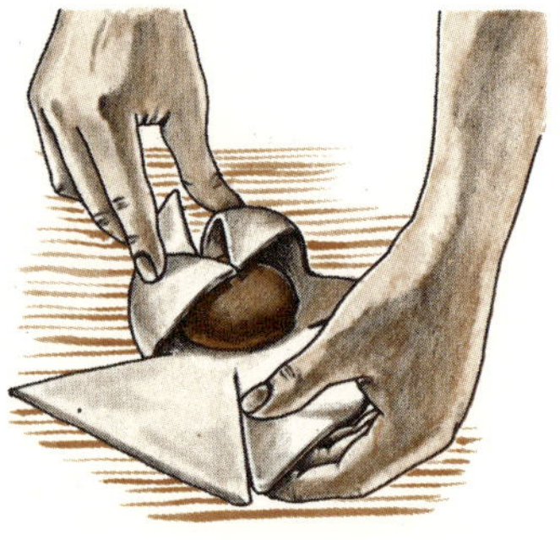

Cut the dough from the corners to the filling. Fold one corner of each triangle into the centre.

Put the filling along the centre line of the dough square and fold in the other two sides.

ALMOND FILLING

2 teaspoons butter
1 oz (25 g) castor sugar
1 oz (25 g) ground almonds
2 drops almond essence
1 egg yolk, lightly beaten

GLAZE

1 small egg
2 tablespoons hot water
2 teaspoons castor sugar

Mash the yeast with ¼ teaspoon of the sugar in a small bowl. Mix in 2 tablespoons warm water. Set aside in a warm place for 15 minutes or until the mixture is puffed up and frothy.

Sift the flour, a pinch of salt and the remaining sugar into a bowl. Make a well in the centre and pour in the yeast mixture, the remaining water and the eggs. Mix to a soft dough, adding more water if necessary.

Cover the dough and put in the refrigerator for 10 minutes.

Allow the butter to soften slightly and spread it on greaseproof paper into a 3- by 9-inch (8- by 23-cm) rectangle ½ inch (1 cm) thick. Put in the refrigerator to chill.

Roll the dough into a 10-inch (25-cm) square. Put the butter in the middle and fold over the two sides to just overlap in the middle. Seal the open ends.

Roll the dough into a 6- by 18-inch (15- by 45-cm) rectangle. Fold in three. Wrap in greaseproof paper or put in a polythene bag and refrigerate for 10 minutes.

Roll out the dough, with the narrow end facing you, to the same size. Fold in three, wrap and refrigerate.

Repeat the rolling and folding once more and put in the refrigerator for at least 2 hours before using.

Meanwhile make the filling. Cream the butter with the sugar. Beat in the ground almonds, almond essence and the egg yolk. Mix to firm paste.

Roll out the dough into a 16- by 8-inch (40- by 20-cm) rectangle. Cut it into eight 4-inch (10-cm) squares. Place a ¾-inch (2-cm) round of almond filling in the centre. Using a sharp knife cut from each corner to the almond filling. Fold one corner of each triangle thus formed to the centre and press the points firmly into the almond paste. Put half a glacé cherry in the centre and press down lightly.

Make the glaze by beating the egg with the water and the castor sugar. Brush the glaze over the pastries.

Preheat the oven to 425°F (210°C, Gas Mark 7). Lightly grease a baking sheet and put the pastries on it. Slip the baking sheet into a greased polythene bag and set aside in a warm place for 20 to 25 minutes or until the pastries are puffed up and doubled in size.

Bake the pastries for 15 minutes or until golden brown. Transfer the pastries to a wire rack to cool.

CUSTARD FILLING

1 tablespoon flour
1 tablespoon sugar
¼ pint (150 ml) single cream or milk, boiling
2 egg yolks
Salt
Vanilla essence
1 teaspoon gelatine dissolved in 1 tablespoon hot water

Blend the flour and sugar in a saucepan. Gradually pour in the boiling cream or milk, stirring constantly. Bring back to the boil, stirring, and cook until thick. Remove the pan from the heat.

Whisk the egg yolk with a pinch of salt and 2 to 3 drops of vanilla essence. Whisk in 2 tablespoons of the hot cream mixture then whisk it all in. Return the mixture to the pan and cook over very low heat for 1 minute. Stir in the gelatine and set aside to cool.

APPLE FILLING

1 large cooking apple, peeled, cored and sliced
1 tablespoon brown sugar
¼ teaspoon ground cinnamon

Put the apple, brown sugar and 2 teaspoons of water in a saucepan and simmer until the apple is soft. Add the cinnamon and beat until smooth.

RAISIN FILLING

2 oz (50 g) butter
4 tablespoons sugar
2 tablespoons raisins
2 teaspoons ground cinnamon

Cream the butter and sugar. Mix in the raisins and cinnamon.

PINWHEELS
Roll out the dough to a 16- by 6-inch (40- by 15-cm) rectangle. Fill with the raisin or apple filling and roll from the short end. Cut the roll across in 1-inch (2-cm) slices.

COCKSCOMBS
Roll out the dough to an 8- by 16-inch (20- by 40-cm) rectangle. Cut the rectangle into 4-inch (10-cm) squares. Spread 2 teaspoons of apple filling across the centre of each square. Fold in half and with a sharp knife make 7 slits on the folded side. Bend the pastry slightly to fan out the "teeth". Brush with the glaze and sprinkle with chopped blanched almonds.

TRIANGLES
Roll out the dough and cut as for cockscombs. Put 2 teaspoons of filling in the centre and fold over diagonally to make triangles. Brush with the glaze and sprinkle with chopped nuts.

Victoria sandwich
This is the basic recipe for cakes made by the creaming method. Whatever the size of the cake the proportion of the other ingredients to the eggs never changes—it is the weight of the eggs (in this case 2 ounces/50 g each) in flour, sugar and fat.
MAKES ONE 7-INCH (18-CM) CAKE
¼ lb (100 g) self-raising flour
Salt
¼ lb (100 g) unsalted butter
¼ lb (100 g) castor sugar
2 eggs
½ teaspoon vanilla essence
3 tablespoons raspberry jam
Icing sugar

Preheat the oven to 350°F (180°C, Gas Mark 4). Grease and dust with flour two 7-inch (18-cm) sandwich cake tins.

Sift the flour and a pinch of salt into a bowl. Cut the butter into pieces and put into a warm mixing bowl. Cream the butter until softened, add the sugar and continue to beat until light and fluffy.

Add the eggs one at a time with a tablespoon of the flour, beating well after each addition. Mix in the vanilla essence.

Fold in half the remaining flour, using a large metal spoon to cut it into the batter. When mixed fold in the other half. Spread the mixture into the cake tins. Bake for about 20 minutes or until the cakes are done. Test by inserting a thin skewer into the centre of one cake—if it comes out clean the cake is ready. Cool the cakes in the tins for a few minutes before turning them on to a wire rack to cool.

When the cakes are cold spread one cake with the jam and put the other on top. Dust the top with a little icing sugar.

Orange Victoria cake
Add the rind of 1 orange to the butter mixture. Use the juice for making a glacé icing.

Coffee and walnut cake
Mix 2 teaspoons instant coffee with the flour. Fold 2 ounces (50 g) of chopped walnuts into the batter mixture.

Sandwich with butter cream to which 1 teaspoon of very finely powdered coffee is added. Ice with glacé icing made with black coffee. Decorate with walnuts.

Spice cake
Add 2 teaspoons of mixed spice to the flour before mixing. Decorate with plain glacé icing.

Seed cake
Add 2 teaspoons caraway seeds to the mixture. Bake in a 6-inch (15-cm) cake tin for 50 minutes.

Chocolate cake
Substitute 1 ounce (25 g) of cocoa powder for 1 ounce (25 g) of flour and sift with the flour. Ice with chocolate frosting.

Basic sponge cake
For two 9-inch (23-cm) cakes increase the eggs to 4 and the flour and sugar by 1 ounce (25 g) each.

The sponge can be made with separated eggs, the whites being whisked until stiff and then folded in after the flour has been added. This makes the sponge drier but lighter.

MAKES ONE 7-INCH (18-CM) CAKE
3 eggs
3 oz (75 g) castor sugar
1 tablespoon water
½ teaspoon vanilla essence
3 oz (75 g) self-raising flour
¼ pint (150 ml) double cream, whipped

Preheat the oven to 350°F (180°C, Gas Mark 4).

Lightly grease the bottoms and sides of two 7-inch (18-cm) sandwich cake tins. Line the bottom of each tin with a round of greaseproof paper and grease lightly. Dust with flour, knocking out any excess. Put the eggs and sugar in a bowl and place in a pan of hot water. Whisk for 10 minutes or until the mixture is very thick and creamy. Whisk in the water and vanilla essence. Fold in half the flour, cutting and folding with a metal spoon. Then fold in the remaining flour. Turn the mixture into the tins and bake for 10 to 12 minutes, or until a fine skewer inserted into the centre comes out clean. Leave in the tins for a few minutes before turning out on to a wire rack to cool. When cold sandwich the two sponges together with whipped cream.

Swiss roll
MAKES ONE SWISS ROLL
Flour
Castor sugar
Basic sponge cake mixture

Preheat the oven to 350°F (180°C, Gas Mark 4).

Brush a 12- by 8-inch (30- by 20-cm) Swiss roll tin with oil. Line the base only with greaseproof paper, brush lightly with oil and dust with a mixture of flour and castor sugar. Pour the sponge mixture into the tin and bake for 12 minutes.

Sprinkle a large sheet of greaseproof paper with castor sugar and turn the tin and cake upside down on to this. Lift off the tin and peel off the paper quickly. Trim the edges, spread with warmed jam and roll up the sponge. If the Swiss roll is to be filled with cream or butter cream roll up the sponge with the greaseproof paper and leave to cool completely before unrolling, removing the paper and filling with the cream mixture.

Génoise sponge
This is the classic French sponge cake. It may be cut into small squares or oblongs and iced or served as a large cake with whipped cream or crême pâtissière as a filling.
MAKES ONE 8-INCH (20-CM) CAKE
6 oz (175 g) unsalted butter
6 eggs
½ lb (225 g) castor sugar
½ teaspoon vanilla essence
6 oz (175 g) flour

Preheat the oven to 375°F (190°C, Gas Mark 5). Lightly grease and dust with flour two 8-inch (20-cm) sandwich cake tins.

Gently melt the butter over a pan of hot water. Leave to cool. Put the eggs, sugar and vanilla essence in a bowl. Place the bowl over a pan of hot water over low heat. Using a wire whisk or rotary beater whisk the mixture for about 20 minutes, or until it is pale and thick and will leave a ribbon trail when the whisk is lifted. Remove from the heat.

Sift the flour into the egg mixture and fold it in carefully with a large metal spoon. Pour in the butter and quickly and lightly mix it in.

Pour the batter into the cake tins and bake for 20 to 30 minutes or until the sponge has shrunk slightly and a thin skewer inserted into the centre comes out clean.

Leave the cakes in the tins for 5 minutes before turning them out on to wire racks to cool.

Date and walnut loaf
MAKES ONE LOAF
½ lb (225 g) flour
1 teaspoon baking powder
¼ lb (100 g) butter, cut into small pieces
¼ lb (100 g) castor sugar
¾ lb (350 g) stoned dates, chopped
2 oz (50 g) walnuts, chopped
1 teaspoon bicarbonate of soda, mixed with 7 tablespoons slightly warmed milk
1 large egg, beaten

Preheat the oven to 350°F (180°C, Gas Mark 4).

Grease a medium-sized loaf tin and set it aside.

Sift the flour and the baking

powder into a mixing bowl. Add the butter and rub it in with your fingertips until the mixture resembles coarse breadcrumbs. Stir in the sugar, dates and walnuts. Make a well in the centre and pour in the bicarbonate mixture and the egg. Stir the liquids together with a wooden spoon, gradually drawing in the flour mixture. Continue stirring until the mixture is smooth and fairly moist, adding a little more milk if necessary.

Spoon the mixture into the loaf tin, smoothing the top down with the back of the spoon. Put the tin in the oven and bake for about 1 hour, or until the loaf has risen and is golden brown on top. Insert a thin skewer into the centre to check that it is cooked all the way through—the skewer should come out dry.

Turn the loaf out on to a wire rack and cool completely before serving.

Crostata di ricotta

If ricotta cheese is not available for this Italian cheesecake use curd cheese instead.

SERVES SIX

½ lb (225 g) flour
Salt
¼ lb (125 g) butter
Grated rind of 1 lemon
1 tablespoon castor sugar
2 egg yolks
1 tablespoon iced water

FILLING

2 lb (900 g) ricotta cheese
4 tablespoons cream
¼ lb (125 g) sugar
Grated rind and juice of 2 lemons
4 egg yolks
4 tablespoons raisins
2 tablespoons pine nuts
Milk

Sift the flour and a pinch of salt into a bowl. Add the butter and cut it into the flour. Rub the butter into the flour until the mixture resembles coarse breadcrumbs. Mix in the lemon rind, sugar, egg yolks and water. Knead lightly to make a smooth dough. Cover the dough and refrigerate for at least 1 hour.

Lightly butter a 9-inch (23-cm) flan dish. Remove a quarter of the dough, cover it and return it to the refrigerator. Roll out the remaining dough on a lightly floured board and line the flan tin with it. Prick the bottom of the dough and put it in the refrigerator for 30 minutes.

Preheat the oven to 425°F (220°C, Gas Mark 7). Put the flan tin in the oven and bake blind.

Meanwhile make the filling. Sieve the ricotta cheese into a bowl. Beat in the cream, sugar, lemon rind and juice and egg yolks. Mix in the raisins.

Remove the pastry case from the oven and reset the temperature to 350°F (180°C, Gas Mark 4).

Roll out the remaining dough into a square a little larger than the diameter of the flan tin and cut it into thin strips with a sharp knife.

Spoon the ricotta filling into the pastry case and smooth it down. Sprinkle the nuts on top. Arrange the pastry strips in a lattice pattern over the filling. Brush the strips with a little milk. Bake for 50 to 55 minutes or until the filling is firm and golden brown on top.

Cool before serving.

Black Forest cherry cake

If fresh cherries are not available use two 1-pound (450-g) cans of cherries—to make the syrup use the juice from only one can, and add 3 tablespoons of castor sugar.

MAKES ONE 10-INCH (25-CM) CAKE

¼ lb (125 g) flour
2 oz (50 g) butter
3 tablespoons castor sugar
1 tablespoon ground almonds
Grated rind of ½ lemon
1 egg yolk

From left to right: marzipan roll, rum baba, white Christmas cake, plum cake or bride's cake, cassata alla Siciliana, and Black Forest cherry cake.

CAKE
8 eggs
½ lb (225 g) castor sugar
1 teaspoon vanilla essence
6 oz (175 g) flour
2 teaspoons baking powder
3 oz (75 g) cocoa powder
¼ lb (100 g) butter, melted

FILLING
1½ lb (700 g) black cherries, pitted
¼ lb (125 g) plus 4 tablespoons castor sugar
1½ pints (900 ml) double or whipping cream
5 tablespoons Kirsch

DECORATION
½ lb (225 g) block chocolate
24 cherries, with stalks

To make the pastry base, sift the flour into a mixing bowl. Rub in the butter until the mixture resembles fine breadcrumbs. Stir in the sugar, ground almonds and lemon rind. Add the egg yolk and mix to a firm dough. Cover the dough and put it in the refrigerator for 30 minutes.

Preheat the oven to 350°F (180°C, Gas Mark 4). Lightly butter a 10-inch (25-cm) spring-form cake tin.

Roll the dough out thinly and line the bottom of the cake tin. Bake for 20 minutes. Leave the pastry in the tin for a few minutes. Transfer the pastry to a wire rack to cool.

Wipe out or wash the cake tin and grease it again with butter.

To make the cake, put the eggs, sugar and vanilla essence in a bowl and beat with a wire whisk or rotary beater until the mixture is pale and thick and leaves a ribbon trail when the whisk is lifted.

Sift the flour, baking powder and cocoa on to the egg mixture and fold it in gently with a large metal spoon. Gently stir in the melted butter, a spoonful at a time.

Pour the mixture into the cake tin and bake for 40 minutes or until the cake is well risen and has shrunk slightly from the sides. Test by inserting a thin skewer into the centre of the cake. If it comes out clean the cake is done.

Leave the cake in the tin for a few minutes before turning it out on to a wire rack to cool.

To make the filling, put the cherries and ¼ pound (125 g) of the sugar in a saucepan and cook, stirring, until the sugar has dissolved. Bring to the boil slowly then remove the pan from the heat. Drain the cherries, return the juice to the pan and boil vigorously until it has reduced to a thick syrup. Pour the syrup over the cherries and set aside to cool.

Put the cream, the remaining sugar and the Kirsch in a bowl and whip until stiff.

To make the decoration, put the chocolate on greaseproof paper and, using a swivel-blade vegetable peeler, shave off curls. Put the chocolate curls in the refrigerator until they are required.

To assemble the cake, cut the cake in half horizontally. Put the pastry base on a serving dish. Spread it with a ½-inch (1-cm) layer of cream. Spoon half the cherries and syrup over the top. Cover with a layer of cake. Spread with a ½-inch (1-cm) layer of cream followed by the remaining cherries and syrup. Put the second layer of cake on top. Spread the top and sides with the remaining cream, reserving a little for decoration. Cover the sides with the chocolate curls. Arrange the cherries and the remaining chocolate curls in circles on top and pipe the remaining cream decoratively around them.

Cereals/cakes

Cassata alla Siciliana

MAKES ONE 8-INCH (20-CM) CAKE

1 génoise sponge made with 3 eggs

FILLING

¾ lb (350 g) mixed crystallized fruit
1½ lb (700 g) ricotta cheese
3 oz (75 g) castor sugar
¼ lb (125 g) plain chocolate, coarsely grated
¼ lb (125 g) pistachio nuts, chopped
8 tablespoons Maraschino

To make the filling, reserve a few crystallized fruit for decoration and chop the remainder coarsely. Beat the ricotta cheese and the sugar until smooth. Mix in the grated chocolate, chopped crystallized fruit and nuts.

Cut the cake into three layers horizontally. Put one layer on to the base of a spring-form cake tin. Sprinkle the sponge with 2 tablespoons Maraschino and spread with ½ inch (1 cm) of the filling. Put the second layer on top, sprinkle with 2 tablespoons of the liqueur and spread with ½ inch (1 cm) of filling. Put the third layer on top and sprinkle with the remaining liqueur. Clip the sides of the cake tin into place. Cover and refrigerate for 3 hours.

Remove the cake from the tin and put it on a plate. Spread the remaining ricotta mixture over the top and sides. Decorate with the reserved crystallized fruit.

Rum babas

MAKES SIXTEEN

1 oz (25 g) yeast
6 tablespoons warm milk
½ lb (225 g) strong white flour
½ teaspoon salt
1 oz (25 g) castor sugar
4 eggs, lightly beaten
¼ lb (100 g) butter, softened
4 tablespoons clear honey
4 tablespoons water
2 tablespoons rum
1 lb (450 g) strawberries
½ pint (300 ml) cream

Grease 16 small ring moulds.

Mash the yeast with the milk in a large bowl. Mix in 2 ounces (50 g) of the flour and set aside in a warm draught-free place for 20 minutes or until the mixture is puffed up and frothy.

Preheat the oven to 400°F (200°C, Gas Mark 6).

Beat the remaining flour, the salt, sugar, eggs and butter into the yeast mixture. Beat well for 3 to 4 minutes.

Half fill the ring moulds with the batter. Cover with a cloth and set aside in a warm place until the batter has risen and the moulds are two-thirds full.

Bake in the top part of the oven for 12 to 15 minutes or until the babas are well risen and golden brown. Take the babas out of the oven and leave them in the moulds for a few minutes, then turn them out on to a wire rack.

To make the syrup put the honey, water and rum in a saucepan and warm over low heat.

Put the babas on a serving dish while still hot and spoon the syrup over them. When the babas are cool and you are ready to serve them put some of the strawberries in the middle of each baba and pour a little cream over the top.

Marzipan roll

MAKES ONE 12-INCH (30-CM) ROLL

4 tablespoons brandy
3 oz (75 g) glacé cherries, halved
1 oz (25 g) candied angelica, chopped
1 strip each candied lemon and orange peel, chopped
2 oz (50 g) walnuts, chopped
2 oz (50 g) hazelnuts, chopped
1 lb (450 g) castor sugar
¾ lb (350 g) ground almonds
¼ teaspoon almond essence
2 eggs, well beaten
¾ lb (350 g) puff pastry
1 egg yolk mixed with 2 tablespoons milk

Put the brandy, cherries, angelica, lemon and orange peel, walnuts and hazelnuts in a bowl and marinate for 2 hours, stirring to coat the fruit with the brandy from time to time.

Meanwhile, make the marzipan. Put the sugar and ground almonds in a bowl and mix well. Make a well in the centre and pour in the almond essence and eggs. Gradually incorporate the dry ingredients, finally mixing with your hands until the mixture is smooth and quite sticky. Mix in the fruit and brandy.

Preheat the oven to 425°F (220°C, Gas Mark 7). Lightly grease a baking sheet.

Roll the pastry dough out on a lightly floured board into an oblong approximately 12 by 4 inches (30 by 10 cm). Put the marzipan mixture on the dough and shape it to an oblong almost, but not quite, as wide or as long as the dough. Moisten the edges of the dough with a little water and bring the long edges up and over to seal the filling. Tuck both ends under. Make leaves out of the dough trimmings and moisten the undersides with a little water. Arrange them along the join to cover. Paint the dough with the egg and milk mixture and very carefully transfer the roll to the baking sheet.

Bake for about 35 minutes, or until the pastry is puffed up and golden brown. Remove the roll from the oven and let it cool completely on the baking sheet before cutting into slices.

Plum cake or bride's cake

To make a white Christmas cake, replace the brown sugar by white, the currants by candied pineapple, and the raisins by chopped angelica and chopped blanched almonds. Increase the glacé cherries by ¼ pound (125 g). If you want to add more brandy, pierce holes in the bottom of the warm cake and pour in 3 to 4 tablespoons of brandy.

MAKES ONE 10-INCH (25-CM) CAKE

1 lb (450 g) flour
1 teaspoon baking powder
¾ lb (350 g) butter
1 lb (450 g) soft brown sugar
1 lb (450 g) currants, washed and dried
1 lb (450 g) raisins, washed and dried
½ lb (225 g) candied peel, chopped
½ lb (225 g) citron peel, chopped
¼ lb (100 g) candied cherries
1 teaspoon ground mace
6 eggs, beaten
¼ pint (150 ml) brandy
2 tablespoons apricot jam
2 tablespoons water
2½ lb (1 kg) marzipan
1½ lb (700 g) royal icing

Preheat the oven to 300°F (150°C, Gas Mark 2).

Grease a 10-inch (25-cm) cake tin. Line it with a double thickness of greaseproof paper and grease the paper.

Mix the flour and baking powder together in a large bowl. Rub in the butter with your fingertips. Stir in the sugar, dried fruit, peel, cherries and mace. Mix the eggs and brandy together. Using a wooden spoon or your hand mix the eggs and brandy into the flour and fruit. When thoroughly mixed turn into the cake tin. Spread the cake mixture evenly, hollowing out the centre slightly with the back of a tablespoon dipped in cold water.

Bake for 2 hours then reduce the heat to 275°F (140°C, Gas Mark 1) and bake for a further 1½ to 2 hours or until the cake is dark and firm to the touch. Switch off the oven and leave the cake for a further 30 minutes before turning it out on to a wire rack to cool. When the cake is cold, wrap it in foil and put it in an airtight tin for at least 30 days.

Before covering the cake with marzipan, make the jam glaze. Put the jam and water in a small saucepan and simmer for 3 to 4 minutes. Sieve the mixture and keep warm.

Trim the top of the cake to straighten it and turn it upside down. The bottom of the cake will now be on the top. Brush the top of the cake with the warm glaze. Dust the work surface with a little icing sugar. Take a little less than half the almond paste and roll it out into a circle the same size as the cake. Invert the cake on to the almond paste. Trim the edges and press down firmly. Upturn the cake.

Roll the remaining paste into an oblong twice as wide as the side of the cake and half the circumference. Cut the oblong in half lengthways and brush with the jam glaze. Roll the cake, like a wheel, along the strips of almond paste and press and smooth over the joins. Leave the almond paste to dry for 48 hours before covering with icing.

To ice the cake, spread two-thirds of the icing thickly over the top and sides using a palette knife dipped in hot water to smooth it down. Leave the icing on the cake to harden before piping the remaining icing decoratively over the top and sides.

Crème pâtissière or confectioner's custard

This custard is used as a filling for many cakes and flans.

MAKES ABOUT 1 PINT (575 ML)

3 egg yolks
3 oz (75 g) castor sugar
2 oz (50 g) cornflour
¾ pint (450 ml) milk
Vanilla essence
1 egg white

Cream the egg yolks with the sugar in a bowl. Beat in the cornflour, ¼ pint (150 ml) of the milk and a few drops of vanilla.

Bring the remaining milk to just under boiling point in a saucepan. Pour it gradually on to the egg mixture, stirring constantly.

Pour the mixture back into the pan and bring back to just under boiling point, stirring constantly. Remove the pan from the heat and beat until smooth. Leave to cool slightly.

Whip the egg white until stiff. Put one-third of the egg and milk mixture in a bowl and fold in the egg white. Fold this mixture into the rest of the egg and milk mixture and return to low heat. Cook for 2 to 3 minutes, stirring. Cool completely.

Butter cream 1

This amount will fill an 8- or 9-inch (20- or 23-cm) cake.

¼ pint (150 ml) milk
2 egg yolks
¼ lb (100 g) castor sugar
½ lb (225 g) unsalted butter

Put the milk in a saucepan and bring to just under boiling point.

Mix the egg yolks with the sugar in a bowl. Mix in the hot milk.

Put the bowl over a pan of barely simmering water and cook, stirring, until the custard is thick enough to coat the back of the spoon. Strain and cool the custard.

Beat the butter in another bowl until soft. Beat in the custard a little at a time. Add the flavouring and use.

Butter cream 2

You will need a sugar thermometer to make this butter cream. This quantity will fill an 8- or 9-inch (20- or 23-cm) cake.

2 oz (50 g) sugar
2 fl oz (50 ml) water
2 egg yolks
¼ lb (100 g) unsalted butter

Dissolve the sugar in the water in a saucepan. Bring to the boil and boil rapidly until the syrup reaches a temperature of 215° to 220°F (101° to 104°C). Remove the pan from the heat.

Meanwhile lightly beat the egg yolks in a bowl. Pour in the syrup, whisking constantly, until the mixture is thick and fluffy.

Beat the butter until soft in another bowl. Gradually beat in the egg mixture. Add the flavouring and use.

Marzipan

MAKES 2½ POUNDS (1 KG)

½ lb (225 g) icing sugar
1 lb (450 g) ground almonds
½ lb (225 g) castor sugar
2 eggs, beaten
1 tablespoon lemon juice
1 teaspoon almond essence

Sift the icing sugar into a bowl with the ground almonds and castor sugar. Stir in the eggs, lemon juice and almond essence. Using your hands, form the mixture into a ball. Dust the working surface with icing sugar and turn the paste out on to it. Knead for a few minutes until the paste is smooth.

Royal icing

This amount of icing will cover a 10-inch (25-cm) cake.

3 egg whites
1½ lb (700 g) icing sugar, sifted
1 teaspoon lemon juice
1 teaspoon glycerine

Lightly beat the egg whites. Stir in the icing sugar, mixing it in with a wooden spoon a little at a time. Stir in the lemon juice and glycerine. Using a wire whisk or rotary beater, beat the icing until it is smooth. It is now ready to use; or cover the bowl and leave for up to 2 hours.

Glacé icing

This amount of icing will cover an 8- or 9-inch (20- or 23-cm) cake.

2½ fl oz (65 ml) water
¾ lb (350 g) icing sugar
5 drops tasteless cooking oil
Flavouring

Put the water in the top of a double saucepan and gradually beat in the icing sugar, the oil and the desired flavouring. Stir over barely simmering water until the icing is warm. It should be smooth, glossy, thick and of a pouring consistency.

To use, put the cake on a wire rack, pour the icing over the top and use a palette knife dipped in hot water to spread the icing evenly. Do not overwork the icing or it will lose its gloss.

Chocolate frosting

This amount will cover one 7-inch (18-cm) cake.

¼ lb (100 g) icing sugar
1 oz (25 g) cocoa powder
2 oz (50 g) butter
2 tablespoons prepared black coffee
2 oz (50 g) soft brown sugar

Sift the icing sugar and cocoa together. Put the butter, coffee and the brown sugar into the top of a double saucepan over simmering water. Stir to dissolve. Add the icing sugar and cocoa, and whisk until smooth. Remove the pan from the heat and continue whisking until cool and thick enough to spread.

Boiled frosting

This amount of frosting will fill and ice an 8-inch (20-cm) cake.

MAKES ABOUT 1 PINT (575 ML)

¾ lb (350 g) sugar
4 fl oz (125 ml) water
Cream of tartar
2 egg whites
Flavouring

Dissolve the sugar in the water over low heat. Stir in a pinch of cream of tartar and bring to the boil. Boil rapidly until the syrup reaches 240°F (115°C) on a sugar thermometer.

Meanwhile whisk the egg whites in a bowl until stiff. Whisking constantly, pour the syrup on to the egg whites. Continue whisking until the icing is thick enough to spread. Whisk in the flavouring.

To use, spread on the cake with a palette knife dipped in hot water. Swirl icing to imitate a snow drift, or spread smoothly.

Covering and icing a cake

Brush the cake with jam glaze and cover the top with marzipan.

Roll the cake along the strip of marzipan to cover the sides.

Using a palette knife, smooth the icing on the top and sides.

Decorate the cake with more icing, using a forcing bag.

Cereals/bread

Bread dough may be cooked in a well-greased loaf tin, a cake tin, a ring mould or an earthenware flowerpot. Alternatively make the dough into one of the traditional shapes—cob, cottage loaf, French stick or plait—and cook it on a greased baking sheet. Sprinkle a little flour over the top of the loaf before putting it in the oven, or glaze it with beaten egg and milk for a glossy finish, or salted water for a really crisp crust. Toppings of poppy seeds, sesame seeds or crushed wheat add taste and texture.

Experiment with additions to the dough—add prunes, dried apricots, nuts, grated cheese, olives or herbs, or mix different flours together to vary the flavour.

Sweet white bread

This sweet white bread recipe can be made into a fruit loaf by adding currants, sultanas or raisins and any other chopped candied fruit. It can be plaited or shaped into buns.

MAKES ONE PLAITED LOAF

½ oz (15 g) fresh yeast
¼ lb (100 g) plus ¼ teaspoon sugar
2 tablespoons lukewarm water
1½ lb (700 g) strong white flour
¼ lb (100 g) butter
8 fl oz (225 ml) lukewarm milk
1 teaspoon salt
2 eggs, lightly beaten

GLAZE

1 egg yolk, lightly beaten with 1 teaspoon castor sugar and 1 tablespoon warm milk

Put the yeast into a small bowl and mash it with ¼ teaspoon of the sugar. Add the water and cream the mixture until it is smooth. Set aside in a warm, draught-free place for 15 minutes, or until the yeast mixture is puffed up and frothy.

Put the flour in a large mixing bowl. Add the butter and cut it into small pieces with a knife. Lightly rub the butter into the flour.

Stir the remaining sugar into the milk with the salt. Continue stirring until the sugar has dissolved. Beat in the eggs.

Make a well in the centre of the flour mixture and pour in the yeast mixture and the egg and milk mixture. Stir the liquids together, gradually incorporating the flour. When the dough is well mixed and coming away from the sides of the bowl, turn it out on to a lightly floured working surface and knead it for at least 10 minutes, or until it is smooth and glossy.

Rinse out and dry the mixing bowl and grease it lightly. Shape the dough into a ball and place it in the bowl. Cover the bowl with a clean, damp cloth and set aside in a warm, draught-free place for about 1 hour, or until the dough has doubled in bulk.

Turn the dough out on to the work surface and knead it vigorously for 5 minutes.

Divide the dough into 3 equal pieces and shape each piece into a long, thin roll. The pieces must be of equal length. Press the 3 pieces together at one end and tuck them under. Plait the pieces together and press the ends together, tucking them under as before.

Carefully transfer the plait to a greased baking tray and brush it with the glaze. Set aside in a warm, draught-free place for 40 minutes or until the plait has doubled in bulk.

Meanwhile preheat the oven to 475° (240°C, Gas Mark 9).

Place the bread in the oven and bake for 15 minutes. Reduce the heat to 425°F (220°C, Gas Mark 7) and bake for a further 25 to 30 minutes, or until the bread is cooked and sounds hollow when the underside is rapped with your knuckles. Cool the bread on the baking sheet, or transfer it to a wire rack.

Granary bread

This bread can be baked in a loaf tin or shaped into a ball with a deep cross cut in the top before rising for the second time. It can also be baked as two small loaves.

MAKES ONE LARGE LOAF

¾ oz (20 g) fresh yeast
¼ teaspoon sugar
¾ pint (450 ml) half milk, half water, lukewarm
2 tablespoons malt
1 tablespoon melted butter
1¾ lb (800 g) granary flour
¼ lb (125 g) cracked wheat
2 teaspoons salt

Crumble the yeast into a small bowl and mash in the sugar. Add 2 tablespoons of the lukewarm liquid and blend them together until smooth. Set aside in a warm, draught-free place for 15 minutes, or until the yeast is puffed up and frothy.

Mix the remaining liquid with the malt and butter, and set aside.

Put the flour into a large mixing bowl and mix in the cracked wheat and salt. Make a well in the centre of the mixture and pour in the yeast mixture and the malt mixture. Stir the liquids together, gradually incorporating the flour. When the dough begins to come away from the sides of the bowl, turn it out on to a lightly floured surface and knead vigorously for at least 10 minutes, or until it is smooth.

Rinse out and dry the mixing bowl and grease it lightly. Shape the dough into a ball and place it in the bowl. Cover with a clean, damp cloth and set aside in a warm, draught-free place for at least 1 hour, or until it has doubled in bulk.

Turn the dough out on to the work surface and punch it once or twice to knock out the air. Knead it thoroughly and then either shape it or place it in a greased loaf tin. Put it back in a warm place and leave it to rise for 30 to 40 minutes, until it has doubled in size or risen to the top of the tin.

Preheat the oven to 425°F (220°C, Gas Mark 7).

When the dough has risen, brush the top lightly with a little milk and place it in the oven. Bake for 10 minutes, then reduce the temperature to 375°F (190°C, Gas Mark 5) and bake for a further 20 to 25 minutes, or until the bread is cooked. Test it by rapping the underside with your knuckles—it should have a hollow sound. Turn the bread out and cool on a wire rack.

Wholewheat bread

This bread is often baked in 2 medium-sized, tall flower pots. For added texture knead in a handful of rolled oats.

MAKES ONE LARGE LOAF

¾ oz (20 g) fresh yeast
¼ teaspoon sugar
12 fl oz (350 ml) warm water
1 tablespoon soft brown sugar or honey
2 teaspoons salt
1½ lb (700 g) wholewheat flour

Put the yeast and sugar in a small bowl and mash them until smooth with 2 tablespoons of water. Set aside in a warm, draught-free place for 15 minutes, or until the mixture is puffed up and frothy.

Meanwhile, mix the brown sugar or honey, salt and the remaining water together.

Put the flour in a large mixing bowl and make a well in the centre. Pour in the yeast and water mixtures and mix them together, gradually incorporating the flour. When the dough is well mixed and coming away from the sides of the bowl, turn it out on to a lightly floured work surface and knead for at least 10 minutes, or until the dough is smooth.

Rinse out and dry the mixing bowl and grease it lightly. Shape the dough into a ball and place it in the bowl. Cover the bowl with a clean, damp cloth and set aside in a warm, draught-free place for about 1 hour, or until the dough has risen and doubled in bulk.

Turn the dough out on to the work surface and punch it once or twice to knock out the air. Knead it for about 5 minutes, then shape it or put it into a greased loaf tin.

Set aside in a warm, draught-free place for about 30 minutes, or until it has doubled in bulk or risen to the top of the tin.

Meanwhile, preheat the oven to 475°F (240°C, Gas Mark 9).

Place the loaf in the oven and bake for 15 minutes. Reduce the heat to 425°F (220°C, Gas Mark 7) and bake for a further 20 to 30 minutes, or until the loaf sounds hollow when the underside is rapped with your knuckles.

Lardy cake, white bread, Chelsea buns and crisp white rolls are just a few of the good things you can make from a yeast dough.

Cereals/bread

Malt loaf

MAKES TWO SMALL LOAVES

1 oz (25 g) fresh yeast
¼ teaspoon sugar
¼ pint (150 ml) plus 2 tablespoons lukewarm water
1 oz (25 g) butter
2 heaped tablespoons malt
2 tablespoons treacle
1 teaspoon salt
1 lb (450 g) strong white flour
½ lb (225 g) sultanas

Crumble the yeast into a small bowl and mash in the sugar. Stir in the 2 tablespoons of water to make a smooth mixture. Set the bowl aside in a warm, draught-free place for 15 minutes, or until the mixture is puffed up.

Melt the butter in the remaining water and mix in the malt, treacle and salt.

Put the flour into a large mixing bowl. Make a well in the centre and pour in the yeast mixture and the malt mixture. Mix the liquids together, gradually incorporating the flour. When the dough is well mixed and beginning to come away from the sides of the bowl, turn it out on to a lightly floured surface and knead it vigorously for 10 minutes, or until it is smooth and elastic. If the dough is sticky knead in a little more flour.

Rinse and dry the mixing bowl and grease it lightly. Shape the dough into a ball and place it in the mixing bowl. Cover the bowl with a clean, damp cloth and set it aside for 1½ hours, or until the dough has risen and doubled in bulk. Turn the dough out on to the working surface and punch it a few times to knock out the air. Spread out the dough and work in the sultanas. Shape the dough into two loaves and put it into two small, greased loaf tins. Set aside in a warm, draught-free place for about 40 minutes, or until the dough has risen to the top of the tins.

Meanwhile, preheat the oven to 425°F (220°C, Gas Mark 7). Bake the loaves for 10 minutes, reduce the oven temperature to 375°F (190°C, Gas Mark 5) and continue baking for a further 20 to 30 minutes or until the loaves have shrunk slightly from the sides of the tin and sound hollow when the undersides are rapped with your knuckles.

Lardy cake

MAKES ONE LARGE CAKE

¾ oz (20 g) fresh yeast
1½ oz (40 g) plus ¼ teaspoon sugar
8 fl oz (225 ml) plus 2 tablespoons lukewarm water
1 tablespoon honey
1 tablespoon melted butter
1 teaspoon salt
1 lb (450 g) strong white flour
¼ teaspoon grated nutmeg
¼ teaspoon ground allspice
1 teaspoon ground cinnamon
¼ lb (100 g) lard, cut into small pieces
½ lb (225 g) currants
2 oz (50 g) sultanas
2 oz (50 g) raisins

GLAZE

1 tablespoon honey and 1 tablespoon sugar mixed with 2 tablespoons water

Crown loaf

To make a crown loaf, arrange even-sized balls of white dough in a round cake tin.

Brioche

To shape a brioche, insert a small ball of dough into the larger ball in the brioche tin.

Crumble the yeast into a small mixing bowl and mash in the ¼ teaspoon of sugar. Add the 2 tablespoons of water and mix until smooth.

Set the bowl aside in a warm, draught-free place for 15 minutes, or until the yeast is puffed up and frothy.

Meanwhile, mix the honey, butter, salt and the remaining water together.

Put the flour into a large mixing bowl and make a well in the centre. Pour in the yeast mixture and the honey and water mixture. Mix the liquids together, gradually drawing in the flour. Add a little more water if the dough is too dry.

When the dough is well mixed and beginning to come away from the sides of the bowl, turn it out on to a lightly floured working surface and knead it for about 10 minutes, or until it is smooth and elastic.

Rinse out and dry the mixing bowl and grease it lightly. Shape the dough into a ball and put it in the bowl. Cover the bowl with a clean, damp cloth and set it aside in a warm, draught-free place for about 1 hour, or until it has risen and doubled in bulk.

Meanwhile, put the rest of the sugar, the nutmeg, allspice, cinnamon, lard and fruit into a mixing bowl and stir well to mix. Set aside.

Turn the dough out of the bowl and punch it once or twice to knock out the air. Knead it for 5 minutes. Roll the dough out into a large oblong. Sprinkle half the fruit mixture over two-thirds of the dough. Fold the remaining one-third of dough over the fruit and fold again to make a parcel. Press down on the edges to seal them. Roll the dough out and repeat the process all over again using the remaining dried fruit mixture.

Preheat the oven to 400°F (200°C, Gas Mark 6).

Shape the dough into an oblong to fit a large, greased, oblong loaf tin and put it in the tin. Set the dough aside in a warm, draught-free place for 40 minutes, or until it has risen to the top of the tin.

Place the cake in the oven and bake for 30 minutes. Brush the top of the cake liberally with the glaze and bake for a further 10 to 15 minutes, or until it is well risen and golden brown.

Cool on a rack.

Chelsea buns

The Chelsea bun mixture may also be baked as one large round.

MAKES NINE BUNS

½ oz (15 g) fresh yeast
2 oz (50 g) plus ¼ teaspoon sugar
2 tablespoons lukewarm water
2 fl oz (50 ml) lukewarm milk
3 oz (75 g) melted butter
1 teaspoon salt
1 egg, lightly beaten
½ lb (225 g) strong white flour
1 teaspoon ground mixed spice
2 oz (50 g) currants
1 oz (25 g) glacé cherries, chopped
1 oz (25 g) mixed peel

Crumble the yeast into a small bowl and mash in the ¼ teaspoon of sugar. Add the water and stir to make a smooth mixture. Set the bowl aside in a warm, draught-free place for about 15 minutes, or until the yeast is puffed up and frothy.

Mix the milk, 2 ounces (50 g) of the melted butter, the salt, the remaining sugar and egg together.

Put the flour into a large mixing bowl and make a well in the centre. Pour in the yeast mixture and the milk mixture. Mix the liquids together, gradually drawing in the flour. When the dough is well combined and beginning to come away from the sides of the bowl, turn it out on to a lightly floured surface and knead for 10 minutes, or until it is smooth and elastic.

Rinse out and dry the mixing bowl and grease it lightly. Shape the dough into a ball and put it in the bowl. Cover the bowl with a clean, damp cloth and set it aside in a warm, draught-free place for about 1 hour, or until the dough has risen and doubled in size.

Turn the dough out of the bowl and knead it for 5 minutes. Roll the dough into a large oblong and brush it liberally with some of the melted butter. Sprinkle over the spice and fruit and roll up the dough from the long end fairly tightly. Slice the roll quite thickly and lay each slice, cut side down, in a greased baking tin. Brush the tops with the remaining melted butter and set aside in a warm, draught-free place for about 30 minutes, or until the buns have risen and almost doubled in bulk.

Meanwhile, preheat the oven to 375°F (190°C, Gas Mark 5). Put the buns in the oven and bake for about 25 to 30 minutes, or until they are cooked and golden brown. Cool the buns on a wire rack.

Croissants

MAKES ABOUT TWELVE

$\frac{1}{4}$ pint (150 ml) milk
5 oz (150 g) butter
1 oz (25 g) fresh yeast
1$\frac{1}{2}$ tablespoons sugar
2 tablespoons warm water
$\frac{3}{4}$ lb (350 g) flour
1 teaspoon salt
1 egg yolk, lightly beaten with 1 tablespoon milk

Put the milk in a saucepan and bring it to just under boiling point. Remove the pan from the heat and add 1 ounce (25 g) of the butter. Leave the butter to melt and the mixture to cool to lukewarm.

Mash the yeast with $\frac{1}{4}$ teaspoon of the sugar and the water to a smooth cream. Set aside in a warm place for 15 minutes or until the mixture is puffed up and frothy.

Sift the flour, salt and remaining sugar into a large warmed bowl. Make a well in the centre and pour in the yeast mixture and the milk and butter mixture. Using your hand, mix the ingredients to a dough. Turn the dough out on to a lightly floured board. Knead for 10 minutes or until the dough is smooth and elastic.

Rinse out and dry the bowl and grease it lightly. Shape the dough into a ball and put it into the bowl. Cover with a damp cloth and set aside in a warm place for 1$\frac{1}{2}$ to 2 hours, or until the dough has doubled in bulk.

Punch the dough to knock out the air and re-form it into a ball. Cover it and put it in the refrigerator for 30 minutes.

Put the remaining butter between two pieces of greaseproof paper. Using a rolling-pin, roll it out to a 6-inch (15-cm) square.

Roll out the dough on a lightly floured board to about a 12- by 8-inch (30- by 20-cm) rectangle. Put the butter in the middle. Fold the dough over the butter to enclose it completely. Roll the dough out again to a strip three times as long as it is wide. Fold the bottom third of the dough upwards and the top third downwards. Wrap the dough in cling wrap or greaseproof paper and refrigerate for 30 minutes. Repeat the rolling out and folding twice more with the same interval of 30 minutes in the refrigerator.

After the final rolling and folding cover with a damp cloth and leave the dough in the refrigerator for at least 1 hour or overnight.

Preheat the oven to 425°F (220°C, Gas Mark 7). Lightly grease two baking sheets.

Roll out the dough $\frac{1}{4}$ inch ($\frac{1}{2}$ cm) thick on a lightly floured board. Cut the dough into 7-inch (18-cm) squares. Cut the squares in half diagonally to make triangles. Roll each triangle from the base to the apex. The pointed ends will be in the centre. Shape into crescents and put on the baking sheets with the pointed end underneath. Brush with the egg mixture and bake for 15 minutes or until golden.

Brioche

Small brioche tins can be used to make individual brioches.

MAKES ONE BRIOCHE

$\frac{1}{2}$ oz (15 g) fresh yeast
2 tablespoons warm water
$\frac{1}{2}$ lb (225 g) flour
1 teaspoon salt
2 teaspoons sugar
2 eggs, lightly beaten
Warm milk
6 oz (175 g) butter, melted

Mash the yeast in a bowl with the water. Add one-quarter of the flour and mix to a soft dough. Shape the dough into a ball and cut a cross on the top. Put the dough into a bowl of warm water for about 5 minutes or until the dough rises to the top and doubles in bulk. Lift out the dough, drain it, cover and set aside.

Meanwhile sift the remaining flour, salt and sugar into another bowl. Make a well in the centre and pour in the eggs—reserving a little for the glaze—and a little warm milk. Using your fingers mix the egg and milk and then draw in the flour to make a sticky dough. Add more milk if necessary. Beat with your fingers by lifting the dough, throwing it down and gathering it up again. Beat for 10 minutes.

Gradually work in the butter a little at a time, beating between additions. The dough should now be smooth and less sticky. Blend the yeast ball into the dough until it is well mixed.

Lightly flour a large bowl. Put the dough into the bowl, cover with a damp cloth and leave in a warm place for 3 hours or until doubled in bulk. Punch down the dough, cover and refrigerate for at least 4 hours, or overnight.

Take the dough out of the refrigerator and knead it very gently for 2 to 3 minutes. Remove a quarter of the dough and roll the rest into a ball and put it in a lightly greased brioche mould. Make a hole in the middle with your fingers. Shape the remaining dough into a ball, then taper one end and fit it into the hole in the brioche. Cover and set aside to prove in a warm place for 30 minutes or until well risen.

Preheat the oven to 450°F (230°C, Gas Mark 8).

Brush the top of the brioche with the reserved beaten egg and bake for 20 minutes. Reduce the oven temperature to 350°F (180°C, Gas Mark 4) and continue baking for 30 minutes or until the top is golden brown and a skewer inserted into the brioche comes out clean.

Remove from the oven and leave the brioche in the mould for 30 minutes before transferring it to a wire rack to cool.

Croissants

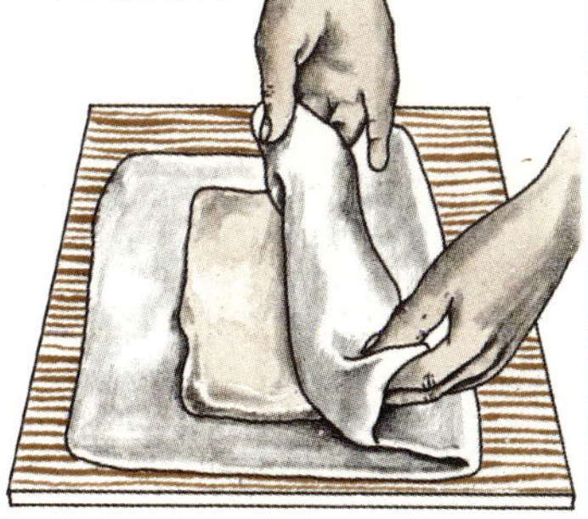

Roll the dough into an oblong. Put the butter on the dough and fold over the edges.

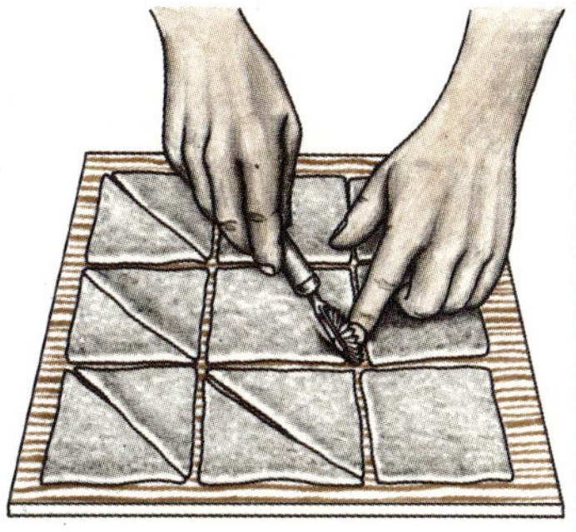

Roll the dough out thinly and cut it into squares. Cut the squares into triangles.

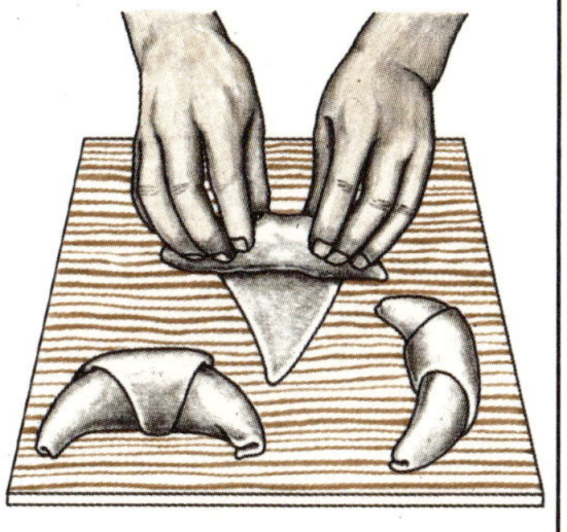

Roll each triangle from the base to the apex, then shape the rolls into crescents.

Soda bread

MAKES ONE ROUND LOAF

1 lb (450 g) flour
1 teaspoon salt
1 teaspoon bicarbonate of soda
1 oz (25 g) butter
$\frac{1}{2}$ pint (300 ml) buttermilk

Preheat the oven to 400°F (200°C, Gas Mark 6).

Lightly grease a baking sheet. Sift the flour, salt and bicarbonate of soda into a bowl. Rub in the butter with your fingertips. Make a well in the centre and pour in the buttermilk. Mix to form a spongy dough.

Turn the dough out on to a floured board and shape it into a round about 2 inches (5 cm) thick. Put the loaf on the baking sheet and score the top into quarters with a sharp knife. Bake for 30 to 35 minutes or until the top is golden brown. Transfer the bread to a rack to cool completely before serving.

Eggs and dairy produce

Baked eggs, custards and soufflés should never be overcooked or they will be spoiled, so it is important to remember that because the heat is retained in the dish in which they are cooked and served they will continue to cook after they have come out of the oven.

Baked eggs are cooked in heatproof ramekins at a temperature of 350°F (180°C, Gas Mark 4) for about ten minutes or until the whites have just set.

Baked custards are cooked in a slightly cooler oven, about 325°F (170°C, Gas Mark 3), for between thirty minutes and one hour, depending on whether the custard is in individual ramekin dishes or in a large baking dish. Bake in a bain-marie until a knife inserted in the centre of the custard comes out clean. Leave to cool before serving.

Soufflés should be cooked in a special straight-sided soufflé dish. Pour the soufflé mixture into the buttered dish, set it on a baking tray in the oven and cook until the soufflé is brown on top and well risen.

Tarte au Gruyère

SERVES FOUR

6 oz (175 g) rich shortcrust pastry
1 oz (25 g) butter
1 oz (25 g) flour
¼ pint (150 ml) milk
Salt and pepper
Cayenne pepper
3 oz (75 g) Gruyère cheese, grated
2 eggs, separated
1 tablespoon grated Parmesan cheese

Preheat the oven to 425°F (220°C, Gas Mark 7).

Roll out the pastry dough and line a buttered 9-inch (23-cm) flan tin. Bake blind for 20 minutes. Remove from the oven and set aside. Reset the oven to 375°F (190°C, Gas Mark 5).

Melt the butter in a saucepan. Stir in the flour to make a roux. Draw the pan off the heat and gradually add the milk, stirring constantly. Return the pan to the heat and bring the sauce to the boil, stirring, until very thick. Season with salt, pepper and a pinch of cayenne. Stir in the Gruyère and remove the pan from the heat.

Beat in the egg yolks and set aside until cool.

Beat the egg whites until stiff and fold them into the cheese mixture. Pour the mixture into the pastry shell, sprinkle the Parmesan on top and bake for 20 minutes or until the top is puffed up and golden brown.

Three light and delicious baked dishes, all made with eggs: Quiche Lorraine, cheese soufflé and, for dessert, caramel custard.

Quiche Lorraine

Serve this classic regional dish warm or cold, either by itself as a first course or with a green salad for a light lunch or supper.

SERVES FOUR AS A MAIN COURSE

6 oz (175 g) rich shortcrust pastry
¼ lb (125 g) streaky bacon, diced
½ pint (300 ml) cream
1 egg plus 3 egg yolks
Salt and pepper
Nutmeg

Preheat the oven to 425°F (220°C, Gas Mark 7).

Line a 9-inch (23-cm) flan tin with the pastry dough. Bake blind for 20 minutes then set aside.

Reset the oven to 375°F (190°C, Gas Mark 5).

Fry the bacon gently for about 5 minutes until the fat begins to run. Using a slotted spoon transfer the bacon to the pastry case.

Beat the cream with the egg, egg yolks and seasoning. Pour the custard into the pastry case, grate a little nutmeg on top and bake for 30 to 40 minutes or until the top is golden brown.

Oeufs sur le plat

Bacon and eggs are extremely good cooked in this way. The bacon is first lightly fried and the fat reserved. The rashers are laid on the buttered dish, the eggs broken on top and the bacon fat poured over the eggs.

SERVES TWO

1 oz (25 g) butter
4 eggs
Salt and pepper
4 teaspoons melted butter

Preheat the oven to 350°F (180°C, Gas Mark 4).

Put the butter into two small ovenproof dishes and melt it in the oven.

Break the eggs carefully into the dishes, season well and pour 1 teaspoon of melted butter over each egg.

Bake for 5 to 6 minutes, or until the whites are just set. The eggs will continue to cook in the heat of the dish and it is therefore important to remove them from the oven just before they are done.

Serve at once.

Cheese soufflé

The mixture can be baked in one large soufflé dish or four individual ones. Serve the soufflé as soon as it is cooked, before it has time to collapse.

SERVES TWO TO FOUR

1½ oz (40 g) butter
1 oz (25 g) flour
8 fl oz (225 ml) milk
Salt and pepper
Cayenne pepper
4 egg yolks
1½ oz (40 g) Cheddar or Gruyère cheese, grated
1 oz (25 g) Parmesan cheese, grated
5 egg whites

Preheat the oven to 350°F (180°C, Gas Mark 4) and put a baking sheet on the middle shelf.

Butter a 1-quart (1-litre) soufflé dish.

Melt the butter in a saucepan over low heat, stir in the flour and cook for 1 minute. Add the milk gradually, stirring constantly, and bring to the boil.

Draw the pan off the heat and season well. Cool the sauce a little, then beat in the egg yolks and cheese. Set the sauce aside to cool completely.

Eggs and dairy produce

Whisk the egg whites until stiff but not dry. Work a spoonful of the egg whites into the sauce and then fold in the remainder with light, quick strokes.

Pour the mixture into the soufflé dish, put the dish on the baking sheet, and bake for 35 to 45 minutes or until the soufflé is well risen and golden brown.

Serve immediately.

Chocolate soufflé

For a delicious variation stir a teaspoon of grated orange rind or a tablespoon of finely chopped bitter marmalade peel into the chocolate before the whites are incorporated.

SERVES FOUR

6 oz (175 g) plain chocolate, broken in pieces
2 tablespoons coffee or rum
4 egg yolks
5 egg whites
½ pint (300 ml) cream or sauce sabayon

Put a baking sheet on the middle shelf of the oven and preheat the oven to 400°F (200°C, Gas Mark 6). Butter a 1-quart (1-litre) soufflé dish.

Melt the chocolate in the coffee or rum in a bowl over simmering water. Remove the bowl from the heat, cool for 1 minute and beat in the egg yolks. Let the mixture cool.

Beat the egg whites until stiff. Stir a spoonful of egg white into the chocolate and then quickly fold in the remainder.

Pour the mixture into the soufflé dish, put the dish on the baking sheet, and bake for 15 to 20 minutes or until the soufflé is well risen with a light crust on the surface.

Serve immediately with the cream or sauce.

Baked custard

The milk may be infused with other flavours such as orange rind, crushed coffee beans or chocolate.

SERVES FOUR

1 pint (575 ml) milk
1 vanilla pod
2 whole eggs plus 2 yolks
1½ oz (40 g) castor sugar
Nutmeg

Preheat the oven to 325°F (170°C, Gas Mark 3).

Lightly butter a 1½-pint (900-ml) baking dish.

Scald the milk in a saucepan and add the vanilla pod. Remove the pan from the heat and leave to infuse.

Beat the eggs, egg yolks and sugar together and pour on the warm milk. Strain the custard into the baking dish. Dust the top with grated nutmeg, stand the dish in a bain-marie of warm water and cook for 45 to 60 minutes or until a knife inserted into the custard comes out clean.

Remove the baking dish from the oven and serve warm or chilled.

Caramel custard

If you prefer, make the custard in a 1½-pint (900-ml) heatproof dish instead of in the individual custard cups and bake for about 1 hour. For a richer custard use half milk and half cream.

SERVES FOUR

¼ lb (125 g) castor sugar
2 tablespoons water
2 eggs plus 2 egg yolks
½ teaspoon vanilla essence
1 pint (575 ml) milk

Preheat the oven to 325°F (170°C, Gas Mark 3). Heat the custard cups.

Put 3 ounces (75 g) of the sugar with the water in a small pan. Cook over moderate heat, stirring constantly, until the syrup is a rich brown.

Pour the caramel into the custard cups. Turn them so that the bottom and sides are coated with the caramel.

Beat the eggs, egg yolks and vanilla essence with the remaining sugar. Scald the milk and pour it over the eggs, stirring.

Strain the custard into the custard cups. Stand the cups in a baking tin. Pour in warm water to come half-way up the sides of the cups. Bake for 30 to 40 minutes or until the custard has set but is still slightly wobbly.

Leave to cool. When the custard is quite cold, cover and refrigerate. Unmould on to plates and serve.

Petits pots de crème au chocolat

Other flavours such as coffee or vanilla may be used instead of the chocolate.

SERVES SIX

¼ lb (125 g) plain chocolate, broken into pieces
½ pint (300 ml) milk
½ pint (300 ml) cream
3 egg yolks plus 1 whole egg
1 oz (25 g) vanilla sugar

Preheat the oven to 325°F (170°C, Gas Mark 3).

Melt the chocolate in the milk and cream. Mix the egg yolks, the whole egg and sugar in a large bowl. Pour in the milk and chocolate mixture and stir to mix. Strain the custard into 6 custard cups, cover with lids or buttered paper and stand in a bain-marie of warm water.

Bake for about 30 minutes, or until a knife inserted into the custard comes out clean. Serve cold.

Meringues

MAKES ABOUT SIXTEEN SHELLS

4 egg whites
½ lb (225 g) plus 2 tablespoons castor sugar, sifted
¾ pint (450 ml) double cream, whipped

Preheat the oven to 250°F (130°C, Gas Mark ½). Line two large baking sheets with non-stick paper or lightly oiled greaseproof paper.

Beat the egg whites in a large bowl with a wire whisk or rotary beater. When the egg whites form stiff peaks beat in 1 ounce (25 g) of the sugar. Beat until stiff and glossy. Using a large metal spoon fold in the remaining 7 ounces (200 g) of sugar.

Spoon the meringue mixture into a forcing bag fitted with a plain nozzle and pipe out the meringue shells on to the baking sheets, or use two large spoons to shape the shells. Dredge the meringues with the remaining 2 tablespoons of sugar and leave to stand for 5 minutes.

Bake for 1½ hours or until the meringues are a pale beige in colour and are set on the outside but sticky on the inside. Look at the meringues from time to time to check that they are not colouring too quickly. If they are, turn off the oven and leave the meringues to cook more slowly.

Gently lift the meringues from the paper, using a palette knife. Press the base of each meringue with your fingertips to make a dent for the cream filling.

Return the meringues, on their sides, to the baking sheets and bake for 20 to 30 minutes.

Cool on a wire rack and when cold either fill with whipped cream just before serving or store in a completely airtight container.

Meringue baskets

This is a stiffer meringue, which will hold its shape well.

MAKES ONE NINE-INCH (23-CM) BASKET

4 egg whites
½ lb (225 g) icing sugar, sifted
Vanilla essence

Line a large baking sheet with non-stick paper.

Preheat the oven to 250°F (130°C, Gas Mark ½).

Beat the egg whites with a wire whisk or rotary beater until they are frothy but not stiff. Place the bowl over a pan of hot water over low heat and gradually whisk in the sugar. Add 2 drops of vanilla essence and continue whisking until the meringue is very thick.

Trace several small circles or one 9-inch (23-cm) circle on to the non-stick paper.

Using a forcing bag, pipe out the meringue in concentric circles to form the base. Then pipe around the edge to make the sides.

Bake for about 1½ hours. Cool on a wire rack and either use at once or store in an airtight container.

Pavlova

Once assembled this dessert should be served immediately or the meringue will become soft.

SERVES FOUR TO SIX

½ pint (300 ml) double cream
1 tablespoon Cointreau
1 tablespoon brandy
One 9-inch (23-cm) meringue basket
1 lb (450 g) fresh fruit, weight after preparation
1 tablespoon castor sugar

Whip the cream until thick. Beat in the Cointreau and brandy and beat until stiff. Spread the cream on the base of the meringue basket.

Cut large fruit into cubes, remove pips and stones. Toss the fruit in the sugar and pile decoratively on top of the cream. Serve immediately.

Meringue hazelnut gâteau

SERVES SIX TO EIGHT

6 egg whites
¾ lb (350 g) castor sugar
2 teaspoons lemon juice
6 oz (175 g) ground hazelnuts
¾ pint (450 ml) double cream
1 tablespoon icing sugar
1 to 2 tablespoons coffee essence
Whole hazelnuts or coffee beans

Preheat the oven to 325°F (170°C, Gas Mark 3).

Line 3 baking sheets with greaseproof paper. Trace three 9-inch (23-cm) circles on the paper, then lightly oil the paper.

Using a wire whisk or rotary beater, whisk the egg whites in a bowl until stiff. Add 2 tablespoons of the sugar and the lemon juice and beat for a further 30 seconds. Fold in the remaining sugar and the ground hazelnuts.

Spread equal amounts of the meringue mixture on to the traced circles on the baking sheets. Bake for 25 to 30 minutes or until the meringues are lightly coloured and firm to the touch. Carefully transfer the meringues to wire racks to cool.

Meanwhile whip the cream with the icing sugar until stiff, adding the coffee essence to taste. Sandwich the meringue layers with half the cream mixture. Spread the remaining cream over the top and sides. Decorate with the hazelnuts or coffee beans. Put the gâteau in the refrigerator for 30 minutes before serving.

Baked Alaska

The secret of a successful baked Alaska is that the ice-cream should be very cold and the oven temperature high enough to colour the meringue quickly without melting the ice-cream. Use a really good-quality ice-cream.

SERVES SIX

1½ pints (900 ml) good-quality chocolate ice-cream
1 sponge cake, 8 inches (20 cm) in diameter
4 tablespoons rum
4 large egg whites
Pinch cream of tartar
6 oz (175 g) castor sugar

Put the ice-cream on a sheet of foil and shape it into a round the same size as the cake. Wrap the foil around the ice-cream and put it in the ice-making compartment of the refrigerator to harden.

Preheat the oven to 450°F (230°C, Gas Mark 8).

Put the cake on an ovenproof plate and sprinkle it evenly with the rum. Leave to soak for 30 minutes.

Beat the egg whites with the cream of tartar until stiff. Whisk in the sugar, a tablespoonful at a time, until the whites form glossy peaks.

Very quickly, put the ice-cream on to the cake and cover both completely with the meringue, leaving no spaces or the ice-cream will melt.

Bake the Alaska for 3 to 5 minutes, or until the meringue is golden. Serve at once.

Queen of puddings

Serve this delightful pudding with plenty of cream.

SERVES FOUR

1 pint (575 ml) milk
2 oz (50 g) butter
2 oz (50 g) granulated sugar
Grated rind of 1 lemon
¼ lb (125 g) fresh white breadcrumbs
3 eggs, separated
4 tablespoons of jam (blackberry, apricot, strawberry or blackcurrant), warmed
3 oz (75 g) castor sugar

Butter a 2½-pint (1¼-litre) shallow baking dish.

Heat the milk, butter, granulated sugar and lemon rind slowly in a covered saucepan, stirring once as the butter melts. When the milk is just warmed through, turn off the heat but leave the pan on the cooker for 10 minutes.

Put the breadcrumbs in a large bowl and pour the milk over them. Leave to soak for at least 20 minutes.

Preheat the oven to 350°F (180°C, Gas Mark 4).

Beat in the egg yolks and pour the mixture into the baking dish.

Bake the pudding for 30 minutes, or until lightly set. Remove the pudding from the oven and spread the warm jam evenly over the top.

Whisk the egg whites until they are stiff. Beat in 2 tablespoons of the castor sugar, and when the mixture is glossy fold in the remaining sugar.

Pile the meringue on top of the pudding and bake for 10 minutes or until the top is set and lightly coloured.

Serve hot.

Raspberry tart

SERVES FOUR TO SIX

½ lb (225 g) unblanched almonds, washed and dried
½ lb (225 g) castor sugar
4 egg whites
¾ lb (350 g) raspberries
½ pint (300 ml) double cream, whipped
½ oz (15 g) flaked almonds, toasted

Preheat the oven to 350°F (180°C, Gas Mark 4). Line the bottom of a shallow 9-inch (23-cm) cake tin with lightly oiled greaseproof paper.

Grind the almonds in a liquidizer. Put them in a bowl and mix in the sugar. Whisk the egg whites in another bowl until stiff. Fold in the almond and sugar mixture. Spread the meringue smoothly in the cake tin. Bake for 35 minutes or until lightly coloured and firm to the touch.

Turn the meringue out carefully on to a wire rack to cool.

Just before serving, cover the meringue with the raspberries, reserving a few for decoration. Swirl the cream over the top and decorate with the reserved raspberries and toasted almonds.

The cold table

These specially selected hors d'oeuvre, pâtés, salads, ices and desserts are additional to the cold dishes included earlier in the book to illustrate the various cooking methods.

Hors d'oeuvre

Pan bagna
Other ingredients which may be included in a pan bagna are cooked, diced artichoke hearts, a few sliced gherkins or a small portion of mushrooms à la Grecque. Salami is not a traditional part of this provençal sandwich, but it adds an interesting flavour.

If the loaf is awkward to handle cut it in two or three pieces after filling it. A round, flat country loaf may also be used.

Pan bagna is excellent to take on a picnic.

SERVES FOUR TO SIX

1 long French loaf
4 to 6 tablespoons olive oil
1 garlic clove, cut in half
¼ lb (125 g) black olives, pitted and sliced
2 oz (50 g) capers
¾ lb (350 g) tomatoes, sliced
2 oz (50 g) anchovy fillets, cut into small pieces
6 oz (175 g) salami, diced

Cut the loaf in half lengthways. Remove some of the bread from both halves and put it in a large bowl.

Lay the two halves of the loaf, crust side down, on a dish. Dribble the oil over the insides, rub with the garlic and set aside for about 1 hour.

Add the olives, capers, tomatoes, anchovies and salami to the bread in the bowl. Stir the mixture well, then pile it into the bottom half of the loaf. Cover with the other half of the loaf, then wrap tightly in aluminium foil.

Put a heavy weight on top of the loaf and leave for several hours or overnight.

To serve, remove the foil and cut the loaf into thick slices.

Crudités
Crudités are raw, young vegetables trimmed and washed and eaten dipped in garlic mayonnaise. Use whichever vegetables are available.

SERVES FOUR TO SIX

½ pint (300 ml) aioli
1 cauliflower, washed and cut into florets
10 young carrots, scrubbed
6 celery stalks, washed and cut into strips
12 spring onions, trimmed
1 head of chicory, separated into leaves
1 green pepper, seeded, cored and cut into strips

Pour the aioli into a bowl, cover it and chill for at least 1 hour.

Arrange the vegetables on a large serving dish. Serve with the aioli.

Stuffed eggs
Serve stuffed eggs on a bed of watercress as a first course, as part of an hors d'oeuvre, or as a garnish for a salad.

SERVES FOUR

8 hard-boiled eggs, shelled
2 tablespoons mayonnaise
8 anchovy fillets, diced
16 capers
2 tablespoons chopped fresh parsley
Salt and pepper

Cut the eggs in half. Remove the yolks and put them into a bowl.

Mash the yolks with a fork, then add the mayonnaise, anchovies, capers and parsley. Mix well and season to taste with salt and pepper.

Fill the eggs with the stuffing.

Chill for at least 30 minutes before serving.

Egg mayonnaise
Serve egg mayonnaise with thin slices of brown bread and butter.

SERVES FOUR

1 small lettuce, washed
6 hard-boiled eggs, shelled and cut in half lengthways
½ pint (300 ml) thick mayonnaise
6 anchovy fillets, diced
1 tablespoon chopped parsley

Divide the lettuce between four plates, and lay three egg halves on each plate. Spoon the mayonnaise over the eggs, and garnish with the anchovies and parsley. Chill for at least 30 minutes before serving.

Pears with cream cheese
If the pears are not absolutely ripe, prepare them the previous day and let them marinate in the dressing overnight.

SERVES FOUR

Salt and pepper
1 tablespoon lemon juice
3 tablespoons olive oil
4 pears
½ lb (225 g) cream cheese
1 tablespoon chopped fresh parsley

To make the dressing, mix the salt, pepper and lemon juice in a bowl. Add the oil a little at a time and beat gently until it has amalgamated with the lemon juice.

Peel, core and slice the pears and put them immediately into the dressing. Cover the bowl and put it in the refrigerator for at least 2 hours. Baste the pears with the dressing every 30 minutes.

Shape the cheese into small balls. Roll the cheese balls in the chopped parsley and put them in the refrigerator.

To serve, divide the pears between 4 plates and top each portion with the cheese balls.

Seviche
Although the fish is never actually cooked, the lime juice marinade breaks down the fibres, making it deliciously tender. Use any firm-fleshed white fish.

SERVES FOUR

¾ pint (450 ml) fresh lime juice
2 onions, thinly sliced
1 red chilli, seeded and chopped
1 garlic clove, crushed
1½ teaspoons salt
Black pepper
1½ lb (700 g) fish fillets, cut into ½-inch (1-cm) pieces
Black olives, to garnish

Combine the lime juice, onions, chilli, garlic, salt and a sprinkling of pepper in a bowl.

Add the fish and stir to make sure it is well coated with the marinade.

Cover the bowl and refrigerate for at least 24 hours or until the fish is opaque and tender. Serve garnished with black olives.

Rollmops
Rollmops, or raw pickled herrings, should be left to marinate for at least a week, or a few days longer, if possible. Serve them with the onion rings and a little of the pickling liquid, which should first be strained.

SERVES FOUR

12 salt herring fillets
¾ pint (450 ml) white wine vinegar
½ pint (300 ml) water
2 oz (50 g) castor sugar
Dijon mustard
1 oz (25 g) capers
12 small gherkins
3 medium-sized onions, sliced and pushed out into rings
8 peppercorns
½ oz (15 g) mustard seeds
6 juniper berries
Finely grated rind of ½ lemon

Soak the herring fillets in cold water for 12 hours. Drain the fillets, rinse them under cold

Use a sharp, pointed knife to cut a tomato in half decoratively.

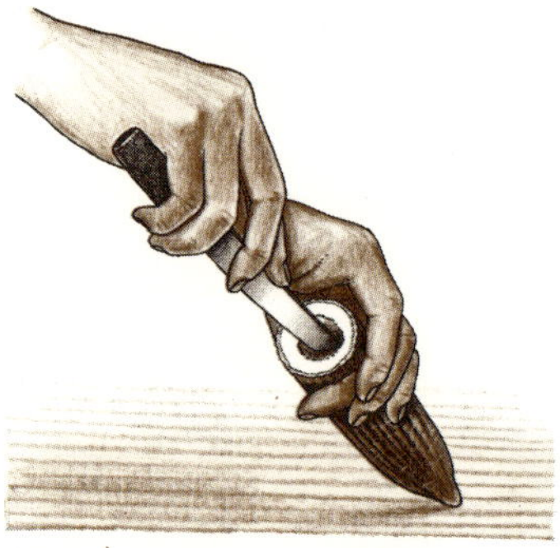

Cut a cucumber into lengths then scrape out the seeds.

Before serving cut the stuffed, chilled cucumber into slices.

running water and dry on kitchen paper towels.

To make the pickling mixture, put the vinegar, water and sugar in a saucepan. Stir to dissolve over low heat then bring to the boil, stirring constantly. Remove the pan from the heat and set aside.

Lay the fillets skin side down. On each fillet put a little mustard, a few capers and a gherkin. Roll the fillets up and secure each one with a cocktail stick.

Put alternate layers of onion rings and herrings into a large screw-top jar or deep bowl, sprinkling the layers with the peppercorns, mustard seeds, juniper berries and lemon rind.

Pour the pickling liquid into the jar or bowl, cover and refrigerate.

Curried rice salad

This is a very luxurious salad that may be served on its own as a first course or as a main dish accompanied by other salads.

Use a good-quality long-grain rice such as basmati.

SERVES SIX TO EIGHT

3 fl oz (75 ml) mayonnaise, made with lemon juice
4 tablespoons double cream
1 tablespoon curry paste or powder
Salt and freshly ground black pepper
1 tablespoon lemon juice
1 garlic clove, crushed
2 spring onions, chopped
1 green pepper, cored, seeded and chopped
2 avocado pears, peeled, stoned and sliced
½ lb (225 g) fresh pineapple, chopped
2 oz (50 g) halved blanched almonds
½ lb (225 g) peeled prawns
½ lb (225 g) cooked chicken, diced
½ lb (225 g) long-grain rice, washed, soaked, cooked and cooled

Put the mayonnaise, cream, curry paste or powder, seasoning, lemon juice and garlic into a large salad bowl and stir well. Add the remaining ingredients and toss the salad to coat the ingredients with the dressing. Chill in the refrigerator for 1 hour before serving.

Stuffed tomatoes

SERVES FOUR

4 large, firm tomatoes
¼ pint (150 ml) mayonnaise
1 tablespoon lemon juice
1 tablespoon double cream
½ lb (225 g) cooked white crab meat
1 green pepper, seeded, cored and finely chopped

Slice the tops off the tomatoes. Scoop out the flesh then turn the empty tomato cases upside down to drain. Reserve the tops.

Mix the mayonnaise with the lemon juice and cream. Stir in crab meat mixture, and replace

Fill the tomato cases with the crab meat mixture, and replace the tops. Chill for at least 30 minutes before serving.

Avocados stuffed with prawns

SERVES FOUR

¼ pint (150 ml) mayonnaise
2 tablespoons cream
1 tablespoon lemon juice
2 drops Tabasco sauce
½ lb (225 g) prawns, cooked and peeled
2 large, ripe avocados, halved and stoned
½ lemon

Combine the mayonnaise, cream, lemon juice and Tabasco in a bowl. Add the prawns and stir until they are well coated. Rub the avocados with the lemon.

Spoon the mixture into the avocados and chill for at least 30 minutes before serving.

Stuffed cucumber

SERVES FOUR TO SIX

1 large cucumber, peeled and cut crossways into pieces
¼ lb (125 g) canned tuna fish
½ oz (15 g) butter
1 oz (25 g) cream cheese
1 tablespoon chopped parsley
1 teaspoon fresh thyme
1 teaspoon fresh oregano
1 teaspoon fresh tarragon
1 teaspoon chopped fresh chives
½ teaspoon lemon juice
Salt and pepper

Using a sharp knife or a teaspoon, scoop the pulp and seeds from the centre of each piece of cucumber. Pat dry with kitchen paper towels.

Drain the tuna fish and put it in a bowl. Add the butter, cheese, herbs and lemon juice and mash well with a fork. Season to taste.

Stuff the cucumber pieces with the tuna fish mixture, and put in the refrigerator for at least 1 hour. Before serving, cut each piece of cucumber into slices.

Cheese ring

SERVES SIX

2 teaspoons flavourless cooking oil
6 oz (175 g) dolcelatte cheese
½ lb (225 g) cream cheese
Cayenne pepper
1 tablespoon chopped chives
½ oz (15 g) gelatine dissolved in 2 fl oz (50 ml) hot water
¼ pint (150 ml) mayonnaise
¼ pint (150 ml) double cream
6 radishes, thinly sliced

Grease a 1½-pint (900-ml) ring mould with the oil, and set aside.

Push the dolcelatte through a sieve into a bowl. Beat in the cream cheese, a pinch of cayenne pepper and the chives. Mix thoroughly, then add the dissolved gelatine and continue to stir the mixture for a few minutes more.

Fold in the mayonnaise and cream then spoon it into the ring mould. Chill in the refrigerator for 2 hours or until the mixture has set.

To serve, turn the mould out and garnish with radish slices.

Salade de Charentais

SERVES FOUR

2 Charentais melons
½ cucumber, peeled
2 ripe dessert pears, peeled and cored
6 tablespoons vinaigrette
4 tablespoons soured cream
2 tablespoons lemon juice
2 teaspoons sugar
Salt and pepper

Cut the melons in half and remove the seeds. Scoop out the flesh leaving ¼-inch (½-cm) thick shells. Dice the flesh and put it into a bowl.

Cut the cucumber and pears into dice of the same size and mix with the melon. Pour in the vinaigrette, toss well to mix and set aside for 1 hour in the refrigerator.

Drain the fruit and cucumber and pile into the melon shells.

Beat the soured cream with the lemon juice and sugar and season to taste. Spoon the dressing over the salad and serve.

Grapefruit with prawns

SERVES FOUR

2 grapefruit, chilled
½ lb (225 g) peeled prawns, chilled
¼ pint (150 ml) mayonnaise, chilled
4 mint sprigs

Cut the grapefruit in half. Using a sharp knife, carefully detach the grapefruit segments. Reserve the shells.

Combine the grapefruit segments, prawns and mayonnaise. Pile the mixture into the grapefruit shells, garnish with the mint sprigs and serve.

Shellfish cocktail

SERVES FOUR

1 lb (450 g) mixed cooked lobster, crab meat and peeled prawns
1 tablespoon chopped walnuts
4 tablespoons chopped celery
8 fl oz (225 ml) well-seasoned mayonnaise
4 tablespoons double cream
1 teaspoon tomato purée
Tabasco sauce
½ teaspoon grated horseradish
Lemon juice
4 watercress sprigs

Cut the lobster into small pieces and shred the crab meat. Put the shellfish into a bowl and mix in the walnuts and celery.

Combine the mayonnaise, cream, tomato purée, a few drops of the Tabasco sauce and the horseradish. Taste the sauce and add a little lemon juice if necessary.

Pour the sauce over the shellfish mixture and toss well to mix. Cover the bowl and refrigerate for at least 30 minutes.

To serve, spoon the mixture into 4 glass bowls. Garnish with the watercress and serve.

Pâtés

Smoked mackerel pâté

SERVES FOUR

1 smoked mackerel (approximately 1 pound/450 g), skinned and boned
2 oz (50 g) unsalted butter, melted
Grated rind and juice of 1 lemon
1 shallot
$\frac{1}{4}$ teaspoon salt
Black pepper
Sliced cucumber

Break up the mackerel fillets and put them in the liquidizer with all the other ingredients except the cucumber. Blend until smooth. Taste and add more salt, pepper or lemon juice if necessary. Chill the pâté.

Arrange the cucumber slices overlapping in a circle on a dish. Spoon the pâté into the middle and serve.

Game pâté

Line the terrine with fat.

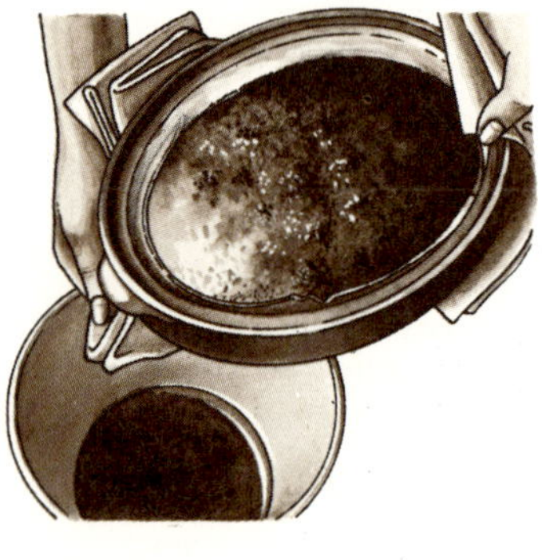

Pour away excess liquid.

Spoon over the jellied stock.

Danish liver pâté

SERVES FOUR TO SIX

1 lb (450 g) pig's liver
$\frac{1}{4}$ lb (125 g) back fat
5 anchovy fillets
$\frac{1}{2}$ pint (300 ml) béchamel sauce, cooled
1 garlic clove, crushed
$\frac{1}{2}$ teaspoon salt
Pepper
$\frac{1}{4}$ teaspoon ground mace
$\frac{1}{4}$ lb (125 g) streaky bacon rashers

Preheat the oven to 350°F (180 °C, Gas Mark 4).

Mince the liver, back fat and anchovy fillets very finely or put in a liquidizer a little at a time and blend until smooth. Put the mixture into a bowl and beat in the béchamel sauce, a little at a time. Mix in the garlic, salt, pepper and mace.

Line a 1-pint (575-ml) baking dish or small loaf tin with the bacon rashers. Spoon in the mixture. Cover the top with buttered greaseproof paper or foil. Put the dish in a baking tin half filled with water. Bake for 1 hour or until the pâté is firm to the touch.

Take the dish out of the oven and leave to cool. When cool cover with fresh foil and chill for 12 hours before serving.

Game pâté

SERVES SIX

$\frac{1}{4}$ lb (125 g) streaky bacon or back fat
2 pheasants, or wild ducks, roasted
$1\frac{1}{2}$ lb (700 g) pork belly, minced
$\frac{1}{2}$ lb (225 g) pig's liver, minced
2 oz (50 g) back fat, diced
1 teaspoon grated orange rind
1 teaspoon dried thyme
1 teaspoon dried marjoram
1 teaspoon salt
1 teaspoon black peppercorns, coarsely crushed
4 tablespoons white wine
2 tablespoons brandy
Clarified stock made from the bird carcasses, cold

Line a 1-quart (1-litre) terrine with the bacon or fat. Strip the meat off the game birds and chop it coarsely. Mix the meat with all the remaining ingredients except the cold stock. Put the mixture into the terrine and set aside for 1 hour.

Preheat the oven to 325°F (170°C, Gas Mark 3).

Put the terrine into a roasting tin. Half fill the tin with boiling water. Bake the pâté for $1\frac{1}{2}$ to $1\frac{3}{4}$ hours or until the top is brown and the pâté has shrunk slightly from the sides.

Remove the terrine from the oven. Pour out any liquid. Leave to cool. Cover the top with foil and put a weight on top. When the pâté is cold pour a thin layer of the cold stock over the top and refrigerate until set.

Hare pâté

The meat may be taken from a roasted or casserolled hare. One large hare will provide enough meat for a roast as well as for a pâté for four people.

SERVES FOUR

1 lb (450 g) cooked, boned hare, minced
$\frac{1}{2}$ lb (225 g) pork, minced
1 lb (450 g) streaky bacon
2 garlic cloves, crushed
$1\frac{1}{2}$ teaspoons dried basil
$1\frac{1}{2}$ teaspoons dried marjoram
4 fl oz (125 ml) red wine or brandy
$\frac{1}{2}$ teaspoon salt
1 teaspoon black peppercorns, coarsely ground
Grated rind of $\frac{1}{2}$ lemon

Preheat the oven to 325°F (170°C, Gas Mark 3).

Mix the hare and pork together in a bowl. Chop $\frac{1}{2}$ pound (225 g) of the bacon and mix it in. Stir in the garlic, herbs, wine or brandy, salt, pepper and lemon rind.

Line a 1-quart (1-litre) terrine or loaf tin with half the remaining bacon rashers. Spoon in the hare mixture and cover the top with the remaining bacon.

Put the terrine in a baking tin half filled with boiling water and bake for $1\frac{3}{4}$ hours or until the sides have shrunk slightly.

Remove the terrine from the oven and leave to cool. When cool, cover with foil and refrigerate for at least 3 hours before serving.

Gelée de saumon

SERVES FOUR

$\frac{1}{2}$ oz (15 g) gelatine
4 fl oz (125 ml) boiling water
2 tablespoons lemon juice
1 small onion, sliced
4 fl oz (125 ml) mayonnaise
1 teaspoon dried dill weed
1 lb (450 g) cooked salmon, boned and skinned, or 1 lb (450 g) canned salmon, drained
8 fl oz (225 ml) double cream
1 teaspoon salt

Lightly oil a 1-quart (1-litre) mould or loaf tin. Dissolve the gelatine in the water and pour it into a liquidizer with the lemon juice and onion. Blend at high speed for 40 seconds. Add the mayonnaise, dill and salmon and blend for a few seconds. Add the cream one-third at a time, blending for a few seconds after each addition. Taste the mixture and if necessary add a little salt. Blend for 30 seconds.

Pour the mixture into the mould. Cover and chill for at least 2 hours before turning it out on to a serving dish.

Veal and ham pâté

SERVES SIX

$\frac{1}{2}$ lb (225 g) veal, minced
$\frac{1}{2}$ lb (225 g) pork, minced
$\frac{1}{2}$ lb (225 g) back fat, minced
$\frac{1}{4}$ lb (125 g) prosciutto ham, cut in dice
2 oz (50 g) capers
2 oz (50 g) pistachio nuts
4 tablespoons dry sherry
1 teaspoon salt
1 teaspoon peppercorns, coarsely crushed
1 garlic clove, crushed
2 teaspoons chopped basil
$\frac{1}{4}$ lb (125 g) streaky bacon

Mix all the ingredients except the bacon in a bowl. Spoon the mixture into a 1-quart (1-litre) terrine. Lay the bacon over the top and set aside for 1 hour.

Preheat the oven to 325°F (170°C, Gas Mark 3).

Put the terrine in a roasting tin half filled with water and bake for $1\frac{3}{4}$ hours.

Remove the terrine from the oven and leave to cool. Cover the top with foil and put a weight on top.

When completely cold refrigerate for 12 hours before serving.

Pâté au cognac

Once the pâté has been cooled, it can be finished off with a thin coating of meat glaze or melted butter.

SERVES SIX

3 oz (75 g) butter
2 shallots, finely chopped
½ fresh bay leaf
2 garlic cloves, crushed
1½ lb (700 g) chicken livers, cleaned, trimmed, washed and dried
1 to 2 tablespoons brandy
2 egg yolks

Melt the butter in a medium-sized saucepan over low heat. Add the shallots, bay leaf and garlic and cook, stirring occasionally, until the shallots are soft but not coloured. Add the chicken livers and cook them until they are tender. Mash them with a fork and cook for a further 5 minutes, stirring constantly. Remove the pan from the heat.

Preheat the oven to 350°F (180°C, Gas Mark 4). Grease a terrine or medium-sized baking dish and set it aside.

Put the chicken liver mixture into a liquidizer and blend until smooth. Alternatively, rub the mixture twice through a fine strainer. Beat in the brandy and egg yolks and pour the mixture into the baking dish. Place the dish in a baking tin half filled with water and bake for 1 hour, or until the pâté is firm to the touch.

Cool before serving.

Taramasalata

In Greece this delicious pâté is made from the roe of the grey mullet, but it can also be made from smoked cod's roe. Garnish the pâté with black olives and serve with toast or hot pitta.

SERVES SIX TO EIGHT

¾ lb (350 g) smoked cod's roe
4 slices white bread, crusts removed
6 tablespoons milk
2 garlic cloves, crushed
¼ lb (125 g) cream or curd cheese
9 tablespoons olive oil
Juice of 1 large lemon
Salt and pepper

Using a teaspoon scoop the roe out of its skin into a bowl. Soak the bread in the milk. When the bread is soft squeeze out any excess milk and add the bread to the roe. Beat in the garlic and cheese. Add the oil and lemon juice a spoonful at a time, beating well between each addition.

Put the mixture into a liquidizer a little at a time and blend until smooth. Season to taste and add more lemon juice if necessary.

Meat loaf

SERVES SIX

½ lb (225 g) pork, minced
½ lb (225 g) veal, minced
1 lb (450 g) gammon, minced
2 garlic cloves, crushed
1 tablespoon chopped mint
½ teaspoon salt
½ teaspoon coarsely ground black pepper
2 eggs
3 large hard-boiled eggs

Preheat the oven to 350°F (180°C, Gas Mark 4).

Combine all the ingredients except the hard-boiled eggs in a mixing bowl. Stuff the mixture into a straight-sided, wide-mouthed, heatproof jar. Push the eggs in down the centre, nose to tail. If a jar is not available use a 2-pound (900-g) loaf tin. Put half the mixture in the bottom of the tin, lay the hard-boiled eggs in a row down the centre and cover with the rest of the mixture. Cover the tin or jar with foil, stand it in a roasting tin half-filled with boiling water and bake for 1¾ hours.

Remove the meat loaf from the oven and leave to cool. Cover with fresh foil and refrigerate.

Pâté de campagne

SERVES SIX

1 lb (450 g) veal, minced
1 lb (450 g) pork belly, minced
½ lb (225 g) pig's liver, minced
2 garlic cloves, crushed
2 oz (50 g) back fat, diced
½ teaspoon coarsely ground black pepper
1 heaped teaspoon salt
8 juniper berries, lightly crushed
4 tablespoons brandy
¼ lb (125 g) streaky bacon, cut in half lengthways

Mix all the ingredients except the bacon and put into a 1-quart (1-litre) terrine or loaf tin. Lay the bacon over the top and set aside for 1 hour.

Preheat the oven to 325°F (170°C, Gas Mark 3).

Put the terrine in a roasting tin. Pour some water into the tin and bake the pâté for 1¾ hours.

Remove the terrine from the oven and leave to cool. Cover the top with foil and leave to become completely cold. Chill in the refrigerator before serving.

Pork terrine

SERVES SIX TO EIGHT

½ lb (225 g) streaky bacon
1½ lb (700 g) pork fillet, beaten out into thin escalopes
1½ lb (700 g) ham, thinly sliced
2 tablespoons chopped parsley
2 tablespoons chopped onion
2 tablespoons sliced stuffed olives
Salt and pepper
¼ pint (150 ml) white wine
2 fl oz (50 ml) brandy

Preheat the oven to 325°F (170°C, Gas Mark 3).

Line a 2-pound (900-g) loaf tin or terrine with half the bacon. Layer the pork and ham, sprinkling the layers with the chopped parsley, onion, sliced olives and seasoning.

Mix the wine and brandy together and pour it over the meat. Cover the top with the remaining bacon.

Bake in a roasting tin half-filled with water for 2 hours.

Remove the terrine from the oven, cover with foil and put a weight on top. Leave overnight or until completely cold. Chill and serve thinly sliced.

Ham mousse

SERVES FOUR TO SIX

½ oz (15 g) gelatine
½ pint (300 ml) chicken stock
2 eggs, separated
¼ pint (150 ml) mayonnaise
½ lb (225 g) cooked ham, cut into pieces
1 tablespoon chopped chives
2 teaspoons Dijon mustard
½ teaspoon paprika
¼ pint (150 ml) double cream

Lightly oil a 1-quart (1-litre) round mould. Dissolve the gelatine in 3 tablespoons of the chicken stock over low heat. Put the gelatine, the remaining stock, egg yolks, mayonnaise, ham, chives, mustard and paprika into a liquidizer and blend until smooth. Pour in the cream and blend for a few seconds. Pour the mixture into a bowl.

Whisk the egg whites until stiff but not dry and fold into the ham mixture. Turn the mixture into the mould, cover and chill for at least 2 hours.

Chopped liver

Serve chopped liver with thin slices of buttered toast.

SERVES FOUR TO SIX

1 lb (450 g) chicken livers, carefully cleaned
1 large onion
2 hard-boiled eggs
1 oz (25 g) butter
Salt and pepper

Preheat the grill to moderate. Grill the chicken livers for 1 minute on each side.

Chop the onion coarsely in a large wooden chopping bowl. Add the liver and chop until the mixture is fairly smooth.

Add the eggs and chop them coarsely. Mix in the butter and season to taste. Serve immediately or store in the refrigerator.

Avocado and shrimp cream

Serve as a first course with melba toast. The cream must be eaten very soon after it has been made, as avocados discolour quickly.

SERVES FOUR TO SIX

3 large, very ripe avocados, peeled and stoned
2 garlic cloves, crushed
1 tablespoon lemon juice
¼ teaspoon cayenne pepper
Salt and pepper
¼ pint (150 ml) soured cream
½ lb (225 g) fresh shrimps, cooked and peeled

Put a strainer over a mixing bowl and rub the avocados through the strainer with the back of a wooden spoon. Clean out the strainer and rub the avocados through again. Beat in the remaining ingredients and spoon the mixture into a serving bowl.

Salads

Celeriac salad

SERVES FOUR

¾ lb (350 g) celeriac root, peeled
¼ pint (150 ml) mayonnaise made with extra mustard
½ red pepper, cored and sliced thinly in rings
½ green pepper, cored and sliced thinly in rings
½ onion, sliced thinly in rings

Cut the celeriac in slices and then in strips. Combine the mayonnaise with the celeriac strips. Pile the mixture into a bowl and garnish with the peppers and onion.

Russian salad

SERVES FOUR

½ lb (225 g) potatoes, cooked
½ lb (225 g) carrots, cooked
½ lb (225 g) green beans, cooked
¼ lb (125 g) peas, cooked
2 tablespoons chopped chives
4 tablespoons vinaigrette
4 fl oz (125 ml) mayonnaise
6 anchovy fillets
2 hard-boiled eggs, cut in quarters
2 tablespoons capers

Cut the potatoes and carrots into ¼-inch (½-cm) cubes. Cut the beans into ¼-inch (½-cm) lengths. Put the vegetables and the chives into a bowl, pour in the vinaigrette and toss to mix. Leave for 1 hour to marinate.

Drain the vegetables and put them in another bowl. Pour in the mayonnaise and toss to mix. Garnish with the anchovy fillets, hard-boiled eggs and capers.

Serve chilled.

Coleslaw

SERVES FOUR

1 small white cabbage, finely shredded
6 fl oz (175 ml) mayonnaise
3 fl oz (75 ml) soured cream
2 teaspoons castor sugar
1 teaspoon prepared mustard
Juice of ½ lemon
Salt and pepper

Put the cabbage in a bowl. Mix all the remaining ingredients together and pour over the cabbage. Toss well. Serve well chilled.

Rice salad

SERVES FOUR

½ lb (225 g) rice, cooked
3 fl oz (75 ml) vinaigrette
2 tablespoons chopped parsley
¼ cucumber, diced
6 spring onions, chopped
2 oz (50 g) stuffed olives, sliced
2 celery stalks, chopped
2 carrots, diced
2 hard-boiled eggs, quartered
2 tomatoes, quartered

Put the rice, while it is still hot, into a salad bowl. Mix in the vinaigrette, parsley, cucumber, spring onions, olives, celery and carrots. Garnish with the eggs and tomatoes. Serve chilled.

Spinach and mushroom salad

SERVES FOUR

2 fl oz (50 ml) vinaigrette
½ lb (225 g) mushrooms, cleaned
½ lb (225 g) fresh spinach, washed and drained
Lemon juice

Put the vinaigrette in a salad bowl. Slice the mushrooms fairly thickly and put them in the bowl.

Remove the central vein from each spinach leaf. If the leaves are large tear them into bite-sized pieces. Put the leaves on top of the mushrooms. Add a squeeze of lemon juice and toss.

Aubergine salad

Serve with Greek bread or toast as an appetizer.

SERVES FOUR TO SIX

4 large aubergines
2 garlic cloves, crushed
4 fl oz (125 ml) olive oil
Juice of 1 lemon
Salt and pepper
4 tablespoons chopped parsley

Preheat the oven to 350°F (180°C, Gas Mark 4).

Wrap the aubergines in foil or oiled greaseproof paper. Put them on a baking sheet and bake for 40 minutes.

Remove the aubergines from the oven and when they are cool enough to handle cut them in half. Scrape out all the flesh into a bowl. Mix in the garlic. Beat in the olive oil a few drops at a time as you would for mayonnaise. Mix in the lemon juice and season with salt and pepper to taste. Mix in the parsley. Chill before serving.

Mushrooms à la Grecque

SERVES FOUR

¾ pint (450 ml) water
2 garlic cloves, crushed
Juice of 2 lemons
2 fl oz (50 ml) olive oil
6 peppercorns
Salt
1 tarragon sprig
1 parsley sprig
1 lb (450 g) mushrooms, stalks removed
Chopped parsley

Put the water, garlic, lemon juice, olive oil, peppercorns and a large pinch of salt in a saucepan and bring to the boil. Reduce the heat and simmer for 10 minutes. Add the tarragon, parsley sprig and mushroom caps and simmer for 10 minutes.

Drain the mushrooms and put them in a dish. Return the marinade to the pan and boil rapidly to reduce to ¼ pint (150 ml). Strain the marinade over the mushrooms. Cover the dish and refrigerate. Serve garnished with the chopped parsley.

Green bean salad

SERVES FOUR

1 lb (450 g) green beans, trimmed and washed
Salt
8 tablespoons vinaigrette
8 anchovy fillets
4 tablespoons thick mayonnaise
8 black olives, pitted

Drop the beans into salted boiling water. When the water returns to the boil, reduce the heat and simmer for 5 minutes. Drain and refresh the beans under cold running water.

Drain the beans well and put in a bowl. Pour in the vinaigrette and leave for 1 hour.

Arrange the beans neatly in stacks on 4 plates. Slit the anchovy fillets in half lengthways and lay them across the beans. Spoon the mayonnaise in between the anchovies. Put the olives on top. Serve chilled.

Celery, apple and walnut salad

SERVES FOUR

½ pint (300 ml) yogurt
2 tablespoons honey
1½ teaspoons dried mint
1 head of celery, washed and sliced
2 apples, cored and sliced
2 oz (50 g) walnuts, coarsely chopped

Whisk the yogurt in a bowl. Add the honey, a little at a time, and continue to whisk until the ingredients are well blended. Stir in the mint.

Put the celery, apples and walnuts in a large bowl, pour over the yogurt dressing and serve.

Carrot and apple salad

SERVES FOUR

½ lb (225 g) carrots, coarsely grated
2 well-flavoured unpeeled dessert apples, coarsely grated
2 oz (50 g) sultanas
1 oz (25 g) peanuts
¼ pint (150 ml) vinaigrette

Mix all the ingredients together in a salad bowl.

Chicory, orange and watercress salad

This salad, which may be garnished with black olives, goes particularly well with duck.

SERVES FOUR

1 tablespoon lemon juice
Salt and pepper
½ teaspoon French mustard
1 teaspoon sugar
Tabasco sauce
3 tablespoons olive oil
2 oranges, peeled and sliced
4 heads chicory, sliced crossways
1 bunch watercress, washed

Combine the lemon juice, salt and pepper to taste, mustard, sugar and a few drops of Tabasco in a bowl. Add the oil a little at a time, beating constantly, until the dressing is smooth.

In a large salad bowl, put the orange slices, chicory and watercress. Pour over the dressing, toss well and serve immediately, or chill for about 30 minutes before serving.

Tomato salad

A simple tomato salad can be made with peeled, sliced tomatoes, sprinkled with salt, black pepper and chopped fresh basil. Dress with a vinaigrette or omit the basil and use an English salad dressing. This variation comes from Greece. If you are unable to buy feta cheese, mozzarella is a good substitute.

SERVES FOUR

3 oz (75 g) feta cheese, cubed
2 lb (900 g) tomatoes, peeled and sliced
1 green pepper, cored, seeded and sliced
1 small onion, finely chopped
Salt and pepper
1 teaspoon dried mint
1 garlic clove, crushed
1 tablespoon lemon juice
3 tablespoons olive oil
¼ lb (125 g) black olives, pitted

Put the cheese, tomatoes, pepper and onion in a salad bowl.

In another bowl mix the salt, pepper, mint, garlic and lemon juice. Gradually add the olive oil and beat until all the ingredients are amalgamated.

Pour the dressing over the cheese and vegetables and toss well. Scatter the olives over the salad and serve.

Waldorf salad

This salad is excellent served with cold roast chicken.

SERVES FOUR

1 lb (450 g) apples, diced
2 celery stalks, diced
½ lb (225 g) grapes, halved and seeded
2 oz (50 g) walnut or pecan pieces
¼ pint (150 ml) mayonnaise

Mix all the ingredients together in a bowl. Chill well before serving.

Green salad with blue cheese dressing

SERVES FOUR

2 oz (50 g) blue cheese
2 tablespoons wine vinegar
½ to 1 teaspoon French mustard
Sugar
Salt and pepper
5 tablespoons olive oil
1 head of chicory, sliced crossways
1 cos lettuce
1 endive, coarsely chopped
A few dandelion leaves (optional)

To make the dressing mash the cheese in a bowl. Beat in the vinegar, mustard and sugar, salt and pepper to taste. Add the oil a little at a time, beating well to mix.

Put the chicory, lettuce, endive and dandelion leaves, if you have them, in a salad bowl. Pour over the dressing, toss the salad well and serve.

Avocado salad

SERVES FOUR

1 cos lettuce heart
3 avocados, peeled and sliced lengthways
2 oranges, peeled and segmented
1 grapefruit, peeled and segmented
4 fl oz (125 ml) vinaigrette made with lemon juice

Tear the lettuce into pieces and put in a salad bowl with the avocados, oranges and grapefruit. Pour over the dressing and toss. Serve immediately.

Cold desserts

Lemon curd

This recipe is equally delicious made with oranges instead of lemons.

MAKES TWO POUNDS (900 G)

6 oz (175 g) unsalted butter, cut into small pieces
1 lb (450 g) castor sugar
Thinly pared rind and juice of 4 lemons
4 eggs, beaten

Put the butter, sugar, lemon rind and juice in a heatproof mixing bowl. Set the bowl over a pan of barely simmering water and cook the mixture, stirring occasionally, until the sugar has dissolved.

Stir in the eggs and cook the lemon curd, stirring frequently, for about 25 minutes, or until it has thickened enough to just coat the back of the spoon.

Remove the pan from the heat and lift out the lemon rind with a slotted spoon. Pour the curd into jam jars and let it cool. When it is completely cold, cover with a disc of waxed paper. Then cover each jar with cellophane and fasten with a rubber band. Store in a cool place.

Lemon curd tartlets

MAKES TWELVE

2 teaspoons butter
6 oz (175 g) pâte sucrée pastry dough
8 tablespoons lemon curd
4 fl oz (125 ml) double cream, whipped until thick
1 tablespoon finely chopped pistachio nuts (optional)

Preheat the oven to 375°F (190°C, Gas Mark 5). Using the butter, grease twelve 3-inch (8-cm) patty tins.

Roll the dough out thinly on a lightly floured board and use it to line the patty tins. Prick the bottoms with a fork and bake for 10 to 12 minutes, or until the pastry is crisp and golden. Remove the tins from the oven, let the pastry cool thoroughly and then turn the tartlets out of the tins.

Spoon about 2 teaspoonfuls of the lemon curd into each tartlet. Fill a forcing bag fitted with a star nozzle with the cream and pipe it over the lemon curd to cover it completely. Sprinkle over the pistachio nuts, if you are using them, and serve.

Apricot tart bourdaloue

SERVES SIX

5 oz (150 g) almond pastry
¼ lb (125 g) sugar
½ pint (300 ml) water
1½ lb (700 g) apricots, halved and stoned
1 pint (575 ml) crème pâtissière, flavoured with grated orange rind
1 oz (25 g) flaked almonds, toasted

Preheat the oven to 375°F (190°C, Gas Mark 5).

Press the pastry dough into an 8-inch (20-cm) flan ring to line it. Bake blind for 25 to 30 minutes, uncovering the pastry for the last 10 minutes to brown. Remove from the oven and set aside to cool.

Meanwhile dissolve the sugar in the water. When the sugar has dissolved bring the syrup to the boil and boil for 5 minutes. Add the apricots and simmer for 5 minutes or until the apricots are tender but not mushy.

Drain the apricots and return the syrup to the pan. Boil for 5 minutes or until thick.

Put the pastry case on a plate. Spread the crème pâtissière over the bottom of the case, rounding it slightly in the centre. Cover the crème pâtissière completely with the apricot halves, cut sides down. Brush the apricots with the syrup. Scatter the flaked almonds on top and serve.

Lining patty tins

Roll out the dough. With a biscuit cutter, cut out circles the same size as the patty tins.

Lift the dough on to the patty tins. Using your fingertips, ease it in to the bottom and sides.

Lemon jelly

For a sparkling fruit jelly clarify the jelly in the same way as for aspic.

SERVES FOUR

½ oz (15 g) gelatine
¾ pint (450 ml) water
¼ lb (125 g) sugar
¼ pint (150 ml) lemon juice
Pared rind of 2 lemons

Put the gelatine and 4 tablespoons of the water in a cup and leave to soften.

Put the remaining water, sugar, lemon juice and rind into a saucepan. Stir to dissolve the sugar over low heat. Leave to infuse for 30 minutes. Stir in the gelatine and stir until it has dissolved. Strain the mixture into a wet 1-pint (575-ml) jelly mould. Chill for 4 hours or until set.

Orange jelly

Make orange jelly in the same way as lemon jelly, using ¾ pint (450 ml) of orange juice, juice of 1 lemon, thinly pared rind of 1 orange, 2 to 3 ounces (50 to 75 g) of sugar, 3 fluid ounces (75 ml) of water and ½ ounce (15 g) of gelatine.

Syllabub

SERVES FOUR

Finely pared rind and juice of 1 lemon
3 fl oz (75 ml) sherry
2 tablespoons brandy
3 to 4 tablespoons castor sugar
½ pint (300 ml) double cream

Put the lemon rind and juice, sherry and brandy into a small bowl or jug. Cover and leave overnight.

Strain the lemon mixture into a bowl and mix in the sugar to taste. Stir in the cream. Then using a wire whisk or rotary beater whisk until the mixture is thick and will hold its shape. Serve the syllabub in small cups or glasses.

Lemon snow

SERVES FOUR

Juice and thinly pared rind of 2 lemons
½ pint (300 ml) water
3 oz (75 g) sugar
½ oz (15 g) gelatine
2 egg whites

Put the lemon rind and water in a saucepan and heat gently. The water must not boil or simmer. Cover the pan and leave to infuse for 30 minutes. Strain and mix in the sugar and lemon juice. Stir until the sugar has dissolved.

Meanwhile dissolve the gelatine in 3 tablespoons of water over low heat. Mix the gelatine with the lemon juice mixture and pour into a bowl. Chill until nearly set.

Whisk the egg whites until stiff but not dry and fold them into the lemon jelly. Put the bowl back into the refrigerator.

Remove from the refrigerator 1 hour before serving.

Pears sabayon

SERVES FOUR

2 eggs, separated
2 tablespoons castor sugar
3 tablespoons Marsala wine
¼ pint (150 ml) double cream, whipped
2 large, ripe dessert pears

Whisk the egg yolks with the sugar in the top of a double saucepan. Add the Marsala and continue whisking over barely simmering water until the mixture is smooth and thick.

Remove the pan from the heat and continue whisking until the mixture is cool.

Fold in the cream. Whisk the egg whites until stiff but not dry and fold them in gently.

Peel, core and slice the pears. Divide the pear slices between 4 serving bowls or glasses. Pour the sabayon over the pears and refrigerate for at least 3 hours before serving.

Trifle
If preferred use a fresh fruit purée instead of the jam—raspberry, strawberry or apricots are best.

SERVES SIX

1 day-old sponge cake, made with 3 eggs
Strawberry or raspberry jam
3 fl oz (75 ml) sherry
2 tablespoons brandy
1 pint (575 ml) cream
1 vanilla pod
2 whole eggs plus 2 egg yolks
3 tablespoons castor sugar
1 tablespoon cornflour
½ pint (300 ml) double cream
Vanilla essence
Ratafia biscuits
Toasted split almonds or crystallized violets

Split the sponge cake in half and cut into pieces. Sandwich the pieces of cake with jam and put them in a glass bowl. Mix the sherry and brandy together and pour the mixture over the sponge. Cover the bowl and set it aside for 1 hour.

Meanwhile make the custard. Put the cream and vanilla pod in a saucepan and bring to just under boiling point. Remove the pan from the heat, leave to infuse for 15 minutes and strain.

Beat the eggs and egg yolks with 2 tablespoons of the sugar and the cornflour in a bowl. Pour in the cream, beating constantly. Put the bowl over a saucepan of barely simmering water and cook, stirring, until the custard is very thick and smooth. Taste it and add more sugar if necessary.

Pour the hot custard over the sponge and leave to cool. When cool cover the bowl and put it in the refrigerator until well chilled.

Whip the double cream in a bowl with half the remaining sugar. Taste the cream and add the rest of the sugar if necessary. Mix in a few drops of vanilla.

Spread the cream over the custard and decorate the top with the ratafia biscuits and almonds or violets.

Strawberry cheesecake
If you like, cut the cheesecake across in half and cover the bottom half with a little whipped cream and some sliced strawberries. Replace the top half of the cake and cover with more cream and sliced strawberries.

SERVES FOUR

6 oz (175 g) digestive biscuits
1½ oz (40 g) butter
¾ lb (350 g) curd or cream cheese
2 eggs
3 tablespoons castor sugar
1 teaspoon grated lemon rind
¼ pint (150 ml) double cream, whipped until thick
½ lb (225 g) strawberries, hulled

Preheat the oven to 350°F (180°C, Gas Mark 4). Lightly grease a 7-inch (18-cm) springform cake tin and set it aside.

Put the digestive biscuits in a plastic bag and knot the end. Beat on the bag with a rolling pin until the biscuits are reduced to crumbs.

Melt the butter in a saucepan over moderate heat. Remove the pan from the heat and stir in the biscuit crumbs to coat them thoroughly with the butter. Press the mixture into the bottom of the cake tin, smoothing it down well with the back of a spoon.

Put the cream cheese into a mixing bowl and beat it with a wooden spoon until it is smooth. Gradually beat in the eggs, being careful to avoid lumps. Beat in 2 tablespoons of the sugar and the lemon rind. Spoon the mixture into the cake tin, smoothing the top down, and bake for 30 to 40 minutes, or until the centre is firm when lightly pressed. Do not worry if a few small cracks appear on the top.

Remove the cheesecake from the oven and let it cool completely in the tin. Very carefully remove the cooled cheesecake from the tin and slide it on to a serving plate. Spread over the whipped cream and embed the strawberries in the cream. Sprinkle over the remaining sugar and serve.

Strawberry shortcake
This popular American dessert may also be served with coffee.

SERVES EIGHT

½ lb (225 g) flour
1 teaspoon baking powder
Pinch salt
¼ lb (125 g) butter
3 tablespoons castor sugar
1 egg yolk
2 to 3 tablespoons milk

FILLING
½ pint (300 ml) double cream
1 tablespoon castor sugar
1 lb (450 g) strawberries

Preheat the oven to 375°F (190°C, Gas Mark 5). Lightly grease two baking sheets with butter.

Sift the flour, baking powder and salt into a mixing bowl. Cut in the butter then rub it into the flour with your fingertips until the mixture resembles breadcrumbs.

Mix in the sugar. Make a well in the centre. Mix in the egg yolk and enough milk to make a soft dough. Turn the dough out on to a lightly floured surface and knead gently.

Divide the dough in half and roll out two 9-inch (23-cm) circles. Score one circle into 8 pieces. Put the circles on the baking sheets and bake for 12 minutes or until the shortcake is just beginning to brown. Transfer the shortcakes carefully to a wire rack to cool.

To make the filling, whip the cream and sugar until stiff. Slice the strawberries, reserving a few for decoration, and fold them into the cream.

Put one shortcake on a serving plate. Spread the cream and strawberry mixture on top and smooth it down evenly. Cut the other shortcake along the score marks. Place the segments on top, decorate with the reserved strawberries and serve.

Chestnut cake

SERVES SIX TO EIGHT

2 lb (900 g) chestnuts, boiled and peeled
Milk
¼ lb (125 g) sugar
6 oz (175 g) butter
6 oz (175 g) plain chocolate, broken into pieces
3 tablespoons brandy or rum

Put the chestnuts in a saucepan. Pour in enough milk to cover and bring to the boil. Cover the pan, reduce the heat to low and simmer for 40 to 60 minutes or until the chestnuts are soft.

Drain the chestnuts and purée them in a liquidizer or push them through a sieve. Beat in the sugar and ¼ pound (125 g) of the butter.

Lightly oil a small loaf tin and line the base with greaseproof paper. Oil the paper.

Spoon the mixture into the tin and smooth it down. Cover the tin with foil and put the tin in the refrigerator for 12 hours.

Run a knife around the edges of the tin and turn out the chestnut cake on to a plate.

Put the chocolate into a bowl with the brandy or rum and melt it over hot water. The chocolate must have the consistency of thick cream so add a little water if the mixture is too thick. Remove the bowl from the heat and stir the remaining butter into the chocolate, a piece at a time. When the chocolate is smooth and glossy spread it over the cake, using a knife dipped in hot water.

Set aside for 30 minutes or until the chocolate has set.

Chocolate torrone
This marvellously rich Italian dessert can be made one or two days in advance and kept in the refrigerator.

SERVES SIX TO EIGHT

½ lb (225 g) plain chocolate, broken into pieces
4 tablespoons rum
½ lb (225 g) butter
1 oz (25 g) castor sugar
2 egg yolks
¼ lb (125 g) hazelnuts, coarsely chopped
4 egg whites
Salt
12 plain, crisp sweet biscuits, broken into pieces

Lightly butter a 1-quart (1-litre) bowl.

Melt the chocolate in the rum in a heatproof bowl over hot water. When the chocolate has melted remove the bowl from the heat and let the mixture cool.

Cream the butter with the sugar until smooth, then add the egg yolks one at a time. Stir in the nuts and the chocolate.

Beat the egg whites with a pinch of salt until they form stiff peaks. Using a large metal spoon, fold the egg whites into the chocolate mixture. Carefully mix in the biscuits.

Pour the torrone into the bowl, cover with aluminium foil and refrigerate for several hours before serving.

Ice-creams

There are two kinds of ices—ice-creams and water-ices. Ice-creams are divided into two main types: egg-mousse-and-cream-based and custard-based. Water-ices, or sorbets, are made with well-flavoured fruit juice, black coffee or wine, mixed with sugar and water.

The best ices are made in a churn—electrically operated models are now available, but the smallest of these has a one-gallon (4-litre) capacity. If you have a refrigerator with a large ice-making compartment, or a freezer, you can also obtain excellent results with a sorbetière, a metal box (1 quart/1 litre capacity) fitted with electrically operated plastic paddles, which stop moving when the ice is the right consistency.

Good ices can also be made in the ice-making compartment of the refrigerator without special equipment which churns or stirs automatically. These "still-frozen" ices take a long time to freeze, however, and must be thoroughly beaten at least twice during the freezing period to avoid ice crystals forming and spoiling the texture.

To still-freeze successfully, set the refrigerator at its coldest temperature one hour in advance, and chill the ingredients and utensils before using them. The ice-cream mixture should have a fairly thick consistency before being frozen and water-ices should include gelatine or egg white to ensure a smoother result.

When the mixture is ready and well chilled put it into an ice-cube tray or any other suitable container, cover with foil and put it in the ice-making compartment of the refrigerator. After about forty-five minutes the mixture should be firm around the edges. Turn it out into a well-chilled bowl and whisk well with a rotary beater. An electrically operated hand-held beater is the easiest to use. Return the mixture to its container. Cover and freeze for another thirty minutes, then repeat the process. After another hour the mixture should be frozen through.

Reset the temperature control to its normal setting and leave the ice in the ice-making compartment for at least one hour but preferably for three hours or more. This "ripening" improves the flavour of the ice.

The general rules for making ices are the same whether they are made in a machine or still-frozen:

Because freezing diminishes flavours it is necessary to flavour and sweeten the mixture well. If you use too little sugar the ice will be hard and unpalatable; if you use too much the ice will not set properly. The maximum amount that may be used for an ice-cream flavoured only with an essence, vanilla for example, is about one part sugar to four parts custard or cream (volume measure), or $\frac{1}{4}$ pound (125 g) sugar to one pint (575 ml) custard or cream.

It is best to add sugar in the form of syrup, unless you are making a custard-based ice-cream. The syrup is boiled until the temperature reaches 220°F (104°C) on a sugar thermometer. If you do not have a thermometer boil the syrup for 6 minutes. If you are using a liqueur, pour it over the ice just before serving, instead of including it in the mixture.

Containers should be only three-quarters filled with the mixture to allow for expansion during freezing.

Cream-based vanilla ice-cream

Use double cream if the mixture is to be still-frozen.

SERVES FOUR TO SIX

1 pint (575 ml) single or double cream
1 vanilla pod
4 egg yolks
3 oz (75 g) sugar
$\frac{1}{4}$ pint (150 ml) water

Put the cream and vanilla pod into a small saucepan and bring to just under boiling point. Remove the pan from the heat and allow the mixture to infuse for 5 minutes. Remove the vanilla pod, pour the cream into a bowl and set aside to cool. When cool chill over ice cubes.

Beat the egg yolks in a heatproof bowl. Dissolve the sugar in the water over low heat. When the sugar has dissolved increase the heat and boil the syrup until it reaches a temperature of 220°F (104°C). Remove the pan from the heat, wait 30 seconds then pour in a steady stream over the yolks, beating all the time with a rotary beater—a hand-held electrically operated one is easiest to use. Beat until the mixture is thick and mousse-like, then cool.

If you are using double cream whisk it until it is thick but not stiff. Fold the cream into the egg and sugar mixture. For still-freezing chill the mixture then pour into the freezing tray or container and freeze.

Chocolate ice-cream

Melt 6 oz (175 g) dark chocolate with 1 tablespoon of rum and fold it in to the cooling cream mixture, but halve the sugar.

Blackcurrant ice-cream

Put 1 pound (450 g) of blackcurrants, 1 tablespoon of water and 1 tablespoon of sugar in a pan and cook over low heat for 10 minutes, stirring occasionally. Sieve into the ice-cream mixture, taste and add more sugar if necessary.

Strawberry ice-cream
Purée 1½ to 2 lb (700 to 900 g) strawberries and combine with the egg mixture before folding in the double cream.

Custard-based vanilla ice-cream
SERVES FOUR TO SIX

½ pint (300 ml) milk
1 vanilla pod
1 teaspoon cornflour
2 whole eggs
2 egg yolks
3 oz (75 g) castor sugar
½ pint (300 ml) double cream

Put the milk and the vanilla pod into a saucepan and bring to just under boiling point. Remove the pan from the heat and set aside to infuse for 5 minutes. Remove the vanilla pod.

Beat the cornflour with the eggs, egg yolks and the sugar until well mixed. Pour in the milk, stirring constantly. Pour the mixture into the top of a double saucepan and cook, stirring, over hot water until the custard is smooth and thick.

Strain the custard into a bowl and set aside to cool, stirring occasionally.

Put the cream into another bowl and whisk until thick but not stiff. Fold the cream into the custard and chill before freezing.

Orange ice-cream
Rub 2 oranges all over with 6 sugar lumps. When the sugar has absorbed all the zest, crush the cubes and dissolve them in 1 tablespoon of water.

Make the custard, replacing some of the milk with the orange juice and some of the sugar with the dissolved sugar cubes.

Lemon water-ice
The syrup given in this recipe makes 1¼ pints (725 ml) and can be used for all water-ice recipes. You may use 2 teaspoons gelatine dissolved in a little water instead of the egg white or in addition to it. The gelatine helps to prevent ice crystals from forming when the water-ice is still-frozen. Three heads of elderflowers infused in the syrup after it is taken off the heat will give this ice a delicious flavour.

SERVES FOUR

1 pint (575 ml) water
6 oz (175 g) sugar
Rind and juice of 3 lemons
1 egg white, stiffly beaten

Put the water, sugar and lemon rind in a saucepan and cook over low heat, stirring, until the sugar dissolves. Increase the heat to high and boil the syrup, without stirring, until the temperature reaches 220°F (104°C) on a sugar thermometer or for 6 minutes, if you do not have a thermometer. Remove the pan from the heat and add the lemon juice. Cool the mixture and then chill it.

Strain the mixture into an ice-cube tray and freeze until it becomes mushy in the middle and hard around the edges.

Turn the mixture into a bowl and whisk until it is smooth. Whisk in the beaten egg white, return the mixture to the freezer compartment and freeze for 30 minutes. Whisk again and then freeze for 1 to 1½ hours, or until the water-ice is frozen through.

Grapefruit water-ice
Use 2 grapefruit and 1¼ pints (725 ml) of sugar syrup.

Orange water-ice
Use 3 oranges, the juice of ½ lemon and 1 tablespoon orange blossom water to 1¼ pints (725 ml) sugar syrup.

Berry water-ice
Make ½ pint (300 ml) fruit purée from any berry fruit—raspberries, blackcurrants, redcurrants or gooseberries (use double the amount of strawberries). Use ½ pint (300 ml) sugar syrup and 2 egg whites.

Coffee granita
The ice crystals which form during freezing gives coffee granita its distinctive texture.

SERVES FOUR

½ lb (225 g) dark roast coffee beans, finely ground
¼ lb (125 g) sugar
1 quart (1 litre) boiling water

Put the coffee and sugar into a heatproof glass or ceramic coffee jug. Pour the boiling water into the jug. Put the jug on an asbestos mat on the lowest heat and leave for 1 hour.

Allow the coffee to cool, then strain it through a sieve lined with muslin. Chill before freezing. Whisk three times during the freezing process.

Coffee ice-cream
If this ice-cream is made in a sorbetière or churn, reduce the cornflour to 1 teaspoon.

SERVES FOUR TO SIX

2 oz (50 g) dark roast coffee beans, bruised
½ pint (300 ml) cream
5 oz (150 g) sugar
Salt
1 tablespoon cornflour
3 tablespoons milk
3 egg yolks
½ pint (300 ml) double cream

Put the coffee beans and cream in a saucepan and bring to just under boiling point. Reduce the heat to very low, cover the pan and leave the cream to infuse for 1 hour. The cream should remain hot, but not come to the boil. Strain the cream.

Combine the sugar, pinch of salt and cornflour with the milk. Beat in the egg yolks and gradually stir in the coffee cream. Cook over barely simmering water until the custard thickens.

Remove the custard and set aside to cool. Stir occasionally as it cools to prevent a skin forming.

Whip the double cream in a bowl until it is thick but not stiff and fold it into the custard. Chill the mixture before freezing.

Tutti frutti
This is a good mixture for still-freezing.

SERVES FOUR

1 oz (25 g) glacé cherries, chopped
1 oz (25 g) angelica, chopped
1 oz (25 g) crystallized pineapple, chopped
1 oz (25 g) sultanas
4 fl oz (125 ml) rum
2 egg whites
¼ lb (125 g) sugar
¼ pint (150 ml) water
¼ oz (10 g) gelatine dissolved in 2 tablespoons warm water
½ pint (300 ml) double cream
½ teaspoon vanilla essence

Put the fruit in a bowl. Pour over the rum. Cover the bowl and set aside for 1 hour.

Have the egg whites ready in a heatproof bowl.

Put the sugar and water in a saucepan and stir to dissolve over low heat. Increase the heat and boil the syrup for 6 minutes or until the temperature reaches 220°F (104°C) on a sugar thermometer.

Using a rotary beater, preferably electrically operated, beat the egg whites until stiff but not dry. Pour the syrup over the egg whites in a steady stream, beating constantly. Pour in the gelatine and beat until thick.

Beat the cream and vanilla essence until thick but not stiff. Fold the cream into the egg white mixture and freeze, beating twice. Drain the fruit and add it after the final beating.

Pistachio ice-cream
SERVES FOUR TO SIX

¼ lb (125 g) shelled pistachio nuts
½ pint (300 ml) single cream
3 oz (75 g) sugar
¼ pint (150 ml) water
4 egg yolks
Almond essence
Green food colouring
½ pint (300 ml) double cream
4 egg whites

Put the nuts in a liquidizer with just enough of the cream to prevent the machine clogging and blend until smooth.

Put the sugar and water in a saucepan and stir to dissolve over low heat. When the sugar has dissolved boil rapidly for 6 minutes or until the temperature reaches 220°F (104°C) on a sugar thermometer. Remove the pan from the heat.

Using a rotary beater, whisk the egg yolks in a bowl. Pour in the syrup in a steady stream whisking all the time until the mixture is thick and fluffy. Mix in the pistachio cream, the remaining single cream, a few drops of almond essence and 1 to 2 drops of food colouring.

Whisk the double cream until thick but not stiff and mix it into the custard. Chill the mixture.

Whisk the egg whites until stiff. Fold into the mixture and freeze.

Glossary

Acidulated water. Water to which lemon juice or vinegar has been added. Cut fruit and vegetables are dropped into acidulated water to prevent them discolouring. Add 1 tablespoon of lemon juice or vinegar to 1 pint (575 ml) of water.

Aspic. Clear jelly made from meat, chicken or fish stock, used to coat food or chopped and used to garnish a cold dish.

Au bleu. A method of cooking live freshwater fish. The fish is stunned and put in a pan. It is then sprinkled with vinegar and cooked in a court bouillon.

Au gratin. Food which is covered with a sauce, breadcrumbs and/or grated cheese and then baked or grilled.

Back fat. Pork fat used for larding or barding; also used in the making of pâtés.

Bain-marie. A large pan (a roasting or baking tin or dish may be used) filled with hot water in which smaller pans or pots can be placed. It is used to cook or heat custards and sauces that are too delicate to be put over direct heat.

Baking blind. Baking pastry cases without a filling.

Barding. Covering joints of lean meat and the breasts of poultry or game birds with strips of back fat or fat bacon, to prevent them from drying out during roasting.

Basting. Moistening meat, game, poultry or fish with fat, stock or other liquids.

Beurre manié. A paste made from equal quantities of flour and butter kneaded together. It is used to thicken soups, sauces and stews.

Blanching. Plunging food—fruit, vegetables, nuts or meat—briefly into boiling water, or putting them in cold water, bringing them to the boil and, sometimes, boiling them for a few minutes. This is done to loosen the skin prior to peeling; to reduce strong flavours, saltiness or bitterness; or to set the colour and prepare food for freezing.

Blending. Mixing ingredients together with a spoon or in a liquidizer until thoroughly amalgamated and smooth.

Bouquet garni. Various herbs, including parsley, bay and thyme, sometimes contained in a muslin bag. It is used to flavour soups, stews and sauces.

Braising. Cooking meat, game, fish or vegetables first on top of the cooker and then with very little liquid in a slow oven.

Clarified butter. Butter melted, cooked gently and strained to eliminate salt, milk solids and moisture. This gives a clear fat that can be heated to a higher temperature than butter without burning.

Compound butters. Butter to which various savoury flavourings have been added. They are always chilled and served with hot food.

Court bouillon. A seasoned, acidic liquid used for poaching fish.

Croustade. A fried or baked bread case.

Croûtons. Small cubes of bread which are fried or toasted and used to garnish soups and some salads. The term also applies to larger pieces of fried or toasted bread used as a base for steaks or small birds.

Deglazing. Dissolving the sediments left in a pan after frying or roasting. A little liquid is poured in, stirred and mixed with the sediments, then brought to the boil and used as gravy.

Degorging. A process used to draw out the juices and bitterness from such vegetables as aubergines or cucumbers before they are cooked. The vegetables are sliced, sprinkled with salt and left to drain, weighted down with a plate, for 30 minutes.

Degreasing. Removing the grease from a cooked liquid, such as stock. The liquid is cooled. When the grease rises to the surface it is skimmed off.

Dice. To cut food into small cubes.

Dripping. Fat that has dripped into the pan from meat or poultry during roasting.

Duxelles. A paste made from finely chopped mushrooms and/or mushroom stalks that is used to flavour soups, stews and various other dishes. It can be stored in a screwtop jar in the refrigerator for 1 month and in the freezer for 3 months.

En croûte. A term used to describe meat that is cooked wrapped in pastry or bread dough. The pastry is not eaten.

En papillote. A term used to describe food that is cooked and served wrapped in paper.

Flambé. To pour alcohol over food and set light to it. The food and the alcohol must be warm before being ignited.

Fondue. Pieces of bread or other food speared on long-handled forks and dipped into a cheese or chocolate sauce or hot oil.

Garam masala. A mixture of ground dried spices used mainly in Indian dishes. Not to be confused with curry powder.

Giblets. Edible entrails, such as the liver, heart and gizzard, that are removed from poultry or game birds.

Glaze. A glossy finish given to food by coating it with egg, water, syrup, puréed jam or concentrated stock.

Jam glaze. Jam heated with a little water and lemon juice, then sieved.

Julienne. A term used to describe any food that is cut into narrow strips.

Lard. Pork fat that is melted down, clarified and used as a cooking fat.

Larding. Threading pieces of back fat through joints of lean meat that are to be roasted.

Liaison. The thickening agent—for example a roux, egg yolks and cream, or blood—used to bind sauces.

Marinade. An acidulated or seasoned liquid, often a mixture of oil and wine or vinegar, spices and herbs, that is used to tenderize and give flavour to food. Yogurt is used as a marinade in many Eastern countries.

Marinate. To soak food in a marinade.

Mask. To coat food completely with a sauce or aspic.

Meat glaze. Brown stock, degreased and boiled until it is reduced to a clear, dark brown, syrupy glaze. 1 to $1\frac{1}{2}$ quarts (1 to $1\frac{1}{2}$ litres) of stock will make $\frac{1}{4}$ pint (150 ml) of glaze. It is used to enrich gravies, sauces and stocks.

Mirepoix. Diced or sliced root vegetables and, sometimes, diced bacon, cooked in butter until tender and used to enhance the flavour of fish, poultry and meat.

Oeufs mollets. Eggs boiled for $4\frac{1}{2}$ to 5 minutes, or until the yolks are soft but the whites firm.

Panade. A thick paste made either with flour, butter and water or milk, or with breadcrumbs soaked in milk or water, and used to bind and thicken quenelles and forcemeat.

Paper collar. A strip of paper tied around a soufflé dish to support a hot soufflé as it rises and a cold soufflé or mousse until it sets.

Par-boiling. Cooking food in boiling water for a short time before continuing to cook it by another method, such as baking.

Pickling onions. Small button or pearl onions used whole for pickling, garnishing and in stews and sautés.

Reducing. Boiling liquid rapidly until it has reduced in volume and strengthened in flavour.

Rendering fat. The process of slowly melting down fat from its solid to its liquid state.

Roux. A base for sauces made of flour mixed with hot fat.

Sautéing. From the French verb sauter, to jump. Cooking food briskly in a little fat until it is brown on all sides. Often, after a preliminary sautéing, a little liquid is added, the pan covered and the food cooked gently until it is tender.

Scalding. Heating liquid to just under boiling point.

Scoring. Making incisions in fish or meat.

Seasoned flour. Flour seasoned with salt and pepper and sometimes cayenne pepper or herbs, and used to coat food for frying.

Stir-frying. A method of frying perfected by the Chinese. Meat, poultry, fish or vegetables are cut into small pieces of equal size and fried quickly in hot oil. The food must be stirred constantly to prevent burning and to ensure that it is cooked evenly.

Trussing. Tying up a bird with trussing string so that the legs and wings are kept neatly in place during cooking.

Vanilla sugar. Sugar that has been put in a jar with a vanilla pod so that it absorbs the vanilla flavour.

Wok. A large frying-pan with a rounded base, used in Chinese cooking.

Zest. The coloured part of orange or lemon skin, which can be thinly pared with a potato peeler. The word zest is also used to mean the oil that can be extracted from the skin if a lump of sugar is rubbed over it.

Index

Recipe titles and page numbers are in bold type. Illustrations are denoted by italic numerals.

Index

Index

Index